The State of Citizen Participation in America

A volume in
International Civic Engagement
Erik Bergrud and Kaifeng Yang, *Series Editors*

The State of Citizen Participation in America

edited by

Hindy Lauer Schachter
New Jersey Institute of Technology

Kaifeng Yang
Florida State University

INFORMATION AGE PUBLISHING, INC.
Charlotte, NC • www.infoagepub.com

Library of Congress Cataloging-in-Publication Data

The state of citizen participation in America / edited by Hindy Lauer Schachter.
        p. cm. – (Research on international civic engagement)
    Includes bibliographical references.
    ISBN 978-1-61735-835-7 (hardcover) – ISBN 978-1-61735-834-0 (pbk.) –
    ISBN 978-1-61735-836-4 (ebook) 1. Political participation–United States.
    2. Public administration–United States–Citizen participation. 3. Public
    administration–United States–Citizen participation–Case studies. 4.
    Political planning–United States–Citizen participation. 5. Political
    planning–United States–Citizen participation–Case studies. I. Schachter,
    Hindy Lauer.
    JK1764.S84 2012
    323'.0420973–dc23

                                                                 2012011833

Printed in the United States of America

CONTENTS

PART III

CITIZEN PARTICIPATION: TRENDS AND ASSESSMENTS

PART IV

CITIZEN PARTICIPATION: INNOVATIVE CASES

PART V
RESEARCH REFLECTIONS

PART VI
CONCLUSION

PREFACE

This book offers state-of-the-art assessment of citizen participation practice and research in the United States. With contributions from a stellar group of scholars, it provides readers an overview of a subject at the heart of democratic governance. Individual chapters trace shifts in participation philosophy and policy, examine trends at different government levels, analyze technology/participation interactions, identify the participation experiences of minority populations, and explore the impact of voluntary organizations on this topic. A five-chapter section illustrates innovative cases. Another section explores the role of various methodologies in advancing participation research.

In developing the volume, the two editors have collected a set of debts. One is to Margaret Stout, who reviewed material and made suggestions for revision. Another is to Youngmin Oh, who helped format the files and figures.

The State of Citizen Participation in America, page ix
Copyright © 2012 by Information Age Publishing
All rights of reproduction in any form reserved.

PART I

CIVIC PARTICIPATION IN AMERICA

CHAPTER 1

INTRODUCTION

American Civic Participation
in the 21st Century

Hindy Lauer Schachter
New Jersey Institute of Technology

Although civic engagement has always been an important topic in American public administration (PA) and political science, the past 20 odd years have seen an unusual concentration of citizen participation scholarship in both fields. In the late 1970s and early 1980s, few American Society for Public Administration (ASPA) national conferences featured separate citizen participation tracks; in the first decade of the 21st century, such offerings were common. Kerrigan and Hinton's 1980 article on the educational needs of public administrators made no mention of citizen interaction skills. By the 1990s, many writers argued that effective administrators needed to understand citizen engagement (e.g., Box, 1998; King, Kathryn, & O'Neill Susel, 1998; Schachter, 1997; Thomas, 1995). Walsh's (1997) International City/County Management Association (ICMA) training workbook featured tools to enhance citizen interaction skills. When Robert Behn (1995) argued that micromanagement, motivation, and measurement were the big questions

The State of Citizen Participation in America, pages 3–20
Copyright © 2012 by Information Age Publishing
All rights of reproduction in any form reserved.

of public management, John Kirlin (1996) responded that in reality, the key questions concerned citizenship. The most important queries focused on how to develop and nurture a democratic polity.

Renewed interest in citizenship emerged simultaneously in political science. That discipline had always had a lively interest in who participated, particularly as voters (e.g., Verba & Nie, 1972). In the 1990s, theorists such as Sandel (1996), Barber (1998), and Warren (2001) supplemented this concern with a call for association and deliberation to enhance collective self-governance. Several theorists argued that deliberation was key to increasing the legitimacy of political decisions and helping citizens understand public issues (Ackerman & Fishkin, 2004; Fishkin, 1997).

Further support for the importance of this topic came from the highest disciplinary levels. In 1996, Elinor Ostrom, then president of the American Political Science Association (APSA), appointed a Task Force on Civic Education for the Next Century as a response to a perceived participation decline and emphasized the importance of this normative endeavor for the discipline (Schachter, 1998). Two other APSA presidents—Robert Putnam (2000) and Theda Skocpol (2003)—were leaders in publicizing the need to enhance social capital through voluntary-sector participation opportunities so that citizens would have the necessary communication skills and trust to get involved.

In a sense, this explicitly value-laden interest in citizenship brought American PA and political science back to their origins. The progressive founders of what was then a single intertwined enterprise had a strong sense of citizen responsibility; many of their leaders were political reformers and members of an activist social science community (Mosher, 1968; Recchuiti, 2007). The citizen participation emphasis of a Kirlin or Barber showed that at least some contemporary scholars had begun "a return to an emphasis on the *public* aspects of the field and to the basic issues of democratic theory"—a development that Frederickson (1982, p. 503) had called for at the start of the 1980s.

This scholarly interest followed unprecedented political developments to encourage participation, so that commentators have argued that in some sense, "practice is leading theory" (Bingham, Nabatchi, & O'Leary, 2005, p. 547). Starting in the 1960s and 1970s, the civil rights and women's movements produced new concern with representativeness, both in terms of having diverse officials and getting a more diverse set of citizens involved. This concern emerged first in War on Poverty statutes that mandated citizen involvement in local boards running federally funded community action, model cities, and community health programs in poor urban areas. A symbiotic relationship emerged between the world of practice and research. While academics studied new developments as they emerged from innovative policies, political leaders were often receptive to learning from academic/think-tank analyses, as was shown most clearly in the 1990s when the Clinton administration borrowed ideas from the literature on reinventing government.

The public administration/political science communities never had a single prescriptive participation agenda. While almost all late 20th-/early 21st-century writers on citizenship encouraged some form of popular engagement, ambivalence was rampant about the kind of participation America's polities required. No scholarly or practitioner consensus has ever existed on the aims of involvement or how to reconcile the type of participation envisioned historically by the Constitution and the Founders with modern problems and technologies. None has existed on preferred participation loci, whether federal, state, or local, as well as the effective extent of participation. No consensus existed on whether participation needed a strong deliberative focus. None existed on whether it is useful to get citizens involved in technical issues such as where to build mass transit. On one end of a continuum, writers such as Irvin and Stansbury (2004) or Thomas (1995) argue that citizen participation may be ineffective and even wasteful for technical decisions. On the other side, writers such as Barber (1990) and Schachter and Liu (2005) call for strong participation across issue areas.

No consensus existed on which participation forums were most effective. Governments offer citizens different rosters of participation forums for different issues, sometimes based on federal statute and sometimes on local preference. The most common administrator-provided forums are surveys and public hearings, neither of which involve two-way communication or deliberation. Other opportunities may include citizen advisory committees, panels, discussion groups, and electronic interchange. Analysts differ on the worth of each of these techniques. For example, King et al. (1998) say that public hearings do not work to give people an authentic policy voice. Adams (2004) argues that hearings "can complement the structures that foster citizen deliberation" (p. 43). Case studies show that sometimes public hearings do not seem to sway outcomes and other times they do (Cole & Caputo, 1984; Rosener, 1982, respectively); context matters.

Analysts' perspectives differ also on who should initiate and control involvement processes. Some commentators argue that administrators have to make the decision to involve citizens (e.g., Thomas, 1995). Other writers consider a citizen-driven agenda crucial because "citizens are governors...masters of their own fates" (Barber 1990, p. xvii); they know which issues interest them. The ambiguities are not much diminished from when Frederickson (1991) noted that PA had no coherent model of the public. Key unresolved questions continue to include, "How do citizens interact effectively with their governments?" and "What constitute the responsibilities and actions of effective citizens?"

Difficulties in answering these questions arise from each analyst's perspective being based at least partly on individual values—what kind of participation the particular person thinks is important in a democracy. Value problems emerge in reconciling the individualistic/rights and communitarian/republican aspects of our tradition. Allied are difficulties in using the traditional citizen responsibility of voting as the bedrock of self-government and the need to supplement the vote in some way to achieve effective policy involvement. But which way? Which roles should American citizens play to gain authentic participation? Are citizens customers of government as some analysts propose, or are they its active owners? Much of the contemporary citizen participation literature investigates one or another of the voter, customer, or owner roles. Yet, as the following sections show, problems arise in trying to operationalize the voter, customer, and active citizen roles and using any of them as a mechanism for anchoring participation.

VOTERS

Elections are crucial for the American model of representative government. While America's theory of democratic representation assumes that elections are a necessary prerequisite for self-government, in actuality, elections turn out to be a necessary but insufficient condition. In theory, voters go to the polls at set intervals. Majorities elect executives, legislatures, and in some jurisdictions, judges. Elected officials are supposed to hold views compatible with citizen predilections, thus ensuring that policy follows citizen desires. These elected executives appoint and supervise agency heads who adhere to popularly supported policy prescriptions. The federal, state, and local executives then watch carefully that their own subordinates, the agency managers, and entry-level employees follow the citizen-mandated line.

Tidy as this flowchart of responsibilities is, it suffers from being aslant from reality at every stage. First, elections do not necessarily ensure that officials follow (or even know) citizen desires. At a minimum, elections can only involve people who vote. In most contemporary American elections, a majority of eligible voters stay home, thus ensuring that almost no contest can claim to express a majority preference. In addition, hard-fought contests can bring victory to the person who amasses 55% or 60% of the vote. Are we to say that the other 45% or 40% are to have no policy input at all?

The demographic characteristics of voters differ from the population at large. Voters tend to be older (Plutzer, 2002). They have higher socioeconomic status and more formal education, factors that could well make their preferences differ from those of citizens in general (Nie, Jane, & Stehlik-Barry, 1996; Verba, Schlozman, Brady, & Nie, 1993). Older people, for example, are likely to have different attitudes toward social security policies than young workers (Campbell, 2002).

A considerable political science literature shows gaps in citizen policy knowledge; this means that many voters may not even know the various candidates' policy preferences (e.g., DelliCarpini & Keeter, 1996). Some may select candidates for reasons other than policy congruence, such as party affiliation, good looks, or ethnic ascription. In addition, between elections, citizen opinion may change or new issues may arise that the election could not adjudicate. It should not be surprising, therefore, that discrepancies exist between officials' beliefs about citizen preferences and preferences citizens articulate themselves. Such discrepancies appear in a recent survey in North Carolina, which found that most elected officials identified themselves as seeking citizen participation on budget issues, but most citizens did not believe that officials sought their participation (Berner, Amos, & Morse, 2011).

But even if elections did ensure that political officials embraced popular sentiment, this symmetry would not guarantee citizens sufficient input into policy development or implementation. A tenet of public administration is the considerable independence and discretion agency employees possess right down to the street level (Lipsky, 1980). To have an impact on policy, citizens have to connect in some way with the administrators implementing policies over time.

However, as Breyer (2009) found in a study of Los Angeles agencies, departments differ in their responsiveness to citizen interaction; some organizations insist on maintaining their role as experts, while others embrace partnership with neighborhood councils. At least some administrators are ambivalent about engaging citizens in dialogue and do not seek participation that they see as inefficient and a waste of time (King et al., 1998). A recent survey of New Jersey administrators found that while a majority supported citizen-driven performance measurement, over a quarter of the respondents did not (Yang, 2007). Two different surveys of Georgia administrators found that many could not identify citizen opinion correctly, instead rating citizens as more pessimistic about services than actual survey data warranted (Melkers & Thomas, 1998; Poister & Thomas, 2007). This type of discrepancy might not occur if people had some way of sharing their ideas and concerns directly with administrators.

The bottom line is that elections alone are insufficient to provide meaningful citizen input to the policy process. As Arendt (1963) has noted, at best they give citizens power on election day. To combat this inadequacy, PA writers have turned their attention to two other citizen roles, those of consumer/customer and of active citizen. Reflections on each role have led to two radically different concepts of citizen involvement.

CUSTOMERS

In the 1990s, proponents of reinventing government (REGO) argued that efficiency required customer-driven management (Osborne & Gaebler, 1992; Osborne & Plaistrik, 2000). Administrators had to stop concentrating on pleasing their political superiors, particularly legislators, and learn instead to please their customers. REGO proponents borrowed the utility of the entrepreneurial manager/customer relationship from business practice, which they considered superior to public sector ways. They learned from total quality management (TQM) theory the key mantra that firms should delight their customers (Swiss, 1992).

This new dispensation required that agencies obtain information on preferences and complaints from the public so that administrators could know customer choices. To get such information, administrators had to identify their customer base (not always an easy task with public services) and gauge its satisfaction (Poister, 2003). The participation technique most often proposed to gain this knowledge was the citizen survey, in which administrators asked respondents to indicate their service preferences or evaluate existing services (Gore, 1994). Some jurisdictions had used this technique since the 1970s, but REGO's influence sparked additional analysis of its role as a tool to get customer feedback. As President Clinton's federal-level National Performance Review noted in expanding survey programs, "only the customer knows what the customer wants" (National Performance Review, 1994, p. 49).

Some commentators have concluded that the citizen survey does empower people. It provides an effective channel for people to impact policy development by communicating service preferences and then allowing administrators to recalibrate offerings to meet popular desires. Watson, Robert, and Johnson (1991, p. 238) argued, based on evidence from Auburn, Alabama, that "citizen surveys can be an efficient and productive linkage mechanism between public officials and citizens." When citizens gave low grades to Auburn's public light fixtures, administrators changed the lighting.

Epstein, Coates, Wray, and Swain (2006) commended the Des Moines Digital Survey in Iowa; the city directly downloaded data into its electronic complaint tracking system, allowing respondents to check how administrators handled issues. The ICMA's manual for local governments on how to produce effective surveys reported that more than half of the city managers contacted said they used their jurisdiction's survey results to evaluate programs and guide policy decisions (Miller, Kobayashi, & Hayden, 2008).

Surveys, however, have met two quite different critiques. The first emanates from some analysts' questioning whether respondents know enough about service quality to give accurate assessments; in other words, they question how much administrators can rely on the answers of what these commentators call a subjective, not well-informed public. Such commentators argue that citizens rate services based on their own sociodemographic characteristics or their opinions about other matters such as the worth of the jurisdiction's entire policy lineup (e.g., Licari, McLean, & Rice, 2005). More recently, Van Ryzin, Immerwahr, & Altman (2008) have countered this critique with research showing similarities between citizen ratings and agency measurements of services such as street cleaning. Schachter (2010) questioned the downgrading of citizen surveys because they are subjective, with analysis focusing on the subjective nature of all performance measures, including those developed by agency experts.

A second critique emanates from analysts who find surveys problematic because they keep control of the agenda in administrative hands and eliminate co-creation of meaning. Surveys allow no room for deliberation and communal learning among respondents. Their proponents seem to assume that each individual can have fully formed opinions about service quality before hearing what other citizens have to say and seeing how different options affect the community. Yet political scientists such as James Fishkin (1997) and Jason Barabas (2004) have shown that people refine their policy views if they have a chance to deliberate with others and get new information. People deliberating under fair conditions of argument can change their minds as they see how their old positions affect different interests (White, 2010). In addition, citizens in focus groups sponsored by the Kettering Foundation critiqued surveys for being "impersonal," which seems to say that surveys did not capture their real concerns (Harwood Group, 1991, p. 16).

Many democratic theorists believe that public opinion is formed in intersubjective processes of reason-giving and response (e.g., Warren, 2001). Helping to evaluate good customer service from a list of expert-arranged choices is not how such analyst's define effective citizen participation. Writers in this camp crave a more thorough role change—"a move from seeing citizens as voters, volunteers, clients, or consumers to viewing citizens as problem solvers and cocreators of public goods" (Boyte, 2005, p. 537). These analysts want the citizen to have a hand in constructing lists of planned programs. They want citizens involved at every stage from problem definition to decision making. They want deliberative, active citizenship.

ACTIVE CITIZENS

Active citizens are "people engaged in deliberation to influence public-sector decision making, animated, at least in part, by concern for the public interest, a concept that each individual may define in a different way" (Schachter, 1997, p. 1). Active citizens join together to take a hand in setting the political agenda through common talk, decision making, and action; their concern extends to public-sector aims as well as evaluating the merits of current programs (Barber, 1990). At their best, they use deliberation to engage in generative learning that "opens up new ways of looking at the world and encourages a deeper understanding of a system and its underlying dynamics" (Roberts, 1997, p. 125). Schachter (1997) suggests that active citizens behave as if they are the owners rather than the customers of government; they care about the enterprise as a whole rather than only about the transactions that involve them personally. They feel a sense of civic responsibility (Candler & Dumont, 2010).

Some commentators have wondered if active citizenship is practical, given the time constraints endemic to most people's busy lives (Burtt 1993; Smith & Huntsman, 1997). A survey of county and city chief administrative officers showed that almost three quarters of respondents saw lack of time as a key reason for low citizen involvement (Yang & Callahan, 2007).

The feasibility of active citizenship is a fair concern. But low participation rates in our current system do not indicate that these rates are the only ones possible for human society. Different socialization patterns or involvement forums might alter involvement patterns. Participation patterns have varied widely over the course of American history. We cannot definitely know what participation might look like in a system that adequately socializes people for an active role until we get such a system. If greater deliberation opportunities changed participant knowledge and ability to provide logical and consistent opinions, this shift might increase the desire of citizens to make time for getting involved. A number of experiments in the political science literature show that voting numbers rise and fall based on social factors—what people believe their neighbors are doing and whether they think others know about their voting patterns (Grosser & Schram, 2006). Social construction of participation is almost certainly not limited to voting patterns. Social and political factors are likely to affect participation in deliberative forums as well.

At present, we only have examples of limited, often self-chosen, groups of citizens coming together to deliberate on public problems. In these examples, statute, administrative action, or a privately developed project created the space for deliberation. To get some idea of the range of deliberative venues created in these three ways in the last 30 years, we can examine a few case studies of each type of involvement in turn. The following chapter subsections do not attempt to provide anything resembling a complete list of cases, but even sampling a restricted group gives some idea of the range of policies appropriate for deliberation and the factors that affect the impact of actual deliberation efforts, including the context dependency of results. A key question still remains on how to motivate extensive participation for the population at-large to counter the class and education biases rampant in current participation patterns. Increasing participation across the board must be resolved if active citizenship is to involve a representative body of Americans.

Statute-Mandated Deliberation

Sometimes federal statutes set up the space for deliberation by requiring that citizen boards make at least some decisions for specific social programs. For example, federal law dating from the War on Poverty in the 1960s requires neighborhood participation in Community Action Agencies (CAA), model cities programs, and community health center boards. Reports on the impact of these mandates show that the actual participation that the statute enabled depended on various contextual factors. First, participation differed by program. Strange (1972) reported that over time, the impact of CAA board participation diminished as federal-agency administrators made more and more decisions in Washington and then sent local agencies one-size-fits-all packaged programs. On the other hand, Stivers (1990) reports that in community health centers, citizen boards did make important decisions about services and personnel.

Participation also differed based on local political context. Greenstone and Peterson (1973) found almost no genuine participation in Chicago, where community boards were controlled by city machines. In Detroit and New York, boards did transfer important organizational resources to neighborhood groups.

Federal statutes also sometimes require a citizen component for temporary study panels. In 1990, when Congress established the Northern Forest Lands Council to study forest use in New York and New England, it prescribed innovative public involvement processes such as open meetings and citizen advisory committees. Interviews with citizens who participated indicated satisfaction with the process. It gave them an opportunity to speak, some chance to influence outcomes, a structure that facilitated interaction (e.g., accessible time, location, seating arrangement, personality of agency facilitators), and access to information. It also enabled future processes for involvement (Webler & Tuler, 2000).

Administrator-Conceived Deliberation

Space for deliberation can also arise if individual administrators take the lead in developing successful opportunities for citizens to talk together. As a school superintendent in Minnesota, Ruth Randall used citizen deliberation as one tactic to administer budget cuts in a way that minimized operational disruption. Over a period of four months, beginning in December 1981, she held citizen meetings in 10 elementary schools where over 2,000 people came to speak out, listen, and comment on recommendations that had been developed by the educational staff. Principals and district administrators reviewed the citizen suggestions and forwarded them to Randall. She in turn used this material in preparing her submission to the Board of Education, which accepted all her proposals (Roberts, 1997).

As Minnesota's commissioner of education, Ruth Randall invited anyone who wanted, to join a Governor's Discussion Group on schools, which eventually included 61 people. Although Randall encountered pressure to restrict admission to representatives of organized groups, she did not accept this limit on who could participate. A group with organizational representatives and other interested individuals met monthly in the late 1980s for a total of 22 sessions. A case study of Randall's initiative indicated that the group was a success in terms of process and effect. The author concluded that "members came to understand that addressing the problems of education would require their combined efforts, not just their individual solutions" (Roberts 2002, p. 662). When the group submitted a proposal for educational change, the governor incorporated most of its contents into his legislative package.

Voluntary Organization Projects

Voluntary organizations with an interest in citizen deliberation have also initiated participation forums. In the 1980s, the Center for New Democratic Processes developed Citizen Panels, a participation forum based on the jury system. The group's Agriculture/Water Quality Project in Minnesota was the first to use randomly selected groups of citizens to study a political issue and make recommendations to public administrators and elected officials. Project leaders chose panel members on a stratified random basis from people who either had attended informational meetings on conflicts between agricultural practices and water quality or had taken part in a statewide telephone survey. Panel members heard testimony from expert witnesses on ways to deal with agriculture's impact on water. The panel then deliberated and developed recommendations. An analysis of the project concluded that the panel was successful as a start, although it did not actually influence legislation. Relevant administrators did read its reports, although the state legislature did not adopt the bulk of the recommendations (Crosby, Kelly, & Schaefer, 1986).

Another example comes from the Loka Institute, a private research and advocacy group, which helped set up a deliberation forum on genetically modified (GM) food at the University of New Hampshire in 2002. The aim was to provide a group of citizens with presentations from different points of view and then afford the participants time to deliberate on the issues. Unfortunately, the organizers were not able to secure pro-GM speakers (possibly because Loka was seen as anti-GM), and the conference had little policy impact. That outcome underscores the need for forum enablers to appear to potential participants as people who operate outside a partisan political agenda (Dryzek & Tucker, 2008).

ENABLING ACTIVE CITIZENSHIP

One problem with projects initiated by individuals, whether they be administrators or outside leaders, is that when the founder departs or loses interest, the forum may disappear as well. As David Mathews (2010) has noted, replacing civic entrepreneurs who leave or retire is a constant challenge. Because administrators vary in their orientation to participation, not every Minnesota education commissioner will continue Randall's innovations. The Center for New Democratic Processes, currently called the Jefferson Center for New Democratic Processes, spearheaded only one citizen jury project in 2009 and two in 2010.

In addition, even at their best, these exercises involve relatively few citizens. Most Minnesotans never attended Randall's deliberations or participated in the Center for New Democratic Processes' panels. As Dryzek and Tucker (2008) noted, "American public interest foundations . . . and the deliberative innovations they sponsor are just one kind of voice in a pluralist cacophony, and it is a struggle for them to get their ideas noticed" (p.872). Without a legal mandate, these initiatives are at the whim of any need to prune budgets of agencies and voluntary groups. In addition, as long as much deliberative participation remains at the project level, the people involved will inevitably be skewed to those who have more time and income. This lack of representation mirrors the overrepresentation of people with higher socioeconomic status as voters and as speakers at public hearings (Halverson, 2006).

Entrenching deliberative participation requires institutional commitment. It requires finding public places for citizens and officials to discuss policy issues (Harwood Group, 1991). It requires capacity-building efforts for citizens and administrators alike (Musso, Christopher, Bryer, & Cooper, 2011). As Bingham et al. (2005, p. 555) noted, deliberative techniques have been used off and on for over 20 years. The time has come to ask, "What steps need to be taken to institutionalize these processes?"

The importance of continuity in providing deliberative space undergirds Box (1998) and Leib's (2004) calls for institutionalizing citizen forums at the constitutional level so that they are not dependent on the vagaries of incumbent support. Box focuses on the local level. He envisions moving elected legislative bodies from a decision-making to a coordinating status, with citizen advisory boards assisting in developing policy for every function. Leib wants nothing less than the creation of a new branch of government—the popular branch—at state and federal levels. In this branch, randomly selected groups of citizens come together to deliberate public issues and, by a two thirds vote, enact laws. He also insists that participation in these deliberations be compulsory (as is current jury service) to achieve representative involvement.

Neither of these two fantasies is likely to become reality anytime soon. But they both challenge the notion that the structural reality we have today is the only pattern our society can stomach. In fact, possibilities for innovative forums are multiplying in the age of the Internet and Web 2.0 as technological developments allow new and fewer time-dependent ways of involvement. Online participation will not solve all current representation problems. The problem of an income- and education-based digital divide is real, but for the age variable, technology may actually increase participant diversity and foster involvement from the traditionally marginalized youth sector (Schlozman, Verba, & Brady, 2010). When the Alfred P. Sloan Foundation funded several projects in which lower-income high schools received handheld computers to monitor neighborhood infrastructure problems, the lure of the technology itself may have been one reason younger citizens (often absent from involvement forums) participated. In a recent poll, younger people, racial minorities, and lower-income people actually expressed more interest than other respondents when asked if they wanted to participate in an online deliberative session on political issues (Neblo, Ryan, Kennedy, & Anand, 2010).

While futuristic scenarios from Box (1998) or Leib (2004) almost certainly do not depict the actual future, they set the stage for asking, How can we change the system to give us the citizen roles we think appropriate now. Each chapter in the book you are reading provides information that may help answer this question.

ORGANIZATION OF CHAPTERS

As any historically grounded analysis of American participation must start with the nation's founding, Masami Nishishiba, Margaret Banyan and Douglas Morgan open the discussion with an analysis of how the founder's conception of "libertarian" democracy influences current participation patterns. They draw linkages between libertarian thought with its emphasis on the private sector and the civic engagement role of voluntary organizations that commentators from Alexis de Tocqueville on have seen as key to

American political involvement. Voluntary organization patterns identified in this historical analysis will emerge as important in many current trends described in other chapters as well.

As my introductory chapter shows, government policies help produce participation forums, techniques, and involvement. The next two chapters explore further how policy influences participation modes. Looking at the national policy level, Thomas Bryer analyzes presidential records to learn the different ways in which various recent administrations have encouraged citizenship. Suzanne Piotrowski and Yuguo Liao then explore the importance of information policies to produce the transparency that participation requires.

Participation trends have multiple dimensions. Three chapters focus on aspects of local involvement. Elaine Sharp provides an analytic overview of participation trends at the local level. Desirai Anderson Crow and J. Richard Stevens examine how information deficits influence the low involvement endemic in local environmental forums. Bill Barnes and Brian Williams explore the role of new technologies in enhancing city and county participation.

We know that the current playing field for civic engagement is far from level. Each racial and ethnic group encounters its own barriers and opportunities that vary among jurisdictions. Patria de Lancer Julnes examines how one group confronts problems and opportunities in her examination of Hispanic participation in Utah. She ties her analysis to a provocative critical theory on the social construction of minority groups.

The next two chapters return to the important role of voluntary organizations in molding participation. Alicia Schatteman examines how Illinois nonprofits have fostered online participation. Angela Eikenberry and Courtney Jensen analyze shifts in the roles nonprofit organizations and voluntary associations have played in civic engagement from Alexis de Tocqueville's era to our own time, sometimes with consequences that limit widespread involvement.

A look at five innovative participation cases follows. These narratives suggest what involvement may accomplish (or fail to accomplish) in particular situations. Larkin Dudley analyzes a mock courtroom experiment on health care costs, Alan Kopetzky looks at citizen participation in urban planning in Nebraska, and Jeremy Harris Lipschultz focuses on deliberative polling as a civic engagement technique.

Contemporary public administration literature contains important debates on the role of citizens in performance-measurement programs. Marc Holzer and Lauren Bock Mullins further this discussion by exploring the advantages that accrue when jurisdictions assign citizens important roles in planning performance measurement. They adumbrate a performance management model that provides a key citizen role.

A succeeding chapter by Holzer, Mullins, Rusi Sun, and Jonathan Woolley analyzes criteria for constructing collaborative governance models involving citizens. Using 21 exemplary cases, they look at issues such as who funds the organizations, who joins, and how such criteria lead to collaborations that can catalyze local reform and development.

Interesting research depends on appropriate and innovative methodologies. But what are the appropriate methods in such a heavily contested field as participation studies? Maria Elías makes a case for the advantages of interpretive phenomenology and provides supporting evidence from a case study. Walt Kuetzel and Curtis Ventriss explore the importance of the sociopsychological literature with its attendant methodologies in this field.

In summarizing the diverse approaches of the various chapters, Kaifeng Yang offers conclusions on the key role of theory building and testing in any intellectual enterprise. He reviews the major findings of these essays, relates their concerns, and identifies some research gaps that need further explication.

Engaging and empowering citizens is a core activity of any democratic polity. These chapters offer much food for thought for researchers intent on understanding the crucial role of citizen participation in America today.

REFERENCES

Ackerman, B., & Fishkin, J. S. (2004). *Deliberation day*. New Haven, CT: Yale University Press.

Adams, B. (2004). Public meetings and the democratic process. *Public Administration Review, 64*(1), 43–54.

Arendt, H. (1963). *On revolution*. New York, NY: Viking.

Barabas, J. (2004). How deliberation affects policy opinions. *American Political Science Review, 98*(4), 687–702.

Barber, B. R. (1990). *Strong democracy: Participatory politics for a new age*. Berkeley: University of California Press.

Barber, B. R. (1998). *A place for us: How to make society civil and democracy strong*. New York, NY: Hill and Wang.

Behn, R. B. (1995). The big questions of public management. *Public Administration Review, 55*(4), 313–324.

Berner, M. M., Amos, J. M., & Morse, R. S. (2011). What constitutes effective citizen participation in local government? Views from city stakeholders. *Public Administration Quarterly, 35*(1), 128–163.

Bingham, R. B., Nabatchi, T., & O'Leary, R. (2005). The new governance: Practices and processes for stakeholder and citizen participation in the work of government. *Public Administration Review, 65*(5), 547–558.

Box, R. (1998). *Citizen governance*. Thousand Oaks, CA: Sage.

Boyte, H. (2005). Reframing democracy: Governance, civic agency, and politics. *Public Administration Review, 65*(5), 536–546.

Breyer, T. (2009). Explaining responsiveness in collaboration: Administrator and citizen role perceptions. *Public Administration Review, 69*(2), 271–283.

Burtt, S. (1993). The politics of virtue today: A critique and a proposal. *American Political Science Review, 87*(2), 360–368.

Campbell, A. (2002). Self-interest, social security, and the distinctive participation patterns of senior citizens. *American Political Science Review, 96*(3), 565–574.

Candler, G., & Dumont, G. (2010). The price of citizenship: Civic responsibility as the missing dimension of public administration theory. *Public Administration Quarterly, 34*(2), 169–201.

Cole, R., & Caputo, D. (1984). The public hearing as an effective citizen participation mechanism. *American Political Science Review, 78*(2), 404–416.

Crosby, N., Kelly, J. M., & Schaefer, P. (1986). Citizen panels: A new approach to citizen participation. *Public Administration Review, 46*(2), 170–178.

DelliCarpini, M. X., & Keeter, S. (1996). *What Americans know about politics and why it matters.* New Haven, CT: Yale University Press.

Dryzek, J., & Tucker, A. (2008). Deliberative innovations to different effect: Consensus conferences in Denmark, France, and the United States. *Public Administration Review, 68*(5), 864–876.

Epstein, P. D., Coates, P. M., Wray, L. D, & Swain, D. (2006). *Results that matter: Improving communities by engaging citizens, measuring performance, and getting things done.* San Francisco, CA: Jossey-Bass.

Fishkin, J. (1997). *The voice of the people: Public opinion and democracy.* New Haven, CT: Yale University Press.

Frederickson, H. G. (1982). The recovery of civism in public administration. *Public Administration Review, 42*(6), 501–508.

Frederickson, H. G. (1991). Toward a theory of the public for public administration. *Administration and Society, 22*(4), 395–417.

Gore, A. J. (1994). The new job of the federal executive. *Public Administration Review, 54*(4), 317–321.

Greenstone, J. D., & Peterson, P. (1973). *Race and authority in urban politics.* New York, NY: Russell Sage.

Grosser, J., & Schram, A. (2006). Neighborhood information exchange and voter participation: An experimental study. *American Political Science Review, 100*(2), 235–248.

Halverson, K. (2006). Critical next steps in research on public meetings and environmental decision making. *Human Ecology Review, 13*(2), 150–160.

Harwood Group. (1991). *Citizens and politics: A view from main street America.* Dayton, OH: Kettering Foundation.

Irvin, R., & Stansbury, J. (2004). Citizen participation in decision making: Is it worth the effort? *Public Administration Review, 65*(5), 55–65.

Kerrigan, J., & Hinton, D. (1980). Knowledge and skill needs for tomorrow's public administrators. *Public Administration Review, 40*(5), 469–473.

King, C. S., Kathryn, K. M., & O'Neill Susel, B. (1998). The question of participation: Toward authentic participation in public administration. *Public Administration Review, 58*(4), 317–326.

Kirlin, J. (1996). The big questions of public administration in a democracy. *Public Administration Review, 56*(5), 416–423.

Leib, E. (2004). *Deliberative democracy in America.* University Park: Pennsylvania State University Press.

Licari, M., McLean, W., & Rice, T. (2005). The condition of community streets and parks: Comparison of resident and nonresident evaluations. *Public Administration Review, 65*(3), 360–368.

Lipsky, M. (1980). *Street level bureaucracy.* New York, NY: Russell Sage.

Mathews, D. (2010). *Preface. In doing democracy: How a network of grassroots organizations is strengthening community, building capacity, and shaping a new kind of civic education* (S. London, Ed.). Dayton, OH: Kettering Foundation.

Melkers, J., & Thomas, J. C. (1998). What do administrators think citizens think? Administrator predictions as an adjunct to citizen surveys. *Public Administration Review, 58*(4), 327–334.

Miller, T., Kobayashi, M. M., & Hayden, S. (2008). *Citizen surveys for local government: A comprehensive guide to making them matter.* Washington, DC: International City/County Management Association.

Mosher, F. (1968). *Democracy and the public service.* New York, NY: Oxford University Press.

Musso, J., Christopher, W., Bryer, T., & Cooper, T. (2011).Toward "strong democracy" in global cities? Social capital building, theory-driven reform and the Los Angeles neighborhood council experience. *Public Administration Review, 71*(1), 102–111.

National Performance Review. (1994). *Putting customers first: Standards for serving the American people.* Washington, DC: U.S. Government Printing Office.

Neblo, M., Ryan, K., Kennedy, D. L., & Anand, S. (2010).Who wants to deliberate— And why? *American Political Science Review, 104*(3), 566–583.

Nie, N., Jane, J., & Stehlik-Barry, K. (1996). *Education and democratic citizenship.* Chicago, IL: University of Chicago Press.

Osborne, D., & Gaebler, T. (1992). *Reinventing government: How the entrepreneurial spirit is transforming government from schoolhouse to state house, city hall to pentagon.* Reading, MA: Addison-Wesley.

Osborne, D., & Plastrik, P. (2000). *The reinventor's fieldbook: Tools for transforming your government.* San Francisco, CA: Jossey-Bass.

Plutzer, E. (2002). Becoming a habitual voter. *American Political Science Review, 96*(1), 41–56.

Poister, T. (2003). *Measuring performance in public and nonprofit organizations.* San Francisco, CA: Jossey-Bass.

Poister, T., & Thomas, J. (2007). The wisdom of crowds: Learning from administrators' predictions of citizen perceptions. *Public Administration Review, 67*(2), 279–289.

Putnam, R. (2000). *Bowling alone.* New York, NY: Simon and Schuster.

Recchuiti, J. (2007). *Civic engagement: Social science and progressive-era reform in New York City.* Philadelphia: University of Pennsylvania Press.

Roberts, N. (1997). Public deliberation: An alternative approach to crafting policy and setting direction. *Public Administration Review, 57*(2), 124–132.

Roberts, N. (2002). Keeping public officials accountable through dialogue: Resolving the accountability paradox. *Public Administration Review, 62*(6), 658–669.

Rosener, J. (1982). Making bureaucracy responsive: A study of the impact of citizen participation and staff recommendations on regulatory decision making. *Public Administration Review, 42*(4), 339–345.

Sandel, M. (1996). *Democracy's discontent.* Cambridge, MA: Belknap Press of Harvard University Press.

Schachter, H. L. (1997). *Reinventing government or reinventing ourselves: The role of citizen owners in making a better government.* Albany: State University of New York Press.

Schachter, H. L. (1998). Civic education: Three early American Political Science Association committees and their relevance for our times. *PS:Political Science and Politics, 31*(3), 631–635.

Schachter, H. L. (2010). Objective and subjective performance measures: A note on terminology. *Administration and Society, 42*(5), 550–567.

Schachter, H. L., & Liu, R. (2005). Policy development and new immigrant communities: A case study of citizen input in defining transit problems. *Public Administration Review, 65*(5), 614–623.

Schlozman, K., Verba, S., & Brady, H. (2010). Weapon of the strong? Participatory inequality and the Internet. *Perspectives on Politics, 8*(2), 487–510.

Skocpol, T. (2003). *Diminished democracy.* Norman: University of Oklahoma Press.

Smith, G., & Huntsman, C. (1997). Reframing the metaphor of the citizen-government relationship: A value-centered perspective. *Public Administration Review, 57*(4), 309–318.

Stivers, C. (1990). The public agency as polis: Active citizenship in the administrative state. *Administration and Society, 22*(1), 86–105.

Strange, J. (1972, September). The impact of citizen participation on public administration. *Public Administration Review, 32*(Special Issue), 459–470.

Swiss, J. (1992). Adapting total quality management (TQM) to government. *Public Administration Review, 52*(4), 356–362.

Thomas, J. C. (1995). *Public participation in public decisions.* San Francisco, CA: Jossey-Bass.

Van Ryzin, G. G., Immerwahr, S., & Altman, S. (2008). Measuring street cleanliness: A comparison of New York City's scorecard and results from a citizen survey. *Public Administration Review, 68*(2), 295–303.

Verba, S., & Nie, N. (1972). *Participation in America: Political democracy and social equality.* Chicago, IL: University of Chicago Press.

Verba, S., Schlozman, K. L., Brady, H., & Nie, N. (1993). Citizen activity: Who participates? What do they say? *American Political Science Review, 87*(2), 303–318.

Walsh, M. (1997). *Building citizen involvement: Strategies for local government.* Washington, DC: International City/County Management Association.

Warren, M. (2001). *Democracy and association.* Princeton, NJ: Princeton University Press.

Watson, D., Robert, J., & Johnson, G. (1991). Institutionalized use of citizen surveys in the budgetary and policy-making processes: A small city case study. *Public Administration Review, 51*(3), 232–239.

Webler, T., & Tuler, S. (2000). Fairness and competence in citizen participation: Theoretical reflections from a case study. *Administration and Society, 32*(5), 566–595.

White, S. (2010). Fullness and dearth: Depth experience and democratic life. *American Political Science Review, 104*(4), 800–816.

Yang, K. (2007). Making performance measurement relevant? Administrators' attitudes and structural orientations. *Public Administration Quarterly, 31*(3), 342–383.

Yang, K., & Callahan, K. (2007). Citizen involvement efforts and bureaucratic responsiveness: Participatory values, stakeholder pressures, and administrative practicality. *Public Administration Review, 67*(2), 249–262.

CHAPTER 2

LOOKING BACK ON THE FOUNDING

Civic Engagement Traditions in the United States

Masami Nishishiba
Portland State University

Margaret Banyan
Florida Gulf Coast University

Douglas F. Morgan
Portland State University

INTRODUCTION

In the United States . . . [there is a widely held belief that] providence has given to each individual, whoever he may be, the degree of reason necessary for him to be able to direct himself in things that interest him exclusively. . . . Extended to the entirety of the nation, it becomes the dogma of the sovereignty of the people.

—de Tocqueville, 2000, p. 381

The State of Citizen Participation in America, pages 21–52
Copyright © 2012 by Information Age Publishing
All rights of reproduction in any form reserved.

21

Tocqueville did not view private voluntarism as an amusing carnival midway of private intentions, but as a fundamental part of a national power system.

—Hall, 1992, p. 85

The American founding experience uniquely frames the role of citizen participation and civic engagement[1] in the United States. While there is ongoing debate over the meaning of this experience, there is widespread consensus that the primary goal of the Declaration of Independence and the U.S. Constitution was to create a system of government that would maximize the enjoyment of individual liberty (Arendt, 1963; Morgan, Green, Shinn, & Robinson, 2008). This libertarian focus of the American political system is commonly understood as negative freedom (Berlin, 1969), which means "freedom from interference, from being pushed around, restricted, locked up" (Held, 1984, p. 124). This negative approach to liberty has three important implications for understanding the debate over citizen participation and civic engagement throughout the course of American history.

First, one's definition of "good citizenship" depends largely on the role that citizens need to play in guarding the political system from the chief threats to liberty. Are these threats most likely to come from the abuse of power by government officials? Are they to come from a system that has too little capacity to enforce the laws needed to protect individual liberty from internal and external threats? Or finally, will *doux commerce*[2] undermine the republican spirit upon which liberty itself rests? In Part I of this chapter, we will review answers to these questions, showing how each set of answers creates a quite different framework for thinking about "good citizenship."

A second implication of the libertarian focus of the American political system is that the public sphere is viewed as quite small and of lesser importance than the private spheres of economic and civic activity. This results in a truncated view of public life and those who spend time making it work.

> The public stage is not regarded as a place where men gather to seek self-understanding and self-enlargement by presenting themselves to others in an open dialogue of thought and action. The citizen is expected to disclose but a fraction of himself to the public gaze ... and regard it as entirely legitimate that he will seek to translate his private will into public policy through whatever political instruments are available to him and we assume that he has a right to keep his political opinions and conclusions to himself. Politics quickly comes to be thought of as a distinctly second-order and instrumental activity and occupation, subordinate to the primary concerns of the private life. (Schaar, 1964, p. 888)

In Part II of this chapter, we will show how these libertarian assumptions have shaped American views of the appropriate relationship of citizens to their governing institutions, resulting in four different models for defining the meaning of "good citizenship."

Finally, in Part III, we will explore the third important implication of the libertarian focus of the American political system, namely, the assumption that citizens will spend the most meaningful part of their life engaging in economic activity and participating in voluntary associations. Alexis de Tocqueville was especially struck in his travels across the United States in the 1830s by the vibrancy and abundance of voluntary associations and the importance they have in facilitating a shared sense of the common good.

> Everywhere...at the head of a new undertaking count on it that you will perceive an association in the United States....The free institutions that the inhabitants of the United States possess...recall to each citizen constantly and in a thousand ways that he lives in society. At every moment they bring his mind back to [the] idea that the duty as well as the interest of men is to render themselves useful to those like them....Sentiments and ideas renew themselves, the heart is enlarged and the human is developed [through participation in these associations]. (de Tocqueville, 2000, pp. 489, 488, 491)

But we have come to discover over the last 150 years that not all associations are equally salutary to the public good, especially in an age of technology in which advocacy groups can be created and multiplied without ever "enlarging the heart." In Part III of this chapter, we will further explore these considerations and present four different models for better understanding how participation in the voluntary sector contributes to our understanding of what "good citizenship" means in the context of the civic sphere.

PART I. THE AMERICAN FOUNDING: IMPLICATIONS OF LIBERTARIAN DEMOCRACY FOR CITIZEN PARTICIPATION AND CIVIC ENGAGEMENT

As we suggested in the introduction to this chapter, one's definition of "good citizenship" in the American context depends on what kind of role citizens want government to play in securing their liberty. This debate is framed by two simple questions: "Who should govern?" and "What is the proper role of government?" But as the Founders discovered, answers to these questions are not so simple, mainly because of the multitude of ways in which individual liberty can be undermined (Morgan, 2001; Morgan et al., 2008).

The American Revolution began with the Boston Tea Party and the mantra "No taxation without representation." This mantra reflected deep-seated unhappiness with King George and the perception that he was exercising arbitrary and capricious power. To correct this abuse, the colonists not only declared their independence from Great Britain, but they created a corrective against the future tyrannical abuse of executive power by establishing both national- and state-level systems of government that placed controlling power in the hands of the legislative branch (Thach, 1969). This effort to create more citizen-centered governance quickly succumbed to the reality that without adequate capacity at the executive level, General George Washington could not be supplied with the troops and logistical support necessary to win the war. This prompted a call for a Constitutional Convention to fix the inadequacies of the Articles of Confederation. On the road to the Philadelphia convention, delegates were reminded of the problem of "majority tyranny" by an armed rebellion of farmers in western Massachusetts, who took up arms to forestall foreclosures on their property by local courts (known as Shay's Rebellion). The farmers surrounded the courthouse, threatening to shoot any judge who rendered a foreclosure decision.

The founding deliberations were significantly shaped by the Anti-Federalists who argued against a strong central government, especially one that encourages the private pursuit of material gain and is dependent on a professionalized cadre of experts. Such a government would tend to discourage civic engagement. Once ordinary citizens become disengaged and started to "bowl alone" (Putnam, 2000), the Anti-Federalists believed that this would undermine the kind of eternal vigilance needed to prevent government from pursuing grand, glorious, costly, and elusive adventures at home and abroad, and result in policies that disproportionately advantage the few at the expense of the many (Storing & Dry, 1981a, 1981b).

These contending arguments about what was needed to secure liberty against a multiplicity of dangers resulted in the creation of a complex system of government that significantly confounds the meaning and requirements of "good citizenship." We have summarized this complexity in Table 2.1 below. The left-hand column lists the source of danger to liberty. The middle column summarizes how each of the dangers was addressed by members of the Constitutional Convention. The right-hand column summarizes the implications of the solutions for democratic citizenship. As Table 2.1 suggests, the framers produced two models of "good citizenship," which have been characterized as the "procedural republic" model and the "civic republic." model The contrasting characteristics of these two models are summarized in Table 2.2 (Morgan, et al., 2008, p. 53).

As Tables 2.1 and 2.2 indicate, for the Founding generation, the role of citizens in promoting the public good was problematic because each of the four sources of danger to liberty could not be corrected without making the other problems worse. There was an irreconcilable four-way tension among the need for government competence, popular sovereignty, the preservation of minority rights, and an engaged citizenry. For the Federalists, too little governmental power at the center and majority tyranny were

TABLE 2.1   How to Address the Multiple Threats to Individual Liberty

Sources of Danger to Liberty	Solutions	Citizenship Implications
Arbitrary abuse of power by government officials: "The King George Problem"	• "Rule of Law" prophylactics such as the Bill of Rights • Separation of powers • Checks and balances • Federalism • Strong representative government and frequent elections • Limited and enumerated government powers	• Reliance on representational institutions by which citizens exercise control through periodic elections • Reliance on the "auxiliary precautions" of formal legal structures and processes, which reduce citizenship demands
Weak, incompetent, and fickle government: "The George Washington Problem"	• Strong executive branch • Reliance on experienced leaders with expertise • Separation of powers • Checks and balances • Structural incentives to encourage continuity in office and independent and informed judgment	• Creation of mediating structures that reduce dependence on highly active and knowledgeable citizenry (i.e., Senate chosen by the states, court with life tenure, president elected by an electoral college with no term limits)
Majority tyranny: "The Shay's Rebellion Problem"	• Structural checks and balances, both internally in the government and externally in the socioeconomic setting • Foster a large commercial republic that would create a multiplicity of interests • Bill of Rights	• Reliance on a procedural democracy that places few demands on citizens except to pursue their own interests within a limited legal framework that protects rights
Disengaged citizens and loss of republican virtue: "The Bowling Alone Problem"	• Small, simple, and limited government • Large representative body composed of the "those in middling circumstances" • Constraints on the "emergence of a large commercial republic"	• Reliance on a civic republic in which small, local, and direct democracy is sufficient to address the major problems faced by citizens

far more deleterious to the public interest than the Anti-Federalists' fear of too much power at the center and lack of a spirited and engaged citizenry. In the next section, we use the libertarian focus of the American founding to create four models for describing the relationship of citizens to their formal institutions of government.

TABLE 2.2   Good Citizenship Traditions

	Civic Republic Tradition	Procedural Republic Tradition
Origins	• Anti-Federalists • small agrarian republic	• Federalists • interest group pluralism
Characteristics	• face-to-face communication • emphasis on substantive equality • emphasis on substantive agreement and consensus • emphasis on action, i.e., doing things together rather than getting formal agreement • community good is socially constructed • emphasis on importance of place	• reliance on indirect representation • reliance on procedural equality • emphasis on voting and majority rule principle • community is a legal agreement • emphasis on procedural fairness with open access and right to participate • rule of law orientation • emphasis on rights over duties
Citizenship requirements	• high level of deliberative skills • development of relevant knowledge and expertise • personal participation • citizen ownership and control of decision making	• voting • heavy reliance on interest group participation • opportunity for individuals to give advice and counsel • heavy reliance on elected officials and career administrators
Legitimating criteria	• degree of participation • degree of citizen control • sense of ownership of both process and outcome	• electoral oversight • due notice of important decisions and open access to decision making • opportunity for a "hearing" and right to be heard • procedural fairness in gathering and assessing information

Source: Adapted from Morgan, et al., 2008, p. 53.

PART II. FRAMING CIVIC ENGAGEMENT TRADITIONS IN THE UNITED STATES: "WHO SHOULD GOVERN?" AND "WHAT IS THE PROPER ROLE OF GOVERNMENT?"

As we described in the previous section, civic engagement has been significantly shaped by the way in which the Founders chose to answer the following two questions: "Who should govern?" and "What is the proper role of government?" These two questions in Figure 2.1 below serve as the building blocks of our four models for describing the relationship of citizens to their formal institutions of government. Debate over these core questions has produced some enduring patterns that reflect the kind and quality of civic engagement that is most needed to preserve individual liberty. These

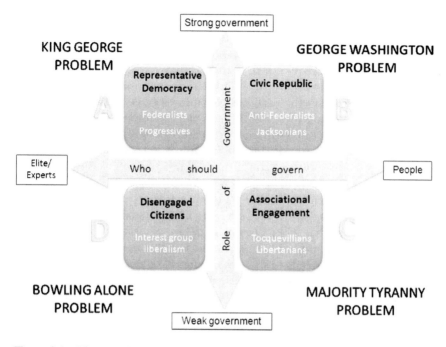

Figure 2.1 The founding debate: How to make democracy successful.

patterns have acquired the institutional status of traditions, which we have organized into four models that are described in greater detail in the sections that follow.

"Who Should Govern?" Dimension (X axis)

The horizontal axis in Figure 2.1 summarizes the range of possible answers to the question of "Who should govern?" The left end of the axis represents those who believe that liberty is best protected by relying on governing experience and expertise. The right end of the axis represents those who believe that democracy is safest when decision making and policy implementation is placed directly in the hands of the people rather than with experts.

As we saw in Part I, the American Revolution celebrated the principle that government should be based on "We the People," which is memorialized in both the Declaration of Independence and the Preamble to the U.S. Constitution. But this "ode to the people" was tempered by the experience of unsuccessfully trying to levy and collect taxes, raise and supply an army, and negotiate complicated relations with foreign nations without an experienced cadre of governing agents who could devote full time to their work. The issue of citizen versus expert-centered governance came into sharp focus in the Constitutional Convention, as delegates debated the kind of government that was most needed to preserve liberty. As an accommodation to control the tyranny of the majority and a lack of energetic government, the framers sought to have the best of both worlds. The establishment of three branches of government (the U.S. Senate, the Presidency, and the Supreme Court) would attract those with more experience and give these individuals the independence to exercise judgment without fear of immediate retribution by voters at the polls. To control for too much power at the center and to ensure that government rested on the "consent of the governed," the rule of experts was tempered by reliance on regular elections, the enumeration of government powers, the development of a system of checks and balances within a federal system, and the adoption of a Bill of Rights.

The American constitutional system of indirect democracy doesn't assume that everyone needs to spend considerable time and energy overseeing the work of their elected representatives. Through a combination of regular elections and institutional checks and balances, the majority of the founding generation believed that liberty could be secured from a multiplicity of dangers. The framers bet on Alexander Hamilton's assumption that the confidence of the people in, and obedience to, a government "will commonly be proportioned to the goodness or badness of its administration," and that the federal institutions they had designed would on the whole produce better administration over time than their state counterparts (Hamilton, Madison, & Jay, 1961, p.174). This Federalist emphasis on expertise as the best security for preserving a regime of ordered liberty has been constantly renewed over the course of American history, first by the Progressive Movement's emphasis on "scientific management" of the business of government and the need for leaders to serve as moral exemplars for the masses. It was refueled again during the New Deal period and kept alive by both World War II and the expansion of the regulatory role of the government, all of which required a growing cadre of trained experts who devoted their careers to public service (Morgan et al., 2008, ch. 4).

As the role of experts in making democracy work has grown over the course of American history, ironically, this has not necessarily come at the expense of those who share the Anti-Federalist and Jeffersonian view of a citizen-centered democracy. This view is represented by the right side of the X axis in Figure 2.1. This side of the axis emphasizes the importance of decentralized government, with a focus on local face-to-face governance in which people take personal responsibility for decision making and policy implementation rather than depending entirely on career experts to do the public's work (Box, 1998). In its extreme form, this model is similar to direct democracy (in contrast to representative democracy), which is found in small geographic areas, such as the New England town meetings, local neighborhood associations, or is represented by co-produced public services in local government (i.e., community policing). This Jeffersonian vision has occasionally captured the hearts and minds of a national constituency and taken on the characteristics of a movement. This has occurred at several key points in American history, starting with the Jacksonian revolution in the 1830s, which introduced the principle of "rotation in office" as an antidote to rule by the rich and privileged elites. It resurfaced during the Populist era in the 1890s as the initiative, referendum, recall, the "long ballot," civil service reform, regulatory control over corruption, and nonpartisan elections were popularized. During this period, the Pendleton Act was passed. The Act created a merit system for the appointment and promotion of career public servants. Reformers argued that such a system was needed to counter the corruption of the principle of "rotation in office," which had deteriorated into the "spoils system," which rewarded individuals for their loyalty to various kinds of ruling elites. The Jeffersonian model resurfaced once again as an important influence in structuring the implementation of President Johnson's antipoverty programs in the 1960s and more recently has been a galvanizing force for the antitax revolt in the West and the Tea Party movement in the 2010 congressional elections.[3]

To summarize, the answer to the question of "Who should govern?" has shifted over the course of American history, much like a pendulum that shifts toward one end of the X axis more than the other, but never to the exclusion of the claims represented by the countervailing antagonist. In this swing, the Federalist emphasis on the importance of experience and expertise has been the protagonist, with the Jeffersonian tradition constantly serving as the preeminent antagonist. As we will see in the next section, a similar story can be told of the answer to the second critical question that has shaped the American civic engagement tradition: "What is the proper role of the government?"

"What is the Proper Role of Government?" Dimension (Y axis)

In Figure 2.1, the vertical Y axis represents contending views regarding the proper role of government within American democracy. The upper end of the Y axis represents the view that the government should be taking an active role in protecting individual liberty. For the purpose of this chapter, we refer to this idea as a "strong government" role. The bottom end of the Y axis represents the view that institutions other than the government should take an active part in the protection of individual liberty, with government playing a minimum role. In this chapter, we refer to this idea as a "weak government" role.

As we noted earlier in Part I, American democracy rests on the principle that the most important goal of government is to protect individual liberty. But this begs the question of what most endangers liberty—too little or too much government? The answer to these questions has resulted in dynamic shifts in the extent to which government is treated as a separate but limited actor within a larger system of market and civil society actors and the extent to which the market and civil society play a distinctively separate role in preserving individual liberty.

Framework for Civic Engagement Traditions: Four Quadrants

When the two dimensions in Figure 2.1 (Who should govern? and What is the proper role of government?) are laid out orthogonally, it produces four quadrants. The upper left corner of the coordinate, labeled Quadrant A, represents the idea that "Elite/experts should govern under strong government." The upper right corner of the coordinate, labeled Quadrant B, represents the idea that "People should govern under strong government." The lower right corner of the coordinate, labeled Quadrant C, represents the idea that "People should govern under weak government." And finally, the lower left corner of the coordinate, labeled Quadrant D, represents the idea that "Elite/expert should govern under weak government." To each of these quadrants we have added the particular threat to individual liberty that the quadrant is seeking to address, which we have discussed in our summary of the Founding debates.

In the following sections, we will explain how each one of these ideas was represented by different political philosophies at play during the founding era, what institutional problems each quadrant creates, and the implications each quadrant has for the American civic engagement traditions.

Elite/Experts Govern Under Strong Government—Representative Democracy Model (Quadrant A)

The reign of King George at the end of the colonial period represents the extreme case of elite/experts governing under a strong government model. But as described in the Declaration of Independence, this governing elite abused its power, resulting in oppression of the people. Reaction to this "King George Problem" spawned the Boston Tea Party and the famous "Ride of Paul Revere," calling for the creation of a new system that would check the abusive exercise of government power by domineering officialdom. As a consequence, the newly adopted state constitutions (with New York the exception) and the Articles of Confederation focused on limiting the power of the executive branch of government by creating strong legislative authority in an effort to give more power to the people through indirect representation (Thach, 1969). This resulted in a shift from the *elite/expert* end of the "Who should govern continuum" toward the *citizen* end of the continuum. In making this shift during the early days of the Revolutionary War period, the states were assumed to be the primary agents of governing through their systems of indirect rather than direct representation. The states were held together under a weak confederation model that embodied the procedural republic and representative democracy assumptions of the Federalist tradition.

People Govern Under Strong Government—Civic Republic Model (Quadrant B)

The shift of power from the executive to the legislative branch of government was short-lived. The excitement of "giving all power to the people" soon foundered on the shoals of trying to raise and collect taxes, field and support an army, and conduct sensitive foreign relations under a citizen-centered system of government. Realizing that more power was needed at the executive level to solve the "George Washington Problem" resulted in the call for a Constitutional Convention to revise the Articles of Confederation. This "call" produced a shift back toward a strong expert-centered government or the middle of Quadrant A, which was fiercely opposed by the Anti-Federalist antagonists who held on to what has come to be called a civic republican model of democratic governance.

The civic republic tradition argues that strong and safe government is only possible if it is nurtured by three sets of conditions, one having to do with geography, one having to do with the complexity of the "business of government," and one having to do with the character of the people themselves. First, the Anti-Federalist antagonists continually reminded their Federalist colleagues that liberty could not be maintained over a large and extended territory like the United States. This was because a large and bountiful territory would require a large standing army to protect the frontiers from invasion by greedy and envious foreign powers. A standing army would be costly to maintain and eventually would develop a will of its own that would endanger the liberty of the people. For these reasons, the Anti-Federalists defended a federal system that preserved states as the more important governing unit for meeting the basic needs of citizens.

An important part of the civic republican argument of the Anti-Federalists was a long-standing fear that is reflected in Lord Acton's famous observation that "power tends to corrupt and absolute power corrupts absolutely" (Acton Institute, 2012; originally appeared in *Letter to Bishop Mandell Creighton*, 1887). Another version of this fear is captured by Michel's "iron law of oligarchy" (Michels, Paul, Paul, & Lipset, 1968, p. 224), which argues that the self-serving goals of leaders displace the goals of the organization the longer they hold office. This perspective argues in favor of short and limited terms of office, keeping the business of government simple such that, in the words of Andrew Jackson, "the duties of all public offices are, or at least admit to being made, so plain and simple that men of intelligence may readily qualify themselves for their performance" (Richardson, 1899, p. 448).

Finally, the civic republic model requires the right kind of moral character among the citizenry. The Anti-Federalists worried that the energies of the people in a large commercial republic would be mobilized to increase trade and commerce in the service of what Patrick Henry in the Virginia ratifying convention characterized as "grandeur, power and splendor," rather than in guarding their liberties. "Those nations who have gone in search of grandeur, power and splendor have also fallen a sacrifice, and been the victims of their own folly. While they acquired those visionary blessings, they lost their freedom" (Storing & Dry, 1981a, p. 214). Needed most was a vigilant temperament, and this was thought to exist especially among those in "middling circumstances," who "are inclined by habit, and the company with whom they associate, to set bounds to their passions and appetites." The substantial yeomanry of the country were thought to be "more temperate, of better morals, and less ambition, than the great" (Storing & Dry, 1981a, p. 158).

In summary, the civic republic tradition of government places a high value on individual liberty, to be sure, but this is nurtured "within the fabric of a relatively small and homogenous community whose citizens operate according to a shared moral code and a respect for social norms" (Brinkley, Polsby, Sullivan, & Lewis, 1997, p. 93). The civic republic tradition recognizes the "strong" role of government in protecting the liberty of the citizens. However, the power and authority of the government is "less trustworthy the more it [is] dissociated from the participatory practice of local politics" (Wolin, 1989, p. 188). But the chief danger of the civic republic model is that it provides little protection against popular mobs like Shay's Rebellion and more generally, majority tyranny, which we will discuss further in the next section.

People Govern Under Weak Government—Associational Engagement Model (Quadrant C)

Another important long-standing governance tradition relies on the libertarian foundations of the American political system to argue that citizens have the wisdom and decency to govern themselves and that government needs only to stay out of their way (Brinkley et al., 1997). This libertarian view relies on private social institutions and the market economy to protect individual liberty and maintain social order.

Alexis de Tocqueville was struck by this libertarian quality of American life in his travels across the United States in the 1830s.

Americans of all ages, all conditions, all minds constantly unite. Not only do they have commercial and industrial associations in which all take part, but they also have a thousand other kinds: religious, moral, grave, futile, very general and very particular, immense and very small. (de Tocqueville, 2000, p. 489)

De Tocqueville believed that this active associational participation among American citizens was due to "the extraordinary fragmentation of administrative power" (de Tocqueville, 2000, pp. 494–495), which requires citizens to gather with others to meet their personal needs and solve common problems rather than rely on the government.

De Tocqueville believed he was witnessing the formative stages of an entirely new social order that had never existed in previous history, in which the cohering glue was provided by people taking control of their own liberty without any seemingly direct influence of formal governing authority. Instead, the cohering forces of society seemed to be operating informally as a result of the free association of individuals exercising their liberty to engage in commerce, practice their religion, and join with other like-minded individuals to share beliefs and advocate causes within a rule of law system.

This libertarian model has gathered renewed support from many contemporary civic-minded libertarians who are advocating a return to the Tocquevillian ideal that is "egalitarian," "individualistic," "decentralized," "religious," "property loving," and "lightly governed" (Barone, 1996). This ideal assumes that many of the functions performed by the government can be transferred to the multicolored cloth of voluntary associations.

One of the weaknesses of the Tocquevillian ideal was prominently on the minds of the Founders during the debates at the Constitutional Convention in 1787. As we observed in Part I of this chapter, the specter of Shay's Rebellion hung in the background of the founding debates. The Framers were keenly aware that the free association of individuals in civil society and the private market place can result in "tyranny of the majority" expressing its will through an unchecked legislative majority. This fear guided the Framers' thinking in constructing a system of checks and balances, separation of powers, and designing other strategies that would confound, confuse, and check the ability of tyrannous majorities to organize and act to achieve their goals.

According to James Madison, the single most important safeguard against tyrannous majorities was to "enlarge the orbit" by expanding the geographic boundaries of the United States and encouraging unfettered access to the development of its resources. This model of a large commercial republic has provided the basis for the rise of "interest group liberalism" (Lowi, 1979, pp. 50–63) with the attendant problems of "bowling alone" (Putnam, 2000). This will be the focus of our discussion of the last quadrant in the next section.

Elites/Experts Govern Under Weak Government—Disengaged Citizens Model (Quadrant D)

Perhaps the most unique contribution to the Constitutional Convention debates was made by James Madison. He argued that liberty could be more confidently secured in a large commercial republic than if it were left in the attendant hands of the existing states. He developed this argument more fully in the now famous *Federalist* #10, in which he reasoned that by "enlarging the orbit," the federal government would spawn a greater multiplicity of interests and that the growth of these interests within a large commercial republic would make it more difficult for any single interest to see what it had in common with others. And if a common interest were to coalesce into some kind of tyrannous majority, the sheer expanse of territory would make it more difficult for a tyrannical majority to take common action that would threaten the rights of the minority (see Hamilton, Madison, Jay, 1961, *Federalist* #10). In short, a large and commercially diverse territory with open access to development would fragment opinion, multiply sectarian organizations, and balkanize the formation of interest groups.

Madison's model requires that government play only a relatively small but critical role in providing the infrastructure that "greases the skids" for the expansion and growth of civil society and the market economy. Alexander Hamilton's *Report on Manufacturers* (Hamilton, 1791) and his early efforts as Secretary of Treasury to create a system of public credit and debt management helped stabilize the young American economy and set it on a course for prosperous commercial and agricultural development. The regulation of the economy through the Federal Reserve Board's use of refined monetary policies to manipulate interest rates exemplifies the exercise of this "soft" and unobtrusive use of government power at work today.

Various authors (e.g., John, 1995; Lowi, 1979; Skocpol, 1997) have reminded us that this kind of facilitative role on the part of government has played an important part not only in the development of America's system of commerce but also in the robust development of associations. For example, John (1995) points out that during the 1830s and 1840s, the U.S. Postal System was one of the biggest government operations in the United States. The institutional structure of the U.S. government and U.S. postal rules contributed to the spread of a postal network, and the resultant active use of information exchange among civic associations through mail and newspapers (Skocpol, 1997).

This underlying reliance on government infrastructures by civic associations continued through the late 19th century and most of the 20th century. Small local associations spread geographically and expanded their network in order to take advantage of "the opportunity to join together with like-minded others in crusades, associations, and parties that could make a difference—even at the level of the entire nation" (Skocpol, 1997, p. 472).

As the associations' networks expanded, their need to develop stronger ties with the extra-local government also grew. Unless they were purely local, many of these associations moved their headquarters to New York City and Washington, DC, where their professional staff could work directly with government policymakers. Consequently, many civic associations became disassociated from the local citizens as the associational activities were taken over by the professional staff (i.e., the experts). Professionalization of civic associations resulted in the rise of what has come to be called "interest group liberalism."

Interest group liberalism is a system of powerful interest groups that are run by professional experts who have close working relationships with government officials at the legislative and executive levels of government. Sometimes called the "iron triangle," the three sides of the triangle consist of key members of congress who are responsible for funding and providing oversight of a particular program, a federal agency that administers the program, and last, the trade associations and lobbying groups that are the chief beneficiaries of the program. There is a common interest among these three sets of participants to craft solutions to problems that result in a weak role for government and policy without the teeth of law (Lowi 1979, see especially ch. 5). This condition is represented in Quadrant D of Figure 2.1.

One of the implications of interest group liberalism for civic engagement is that ordinary citizens are not a part of this system of governance. Over time, citizens may become cynical and feel disenfranchised. Despite elections, the same groups of insiders end up being the "real decision makers." As a result, citizens may start to feel that they can no longer "band together to get things done either through or in relationship to government" (Skocpol, 1997, p. 472). When the frustration mounts to a boiling point, they may decide to form a movement to throw the rascals out. But a more likely result is that citizens decide to largely disengage from political and civic life. As Putnam (2000) and others note, American citizens over the last two decades have significantly reduced their participation in political and civic organizations. Instead, they have opted to live in gated communities, become couch potatoes, and metaphorically, "bowl alone."

Section Summary

The history of American civic engagement is a story of enduring uncertainty and disagreement about "Who should govern?" and "What is the proper role of government?" While answers to these two questions have changed over the course of American history, they have resulted in four different models that norm the behavior of citizens toward their governing institutions. The upper Quadrants A and B in Figure 2.1 represent two models that establish strong norms in favor of active participation in political and civic life, with the *civic republic* model setting a higher standard than the *representative democracy* model. The lower Quadrants C and D represent two models that create weak norms in favor of citizen participation in the formal institutions of governance. For the *associational engagement* model, the norm is weak because the greatest source of security for individual liberty is believed to reside in associations, not in government. For the *disengaged citizen* model, the participation norm is weak because people assume that the real decision-making power is in the hands of a small group of professional experts and "insider elites." As we will see in the next section, the complexity of what it takes to make democratic governance work has grown even more complicated as a result of the powerful role that civic associations play in the civic sector.

PART III. THE CIVIC SECTOR

As we described in the previous section, civic engagement has been significantly shaped by the way in which the Founders chose to answer the following two questions: "Who should govern?" and "What is the proper role of government?" The libertarian focus of the American founding has not only had a profound influence in shaping our various definitions of citizenship, but it has also shaped the way in which we view the proper role of civic associations in their relationship to governing institutions. This relationship has received much greater attention over the last two decades both because of the increased reliance on civic associations to provide government services and also because the United State houses the largest and most diverse array of civic associations than is found anywhere else in the world. In 2010, there were 1,569,572 tax-exempt nonprofit organizations, which included public charities, private foundations, and other types. In 2006, these organizations had more than $4 trillion in assets and paid out 8.11% of all wages and salaries in the United States (National Center for Charitable Statistics, 2010).

Civic associations have long been considered especially important in America's individualist-centered system of government for the role they play in the development of a commitment to the larger community good. In pursuit of a common goal with others, citizens learn to resolve problems, build civic skills, and create social capital (Putnam, 1993; Smidt, den Dulk, Penning, Monsma, & Koopman, 2008). By facilitating an environment that is relational and dialogic, associations perform a mediating function between citizens and government by collecting the interests of their members and transforming these interests into values that are expressed to governing institutions (Berger & Neuhaus, 1996; Couto, 1999; Pinkerton, 1996; Reid, 1999).

While civic associations are generally viewed as important for developing public, spirited, and engaged citizens, it would be wrong to conclude that all forms are mediating institutions and equally contribute to the social and civic engagement of Americans. We offer several observations as evidence for this conclusion. First, the rise in nonprofit organizations has not resulted in a similar rise in civic participation. In fact, civic engagement has steadily declined in the United States, especially since 1985, with the largest decline occurring among those who are the most educated (Putnam, 2000). The second is the observation that modern nonprofit organizations are tasked with providing public services to clients rather than merely meeting the dialogical and associational needs of their members (Hall, 1992; Smith & Lipsky, 1993). Further, international comparisons of civic engagement suggest that institutions greatly influence patterns of civic engagement. For example, Schofer and Fourcade-Gourinchas (2001) point out that civic engagement in Germany is largely expressed through the institutional tradition of participating in unions and political parties, compared to the United States where citizens have higher levels of participation in religious organizations. Francis Fukuyama's (1995) comparative study of trust demonstrates the importance of family relationships in Asian countries, which lessens the importance of civic engagement in favor of "relationship-based" approaches to governance.

In this section, we critically examine the broad assumption that all civic associations are the "backbone of political voice in communities across the country" (Reid, 1999, p. 2). We argue that there are two sets of conditions that determine how well associations serve this "backbone" role: the institutional role of civic associations within the larger political arena and the manner in which these associations collect the values of their members. These two dimensions are illustrated in Figure 2.2. The horizontal axis represents the degree to which a civic association serves the narrow interests of its members on the far left of the X axis or has an expressed commitment to integrating the diverse values of the community into a larger shared sense of the common good. The vertical axis represents the degree to which a civic association defines its mission narrowly at the bottom of the Y axis or has a larger goal of making public policy changes in the external political environment. As in the previous section, we will use these two dimensions as the building blocks for developing four models for describing the relationship of civic associations to the formal institutions of government and to the communities within which they do their work. In the following section, we address the Y axis, which describes the role of civic associations in policymaking within the larger external political environment. The top of the Y axis represents a strong role for civic associations in influencing policy. The bottom represents a weakened role for civic associations in policymaking and focuses on their contribution to service delivery.

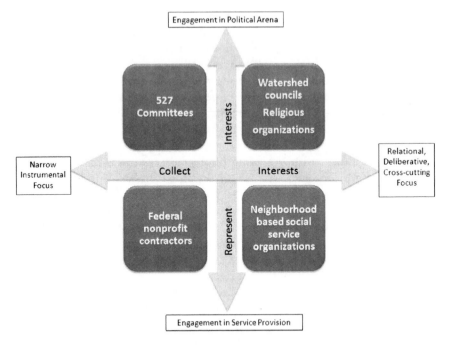

Figure 2.2   The civic role of nonprofit organizations.

"The Role of Associations in Relationship to Government" Dimension (Y axis)

The early history of charitable associations illustrates considerable differences of opinion as to whether government should encourage their development and how valuable they were to society.[4] Some associations "were unquestionably more important than others in the nation's economic and cultural development" (Hall, 1992, p. 32). The history of civic associations in the United States is characterized by two key debates surrounding the sector's involvement in political affairs. At the center of the first debate is the question of whether associations are primarily self-serving organized factions or whether they on the whole contribute to the development of civic virtue and allegiance to the state. At the center of the second and more recent debate is the question of whether government should encourage extensive reliance on civic associations for the delivery of public services.

Unsettled Ideas and Undemocratic Roots

In Hall's history of the development of the nonprofit sector in the United States, he observes that Americans have constantly

> argued about whether voluntary associations threatened democracy by permitting small groups of citizens, particularly the wealthy, to exercise power disproportionate to their numbers, or whether such bodies were essential to a citizenry that, without them, would be powerless to influence the state. (Hall, 1992, p. 15)

Early on, the issue of granting charters to corporations was of central importance to this debate. Control over corporate charters affected educational institutions and charitable foundations. Some of the early American colonies expressed different levels of anxiety over whether to give corporations control over their charters. Due to a fear of faction and excessive control, some colonies denied charters to anyone other than "politically and religiously reliable leaders" (Hall, 1992, p. 21). States such as Virginia repealed the Elizabethan Statute of Charitable Uses, seized the endowment funds of the Anglican church, and redistributed their assets to the county.

The perceived value of associations and who they served framed part of this debate. The Federalists and elite proponents of corporations saw civic associations as a means to counteract the electoral majority and tyranny of the majority. They "disparaged democratic institutions through which the majority pursued its purposes" and believed that the associations being formed by industrial workers were dangerous alliances of "'weak,' 'narrow minded' and 'dependent'" people (Hall, 1992, p. 32). These elites viewed corporations as an opportunity to serve as the moral keepers of the republic, as they alone would possess greater wisdom in determining civic affairs. They also viewed corporations as a means to preserve liberty by proliferating interests that would serve to counterbalance other interests. Others saw associations as a means to counter elite power and place more power in the hands of the people.

Over time, the federal courts, then the states, upheld the rights of charitable corporations. The rights of corporations were first upheld on the basis of contract law and then later on the basis of the right to hold funds. Part of the reason for this reversal was the Federalist influence, which saw charitable corporations as important for pluralism with the ability to temper excessive democracy. Where once the church controlled the vices of the citizens, a looser set of social restrictions endangered traditional sources of power. As a result, "conservatives began to cast about for alternatives to political power—and one area of interest was the law, especially laws that permitted individuals and groups to act in the name of the public without being directly accountable to the public" (Hall, 1992, p. 171). Over time, the rights of all corporations—business, associational, and charitable—became firmly and legally entrenched. Civic associations began to control significant wealth and as a result, enlarged their role in making policy. For example, the Russell Sage Foundation, the Brookings Institution, and the Twentieth Century Fund directed their wealth at research activity that would influence public policy. Although the institutional development of the sector highlights the deep fear of faction, associations became deeply imbedded in the legal system and an increasingly institutionalized source of elite influence over public policy.

Demands for Service Delivery, the Fear of Socialism, and Interpenetration of Government and Associations

As the role of associations in influencing public policy grew, government dependence on the charitable sector also increased. Prior to the Civil War, civic associations, especially religious institutions, were the source of morality and voluntarism (Smidt et al., 2008). They were also a source of considerable organization and energy. As Progressives began to demand an increased role on the part of the national government in providing clientele-serving programs, there was a significant dearth of government expertise. At the same time, however, a fear of socialism was instrumental in deterring massive government intervention. This fear emanated from the belief, discussed above, that government intervention itself was a threat to liberty (Karl, 1998). The increased push for expertise at the federal level caused the government to turn to religious institutions, which had the expertise that was needed. As owners and operators of hospitals and universities, they had experience and skill in professional management. From the 1920s to the 1950s, the number of nonprofit organizations grew and took on an expanded role in delivering public services. The Roosevelt administration added momentum to this development by reforming the tax code with the goal of increasing the level of wealth and corporate giving. This stimulated a significant rise in the number of civic associations, which continued throughout the 1950s–1990s as the federal government invested in institutions such as the National Science Foundation, the National Institute of Health, and universities. The role of civic associations in delivering government services continued to increase even as President Ronald Reagan attempted to divest the government from funding social services. His attempts to reduce funding and hand over the responsibility to civic associations proved to be ineffective. Reagan's attempts made it clear that much of the sector was so heavily dependent upon federal funding that it did not have the financial capacity to stand on its own without government's continued support. As a result, the federal government continued its public funding of services through private nonprofit organizations.

The increased reliance on the charitable sector to provide government-funded services had a profound impact on the sector. In order to compete successfully for federal dollars, the sector began to orient itself toward increased professionalism and became less dependent on volunteers. This shifted control downward from volunteer boards to staff and caused some organizations to change their missions to meet federal contract requirements (Smith & Lipsky, 1993).

The evolution of the charitable sector has several implications for understanding the institutional context of civic engagement. First, as outlined above, there remains a deep ambivalence regarding the relationship of the sector to government. This ambivalence stems from a concern that associations, on the one hand, can become factions that are dangerous to the well-being of the state. On the other hand, associations can serve as a powerful inspiration for civic and moral action as well as efficient agents for the delivery of social services. A second source of ambivalence is the emergence of increasingly dependent and professionalized organizations, which has resulted in a homogenization of values and deference to the priorities of government rather than concern for the dialogical and affiliation needs of association members (Hall, 1992; Smith & Lipsky, 1993). For this reason, some have argued that civic associations should be truly independent of the state (Besharov, 1996; Green, 1996), especially if they are to be successful in performing their advocacy role on behalf of their members in the public policy arena. Still others have argued that independence for some nonprofit organizations while funding others might result in a political landscape that is dominated by wealthier interests (Reid, 1999). Wealthier organizations that might not depend on the state for support are most able to freely express their political interests. Those that represent lower income interests and are funded by government have limited flexibility to advance the policy goals of their members.

To summarize, there is a range of relationships that civic associations can have with the formal structures of government. At one end are policy-driven relationships in which the primary purpose of the association is to shape the values of citizens and mobilize citizen support to influence public policy. At the other end of spectrum are contract-driven relationships in which the main goal of the association is to provide public services. Should we be concerned that using nonprofits as agents of government service delivery can seriously undermine their role in facilitating democratic engagement, or should we be more concerned that aggressively promoting their involvement will unleash an unhealthy spirit of faction? A lot is at stake in how we answer this question, but in the end, it may be a false choice. As was clearly demonstrated by the 2010 congressional campaigns, the newly found right of corporations to freely spend money to influence campaign outcomes reminds us that access to, and use of, money may be more important than either political independence or commitment to use that independence to facilitate civic engagement. In the next section, we will continue to explore the role of associations in facilitating civic engagement by examining the role they play with citizens in the community.

"The Role of Associations in Engaging Citizens" Dimension (X Axis)

In this section, we turn from the vertical relationship of civic associations to the formal institutions of governance to the horizontal relationship these associations have with citizens in the community. As noted above in Figure 2.2, the horizontal axis represents the degree to which a civic association serves the narrow interests of its members on the far left of the X axis or has an expressed commitment to integrating the diverse values of the community into a larger shared sense of the common good at the far right of the X axis.

Several scholars have been particularly concerned with how well-connected organizations are to the larger community of which they are a part. The relationship to the community is critically important, for it is the organization that teaches civic skills, provides the forum for engagement, and has "a role in shaping the quality of a citizen's interaction with the state" (Smidt et al., 2008, p. 37). Generally, these scholars focus on the "embeddedness" of the organization within the community (Berger & Neuhaus, 1996; Couto, 1999; Selznick, 1992; Wogaman, 1980). The horizontal axis in Figure 2.2 represents the scope and manner in which community interests are collected: deeply relational or instrumental, deliberative or unreflective, and cross-cutting or specific. Each of these factors will be discussed more thoroughly in the sections to follow.[5]

Relational, Deliberative, and Cross-Cutting

Relational

It is no surprise that associations have been heralded as the locus of democratic engagement, especially since many of the associations that de Tocqueville described were deeply tied to their respective communities. They were, as Smith and Lipsky (1993) wrote, "essential to a democratic way of life" (p. 26). This "essence" was due to their unique claim to legitimacy through an imbedded relationship with the community (Smith & Lipsky, 1993). Selznick (1992) describes these kinds of organizations as being "thickly institutionalized." By that he means organizations whose goals are functionally and morally intertwined with their community. For example, a community may have a civic organization that serves as the collective memory and conscience of the community, providing a forum for the exchange of information and debate on issues that are central to the well-being of the community and its citizens. There are three factors that characterize this kind of thickly institutionalized association: the organization acts as a moral agent for the community, it plays a role in constituting community, and it is interactive with other community organizations (Selznick, 1992). At the other extreme, we can identify examples of civic associations whose "animating purpose" (Selznick, 1992, p. 238) is instrumental. These organizations make no claim to a community-based moral authority and exist merely to achieve a singular goal. Lacking this fundamental relationship with a community, it is difficult or impossible for citizens to influence the organization's mission in any meaningful way. A lack of a relationship with the community makes it unlikely, or impossible, for the organization to collect member's values.

Deliberative

The organization's relationship with the community is, in part, driven by its deliberative qualities. De Tocqueville recognized this quality in the early Protestant religious organization in New England. Allen (2006) noted that the Protestants had a core belief in shared authority and social unity. "The sum of these qualities produced not only the striving, voluntaristic societies about which Tocqueville read but also polities characterized by a tremendous amount of individual reflection, collective deliberation, and constitutional and collective choice" (pp. 13–14). The deliberative quality is considered to be essential as a developmental tool for civic judgment. Civic judgment is important for creating a shared language of the common good as well as for negotiating conflicts among values (Etsioni, 1988; Fox & Miller, 1996; Matthews, 1996; Smidt et al., 2008; Steinberger, 1993).[6] What is important is the way in which the organization collects values rather than the purpose for which it was formed. At the same time, however, those nonprofit organizations that primarily deliver services might, by necessity, focus less on the deliberative aspects of their work.

Cross-cutting

It should be no surprise that religion and volunteering are strongly linked, given the importance of religion to the formation of republican and civic virtue (Smidt et al., 2008). For example, Greeley noted that in 1992, some 28% of volunteers freely donated time for religious purposes. Further, he pointed out that religious involvement in volunteering went far beyond church-related issues, but included education, politics, human services, and health (Greeley, 1997). Though de Tocqueville worried about vapid American faith traditions, they no doubt played an important role in establishing a culture of engagement that was focused on the cross-cutting community needs (Smidt et al., 2008).

Secular examples of organizations that demonstrate the two ends of the X axis are found in watershed councils and 527 committees. Watershed councils began as narrowly focused organizations interested in water quality. Over time, however, they began to become institutionalized and found that the good of the watershed was tied to the good of the community. Community and watershed health depended on the engagement of citizens in diverse policy arenas, multiple jurisdictions, across sectors, and broad social concerns (Rogue Basin Watershed, 2008). This is contrasted with those organizations in which activity is limited to narrow and specific issues. For example, 527 committees are tax-exempt organizations whose purpose is to collect money for political activity. While they are prohibited from endorsing particular candidates, they are allowed to engage in voter mobilization and purchase political ads. Reports on 527 committees shows that in 2010, the top five committees expended over $70 million dollars on political activity (Open Secrets.org, 2010) directed at narrow interests that ranged from conservative to liberal but were not cross-cutting in their influence over broad community needs.

As discussed above, civic associations have framed the institutional environment in which citizens participate. Organizations that mediate between individuals and society are relational, deliberative, and cross-cutting. They provide the framework in which civic engagement is learned, developed, and practiced.

Section Summary: Representing and Collecting the Public Interest

Our discussion of civic associations has emphasized that certain organizations are better-suited at collecting and representing the public interest than others. We have identified two dimensions we believe are important in helping to classify civic associations with respect to their "public interest" potential. As noted above, the vertical dimension focuses on the role of civic associations in expressing collective interests through policy advocacy. The ongoing debate and conflict over this role is reflected in the diversity of organizations that compose the civic sector. The horizontal dimension accounts for how the civic association collects the interests of its members. The two extremes of this dimension help account for the differences among organizations in terms of the extent to which they are relational, deliberative, and cross-cutting. Using these dimensions, we can begin to build a preliminary typology of organizations based on the extent to which they facilitate civic engagement at the organizational level of analysis. We have provided exemplary organizations that illustrate the range of possibilities represented by the four quadrants in Figure 2.2. Certainly, there are specific organizations that do not neatly fall within the quadrants we have assigned. For example, plenty of neighborhood social service organizations are deeply engaged in policy advocacy, and many religious organizations steer clear of political work. However, the value of the model is that it helps us frame the question about what kinds of organizations are best-suited to facilitate civic engagement. This is particularly important for those who argue that "the relationship to the community depends upon the relationship to government" (Smith & Lipsky, 1993, p. 40).

If ensuring liberty through greater civic engagement is a matter best left to civil society, we should then be keenly aware of the impact of the legal and institutional choices made with respect to the nonprofit sector. Absent reflection and specificity, we have a vague general notion that civic associations will deliver services, engage members, advocate on behalf of policy issues, and enhance pluralism. Yet these roles are often in conflict with each other and are in conflict with "enlarging the heart" or "developing humans." How this question is resolved for civic associations and the nonprofit sector depends on how we answer the question about the role of citizens in government: What kind and how much engagement is needed to preserve liberty?

CONCLUSION

Over the course of American history, the debate over what kind and how much civic engagement is needed to preserve a regime of ordered liberty has for the most part mirrored the founding debates over what dangers are most likely to sink the ship of democratic liberty. For the Founding generation, the role of citizens in promoting the public good was problematic because each of the four sources of danger to liberty could not be corrected without making the others worse. There was an irreconcilable four-way tension among the need for government competence, popular sovereignty, the preservation of minority rights, and an engaged citizenry. For the Federalists, too little governmental power at the center and majority tyranny were far more deleterious to the public interest than the Anti-Federalists' fear of too much power at the center and lack of a spirited and engaged citizenry. The tensions among these competing dangers are nicely summarized by the following "Beatitudes."

The Founding Beatitudes

Too much power begets usurpation, to which majority rule is a corrective;

Too much majority rule begets majority tyranny, to which separation of powers and checks and balances is a corrective;

> Too much separation of powers and checks and balances begets incompetent government, to which unity at the center is a corrective;
>
> Too much unity at the center begets usurpation, to which civic engagement is a corrective. (Morgan et al., 2008, p. 56)

Over the course of American history, there has been a tendency for swings toward a stronger role for government to coincide with greater reliance on experts and conversely, for swings toward a weaker role for government to coincide with a greater reliance on citizens. For example, the Progressive Era, the New Deal, the New Frontier, and the Great Society periods of American history are marked by the desire to increase the role of government by relying upon a cadre of professional experts to achieve the goals of a stronger central government. Likewise, the Jackson and Reagan presidential periods were marked by pushes to weaken the regulatory role of the central government in favor of relying more on the voluntary action of citizens and associations at the local levels of government. But this "mirroring" of the two dimensions of our model in Figure 2.1 is misleading. What is particularly interesting about these pendulum swings is the results that are produced when the advocates for strengthening the role of the central government do so because they want to empower the role of citizens over experts, or conversely, when they want to weaken the role of government in order to strengthen the role of experts. The "taxpayer revolt" in the western United States over the last several decades, the Tea Party Movement in the 2010 Congressional elections, and the debate over public support of religious institutions reflect the desire to use the full power of the federal government to strengthen citizen control at the grassroots level. Conversely, there are strong defenders of weakening the role of government because they know it will strengthen the influence of insider experts in the key decision-making processes of government. This view is reflected in the recent debates over health care, banking regulation, and strategies for economic recovery. These complex and, perhaps, counterintuitive outcomes are brought into sharper focus by examining the four quadrants that result from our two-dimensional framework for understanding the role of citizens in interacting with their governing institutions.

Implicit in this analysis is that no matter where one places the locus of power—with experts or citizens or with government or civil society—there are risks to liberty. Our basic notions of the role of government are in conflict with each other but are deeply rooted in American political theory and imbedded in institutional traditions. The Hobbsean liberal tradition, which makes personal security against violent death the preeminent goal, produces a strong government. The Lockean liberal tradition, which makes liberty to pursue one's personal interests the preeminent goal, produces a more benign government whose role is to provide the enabling conditions for this liberty to be enjoyed. But this libertarian consensus still results in roles that are confusing, disjointed, and conflicting for citizens, for government, as well as for civic associations. The models presented in Parts II and III illustrate the tensions that keep our system in balance, much like a centripetal force that pulls objects toward the middle.

There are four major contributions that this chapter makes to the ongoing discussion on civic engagement in the United States. First, most models of political and civic engagement are not that useful in the American setting because of their generic assumption that participation can be organized on a continuum that puts direct democracy on one end of the spectrum and representative government on the other end.[7] But as this chapter illustrates, such a view obscures the peculiar American preoccupation with creating a system that secures liberty from a multitude of dangers. This preoccupation with creating a system of government that could secure individual liberty from multiple dangers resulted in treating citizen participation and civic engagement as means that are subservient to the larger end of preserving individual liberty.

Second, this chapter calls into question the remarkable consensus that has emerged "around Alexis de Tocqueville's view that the virtues and viability of a democracy depend on the robustness of its associational life" (Warren, 2001, p. 4). As we illustrated in Part III of this chapter, this is a view that has not been necessarily shared by the partisans of American democracy over the course of its history. This is not because they disagree with de Tocqueville's emphasis on the importance of associational life, but because they do not necessarily believe that strengthening associational life is the thing most needed to make American democracy work at a given period of its development. The current status of the American nonprofit sector is a good example to illustrate the point. While the number of nonprofits in the United States has roughly doubled in the last 30 years to 1.4 million (Berry, 2005; Lohmann, 2007), this growth is not necessarily viewed as a sign of improved associational or democratic health. Scholars remind us that the increased reliance on wealthy donors as board members and professional staff to run these organizations has not done much to improve civic engagement (Putnam, 2000; Schachter, 1997; Smith & Lipsky, 1993). In short, we can't make informed judgments about what counts for good kinds of civic engagement without knowing the political ends that these activities are intended to serve.

Third, this chapter presents a "political economy approach" to citizen participation and civic engagement. By that, we simply mean that the market economy, the public sector, and civil society have a mutually interdependent influence on one another. The amount and kind of participation in one sector has consequences for both the amount and quality of participation that occurs in the other sectors. For example, as we described in

Section III of this chapter, the growth of corporate philanthropy has fundamentally altered volunteerism and the role of associations in supporting democratic governance.

Finally, this chapter emphasizes the importance of taking an institutional perspective in our thinking about citizen participation and civic engagement. By institutional we simply mean that political institutions act as opportunity structures that influence individual behavior. Experiences with these institutions "allow individuals to learn and to adapt their behavior to the logic and mechanisms of the political context in which they live" (Stadelmann-Steffen & Freitag, 2010). They edify citizens as to what "good citizenship" means and requires. Therefore, differences in the conceptions of democracy and in the importance of volunteering and participating in the political process provide individuals with specific experiences from which to learn. Over the course of American history, models of what being a good citizen means have been shaped by the evolutionary political forces that have acquired institutional meaning and are deeply embedded in the local cultures in which individuals choose to live out their lives. In short, this chapter is premised on the institutional assumption that there is an organic legal framework to one's engagement, whether that activity occurs in the political or in the civil society. This legal framework both determines and is shaped by the institutional forces that over time define the meaning of a given political community.

ENDNOTES

1. For purposes of this chapter, we use the phrase "citizen participation" to denote the relationship between citizens and their legally constituted governing institutions. We use the phrase "civic engagement" to denote the relationship between citizens and voluntary associations in civic society as well as the relationship between voluntary associations and the legally constituted governing institutions. There is good reason to add corporations to the discussion of citizen participation and civic engagement. Over the years, decisions by U.S. courts have extended to corporations many of the same rights of free speech and assembly that have traditionally been extended to individuals and voluntary associations (see especially *Citizens United v Federal Election Commission*, 130 S.Ct. 876 [2010], which provides an excellent history of this evolution). Corporations now are able to use the first amendment right of free speech and assembly and the 5th and 14th amendment due process provisions as a bar against various kinds of regulatory initiatives by government. These developments have changed the dynamic interrelationship among the private, nonprofit, and public sectors and in so doing are likely to alter our understanding of what "good citizenship" means.

2. *Doux commerce* refers to the idea that increasing trade and wealth (i.e., capitalism) leads to less violent and warlike societies (Hirschman, 1977, 1981). This

issue is discussed more fully in our elaboration of the civic republic model of democracy that was advanced by the Anti-Federalists (see discussion of Quadrant B of Figure 2.1).

3. The rhetoric of the antitax revolt and the Tea Party movement have been populist in tone; however, it is a matter of debate whether the motivation is solely to put more power in the hands of citizens. Rather, these movements are loosely organized and may or may not share a consistent philosophy across issues.

4. For the development of this section on the history of nonprofit associations, we rely heavily on Peter Dobkin Hall's 1992 book, *Inventing the Nonprofit Sector*. To encourage a narrative flow, we have removed the in-text citations and retained only direct quotations.

5. This discussion leaves aside for the moment the questions of faction and contracting, and focuses only on the quality of civic engagement between civic organizations and citizens.

6. Organizations that facilitate deliberation cannot neatly be judged by the sector in which they exist. For example, Pateman (1970) showed that democratic organizations are quite possible in the private for-profit sector. On the other hand, de Tocqueville recognized that the American style of religion was not sufficient to build individuals' habits of the heart. He worried that American religion was too "vapid," "weak," and "self-centered" to fill the void in a liberal civil society (Allen, 2006).

7. See especially Barber, 1984, 1998; Berger 2009; Box, 1998; Burtt, 1993; Crosby, Kelly, & Schaefer, 1986; Fishkin, 1997; King, Feltey, & Susel, 1998; Leib, 2004; Meier &Bohte, 2007; Posner 2003; Schachter, 1997; Skocpol & Fiorina, 1993; Smith & Huntsman, 1997; Stadelmann-Steffen & Markus Freitag, 2010; Verba, Schlozman, Brady, & Nie, 1993; Warren, 2001.

REFERENCES

Acton Institute. (2012). Retrieved January 2, 2011, from http://www.acton.org/research/lord-acton-quote-archive

Allen, B. (2006, August 30–September 3). *Hope and zeal on the democratic frontier: The problem and promise of civic enlightenment.* Paper presented at the American Political Science Association, Philadelphia, PA.

Arendt, H. (1963). *On revolution.* New York, NY: Viking.

Barber, B. (1984). *Strong democracy: Participatory politics for a new age.* Berkeley: University of California Press.

Barber, B. (1998). *Place for us: How to make society civil and democracy strong.* New York, NY: Hill and Wang/Farrar & Strauss.

Barone, M. (1996, January 15). The road back to Tocqueville: At last, 19th century values stage a revival [Commentary]. *The Washington Post,* pp. 21–23.

Berger, P. L., & Neuhaus, R. J. (1996). To empower people: From state to civil society. In M. Novak (Ed.), *To empower people* (2nd ed., pp. 145–208). Washington, DC: Free Press.

Berlin, I. (1969). *Four chapters on liberty.* London, England: Oxford University Press.

Berry, J. M. (2005). Nonprofits and civic engagement. *Public Administration Review, 65*(5), 568–578.

Besharov, D. J. (1996). Bottom-up funding. In M. Novak (Ed.), *To empower people: From state to civil society* (20th anniv. ed., pp. 124–131). Washington, DC: American Enterprise Institute for Public Policy.

Box, R. C. (1998). *Citizen governance: Leading American communities into the 21st century.* Thousand Oaks, CA: Sage.

Brinkley, A., Polsby, N. W., Sullivan, K. M., & Lewis, A. (1997). New Federalist papers: Chapters in defense of the Constitution. *The New York Times Book Review, 18.*

Burtt, S. (1993). The politics of virtue today: A critique and a proposal. *American Political Science Review, 87*(2), 360–368.

Crosby, N., Kelly, J. M., & Schaeffer, P. (1986). Citizens panels: A new approach to citizen participation. *Public Administration Review, 46*(2), 170–178.

Couto, R. (1999). *Making democracy work better: Mediating structures, social capital, and the democratic prospect.* Chapel Hill: University of North Carolina Press.

de Tocqueville, A. (2000). *Democracy in America: The complete and unabridged volumes 1 and 2.* New York, NY: Bantam.

Etzioni, A. (1988). *The moral dimension: Toward a new economics.* New York, NY: Free Press.

Fishkin, J. S. (1997). *When the people speak: Deliberative democracy and public consultation.* New York, NY: Oxford University Press.

Fox, C. J., & Miller, H. T. (1996). *Postmodern public administration: Toward discourse.* Thousand Oaks, CA: Sage.

Fukuyama, F. (1995). *Trust: The social virtues and the creation of prosperity.* New York, NY: Free Press.

Greeley, A. (1997). The other civic America: Religion and social capital. *American Prospect, 32,* 68–73.

Green, D. G. (1996). Community without politics—A British view. In M. Novak (Ed.), *To empower people: From state to civil society* (pp. 30–48). Washington, DC: American Enterprise Institute for Public Policy.

Hall, P. D. (1992). *Inventing the nonprofit sector and other chapters on philanthropy: Voluntarism, and nonprofit organizations.* Baltimore, MD: Johns Hopkins University Press.

Hamilton, A. (1791/1969). Report on manufactures. In H. C. Syrett & J. E. Cooke (Eds.), *Volume 10 of The Papers of Alexander Hamilton.* New York, NY: Columbia University Press.

Hamilton, A., Madison, J., & Jay, J. (1961). *The Federalist papers* (C. Rossiter, Ed.). New York, NY: New American Library.

Held, V. (1984). *Rights and goods.* New York, NY: Free Press.

Hirschman, A. O. (1977). *The passions and the interests: Political arguments for capitalism before its triumph.* Princeton, NJ: Princeton University Press.

Hirschman, A. O. (1981). *Chapters in trespassing: Economics to politics and beyond.* Cambridge, England: Cambridge University Press.

John, R. R. (1995). *Spreading the news: The American postal system from Franklin to Morse.* Cambridge, MA: Harvard University Press.

Karl, B. D. (1998). Volunteers and professionals: Many histories, many meanings. In W. W. Powell & E. S. Clemens (Eds.), *Private action and the public good* (pp. 245–257). New Haven, CT: Yale University Press.

King, C. S., Feltey, K. M., & Susel, B. O. (1998). The question of participation: Toward authentic public participation in public administration. *Public Administration Review, 58*(4), 317–326.

Lohmann, R. A. (2007). Charity, philanthropy, public service, or enterprise: What are the big questions of nonprofit management today? *Public Administration Review, 67*(3), 437–444.

Leib, B. (2004). *Deliberative democracy in America: A proposal for a popular branch of government.* University Park: Pennsylvannia State Press.

Lowi, T. J. (1979). *The end of liberalism: The second republic of the United States.* New York, NY: Norton.

Matthews, D. (1996). Why we need to change our concept of community leadership. *Community Education Journal, 9*(18).

Meier, K. J., & Bohte, J. (2007). *Politics and the bureaucracy: Policymaking in the fourth branch of government* (5th ed.). Belmont, CA: Thompson Wadsworth

Michels, R., Paul, E., Paul, C., & Lipset, S. M. (1968). *Political parties: A sociology study of the oligarchical tendencies of modern democracy.* New York, NY: Free Press.

Morgan, D. F. (2001). Ethics and the public interest. In T. L. Cooper (Ed.), *Handbook on administrative ethics* (2nd ed., pp. 151–175). New York, NY: Marcel Dekker.

Morgan, D. F., Green, R., Shinn, C. W., & Robinson, K. S. (2008). *Foundations of public service* Armonk, NY: M.E. Sharpe.

National Center for Charitable Statistics. (2010). *Number of nonprofit organizations in the United States, 1999–2009.* Retrieved December 20, 2010, from http://nccs.urban.org/index.cfm

Open Secrets.org. (2010). *527S Organizations: Top 50 federally focused organizations.* Retrieved December 30, 2010, from http://www.opensecrets.org/527s/527cmtes.php?cycle=2004&level=C

Pateman, C. (1970). *Participation and democratic theory.* Cambridge, MA: Harvard University Press.

Pinkerton, J. (1996). Mediating structures, 1977–1995. In M. Novak (Ed.), *To empower people: From state to civil society* (2nd ed., p. 213). Washington, DC: American Enterprise Institute Press.

Posner, R. (2003). *Law, pragmatism, and democracy.* Boston, MA: Harvard University Press.

Putnam, R. D. (1993). *Making democracy work: Civic traditions in modern Italy.* Princeton, NJ: Princeton University Press.

Putnam, R. D. (2000). *Bowling alone: The collapse and revival of American community.* New York, NY: Simon & Schuster.

Reid, E. (1999). Nonprofit advocacy and political participation. In E. C. Eugene (Ed.), *Nonprofits and government: Collaboration and conflict* (p. 383). Washington, DC: Urban Institute Press.

Richardson, J. D. (Ed.). (1899). *A compilation of the messages and papers of the presidents* (Vol. 10). Washington, DC: U.S. Government Printing Office.

Rogue Basin Watershed. (2008). *Applegate partnership and watershed council.* Retrieved May 24, 2010, from http://www.roguebasinwatersheds.org/Section-Index.asp?SectionID=3

Schaar, J. H. (1964). Some ways of thinking about equality. *The Journal of Politics, 26*(4), 867–895.

Schachter, H. L. (1997). *Reinventing government or reinventing ourselves: The role of citizen owners in making a better government.* Albany: State University of New York Press.

Schofer, E., & Fourcade-Gourinchas, M. (2001). The structural contexts of civic engagement: Voluntary association membership in comparative perspective. *American Sociological Review, 66*(6), 806–828.

Selznick, P. (1992). *The moral commonwealth: Social theory and the promise of community.* Berkeley: University of California Press.

Skocpol, T. (1997). The Tocqueville problem: Civic engagement in American democracy. *Social Science History, 21*(4), 455–479.

Skocpol, T., & Fiorina, M. (Ed.). (1993). *Civic engagement in American democracy.* Washington, DC: Brookings Institution.

Smidt, C. E., den Dulk, K. R., Penning, J. M., Monsma, S. V., & Koopman, D. L. (2008). *Pews, prayers, and participation: Religion and civic responsibility in America.* Washington, DC: Georgetown University Press.

Smith, G. E., & Huntsman, C. A. (1997). Reframing the metaphor of the citizen-government relationship: A value-centered perspective. *Public Administration Review, 57*(4), 309–318.

Smith, S. R., & Lipsky, M. (1993). *Nonprofits for hire: The welfare state in the age of contracting.* Cambridge, MA: Harvard University Press.

Stadelmann-Steffen, I., & Freitag, M. (2010, April). Making civil society work: Models of democracy and their impact on civic engagement. *Nonprofit and voluntary sector quarterly, XX*, 1–26.

Steinberger, P. (1993). *The concept of political judgment.* Chicago, IL: University of Chicago Press.

Storing, H. J., & Dry, M. (1981a). *The complete anti-federalist.* Chicago, IL: University of Chicago Press.

Storing, H. J., & Dry, M. (1981b). *What the anti-federalists were for: The political thought of the opponents of the constitution.* Chicago, IL: University of Chicago Press.

Thach, C. (1969). *The creation of the presidency: 1775–1789.* Baltimore, MD: Johns Hopkins University Press.

Verba, S., Schlozman, K. L., Brady, H., & Nie, N. (1993). Race, raciality, and political resources: Participation in the United States. *British Journal of Political Science, 23*(4), 453–497.

Warren, M. (2001). *Democracy and association.* Princeton, NJ: Princeton University Press.

Wogaman, J. P. (1980). The church as mediating institution: Theological and philosophical perspective. In M. Novak (Ed.), *Democracy and mediating structures: A theological inquiry* (pp. 69–105). Washington DC: American Enterprise Institute for Public Policy Research.

Wolin, S. S. (1989). *The presence of the past: Chapters on the state and the constitution.* Baltimore, MD: Johns Hopkins University Press.

PART II

CITIZEN PARTICIPATION AND POLICY

CHAPTER 3

ENCOURAGING CITIZENSHIP IN U.S. PRESIDENTIAL ADMINISTRATIONS

An Analysis of Presidential Records

Thomas A. Bryer
University of Central Florida

INTRODUCTION

This study examines initiatives by presidents and presidential administrations to promote, encourage, transform, or institutionalize public engagement practices within federal systems and processes. The objective is to craft a history on the use of presidential power and authority to shape civic culture in the United States. This study is not an effort to evaluate the success or impact of presidential efforts but to categorize those efforts over time and across political party affiliations.

Analyzing public participation initiatives across U.S. presidential administrations is a unique undertaking. Through this work, it becomes possible to understand the influence of presidential powers and authorities for shaping both the narrative around what it means to be a citizen in the

The State of Citizen Participation in America, pages 55–75
Copyright © 2012 by Information Age Publishing
55

United States as well as the behaviors of individuals and groups in relation to each other and their government. As such, this study is of potential interest to students and scholars of presidential power as well as of public participation. Broad findings tied to each of these subject areas and identified through the detailed analysis are stated in the remainder of this introduction.

Beginning largely with the Kennedy administration, presidents of the United States have communicated through formal and informal communications what they perceive the role of citizens to be both within society and in relation to their government. The analysis shows a greater emphasis across administrations in what can be characterized as *engaged citizenship*: calling on citizens to act in ways that are beyond their self-interest and beyond simple obedience to the law (Dalton, 2009). This is compared to calls, which occurred less frequently, for *dutiful citizenship*: calling on citizens to act in ways that ensure proper functioning of societal institutions and in support of national identity (Dalton, 2009). Whereas calls for engaged citizenship spanned administrators and presidents with different party affiliations, calls for dutiful citizenship were more pronounced during administrations, regardless of party, during whose time there was a national need (e.g., the energy crisis during the Nixon administration).

The analysis presented in this chapter shows administrations led by presidents belonging to the Democratic Party were more likely than Republican administrations to create mechanisms within federal agencies to involve citizens in the process of governing. These efforts were most pronounced during the Carter and Obama administrations and were virtually nonexistent during administrations led by Republican presidents.

Overall, the analysis shows, dating from the Kennedy administration, presidents have used their powers and authority to pursue an agenda of citizenship. Those agendas have shifted across administrations, and the techniques have varied. Across administrations, it becomes clear the potential for presidents through administrative and managerial action to pursue agendas, with or without legislative involvement (Durant, 2009; Nathan, 1983; Pfiffer, 1999). The tools of presidential administration (Kagan, 2001) include unilateral actions, such as executive orders, executive memoranda, presidential proclamations, and bill signing statements. They also include the power of appointments, both for cabinet-level posts and for lower level advisory committees (Aberback & Rockman, 2009).

Presidents have also varied in their relations with the Congress: some chose direct appeals to Congress in messages or letters to Congressional leaders, or formal addresses. Others sought to create the debate desired by shifting the political and popular environment through communications through the media or direct public remarks. Edwards (1999) distinguished these leadership approaches with Congress as "directors" or "facilitators."

Directors seek to create the policy environment desired to pursue an agenda; facilitators work to achieve an agenda given an existing political context.

Each of these types of tools—administrative, Congressional leadership, and political—are analyzed to capture a history of the pursuit of a citizenship agenda across administrations. The method of agenda pursuit and content of the agenda are captured in the analysis.

METHOD

Presidential documents were searched via the collection maintained by the American Presidencies Project (APP) and coordinated by John Woolley and Gerhard Peters at the University of California, Santa Barbara. The APP collections include nearly 90,000 documents, including (American Presidencies Project, 2010):

- Messages and Papers of the Presidents (Washington 1789 through Taft 1913)
- Public Papers of the Presidents (Hoover 1929 through Obama 2010)
- Weekly Compilation of Presidential Documents (Carter 1977 through G.W. Bush 2009)
- Daily Compilation of Presidential Documents (Obama 2009–2010)
- Annual Messages to Congress on the State of the Union (Washington 1790–Obama 2010)
- Inaugural Addresses (Washington 1789–Obama 2009)
- Saturday Addresses (Radio from Reagan through G.W. Bush; Reagan 1982–Obama 2010)
- Fireside Chats (F. Roosevelt)
- News Conferences (Hoover 1929–Obama 2010)
- Executive Orders (J.Q. Adams 1826–Obama 2010)
- Proclamations (Washington 1789–Obama 2010)
- Presidential Signing Statements (Hoover 1929–Obama 2010)
- Statements of Administration Policy (Clinton 1997–Obama 2010)
- Presidential Nomination Acceptance Addresses (1928–2008)
- Presidential Candidates Debates (1960–2008)

A total of 21 search terms were used to search the APP collection. Seven terms were ultimately included for analysis. The remaining generated either too few or too many results. For those that generated too many results (e.g., volunteerism), future work can analyze these subjects on their own terms, as they represent a significant additional aspect of citizenship (Nesbit & Brudney, 2010) as reflected in the rich history of federal initiatives cat-

TABLE 3.1 American Presidencies Project Data, 1789–2010

Search Term	Records Found	Usage (Range in Years)	Most Cited by Administration
Civic Engagement	16	2000–2010	Obama (×7)
Civic Participation	45	1956–2008	Bush, G. W. (×38)
Neighborhood Partnerships	6	2008–2010	Obama (×6)
Open Government	58	1906–2010	Obama (×11)
Public Engagement	15	1813–2010	Obama (×6)
Public Involvement	37	1966–2009	Carter (×12)
Public Participation	123	1950–2009	Carter (×26)

alogued by the Corporation for National and Community Service (2010). Table 3.1 lists the seven terms included in the final document analysis.

Each record found through the search terms was analyzed to address the following questions: (a) What administration created the record? (b) What kind of record was it (e.g., executive order, press event, etc.)? (c) What was the content of the record? For the last question, records were coded by the author and a research assistant using the following categories: (a) substantive content authorizing or mandating federal agency action, (b) symbolic content that promotes or recognizes civic engagement, or (c) content not relevant to the subject of civic engagement due to an alternative definition usage of one of the keywords. Symbolic content was further subcategorized if it called citizens to action or was a passive statement without any call to action. Last, if symbolic content called citizens to action, it was subcategorized as calling citizens to be dutiful citizens, following the law or voting; or engaged citizens, taking initiative to participate in governance or work for interests other than their own.

FINDINGS

Data are presented in summary format, across time and administrations, and then in greater detail for administrations ranging from pre–Lyndon Johnson through Obama. The Lyndon Johnson through Obama administrations generated the highest quantity of records based on keywords. The Kennedy, George H. W. Bush, George W. Bush, and Obama administrations promoted national and community service to a larger extent than is captured in these data. For a history of these service activities, see the Corporation for National and Community Service (2010).

Figure 3.1 shows total number of records generated through the keyword search. The administration with the greatest overall number was that of

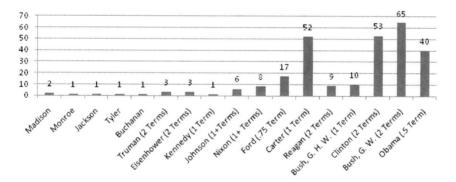

Figure 3.1 Number of records across administrations.
Note: Administrations not listed signifies that zero documents were generated in the search.

George W. Bush, though the 65 records were generated across two terms; this contrasts with 52 records in Jimmy Carter's single term and Barack Obama's 40 records in half a term. Proportionally, then, the Obama administration is on course to generate the greatest number of relevant records, followed by the Carter administration, the George W. Bush administration, and then the Clinton administration, with 53 records across two terms. The administrations of Madison, Monroe, Jackson, Tyler, and Buchanan are included only for the use of the term "public engagement," which was used here to mean public sector/government obligation. The modern-day usage of public engagement as a form of civic engagement was first used in the Eisenhower administration. All remaining analysis excludes records from the Madison, Monroe, Jackson, Tyler, and Buchanan administrations for this reason.

Figure 3.2 shows the total number of records categorized by record type. The three most used documents including one or more of the keywords were public remarks/speeches, messages to Congress, and executive orders—the full range of administrative, Congressional leadership, and political tools. Other popular documents include press events, proclamations, personnel actions, public statements/messages, executive memoranda, and fact sheets.

Figure 3.3 shows records categorized by record type and administration. The Carter, Clinton, and Obama administrations most often used administrative tools (i.e., executive order, executive memo) to pursue civic engagement objectives. These same three administrations made most use of remarks at public events—political tools—to promote civic engagement; the Carter administration utilized messages to Congress more than others in order to encourage legislative action in support of a civic engagement agenda. President George W. Bush made use of fact sheets and interviews with select media to discuss aspects of civic engagement.

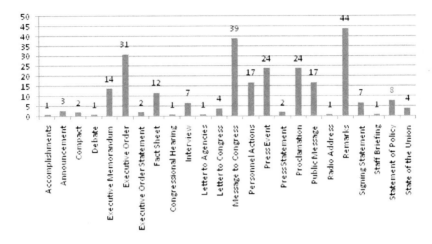

Figure 3.2 Number of records by type of record.

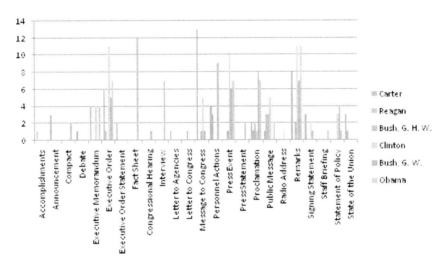

Figure 3.3 Number of records by type of record and administration.

The majority of records generated contained substantive content, as shown in Figure 3.4. These records established a new rule or promoted the passage of a new law, typically through executive orders, executive memoranda, or messages or other correspondence with Congress. Symbolic passive content was second most common, aggregated across administrations, followed by calls to action for engaged citizenship and calls for action for dutiful citizenship. Symbolic passive content is defined as content that does not enact or seek to enact a new rule or law but instead offers casual acknowledgement on the function or importance of an aspect of civic engage-

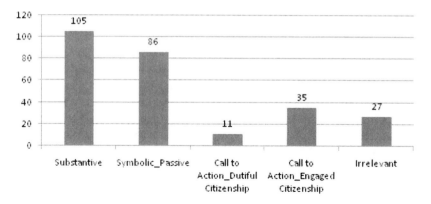

Figure 3.4 Content of records for all administrations.

ment. Calls for engaged citizenship asked citizens to act beyond what is expected of a citizen under the law, to help serve the interests of others, as well as their own and their country's interests. Calls for dutiful citizenship include expressions that citizens ought to follow the law, act in the national interest, or otherwise be patriotic (Dalton, 2009).

The Clinton administration generated the highest absolute number of substantive records. Substantive records were also numerous in the Carter, Obama, and G. W. Bush administrations. The Johnson administration generated the highest proportion of substantive records (83%) relative to all other records it generated. The Clinton administration was the only other to generate more than 50% of its records as substantive, followed by the Carter (45%) and Obama administrations (43%).

The G. W. Bush, Carter, and Obama administrations generated the highest number of symbolic passive records. Excluding the Kennedy administration (which only generated a single record within the search parameters used in the analysis), the Reagan (67%) and Ford (53%) administrations generated the highest proportion of symbolic passive records, relative to the content of other records generated by their administrations. The lowest proportions of symbolic passive records were generated by the Truman (0%), Eisenhower (0%), Nixon (0%), Johnson (17%), and Clinton (15%) administrations.

Across administrations, few records were generated calling citizens to be dutiful. Proportionally, the Truman (33%), Nixon (25%), and G. H. W. Bush (10%) administrations were most likely to call for dutiful citizenship. Calls for engaged citizenship were higher across administrations. The G. W. Bush administration generated the most records of this kind, followed by the Carter and Clinton administrations. Proportionally, the Truman (33%), Nixon (25%), G. W. Bush (23%), Carter (14%), and Clinton (12%) administrations were most likely to call for engaged citizenship.

Pre-Lyndon Johnson Administration

The first modern-day usage of the keywords used in the analysis occurred during the Truman administration. It wasn't until the Kennedy administration before a perceptible philosophy regarding the role of citizens began to truly take shape. Truman spoke in broad terms about the need for public involvement in educational activities (1952), or in service to children and families (1950). Eisenhower (1956) spoke similarly in broad terms about public participation with respect to aging policy.

John F. Kennedy set the stage for a continual focus on engaged citizenship for his successors. Though the keyword analysis did not generate documents that promoted citizenship or launched initiatives regarding the role of citizens, Kennedy's administration sounded the first significant call for citizens to act beyond their self-interest in service to their country. In his inaugural address (1961), he offered words that have inspired generations since: "And so, my fellow Americans, ask not what your country can do for you, ask what you can do for your country."

Couched in the context of an escalating Cold War with the Soviet Union, Kennedy's call served to both inspire citizen volunteers and also to spread the messages of liberty and freedom around the world, particularly in countries that might be susceptible to communist influence. In this spirit, he created the Peace Corp, noting upon its passage into law, "The wisdom of this idea is that someday we'll bring it home to America" (CNCS, 2010). The Peace Corp and the call to citizens to act in support of country inspired engaged citizenship initiatives during future administrations, including the creation of Volunteers in Service to America, launched in the Johnson administration; USA Freedom Corps, launched in the George W. Bush administration; and AmeriCorps, launched in the Clinton administration.

Lyndon Johnson Administration

The Johnson administration generated six documents based on the keywords used in analysis. Some 67% of documents were messages to Congress; letters to Congress and personnel actions each constituted 17% of documents; 83% of documents were substantive; and the balance was symbolic.

As a former legislative leader, Johnson promoted his agenda through communications to Congress and did not use instruments of executive authority (i.e., orders or memoranda). Substantively, he sought an increase in public participation in fighting crime, implementing the Wilderness Act, and conducting the War on Poverty as a "citizens' war." Additionally, he promoted election laws that would enable more citizen participation in federal election processes by, for instance, reducing taxable income through a contribution to fund campaigns for federal offices.

While in office, Johnson was confronted with adversarial citizen actions in the form of Vietnam War protests. These adversarial actions ultimately led to Johnson not seeking a second full term of office. However, beyond the relatively sparse expressions regarding public participation in the document analysis, Johnson did establish institutions that promote the role of citizens as engaged, acting beyond their immediate or self-interest. These efforts developed as part of his War on Poverty.

In 1964, Johnson created a volunteer program that continues to this day: Volunteers in Service to America (VISTA). Additionally, he created a National Teacher Corp, the Job Corp, and University Year of Action—all programs devoted to providing space and some incentive for citizens to volunteer their time in service to individuals and communities in need. By 1966, some 3,600 VISTA members were working throughout the country (CNCS, 2010). During Johnson's years in office, other volunteer-oriented programs were launched as well, including an early version of the Retired Senior Volunteer Program (RSVP), which sought to place seniors in positions in which they can assist individuals and communities in need, in a similar manner that VISTA allowed with young adults. These programs continued a path taken by John F. Kennedy and established a set of institutions that would span generations. Importantly, these programs identified a role for citizens, facilitated by federal initiative: engage with communities and individuals to enhance overall quality of life; government cannot do it alone, but government can help place citizens where they can be of greatest service.

Richard Nixon Administration

The Nixon administration generated eight documents based on the keywords used in analysis. In total, 75% of documents were messages to Congress; executive orders and public messages each constituted 13% of documents; 38% of documents were substantive; 25% called for dutiful citizenship; 25% called for engaged citizenship; and the balance was not relevant to the question of public participation.

Substantive actions were limited in scope and ambiguous in direction. For instance, Nixon signed Executive Order 11644, establishing policy on the use of off-road vehicles on public lands. One section of the order called for agency heads to "ensure adequate opportunity for public participation in the promulgation of such regulations and in the designation of areas and trails" (1972). Similarly ambiguous language was used in a message to Congress regarding patent review policy: "I am recommending that we broaden public participation in the review of patent applications" (1973).

Nixon was more targeted in his appeals to citizens to act in a dutiful manner or to be a citizen who acts in the national interest or in obedience to the law. This message was emphasized most in response to the energy crisis the country was experiencing in 1973/1974. In a special message to Congress, Nixon (1974) stated,

> With the Nation confronting a severe energy shortage, I appealed to the public eleven weeks ago to undertake a major conservation effort on a personal, voluntary basis. My appeal was repeated by public servants across the land.... Most importantly, the people themselves responded positively, lowering the thermostats in their homes and offices, reducing their consumption of gasoline, cutting back on unnecessary lighting, and taking a number of other steps to save fuel.

A focus on engaged citizenship was not as extensive in the Nixon administration as with the Johnson or Kennedy administrations, with their focus on voluntarism. Nixon did call on citizens to act in a manner beyond their self-interest in a couple of instances, though. For instance, in a 1971 statement about national crime prevention week, he stated, "For only the widest civic participation and support can translate the public programs we have launched into the kind of justice under law that is a prerequisite of creativity, abundance and true social progress."

Gerald Ford Administration

The Ford administration generated 17 documents based on the keywords used in analysis. In sum, 53% of documents were messages to Congress; 24% were public remarks; and executive memoranda, letters to Congress, proclamations, and signing statements each constituted 6% of the total. Another 53% of documents were symbolic and passive; 35% were substantive; 6% called for citizens to be dutiful; and 6% called for citizens to be engaged.

Collectively, Ford's statements spanned a variety of policy areas, including energy, environment, federalism/revenue sharing, and education. The majority of statements expressed passive acknowledgement regarding the role of the public; those statements that called for action or were substantive were focused on state/local government, not on participation with federal agencies. For instance, in a special message to Congress regarding revenue sharing from the federal government to state and local governments, Ford (1975) noted, "To strengthen public participation in determining the use of shared revenues, the proposed legislation requires that recipient governments must provide a procedure for citizen participation in the allocation of revenue sharing monies." Similarly, on the issue of health care reform,

Ford (1976) remarked upon signing a special message to Congress, "My proposal is designed to reduce Federal redtape, increase local control over health spending, and expand public participation in health planning."

Overall, Ford's statements and actions were limited and were not federally focused. The philosophy advanced, implicitly, is that the proper place for public participation is with units of government closer to the people. This perspective changed considerably during the Carter administration.

Jimmy Carter Administration

The Carter administration generated 50 documents based on the keywords used in analysis. In all, 25% of documents were messages to Congress; 15% were public remarks; 12% were executive orders; executive memoranda and personnel actions each constituted 8%; announcements, signing statements, and State of the Union addresses each made up 6%; executive order statements and proclamations each made up 4%; and accomplishments, debates, letters to agencies, and public messages each constituted 2% of the total. Overall, 45% of documents were substantive; 35% were symbolic and passive; 14% called for citizens to be engaged; 4% called for citizens to be dutiful; and 2% were not relevant.

Like the Ford administration, the Carter administration developed a linkage between public participation and a plethora of policy areas, consisting of

- regulatory reform,
- technology policy,
- national privacy policy,
- national trails system,
- radioactive waste,
- commission on world hunger,
- water resource programs,
- radiation policy,
- employee retirement income security,
- acid rain,
- review of federal advisory committees, and
- domestic assistance plans/paperwork reductions for state/local governments.

Among the policy areas on this list, regulatory reform received most attention with respect to public participation. Here, Carter sought to provide citizens with more opportunity to provide input during rulemaking processes. Part of these initiatives sought to lower costs for citizens to participate. Focusing on such "mundane" issues such as rulemaking procedures and federal advisory committees was a part of Carter's stated focus on managerial issues when he assumed the presidency (Carter, 2010).

Contrasted with the Ford administration, Carter perceived a direct role citizens could play with federal agencies. During remarks made at the signing of Executive Order 12044, Carter observed (1978a),

> I think this is the first time in history that a Presidential Executive order has been circulated for comment before it was issued, and the comments have been very constructive. We received some very careful and helpful comments from more than 350 people, and I think this is indicative of the interest that is shown in this particular action on my part.

In a letter to heads of independent regulatory agencies regarding the same Executive Order, Carter (1978b) noted, "This Order will open up new opportunities for public participation in the regulatory process, require regulations to be clearer and more understandable, and assure more effective oversight of the development of agency regulations."

Carter devoted more attention to the issue of public participation in the regulatory process with a memo written to agency heads in 1979, in follow-up to the 1978 Order that sought to improve regulatory processes. In this memo, Carter began by noting, "Executive Order 12044 of March 23, 1978, formalized the administration's commitment to public participation in Federal agency proceedings. Widespread participation can improve the quality of agency decisions by assuring that they are made on the basis of more complete and balanced records."

The memorandum continued:

> Experience has shown, however, that citizen groups often find the cost of meaningful participation in agency proceedings to be prohibitive. Many citizen groups are unable to pay the costs of experts and attorneys' fees, clerical costs, and the costs of travel to agency proceedings. As a result, the views and interests of consumers, workers, small businesses, and others often go unrepresented, or underrepresented, in proceedings that may have substantial impacts on their health, safety, or economic well-being.

> In recognition of the cost problems faced by many citizen groups, several agencies have established programs to provide financial assistance to persons (1) whose participation in a proceeding could reasonably be expected to contribute to a fair disposition of the issues and (2) who would be unable to participate effectively in the proceeding in the absence of such assistance. These programs have improved agency decisionmaking, and I believe they should be utilized in other agencies.

The memorandum closed with a dictate to each agency: "Each department and agency that has not already established a public participation funding program should determine whether it has statutory authority to do so," and "Each department and agency that finds it has authority to establish a public participation funding program should assess the extent of its need for such a program." Lastly, Carter noted,

> I have supported, and will continue to support, legislation to create, standardize, and adequately finance public participation funding programs government-wide. Independent of these legislative efforts, there is a current need for public participation funding and I strongly encourage each department and agency with the requisite authority to institute a public participation funding program.

Carter was, to this point in American history, the most proactive in establishing substantive mechanisms and/or requirements for enhancing public participation within federal institutions. While calling for enhanced participation opportunities within the government, Carter also called for citizens to engage in regulatory processes. In a public statement regarding Executive Order 12044, Carter (1978c) reached out to citizens: "We need public participation to make regulatory reform work."

Ronald Reagan Administration

The Reagan administration generated nine documents based on the keywords used in analysis. Personnel actions and public messages each constituted 33% of documents; executive orders, proclamations, and State of the Union addresses each made up 11% of the total; 67% of documents were symbolic and passive; 11% were substantive; and 22% were not relevant.

Reagan's administration made a clean break with the philosophy advanced during the Carter administration, as expressed through efforts and words regarding public participation. Moreover, Reagan reversed the requirements established by Carter to enhance public involvement in the regulatory process (Cooper, Bryer, & Meek, 2006). The one substantive document that emerged from the Reagan administration concerned Arctic research, as expressed in Executive Order 12501 (1985), in which was stated, "The Interagency Committee will provide public notice of its meetings and an opportunity for the public to participate in the development and implementation of national Arctic research policy." All other documents contained passive statements regarding participation, acknowledging in broad form the importance of public involvement without creating opportunities or calling for specific actions.

George H. W. Bush Administration

The George H. W. Bush administration generated 10 documents based on the keywords used in analysis. Public messages composed 30% of documents; public remarks and proclamations each constituted 20%; and letters to Congress, messages to Congress, and press events each constituted 10%. Symbolic/passive and substantive documents each constituted 40% of the total; documents calling for citizens to be engaged and documents calling for citizens to be dutiful each made up 10% of the total.

Bush launched initiatives and developed a focus on volunteer action by citizens, providing renewed emphasis to initiatives launched by Kennedy and Johnson. Specifically, Bush created the Office of National Service in the White House and the Points of Light Foundation, both initiatives to incentivize and promote volunteering (CNCS, 2010). In this same manner, Bush signed the National and Community Service Act of 1990, which authorized grants to support service-learning pedagogy through Serve America.

Bush's focus on volunteering reflects a broader philosophy, much like that advanced by Kennedy and Johnson. A key role for citizens in a democracy is to work through their own efforts and communities to enhance quality of life for themselves and for others. For example, part of his Points of Light efforts was the notion of spreading 1,000 points of light around the country through volunteer activity; this activity included the America the Beautiful Program, through which President Bush sought to attract volunteers to plant a billion trees.

This is a focus on engaged citizenship, as opposed to dutiful citizenship, though the call to action can be classified as dutiful as well. For instance, Bush called for increasing citizen participation in sporting activities (1991), suggesting both an opportunity for citizens to engage but also a duty to be physically fit in order to bring medical costs down for the nation. Overall, Bush presented a view that citizens should engage freely to enhance quality of life through environmental involvement, fitness, and other community-based programs. No mechanisms or initiatives were developed to have citizens active in public policymaking or performance of public agencies.

William Clinton Administration

The Clinton administration generated 56 documents based on the keywords used in analysis. Executive orders and public remarks each made up 21% of the total documents; 19% were press events; messages to Congress and public messages each constituted 9%; another 8% were executive memoranda; 6% were statements of administration policy; 4% were signing statements; proclamations and radio addresses each made up 2% of total documents; 51% of documents were substantive; 15% were symbolic and passive; 11% called on citizens to be engaged; 2% called on citizens to be dutiful; and 21% were not relevant.

Like some of his predecessors (e.g., Kennedy, Johnson, Bush), Clinton sought to promote the role of citizens as volunteers. In 1993, he signed into law the National and Community Service Trust Act, which created AmericaCorp (programmatic home of VISTA, created under Johnson) and a new agency—the Corporation for National and Community Service. The Act further combined RSVP, the Foster Grandparent Program, and the Senior Companion Program into a single effort labeled Senior Corp (CNCS, 2010).

In terms of public involvement with government, Clinton offered generally broad statements to encourage participation but not specific mechanisms to enhance participation. That said, the Clinton administration was the first to launch a Web site for the White House and encouraged using the Web for information dissemination and government transparency. The numerous mentions of the phrase "open government" occurred in this context, as well as in statements regarding the 1995 showdown with Congress that resulted in the government shutting down. Clinton made statements related to the opening up of government following the shutdown.

George W. Bush Administration

The George W. Bush administration generated 65 documents based on the keywords used in analysis. Fact sheets were 18% of documents; 14% were personnel actions; 12% were proclamations; interviews and public remarks each made up 11%; there were 9% press events; 8% were executive orders; 6% were statements of administration policy; compacts and press statements each made up 3%; Congressional hearings, messages to Congress, and signing statements each made up 2% of the total number of documents. Symbolic/passive and substantive documents each constituted 28% of the total; 23% call for citizens to be engaged; 2% called for citizens to be dutiful; and 20% were not relevant.

A number of symbolic documents are coded as such in that they relate to personnel actions for a newly created Council on Service and Civic Participation. This Council created the President's Volunteer Service Award to honor active volunteers around the country (CNCS, 2010). This effort was part of a larger narrative that spanned Bush's time in office, beginning with his first inaugural address, during which he called for a "nation of citizens, not spectators" (2001a). Following the September 11, 2001, terrorist attacks, the importance of volunteer service took on new meaning, and

Bush promoted programs that sought to take advantage of this altruistic spirit. During his 2002 State of the Union Address, Bush called on citizens to devote 2 years or 4,000 hours to volunteer service during their lifetimes. This call was accompanied by the creation of USA Freedom Corp and an expansion of AmeriCorps, as well as the creation of a new White House Office of Faith-Based and Community Initiatives (G.W. Bush, 2001b). The latter office was created to allow faith organizations to receive federal support to meet the needs of their communities.

Overall, the Bush administration more aggressively pursued an agenda of promoting volunteer service, expanding on the records of George H. W. Bush and Bill Clinton. Like his father, Reagan, and Ford, this call for engaged citizenship was not accompanied by the creation of mechanisms for public engagement with federal government actors or agencies.

Barack Obama Administration

The Obama administration, through its first 2 years, generated 40 documents based on the keywords used in analysis. Public remarks made up 28%; executive orders, press events, and proclamations each made up 18%; some 10% were executive memoranda; 5% were public messages; staff briefings and statements of administration policy each made up 3% of the total; 48% of documents were symbolic; 43% were substantive; and calls for citizens to be dutiful and calls for citizens to be engaged each made up 5% of total documents.

On Obama's first full day in office (January 21, 2009), he signed a Presidential Memorandum directed to the heads of the various federal departments and agencies (2009a). In it, he stated his commitment to and expectation for transparency, public engagement, and collaboration across agencies and organizations. On December 9, 2009, Office of Management and Budget Director Peter Orszag signed a memorandum to department and agency heads specifying the actions that needed to be taken to promote the values identified in the president's memorandum. Summarizing the values, Orszag noted,

> The three principles of transparency, participation, and collaboration form the cornerstone of an open government. Transparency promotes accountability by providing the public with information about what the Government is doing. Participation allows members of the public to contribute ideas and expertise so that their government can make policies with the benefit of information that is widely dispersed in society. Collaboration improves the effectiveness of Government by encouraging partnerships and cooperation within the Federal Government, across levels of government, and between the Government and private institutions.

In addition to these memoranda, the administration has experimented with social and Internet technologies to engage citizens with the White House, with Congress, or with each other, similar to the Clinton administration's early efforts in launching the White House Web site. For instance, the administration has twice utilized a process of co-production of citizen participation (Bryer, 2010a). In other words, the administration has asked volunteer citizens to convene community forums at a time and place of their choosing. Volunteer conveners received discussion questions but were otherwise left on their own, with the only request being that they report on the discussions to the administration. In December 2008, during the transition from the Bush to Obama administration, citizens were asked to convene health care community forums. More than 3,200 such forums were convened around the country, and the Department of Health and Human Services issued a report several months later providing a thorough analysis of the information they received (U.S. Department of Health and Human Services, 2009). This process was repeated in December 2009, when the administration asked citizens to convene community forums on the issue of jobs creation.

In addition to these social technologies, the administration has utilized Internet media and technology in various ways. Early in the administration's tenure, officials facilitated an electronic town hall meeting. Citizens were invited to submit questions electronically that they wanted President Obama to answer during the town hall. Empowering citizens to decide which questions should be answered in the limited time of the town hall meeting, the president agreed to answer the questions receiving the most votes by citizens on an interactive Web site. More than 100,000 questions were submitted and 1.5 million votes cast. The president responded, to one degree or another, as promised, even to a question on whether marijuana legalization can be an effective economic stimulant (Bryer, 2010b).

The aforementioned initiatives of the Obama administration are comparable to the efforts made during the Carter administration, in that mechanisms and processes were specifically developed to allow citizens to engage directly with federal actors and agencies. Obama also followed the path first paved by the Kennedy administration, asking citizens to not only help government serve them better but asking citizens to serve their country in more responsive ways as well. One of the first legislative achievements of the Obama administration was the passage of the Edward M. Kennedy Serve America Act, named after the long-time U.S. Senator from Massachusetts and the brother of the former president. The law expanded engaged citizenship programs administered through the Corporation for National and Community Service—an agency created by the Clinton administration and expanded by the Bush administration.

Obama further expanded on an initiative of the George W. Bush administration. In 2001(b), Bush created by Executive Order 13199, the White House Office of Faith-Based and Community Initiatives. Whereas Bush's order focused on the "indispensable" role of faith-based and community organizations to serve as a partner with government to meet community needs, Obama's order focused on the citizens who are the heart of faith-based organizations. In Executive Order 13498 (2009b), Obama noted,

> The American people are key drivers of fundamental change in our country, and few institutions are closer to the people than our faith-based and other neighborhood organizations. . . . The Federal Government can preserve these fundamental [Constitutional] commitments while empowering faith-based and neighborhood organizations to deliver vital services in our communities, from providing mentors and tutors to school children to giving ex-offenders a second chance at work and a responsible life to ensuring that families are fed.

The renamed White House Office of Faith-Based and Neighborhood Partnerships was thus charged with pursuing the same engaged citizenship objectives as expressed through the Serve America Act.

DISCUSSION

Strengthening or otherwise crafting a role for citizens may not be perceived as the function of the President of the United States. For much of U.S. history, it has not been. However, beginning in the mid-20th century, presidents and presidential administrations began to develop and pursue philosophies regarding the role citizens might play in society and with federal actors and agencies. Statements presidents have made, orders and directives they have issued, and remarks they have delivered help to define the political culture throughout the country.

Since Kennedy, administrations have largely pursued a common message promoting engaged citizenship. There have been exceptions, such as with the Reagan, Ford, and Nixon administrations; overall, though, administrations have sought to encourage volunteer service among citizens and behavior that goes beyond self-interest and obedience to the law. Calls for dutiful citizenship have varied according to the needs of particular times in U.S. history, such as times of war or crisis. Administrations have not forcefully pursued through administrative means initiatives to enhance engagement of citizens with federal actors and agencies. In cases in which this has occurred, specifically within the Carter and Obama administrations, efforts have been far-reaching and ambitious.

Tools that have been applied to pursue citizenship agendas have included administrative, political, and Congressional leadership. The Carter administration utilized all three in its efforts to craft a meaningful role for citizens in the regulatory rule-making process. Other administrations were more apt to use one set of tools rather than triangulating across tools. Future work can determine which sets of tools are most efficacious in accomplishing citizenship objectives.

Likewise, future work can trace the historical success of engaged, dutiful, and government-engaged initiatives across administrations. This study has documented the efforts made and the communications conducted in pursuit of agendas; it has not documented the success of those efforts. It is to this question that future work can be most pivotal: if pursued, can presidents find success in promoting various citizenship behaviors? There is substantial history on which to draw, as the analysis in this study reveals.

REFERENCES

Aberback, J. D., & Rockman, B. A. (2009). The appointments process and the administrative presidency. *Presidential Studies Quarterly, 39*(1), 38–59.

American Presidencies Project. (2010). *Presidential documents archive.* Retrieved December 26, 2010, from http://www.presidency.ucsb.edu/index_docs.php

Bush, G. H. W. (1991). *Proclamation 6285—National Physical Fitness and Sports Month.* Retrieved December 26, 2010, from http://www.presidency.ucsb.edu/ws/index.php?pid=47299

Bush, G. W. (2001a). *Inaugural address.* Retrieved December 26, 2010, from http://www.presidency.ucsb.edu/ws/index.php?pid=25853

Bush, G. W. (2001b). *Executive order 13199—Establishment of White House Office of Faith-Based and Community initiatives.* Retrieved December 26, 2010, from http://www.presidency.ucsb.edu/ws/index.php?pid=61481.

Bush, G. W. (2002). *Address before a joint session of the congress on the state of the union.* Retrieved December 26, 2010, from http://www.presidency.ucsb.edu/ws/index.php?pid=29644.

Bryer, T. A. (2010a). Living democracy in theory and practice: Getting dirty in a local government incorporation process. *Public Administration and Management, 15*(1), 259–304.

Bryer, T. A. (2010b). President Obama, public participation, and an agenda for research and experimentation. *International Journal of Public Participation, 4*(1), 5–11.

Carter, J. (1976). *Special message to the congress proposing health care reform legislation.* Retrieved December 26, 2010, from, http://www.presidency.ucsb.edu/ws/?pid=5618

Carter, J. (1978a). *Executive order 12044—Improving government regulations.* Retrieved December 26, 2010, from http://www.presidency.ucsb.edu/ws/index.php?pid=30539

Carter, J. (1978b). *Improving government regulations—Letter to the heads of independent regulatory agencies.* Retrieved December 26, 2010, from http://www.presidency.ucsb.edu/ws/?pid=30542

Carter, J. (1978c). *Improving government regulations: Remarks on signing executive order 12044.* Retrieved December 26, 2010, from http://www.presidency.ucsb.edu/ws/?pid=30538

Carter, J. (1979). *Public participation in federal agency proceedings: Memorandum from the president.* Retrieved December 26, 2010, from http://www.presidency.ucsb.edu/ws/?pid=32344

Carter, J. (2010). *White House diary.* New York, NY: Farrar, Straus and Giroux.

Cooper, T. L., Bryer, T. A., & Meek. J. W. (2006). Citizen-centered collaborative public management [Special issue]. *Public Administration Review, 66,* 76–88.

Corporation for National and Community Service (CNCS). (2010). *Our history and legislation.* Retrieved December 26, 2010, from http://www.nationalservice.gov/about/role_impact/history.asp

Dalton, R. J. (2009). *The good citizen: How a younger generation is reshaping American politics* (Rev. ed.). Washington, DC: CQ Press.

Durant, R. F. (2009). Getting dirty-minded: Implementing presidential policy agendas administratively. *Public Administration Review, 69*(4), 569–585.

Edwards, III, G. C. (1999). Director or facilitator? Presidential policy control of congress. In J. P. Pfiffner (Ed.), *The managerial presidency* (2nd ed., pp. 285–299). College Station: Texas A&M University Press.

Eisenhower, D. D. (1956). *Memorandum concerning establishment and functions of the Federal Council on Aging.* Retrieved December 26, 2010, from http://www.presidency.ucsb.edu/ws/?pid=10772

Ford, G. R. (1975). *Special message to the congress proposing extension and revision of the General Revenue Sharing Program.* Retrieved December 26, 2010, from http://www.presidency.ucsb.edu/ws/?pid=4866

Ford, G. R. (1976). *Special message to Congress proposing elementary and secondary education reform legislation.* Retrieved December 26, 2010, from http://www.presidency.ucsb.edu/ws/?pid=5654

Kagan, E. (2001). Presidential administration. *Harvard Law Review, 114*(8), 2245–2385.

Kennedy, J. F. (1961). *Inaugural address.* Retrieved December 26, 2010, from http://www.presidency.ucsb.edu/ws/?pid=8032

Nathan, R. (1983). *The administrative presidency.* New York, NY: Wiley.

Nesbit, R., & Brudney, J. L. (2010). At your service? Volunteering and national service in 2020. *Public Administration Review, 70*(Suppl. s1), S107–S113.

Nixon, R. M. (1971). *Statement about National Crime Prevention Week.* Retrieved December 26, 2010, from http://www.presidency.ucsb.edu/ws/?pid=3293

Nixon, R. M. (1972). *Executive order 11644—Use of off-road vehicles on the public lands.* Retrieved December 26, 2010, from http://www.presidency.ucsb.edu/ws/index.php?pid=59104

Nixon, R. M. (1973). *Special message to the congress proposing patent modernization and reform legislation.* Retrieved December 26, 2010, from http://www.presidency.ucsb.edu/ws/?pid=3980

Nixon, R. M. (1974). *Special message to the congress on the energy crisis.* Retrieved December 26, 2010, from http://www.presidency.ucsb.edu/ws/?pid=4241

Obama, B. (2009a). *Memorandum on transparency and open government.* Retrieved December 26, 2010, from http://www.presidency.ucsb.edu/ws/?pid=85677

Obama, B. (2009b). *Executive order 13498—Amendments to executive order 13199 and establishment of the President's Advisory Council for Faith-Based and Neighborhood Partnerships.* Retrieved December 26, 2010, from http://www.presidency.ucsb.edu/ws/index.php?pid=85734

Orszag, P. R. (2009). *Open government directive.* Retrieved December 26, 2010, from http://www.whitehouse.gov/open/documents/open-government-directive

Pfiffer, J. P. (1999). *The managerial presidency* (2nd ed.). College Station: Texas A&M University Press.

Reagan, R. (1985). *Executive order 12501—Arctic research.* Retrieved December 26, 2010, from http://www.presidency.ucsb.edu/ws/index.php?pid=38955

Truman, H. S. (1950). *Statement by the president on the midcentury White House conference on Children and Youth.* Retrieved December 26, 2010, from http://www.presidency.ucsb.edu/ws/?pid=13721

Truman, H. S. (1952). *Proclamation 2985—National Employ the Physically Handicapped Week.* Retrieved December 26, 2010, from http://www.presidency.ucsb.edu/ws/index.php?pid=87339

U.S. Department of Health and Human Services. (2009). *Americans speak on health reform: Report on health care community discussions.* Retrieved December 26, 2010, from http://www.healthreform.gov/reports/hccd/

CHAPTER 4

THE USABILITY OF GOVERNMENT INFORMATION

The Necessary Link Between Transparency and Participation

Suzanne Piotrowski
Rutgers University–Newark

Yuguo Liao
Rutgers University–Newark

INTRODUCTION

Transparency has been widely suggested as a driving force for better governance (Justice & Dülger, 2009; Kim, 2010), though this sentiment is now being critically examined. However, the notion of transparency is more discussed than defined. Philosophically, transparency is a state in which appearances correspond to reality (Marks, 2001). In the field of public administration, it refers to narrowing the gap between what a government seems to be doing and what government is actually doing. A growing number of researchers have discussed the multiple dimensions of transparency,

The State of Citizen Participation in America, pages 77–98
Copyright © 2012 by Information Age Publishing
All rights of reproduction in any form reserved.

including maximum social openness, facilitating public participation, improving social morality, deterring corruption, building up political trust, and the realization of other human rights (Bok, 1982; Florini, 2007; Hood, 2007; Kopits & Craig, 1998). Among them, it is argued that government openness or information disclosure is believed to be the prerequisite of all other dimensions.

However, the influence of information disclosure may not be so straightforward that more openness will necessarily lead to more participation, trust, and disciplined government employees. In this chapter, we specifically focus on the relationship between two dimensions of transparency: information disclosure and public participation. We argue that information disclosure alone does not facilitate participation. The information released through transparency measures does not always facilitate participation, and in some cases may obfuscate it. The nature and the quality of the information released are relevant. Within this chapter, we explore this underexamined area—the usability of government information. Government information that is released through transparency measures must have a minimum level of usability to facilitate public participation. We identify six criteria for ideal information usability and present a discussion of each of these. A new typology maps the relationship between the quantity and quality of released information. These criteria and typologies are then applied to two case studies: USASpending.gov and the 1-800-MEDICARE helpline. Our intention is to show how the issues of government openness, information usability, and public participation intersect in both theory and current cases.

UNDERSTANDING GOVERNMENT INFORMATION DISCLOSURE

We examine information disclosure by exploring three questions: (a) In terms of information nature and content, what kinds of information need to be released? (b) To whom should government information be released? and (c) How should government information be disseminated?

The Scope of Information Release

Discussions over the nature of information dissemination vary considerably. Some of the more radical definitions of transparency refer to no or minimal anonymity. Under these definitions of transparency, everyone is under the observation of all others (Hood, 2007; Marks, 2001; Putterman, 2001; Rousseau, 1772). This complete transparency falls into Hood's (2007) category of general transparency under which privacy is minimized.

Citizens are subjected to tight surveillance so that any violation of government-set rules could be reported to authorities. The notion of complete transparency will be achieved only at the expense of individual rights. Indeed, this vision of general or complete transparency is rarely embraced in history. To the contrary, a more liberal definition applies transparency only to the public domain, as opposed to private life. That is, there is a fine line between public and private life, and transparency should be applied only to one's public life (Barnstone, 2005). With the later definition of transparency, what should be available is information that is related to the public sphere and public interests. By drawing a clear line between public and personal life, this particularized definition of transparency ensures that information disclosure encourages enhanced government accountability rather than distrust and society-wide surveillance.

Recipients of Information Release

The ultimate purpose of information disclosure is to fulfill an individual's rights to know. However, different groups of citizens might exhibit different levels of understanding in receiving, digesting, and applying the released information (Gletiman & Gleitman, 1970; Schroder, Driver, & Strenfert, 1967). Hood (2007) noted that there are two strains of transparency. Direct transparency is the more "populist" definition through which information is released, either through direct observation or direct interaction between administrators and citizens. Indirect transparency is another, more technocratic strain. Indirect transparency refers to the fact that some information and its reporting "makes activity or results visible or verifiable ... only to agents or technical experts" (Hood, 2007, p. 194). This perspective emphasizes that government information should be released in a professional way so that information could be interpreted in a precise and technical way. Clearly, while direct transparency sets general citizens as the main recipients of information, indirect transparency essentially excludes the accessibility of citizens at-large in which neutral and competent experts are treated as the primary recipients of government information.

Approaches of Information Dissemination

There are a variety of ways in which government information is released, including government Web sites, newspapers, press conferences, television, and government periodicals. With the advancement of new technologies, the cost of dissemination is lowered. The main avenues of accessing government information, however, could be categorized as proactive information dissemination, individual requests, open public meetings, and whistleblowing and leaked information (Piotrowski, 2009). In the proactive model, government information is released according to statutory or regulatory requirements, tradition, or trust-building efforts. The requestor model is contrasted with the proactive model in which government documents are released only when individuals or organizations file a request. Once a request is filed, the government is required to either release information promptly or withhold information citing legal exemptions.

The Practice of Information Release

In essence, government openness is composed of potentially competing answers to a set of questions we stated earlier: the scale and scope of information disclosure, the recipients of disclosed information, and the process of disclosing information. The level of government openness is a function of the different approaches to the concept. In practice, there is a wide variation of information dissemination policies and practices.

In the U.S. federal government, the Obama administration initiated the Open Government Directive. On January 21, 2009, President Obama released the Memorandum on Transparency and Open Government. The three principles of open government set out in this memo are transparency, participation, and collaboration. The Obama administration has done quite a bit to promote transparency in government through the use of technology and better implementation of the U.S. Freedom of Information Act. There is still a wide variation in practice among the federal agencies of proactively releasing information on Web sites and through online databases.

At the state and local levels in the United States, there is no common standard or practice of transparency and information release. Every state has their own laws governing these practices. Each state has laws and rules governing open public meetings and a state-level freedom of information act, which applies to the state- and local-level governments. Even with common regulations governing these practices within an individual state, the actual implementation of these policies at the various state-level agencies and the local governments varies widely. Some local governments have additional ordinances governing the release of information.

DEFINING GOVERNMENT INFORMATION USABILITY

As we suggested earlier, government information disclosure alone will not facilitate public participation. We argue that usability is the key that links information disclosure and public participation. The usability of government information refers to the extent to which citizens can use information easily and efficiently for their individual purposes. With the increased popularity of result-oriented management in government (Brudney & Wright, 2002; Ingraham & Moynihan, 2001), questions like "Transparency for whom?" need to be posed. In this sense, our discussion on government information usability is a nuanced response to the question, "Who should be the recipients of disclosed information?"

Most of the previous research regarding information usability focuses on online information design or technology efficiency, such as how to design a user-friendly webpage (Baker, 2009; Faiola & McDorman, 2008; van den Haak, de Jong, & Schellens, 2009). However, few studies have assessed government information usability with attention to the issue of the potential manipulation of information. Indeed, to what extent usable government information is released depends largely on the interplay of political concerns within government. Rather than a sole emphasis on the volume of information released by government, the notion of information usability calls for an increased emphasis on information quality. Information recipients should be clearly targeted; there should be an assessment of the recipient's expectations of released information; and an evaluation of the context within which information will be used should be completed.

This line of research is important for several reasons. First, quality information is crucial for holding governments accountable. The rationale of governmental transparency lies in the entitlement of citizens to understand how government is operated. This places government under the scrutiny of the general public. Moreover, government management is operated in an increasingly complex environment in which the definition and solution of problems are hardly definitive. Therefore, it is crucial to communicate with citizens in a timely and understandable way in order to nurture and maintain citizens' interest to engage in public affairs.

Second, the advancement of new technologies brings new opportunities as well as challenges for citizens to take full advantage of open government information. One of the major objectives of e-government is to set up a web portal, making information more accessible for citizens (Ezz, Papazafeiropulou, & Serrano, 2009). The ever-growing amount and depth of information disclosure requires integration, as well as coordination of the information and services across various public agencies. However, structural reorganization and integration will not be easily achieved for public agencies since both involve cultural and management challenges, such as inflexible bureaucratic structures and procedures, lack of standardization across agencies, and the diversity of organizational culture (Ezz et al., 2009; Riediel, 2001). Information released in a user-friendly manner is more than just a straight technology issue for e-government policy. The increased use of technology with respect to information release brings to light other issues such as the digital divide, in which there is a large proportion of population who have only limited Internet access (Dewan & Frederick, 2005). Income, education, and age have all been shown to impact the intention to use e-government services (Bélanger & Carter, 2009). In this way, the purpose of useable information is to maximize the possible benefits of what new technology has to offer.

Third, there is a disparity among information recipients' skills, which are necessary to effectively interact with open government information. Mossenburg, Tolbert, and Stansbury (2003) use the notion of information literacy to describe one's ability to recognize when information can solve a problem or fill a need and effectively employ information resources. Individuals differ in their ability to notice, absorb, retain, and integrate information. Therefore, to make open government information relevant, it is critical to move one step beyond making information available to making information understandable and applicable.

Our discussion on usable information highlights our assertion that information release should be citizen-centric to enhance government accountability by better linking the public's demand and officials' actions. We propose that government information usability should contain the ideal standards expanded upon below. We recognize that it may be unrealistic to simultaneously embrace all principles at the same level due to their inherited trade-offs, we encourage administrators to strike a balance among these potentially competing expectations.

Accurate

In the field of public administration, the term "accuracy" is used to describe how precise is released government information when compared with the underlying and original information. The notion of accurate information has both managerial and political implications. First, inaccuracy could occur when intraorganizational information flow is obstructed. For example, frontline employees without solid training fail to disseminate

TABLE 4.1 Criteria for Ideal Information Usability

Criteria	Key Characteristics
Accurate	precise, factual
Accessible	anyone, anywhere, anytime
Complete	all necessary parts, no intentional concealment
Understandable	clear, comprehensive
Timely	up-to-date
Free or Low Cost	free of charge or at minimal cost

the requested information to citizens. The Government Accountability Office (GAO, 2004) found that when Medicare beneficiaries, their families, and other members of the public called a nationwide toll-free telephone helpline about program eligibility, enrollment, and benefits, more than 30% of calls were answered inaccurately or received no answer by customer service representatives. Information disclosure could also be manipulated to meet political purposes. For example, the reasons originally justifying the Iraq War turned out to be misleading and wrong (Goldenberg, 2008). According to the Center for Public Integrity, the prewar intelligence was a carefully launched campaign of misinformation in order to rally support for the invasion of Iraq (Lewis & Smith, 2008). As such, political objectives outweigh the efforts to make government information accurate and consistent.

Accessible

In principle, government information should be accessible by anyone from anywhere at any time. Accessibility requires that information be disseminated through multiple mechanisms to reach citizens. Each method of information disclosure targets a certain, though overlapping, group of recipients. The employment of multiple dissemination mechanisms, thus, should cover as many recipients as possible. The Internet and emerging technologies have reshaped the way in which information flows between public agencies and the public. However, in reality, universal access does not exist. Some citizens have cognitive or physical limitations, while others may have limited access to new technology devices (Chesi, Pallotti, & Signore, 2005). The traditional avenues of information dissemination, such as physical service facilities, need to be maintained.

Complete

Information disclosure should not omit any portion due to intentional concealment. In practice, there are limits to this principle. Information dealing with national security, law enforcement, and personal privacy are all well-established areas for limiting release. Helen Darbishire (2010) proposes a minimum standard for public information release. Her discussion of proactive dissemination includes institutional information, organizational information, operational information, decisions and acts, public services information, budget information, open meetings information, decision-making and public participation information, subsidies information, public procurement information, lists, registers and databases, information about information held, publication information, and information about the right to information.

Incomplete information cannot provide a satisfactory basis for policy analysis. Adrian Fozzard (2002) discusses how the structure of budget reporting could distort policy priorities. He noticed that ministerial financial reporting in Mozambique only uses broad functional classification (such as education), without a breakdown of ministries' accounts at departmental level. "Consequently, while it is possible to determine how much has been allocated to and spent on education, it is not possible to determine, on the basis of budget documentation and accounts, what proportion is intended for or delivered to primary education" (Fozzard, 2002, p. 32). This incomplete financial reporting would hinder the consistency and monitoring of public expenditures. Along the same lines, Mark Schacter (1999) outlines four types of performance measures that a complete performance information system should include: input measures, output measures, efficiency measures, and outcomes measures. In sum, complete information provided by government is a crucial precondition of objective decision making.

Understandable

Government information reporting should be clear and comprehensive for citizens from various backgrounds. Many members of the public are nonexpert users of government information. To make released information understandable to individuals, the information must be compelling and responsive to citizen concerns in a straightforward way. However, being understandable is at times at odds with the requirement of being accurate and complete. Take performance measurement as an example. With the development of measurement skills, performance measurement has become more sophisticated and elaborate. This is a result of the efforts to make performance measurement more scientific, reliable, and valid. Over time, the primary users of performance information have been policymakers and legislators (Melkers & Willoughby, 2001). In many cases, citizens are gradually excluded from actively participating and benefiting from performance measurement programs. In order to assure the original objective of transparency—to hold government accountable to citizens—one possible way to meld the interests of administrators and citizens is to encourage governments to solicit citizen input in the decision-making process (Cooper, Bryer, & Meek, 2006; Ebdon & Franklin, 2006; Franklin, Ho, & Ebdon, 2009). By receiving citizen input, public officials can more effectively differentiate what information should be used for internal consumption and what information should be disseminated publicly in a citizen-centered way (Ho, 2007). The key to managing the trade-offs between understandability, accuracy, and completeness is that the public interest and government accountability should always be the guiding principles regarding what and how information should be disseminated.

Timely

Information should be available and updated as quickly as possible. Material available in electronic or hard copy form should indicate when the information was released or updated. Citizens should also be informed of how often the information is being updated. However, this requirement of timeliness may conflict with criteria of accuracy and completeness (Ballou & Pazer, 1995; Hilton, 1981). This tension is especially true when the information is used for strategic planning purposes. In many cases, the quality of information utilized for decision-making and planning purposes becomes increasingly more valid and reliable with the passage of time. The timely release of the preliminary information is based on the available data and a changing environment. In the same vein, when the information about a fixed point becomes more accurate and complete over time, it becomes less current and relevant since most of the policy issues are time sensitive. For example, cost estimates for an infrastructure project are made based on available data. The estimated costs are more accurate as the project progresses. However, with the passage of time, the actual cost becomes less relevant for decision-making and planning purposes. Thus, public managers need to strike some balance between updated but not-very-accurate or complete information, and accurate or complete information that is not current.

Free or Low Cost

Information should be available to the public free of charge or at a low cost. Added value is most likely to be created when the public has access to the government information free of charge or at consistently low cost. Darbishire (2010) argues that information available electronically should be free of charge. There should not be a charge for core information related to law, the budget, annual reports, or forms of governmental services whether they are available electronically or in hard copy (Darbishire, 2010).

THE RELATIONSHIP BETWEEN THE QUANTITY AND QUALITY OF INFORMATION DISCLOSURE

Government openness and information usability constitute two related but distinct aspects of the efforts to counter government secrecy. Gener-

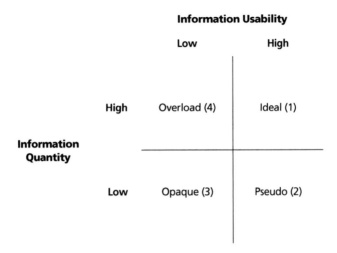

Figure 4.1 Typology of four variants of information quantity and quality.

ally, openness or information disclosure is a requisite of usable information. In a society dominated by administrative secrecy, high quantity and quality open government information is hard to obtain. Openness is necessary but is far from sufficient to facilitate accountability. The notion of usable information coupled with government openness embodies a higher expectation than government openness alone. As Bok (1982) noted, to counter the tendency of secrecy, publicity requires more than mere openness with respect to actual practices. Information usability coupled with openness could serve as one prescription for better governance and accountability.

Figure 4.1 is a straightforward combination of information usability (i.e., quality of information) and quantity of information released. Four different variants have been identified to illustrate the relationship between the quantity and quality of disclosed information.

Ideal (Quadrant 1: High Quantity, High Usability)

The *ideal* variant signifies that a great deal of information is readily available for public decision making. Information disclosure is in accord with the usability principles of accurate, accessible, complete, understandable, timely, and low cost information. This variant represents the most ideal combination of information quantity and quality. With complete and undistorted information, citizens (for whom transparency should ultimately serve) could scrutinize government activities and evaluate government performance. In this sense, this variant is best for nurturing public value, building up public trust, and reconciling public accountability and administrative effectiveness.

Pseudo (Quadrant 2: High Usability, Low Quantity)

The second variant, *pseudo*, refers to governments that have provided some simple and partial information to individuals. The material that is released may have been provided promptly, however the extent to which information is disclosed is still within the tight control of public officials. For example, when public officials are dealing with open government information regulations, they might be interested in disseminating institutional procedures and decision rules completely and timely through multiple channels (Hood, 2007). More politically salient information, such as that which could decrease corruption, is still safely kept in a black box. Open government information regulations operate in controlled and incremental ways, which excludes active citizen engagement. Citizens are discouraged to request government information based on their specific needs and are confined to oversimplified and, at times, a biased segment of information. The pseudo variant violates many of the criteria for ideal information usability discussed above.

Opaque (Quadrant 3: Low Quantity, Low Usability)

This variant represents the least optimal combination of information quantity and quality. The opaque variant represents the situation in which a minimum of government openness is permitted and the process of information release is politically manipulated to best serve the people who have control over it. Some theorists have argued that secrecy can serve rationality and efficiency in administration (Weber, 1968). Full disclosure regarding operational aspects of process could hinder administrators from working in a safe and creative way (Heald, 2006; Prat, 2006). However, the immense destructive power of secrecy repeatedly shows us that secrecy could not only increase the chance of power being abused, but also hamper rational decision making due to inadequate understanding of public policy's context, alternatives, and consequences (Bok, 1982; Mathews, 1978; Rourke & Christoph, 1975). As Bok (1982, p. 181) warned us, "There should be a strong presumption against government control over secrecy because of the abuses it can conceal, the power governments exercise, and their special obligations of accountability."

Overload (Quadrant 4: High Quantity, Low Usability)

This variant refers to the situation in which government information is disclosed in large amounts, but without sufficient attention to information usability. Previous research has focused on the amount of information disclosed rather than the quality or effectiveness of the information disclosed. A notable example of this variant would be reporting problems observed in performance measurement efforts. Metzenbaum (2009) noted that even though Web sites have been extensively established to facilitate access to agency performance information, there is a lack of effective reciprocal communication to make performance information relevant to citizens. Along the same lines, more in-depth analysis on what factors make performance decline or improve is encouraged in performance reporting (Liner et al., 2001). A simple display of performance results without explanation and comparison or a mere focus on what is easiest to measure means users will not have a complete understanding of what has happened and why it has occurred. At the municipal government level, a common example of information overload is when the town's mayor or city manager sends out a newsletter that is extremely long with the most important information, such as the time and date of a planning board meeting, buried in the middle.

USASPENDING.GOV

President Obama has made transparency of government a focus of his administration. The first executive order he issued when taking office was one on transparency and openness (Obama, 2009), and he went on to establish the Open Government Initiative. With respect to proactively released information, the Obama administration has made great strides in posting an increasing number of government datasets online. The Federal Funding Accountability and Transparency Act, a law promoted by then-Senator Obama, established USASpending.gov. The stated purpose of the USAspending.gov is

> to provide the public with information about how their tax dollars are spent. Citizens have a right and a need to understand where tax dollars are spent. Collecting data about the various types of contracts, grants, loans, and other types of spending in our government will provide a broader picture of the Federal spending processes, and will help to meet the need of greater transparency. The ability to look at contracts, grants, loans, and other types of spending across many agencies, in greater detail, is a key ingredient to building public trust in government and credibility in the professionals who use these agreements. (USASpending.gov, n.d.)

The Web site allows you to search or browse through how money is spent by the U.S. federal government. In December 2010, subcontractor spending was added to the body of data that could be searched online (Moore, 2010). In the following section, we analyze the USASpending.gov initiative by applying the six criteria for ideal information usability.

Accurate

While USASpending.gov was introduced with great fanfare, it has received a fair amount of criticism for the quality of the data it relies upon. ClearSpending, an initiative of the Sunlight Foundation, has raised questions regarding the accuracy of the agency data available on USASpending.gov. ClearSpending compared the data available on USASpending.gov to the Catalog of Federal Domestic Assistance and found many inconsistences between the two, leading to the conclusion that some of the data provided through USASpending.gov was inaccurate.

ClearSpending and the Sunlight Foundations have themselves been criticized for their harsh review of USASpending.gov. One technology blogger stated, "Sunlight has, I think, dangerously conflated transparency for reform. You get transparency first and that compels reform. That's the whole point. You don't ask for perfection right out of the gate; it's unreasonable" (Gunnar Hellekson, as quoted in Lipowicz, 2010). The issue of data accuracy is one with which the federal agencies and USASpending.gov are still struggling.

Accessible

If you have access to a computer with the Internet, USASpending.gov is extremely accessible. It is available online with no restrictions. A user can also download datasets from the Web site to analyze on their own computer. If you are one of the millions of Americans without consistent Internet access, your ability to use this data site is limited.

Complete

With the addition of the subcontractor data, USASpending.gov has moved closer to publishing a complete dataset of federal spending. In its review of USASpending.gov, ClearSpending showed that many of the fields reported on the Web site were incomplete. The Office of Management and Budget (OMB) has begun to address this problem by having agencies develop plans to improve the quality of their spending data (OMB Watch, 2010; Struther, 2010). While USASpending.gov does not currently meet the principle of complete information, there is movement in that direction.

Understandable

With some knowledge about the U.S. federal government and budgeting, the USASpending Web site is clear and comprehensive to an enduser. The Web site has a FAQs section and provides definitions for the different categories. If the enduser did not have some basic understanding of the missions of the different agencies and the differences between grants and contract, navigating the Web site and understanding the search results would prove more difficult.

Timely

The Federal Funding Accountability and Transparency Act requires federal spending to be posted within 30 days of its obligation. ClearSpending reports that the postings were usually late. They found that at least 60% of recorded obligations reported were posted more than 45 days after the obligation was made. Of the data they analyzed, Clearspending found that the average submission time was 55 days after obligation (Sunlight Foundation, n.d.). While these findings show that there needs to be improvements to meeting the statutory requirements set out in the Federal Funding Accountability and Transparency Act and that the data is currently available mere months after obligation, this does in many ways embrace the principle of timeliness.

Free or Low Cost

The biggest financial barrier to accessing the data on USASpending.gov is the need to have access to the Internet either at home or through a public computer, such as those available at public libraries. To make good use of the Web site, a user would need to have at least a couple of hours of access to the site. Unlimited computer and Internet access is typically limited at public sites and thus limits a user's ability to search the site. But once Internet access is obtained, searching online and downloading datasets are free.

USASpending.gov is a project that has the potential to have high levels of transparency and high levels of information usability, falling into Quadrant 1 of Figure 4.1, ideal. At the present time though, this project does not fall into the ideal category due to problems with data accuracy and completeness and is relegated to Quadrant 2, pseudo. This example also indicates that if information is released but not accurate, public participation may play a corrective role. Individuals can access the database, spot the inconsistencies, omissions, or inaccuracies and then provide feed to the USAspending.org or the relevant agency. In the case presented, we see how inaccuracies in the data identified by nongovernmental actors lead to new government data management policies.

1-800-MEDICARE HELPLINE

Medicare is a federal insurance program providing health insurance coverage to people who are 65 years old or above. In 1999, a nationwide toll-free Medicare helpline, 1-800-MEDICARE, was launched to answer beneficiaries' questions regarding their program eligibility, enrollment, and benefits (GAO, 2004). Since then, overall call volume has increased dramatically from 1.6 million calls in July 2005 to more than 2 million calls in July 2008 (GAO, 2008). The major responsibilities of the Medicare helpline especially are to:

- Provide general information and printed materials on Medicare and the Medicare Health Plan options as well as plan quality and satisfaction information in English or Spanish.
- Find out information about the new Medicare Prescription Drug, Improvement, and Modernization Act of 2003.
- Provide information on the Medicare-approved drug discount card sponsors.
- Find out the names of Medicare providers and suppliers in customer area.
- Find out specific Medicare coverage information.
- Accept requests for various Medicare publications.
- Help customers disenroll from Medicare+ Choice organizations (managed care plans).
- Obtain phone numbers for SSA, local State Health Insurance Assistance Program (SHIP), State Medicaid Office, and more (Centers for Medicare & Medicaid Services, 2005).

Due to the importance of health insurance and the complexity of Medicare policy for 43 million senior citizens, it is extremely crucial for customer service representatives to provide answers correctly and efficiently to beneficiaries. Again, we will use the criteria of usable public information to assess the 1-800-MEDICARE helpline.

Accurate

Inaccurate answers from the customer service representatives is a major concern in reviewing the performance of the Medicare helpline (GAO, 2004, 2008). According to a survey conducted by the U.S. Senate in 2007, around 90% of Medicare service representatives could not answer the callers' questions or just gave the wrong answers (De Nies & Weber, 2008). The GAO's study (2004) provides a more favorable, but still not satisfactory outcome, with 29% of the callers being provided with incorrect information. The 1-800-MEDICARE helpline provides customer service representatives with written answers that they could use during a call. Therefore, the major reason for inaccurate information is that customer service representatives did not effectively use the scripts (GAO, 2004). Enhanced training and consistent updates of the scripts need to be conducted to ensure the accuracy of information.

Accessible

Currently, the 1-800-MEDICARE helpline operates 24 hours a day, 7 days a week (GAO, 2008). Due to the popularity of telephone and cell phone use, the Medicare helpline is highly accessible for Medicare beneficiaries and their family members.

Complete

Since the launch of the helpline in 1999, changes in the Medicare program have resulted in more and more program information available through 1-800-MEDICARE. From January 2002 through May 2004, the "Medicare & You" program assessed the Medicare helpline in terms of whether it could provide fully responsive answers. They found that the average percentage of calls that received fully responsive answers—which are complete and accurate—ranged from under 40% to over 90%, depending on the question and the period of time studied (GAO, 2004). Studies are needed to identify which kind of questions the customer service representatives could answer more completely and how this could be facilitated.

Understandable

In addition to English, the contractor providing the helpline hired bilingual customer service representatives to provide service to Spanish-speaking callers. As of 2007, slightly more than 7% of customer service representatives are bilingual (GAO, 2008). Also, the contractor established a telephone interpretation service to provide services for callers speaking other languages. Statistics show that the number of languages used on the Medicare helpline has reached 73 as of March 2008 (GAO, 2008). All these measures have broadened the scope that the helpline could serve and make the helpline understandable to more callers.

Timely

To provide timely information is another major challenge. Some customer service representatives could not respond to questions when beneficiaries called. The GAO (2004) found that around 10% of the helpline callers did not receive any answer to their question. Long wait times is another major complaint of the helpline users. Some customers complained that the wait time of the helpline could reach 45 minutes (De Nies & Weber, 2008). Another survey conducted by U.S. Senate Special Committee on Aging found that callers were put on hold for an average of 16.6 minutes, and only half of the calls got through to a real person (Pope, 2008).

Free or Low Cost

The 1-800-MEDICARE helpline is toll free. The only financial cost for callers is access to a telephone. In this sense, to acquire information from the Medicare helpline service is very low cost.

In sum, the 1-800-MEDICARE helpline provides millions of Medicare beneficiaries with opportunities to readily seek answers for their questions. However, based on caller feedback and the assessment of information usability, this helpline does not fully satisfy caller demands and still has much room for improvement. Generally, it could be regarded as an overload model, with the characteristics of both easy access and relatively low information usability. Due to the high quantity and low usability, Medicare beneficiaries may not be fully informed about Medicare policy. They may not be able to understand the details of the Medicare policy when they have questions. As a result, feedback from beneficiaries cannot accurately reflect implementation of the policy. This will further hinder the dialogue and exchange between policymakers and the beneficiaries regarding how to adjust the policy in order to better serve the public, thus obfuscating public participation.

IMPLICATIONS FOR PARTICIPATION

The usability of information released through transparency mechanisms is vital for the scale and level of public participation. If there is a high level of information usability, participation is facilitated. First, releasing more usable information will help governments reach out to the affected public so that an increased number of individuals could become involved. Usable information can bring more citizens affected by a current or proposed government policy to the table because individuals will be better able to digest and respond to information. The release of understandable information could encourage different groups of citizens to participate. Less usable and lower quality information that is publicized adversely affects all citizens but particularly disadvantaged (e.g., less-educated or poor) groups since they have fewer skills and resources to identify, locate, and absorb government information. Information dissemination with low usability will further enhance marginalized groups' exclusion from the policymaking process. For instance, information that is available at a high cost restricts the number of individuals and groups that have access to it and use it to inform their participatory actions. As a consequence, their voices are less likely to be heard by the policymakers or reflected in the final decisions. In this sense, the quality of information is associated with maximizing the number of relevant participants.

Second, quality of information is associated with the outcomes of public participation. Citizen participation in public affairs is composed of several tiers. For example, Arnstein (1969) provided a ladder of citizen participation, including citizen authority over decisions or delegated authority, negotiated decisions, shared partnership in decision making, opportunity to offer advice, opportunity to develop self-confidence, and a channel for citizen support of programs already planned. Similarly, Ebdon and Franklin (2004) identify five goals of citizen participation in budgeting: (a) informing decision making, (b) educating participants on the budget, (c) gaining support for budget proposals, (d) influencing decision making, and (e) enhancing trust and creating a sense of community. Implied is that the influence of citizen participation in decision making could range from low (such as getting citizens educated) to high (such as influencing decision making). Indeed, government information that is released in a usable way has the potential to influence each tier of the participation outcome and help advance public participation from lower tiers to higher ones.

As we illustrated in our case studies, the release of quality information requires the simultaneous utilization of various communication techniques since each method has its own strengths as well as weaknesses. For example, information sent out by e-newsletter might be very timely but not very complete. A citizen advisory committee might be an ideal avenue for sharing information completely, but it may not be easily accessible for every citizen. Multiple mechanisms ensure that the causes, consequences, and contexts of policy issues are explicitly and fully disseminated to all potentially affected citizens. During this process, the public has the opportunity to become educated and understand policy issues, subsequently express demands, and become involved.

How a government shares or releases information has considerable impact on how much influence participants could eventually have on final policy decisions. In fact, a symbolic process of citizen participation could take place when the government does not provide accurate, complete, and understandable information. Usable information can help citizen voices be heard at the right time. The timely release of government information helps citizens provide input earlier in the policymaking process and provide feedback before the final policy is adopted (Ebdon & Franklin, 2004; Franklin & Ebdon, 2005). Information that is accurate and understandable makes the exchange between government officials and citizens possible and more productive. In sum, all six of the criteria for usable information have an impact on public participation. Simple access to government information is not enough. A high level of information usability is essential to facilitate public participation.

REFERENCES

Arnstein, S. (1969). A ladder of citizen participation. *Journal of the American Institute of Planners, 35*(4), 216–224.

Baker, D. L. (2009). Advancing e-government performance in the United States through enhanced usability benchmarks. *Government Information Quarterly, 26*(1), 82–88.

Ballou, D. P., & Pazer, H. L. (1995). Designing information systems to optimize the accuracy-timeliness tradeoff. *Information Systems Research, 6*(1), 51–72.

Barnsone, D. A. (2005). *The transparent state: Architecture and politics in postwar Germany*. London, England: Routledge.

Bélanger, F., & Carter, L. (2009). The impact of the digital divide on e-government use. *Communications of the ACM, 52*(4), 132–135.

Bok, S. (1982). *Secrets: On the ethics of concealment and revelation*. New York, NY: Pantheon.

Brudney, J., & Wright, D. (2002). Revisiting administrative reform in the American states. *Public Administration Review, 62*(3), 353–361.

Centers for Medicare & Medicaid Services. (2005). *Overview: 1-800-MEDICARE help line*. Retrieved December 25, 2010, from http://www.cms.gov/1800medicare/

Chesi, F., Pallotti, M., & Signore, O. (2005). E-government challenges and the CiTel experience. In A. Aurigi, P. van den Besselaar, F. De Cindio, G. Gumpert, & S. Drucker (Eds.), *Digital cities: The augmented public space workshop. In conjunction with the second international conference on communities and technologies proceedings* (pp. 65–70). Milan, Italy: Università degli Studi di Milano.

Cooper, T. L., Bryer, T. A., & Meek, J. W. (2006). Citizen-centered collaborative public management [Special issue]. *Public Administration Review, 66,* 76–88.

Darbishire, H. (2010). *Proactive transparency: The future of the right to information?* World Bank Institute Working Paper.

De Nies, Y., & Weber, V. (2008). *Critics: Medicare helpline not so helpful.* Retrieved December 25, 2010, from http://abcnews.go.com/GMA/OnCall/story?id=5779840

Dewan, S., & Frederick, J. R. (2005). The digital divide: Current and future research directions. *Journal of the Association for Information Systems, 6*(12), 298–336.

Ebdon, C., & Franklin, A. (2004). Searching for a role for citizens in the budget process. *Public Budgeting and Finance, 24*(1), 32–49.

Ebdon, C., & Franklin, A. (2006). Citizen participation in budgeting theory. *Public Administration Review, 66*(3), 437–447.

Ezz, I., Papazafeiropulou, A., & Serrano, A. (2009). Challenges of interorganizational collaboration for information technology adoption: Insights from a governmental financial decision-making process in Egypt. *Information Technology for Development, 15*(3), 209–223.

Faiola, A., & Matei, S. A. (2005). Cultural cognitive style and web design: Beyond a behavioral inquiry into computer-mediated communication. *Journal of Computer-Mediated Communication, 11*(1), article 18. Retrieved March 23, 2012, from http://jcmc.indiana.edu/vol11/issue1/faiola.html

Florini, A. (Ed.). (2007). *The right to know: Transparency for an open world.* New York, NY: Columbia University Press.

Fozzard, A. (2002). *How, when and why does poverty get budget priority: Poverty reduction strategy and public expenditure in Mozambique.* ODI Working Paper.

Franklin, A., & Ebdon, C. (2005). Are we all touching the same camel? Exploring a model of participation in budgeting. *American Review of Public Administration, 35*(2), 168–185.

Franklin, A. L., Ho, A. T., & Ebdon, C. (2009). Participatory budgeting in midwestern states: Democratic connection or citizen disconnection. *Public Budgeting and Finance, 29*(3), 52–73.

Gleitman, L. R., & Gleitman, H. (1970). *Phrase and paraphrase.* New York, NY: W.W. Norton.

Goldenberg, S. (2008, December 2). Iraq war my biggest regret, Bush admits. *The Guardian.*

Government Accountability Office (GAO). (2004). *Medicare: Accuracy of responses from the 1-800-medicare help line should be improved, GAO-05-130.* Washington, DC: Government Accountability Office.

Government Accountability Office (GAO). (2008). *Medicare: Callers can access 1-800-medicare services, but responsibility within CMS for limited English proficiency plan unclear, GAO-09-104.* Washington, DC: Government Accountability Office.

Heald, D. (2006). Varieties of transparency. In C. Hood & D. A. Heald (Eds.), *Transparency: The key to better governance?* Oxford, England: British Academy/Oxford University Press.

Hilton, R. W. (1981). The determinants of information value: Synthesizing some general results. *Management Science, 27*(1), 57–64.

Ho, A. T. (2007). *Engaging citizens in measuring and reporting community conditions: A manager's guide.* Washington, DC: IBM Center for the Business of Government.

Hood, C. (2007). What happens when transparency meets blame-avoidance. *Public Management Review, 9*(2), 191–210.

Ingraham, P., & Moynihan, D. (2001). Beyond measurement. In D. Forsyth (Ed.), *Quicker, better, cheaper: Managing performance in American government.* New York, NY: Rockefeller Institute.

Justice, J. B., & Dülger, C. (2009). Fiscal transparency and authentic citizen participation in public budgeting: The role of third-party intermediation. *Journal of Public Budgeting, Accounting and Financial Management, 21*(2), 254–288.

Kim, S. (2000). Public trust in Japan and South Korea: Does the rise of critical citizens matter? *Public Administration Review, 70*(5), 801–810.

Kopits, G., & Graig, J. (1998). *Transparency in government operations.* Occasional Paper 158, International Money Fund.

Lewis, C., & Smith, M. R. (2008). *False pretenses, Center for Public Integrity.* Retrieved October 1, 2010, from http://www.iwatchnews.org/2008/01/23/5641/false-pretenses

Liner, E. B., Harry, P. H., Elisa, V., Ryan, A., Pat, D., Scott, B., & Ron, S. (2001). *Making results-based state government work.* Washington DC: Urban Institute.

Lipowicz, A. (2010). *Sunlight Foundation taking heat for usaspending.gov critique.* In Government 2.0. Falls Church, VA: Washington Technology.

Marks, J. (2001). Jean-Jacques Rousseau, Michael Sandel and the politics of transparency. *Polity, 33*(4), 619–642.

Mathews, A. S. (1978). *The darker reaches of government: Access to information about public administration in the United States, Britain and South Africa.* Berkeley: University of California Press.

Melkers, J. E., & Willoughby, K. G. (2001). Budgeters' views of state performance budgeting systems: Distinctions across branches. *Public Administration Review, 61*(1), 54–64.

Metzenbaum, S. (2009). *Performance management recommendations for the new administration.* Washington, DC: IBM Center for the Business of Government.

Moore, J. (2010, December 8). *Usaspending.gov offers subcontract data for first time.* Retrieved March 23, 2012, from http://www.executivegov.com/2010/12/usaspending-gov-offers-subcontract-data-for-first-time/"

Mossenburg, K., Tolbert, C., & Stansbury, M. (2003). *Virtual inequality: Beyond the digital divide.* Washington, DC: George Washington University Press.

Obama, B. (2009). *Memorandum for the heads of executive departments and agencies: Subject: Transparency and open government.* Retrieved March 23, 2012, from http://www.whitehouse.gov/the_press_office/TransparencyandOpenGovernment

OMB Watch. (2010, December 4). *The teas of transparency.* Retrieved December 25, 2010, from http://www.ombwatch.org/node/11415

Piotrowski, S. J. (2009). *Transparency and secrecy: A reader linking literature and contemporary Debate.* Lanham, MD: Rowman & Littlefield.

Pope, C. (2008, August 3). "Kick in the backside" urged for Medicare help line: Lawmakers, audits find anemic service. *Chicago Tribune.*

Prat, A. (2006). The more closely we are watched, the better we behave? In C. Hood & D. A. Heald (Eds.), *Transparency: The key to better governance?* Oxford, England: British Academy/Oxford University Press.

Putterman, E. (2001). Realism and reform in Rousseau's constitutional projects for Poland and Corsica. *Political Studies, 49*(3), 481–494.

Riedel, R. (2001). Limitations for interstate e-government and interdisciplinary projects. *Proceedings of the 12th International Workshop on Database and Expert Systems Applications.* IEEE Computer Society, Washington, DC.

Rourke, F. E., & Christoph, J. B. (1975). A comparative view: Secrecy in Britain. *Public Administration Review, 35*(1), 23–32.

Rousseau, J. (1772). *Considerations on the government of Poland and on its proposed reformation.* Retrieved July 10, 2010, from http://www.constitution.org/jjr/poland.htm

Schacter, M. (1999). *Means... ends... indicators: Performance measurement in the public sector.* Policy Brief, No. 3. Institute on Governance, Ottowa, Ontario, Canada.

Schroder, H. M., Driver, M. J., & Strenfert, S. (1967). Human information processing. New York, NY: Holt, Rinehart & Winston.

Struther, R. (2010). Administration releases framework for spending data quality. In *The Fine Print: OMB Watch.* Retrieved March 23, 2012, from http://www.ombwatch.org/node/10765

Sunlight Foundation. (n.d.) *Clearspending. Results.* Retrieved December 25, 2010, from http://sunlightfoundation.com/clearspending/results/

van den Haak, M. J., de Jong, M. D. T., & Schellens, P. J. (2009). Evaluating municipal Web sites: A methodological comparison of three think-aloud variants. *Government Information Quarterly, 26*(1), 193–202.

USASpending.gov. (n.d.). *Learn about usaspending.gov.* Retrieved December 25, 2010, from http://www.usaspending.gov/learn?tab=FAQ#1

Weber, M. (1968). *Economy and society: An outline of interpretive sociology.* New York, NY: Bedminster.

PART III

CITIZEN PARTICIPATION: TRENDS AND ASSESSMENTS

CHAPTER 5

CITIZEN PARTICIPATION
AT THE LOCAL LEVEL

Elaine B. Sharp
University of Kansas

Looming over the topic of citizen participation are two sobering "big picture" views. One stems from Robert Putnam's landmark study *Bowling Alone*
(2000), which documented seemingly inexorable declines in political and
civic engagement since the mid-1970s and linked those to declining social
capital—declining participation in networks of social groups that reinforce
norms of trust and reciprocity. Putnam charted decline in a broad array
of types of participation, including not only voting in national elections,
participation in other electoral or partisan activity, but also attendance at
local public meetings, leadership or committee service in a local organization, signing petitions, writing a letter to the newspaper, and membership
in a broad array of organizations in civil society. While Putnam found differences across these types of participation in both level of activity and rate
of decline, the across-the-board pattern of decline suggests that forms of
political participation and civic engagement that were not tracked would
also show decline.

The other sobering perspective about political participation is the issue
of bias. Across a broad and deep array of scholarship on virtually all forms

The State of Citizen Participation in America, pages 101–129
Copyright © 2012 by Information Age Publishing
All rights of reproduction in any form reserved.

of political participation in the United States stretches the common and troublesome finding that there are systematic inequalities in who participates. Racial and socioeconomic differences in virtually all forms of participation have been documented by numerous studies. The bottom line is nicely articulated by Rosenstone and Hansen (1993, p. 43): "There are racial disparities across every form of political activity in both the electoral and governmental [participation] arenas...In addition, wealthy Americans are more likely than poor Americans to take part in political activities."

This chapter traces contemporary scholarship on political participation *at the local level*. It rests upon a broad definition that sees political participation as any form of involvement in community affairs that has the potential to shape the allocation of public resources or the resolution of community issues. This broad definition includes explicitly electoral activity such as voting and campaign involvement as well as nonelectoral activity such as citizen-initiated contacting of public officials, involvement in neighborhood organizations, and various forms of civic engagement, such as coproduction or discussion of public issues. Most important, the discussion proceeds against the backdrop of the pair of troublesome matters just acknowledged: declining and biased participation. But are these phenomena as evident in local forms of participation as they are in national forms of participation, where they have been substantially documented?

In this chapter, two themes are featured in a review of what is known about this question. These two featured themes are the growth of knowledge about distinctively local forms of political participation, and the importance of various organizations, from religious to governmental, in mobilizing citizen participation. Each theme points us to phenomena that have the *potential* to temper both the Putnam-like view that the extent of civic and political engagement has slid into a trough from which recovery is unlikely and the characterization of participation in America as inherently biased on racial and socioeconomic grounds.

PARTICIPATION AT THE LOCAL LEVEL: HOW MUCH? HOW BIASED?

Voting in national elections is one of the most visible and heavily studied forms of political participation. But by now there is a voluminous body of research examining various forms of citizen participation apart from voting. Indeed, perhaps what is most distinctive about citizen participation at the local level is that, while voting turnout in local elections is typically far below even the disappointing levels of voting in national elections, there are other avenues for distinctively local forms of citizen participation that have the distinct potential for meaningful involvement. As Macedo (2005) argues,

Important as they are, elections and the activities that precede them are but one aspect of political activity. Protesting and marching, attending a public meeting, lobbying a government official, writing to a newspaper about a public issue, signing an e-mail or written petition, boycotting, canvassing a neighborhood, or engaging in political mobilization and debate are all forms of civic engagement. (p. 7)

Acknowledging differences in types of participation is important for many reasons. For one thing, simply acknowledging the wide array of ways in which citizens might participate at the local level is important in the context of discussions about declines or disappointingly low levels of political participation. It is possible that disappointingly low levels of some forms of political participation coexist with unexpectedly high levels of other forms of political participation. In addition, the factors that shape participation may differ across the types, and as a result the characteristics of participants and nonparticipants may also differ across the types. This means that the existence of bias in who participates may differ across different forms of participation. Furthermore, the capacity of governmental and nongovernmental organizations to mobilize participation may differ depending upon the type of participation at issue. Even the impact of participation on local governance may depend on the type of participation.

But what are the different forms of political participation at the local level? Contemporary literature features research on many different forms; and as noted at the outset, this chapter is based upon a broad definition of political participation. However, this chapter will focus on the most heavily researched forms of local participation: (a) contacting public officials; (b) neighborhood organization involvement and closely linked activities such as working on community projects and co-production of urban services; (c) attendance at public meetings as well as the more elaborate version of this: deliberative democracy; and (d) voting in local elections. A brief review of research on each of these forms illustrates that conclusions about the level of political participation and patterns of involvement, including possible socioeconomic and racial bias in participation, depends in part on the form of participation.

Contacting Local Public Officials

Contacting a public official to register a request, complaint, or policy preference can be viewed as a participatory behavior generating the local level equivalent of constituency casework among members of Congress; it can also be the occasion for citizen-bureaucrat interaction when new policies are being implemented or routine services are being delivered. Research on contacting public officials emphasizes that this is a more difficult act than, say, voting. Except in cities that establish specialized complaint-handling units, neither the venue nor the mechanism are laid out for would-be contactors, and the occasion for contacting is also left for the individual to define. Hence, although some earlier research focusing on particular cities suggested that 40% or more of citizens contact their local government in a given year (Thomas & Melkers, 1999; Vedlitz & Veblen, 1980), a definitive study based on a national sample survey conducted in 1989–1990 showed that only 25% of respondents had contacted a state or local elected official, and only 13% had contacted a nonelected official at the subnational level (Verba, Schlozman, & Brady, 1995). More contemporary research from national sample surveys shows similar levels of contacting targeted at local officials; typically in the range of 18% to 30% of those surveyed report having done this in the past year (Jacobs, Cook, & Delli Carpini, 2009, p. 40; Zukin, Keeter, Andolina, Jenkins, & Delli Carpini, 2006).

Early research on citizen-initiated contacting of local officials exhibited a lack of consensus over the question of bias in patterns of contacting. Some research (Sharp, 1982; Hero, 1986) suggested the usual participatory bias (lower propensities for contacting from the disadvantaged and racial minorities); some suggested a curvilinear pattern, with the bulk of contacts coming from middle-class areas rather than advantaged or disadvantaged areas (Jones,Greenberg, Kaufman, & Drew, 1977). Still other research suggested that the institutional arrangements in place for handling contacts shape socioeconomic patterns of contacting. In particular, a city with a specialized complaint-handling unit may level the playing field, such that the usual socioeconomic bias in participation either diminishes or disappears entirely (Sharp, 1986).

Recently, there has been a surge of research on web-based forms of contacting city officials, or "E-government" (Reddick, 2005; Thomas & Streib, 2003;Tolbert & Mossberger, 2006). Some of this research suggests the potential for important benefits from this version of contacting. Reddick (2005), for example, finds that if given a choice, citizens would prefer to use the Web rather than the telephone to contact officials. Scott's (2006, p. 349) study of government Web sites in the core cities of the 100 largest U.S. metropolitan areas finds that, while the sites were generally not structured to enhance online public dialogue, they did provide a great deal of "information, communication and transaction services"—qualities that could facilitate citizen-initiated contacting of government officials. And Tolbert and Mossberger's (2006) analysis of Pew survey data from 2001 suggests that "contacting" local government in the sense of using its Web sites is linked with improved perceptions of government accessibility and responsiveness.

On the other hand, the lingering issue of the digital divide in the United States means that the introduction of web-based methods for contacting government is likely to exacerbate rather than minimize any preexisting socioeconomic biases in who contacts local government officials (Reddick, 2005). In fact, Thomas and Streib's (2003) study of Georgia residents found that while White, wealthy, and younger individuals are unsurprisingly more likely to use the Internet than non-White, nonwealthy, and older individuals, these digital divide characteristics are even greater when use of government Web sites is at issue.

Neighborhood Organizations and Co-production

Research on political participation at the local level has always featured considerable attention to participation in neighborhood organizations of various kinds. This includes a voluminous and ever-growing body of case studies of neighborhood organization activity, typically featuring neighborhood-based activism over objectionable proposed land uses or other development issues (Goetz & Sidney, 1997), gentrification (Boyd, 2008), problematic city service delivery, or other contested matters (Goetz & Sidney, 1994). Neighborhood organizations clearly emerge as key organized interests in city politics, and participation in such organizations can therefore, in part, be viewed as the local level equivalent of lobbying (Mesch & Schwiriam, 1996).

Apart from their role as organized interests lobbying for preferred policy or administrative outcomes, neighborhood organizations are also important for their role in aggregating citizen inputs into co-production. Co-production refers to the process by which citizens and government officials jointly contribute to the production of urban services (Sharp, 1980). For example, citizen participation of the co-production sort can involve the efforts of community volunteers who engage in clean-up campaigns, tree planting, or other activities that help government professionals to produce park and recreational services. Another common example is that of neighborhood residents engaging in property marking and block-watching activities in collaboration with the local police, such that public order and security are co-produced. Bovaird (2007) extends the co-production concept by distinguishing a full set of scenarios differentiated by whether professionals, service users, or both plan the service and whether professionals, service users, or both are involved in service delivery.

While less common than self-reported voting in national elections, the prevalence of participation in neighborhood-based organizations is far from trivial in the United States. For example, Robert Putnam's Social Capital Benchmark Communities (SCBC) survey conducted in 2000 asked if the respondent had "participated in a neighborhood association" in the previous year. Overall, 23% had done so. However, a breakdown of the SCBC survey data, which is available through the Roper Center (http://

www.ropercenter.uconn.edu/), shows that there is substantial city-by-city variation in the propensity of residents to participate in neighborhood associations. In some SCBC cities such as Baton Rouge and Minneapolis, the reported rate of neighborhood association involvement approaches 40%; by contrast, the rate is only 18% in Cincinnati, 16% in Yakima, and 11% in Lewiston, Maine.

Much of the research on participation in neighborhood organizations (and by extension, co-production) suggests that the usual participatory bias is evident here—a bias toward greater participation by the better educated, by those who are better off, and by homeowners (Thomas, 1986; Goetz & Sidney, 1997). Putnam's Social Capital Benchmark Communities survey (SCBC) reveals much the same. With individuals from all community samples and the national sample included, bivariate analysis reveals a definite link between education level and propensity to participate in a neighborhood association. The percentage who report participating in a neighborhood association within the past year is a little over 30% for those with at least a bachelor's degree, drops to 23% for those with some college experience, to 18% for those with a high school diploma, and only 12% for those with less than a completed high school education. Similarly, while 37% of those with an income over $100,000 have participated in a neighborhood association, only 21% earning between $30,000 and $50,000 have done so, and only 14% of those earning less than $20,000 are neighborhood association participators.

On the other hand, some research suggests that the racial aspect of participation bias is reversed when neighborhood association involvement is at issue; Black residents of American cities are at least if not more likely to exhibit civic engagement in the form of neighborhood association involvement (Alex-Assensoh, 1998; Thomas, 1986). Consistent with that research, the SCBC survey reveals Black respondents are slightly more likely than White respondents (29% versus 23%) to report involvement with a neighborhood organization.

Measuring co-production in all its many possible manifestations is not as straightforward as measuring involvement with neighborhood associations, which can include co-production. However, the SCBC survey does include a question on whether the individual had "worked on a community project in the last 12 months." To the extent that this is a viable proxy measure of co-production, it reveals fairly substantial levels of such participation—37% said that they had worked on a community project in the previous year.

However, like neighborhood association involvement, the propensity to work on a community project exhibits the usual socioeconomic bias. The percentage who report this form of civic engagement drops steadily and dramatically from 58% for graduate or professional degree holders to 17% for those with less than a completed high school education and from 54%

for those with an annual income over $100,000 to 23% for those with an income under $20,000. On the other hand, there is a negligible and statistically insignificant difference between the 38% of White respondents and the 34% of African American respondents who worked on a community project.

Attending Public Meetings and Deliberative Democracy

Attending meetings on local issues is another obvious form of participation at the local level. In one sense, simple attendance at a public meeting may not seem all that participatory, particularly if it only involves passive intake of information. However, attendance at a public meeting can be an expressive act, either if the individual chooses to make comments at the meeting or if orchestrated attendance by a large number of stakeholders constitutes an influence attempt (as in showing the strength of one's numbers or the depth of a stakeholder group's interest). In addition, attending a public meeting in many cases can involve relatively intense involvement in planning, "visioning," or other "discursive participation" (Jacobs et al., 2009), a topic to be discussed further below.

Despite its multifaceted character, there is relatively plentiful evidence about the magnitude of citizen participation in the form of attendance at a local public meeting. This is the case because various national sample surveys have included questions about it. For example, drawing from the Roper Center's results for their poll question asking individuals whether they had "attended a public meeting on town or schools affairs" in the past year, Putnam (2000, p. 45) reports a 35% drop from 1973–1974 to 1993–1994 in propensity to attend such a meeting, a drop that took the already low level of this type of political involvement in the 1970s to below 16% by 1990 (Rosenstone & Hansen, 1993, p. 65). Putnam's Social Capital Benchmark Survey, administered in 2000, asks how many times an individual has *ever* attended such meetings. From this lifetime perspective, there is somewhat more participation in public meetings—42% of national sample respondents indicated that they had attended such a meeting at least once; however, 58% had never attended such a meeting, and another 24% had done so only three or fewer times in their life.

There is also evidence of some of the same sorts of biases in public meeting attendance that have been discussed with respect to other forms of participation. A simple modeling exercise applied to Putnam's 2000 survey shows that the number of meetings an individual has attended increases with income, education level, length of residence in the community, and homeownership. On the other hand, bias in propensity to attend a public meeting may be contingent upon the type of meeting at issue. Marschall's (2004) analysis of survey data from the 1989 Detroit Area Study suggests that representational biases in who attends public meetings not only varies city by city within the metro area but is also contingent upon issue. While she included no measure of income, her otherwise elaborate modeling shows that the bias toward the better educated participating more is evident when school-related meetings are asked about, but not public safety-related meetings; neither employment status nor homeownership shaped propensity to participate in either type of meeting.

In recent years, there has been an upsurge of interest in a heretofore unrecognized or at least underacknowledged type of participation that lies in the shadow of attendance at public meetings. When ordinary citizens talk with other citizens about public issues, even if it is in informal social settings, they are exhibiting a form of civic engagement that Jacobs et al. (2009) call discursive participation. In contrast with most traditionally studied forms of participation, which tend to involve attempts to influence public policy, discursive participation features deliberative communication behaviors that allow citizens to formulate and revise their preferences (i.e., learn about what they should want from policymakers).

Discursive participation itself can be decomposed into several subtypes. These include one-on-one conversations with other individuals about public issues ("informal public talk"), communications specifically intended to persuade someone on a public issue or candidate ("political persuasion"), and relatively formal communication with groups of other individuals, either face-to-face or via the Internet ("public deliberation") (Jacobs et al., 2009, p. 37). The "public deliberation" form of discursive participation and particularly the face-to-face version of it, have recently inspired a great deal of attention. A variety of proponents of deliberation processes have emerged to extol the potential for such citizen deliberations to "transform individuals into enlightened citizens and restore democratic policymaking" (Jacobs et al., 2009, p. 9). Public deliberation will be considered more fully in a later section on mobilizing organizations.

For the moment, however, it is important to acknowledge that distinguishing the various subtypes of discursive participation is important with respect to the question of how prevalent this form of political participation is. Based on results from their national sample poll in the spring of 2003, Jacobs et al. (2009) suggest that, while face-to-face deliberation on a public issue with a group of others is relatively rare (25% say they have done so) compared with the more than 60% who report voting in national elections, it is about on par with some nondeliberative forms of participation such as contacting public officials (28%). There is even more frequent participation in "informal public talk" about a public issue—the less formal and less demanding version of discursive participation. Indeed, the 68% reporting this behavior puts it at the same magnitude as reported voting behavior.

Voting in Local Elections

Much less is known about patterns of voting in local elections than is known about voting at the national level. However, what is known suggests that there are disappointingly low levels of this iconic form of political participation. A recent study, for example, suggests that in the United States "only about 27 percent of voting-age adults (or 39 percent of registered voters) participate in city council elections" (Hajnal, 2010, p. 35). This evidence of disappointingly low turnout is admittedly quite dated. Reflecting the difficulty that scholars of local government have in obtaining data on the thousands of elections that occur at the local level in the United States at any given time, Hajnal was forced to rely upon a 1986 survey of city clerks to get data on voter turnout for city council elections, because that is the most recent nationally representative survey that has data on turnout and registration!

One might expect that mayoral elections (in cities with strong mayoral forms of government) would generate somewhat higher levels of voting participation given the greater visibility of this office compared with a city council seat. A scattering of case study evidence suggests that, in some places and under some circumstances, mayoral elections may indeed yield substantial turnouts. In Chicago, for example, the 40% turnout of registered voters for the spring 1995 election that gave Richard M. Daley his second full term as mayor was by local standards a low turnout—indeed the lowest in half a century (Chicago's Mayor, 1995). By contrast, turnout in the April 1983 election that yielded Harold Washington as the city's first Black mayor was a record-setting 79% of registered voters. More generally, mayoral races pitting a Black candidate against a White candidate have been shown to yield unusually high turnouts, in part due to the mobilization of the Black community behind the Black candidate and in part due to a reactionary surge in turnout among White voters who may see the Black candidate as a threat. For example, about 65% of registered voters turned out in the 1991 mayoral election in Memphis—an election that yielded the city's first elected Black mayor as the normally splintered Black community joined forces behind a consensus candidate, Willie Herenton (Vanderleeuw, Liu, & Marsh, 2004).

Evidence about participation in local elections can also be obtained from random sample surveys of the public, although the public's tendency to overreport voting participation is legendary. One of the most definitive large-scale surveys of a representative sample of Americans that asked about local elections was the American Citizen Participation Study (ACPS), conducted in late 1989. When asked about local elections "that have been held since you were old enough to vote," a little over half of respondents claimed to have voted in either all (24%) or most (31%) such elections; but about 22% never or rarely voted (Verba, Schlozman, Brady, & Nie, 1995). As Hajnal's (2010, p. 37) analysis of the ACPS data shows, there is strong evidence of bias in local voting participation. More than 60% of Whites are local voters (defined as those saying they "always" or "often" vote in local elections); by contrast, about 55% of Blacks, 39% of Latinos, and 36% of Asians are local voters. Differences across education groups are even more dramatic: over 70% of those with at least a college degree are local voters compared to about 50% of those with a high school degree and less than 40% of those with less than a high school degree. Mirroring a pattern that is evidenced in national elections, there are also very striking age differences in local voting participation. Nearly 80% of those 65 years old or older always or often vote in local elections; for those aged 25–64, the percentage who are voters drops to about 68%; and for young voters (18–24 year olds), the propensity to vote in local elections is only 30%.

How Much, How Biased? A Preliminary Assessment

For those who might hope that political participation at the local level would be more prevalent and less biased toward greater participation by those with more resources, the results reported so far in this chapter are likely to be somewhat disappointing. Americans are by and large participating at even lower levels at the community level than they do in national politics, at least if the 50% or so (and as of 2008 the 61%) turnout rate for voting in national elections is the standard. Furthermore, socioeconomic biases that are apparent in national level politics are present at the local level as well.

But such a broad-brush overview ignores some noticeable distinctions among types of participation at the local level. Generally, participation via voting in local elections, contacting local public officials about problems or issues, or attending local meetings is not very prevalent. On the other hand, there is evidence of relatively high levels of the more informal versions of discursive participation, such as trying to persuade someone on a public issue; and nearly half of survey respondents indicated some involvement in co-production in the sense of working informally with others on community problems (Jacobs et al., 2009, p. 40) or working on community projects. While not highly prevalent overall, in many communities, participation in neighborhood organizations is also at quite high levels.

To borrow a distinction offered by Zukin et al. (2006), it seems that there is more in the way of civic engagement than political engagement in American communities:

> Political engagement is activity aimed at influencing government policy or affecting the selection of public officials... Civic engagement, on the other

hand, refers to participation aimed at achieving a public good , but usually through direct hands-on work in cooperation with others...The most obvious example of this kind of participation is volunteer work in one's community. (p. 51)

Political engagement is the realm in which socioeconomic biases in participation are most strikingly obvious. Indeed, the relative absence of less educated, lower income individuals from this realm of participation may be a major reason for the uninspiring magnitude of these types of participation. And if Zukin et al.'s (2006) findings about the special distaste for political engagement among younger generations hold up, participation in this form of political engagement may become even less prevalent in the future. By contrast, civic engagement, including some of the most distinctive forms of local participation (such as co-production and some aspects of neighborhood organization activity), is more prevalent in American communities and is of special importance to racial minorities.

But why is the pattern of socioeconomic bias in participation evident on both the political engagement side and on the civic engagement side? Indeed, apart from the generational replacement concerns that are the focus of Zukin et al.'s (2006) work, how might we understand variation across individuals and across places in the rate of political and civic engagement? The next section takes up this question, with special emphasis on the organizations that mobilize individual involvement at the community level.

MOBILIZING ORGANIZATIONS

Several theoretical approaches have been used to explain who participates in politics or civic affairs and under what circumstances. One theoretical approach emphasizes attitudes, values, and other psychological predispositions. Whether or not the individual has a sense of political efficacy, for example, serves as an important predictor in this approach. Another approach emphasizes individual self-interests and rational choices made in the pursuit of those self-interests. Perhaps the oldest approach used to account for variation is a sociological one that depicts political participation as being shaped by the social groups, contexts, and networks within which individuals are located (Mettler & Soss, 2004).

But in the early 1990s, a "political mobilization" explanation, building primarily upon the insights of the sociological approach, rose to special prominence. Political mobilization is defined by Rosenstone and Hansen (1993) as the "process by which candidates, parties, activists, and groups *induce other people to participate*" (p. 25, my emphasis). Mobilization can either be "direct," as when mobilizing agents "contact citizens personally and encourage them to take action"; or it can be "indirect" when mobilizing agents "contact citizens through mutual associates, whether family, friends, neighbors, or colleagues" (Rosenstone & Hansen, 1993, p. 26) or through various organizations in civil society (clubs, churches, and the like). Mobilization increases the likelihood of participation for those who are the target of mobilization by subsidizing political information that individuals would otherwise not have the motivation to obtain, underwriting other costs of participation, and generally creating "opportunities for citizens to participate" (Rosenstone & Hansen, 1993, pp. 26–27). As we will see when we consider city government itself as a mobilizing agent, another form of indirect mobilization occurs when a mobilizing agent creates institutions or structural arrangements that provide occasions for participation for specific individuals—occasions that would not otherwise exist.

Recent research has confirmed the importance of mobilization as an explanation for who engages in political participation at the local level. Reporting on the results of their National Civic Engagement Survey, conducted in the spring of 2002, Zukin et al. (2006) find that "the effects of being personally asked to participate in the political process...are powerful and operate above and beyond the boost provided by traditional political capital" (p. 131). Across all 19 measures of civic engagement that they studied, "those who have been invited to participate were significantly more likely to have done the activity than were those who didn't receive an invitation" (p. 131). Similarly, in her study of two forms of political participation (contacting officials and attendance at meetings) with respect to school-related or public safety issues, Marschall (2004) found that direct recruitment in the sense of being contacted by leaders about a crime or schools problem is a powerful predictor of participation. Depending upon the issue and the type of participation, direct mobilization increased the probability of participation at least 9.4 percentage points and as much as 20.9 percentage points.

While experimental studies of mobilization are relatively rare, there is some strong experimental evidence of the power of mobilization to increase one form of political participation: turnout in municipal elections. Green, Gerber, and Nickerson (2003) report on a set of randomized voter mobilization experiments conducted in Bridgeport, Columbus, Detroit, Minneapolis, Raleigh, and St. Paul. Just prior to election day in 2001, individuals in treatment groups defined by random selection from official registered voter lists were contacted face-to-face by someone from a coalition of nonpartisan student and community groups. During the contact, the individual was encouraged to vote. Green et al. (2003) reported that this simple form of mobilization did effectively increase voter turnout. Across all the sites, face-to-face mobilization increased the probability of voting by 7.1 percentage points; in St. Paul and Bridgeport, face-to-face mobilization increased the probability of voting by 14.4 percentage points. In a related vein, experimental research by Gerber, Green, and Larimer (2008) revealed that social pressure evoked by information that one's voting turn-out (or lack thereof) will be revealed to others in the neighborhood yields equally dramatic increases in the probability of voting, even in a primary election featuring mostly local offices and ballot proposals.

As Zukin et al. (2006, pp. 131–132) noted, however, "the decision by groups or individuals to ask someone to participate is not a random act, and is often related to judgments about the likelihood that the request will yield a positive response" or to "judgments about the effectiveness of the participa-tion likely to be undertaken by the person asked." In particular, they found that younger people are much less likely than older individuals to be the tar-get of mobilization efforts in this sense of being invited to participate.

This point illustrates an important aspect of mobilization. On the one hand, mobilization can serve to exacerbate existing sociodemographic bias-es in who participates. For example, young people are less inclined toward political participation than older people; and to the extent that this is so, they are a less attractive target for mobilization. On the other hand, mobi-lization campaigns can be specifically designed to overcome existing biases in who participates. Mobilizing those who traditionally are *not* predisposed toward political participation is presumably more difficult than mobilizing the already-predisposed. But efforts to do just this are relatively plentiful at the local level. In the sections that follow, a variety of key examples of such mobilizing efforts will be described. The obvious questions about efforts to counteract the usual biases in political participation via mobilization of the underinvolved is whether such efforts can succeed, and if so, for what forms of political participation and under what circumstances. Recent research has yielded interesting findings with respect to these questions.

In order to tackle such questions, it is important to consider first the mat-ter of what types of organizations serve as the mobilizing agents for the vari-ous forms of local level participation that have been outlined so far? A variety of social and political organizations, including political parties, Chambers of Commerce, labor groups, civil rights organizations, and many others are regularly involved as mobilizing agents. However, this section features three types of mobilizing organizations that are of particular interest for one or more of the distinctively local forms of political participation that were out-lined in the previous section. The three types are religious groups or institu-tions, deliberative democracy organizations, and local government itself.

Religious Groups as Mobilizing Organizations

In the broadest sense, religion and religious groups can be said to mo-bilize political participation at the local level because religious organizations shape politically relevant attitudes on local issues. Michael Lee Owens (2010), for example, shows that religious affiliation shapes the extent to which individuals (in the Atlanta area at least) support a resource-sharing, regionalist perspective rather than a defensive localist view. These differing views will presumably have direct implications for the willingness of residents to work on metropolitan level problems rather than restricting their participation to neighborhood level matters.

But churches and other religious-based organizations are even more directly involved in mobilizing citizen participation in government and politics at the local level. There is, of course, a long-acknowledged view of the importance of Black churches in electoral politics and in protest politics, particularly with regard to civil rights organizing. Contemporary research shows that, at least in cities with large Black populations, Black churches still are significant in mobilizing electoral participation. In Detroit, for example, there are church-based political action committees that "distribute information to the African-American community, promote chosen candidates, and support voter registration and turnout activities" (Rusch, 2010, p. 494). Nor is it primarily or even predominantly Black churches that are involved in electoral mobilization. For example, Djupe, Neiheisel, and Sokhey's (2007) case study of Columbus, Ohio, reveals that predominantly White, evangelical Protestant churches were more likely to be involved in voter registration than Black Protestant churches, and that Roman Catholic churches far outshined all denominations in propensity for involvement in voter registration.

But contemporary research has moved beyond this to show the important mobilizing role of churches in other local level matters. Not surprisingly, one key line of work examines the role of churches and church leaders in mobilizing citizens for political participation when morality issues become controversial. An obvious example involves the role of religious organizations in mobilizing anti-abortion protest. Woliver's (1999) case study of anti-abortion activism and government response to it in Greenville and Columbia, South Carolina, shows that religious organizations have been mobilizers on this issue at the local level, not just the national level.

Religious organizations are mobilizers of participation on other morality issues as well. For example, Penning and Storteboom (2007) document the role of clergy in mobilizing residents of Allegan County, Michigan, when an Indian tribe proposed to build a casino in the area. A sizable majority of clergy, across all three major types of denominations in the area, discussed the proposed casino with their congregants. Many others included the proposal in their sermons, thus literally using the pulpit to energize opposition; and a few clergy formed church discussion groups around the issue (2007, p. 37). While the evidence is indirect, Button, Wald, and Rienzo's (1999) study of the adoption of gay rights ordinances in U.S. cities suggests that conservative Protestant churches play an important role in mobilizing community members to oppose such ordinances.

A quite different line of scholarship on religious organizations and leaders as mobilizers of citizen participation focuses on faith-based organizations that are involved in community development and local social justice issues. Owens (2007), for example, documents the important role of Black churches in collaborating with governmental redevelopment programs in several New York City neighborhoods. His research documents how Community Development Corporations (CDCs) have been a key vehicle for churches to mobilize faith-based action. Similarly, Rusch (2010) describes the considerations that shape the willingness of Black pastors in Detroit to bring their congregations into broader, multiracial coalitions and networks intended to tackle abandoned housing, crime, and a variety of other redevelopment problems. And Crawford (2007) shows how two Lutheran church ministers organized a coalition of other congregations, nonprofits, and religiously based health systems—a coalition that mobilized a collective response to the problem of lack of health care access in south Omaha.

There is, in fact, a burgeoning literature on "congregation-based community organizing," which Hart (2001, p. 29) claims to be perhaps "the largest coherent contemporary movement for economic justice—either secular or religious—that engages grassroots Americans locally in face-to-face political activity." Melding themes drawn from Alinsky-style community organizing with traditions of religious social activism that are found across many denominations, congregation-based community organizing gets religious adherents involved in the community issues and projects that are part of a broad, progressive agenda (Hart, 2001, pp. 27–28). In this vein, Swarts (2008) shows how religious organizations have forged community organizing alliances in two cities—San Jose and St. Louis—and how those alliances have mobilized residents for political action on issues that are far removed from the culture-war politics of morality issues. Her case study of the community organization PACT in San Jose shows how this religiously based alliance successfully lobbied local officials to commit to affordable housing plans and other innovative programs focusing on youth, drugs, crime, and neighborhood needs.

Of course, not all religious organizations or religious leaders are predisposed to mobilize their congregants for participation on public issues. However, relatively little empirical work has been done on the factors affecting the propensity of religious entities to engage in political mobilization at the local level. There is some research suggesting denominational differences in the propensity of clergy to act as mobilizers on different types of issues. Penning and Storteboom (2007, p. 37), for example, found that conservative/fundamentalist Protestant clergy in the region affected were more likely than clergy from other denominations to discuss a controversial casino proposal with congregants or to include the proposal in a sermon. Similarly, Guth, Kellstedt, Copeland, and Rowland (2007, p. 146) noted that conservative religious forces were more mobilized over various morality issues (such as gay rights, gambling, and adult clubs) than other denominations in Greenville, South Carolina. On the other hand, fundamentalist clergy were out-shadowed in terms of both extent and success of mobilizing efforts by Baptist churches and some Presbyterian and other mainline Protestant churches when the issue of local observance of Martin Luther King, Jr. Day was at stake. Reese and Shields (2000) laid out a set of variables that on theoretical grounds should be expected to affect the involvement of clergy and congregation members on progressive community development issues and projects. For example, denominations and clergy with "this world" theologies, better educated clergy, and clergy with predominantly African American congregations were hypothesized to be more likely to be mobilizers for economic development activities in their community. However, their preliminary study of a limited number of churches in Detroit's empowerment zone area was not able to adequately test these hypotheses.

On the key issue of whether mobilization by religious organizations exacerbates or counteracts existing sociodemographic biases in who participates, there is no definitive study directly testing for this, especially with respect to local forms of political participation. However, taken as a whole, the research does suggest that religious organizations' mobilizing efforts to some extent counteract existing biases. In particular, mobilization in the form of congregation-based community organizing that is directed at community development and social justice issues can be viewed as broadening avenues for political participation by those with limited resources (in terms of education, income, and political sophistication).

Deliberative Democracy Organizations

As noted earlier in this chapter, a complex form of political participation called deliberative democracy has received a great deal of attention in recent years. Much more than simple attendance at a public meeting or contacting a public official about a community issue, deliberative democracy is a complex process in which citizens discuss and debate public issues and problems with other citizens and with government officials. In contrast with most other forms of political participation, the purpose of deliberative democracy is for citizens to develop ideas about what should be done about public problems using high-quality reasoning processes. Citizen participation in such processes is expected to empower citizens to forge effective partnerships with government officials, yielding shared governance arrangements that enhance both democracy and accountability (Jacobs et al.,

2009, pp. 7–9). Calling this the "new urban governance," Bingham (2006, p. 817) outlined the numerous ways in which the collaborative governance that is built on deliberative democracy is being attempted in U.S. communities. She notes that it includes

> e-democracy, public conversations, participatory budgeting, citizen juries, study circles, collaborative policymaking, and other forms of deliberation and dialogue among groups of stakeholders or citizens. . . . focus groups, roundtables, deliberative town meeting forums, choice work dialogues, cooperative management bodies, and other partnership arrangements. All promote a more civil public discourse and more collaborative and deliberative policymaking among citizens. Local government itself may organize the processes or collaborate with nonprofit organizations and other elements of civil society.

Deliberative democracy activity is being actively mobilized by a "loosely affiliated network of organizations" spanning the local level and the national level (Jacobs et al., 2009, p. 137). At the national level, a variety of organizations dedicated to the facilitation of local dialogue on public issues has emerged, often with the support of foundations. This includes organizations such as the National Issues Forums, Everyday Democracy, and AmericaSpeaks. Jacobs et al.'s (2009, p. 137) description of Everyday Democracy aptly conveys the character of such organizations:

> Everyday Democracy . . . is a national organization that harbors a similar mission of "helping local communities find ways for all kinds of people to think, talk, and work together to solve problems." Founded in 1989 with the support of philanthropist Paul Aicher, Everyday Democracy has worked with more than 550 communities to "help people connect public dialogue to real solutions." (http://www.everyday-democracy.org/en/Index.aspx)

Importantly, there is also a local level layer of organizations engaged in bringing residents together for deliberation on public issues. Church groups, civic associations, PTAs, and ad hoc groups formed to discuss specific problems are a rich seedbed of social capital that such national level organizations can informally tap into in order to facilitate deliberative democracy (Jacobs et al., 2009, p. 137). In addition, there is a supranational level of umbrella groups or professional organizations devoted to fostering public participation in discussion of local public issues. This level includes organizations such as the National Coalition for Deliberative Democracy, the Deliberative Democracy Consortium, and the International Association for Public Participation. The full panoply of professional training and conferences are provided by these organizations, which also consult with local governments, encouraging them to take public participation seriously (Jacobs et al., 2009, pp. 138–139).

There is no complete answer to the question of whether the various private organizations that are promoting deliberative democracy exacerbate or counteract the usual bias in who participates in public meetings, although Jacobs et al.'s (2009) study provides evidence that is guardedly optimistic. Noting that organizational membership and political capital are much more important than socioeconomic status in predicting who is most active in "public talking," they go on to suggest that their survey data and case study work show that "Deliberation is not... 'owned' or dominated by the better-off; participation extends beyond personal networks. Organizers of larger face-to-face forums reach out to a wide array of neighbors, often independently of city government" (p. 156). On the other hand, they do acknowledge that socioeconomic status has an important indirect role. Higher status individuals are more likely to join organizations, and this can bias who is invited into deliberative democracy occasions. Taken together with the evidence that deliberative democracy organizations work with local governments to mobilize their citizens for such participation, this means that whether mobilization is bias-sustaining or bias-reversing hinges on the kinds of organizations that local government chooses to work with. And that takes us to the broader question of government as a mobilizing organization.

Government as Mobilizing Organization

Perhaps the most interesting mobilizing agent for political participation at the local level is government itself. This section takes up local government's role as a mobilizing agent, especially with respect to (a) neighborhood-based participation and related co-production and deliberative democracy opportunities and (b) voting in local elections.

Encouraging Neighborhood-Based Participation

Given the importance of neighborhood groups as lobbyists for spatially defined interests, venues for co-production activities, and building blocks for complex deliberative democracy exercises, they have not surprisingly been the focus of numerous waves of policy innovation designed to incorporate neighborhood-based citizen activism into local government projects or to institutionalize neighborhood organizations such that they become part of ongoing governance or service-delivery activities.

In the narrower, function-specific version of this, local governments have adopted programs, especially in the policing area, that are premised on neighborhood-based civic engagement in collaboration with the police. In their most elaborate form, these programs include elements specifically intended to generate interest on the part of neighborhood residents and to mobilize their involvement in various forms of participation, including the contacting of local officials, co-production, and attendance at meetings where policing priorities for the neighborhood are hammered out. Perhaps the best example is community policing—a police reform program adopted by numerous municipal police forces in the 1990s and still functioning in many police departments today. Under community policing, the police department's emphasis is supposed to shift away from responding to crimes, emphasizing instead proactive, crime prevention measures that neighborhood-based police officers develop and implement in collaboration with neighborhood residents. In order for police officers to develop both enhanced knowledge of the neighborhoods that they serve and greater accessibility to residents, departments practicing community policing have adopted a variety of iconic practices such as fixed (i.e., nonrotational) assignment of officers to neighborhood beats, storefront police stations, deployment of officers on foot, bike or horse patrol, neighborhood block watch and business watch programs, victim contact programs, community newsletters, block meetings between the agency and community participants, and citizen surveys (Zhao, Lovrich, & Thurman, 1999, p. 80).

Neighborhood level meetings bringing together neighborhood residents and police officials assigned to the neighborhood have been one of the most important features of community policing. In Chicago, for example, monthly, neighborhood-based meetings of residents, police, and other city officials is, according to Skogan (2006, p. 11) the "most important mechanism for building and sustaining close relationships between police and the public," and the police put a great deal of effort into publicizing the meetings and encouraging a good turnout.

Community policing thus embodies governmental mobilization in that the program creates a variety of institutional arrangements that subsidize political information that would otherwise be costly for individuals to obtain, underwrites other costs of participation, and creates venues for citizen participation. Moreover, as Fung's (2004) case analysis reveals, community policing in places like Chicago involve even more explicit efforts to mobilize the public. To increase awareness and participation, the city used "both mass-media and community organizing techniques" that cost $1.6 million per year in two years in the late 1990s. Television and radio spots, billboards, and the hiring of between 30 and 60 community organizers who visited churches, neighborhood associations, and residences were used to "advertise and educate residents" about opportunities for participation in the community policing program (p. 75).

While acknowledging that community policing has not always involved smooth relationships between the police and the community in Chicago,

Fung (2004) concluded that in this case, government was not only success-ful in mobilizing the public but also able, through that mobilization, to counter the usual biases in who participates. With respect to the former, Fung (2004, p. 103) reported that citywide, in the latter half of the 1990s, over 6,000 residents of Chicago attended neighborhood-police meetings each month and that the average number of attendees at any of these neighborhood level "beat" meetings was 21 residents. With respect to the latter, Fung (p. 110) reported that, in stark contrast with the biases usually found in political participation, neither the racial composition of the police beat nor the education or income levels of the beat nor the prevalence of homeownership in the beat were significant predictors of attendance rates at these beat meetings. Only the personal crime rate influenced turnout at these meetings.

However, other evidence suggests a different pattern of conclusions about government's mobilizing role under the community policing pro-gram. Looking across 26 cities that are part of Putnam's SCBC survey, Sharp (2012) finds that individuals are *not* more likely to attend a public meeting or to work on a community project if they live in a city with more elaborate and extensive community policing practices. Even more sober-ing is her finding of an *inverse* relationship between individuals' propensity to participate in a neighborhood association and the extensiveness of their city's community policing effort. In the light of these findings, it is not surprising that the same study finds no evidence that community policing helps to counteract the usual biases in participation. When the strength of a city's community policing effort is taken into account, attendance at public meetings, work on community projects, and involvement in neigh-borhood associations are still biased toward the better educated and the wealthier; Black residents are more likely than White residents to be in-volved in neighborhood associations, but that is the case whether or not community policing is in place.

There is in fact substantial case study evidence that, as practiced in some communities, community policing can easily yield *selective mobilization* rath-er than broad-based enhancement of citizen participation, thus exacerbat-ing existing biases in political participation and civic engagement. In his study of the early years of community policing in Houston, for example, Skogan (1994) found that the program was implemented in ways that se-lectively mobilized Whites and established interests in the community. By relying primarily on the leadership of a select set of existing community organizations to publicize community policing activities and to choose in-dividuals to attend meetings with the district commander, Houston's com-munity policing programs succeeded in gaining the involvement of some residents, "but less affluent area residents did not hear about the programs and did not participate in them" (pp. 178–179). In addition, community policing officials chose to hold organizing meetings in parts of the community populated primarily by White homeowners; residents of areas populated primarily by Black residents in large rental properties were therefore not mobilized; indeed, such areas were identified as the source of the community's crime problems. As a result, in Houston the beneficial effects of enhanced citizen engagement with the police "were confined to whites and home owners" (p. 179). In a similar vein, case studies of community policing in Seattle showed that the police department initially partnered with a single community organization—one composed of established business interests and not representative of the racial diversity of the area (Lyons, 1999; Reed, 1999). This along with other aspects of community policing in Seattle kept the Black community from being drawn into participation.

Another version of neighborhood-based participation that has been programmatically encouraged by local government involves policy innovations that some cities have undertaken to build citywide systems for neighborhood-based participation in a wide array of matters of importance to the community. Perhaps the best-known scholarly study of this phenomenon is Berry, Portney, and Thomson's (1993) study of five cities that had implemented elaborate citywide systems for neighborhood-based participation. Neighborhood organizations in those five cities had been given important, ongoing powers. In Portland, for example, indigenous neighborhood associations working through seven district boards provided a focal point for reporting neighborhood needs to city officials, lobbying on neighborhood-specific issues, implementing projects funded with self-help development grants, engaging in comprehensive neighborhood-based planning, and engaging in citizen mediation (Berry et al., 1993, p. 13). That study shows that certain program design elements are required if comprehensive, citywide efforts to encourage neighborhood-based civic engagement are to be successful. These requirements include small, neighborhood-sized organizational units that allow face-to-face interaction, citywide coverage so that all areas of the city are included in the system, the designation of roles for neighborhood organizations that are issue- or policy-based but not partisan, and city provision of supportive resources (Berry et al., 1993, pp. 49–51).

Although the five cities' experience is broadly characterized as exemplary, Berry et al. found that mobilization in the form of enhanced levels of participation had not occurred: "The number of citizens involved in community participation activities is not greater in the core study cities than in the cities with which they were matched that have no citywide systems of participation"; in addition, their study shows that such citywide systems to encourage participation "are not able to overcome the very significant socioeconomic biases that are inherently associated with intensive participation" (1993, p. 97).

Later studies document related though by no means identical innovations through which city governments have attempted to tap into the participatory potential of neighborhoods. In Los Angeles, for example, discontent and efforts on the part of the San Fernando section of the city to secede led to charter reform, which (among other things) called for the creation in 1999 of a citywide system of neighborhood councils. The neighborhood councils were to have an official role as advisory bodies, feeding concerns and issue preferences to L.A. city officials, and thereby increasing "stakeholder involvement in urban governance" (Jun, 2007, p. 108).

In an analysis framed by network theory and drawing upon a 2003 survey of Los Angeles neighborhood council board members, Musso, Weare, Oztas, and Loges found that there is a bias in who participates by becoming a neighborhood council board member: "Board members systematically are better educated, wealthier, White, and older than the average person in their communities" (2006, p. 86). In a related study, Musso Weare, Elliot, Kitsuse, and Shiau noted other representational defects manifested in the Los Angeles experience with L.A. neighborhood councils. In particular, "Homeowners with long tenure in the community are most heavily represented" and "Latinos are underrepresented"; and they argue that these representational defects "endanger the political legitimacy of the councils, and raise questions regarding their ability to speak and act on behalf of diverse constituencies" (2007, p. 1).

Much the same story is evident in research on the planning advisory boards that Detroit has put into place. Research on these citizens' district councils shows that "planning advisory boards have the potential to evolve into nodes for grassroots planning and community development. Their promise, however, is often cut short by limited organizational capacity, lack of political power, municipal budget constraints, and shifting political regimes" (Silverman, 2003, p. 12).

Whether the focus is on narrower, function-specific programs, like community policing, through which local government attempts to mobilize civic engagement at the neighborhood level or on broader efforts to encourage civic engagement in citywide systems of multipurpose, neighborhood-based organizations, the research findings to date feature an odd mix of findings: some claims of success along with much evidence that such mobilization efforts fail to enhance citizen participation generally or to counteract the usual racial and socioeconomic biases in participation. However, the research also includes two very important conceptualizations that help to integrate these diverse findings: the distinction between weak participation activities and strong participation activities, and the concept of accountable autonomy.

With respect to the first of these, Portney and Berry (2007, p. 31) argue that while levels of community participation were no higher in places with citywide systems of neighborhood associations than in cities without such systems, residents in the former engaged in more "strong participation activities" than residents of the latter. Strong participation activities are those, like working with neighbors to solve a community problem, that provide opportunities not only for creating localized social capital but also bridging social capital. Localized social capital is the enhanced understanding and bonding that occurs through informal interaction with those who share similar interests. Portney and Berry (p. 31) argue that weaker forms of participation, like involvement in social and service organizations or contacting behavior, generate only this localized social capital. But the development of bridging social capital as well is important for a strong civil society. And Portney and Berry argue that citywide systems of neighborhood empowerment do encourage greater levels of involvement in the types of community participation that yield such bridging social capital. Citywide systems do this by creating explicit organizational arrangements and powers that require what others have called discursive participation, both within neighborhoods and across the tiered organizational structures that tie neighborhood organizations together.

Via the distinction between strong and weak participation activities, Portney and Berry (2007) can therefore make a case that local government efforts to mobilize neighborhood-based civic engagement are successful. The success lies in enhanced participation in strong participatory activities that provide bridging opportunities for participating residents in different neighborhoods. But there is no success in enhancing community participation overall; and while the citywide systems do not introduce any *additional* socioeconomic or racial bias in participation, they are not shown to ameliorate existing socioeconomic and racial biases in participation.

Fung's (2004) concept of accountable autonomy goes one step further to indicate what might be required for government to successfully mobilize neighborhood-based engagement and to counteract socioeconomic and racial bias in patterns of such engagement as well. Fung acknowledges that efforts to empower citizens for neighborhood level civic engagement often involve at best only the provision of some grant of authority or autonomy for a community group to pursue its own problem-solving agenda. By contrast, accountable autonomy includes such a decentralization of authority but also emphasizes a set of key roles for centralized authority (i.e., city government) in the empowerment scheme. These include the provision of support for neighborhood level action in the form of resources, expertise, and cooperation—supports that may require "extensive training for both participating residents and street level officials, changes in the legal and regulatory environment of these efforts, the pooling of knowledge and experience, and provision of technical assistance" (pp. 6–7). Equally important, in an accountable autonomy scheme, centralized authority must hold local groups accountable for both "the effective and democratic use of their discretionary latitude" (p. 8). Under accountable autonomy schemes, centralized authority (i.e., City Hall) can head off the usual inequalities in participation both by targeting the support resources that are provided in a redistributive fashion and by using reviews, audits, and the like to ensure that participatory procedures and outcomes are equitable.

Taken together, the work of Berry et al. (1993), Portney and Berry (2007), and Fung (2004) suggest that local government *can* mobilize residents for important forms of neighborhood-based participation, and *do so* in a way that remedies the usual biases in patterns of political participation, but that it takes a considerable investment of appropriately targeted supportive resources as well as willingness of government leaders to hold neighborhood leaders accountable for equitable and democratic outcomes. This is a tall order, so much so that examples of mobilization that hold up to it might be considered relatively rare.

However, beyond the cases used by these authors, others have appeared. A notable example is Sirianni's (2009) depiction of neighborhood empowerment in Seattle, Washington, which reveals a city with a richly developed citywide system of neighborhood democracy. The account features an impressive array of meaningful roles delegated to neighborhood groups, including a matching-fund program to support neighborhood projects and extensive neighborhood-based planning. It also features a broad array of supportive resources provided by city government, including funding, expert staff support, and leadership training. Most notable of all are the accountable autonomy-style efforts made to ensure that neighborhood empowerment efforts do not simply re-create participatory biases. For example, when the city's Neighborhood Matching Fund was instituted, eligibility for funding was expanded beyond traditional neighborhood organizations to ethnic associations and other organizations in order to "counteract the underrepresentation of immigrants and communities of color in many neighborhood organizations" (Sirianni, 2009, p. 70). When the city created a tiered system with district councils representing community councils and business associations in broader issues that crosscut neighborhoods, the city undertook "continual efforts to broaden the councils' membership in recent years and reduce the kinds of 'participation biases' prevalent in neighborhood representation systems" (Sirianni, 2009 p. 81). And when the city gave neighborhoods important roles in comprehensive planning, the Neighborhood Planning Office required of each neighborhood a "detailed stakeholder analysis and outreach plan to engage the full diversity of its residents;" neighborhood planning groups that were found to exclude any major stakeholders would have their funding for planning projects withheld—a threat that was actually carried out with respect to one neighborhood (Sirianni, 2009, pp. 88–90).

Government as a Mobilizer/Demobilizer of Local Voting

One of the most well-established ways in which government can either mobilize (or demobilize) voting involves the choice of basic governing institutions. So-called reformed institutions of government such as at-large elections, the council-manager plan, and nonpartisanship have long been viewed as depoliticizing features of local government; and part of depoliticizing means a lowering of citizen interest in politics and local elections. Following up on this long-standing insight, Wood's (2002) study of a random sample of U.S. cities over 25,000 in population shows that governing institutions that heighten the political power of the chief executive also increase voter turnout. In particular, direct election of the mayor, expansion of the mayor's executive authority, and a mayor's office with full-time status all enhance voter turnout. Hajnal and Lewis (2003) considered additional institutional arrangements that affect local voter turnout. Although their study was limited to cities in California, their findings for the very large number of municipalities to be found there likewise indicate that the more politicized mayor-council form of government yields higher turnouts than council-manager government, even when controls for various demographic factors are taken into account. More importantly, they found that the timing of local elections is crucial to turnout. Cities that choose to hold local elections off-cycle from presidential elections or midterm congressional elections are virtually guaranteeing a substantially lower turnout.

This relates to an important insight about local governing institutions, political participation via voting, and mobilization. While much contemporary research is framed in terms that suggest the importance of encouraging voter participation, Amy Bridges's (1997) careful historical study of large reform cities of the southwest shows that in some cities, a version of reform was adopted that featured the conscious utilization of institutional arrangements that would ensure a smaller, less participative electorate that was more White and middle-class than the community as a whole. As a result, turnout rates in these cities was strikingly lower than in turnouts in nonreformed cities.

In short, the flipside of local governments' capacity to mobilize citizens to vote via particular institutional arrangements is local governments' capacity to demobilize citizens via other institutional arrangements. And demobilization is typically far from an across-the-board phenomena. Demobilization is targeted by race and class. Once we acknowledge that the mobilization phenomenon has two faces, it becomes clear that capacity of governments to mobilize is by no means always a tool for overcoming racial and socioeconomic biases in participation. Indeed, it can be the instrument for creating and locking in those inequalities.

REFERENCES

Alex-Assensoh, Y. (1998). *Neighborhoods, family, and political behavior in urban America.* New York, NY: Garland.

Berry, J., Portney, K. E., & Thomson, K. (1993). *The rebirth of urban democracy.* Washington, DC: Brookings Institution.

Bingham, L. B. (2006). The new urban governance: Processes for engaging citizens and stakeholders. *Review of Policy Research, 23*(4), 815–826.

Bovaird, T. (2007). Beyond engagement and participation: User and community coproduction of public services. *Public Administration Review, 67*(5), 846–860.

Boyd, M. (2008). Defensive development: The role of racial conflict in gentrification. *Urban Affairs Review, 43*(6), 751–776.

Bridges, A. (1997). Textbook municipal reform. *Urban Affairs Review, 33*(1), 97–119.

Button, J. W., Wald, K. D., & Rienzo, B. A. (1999). The politics of gay rights legislation. In E. Sharp (Ed.), *Culture wars and local politics* (pp. 81–99). Lawrence: University Press of Kansas.

Chicago's Mayor Daley Leads in Polls. (1995, April 5) *Washington Post.* Retrieved November 30, 2010, http://www.highbeam.com/doc/1P2-829345.html

Crawford, S. (2007). Religious interests in community collaboration: The quiet fight for health care in south Omaha. In P. A. Djupe & L. R. Olson (Eds.), *Religious interests in community conflict* (pp. 103–122). Waco, TX: Baylor University Press.

Djupe, P. A., Neiheisel, J. R., & Sokhey, A. E. (2007). Clergy and controversy: A study of clergy and gay rights in Columbus, Ohio. In P. A. Djupe & L. R. Olson (Eds.), *Religious interests in community conflict* (pp. 73–102). Waco, TX: Baylor University Press.

Fung, A. (2004). *Empowered participation.* Princeton, NJ: Princeton University Press.

Gerber, A. S., Green, D. P., & Larimer, C. W. (2008). Social pressure and voter turnout: Evidence from a large-scale field experiment. *American Political Science Review, 102*(1), 33–48.

Goetz, E. G., & Sidney, M. (1994). Revenge of the property owners: Community development and the politics of property. *Journal of Urban Affairs, 16*(4), 319–334.

Goetz, E. G., & Sidney, M. (1997). Local policy subsystems and issue definition: An analysis of community development policy change. *Urban Affairs Review, 32*(4), 490–512.

Green, D. P., Gerber, A. S., & Nickerson, D. W. (2003). Getting out the vote in local elections: Results from six door-to-door canvassing experiments. *Journal of Politics, 65*(4), 1083–1096.

Guth, J. L., Kellstedt, L. A., Copeland, J., & Rowland, C. (2007). Religious interests and the Martin Luther King Jr. holiday in Greenville, South Carolina. In P. A. Djupe & L. R. Olson (Eds.), *Religious interests in community conflict* (pp. 145–172). Waco, TX: Baylor University Press.

Hajnal, Z. L. (2010). *America's uneven democracy.* New York, NY: Cambridge University Press.

Hajnal, Z. L., & Lewis, P. G. (2003). Municipal institutions and voter turnout in local elections. *Urban Affairs Review, 38*(5), 645–668.

Hart, S. (2001). *Cultural dilemmas of progressive politics.* Chicago, IL: University of Chicago Press.

Hero, R. E. (1986). Explaining citizen-initiated contacting of government officials: Socioeconomic status, perceived need, or something else? *Social Science Quarterly, 67,* 626–635.

Jacobs, L. R., Cook, F. L., & Delli Carpini, M. X. (2009). *Talking together.* Chicago, IL: University of Chicago Press.

Jones, B. D., Greenberg, S. R., Kaufman, C., & Drew, J. (1977). Bureaucratic response to citizen initiated contacts: Environmental enforcement in Detroit. *American Political Science Review, 71*(1), 148–165.

Jun, K. (2007). Event history analysis of the formation of Los Angeles neighborhood councils. *Urban Affairs Review, 43*(1), 107–123.

Lyons, W. (1999). *The politics of community policing.* Ann Arbor: University of Michigan Press.

Macedo, S. (2005). *Democracy at risk.* Washington, DC: Brookings Institution.

Marschall, M. J. (2004). Citizen participation and the neighborhood context: A new look at the coproduction of local public goods. *Political ResearchQuarterly, 57*(2), 231–244.

Mesch, G. S. & Schwirian, K. P. (1996). The effectiveness of neighborhood collective action. *Social Problems, 43*(4), 467–484.

Mettler, S., & Soss, J. (2004). The consequences of public policy for democratic citizenship: Bridging policy studies and mass politics. *Perspectives on Politics, 2*(1), 55–73.

Musso, J., Weare, C., Elliot, M., Kitsuse, A., & Shiau, E. (2007). *Toward community engagement in city governance: Evaluating neighborhood council reform in Los Angeles.* Civic Engagement Public Policy Briefing, Los Angeles: University of Southern California Civic Engagement Initiative and USC Neighborhood Participation Project, www.usc-cei.org

Musso, J. A., Weare, C., Oztas, N., & Loges, W. E. (2006). Neighborhood governance reform and networks of community power in Los Angeles. *American Review of Public Administration, 36*(1), 79–97.

Owens, M. L. (2007). *God and government in the ghetto: The politics of church-state collaboration in Black America.* Chicago, IL: University of Chicago Press.

Owens, M. L. (2010). Public support for the "regional perspective": A consideration of religion. *Urban Affairs Review, 45*(6), 745–774.

Penning, J. M., & Storteboom, A. (2007). God and gaming: Community conflict over a proposed Indian casino in west Michigan. In P. A. Djupe & L. R. Olson (Eds.), *Religious interests in community conflict* (pp. 17–50). Waco, TX: Baylor University Press.

Portney, K. E., & Berry, J. M. (2007). Neighborhoods, neighborhood associations, and social capital. In S. A. Ostrander & K. E. Portney (Eds.), *Acting civically: From urban neighborhoods to higher education* (pp. 21–43). Medford, MA: Tufts University Press.

Putnam, R. D. (2000). *Bowling alone.* New York, NY: Touchstone.

Reddick, C. G. (2005). Citizen-initiated contacts with government: Comparing phones and Websites. *Journal of E-Government, 2*(1), 27–53.

Reed, W. E. (1999). *The politics of community policing: The case of Seattle.* New York, NY: Garland.

Reese, L. A., & Shields, G. (2000). Faith-based economic development. *Review of Policy Research, 17,* 84–103.

Rosenstone, S. J., & Hansen, J. M. (1993). *Mobilization, participation, and democracy in America.* New York, NY: Macmillan.

Rusch, L. (2010). Rethinking bridging: Risk and trust in multiracial community organizing. *Urban Affairs Review, 45*(4), 483–506.

Scott, J. K. (2006). "E" the people: Do U.S. municipal government Web sites support public involvement. *Public Administration Review, 66*(3), 341–353.

Sharp, E. B. (1980). Toward a new understanding of urban services and citizen participation: The coproduction concept. *Midwest Review of Public Administration, 14*(2), 105–118.

Sharp, E. B. (1982). Citizen-initiated contacting of government officials and socioeconomic status: Determining the relationship and accounting for it. *American Political Science Review, 76,* 109–115.

Sharp, E. B. (1986). *Citizen demand-making in the urban context.* Tuscaloosa: University of Alabama Press.

Sharp, E. B. (2012). *Does local government matter? How urban policies shape civic engagement.* Minneapolis: University of Minnesota Press.

Silverman, R. M. (2003, Winter). Citizens' district councils in Detroit: The promise and limits of using planning advisory boards to promote citizen participation. *National Civic Review,* 3–13.

Sirianni, C. (2009). *Investing in democracy: Engaging citizens in collaborative governance.* Washington, DC: Brookings Institution.

Skogan, W. G. (1994). The impact of community policing on neighborhood residents: A cross-site analysis. In D. P. Rosenbaum (Ed.), *The challenge of community policing: Testing the promises* (pp. 167–181). Thousand Oaks, CA: Sage.

Skogan, W. G. (2006). *Police and community in Chicago.* Oxford, England: Oxford University Press.

Swarts, H. J. (2008). *Organizing urban America: Secular and faith-based progressive movements.* Minneapolis: University of Minnesota Press.

Thomas, J. C. (1986). *Between citizen and city: Neighborhood organizations and urban politics in Cincinnati.* Lawrence: University Press of Kansas.

Thomas, J. C., & Melkers, J. (1999). Explaining citizen-initiated contacts with municipal bureaucrats: Lessons from the Atlanta experience. *Urban Affairs Review, 34*(5), 667–690.

Thomas, J. C., & Streib, G. (2003). The new face of government: Citizen-initiated contacts in the era of e-government. *Journal of Public Administration Research and Theory, 13*(1), 83–102.

Tolbert, C. J., & Mossberger, K. (2006). The effects of e-government on trust and confidence in government. *Public Administration Review, 66*(3), 354–369.

Vanderleeuw, J. M., Liu, B., & Marsh, G. (2004). Applying Black threat theory, urban regime theory, and deracialization: The Memphis mayoral elections of 1991, 1995, and 1999. *Journal of Urban Affairs, 26*(4), 505–519.

Vedlitz, A., & Veblen, E. (1980). Voting and contacting: Two forms of political participation in a suburban community. *Urban Affairs Quarterly, 16,* 31–48.

Verba, S., Schlozman, K. L., & Brady, H. E. (1995). *Voice and equality: Civic voluntarism in American politics.* Cambridge, MA: Harvard University Press.

Verba, S., Schlozman, K. L., Brady, H. E., & Nie, N. (1995). Codebook: American citizen participation study. *Inter-University Consortium for Political and Social Research.* Retrieved from http://dx.doi.org/10.3886/ICPSR06635

Woliver, L. (1999). Abortion conflicts and city governments: Negotiating coexistence in South Carolina. In E. B. Sharp (Ed.), *Culture wars and local politics* (pp. 21–42). Lawrence: University Press of Kansas.

Wood, C. 2002. Voter turnout in city elections. *Urban Affairs Review, 38*(2), 209–231.

Zhao, J., Lovrich, N. P., & Thurman, Q. (1999). The status of community policing in American cities. *Policing: An International Journal of Police Strategies & Management, 22*(1), 74–92.

Zukin, C., Keeter, S., Andolina, M., Jenkins, K., & Delli Carpini, M. X. (2006). *A new engagement?* New York, NY: Oxford University Press.

CHAPTER 6

CITIZEN ENGAGEMENT IN LOCAL ENVIRONMENTAL POLICY

Information, Mobilization, and Media

Deserai Anderson Crow
J. Richard Stevens
University of Colorado Boulder

INTRODUCTION

The goal of creating more democratic policy processes that inform citizens and are informed by them is at the heart of much policy scholarship (see e.g., A. L. Schneider & Ingram, 1997), and is "the normative core of democracy" (Fischer, 2005, p. 1). While this lofty democratic ambition is vital to understanding and creating better public policies, a number of factors stand in the way of meaningful participation when it comes to local environmental policy processes in particular. Citizens often are not involved in policy discussions when it comes to environmental policies unless mobilized to do so. Those who most often participate are experts who act as influential political elites in the policy process. Research indicates that a

The State of Citizen Participation in America, pages 131–162
Copyright © 2012 by Information Age Publishing

lack of policy information may contribute to this dearth of citizen involvement, and media reportage patterns may prevent citizens from easily accessing the information necessary for participation. This chapter posits that the technical aspect of environmental policies, along with patterns of mass-media coverage of these policies, can help explain why citizens are not involved in their local government policy processes to the degree that scholars may desire.

Environmental and Science-Based Policymaking

While participation will vary with social and political institutions, some trends are endemic to environmental policymaking. Indeed, environmental policy is the definitive example of technocratic policymaking (Fischer, 2005). Around the globe, environmental policies are debated and enacted to tackle the increasing number of problems associated with human activity and the corollary effects on Earth's ecosystems. Environmental policy debates often focus on scientific research, questions of scientific consensus, and the risks associated with human activity. As with some other areas of public policy, such as health policy or transportation policy, the technical nature of environmental policy makes it difficult for many citizens to understand. This reliance on science and technical information puts environmental policy in a distinct category with some other policy issues that are becoming increasingly reliant on technical data to define policy problems, create policy alternatives, and analyze policy implementation. In fact, public policy analysis itself has taken on many of the characteristics of science through its careful analytical approach, cost benefit calculations, specific criteria used to achieve better policy recommendations, and the tendency to defer to policy experts (A. L. Schneider & Ingram, 1997; Weimer & Vining, 1999). These characteristics make environmental policy an important venue for analysis in any compilation of citizen participation scholarship, an area that has potential relevance to other technical areas of public policy.

Americans generally do not possess abundant information related to political processes and issues (Delli Carpini & Keeter, 1996). This is, of course, simplistic, because American knowledge is not a monolithic concept, in fact, some segments of the population are highly informed while others lack even basic information about political and policy processes (Zaller, 1992). In technical policy venues in which there often is not citizen enthusiasm or outrage, and which are highly complex, this lack of knowledge may be especially acute. Citizens simply cannot compete with professionals when it comes to policy or scientific knowledge and expertise (Dryzek & Torgerson, 1993). In these instances, media play a crucial role in raising interest among citizens, informing them of policy issues, and potentially mobilizing them to participate. Downs (1957) stated that citizens "acquire political information for two main reasons 1) to help them decide how to vote, and 2) to form opinions with which they can influence government policy" (p. 238). Most citizens do not have the time, resources, education, or skills to access information and synthesize it accurately. The media must do this for them. While it is true that in the Internet age, citizens have abundant access to information through multiple channels, due to the costs associated with obtaining, filtering, and assessing this information, it is most likely that activists will seek out information through direct government channels, opinion sources, or other nonmainstream media. For the average citizen, traditional media are likely their primary source of information related to local government policy discussions.

While citizens defer their information collection duties to the media, elected officials also defer their responsibilities. When policy discussions are dominated by science and technical data, elected officials "are inclined to leave the arena to the expertise of scientific and professional networks and align themselves with whatever the experts suggest" (A. L. Schneider & Ingram, 1997, pp. 6–7). Fischhoff (1985) argues that people tend to simplify complex issues and ignore evidence that contradicts their previously held beliefs. The average citizen does not have the capacity to sift through technical information to determine their personal political positions. Citizens are, however, interested in science and complex topics (National Science Board, 2010; Pew Center for the People and the Press, 2009). It may simply require effective technical communication to help citizens synthesize the information necessary to meaningfully engage in environmental policy. While much policy literature focuses on the role that scientific data play in policy decisions, technical data of other types are also important to consider, such as law and economics. Rather than hiding behind science and technical jargon as a means to block citizen input, policymakers must communicate these concepts clearly enough for citizens to understand.

In addition to the importance of providing citizens with access to understandable technical information, it is also important to consider that citizens themselves may possess valuable information. It is increasingly common for policymakers and scholars to appreciate the "local knowledge" that citizens bring to bear on policy conversations (Fischer, 2005). With a deep knowledge of local culture and natural resource use, citizens can provide a depth of knowledge that may be as important as expert technocratic knowledge. Rather than a one-way flow of information, it is important to also encourage citizens to provide input into the policy process in order to enlist their knowledge to increase the legitimacy and responsiveness of policies.

Citizen Participation in Policymaking

Citizen participation is a vital component of democracy. "The more participation there is in decisions, the more democracy there is" (Verba & Nie, 1972, p. 1). While it can easily be argued that many citizens are ignorant of complex environmental issues (Fischhoff, 1985), this is not a reason to exclude them from the process. Many environmental decisions are made *for* communities, but much literature points to the importance of making decisions *with* communities. By involving citizens in policymaking, policy outcomes can be superior because they are informed by values, experiences, and priorities of the citizens who will be affected by policy implementation (Fischer, 2005; Roberts, 2008). Despite our belief that democracy is a superior form of government, citizens no longer believe that their elected officials are responsive, or that they can meaningfully participate in the political process (A. L. Schneider & Ingram, 1997). To design more effective and democratic policies, scholars and practitioners must understand how and when citizens participate and how to encourage appropriate participation. The trouble with understanding citizen participation revolves around two issues: who participates, and what facilitates their involvement.

Participation by individuals generally correlates with higher levels of wealth, education, and other socioeconomic status (SES) indicators. This happens due to the fact that higher SES individuals also tend to have the resources available to engage in participatory activities, such as knowledge, money, and group membership (Brady, Verba, & Schlozman, 1995; Verba, Schlozman, & Brady, 1995). Rosenstone and Hansen (1993) found that "the more involved people are in social life, the more likely they are to be mobilized, the more likely they are to be offered the social incentives toward activism, and the more prone they are to take part in politics" (p. 83). This is supported by findings related to individual organizational and religious membership in communities (Verba et al., 1995). If citizen participation is desirable in policymaking, citizens across the SES spectrum should be encouraged to voice their opinions, not only those in higher SES categories.

This also highlights the second issue related to citizen participation: much participation occurs due to mobilization by organizations, not the self-directed behavior that Verba and Nie (1972) first studied. The mobilization model states that "participation is a response to contextual cues and political opportunities structured by the individual's environment" (Leighley, 1995, p. 188). Participation, "results when groups, political parties, and activists persuade citizens to take part" (Jordan & Maloney, 1997, p. 119). Groups that act as mobilization forces include social, religious, political, and professional organizations. Rosenstone and Hansen (1993) argue that "few people spontaneously take an active part in public affairs. Rather, they participate when politicians, political parties, interest groups, and activists persuade them to get involved" (p. 228). The role of government agencies and other deliberative bodies in soliciting citizen input and encouraging participation, then, is vital in understanding the resulting levels of involvement.

Because most policymakers and managers now understand that citizen involvement is desirable, or at least is a necessary evil, processes have begun to reflect the importance of this notion. Environmental management has entered a new era of collaborative planning instead of top-down implementation, which leads to an increased need for "support by policymakers, the public, and industry" (Mazmanian & Kraft, 2001, p. 145). Environmental managers have begun to understand the importance of avoiding conflict in environmental policy. Tools such as alternative dispute resolution, consensus building, and negotiation have become increasingly important (O'Leary, Durant, Fiorino, & Weiland, 1999). Instead of traditional command and control structures, systems such as co-management, adaptive management, and voluntary programs are on the rise and require citizen input as a part of their structures (see e.g., Lee, 1993; O'Leary et al., 1999). Because policymaking is not accepted as solely a government enterprise, citizens demand a transparent process to ensure appropriate measures are taken to protect public health and environmental welfare.

The range of participatory processes that can be implemented to solicit citizen participation vary along a continuum of high to low participation, high to low citizen decision making power, and along a deliberative to nondeliberative spectrum (Beierle, 1998; Steelman & Ascher, 1997). The most common alternative is to hold public hearings. This can be an effective means by which policymakers can elicit opinions and statements from the public and is the most common form of public participation. Hearings provide a forum for citizens to meet face-to-face with government representatives and voice their concerns or grievances. Hearings, however, are criticized for their limitations in providing meaningful participation for citizens. Beyond public hearings, tools such as the Citizen Advisory Committee and the Citizen Jury provide more opportunity for true deliberation, stakeholder involvement, and consensus building (Allen, 1998; Beierle, 1998, 2000). While these forms of in-depth citizen involvement are not always appropriate or desired, it is important for decision makers to consider the varying levels of possible citizen and stakeholder involvement within the structure of policy processes and decisions. The various forms of citizen participatory mechanisms can also, to varying degrees, invoke the local knowledge that citizens possess and that can help construct effective, responsive, and legitimate policies (Fischer, 2005).

The literature above stresses the importance of citizen participation and the significance of mobilization to encouraging participation, and begs the question of whether citizens actually do participate when given the opportunity, resources, and encouragement. A number of studies analyzing the role of citizens in various environmental policy settings demonstrate that citizens are willing to actively participate, even in the most time-consuming citizen advisory roles, in some instances (Busenberg, 2000; Koontz & Johnson, 2004). Other scholars point out the disparity that citizens face with regard to resources and political capital when competing with industry or experts for attention from policymakers (Layzer, 2002a). The dichotomy between citizen participation and elite decision making has been referred to by some as a false construct (Steelman, 2001). It is not uncommon to have both citizen input as well as elite influence in a single policy deliberation. With regard to citizen participation, it seems fair to summarize the literature by emphasizing the potential for citizen participation and deliberative input, but also the barriers to entry and influence with which citizens are faced when they do decide to become involved in the policy process.

Regardless of the tools or processes used, environmental policy literature points to the importance of public involvement to ensure stakeholder support, policy effectiveness, and equal distribution of burdens. Allowing individuals the opportunity to express themselves and present evidence in support of their argument results in a collective view that the process is fair and an increased sense of commitment to the rulemaking authority (Lind & Early, 1992). This satisfies the goal of public support for the policy solution and achieving justice for all groups. Policy effectiveness can be greatly diminished when policies are not considered legitimate by segments of the stakeholder population (Roberts, 2008). Free-riders and defectors from policy regimes are much less likely when parties involved in the process are satisfied with the mechanisms in place (procedural as well as regulatory) (Lind & Early, 1992; Tyler, 1994). A publicly supported policy solution is generally regarded as a higher quality solution.

Participation in environmental policymaking allows for incorporation of the varying interests and stakeholder groups, which may lead to a better end-solution or recommendation (Koontz & Johnson, 2004). This will not only help citizens become better informed, it will help managers become informed about citizen preferences and concerns (Irvin & Stansbury, 2004; Steelman, 2001). Otherwise, the program is reduced to an "inconsequential democratic drama" (Hampton, 1999, p. 173). Finding the balance between citizen input and expert advice is a dilemma, but each is required to make appropriate decisions for environmental quality and public health (Korfmacher & Koontz, 2003; Steelman, 2001). Unfortunately, despite the importance of citizen participation, it is often elites who choose to participate in policymaking. These experts, who are awarded a trusted and respected role in policy decisions and who possess the technocratic knowledge to influence policy outcomes, can exert the most influence over policies when citizens are not involved.

The Role of Entrepreneurs in the Policy Process

While participatory processes are on the rise in environmental policy-making, the literature above suggests citizen participation is unlikely unless active mobilization takes place to encourage participation. Political elites, then, are in a position to dominate the policy process. These elites can assume many roles, one of which is the policy entrepreneur. Experts become political elites because of the tendency for elected officials to disengage when policy issues involve complex technical information (A. L. Schneider & Ingram, 1997). These technical experts are therefore able to exert significant policy influence. Policy entrepreneurs are advocates for policy proposals who may be inside or outside of government, groups, or individuals, but who share the defining characteristic of

> a willingness to invest their resources—time, energy, reputation, and sometimes money—in the hope of future return. That return might come to them in the form of policies of which they approve, satisfaction from participation, or even personal aggrandizement in the form of job security or career promotion. (Kingdon, 1995, pp. 122–123)

These actors can help "change the direction and flow of politics" (M. Schneider & Teske, 1992, p. 737).

Policy entrepreneurs can include actors within and outside of traditional government sources of influence and power. They can include experts, or policy elites, as mentioned above, but they can also include citizens. Citizens, as in the Love Canal, New York, case and many others, have been instrumental in promoting and demanding change throughout U.S. environmental policy history (Fischer, 2005; Layzer, 2002b). As Layzer (2002b) illustrates, this citizen entrepreneurship is frequently seen in cases of NIMBY-ism (not in my backyard) or cases in which communities face hazardous exposure or other health risks associated with environmental contamination. Local bureaucrats, with their leadership and technical knowledge, also act as entrepreneurs when citizens demand or require change and elected officials do not provide that change (Teske & Schneider, 1994). Similarly, scientific elites can act as policy entrepreneurs based on their expertise in a particular field or scientific policy issue (Hart & Victor, 1993). Elites and experts may be particularly influential in policy decisions and innovation to a greater degree than regular citizens. Their expertise may prove to be one way in which entrepreneurs can overcome barriers to entry in local politics that prevent citizens from participating (Teske & Schneider, 1994).

While policy entrepreneurs can promote policy innovation through "the generation, translation, and implementation of new ideas," they cannot do so alone (Roberts & King, 1991, p. 147). While they can help change the flow of policies, they do not control this flow, according to Roberts and

King (1991). The presence of policy entrepreneurs in policy venues does increase the likelihood of political consideration of policy choices (Mintrom, 1997). Mintrom argues that policy innovation, or the spread of new policy ideas, is related directly to policy entrepreneurship. Indeed, these political innovators "generate creative policy solutions, redesign governmental programs, and implement new management approaches" (King & Roberts, 1992, p. 173).

Beyond acting as entrepreneurs directly, citizens can be important tools for entrepreneurs to achieve their policy goals. Baumgartner and Jones (1993) argue that by reframing issues and opening policy subsystems to a greater number of participants, policy change can rapidly take place. They also describe a dual mobilization process through which those who are critical of policies can make change by opening policy venues to more actors. The focus in political mobilization literature on the role that external groups play in motivating participation among mass groups (Jordan & Maloney, 1997; Rosenstone & Hansen, 1993) also alludes to the role that these masses may play as tools for groups or individuals with policy agenda goals. Since citizen participation is unlikely without mobilization, yet desirable in environmental policy deliberation, and experts can dominate technical policy debates when the public is not involved, it is important to understand why and what processes serve as barriers to citizens.

The Role of Media and Information

As with almost every policy issue, environmental policymaking relies on mass media for the communication of complex policy problems, alternatives, and solutions. It is through media framing and simplification that citizens come to understand the complexities of government debates and decisions. Downs (1972) argued that media help to determine the level of societal knowledge about environmental issues and the corollary importance of those issues in the public and policy discourse through an issue-attention cycle. Through reporting on environmental issues, media help not only to raise awareness about issues, but also to define the problems and associated costs of solving those problems (Baumgartner & Jones, 1993). Unfortunately, because media often pay attention to these important issues for only short periods of time (Kingdon, 1995) and cover complex stories in ways that oversimplify, dramatize, or inaccurately portray science and opposing political views (see Boykoff & Boykoff, 2004, 2007), media also prevent lasting concern, accurate understanding, or policy solutions to these same problems. Media coverage patterns are therefore crucial to understanding the level of involvement that citizens have in environmental policymaking.

Mass Media Influence in Policy Decisions and Public Perceptions

Undoubtedly, one of the most important dimensions of media influence over policy issues is the process through which media influence issue salience. Beyond the role that media can play in influencing public opinion and policy agendas, the broader political agenda and climate are also shaped through a process by which "social problems [that] originate on the media agenda... are subsequently transformed into political issues" (Anderson, 1993, p. 25). By directing public attention to certain aspects of the policy process through the transmission of salience, media wield influence over the political process (Kennamer, 1992). Influence over the public issue agenda is vital to understanding which issues are placed at the top of the governmental agenda (McCombs, 2005; McCombs & Shaw, 1972). Media coverage of issues, particularly the quantity, prominence, and frequency of coverage, translates to corollary placement of those issues on governmental and public issue agendas. It is not only the information in media messages that matters in determining the salience of public issues, but the amount and placement of those issues are of utmost importance (Scheufele & Tewksbury, 2007).

Salience as it relates to policy agendas has been summarized into three points: (a) mass media influence the public agenda; (b) the public agenda influences the policy agenda of decision makers; and (c) the policy agenda can have a direct influence on the media agenda (Rogers & Dearing, 2007). Kingdon's (1995) theory of policy change would indicate that by highlighting certain issues and ignoring others, media are more likely to raise awareness about policy problems rather than promote policy alternatives. This cyclical and limited agenda process is important to consider when seeking an understanding of citizen access to policy information and the potential for citizen influence over policy outcomes.

Beyond simple placement on policy agendas, the salience of issues in the public discourse can influence policy outcomes by helping shape public opinion as it relates to particular topics. "The public are recipients, willing or unwilling, passive or active, of this media content, over whose making they have little direct influence" (Paletz, 1999, p. 330). Entman (1989) states that public opinion among citizens is influenced when media "control what they think about" (p. 77). Miller and Krosnick (2000) argue that journalists select stories based on their view of what is important in society. By inference, then, individuals assume that the issues covered by the media are the most important issues facing their communities. "Journalists, selecting and highlighting a few stories each day, determine which issues are treated as important in the news" (Paletz, 1999, p. 141). Through this inference, journalists determine the salience of certain policy issues over others. "Media content is pervasive and rife with explicit and implicit political meaning" (Paletz, 1999, p. 330), and the salience that media create on a given issue can influence public opinion related to policy issues.

Beyond issue salience, media can influence issue agendas by portraying an issue, or framing it, as positive or negative; citizens may then be influenced by media to hold similar opinions (Iyengar, 1990; Iyengar & Kinder, 1987). By discussing local issues in a positive manner, local media can garner support for issues and encourage citizen involvement, while the opposite can also be true. Nicodemus (2004) found that of two newspapers in a single community, one framed a local environmental issue in a positive, communitarian light, while the other emphasized the difficulties of making a difference in the political process and of challenging the environmental wrong-doer. Nicodemus argues that this framing influenced the community's likelihood of collective action toward policy change.

While scholars generally agree with the premise that media coverage of issues determines the importance that citizens and policymakers place on those issues, scholars are far less certain as to the behavioral consequences of such media attention. Iyengar and Kinder (1987) and others argue that media coverage clearly influences opinions that individuals hold, but there is still far less consensus as to whether an influence over opinions changes individual or collective behavior or whether any changes that might take place will prove to be lasting changes (McQuail, 2007). Scholars point to the impossibility with which we can point to one social institution and separate its influence from other societal influences over opinions and behavior. Weber, in his Ideational Model (summarized well by Neuzil & Kovarik, 1996), argued that ideas are effective in creating social change only when also held within other social forces, specifically the power structure and the mass media.

It is therefore most important to consider media influence in the context of its most important role: the establishment of knowledge, which helps to maintain or change social structures and institutions (Donohue, Tichenor, & Olien, 1973). The idea that communication and knowledge are bases of social control has long been argued (e.g., Galbraith, 1978). That media help to create this knowledge and maintain social order through reinforcement of dominant value systems (Gans, 1979) calls into question whether media coverage often brings about significant social change. Media do serve an important role in creating "publics" along the lines of what Dewey (1927) conceived—those that emerged due to a perceived threat to the community through increased knowledge about such threats.

Case studies point to many instances in which media coverage of environmental issues led to social and political change (Layzer, 2002b; Neuzil & Kovarik, 1996; Nicodemus, 2004), but these same scholars also highlight the complexities of the cases and are often reluctant to state with certainty that mass media coverage can directly influence social and political change. While behavior change cannot explicitly be attributed to media coverage in most instances, the role of knowledge formation is undoubtedly influenced by media, which can potentially lead to a more informed and more involved public—" the power of the press is the influence that news-papers exercise in the formation of public opinion and in mobilizing the community for political action" (Park, 1941, p. 1). It is therefore a fair assessment of media influence to state that media help to determine knowledge about current issues, the salience of those issues on the public and policy agendas, and may at times help to influence political mobilization toward creating social change.

Based on this literature, media coverage of policy issues is expected to serve an important role to inform citizens and highlight the important issues of the day. In today's media landscape, there are overwhelming amounts of media messages in local newspapers, on television, and increasingly on the Internet and blogosphere. In the context of local environmental policy, local news sources will likely be the only source of information for citizens. In many cases, this will involve traditional media as the primary news sources since it is generally in larger cities, states, and national contexts in which there is active Internet and blog activity related to policy information. While the media landscape in local communities may not involve new media platforms to the extent that state, regional, or national media analyses would, the changing nature of the news business affects all types of media, in all markets.

Reporting on Science and Environment

Despite the high levels of interest in science (National Science Board, 2010; Nunn, 1979; Pew, 2009), American news organizations tend to treat the reportage of science as a niche or beat subject, leading to uneven coverage by beat reporters, general assignment reporters, and wire stories (Friedman, 1986). Scientists are disappointed at public knowledge of science and blame the media for inadequately covering the issues and reporting inaccurate and distorted versions of technical issues (Dunwoody & Scott, 1982; Pew, 2009; Tankard & Ryan, 1974; Tichenor, Olien, Harrison, & Donohue, 1970). Few journalists covering science topics have scientific backgrounds (Palen, 1994): only 3% of journalists with college degrees major in the areas of mathematics or science, while most major in communication fields (Weaver & Wilhoit, 1996).

Winsten (1985) found that competition among journalists led to a "strong motivation to distort their coverage" (p. 8). "The result has been a spiraling competition, sometimes characterized by exaggerated claims, in which 'science by press conference' has begun to replace the traditional mode of scientific discourse" (pp. 14–15). Dunwoody (1979) found that reporters with multiple story assignments and tight deadlines relied more heavily on press conferences and fewer sources in their reporting than reporters with fewer schedule restraints. These schedule constraints are only growing as newsrooms downsize, and most reporters are now also expected to blog in addition to their daily reporting routines. Reliance on traditional journalistic norms such as personalization, novelty, and balance can at times lead to inaccuracies in reporting because journalists do not know enough about content areas to screen out erroneous statements or misleading claims about science or policy (Boykoff & Boykoff, 2007).

Editors favor conflict frames and sensational story elements more than science writers (Johnson, 1963), a difference Dennis and McCartney (1979) found key to the dissatisfaction science writers have with the priorities of their editors. Editors are driven by the competitive demands of their market, forces that push them to pursue the attention of readers and audiences. The drawbacks of competitive corporate culture to science and environmental coverage have recently become more apparent. As media organizations reduce staff and resources, specialty reporting appears to be one of the first cuts made. Perhaps no greater example of this trend was the decision in December 2008 by CNN to dissolve its entire science, technology, and environment news staff. CNN stated that it wanted to integrate special-topic coverage into the regular editorial divisions of the organization, but the decision drew widespread industry criticism (Brainard, 2008). This trend may continue or escalate as a result of diminishing newsroom profits in the years to come. It highlights the importance of accurate and reliable information about environmental topics, but also points to a growing likelihood that audiences may not receive this type and quality of environmental news.

As environmental problems grow increasingly difficult to solve (Vig & Kraft, 2003), and technical data produce comprehension barriers for the average citizen, the role of environmental reporting becomes more important. When experts dominate the policy process, and media coverage of these policy decisions is minimal, the public will not contribute in meaningful ways to policy decisions (Crow, 2010a, 2010b). Environmental policy literature indicates that, in technical policy venues, experts can dominate discourse and influence policy outcomes if citizens are uninvolved (Baumgartner & Jones, 1993; Hart & Victor, 1993). One hurdle to overcoming this trend is the difficulty journalists face to effectively communicate complex ideas to the public in a manner that promotes understanding and active participation in democratic debate. It is, however, increasingly important to do so because "the public may be highly susceptible to influence by changes in media attention and media characterization" of scientific issues (Nisbet, 2004, p. 139). As scholars and practitioners seek to understand how, when, and why citizens choose to participate in policymaking, analyses of media coverage and provision of adequate policy information are vital to understanding the complete menu of information and choices with which citizens are faced.

RESEARCH METHODS

As previous studies show, while citizen participation might be desirable in a democracy, it is not common in technical policy venues unless extrinsic factors encourage them to do so. There is also considerable evidence to suggest that mass media communication of complex policy issues does not reduce the barriers for citizens to meaningfully understand and participate in their local policy processes. This chapter draws from two separate research studies to form conclusions about citizen participation in local environmental policymaking.

Comparative Case Study Method: Recreational Water Rights in Colorado

The first study was a comparative case study of Colorado communities wherein the communities sought recreational water rights for kayaking and whitewater rafting. This local policy example provides an appropriate case for analysis of the concepts presented in the literature above. This comparative case study involved in-depth analysis of the policy process in all 12 adopter communities as well as 6 non–adopter communities. The data from interviews, legal and legislative document analysis, and media coverage of the policy debates were coded and analyzed to provide a rigorous analysis of policy influences within local communities. Interviews were conducted with policy participants in all communities included in the study,[1] legal documentation was collected in each of the communities, and all local media coverage of the policy issue was coded and analyzed. These cases were then analyzed in a cross-case method to determine common patterns, influences, and processes. This case provides an example of a highly technical policy venue focused on water law and hydrology, and is an appropriate case for exploring the concepts of citizen participation, technical policy debates, and media coverage of such subjects.

Survey Research Methods: A Study of Colorado Journalists

The second study used an online survey of Colorado journalists. Reporters, editors, anchors, producers, and news managers were included in the sample. The survey sample included newspapers and television news media across Colorado, based upon listings provided by the Colorado Press Association (for newspapers) and by individual television stations. A total of 431 potential respondents were contacted, with a response rate of 21.8% (N = 94). The average online survey response rate falls between 32.52% and 41.21%, according to one study (Hamilton, 2003). Daily deadlines, multiple story workload pressures in today's newsrooms, and personnel turnover could easily have pushed the response rate for this online survey lower than desired.

The online survey included questions related to (a) length of employment experience and journalistic training both in formal education settings and postcollege training opportunities, (b) daily journalistic routines with regard to science and environmental coverage of individual journalists, (c) budget cuts and personnel downsizing generally and specifically related to environmental coverage within the newsroom, (d) use of various sources in science and environment reporting, and (e) journalist demographics. These responses were analyzed to understand the nature of science and environmental reporting in Colorado daily news, as indicated by the journalists who cover these topics, the experience and training they have, and the frequency with which they cover these technical topics. This is an important topic for consideration when exploring the factors promoting and preventing citizen participation.

Research Findings: Recreational Water Rights in Colorado

In all American states, a system of granting use rights to water resources has been established. In the western United States, where water resources are variable and less plentiful, these systems are controlled primarily under the system of prior appropriation (Getches, 1997). Under prior appropriation, holders of junior water rights, as determined by the date of appropriation of the resource, are not allowed to take any of their water until the senior water rights holders on the river have fully satisfied their rights. This system has come to be known as "first in time, first in right" due to the priority of water rights based on longevity of use.

All water rights holders must additionally put their water to a beneficial use, as designated by a Colorado water court. Colorado's prior appropriation system first only allowed for irrigation water rights (Hobbs, 1997), but over time has evolved to include many other uses of water including domestic, industrial, mining, snowmaking for ski resorts, environmental protection, and other uses (Colorado Foundation for Water Education, 2004). This evolution of uses has most recently included the development of in-channel recreational use of water for maintaining river flows for kayaking and whitewater boating. This new water right—the recreational in-channel diversion, or RICD—is the focus of the case study presented here.

In 1998, Golden, Colorado, applied for the first such water right in water court. As recreation and tourism have become more important economic drivers in Colorado and in many communities, local governments sought innovative solutions that would help to establish or protect their recreational resources, such as whitewater boating. Golden was followed by Vail, Breckenridge, and nine other communities between 1998 and 2006. Due to intense political opposition to these water rights, the state legislature debated legislation on three separate occasions to codify and restrict the water right, passing two pieces of legislation and defeating a third (Senate Bills 216 [2001]; 62 [2005]; 37 [2006]). The Colorado Supreme Court also heard the cases involving four of these communities before the water rights were granted. Under state statute, only subdivisions of state government (municipalities, counties, water districts, etc.) can own a RICD water right.

Over a decade, this issue rose in importance throughout communities in Colorado. Similar policy debates were held in local communities regarding whether or not to pursue a water right and build the required boating course structures to qualify for such a water right. This not only was a politically controversial issue, but it was also an expensive undertaking for the communities that chose to pursue an RICD. Communities spent hundreds of thousands of dollars in legal fees associated with the water right (mean cost = $276, 714), and many also spent hundreds of thousands of dollars building the boating course structures (mean cost = $378,200). Considering that many of these communities have small tax bases (mean population = 21,385), this is a significant investment and an appropriate case for analysis of local environmental policy decisions and political involvement.

Citizen Involvement in Local Environmental Policy

When asked about the level of involvement by various stakeholders in the case study communities, interview subjects stated that water law and policy is a complex and mundane process for the average citizen and that they rarely see or expect citizen participation.

Water rights for people that even deal with them are pretty obscure. [LG-09]

It's sort of one of those water rights things which seems to be abstract and boring. [LR-05]

Because of the technical nature of water rights, individuals may be unlikely to participate without efforts to encourage them to do so. This section will analyze whether citizens have been involved in the process of policy change in Colorado communities and if so, what the nature of that participation was.

The first question to analyze is whether communities made efforts to encourage citizen input and provide information about policy decisions, or the deliberations that preceded them. Without this effort, based upon political mobilization literature, it can be assumed that levels of citizen involvement would be quite low, especially given the technical nature of water rights mentioned above. Table 6.1 shows that four communities did not attempt to make citizens aware of the issue of RICD water rights. Four other communities did so, but only through the minimal process of city council meetings and public notice thereof. Finally, four communities actively attempted to involve citizens in the policy process.

The next important consideration is whether these limited attempts to solicit citizen participation in some RICD communities resulted in the desired citizen participation and input. Interview subjects reported some citizen involvement, but the focus of these individuals was primarily limited to the process of policy change with regard to decisions to build the recreational amenities upon which RICD water rights are based, not the water rights themselves.

> We had a local paddler club in town that were advocating boating and doing some sort of a boating course. [LG-12]

TABLE 6.1 Effort to Make Citizens Aware or Involved in RICD Decision

Community	Public Notice[a]	Policy Initiator (Crow, 2010a)
Golden	None	Expert (S)[b]
Vail	None	Expert (A)
Breckenridge	None	Expert (A)
Longmont	None	Expert (A)
Pueblo	Minimal	Expert (A)
Gunnison	Active	Expert (S)
Steamboat Springs	Active	City Council and Citizens
Chaffee County	Active	Citizens
Silverthorne	Minimal	Expert (A/S)
Durango	Active	Citizens
Avon	Minimal	City Council
Carbondale	Minimal	Expert (A/S)

[a] Minimal notice involved simply listing the RICD issue as an agenda item in city council notices. Active notice involved city officials holding open meetings, discussing the issue with local journalists, and additional methods of attempting to solicit citizen input into the policy decision.

[b] Expert (S) = Expert government staff such as water managers. Expert (A) = Water attorney.

We were approached by a group of boaters. [LG-01]

The recreational community was very supportive of the whitewater park and were frustrated about the length of time that it took us to come together to actually do it. [LG-05]

The boating community has been talking about it. [EL-06]

There were three exceptions to this rule. In Durango, Chaffee County, and Steamboat Springs, community members and local groups were actively involved in local government hearings and public discussions. However, the groups that were actively involved were limited to a few community members.

They had expressed an interest in...protecting flows in the river for recreation and so we began to explore and talk about it. [LG-19]

The initial proponents of it were the Arkansas River Trust. [LR-01]

The recreation and environmental community and the city was largely supportive of it. [CW-01]

Sort of an activist group of people that were interested in it and I think the rest of the people were probably ambivalent. [LW-09]

In the majority of communities where citizens were involved in the process of policy change, these people were important to the decisions to build the recreational infrastructure upon which the water right was based. The case studies demonstrate citizen group involvement in 10 RICD communities. In seven of these communities, citizens were primarily or only involved in promoting the construction of whitewater parks. These citizens advocated directly for the community to provide an amenity that would benefit their personal recreational interests, but did not continue to do so for the more nebulous benefit of the water right.

In this era of open governance and sunshine laws, there is some degree of expectation that government decision makers see the value in soliciting citizen input, or at least do so in order to be seen as valuing transparency. It may therefore appear incongruous that two thirds of RICD communities either did not attempt to inform citizens or did so only at the statutorily required minimal levels (i.e., providing public notice in city council agendas), as outlined above. This finding may be closely related to the field of water rights and the technical nature of this policy area. Since water rights based on prior appropriation place value on the timing of a water right claim, some argued that public involvement was not desirable.

You typically don't have a public discussion about a water right filing because if you tell everybody we're going to file,...there would have been a just a rush to the courthouse [to file first or oppose the water right application]. [LG-13]

The specific question of the RICD was considered more of a technical detail. [EL-04]

Water rights may be similar in this respect to many other technical environmental policy decisions made within local governments. These findings support the literature presented above and indicate that a lack of citizen input may be pervasive across environmental policy issues beyond RICD water rights, in which technical or complicated information is seen as beyond the scope of individual knowledge or interest and where these policies are seen as details in which citizen input is not required.

Next, based on the public notice that was provided, it does not appear that citizens chose to participate in policy discussions related to the water right issue.

> They wanted the course, they wanted to go boating. They had the course, they were boating. Securing the future of the water, that's something that isn't really real to them. [LG-09]

> There were remarkably few kayakers...who showed up at these meetings. [LW-04]

> There wasn't a lot of discussion about the RICD filing. [LG-13]

While levels of citizen participation differ between RICD communities, overall levels of citizen participation appear to be quite low in recreational water rights policy processes. This suggests that either citizens simply chose not to participate, or there were specific barriers to entry into the political process in these cases. The rest of this chapter analyzes some of the possible reasons for this lack of citizen involvement in RICD local policy decisions. If citizens are not influential actors in local policy processes, as in the cases presented here, seeking opportunities for involvement and input, then it is also vital to understand which actors are influential in these local decisions.

Citizens, Entrepreneurship, and Local Environmental Policy

Within each community, interviews were conducted to understand the process through which the idea of applying for RICD water rights arose and the initiators of the idea. The concept of a policy entrepreneur was not described to interview subjects so as not to bias their responses. Instead, policy entrepreneurs were defined based upon previous policy studies, as outlined in the literature review and were identified during data analysis by referencing these definitions. Policy entrepreneurs were defined in this study as actors who initiated RICD policy ideas and who subsequently fought for the policy within local communities. Interview subjects' responses indicated that entrepreneurship was evident across adopter communities.

The lead proponent of that was a council member. [LW-05]

The idea actually came from one of the council members. [LG-22]

I think the fact that it came from a citizen and not from the government directly says something. [LR-02]

The individuals identified in the case study communities who promoted the idea of applying for recreational water rights fall into three categories, as outlined in the Table 6.1.

These policy entrepreneurs come from within and outside of government and include experts in the field of water rights, as well as citizens. In Colorado, water rights matters are almost always handled by water attorneys who have expertise in the legal and statutory requirements related to water. There are also water managers within communities who are charged with supervising water infrastructure, development, supply, and the community's water portfolio. In six RICD communities, the water rights attorney acted as a policy entrepreneur. These individuals not only gave legal advice to their client communities, but they also advocated for the water right. While professional advice is based on the best interests of the client, there were many interviews that pointed to the overlap in personal and professional support for RICD water rights in client communities. Second, in four communities, technical government staff for the local community acted as policy entrepreneurs. Municipal water managers acted in a similar manner as water attorneys. Only those managers who also personally believed in the RICD promoted it within their communities. In two additional communities, elected officials served as policy entrepreneurs. Elected officials often promoted RICDs based on their personal values as well as their hopes for promoting local economic development through recreational tourism. Finally, in three communities, citizens promoted the idea of filing for RICD water rights. It was only in communities where local governments actively solicited citizen input in which citizens were policy entrepreneurs. Keep in mind, however, that entrepreneurship would generally precede public notice, so there is no causal mechanism at work here. Entrepreneurship is the process through which the idea surfaces and is successful within policy circles, so at the point in which city council officials are discussing the idea openly, it has already made it onto the public issue agenda.

In cases in which experts acted as entrepreneurs, these individuals were hired to provide advice based on their subject expertise. This advisory role of experts is where they were able to influence policy change to the greatest degree. Their skills and knowledge allowed them access to information that is not widely available or understood. Expertise also allowed these actors to capture the trust of elected officials within the communities to promote policy change in favor of RICD water rights to a greater degree than nonexperts.

> [Our attorney] is a tremendous visionary and...he's been given a tremendous amount of free reign and he's got a Midas touch. [LW-06]

It is important to note that while city government managers and staff are experts within city government, the water attorneys presented in this section are all private attorneys. In Colorado, municipal and county governments generally retain a private water attorney to handle water matters exclusively. These attorneys provide counsel and handle water litigation and negotiations, but are not government staff, which is why they are categorized separately.

Based upon the data presented here, Table 6.2 outlines the types of entrepreneurs found in RICD policy in Colorado, the roles that they play, and the corollary literature that speaks to the importance of these actors in the policy process. As indicated in this study, while experts were the most influential to this case, citizens and elected officials can be important sources of innovation in some communities. While many Colorado communities could have benefitted from an RICD water right to protect their invest-

TABLE 6.2 Policy Entrepreneurs by Category (Crow, 2010b)

Policy Entrepreneur Category	Characteristics and Reasons for Entrepreneurship	Related RICD Cases	Supporting Policy Literature
Citizen Entrepreneur	• Personally interested • Possible economic interest • Ideological interests • Effective through group membership	Steamboat Springs Chaffee County Durango	Layzer (2002b) Kingdon (1995) Baumgartner & Jones (1993)
Expert Entrepreneur	• Professionally interested • Personally interested • Access to decision makers • Expertise in relevant policy area • Trusted by decision makers • Access to policy information • Disseminator of policy information	Golden Vail Breckenridge Longmont Pueblo Gunnison Silverthorne Carbondale	Teske & Schneider (1994) Hart & Victor (1993) Kingdon (1995) Baumgartner & Jones (1993)
Elected Entrepreneur	• Ideologically interested • Personally interested • Politically knowledgeable • Policy expertise • Possible subject expertise	Steamboat Springs Avon	Kingdon (1995) Baumgartner & Jones (1993)

ments in whitewater recreation, it was only those communities with active policy entrepreneurs that chose to pursue an RICD water right. The importance of entrepreneurship in these case study communities indicates an important role for individuals in the policy process.

The experts discussed in this section influenced policy debates and outcomes to a much greater extent than citizens, given the data presented on both categories of actors. The expertise and technical skills that these individuals possessed allowed them to build trust and negotiate the policy process in ways that citizens did not. This access allowed them influence that other actors did not enjoy. Experts, and not citizens, were the most involved and influential actors in the local environmental policy case presented here. Next, this chapter will consider the reasons why this may be the case.

Local Media Influence

As the literature and everyday experiences suggest, media coverage of policy issues, or lack of coverage, may be an important factor in understanding citizen involvement in local environmental policy decisions. It is with this understanding that media coverage frequency, timing, and content were analyzed in the case study communities. The content analysis of media coverage from all case study communities indicates that media coverage across communities was skewed toward positive coverage of RICD policy issues and discussions. This means that when analyzing the content of local media, those who supported the water right saw their "side" of the debate framed in a more positive light. Table 6.3 is based upon a content analysis for all media coverage in local newspapers (there were no local television media sources except in the Pueblo/Colorado Springs market) during the period from 1998 through 2006.

Based on this content analysis, media coverage in 10 of the 12 RICD communities was supportive of RICD water rights and the legal cases related to obtaining those water rights. This table is limited to those articles related to local RICD cases (38.8% of total articles) and local editorials (4.6%); the additional articles that were published in local newspapers addressed local kayak courses (13.5%), other communities' legal cases (13.2%), other kayak courses (2.9%), legislation related to RICDs (18.5%), and general RICD issues (7.3%).

For mass-media coverage to help mobilize citizen participation in order to influence policy change within local communities, this media coverage would have had to begin prior to policy decisions being made. This, however, was not the case in RICD communities in Colorado. Table 6.3 depicts the timing of the start of media coverage in each RICD community, and shows that in the 12 RICD communities, media coverage began after the

TABLE 6.3 Local Media Coverage of RICD Water Rights (Crow, 2010a)

Community	# Local RICD Articles	% Positive RICD Paragraphs	% Positive Quotations in RICD Articles	% Positive RICD Editorials	Date of First Local Article	Date of RICD Application
Aggregate Media Data	*168*	*67.7*	*72.3*	*80.1*	*03/01/01*[a]	*12/30/98*[a]
Golden	10	53.5	65.4	85.7	03/01/01	12/30/98
Vail	5	72.0	83.7	—	06/25/02	12/26/01
Breckenridge	6	74.6	92.0	100.0	05/27/01	12/28/00
Longmont	2	80.0	57.1	—	04/13/04	12/27/01
Pueblo	36	68.7	70.8	60.0	11/05/01[b]	12/31/01
Gunnison	9	87.1	85.7	100.0	Fall 2001[b]	03/29/02
Steamboat Springs	23	56.4	61.6	—	09/27/03[b]	12/22/03
Silverthorne	7	66.6	76.9	—	03/09/05	12/27/04
Chaffee County	30	58.4	57.3	40.0	10/25/04[c]	12/30/04
Avon	—	—	—	—	N/A	12/27/05
Durango	31	39.7	50.0	100.0	06/08/04[c]	02/28/06
Carbondale	2	87.9	94.7	—	04/06/06[b]	05/02/06

[a] Earliest media coverage and earliest RICD application are listed here to indicate the starting point for these policy debates across Colorado.
[b] Communities in which local media coverage began before the paperwork had been filed to apply for the RICD water right, but after the policy decision had been made.
[c] Communities in which local media coverage began before the policy decision had been made.

date of RICD application filing in half of the cases. In the six communities where media coverage began prior to RICD application filing, the coverage nonetheless started after the decision to seek an RICD water right in four of the communities (Pueblo, Gunnison, Steamboat Springs, and Carbondale). In fact, the first article in each of these communities focused on the news that decision makers had already decided to apply for the RICD. In both Chaffee County and Durango, there was local coverage related to the issue prior to the decision to file in both communities, perhaps due to the very public nature of the debate over these water rights.

Therefore, based on the data presented here, citizens did not have access through media sources to information related to government deliberations prior to the decisions being made. Across case study communities, media coverage was limited in most communities, skewed positive in relation to RICD water rights coverage, and it began after policy decisions had already been made. The media coverage in these cases was such that critical assessment and analysis of the RICD policy proposals prior to decision making was limited. Only in a handful of communities was there balanced media coverage or coverage prior to final policy decisions. This lack of media coverage, combined with the technical nature of these policy issues, may have limited access to information that would be necessary for citizens to become involved in policy decisions. This also could increase the influence that experts have over an insular policy process.

It is important to note that in three RICD communities (Steamboat Springs, Durango, and Chaffee County), the data show that citizens were actively involved and that local government officials actively solicited input from the public. Two of these three cases are also among the small number of cases in which media coverage began prior to policy decision making. Because of the small N case study method used here, no causal mechanism is argued. However, the narrative formed to explain these cases includes city officials who value or at least actively solicit input, local media that more adequately cover policy issues prior to government decisions (in comparison to their Colorado media counterparts), and citizens who decide to engage in the local policy process. These elements seem to be important to the process of engaging citizens—local government openness and local media coverage of policy processes.

Research Findings: Environmental Reporting in Colorado

While it is clear from the case analysis above that local media coverage plays an important role in providing public access to policy information and influencing corollary participation levels, it is also true that media are experiencing changes that may dramatically alter the nature of their reportage. Mainstream media and academic press coverage is rife with stories of crisis within media industries (see Morton, 2008; Smolkin, 2006; Starr, 2009). It is through this lens of declining newspaper coverage, shuttered newsrooms, and reporter layoffs that this survey sought to understand the current landscape of local environmental media coverage. The survey of Colorado journalists informs the following data analysis related to the current trends in environmental reporting.

The first important area of analysis concerns whether newsroom budget cuts lead to reductions in environmental reporting. Because most news personnel may not be aware of specific budget cuts, respondents were asked if there had been layoffs in their newsroom as a proxy measure for budget cuts. Researchers expected that newsrooms where budgets had been cut and news staff reduced would be the same newsrooms in which coverage of specialized topics such as environment and science would decrease in frequency. The researchers also hypothesized that budget cuts would result in less experienced reporters covering environmental stories as more expensive senior reporters are laid off. As a point of reference, this survey was sent only to Colorado journalists and within months after the *Rocky Mountain News*, Denver's oldest newspaper and one of its two statewide dailies, closed. The presence of real and feared budget cuts was on the minds of Colorado journalists during this time period. As expected, layoffs correlated with specialists being laid off. Additionally, the layoffs of specialists significantly correlated with a reduction in special-section coverage in these Colorado newsrooms, as indicated in Table 6.4.

Beyond simply whether specialists and special-section coverage were reduced in these newsrooms, it is also important to understand whether generalists instead of specialists are now covering these complex environmental topics. Due to the complex nature of these stories, the frequency with which journalists cover science and environmental stories matters, as does the background and specialty training of journalists. When journalists are asked to report as a generalist and therefore only occasionally are asked to cover technical science or environmental stories, it is less likely that they are

TABLE 6.4   Budget Cuts (Layoffs) and Levels of Environmental Coverage

	Special Section Reduction	Environmental Stories No Longer Covered
Layoffs	.17	−.19
Specialist Layoffs	.38**	.08

**$p < .01$

TABLE 6.5   Correlations: Layoffs and Trend to Become More of a Generalist

	More of a generalist
Layoffs	−.016
Specialist layoffs	.179

abreast of the appropriate sources, the context of the story, or how to accurately communicate the technical concepts. It was expected that in newsrooms that were forced to cut personnel, a reporter would experience pressures to become more of a generalist since special-topics coverage would be the responsibility of all personnel, not just specialists.

Surprisingly, according to the data in Table 6.5, there is no significant relationship between layoffs or specialist layoffs and pressure to become more of a generalist. While layoffs did not correlate with a trend toward Colorado reporters becoming generalists, layoffs of specialists correlate with reductions in special-topics section coverage. This likely means that when environmental and science stories are covered, they are no longer assigned to specialist reporters or special sections, and general assignment reporters are increasingly asked to report on these topics.

If general-assignment reporters instead of specialist reporters are covering environmental stories, it is important to determine if these people are less experienced, educated, or trained than their colleagues. Table 6.6 indicates that science and environmental journalists do not look different from their newsroom colleagues in terms of training, education, or experience. This may be good news since journalists covering environmental stories are not less experienced than their colleagues. Keep in mind, however, the fact that these topics require more skills and background to cover well. Therefore, environmental journalists who have the same education, training, and experience as their other newsroom colleagues may actually be

TABLE 6.6   Experience and Training of Environmental Journalists

	Journalism BA/BS/MA	Length of Employment	Total Workshops Attended	Annual Salary
Environmental Reporting	−.19	−.09	.06	.08
Frequent Environmental Reporting	−.13	.13	.10	.06
Journalism BA/BS/MA			.20*	

*$p < .05$

less equipped to cover environmental stories due to the complex nature, science-heavy subjects, and technical content of the stories. These "average" journalists may, therefore, be underprepared to cover stories that require above-average preparation. These trends toward general-assignment reporter coverage of environmental stories, along with the reductions in specialists in Colorado newsrooms, may lead to less accurate, frequent, or informative news coverage of important environmental topics. Without media coverage of such topics that provides necessary information in a comprehensible format, citizens may be limited in their abilities to access the information necessary to participate effectively in technical environmental policy discussions in their local communities.

Citizen Participation in Local Environmental Policy

As the literature indicates and this research supports, citizens are unlikely to participate in their local environmental policy processes unless mobilized to do so and provided the information upon which to act. Despite the significant effect that these local policy debates may have on tax revenue, property values, tourism and recreation, quality of life, and human and environmental health, citizens remain uninvolved when not given the information or motivation to do so. This research concludes that much of the blame rests with the very nature of environmental policy—that these policy issues are highly complex and the average citizen does not have the scientific knowledge or background to understand the complexities involved. Exceptions to this finding, however, are important to note. Case studies demonstrating the powerful NIMBY phenomenon with regard to policy outcomes are common (Layzer, 2002b). These cases also present examples of the powerful knowledge that citizens can possess, even if it is not the same technocratic knowledge with which policymakers have become enamored (Fischer, 2005). The difference presented in this case study research is that there are no overtly hazardous policy outcomes to many environmental decisions. While it can be expected that in cases in which environmental toxins and other hazards are present, citizens will be motivated by NIMBY-ism or outrage; in many other cases, citizens are not as engaged. This disconnect may be a result of the technical dimensions of environmental policies, the nebulous benefits or harms associated with many policies, or the lack of active mobilization of citizens.

It is due to a lack of citizen involvement, according to the case study research presented here, that experts are able to exert such a high degree of influence over local environmental policy decisions. The responsibility for the dearth of participation and lack of environmental knowledge among citizens may also rest with the media coverage of these complex policy topics.

Local media in the case presented here did not critically cover local environmental policy discussions and did not cover the topic prior to policy decision making. Citizens, therefore, did not have the opportunity or information necessary to participate in discussions related to the topic of recreational water rights in their communities. Additionally, while newsroom budgets are being cut, the demands on journalists to communicate important and complex policy issues continue to increase. These processes are taking place and influencing the trend we see in the data presented above, in which the background and experience of journalists covering environmental stories is inadequate for the technical nature of the topics in question.

In a confusing world of conflicting messages, blogs, and social media overload, it is important for citizens to have access to clear, accurate, and understandable information about policy debates. It is likely that the trends presented in this chapter are evident across communities, policy venues, and media platforms. Local media do not appear prepared or fully resourced to fairly and accurately cover environmental policy decisions or provide clear information to their readers and viewers. This lack of information in local communities, in which citizens have limited means for finding information without the assistance of their local media, can and does hamper citizen participation, interest, and knowledge with regard to policy decisions made on their behalf.

Important roles exist both for journalists and for policymakers with regard to engaging citizens to a greater extent. While local media are increasingly faced with limited resources, it may still be necessary for "point people" to be designated as issue experts when it comes to areas that are more technical in nature (akin to designated "beats" but perhaps without the rigidity that restricted coverage of these topics *only* to beat reporters). With familiarity comes a greater degree of expertise and effectiveness in reporting. Through this familiarity, a formerly inexperienced journalist can gain some degree of comfort and efficacy with regard to reporting on science and environmental topics. Additionally, many nongovernmental organizations and government agencies are now providing topical primers for students, journalists, and citizens on a variety of technical topics. A catalog of these easily accessible sources in local newsrooms would help to provide journalists who are on tight deadlines with simple ways in which they can check the accuracy of statements, understand technical nuances, and gain a greater degree of understanding about local environmental issues. While it is not realistic to assume mastery of these topics by general-assignment reporters, easy access to information for journalists may help to improve accuracy, confidence, and reduce "he said, she said" reporting.

Second, local policymakers might consider the importance of actively soliciting citizen input into policy decisions. While it may satisfy sunshine law requirements to simply print a notice in city council agendas, this does not accomplish the goal of providing the public with easily accessible information related to ongoing government policy discussions. The information may technically be available through minimal public notice mechanisms, but it is likely that only community activists will take the time to seek out information, and then only with regard to topics with which they are already concerned. To get beyond this small circle of activists, community leaders need to engage the public through multiple mechanisms, including news media outreach, columns in local media, e-mail newsletters, and perhaps even social media tools. This information provided to the public should include traditional public notices, but also active education campaigns and mass-media outreach (Beierle, 1998). Public managers and elected officials must begin to view local media as partners in their mission to inform the local citizens of government business.

NOTE

1. Each time an interview quotation is used in this chapter, the following coding scheme is used to reference interview subject data: EL = Local elected official; ES = State elected official; CW = Colorado Water Conservation Board employee; CO = Other state agency employee; LR = Local recreation interest; WA = Water attorney; LG = Local government employee; LW = Local water provider; WP = Other water provider; ER = Environmental or recreation interest; RE = Recreation engineer; AD = Water Rights Advocacy Groups. These codes, along with a numerical designation, help identify the subjects used in this research.

REFERENCES

Allen, P. (1998). Public participation in resolving environmental disputes and the problem of representativeness. *Risk: Health, Safety & Environment, 9*(4), 297–308.

Anderson, A. (1993). *Media, culture and the environment.* Rutgers, NJ: Rutgers University Press.

Baumgartner, F. R., & Jones, B. D. (1993). *Agendas and instability in American politics.* Chicago, IL: University of Chicago Press.

Beierle, T. (1998). *Public participation in environmental decisions: An evaluation framework using social goals.* Unpublished discussion paper. Resources for the Future Press.

Beierle, T. (2000). *The quality of stakeholder-based decisions: Lesson from the case study record.* Unpublished discussion paper. Resources for the Future Press.

Boykoff, M. T., & Boykoff, J. M. (2004). Balance and bias: Global warming and the US prestige press. *Global Environmental Change, 14,* 125–136.

Boykoff, M. T., & Boykoff, J. M. (2007). Climate change and journalistic norms: A case study of U.S. mass media coverage. *Geoforum, 38,* 1190–1204.

Brady, H., Verba, S., & Schlozman, K. L. (1995). Beyond SES: A resource model of political participation. *American Political Science Review, 89*(2), 271–294.

Brainard, C. (2008, December 4). CNN cuts entire science, tech team. *Columbia Journalism Review.*

Busenberg, G. J. (2000). Resources, political support, and citizen participation in environmental policy: A reexamination of conventional wisdom. *Society and Natural Resources, 13*(6), 579–588.

Colorado Foundation for Water Education. (2004). *Citizen's guide to Colorado water law.* Denver: Colorado Foundation for Water Education.

Crow, D. A. (2010a). Local media and experts: Sources of environmental policy initiation? *Policy Studies Journal, 38*(1), 143–164.

Crow, D. A. (2010b). Policy entrepreneurs, issue experts, and water rights policy change in Colorado. *Review of Policy Research, 27*(3), 299–315.

Delli Carpini, M. X., & Keeter, S. (1996). *What Americans know about politics and why it matters.* New Haven, CT: Yale University Press.

Dennis, E. E., & McCartney, J. (1979). Science journalists on metropolitan dailies: Methods, values and perceptions of their work. *Journal of Environmental Education, 10*(3), 9–15.

Dewey, J. (1927). *The public and its problems.* Chicago, IL: Swallow.

Donohue, G. A., Tichenor, P. J., & Olien, C. N. (1973). Mass media functions, knowledge, and social control. *Journalism Quarterly, 50,* 652–659.

Downs, A. (1957). *An economic theory of democracy.* Boston MA: Addison-Wesley.

Downs, A. (1972). Up and down with ecology—The 'issue attention cycle.' *The Public Interest, 28,* 38–50.

Dryzek, J. S., & Torgerson, D. (1993). Democracy and the policy sciences: A progress report. *Policy Sciences, 26*(3), 127–137.

Dunwoody, S. (1979). News-gathering behaviors of specialty reporters: A two-level comparison of mass media decision-making. *Newspaper Research Journal, 1*(1), 29–41.

Dunwoody, S., & Scott, B. T. (1982). Scientists as mass media sources. *Journalism Quarterly, 59*(1), 52–59.

Entman, R. M. (1989). *Democracy without citizens: The media and the decay of American politics.* New York, NY: Oxford University Press.

Fischer, F. (2005). *Citizens, experts, and the environment: The politics of local knowledge.* Durham, NC: Duke University Press.

Fischhoff, B. (1985, Fall). Managing risk perceptions. *Issues in science and technology, 2*(1), 83–96.

Friedman, S. M. (1986). The journalist's world. In S. M. Friedman, S. Dunwoody & C. L. Rogers (Eds.), *Scientists and journalists: Reporting science as news* (pp. 17–41). New York, NY: Free Press.

Galbraith, J. K. (1978). *The new industrial state* (3rd ed.). Boston, MA: Houghton Mifflin.

Gans, H. J. (1979). *Deciding what's news.* New York, NY: Vintage.

Getches, D. H. (1997). *Water law: In a nutshell.* St. Paul, MN: West.

Hamilton, M. B. (2003). *Online survey response rates and times: Background and guidance for industry*. Super Survey, Tercent Inc.

Hampton, G. (1999). Environmental equity and public participation. *Policy Sciences, 32*(2), 163–174.

Hart, D. M., & Victor, D. G. (1993). Scientific elites and the making of US policy for climate change research, 1957–74. *Social Studies of Science, 23*(4), 643–680.

Hobbs, G. J. (1997). Colorado water law: An historical overview. *University of Denver Water Law Review, 1*(1), 1–138.

Irvin, R. A., & Stansbury, J. (2004). Citizen participation in decision making: Is it worth the effort? *Public Administration Review, 64*(1), 55–65.

Iyengar, S. (1990). Framing responsibility for political issues: The case of poverty. *Political Behavior, 12*(1), 19–40.

Iyengar, S., & Kinder, D. R. (1987). *News that matters*. Chicago, IL: University of Chicago Press.

Johnson, K. G. (1963). Dimensions of judgment of science news stories. *Journalism Quarterly, 40*, 315–322.

Jordan, A. G., & Maloney, W. A. (1997). *The protest business?: Mobilizing campaign groups*. New York, NY: Manchester University Press.

Kennamer, D. (1992). *Public opinion, the press and public policy*. Westport, CT: Praeger.

King, P. J., & Roberts, N. C. (1992). An investigation into the personality profile of policy entrepreneurs. *Public Productivity & Management Review, 16*(2), 173–190.

Kingdon, J. W. (1995). *Agendas, alternatives and public policies* (2nd ed.). New York, NY: Longman.

Koontz, T. M., & Johnson, E. M. (2004). One size does not fit all: Matching breadth of stakeholder participation to watershed group accomplishments. *Policy Sciences, 37*(2), 185–204.

Korfmacher, K. S., & Koontz, T. M. (2003). Collaboration, information, and preservation: The role of expertise in farmland and preservation task forces. *Policy Sciences, 36*(3–4), 213–236.

Layzer, J. A. (2002a). Citizen participation and government choice in local environmental controversies. *Policy Studies Journal, 30*(2), 193–207.

Layzer, J. A. (2002b). *The environmental case: Translating values into policy*. Washington, DC: Congressional Quarterly Press.

Lee, K. N. (1993). *Compass and gyroscope: Integrating science and politics for the environment*. Washington, DC: Island.

Leighley, J. E. (1995). Attitudes, opportunities and incentives: A field essay on political participation. *Political Research Quarterly, 48*(1), 181–209.

Lind, A. E., & Early, P. C. (1992). Procedural justice and culture. *International Journal of Psychology, 27*(2), 227–242.

Mazmanian, D. A., & Kraft, M. E. (Eds.). (2001). *Toward sustainable communities*. Cambridge, MA: MIT Press.

McCombs, M. (2005). A Look at agenda-setting: Past, present and future. *Journalism Studies, 6*(4), 543–557.

McCombs, M., & Shaw, D. (1972). The agenda-setting function of mass media. *Public Opinion Quarterly, 36*(2), 176–187.

McQuail, D. (2007). The influence and effects of mass media. In D. A. Graber (Ed.), *Media Power in Politics* (5th ed., pp. 19–35). Washington, DC: CQ Press.

Miller, J. M., & Krosnick, J. A. (2000). News media impact on the ingredients of presidential evaluations: Politically knowledgeable citizens are guided by a trusted source. *American Journal of Political Science, 44*(2), 301–315.

Mintrom, M. (1997). Policy entrepreneurs and the diffusion of innovation. *American Journal of Political Science, 41*(3), 738–770.

Morton, J. (2008, February/March). A year marked by change. *American Journalism Review.* Retrieved from http://www.ajr.org/article.asp?id=4473

National Science Board. (2010). *Science and technology: Public attitudes and understanding.* Retrieved from http://www.nsf.gov/statistics/seind10/pdf/seind10.pdf

Neuzil, M., & Kovarik, W. (1996). *Mass media and environmental conflict: America's green crusades.* London, England: Sage.

Nicodemus, D. M. (2004). Mobilizing information: Local news and the formation of a viable political community. *Political Communication, 21*(2), 161–176.

Nisbet, M. C. (2004). Public opinion about stem cell research and human cloning. *Public Opinion Quarterly, 68*(1), 131–154.

Nunn, C. Z. (1979). Readership and coverage of science and technology in newspapers. *Journalism Quarterly, 56*(1), 27–30.

O'Leary, R., Durant, R., Fiorino, D., & Weiland, P. (1999). *Managing for the environment: Understanding the legal, organizational, and policy challenges.* San Francisco, CA: Jossey-Bass.

Palen, J. A. (1994). A map for science reporters: Science, technology and society studies: Concepts in basic reporting and newswriting textbooks. *The Michigan Academician, 26*(3), 507–519.

Paletz, D. L. (1999). *The media in American politics: Contents and consequences.* New York, NY: Longman.

Park, R. (1941). News and the power of the press. *American Journal of Sociology, 47*(1), 1–11.

Pew Research Center for the People and the Press. (2009). *Scientific achievements less prominent than a decade ago: Public praises science; scientists fault public, media.* Washington, DC: Pew Research Center for the People and the Press.

Roberts, N. C. (Ed.). (2008). *The age of direct citizen participation.* London, England: M.E. Sharp.

Roberts, N. C., & King, P. J. (1991). Policy entrepreneurs: Their activity structure and function in the policy process. *Journal of Public Administration Research and Theory, 1*(2), 147–175.

Rogers, E. M., & Dearing, J. W. (2007). Agenda-setting research: Where has it been, where is it going? In D. A. Graber (Ed.), *Media power in politics.* Washington, DC: CQ Press.

Rosenstone, S. J., & Hansen, J. M. (1993). *Mobilization, participation, and democracy in America.* New York, NY: Macmillan.

Scheufele, D. A., & Tewksbury, D. (2007). Framing, agenda setting, and priming: The evolution of three media effects models. *Journal of Communication, 57,* 9–20.

Schneider, A. L., & Ingram, H. (1997). *Policy design for democracy.* Lawrence: University Press of Kansas.

Schneider, M., & Teske, P. (1992). Toward a theory of the political entrepreneur: Evidence from local government. *The American Political Science Review, 86*(3), 737–747.

Senate Bill 216, Colorado General Assembly (2001).

Senate Bill 37, Colorado General Assembly (2006).

Senate Bill 62, Colorado General Assembly (2005).

Smolkin, R. (2006, June/July). Adapt or die. *American Journalism Review, 28*(3), 17–23.

Starr, P. (2009). Goodbye to the age of newspapers (Hello to a new era of corruption). Retrieved March 4, 2009, from http://www.tnr.com/article/goodbye-the-age-newspapers-hello-new-era corruption?id=q4hWPDYjcwFatgm9FD70lq EdHJOYnbGaHX/twe+k1xzCpjCcv+gqc5cJMNkPmAA3

Steelman, T. A. (2001). Elite and participatory policymaking: Finding a balance in the case of national forest planning. *Policy Studies Journal, 29*(1), 71–92.

Steelman, T. A., & Ascher, W. (1997). Public involvement methods in natural resource policy making: Advantages, disadvantages and trade-offs. *Policy Sciences, 30*(2), 71–90.

Tankard, J. W., & Ryan, M. (1974). News source perception of accuracy of science coverage. *Journalism Quarterly, 51,* 219–225.

Teske, P., & Schneider, M. (1994). The bureaucratic entrepreneur: The case of city managers. *Public Administration Review, 54*(4), 331–340.

Tichenor, P. J., Olien, C. N., Harrison, A., & Donohue, G. (1970). Mass communication systems and communication accuracy in science news reporting. *Journalism Quarterly, 47,* 673–683.

Tyler, T. R. (1994). Governing amid diversity: The effect of fair decision-making procedures on the legitimacy of government. *Law & Society Review, 28*(4), 809–832.

Verba, S., & Nie, N. H. (1972). *Participation in America: Political democracy and social equality.* Chicago, IL: University of Chicago Press.

Verba, S., Schlozman, K. L., & Brady, H. E. (1995). *Voice and equality in American politics.* Cambridge, MA: Harvard University Press.

Vig, N. J., & Kraft, M. E. (2003). *Environmental policy: New directions for the twenty-first century* (5th ed.). Washington, DC: Congressional Quarterly Press.

Weaver, D., & Wilhoit, G. C. (1996). *The American journalist in the 1990s.* Mahwah, NJ: Lawrence Erlbaum.

Weimer, D., & Vining, A. (1999). *Policy analysis: Concepts and practice.* Englewood Cliffs, NJ: Prentice-Hall.

Winsten, J. (1985, Spring). Science and the media: The boundaries of truth. *Health Affairs, 4*(1), 5–23.

Zaller, J. R. (1992). *The nature and origins of mass opinion.* Cambridge, England: Cambridge University Press.

CHAPTER 7

APPLYING TECHNOLOGY TO ENHANCE CITIZEN ENGAGEMENT WITH CITY AND COUNTY GOVERNMENT

William (Bill) S. Barnes, Jr.
City of Suwanee

Brian N. Williams
The University of Georgia

INTRODUCTION

What does an engaged citizen look like in the 21st century? Going to a political meeting at the local public library? Or is it something more like "liking" the mayor on Facebook and getting headlines sent to an iPhone? Considering the high tech reality of present-day society, local governments need to embrace technology if they want to ensure their "high touch" ability to engage their residents. Robert Putnam, in his "Bowling Alone" essay stated,

> Recently, American social scientists of a neo-Tocquevillean bent have unearthed a wide range of empirical evidence that the quality of public life and the performance of social institutions (and not only in America) are indeed

The State of Citizen Participation in America, pages 163–194
Copyright © 2012 by Information Age Publishing
All rights of reproduction in any form reserved.

powerfully influenced by norms and networks of civic engagement. (McDonald & Popkin, 2001)

What is Citizen Engagement and Why Does it Matter?

Citizen engagement is associated with governmental attempts to actively seek and involve individual citizens in public policymaking and decision making. Defined by Phillips and Orsini (2002) as "interactive and iterative processes of deliberation among citizens" (p. 1), citizen engagement attempts to bring the theory of democratic governance into practice. Even though it has been described as "an evolving concept in an emerging field," citizen engagement seeks to generate innovative ideas and the active participation of ordinary lay citizens and facilitate the sharing of decision-making power and responsibility between the governed and those who are governing (Sheedy, MacKinnon, Pitre, & Watling, 2008, p. 5). This arrangement is based upon mutual trust and respect among all participants and requires that information and processes be available and transparent to all.

Citizen engagement revolves around community involvement and social networking, which lead to social capital formation. This formation of social capital has been found to have a positive impact on enhancing quality of life. For instance, a crucial "Kids Count" composite index composed of factors such as infant mortality rates, percentage of children in poverty, percentage of families headed by a single parent, and seven other factors, correlates highly positively with Putnam's Social Capital Index (SCI). Per capita murder rates on the state level correlates negatively with the SCI. States scoring higher on the Healthy State Index correlate positively with the Social Capital Index, while the All-Cause Mortality Rate correlates strongly negatively with the SCI (Putnam, 2000).

Citizen engagement or the creation of social capital has also been found to improve government performance. Putnam's (2000) 20-year study of subnational governments in Italy reveals that some perform better than others in such activities as economic development, childcare, family health clinics, and citizen satisfaction. Strong civic traditions contributed to social capital creation in the regions where the governments perform the best.

Similar findings have been found in domestic studies. From small Iowa communities to sometimes even smaller campus communities, there has been recognition that a sense of community enhances achievement of shared group goals. While small Iowa communities are admittedly homogenous and therefore susceptible to creating primarily bonding social capital, research did show a strong positive correlation among towns with high social capital and perceptions by residents that their local government was responsive and effective (Rice, 2001).

So in essence, engaged citizens create social capital, which enhances their quality of life and improves government performance. Technology offers many advantages in aiding the creation of social capital, such as greater efficiency, mass availability of information, public safety, and increasing access to information. New applications enable faster mass communications with feedback, as well as more targeted and even individualized real-time information exchange, as opposed to one-way dissemination of information using older technologies.

This chapter explores the opportunities and challenges of applying technology to enhance citizen engagement with city and county governments within the United States. As Baby Boomers continue to increase their technological savvy, and subsequent generations increasingly rely on social networking technologies to interact with institutions as well as individuals, local government should plan to capitalize on the opportunities offered. Highly cost-effective yet more frequent and personalized engagement can be accomplished. Transparency can be enhanced, and participatory decision making can be achieved. Increasing perceived individual "mattering," measurable quality of life metrics, and community cohesiveness are goals that can be addressed through application of interactive technologies, some new and evolving and others adapted from older previous uses.

This chapter concludes by highlighting that (a) strategic planning is critical so that expensive cutting-edge technology is selected by local governments only when the cost/benefit analysis dictates and resource allocation for the application of technologies is tied to specific goals; and (b) planned assessment with benchmarks should be established prior to technology and program adoption. These prescriptions can aid in demonstrating effectiveness, good stewardship, and in building citizen support for continued or expanded goals relative to citizen engagement.

WHAT IS AN "ENGAGED" CITIZEN?

Classic measures associated with civic engagement have included voting participation, membership in civic organizations, and paying attention to political news. These measures have been much studied and trends identified (Bennett, 2008; McDonald & Popkin, 2001; Putnam, 1995, 2000; Kirlin, 2003). Using these measures, it could appear that engagement has been declining. However consideration of other factors may be needed to round out an understanding of a modern concept of engagement. Generational factors, participation in policy deliberations, "full circle" engagement, two-way communication versus drop-in isolated actions, and one-way communication channels all contribute to a contemporary understanding of engagement in the 21st century.

Engagement in Generational Context

Engagement may be in the eyes of the beholder, and the beholders position (demographic, especially generational) may color their perception. A reduced level of participation in formal civic organizations among younger generations ("Y" and "Z" or the "dotnet" generation) may be replaced with an increased and as yet poorly tracked involvement in communal efforts. These generations may have replaced lower apparent levels of newspaper use with an equal or higher level of consumption of current events and political news via new digital media sources.

Through an extensive review of the literature, Kirlin (2003) identifies three important dimensions for youth civic engagement: intent, membership, and commitment, and indications that there is a strong correlation between youth extracurricular involvement and adult civic participation. Causality is still in question, and many of the older studies reviewed may not account for paradigm shifts in defining engagement.

Bennett (2008) cites movement from a "dutiful citizen" model to an "actualizing citizen model," especially among Millenials, or the "dotnet" generation (those born between 1977 and 1987). Bennett's table contrasting the two perspectives on citizenship is reproduced in Table 7.1.

Pettingill (2008) suggests that youth may be participating differently yet receiving the same benefits of participation previously acquired through more formal organizational activity. The impact of commitment over time and sustained organizational membership may have been overstated. Rather

TABLE 7.1   The Changing Citizenry: The Traditional Civic Ideal of the Dutiful Citizen Versus the Emerging Youth Experience of Self-Actualizing Citizenship

Actualizing Citizen	Dutiful Citizen
Diminished sense of government obligation; higher sense of individual purpose	Obligation to participate in government-centered activities
Voting is less meaningful than other, more personally identified acts such as consumerism, community volunteering, or transnational activism	Voting is the core democratic act
Mistrust of media and politicians is reinforced by negative mass media environment	Becomes informed about issues and government by following mass media
Favors loose networks of community action, often established or sustained through friendships and peer relations and thin social ties maintained by interactive information technologies	Joins civil society organizations and/or expresses interests through parties that typically employ one-way conventional communication to mobilize supporters

than counting the number of City Council meetings attended, for younger generations it may be more important to gauge how many times they have "tweeted" positively regarding service delivery, whether they are a "friend" or "fan" of the county on Facebook, or whether they participated in the latest live online chat with the Planning Department regarding the latest iteration of the comprehensive plan.

Variance among generational expectations of the role of government, the ability of the individual to affect governmental responsiveness, or the role of alternate delivery systems (nonprofits and other nongovernmental organizations) will impact which means of engagement should be employed. Rowe and Frewer (2005) offer an extensive typology of "mechanisms" based on desired outcomes. If this typology could be refreshed with generational applicability dimensions, a menu of strategies could be developed to effectively guide selection of public engagement processes. With the pace of change and development of new technologies increasing, an evolution of the menu will continue to generate new possibilities for targeted engagement of generations.

Public Participation in Policy Deliberations and Governmental Transparency

As noted earlier, Phillips and Orsini (2002) define citizen engagement as interactive and iterative processes characterized by deliberations among citizens with the purpose of contributing, in meaningful ways, to specific public policy decisions in a transparent and accountable manner. In their study of citizen involvement in Canadian federal decision-making processes, they identified eight dimensions of citizen involvement: mobilizing interest, claims making, knowledge acquisition, spanning and bridging, convening and deliberation, community capacity building, analysis and synthesis, and transparency and feedback.

These dimensions can most successfully be carried out in an environment of public trust and invited participation; however, the participation must be more than token and patronizing. The purposes of participation must be transparent. Increasing transparency has been associated with five benefits: enhanced accountability, increased citizen involvement in government, increased performance, boosting of government credibility, and reduction in corruption (Eggers, 2005). In a generation for which information is available in (almost) real time at your fingertips, government transparency and responsiveness become even more vital in establishing trust and satisfaction.

Voice, Action, and Reflection: A Full Circle Process

Raill and Hollander (2006) describe the evolution of three principles of engagement: voice, action, and reflection. Growing out of the collegiate service-learning arena, these scholars maintain that

> engagement is more than just volunteering—although volunteering can be engagement. Engagement is more than just voting—although voting can be engagement. Engagement is a combination of voice, action, and reflection ... Engagement exists when individuals recognize that they have responsibilities not only to themselves and their families, but also to their communities—local, national, and global—and that the health and well-being of these communities are essential to their own health and well-being. They act in order to fulfill those responsibilities and try to affect those communities for the better. Those actions, in turn, give them an even deeper understanding of their independence with communities. (pp. 4–5)

This full-circle process of voice, action, and reflection suggests that participation in a nonpolitical social arena can lead to later participation in the political arena. As such, helping a neighborhood can grow into a desire to help a city. This process can be enhanced by social capital.

Social Capital

Putnam (1995) refers to social capital as "features of social organization such as networks, norms, and social trust that facilitate coordination and cooperation for mutual benefit" (p. 66). Two types of social capital are identified: bonding and bridging. While measuring the distinction between the two types of social capital and their independent impact upon aspects of community development is difficult, they do have differing characteristics.

Bonding social capital is exclusive in nature and is developed through homogenous organizations. Examples are most fraternal organizations, country clubs, and other social groups in which there is little diversity in membership. Bonding capital focuses on similarities, creates strong interpersonal ties based on likeness, and creates unity based on sameness. Putnam emphasizes that bonding social capital is

> good for undergirding reciprocity and mobilizing solidarity ... Dense networks in ethnic enclaves, for example, provide crucial social and psychological support for less fortunate members of the community, while furnishing start-up financing, markets, and reliable labor for local entrepreneurs. (2000, p. 22)

Bridging social capital is more impactful in creating connections across socioeconomic boundaries. Broader networks built on commonalities rooted in causes, values, specific goals, or shared missions can provide positive benefits for economic development, community building, and overall enhancement of quality of life. Beugelsdijk and Smulders (2003) concluded that only bridging social capital has a positive impact on economic development. By participating in networks that bridge communities, trust is developed among network members that reduce opportunistic behaviors toward one another.

There may be identifiable subgroups in each community that tend to engage more readily. While some of these groups may appear to be based on bonding rather than bridging, these groups might serve as a starting place for connecting local government and citizens.

"Mattering"

Rosenberg and McCullough introduced the psychological concept of *mattering* in 1981 as "the feeling that others depend upon us, are interested in us, are concerned with our fate, or experience us as an ego-extension" (p. 165).

While developing a 24-item Mattering Index, Elliott, Kao, and Grant (2004) refine this original definition of mattering as "the extent we make a difference in the world around us. People matter simply because: others attend to them (awareness), invest themselves in them (importance), or look to them for resources (reliance)" (p. 339).

Citizens are more likely to engage with their local government, creating social capital, if they feel like their participation matters.

Citizen/Local Government Engagement Defined

Based on the preceding information, we offer a broad definition of positive engagement between citizen and local government, inclusive of its various caveats.

Engaged citizens desire to have a high level of trust in their government. An engaged citizenry perceives that their government operates with *transparency* and *accountability* in an environment of *public trust*, and balances equity and efficiency while practicing good stewardship of resources. Citizens feel they can express their opinion, that their opinion will be heard, and that they *matter*.

The government provides timely information through media and methods relevant to citizens, on group and individualized levels, as much as practical or desired by the public. Citizens participate through voluntary activity, contributing time and talents to the accomplishment of shared goals. Citizens trust each other and trust their government, expecting ethical conduct of those activities that belong to government for the common good.

Voluntary participation includes group interactions, allowing for more complete understanding of community and individual perspectives. These interactions also provide appropriate channels for citizen participation in policy formation and implementation, and involve interaction with other citizens, staff, and elected officials.

Social capital (primarily bridging capital) is created and channeled to positively benefit the objects of government operations rooted in shared community values and desires. Increased engagement of stakeholders seems to generally enhance efficiency. Examples from systems as disparate as education and economics illustrate this tendency. In a review of studies of community college students and their educational outcomes, McClenney, Marti, and Adkins (2006) report clear positive impact of student engagement. Similarly Svanum and Bigatti (2009) find that a high level of engagement forecasts college success or, as the subtitle of their journal article summarizes, "Engaged Students Are More Likely to Earn a Degree, Do it Faster, and Do it Better."

In an example of economic efficiency, Barth (2007) found in a study of wine shops that those that used interactive engagement methods were more efficient economically. Shops that had customers involved in educational seminars, wine tastings, and cooking demonstrations were able to more efficiently meet their customers purchasing interests and produced higher sales and faster inventory turnover.

However, when disengaged citizens initially attempt to plug-in, their attempts to be heard and desire to "matter" can create a strain on the efficiency of planning and decision-making processes. Citizens can attempt to become engaged without a predisposed trust relationship with their local government. At times, those who feel unheard, maligned, and/or disconnected from decision-making processes search for a means to communicate. Integrating these citizens into engagement activities can be difficult, disruptive, and resource intensive initially. If eventually effectively engaged, these citizens can contribute to an improved community-building process. Otherwise they can continue to be a drain on the efficiency of processes, even causing engagement processes to be eliminated.

The New Digital Media and Other Technologies

Technology is a powerful tool. It can be difficult to incorporate into a government's toolkit because it evolves and changes so rapidly. Communication vehicles of today are replaced tomorrow. Even the three classic mea-

sures associated with civic engagement (voting, civic organizations, and political news) have been impacted. Electronic voting, online organizations,
and the plethora of sources for political news now available are signs that
technology can impact some of the more static and change-resistant norms
of civic engagement.

Generational comfort levels with technology vary, and economic realities
impact accessibility. Groups who adopt technological means of engagement
can even drop them when other groups move in, as Facebook's original
incarnation as a social network for college students was invaded by older
users, college students moved on to Twitter (Smith, 2009).

There are opportunities that should be capitalized on at every level
of government. At the federal and state levels, there is beginning to be a
great deal of information on how money is being spent and laws are being
brought to the floor. At the local level, technology has also impacted how
citizens interact with their government (borough, town, city, and county).
Below, many of the new media applications are categorized and described
as to how they are currently deployed to impact citizen service delivery,
communication, engagement, and political participation with local government. Applications often cross categories and serve multiple functions.

One-Way Mass Communication for Efficiency

E-mail distribution groups are used to be able to send one e-mail to many
people. Following the Columbine High School and Virginia Tech campus
shooting incidents, campus alert systems have been developed allowing
educational institutions to send mass phone calls, e-mails, and now text
messages and "tweets" to mass preassembled distribution groups. Similarly,
Calling Post and other similar commercial competitors allow the building
of phone call distribution trees for sending one message to many people
quickly. Reverse 911 systems can perform the same function in many municipalities, using 911 call databases originally, and now adding geographic
information system integration for rapid development of calling lists built
on specific geographic areas. These systems can be used to inform citizens
about "boil water" advisories, BOLO (Be on the Lookout) warnings, emergency weather advisories, hazmat accident and emergency weather evacuation orders, and other public health and safety notifications.

Another variant of mass distribution is RSS (Really Simple Syndication)
feeds, which allow subscribers to select specific sources from which to receive information. Users can control the topic, channel, and timing of information they wish to receive.

Mass Accessibility of Video Content

YouTube has revolutionized the creation, accessibility, and ability to impact public awareness and opinion through video content. From persuasive

speech, idea promotion, education, and information, YouTube has enabled private citizen as well as organizational use of video. Using the platform of Apple's iPod and other similar products, video content can be recorded, posted on Web sites, and downloaded to these devices for later play. Duke University gave all incoming freshman an iPod prior to the fall of 2004. These iPods were loaded with orientation content and were later used for downloading podcasts of professors' lectures, supplemental educational content, and university resources. The Duke Digital Initiative has expanded to

- connect and collaborate remotely with guest speakers and peers at other campuses using Web and video technologies,
- share comments and build discussions around images and video using VoiceThread,
- explore new, flexible publishing platforms to share digital media and extend learning beyond classroom walls,
- encourage new forms of student reflection and course content engagement with Twitter,
- experiment with new teaching applications for mobile devices, and
- use microprojectors to teach in nontraditional spaces. (http://dukedigitalinitiative.duke.edu/)

Improved Two-Way Interactive Communication

Video conferencing has allowed criminal justice systems to conduct arraignments, bond hearings, and other preliminary proceedings without having to bring defendants from jail to the courthouse. This innovation can create a safer judicial environment, save money by reducing labor intensive transportation, and speed up hearings.

Long distance candidates for jobs can be interviewed without travel expenses thereby allowing governments to expand their pool beyond local talent. Technologies such as Skype can provide access to long distance and international communications. Local government can interactively communicate with benchmark governments to learn about best practices without costly travel.

Using interactive cable methodology, meetings can be conducted and televised, while citizens can provide real-time feedback to opinion polling during the meeting. This process can add a real-time aspect. As many small communities are struggling with severe budget issues, one small-town mayor conducted a series of webcasts. Beginning with a webcast that explored "What makes a healthy city," the mayor followed up with another webcast that focused on being proactive and making sustainable decisions (Young, 2010, p. 4C). This level of transparency should have a positive impact on public perceptions of accountability and stewardship.

Building Social, Professional, and Other Interpersonal Connections

Facebook, Friendster, MySpace, and other social networking competitors provide opportunities for groups (including governments) to create social linkages. The development of bridging capital can be enhanced by encouraging citizens to interact with elected officials and staff, as well as with other citizens. "Friends," "Fans," and other means of connecting provide controlled interaction and information.

LinkedIn and some other networking entities provide more focused professional networking. These networks can be tapped for employee and volunteer recruitment, consultant and contractor sourcing, and reference checks.

A study released in 2010 found that 66% of government workplaces use some type of social networking tool. Of these government workplaces using networking tools, 65% of them are using more than one tool (Human Capital Institute, 2010). According to the 2009 Nielsen Report on Social Networking's Global Footprint, "social networking and blogging sites account for almost 10% of all Internet time" (p. 14).

A study of college students' use of Facebook at Michigan State concluded that there was a "robust connection" between the use of Facebook and related indicators of social capital, especially the bridging type. It concluded that Internet use alone did not predict social capital accumulation, but intensive use of Facebook did (Ellison, Steinfield, & Lampe, 2007).

Free Expression

Blogs provide many citizens the ability to express themselves to others without a great deal of technical knowledge required. Blogs can provide watchdog functions helping to create accountability. Information can be disseminated, from the obscure to the less than credible. Nonetheless, citizens now have a means of reaching others with opinions, ideas, and sometimes less-than-civil expression. Everyone has a voice and an outlet in which to express it.

Increasing Access to Services

Personalized Web portals can be used to control an interface with government. Citizens can set up sections of a Web portal that can allow them to efficiently access the interactions they prefer. Online bill payment, e-mail access, Web-site links, and news feeds can be organized for efficiency, while extraneous content can be removed. In some cases, single sign-on systems can be integrated so that all services can be accessed with one password rather than multiple layers of transactions inhibiting the usability of a government Web site.

Knowing Citizens

Citizen Relation Management (CRM) systems have been adapted from Customer Relations Management systems developed in private sector sales organizations. Sales and service often operated separate silos of information about customers. As computers became commonplace in the 90s in these organizations, companies discovered they could merge these silos and know much more about customer behaviors, needs, and preferences and therefore better market to them (Thompson, n.d.).

Similarly, local government can now know much more about the citizens to which they provide services. Transactions can be archived and information integrated so that interactions do not have to start from scratch each time. Data can be aggregated from various sources so that government can interact more personally with its citizens.

Data-mining techniques can be used in law enforcement, public works, economic development, and other areas to anticipate citizen behaviors. Tracking requests, usage of services, financial transactions, and other interactions with government can provide the data needed for analysis.

Online surveying software and Web sites have emerged that can allow government to conduct more professional survey research and make more accurate and appropriate conclusions than may have been previously possible. Smaller governments may be able to deploy surveys and receive better data analysis without the expense of employing professional market or social research consultants. Web sites such as Survey Monkey, Zoomerang, Question Pro and other survey software can be inexpensive solutions for gathering data on opinions, attitudes, preferences, and satisfaction levels.

Providing More Efficient Services

CRM not only allows local government to know their citizens better, but is a vehicle for providing more efficient services. "CRM combines advanced telephony, internet and computer technology with constituent-focused business processes and an ethos of service to the community" (Kavanagh, 2007). Usually the implementation processes of CRM systems are coupled with process redesign efforts. Metrics are applied to responsiveness activities, and huge improvements can be seen. For example, Chicago reduced by almost 80% the amount of time from a citizen report of a pothole to completion of the repair (Kavanagh, 2007).

The 311 system now provides citizens with the ability to access services during extended hours, diverting many afterhours calls from 911 where they inappropriately clog emergency channels. Associated knowledge bases can allow a 311 call-taker to provide an answer rather than transfer the caller to another department, or worse yet, a voice mail system. Government "run around" can be virtually eliminated, and citizens can talk with a person rather than a machine.

"Push, pull, publish" approaches to systems integration using Web services or XML interface software allows many previously disparate software systems to integrate. Business license data kept in one system can now be fed into fire inspection systems kept in another database in order to facilitate the coordination of work orders, inspections, and processing of the license. Issuance of development permits can connect to site-inspection information, submission of contractor insurance information, and other requirements in order to keep projects moving forward more efficiently.

Electronic voting machines allow faster tabulation of results. While not implemented on a wide scale in the United States, Internet voting has been piloted and studied. Election.com is a for-profit company, partly backed by VeriSign, the Internet security company. One criticism is an inequitable computer ownership situation that could lead to an unintended consequence of impacting the racial make-up of voter participation (Berman, 2000). In 1999, the Arizona Democratic Party contracted with another company, Votation.com, to conduct their primary election via Internet voting, once again using VeriSign security certificate technology (Phoenix Business Wire, 1999). Online voting has also been piloted by the Federal Voting Assistance Program, administered under the auspices of the Uniformed and Overseas Citizens Absentee Voting Act. The VOI (Voting over Internet) Pilot recommendations included further study and a "low risk incremental" development approach toward full implementation (Department of Defense, 2001).

Personal Data Assistants (PDAs) and SmartPhones can keep workers in the field in touch, accessing data, and completing tasks, reducing the frequency of trips back from the field to do paperwork. Eliminating travel time can increase productivity and reduce fuel and vehicle costs.

GPS-enabled devices can provide data for Geographic Information Systems (GIS). From locating missing water valves to tracking movement of city fleet vehicles, efficiencies can be gained, service delivery improved, and costs controlled. GIS analysis can inform planning, economic development, public works, and other departments in their policymaking decisions.

Enhancing Public Safety

Perhaps one of the quickest areas to adopt new technologies has been law enforcement and court systems. Reverse 911 was developed to provide a means to communicate quickly with people in a geographic area. The technology has been applied successfully in issuing fire evacuation orders in California (McKay, 2008), and in the state of Washington, this technology has been employed to locate missing children, help find lost and vulnerable Alzheimer's patients, and evacuate citizens in flood areas (Sclair, 2009).

The 311 system relieves 911 call loads by redirecting nonemergency calls, and has evolved into a centralized number for general government services. In many areas, 211 has now become a centralized social services access point.

Many agencies offer online incident reporting with the ability to attach photos. These applications help citizens become more engaged by reporting code violations, incidents of vandalism such as graffiti, suspicious vehicles in neighborhoods, and other information that police departments struggle to keep up with.

Electronic ticketing and in-field electronic accident investigation technologies allow police to conduct these activities more efficiently and effectively. Line-of-sight angles, distances, and vehicle conditions can be documented immediately and attached to other data used in accident reports. Traffic citations can be generated with in-vehicle systems, complete with court date through integration with case and docket management software integration, as well as eliminating duplicative data entry and handwriting transcription errors.

License plate scanning systems can allow in-vehicle cameras to scan license plates, searching NCIC (National Crime Information Center) databases for wants and warrants, and checking for consistency between the plate and the correct vehicle.

AFIS (Automated Fingerprint Identification Systems) and other biometrics can be used for personal identification. Use of automated fingerprint systems can speed up business, alcohol, and some occupational license application processes. Biometrics can also be used in building access systems.

Arraignment and bond hearings conducted via video can reduce costs and increase personal safety, not to mention increase the efficiency of the system by enabling more hearings to be conducted per session.

RFID (Radio Frequency Identification) tracking tabs have been used in monitoring evidence inventory and movement of items, case files, equipment, and even people. Small tabs with embedded data communication chips are attached, and remote devices can send out signals and retrieve data from the tabs. Other similar technologies have been used for monitoring probationers or others whose movements or location may be restricted.

Increasing Access to Information: Wikis, Web Sites, Web Portals

Wiki's have been deployed to help citizens access information. A system of content management using software to create templates of information, a wiki allows multiple users to contribute information from their expertise in a collaborative publication.

Two of the best examples of city-created wiki's are from Seattle, Washington, and Salt Lake City, Utah. Seattle's wiki is focused around their online Civic Engagement Initiative (http://dowire.org/wiki/Seattle's Online Civic Engagement Initiative). Salt Lake City's wiki was developed as part of the Greater Transparency for Collaborative Government Initiative (http://www.transparencyslcgov.com/wiki/tabid/56/Default.aspx). Both these initiatives are discussed further at the end of this chapter.

Web sites have grown from one-way graphic communications instruments to highly interactive sites that can even enable instant live chats with staff members and streaming video instructional material. Electronic payments, document downloads, and webcasts can all be offered through Web sites for citizen 24/7 accessibility.

Web portals offer the ability to allow citizens to custom create their graphic interface with their local government. Through WYSIWIG editing tools, a citizen can design a portal entry page that contains the government services, activities, or information that they want to frequently interact with. Elements can be managed so that the page provides maximum efficiency.

NEW DIGITAL MEDIA CONCERNS: TRANSPARENCY AND PRIVACY

Any time new technology emerges, there are unintended consequences. When incorporating new technologies into local government services, there are two clear potential consequences: laws that complicate reporting and transparency, and citizens feeling that their privacy is being violated.

The Double-Edged Sword of Transparency

In 2009, Salt Lake City, Utah, embarked on an impressive process of creating and sustaining transparency in government (http://www.transparencyslcgov.com/Home/tabid/36/Default.aspx). Broadened to an "Open Government" initiative including elements other than transparency, the project continued in 2010.

Ken Pulskamp, City Manager of Santa Clara, California, is quoted in an article about local government of new media saying, "The information age creates a greater expectation for transparent government and an even greater expectation that the information is both real-time and easily accessible" (Long, 2009). While use of new digital media can enhance the appearance of transparency with its real-time delivery, a new threat is quickly emerging.

Melinda Catalan, records manager for a city government and an attorney by training, describes what could be "a series of short leaps from text messaging via pagers to electronic communications in general, to electronic communications via external sources" in the courts expectations of accessible records (Opsahl, 2010). The Florida State Attorney General in fact has issued an Advisory Legal Opinion to the City of Coral Springs advising,

Communications on the city's Facebook page regarding city business by city commissioners may be subject to Florida's Government in the Sunshine

Law… Thus, a member of a city board or commission must not engage on the city's Facebook page in an exchange or discussion of matters that forseeably will come before the board or commission for official action. (Farrell, 2009)

The City Attorney for the Florida city of Marco Island states,

If the city official is using their personal computer to communicate city business then the city is required to maintain copies of those communications. In some cases, these communications and the management of these records become difficult, if not impossible. You can expect the state to adopt new legislation to address these very issues.

The possibility that Facebook, Twitter, or other communications may be covered by open government, "Sunshine," or other Freedom of Information Act-type requests raises questions for records managers. Archiving, managing, and producing electronic communications may be a challenge. Governments may choose to use third-party solutions such as TweetTake, ArchiveFacebook, and SocialSafe if the solutions meet archiving requirements. Otherwise the local government may have to take on creation of solutions for archiving and records management for these communications (Opsahl, 2010).

The use of Facebook and Twitter via cell phone opens even more challenges for communications retention and archiving. Whether personal, government owned, or government subsidized communication on cell phones, PDAs, and computers, suddenly the government IT manager can have responsibility for devices that may be beyond his or her network control.

Privacy: Balancing Personal Attention with Perceptions of "Big Brother" Watching

One of the common complaints citizens voice about government service is the anonymity and apparent lack of mattering. Impersonal one-size-fits-all solutions, service provision, and interaction systems do not create a perception that a single citizen is uniquely served by their local government.

At the juncture of biology and computing, there emerges a field of artificial intelligence. Applied to e-commerce and more specifically e-government offerings, intelligence techniques can allow service request systems, e-commerce interaction systems, Web portals, and other means of electronic interaction to "learn" a citizen's tendencies and preferences, and even anticipate needs.

Artificial intelligence techniques, inclusive of conventional intelligence like expert systems, machine learning, case-based reasoning, Bayesian networks, and computational intelligence (e.g., artificial neural networks, fuzzy systems, and evolutionary computation) are playing important roles in e-service applications. Lu and Chang (2007) detail these techniques and their impact on e-service personalization.

Other studies of personalization in the public sector identify trust and privacy as critical elements (Pieterson, Ebbers, & van Dijk, 2007). Balancing the level of personalization with the perception that government is amassing too much information about its citizens is a difficult task.

While social communications and networking Web service Twitter now offers a "Tweet with Your Location Feature," allowing users to add their exact location to their tweets, they provide copious information on the opt-in feature, privacy issues, and a generalized location option rather than the exact latitude and longitude coordinates.

Tracking the location of communications devices has been used by law enforcement, and current litigation is still defining the rules. The Justice Department is currently arguing that warrantless tracking is permitted and that Americans do not have a reasonable expectation of privacy in the use of their phones (McCullagh, 2010).

Technology provides ample opportunity for more personalized service, greater efficiency, and creation of a sense of individual service provision. The degree to which citizens will be interested in a close personal relationship with their local government will depend largely on their level of trust and confidence that privacy can be provided.

OPPORTUNITIES FOR RECOGNITION, CREDENTIALING, DEVELOPMENT OF STANDARDS, AND SOURCES OF FUNDING

Similar to the evolution of new professions, there is a need for the credibility of a recognized body of knowledge, credentials, standards, and recognition of achievement from within and without the community of practitioners. As application of new digital media becomes common within government service and community development, programs will be created to fill these needs.

One such organization is the Public Technology Institute. The description of the organization from its own Web site states,

> As the only technology organization created by and for cities and counties, PTI works with a core network of leading local government officials—the PTI membership—to identify opportunities for technology research, to share solutions and recognize member achievements, and develop best practices that address the technology management, governance and policy issues that impact local government. (http://www.pti.org/index.php)

Currently, the Public Technology Institute's "Citizen-Engaged Community" designation program for "cities and counties in the United States is to recognize excellence in multi-channel contact centers and best practices for the use of Citizen Relationship/Records Management (CRM) systems, 311 systems, web portal technology, telephony systems and mobile communications infrastructure." Focus is on "best practices and standards in four key areas":

> Citizen Participation Processes (information, service requests, complaints, interactive business applications and forms, surveys, focus groups, suggestions, chats)

> Integrated Communication Channels (contact center, self-service Web and automated phone systems, walk-ins, neighborhood stations, contact center linkage with service departments, mobile citizens and mobile crews)

> Integrated Technology (311, CRM, Web 2.0 applications, VoIP telephony, GIS, work management, mobile communications, knowledge-based data repositories)

> Performance Reporting (external citizen metrics, customer driven internal service metrics, use of real-time data, service level agreements for contact center and service departments).

Another entity that has been involved in the application of technology to government is the National Science Foundation's Digital Government Research Program. Three university-based research centers have been established at institutions recognized as some of the premier public administration graduate institutions. Each of these centers sponsors research, provides grants, conducts annual conferences for idea exchange, and advances best practices. These centers are

- Digital Government Research Center (University of Southern California and Columbia University)
- Center for Technology in Government (SUNY Albany)
- National Center for Digital Government (originally at Harvard University, now at University of Massachusetts, Amherst).

eRepublic.com, while admittedly a commercial entity, describes their company as follows:

> e.Republic, Inc. is the nation's leading publishing, research, event and new media company focused on the state and local government and education markets.

> Serving both government and industry for over 20 years, e.Republic publishes the market's leading periodicals and websites, runs the largest intergovern-

mental conferences in the nation and produces over 100 targeted and custom events annually.

e.Republic is also home to the Center for Digital Government and Center for Digital Education, the premier research and market advisory services in their respective fields.

The company publishes among others, "Government Technology" and "Digital Communities" magazines, sponsors the Center for Digital Government, coordinates large trade shows and specialty themed events, produces white papers, provides a subscription grants database, provides contract technical project support, and provides awards and recognition for outstanding applications.

Deeply involved in the creation of the 311 concept is the Department of Justice. Originally conceived as a place to redirect inappropriate 911 calls, 311 quickly became a general government service three-digit dialing service number for government (primarily local) services. Initial funding of pilot programs came from the Department of Justice's COPS (Community Oriented Policing Services) program. Over $6 million has been provided to various programs, resulting in the production of "how-to" manuals and "white papers" to assist replication in other jurisdictions.

The Office of Justice Programs (http://www.it.ojp.gov/jxdm/), another unit of the Department of Justice, has been a major player in the development of the Global Justice XML Data Model. This project seeks to create common mark-up language (XML or Extensible Mark-up Language), data definitions, and standards so that criminal justice and Homeland Security entities can share data across platforms and systems—a critical operational consideration for law enforcement. The Georgia Tech Research Institute Justice XML Research Center (http://justicexml.gtri.gatech.edu/) is another academic center devoted to the development, dissemination, and coordination of the evolution of the data model.

Another organization that has become heavily involved in criminal justice technology exists as a nonprofit organization. The Institute for Justice Information Sharing (IJIS; http://www.ijis.org/) provides training, technical assistance, research, and contracted services such as program planning, process guidance, and project management.

These entities and their initiatives, as well as others, have been laying the groundwork for credibility, creation of a body of knowledge, standards, and means of evaluation that will guide implementation of future applications. From private sector (eRepublic.com), to nonprofit (the IJIS Institute), to government (Department of Justice), to academia (National Science Foundation, GTRI), there are numerous programs underway, many of which are public/private partnership in nature.

A FRAMEWORK FOR ENHANCING ENGAGEMENT

So where should a city or county start when considering how to apply tech-nology to increase citizen engagement? Using the description of engage-ment provided earlier, coupled with applying technological applications with the intent of increasing engagement, the focus should be on activities that

- describe/define an engaged community;
- increase voting participation;
- strengthen organizations that create social capital;
- increase density and extent of networks, especially related to the development of bridging social capital;
- provide access to relevant information and through preferred me-dia channels and vehicles;
- protect and enhance transparency and accountability;
- provide opportunities for voice, action, and reflection;
- provide opportunities for citizens to express their opinion to elected officials, staff, and other citizens;
- provide opportunities for citizens to engage in meaningful discus-sion/debate;
- provide opportunities for citizens to contribute their time, talent, treasure, expert knowledge, or specialized skills to assist the city/ county in achieving its goals;
- improve efficiency or effectiveness of service provision; and
- enhance citizen satisfaction with the range, efficiency, effectiveness, and equity of services provided.

With these focus areas as an underlayment, a full-circle planning, evalu-ation, implementation, and feedback process should be employed. Each subprocess feeds into the next and the circle continues as constant evalua-tion and planning occurs.

This process should be built so that it might survive changes in political leadership or senior management. As leaders and staff change, assuming continued endorsement and support, the program can continue without disruption.

A detailed description of similar processes is available in many process management or project implementation treatises. Graphically presented, this model is not unlike that which should be followed for any major pro-grammatic initiative (see Figure 7.1).

Local political processes will scrutinize and massage the ideas, and lead-ership (both elected and professional management) will decide to champi-on (or not) their funding and implementation. Professional staff members need to provide much of the research as to best practices and underlying

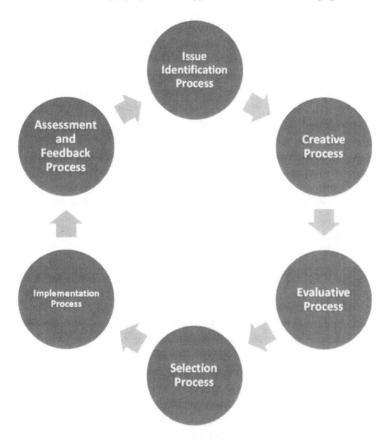

Figure 7.1 Enhancing engagement: A full circle model.

theory, to help educate citizens and political leadership as evaluations of potential impact, efficacy, cost-effectiveness, and equity are conducted.

Issue Identification Process involves identifying from political leaders, professional staff, and citizens the issues that they would like to see addressed. Recognizing the goal of increasing engagement may be one of several goals of an initiative that provides the opportunity; a staff-driven process could help provide success and maintain focus.

Creative Process provides many opportunities to demonstrate technologies, educate participants about cutting edge possibilities, engage with benchmark communities or areas of best practice knowledge, and even break new ground in generating ideas.

Evaluative process will filter ideas and initiatives based on political preferences, community values, and the realities of resource allocation, whether it is skillsets needed or financial resources.

Selection process: Once filtered, remaining possibilities need to survive formal selection processes that may include legislative adoption, budget cycle processes, and possibly even voter referendum.

Implementation process includes funding, accountability reporting, proper project management, and development of champions and community support.

Assessment and Feedback process will provide answers to questions such as return on investment, quantitative and qualitative program evaluation measures, and perceptions of efficiency, effectiveness, equity, and general efficacy.

Issue Identification process: As the circle closes, the process should repeat itself as technology changes at a seemingly ever-increasing pace. CQI (Continuous Quality Improvement) and TQM (Total Quality Management) techniques and processes may be employed to insure good stewardship with allocation of public resources.

SOURCES OF IDEAS FOR INCREASING ENGAGEMENT

During the idea-generation phase, expect some participants to have ideas. Their awareness of the range of ideas, technologies, and the breadth of issues surrounding these potential initiatives may be limited. Here again is where professional staff can help educate and inform.

It will be important to remember that some participants will be more adept and comfortable with technology. Much of the differences may be generational. Peer-to-peer coaching, small group meetings with a technology power user, or other tactics may need to be developed to enhance participation among those who need an increased skillset in order to more fully participate.

Below are several possible sources of information and ideas that can be used to identify the potential areas of technological application specifically focused on increasing citizen engagement with city/county government:

- Citizen participation, especially from those who are not currently "engaged" or from which there is significant underrepresentation in government activities;
- Strategic planning documents and other direction-setting agendas from deliberative bodies;
- Homeowners associations, business associations, religious bodies, PTAs and other school-affiliated advisory bodies, social service networks and nonprofits (individually or collectively);
- Local and regional organizations such as municipal associations, city and county coordinating bodies, as well as their parent organizations such as NACO (National Association of Counties) Information Committee and ICCMA (International City County Manager Association);

- Publications and organizations in the arena (many of which have been mentioned or cited as references in this chapter) such as Public Technology Institute and eRepublic publishers publications;
- Seattle Online Civic Engagement Initiative;
- Salt Lake City Open Government Initiative;
- "Better Together," the report published by the Saguaro Seminar initiative (2001);
- The Web site of the Corporation for National and Community Service, titled "Volunteering in America: Information on Volunteering and Civic Engagement" (http://www.volunteeringinamerica.gov/).

Three of these in particular have not been fully described previously in this chapter and merit a more detailed view as they have particular applicability and significance. These three are the Saguaro Project, and the Seattle and Salt Lake City initiatives. While the Saguaro Project is more general in scope, the Seattle and Salt Lake initiatives are major city government projects.

SAGUARO PROJECT

The Saguaro Project is an initiative driven by Dr. Robert Putnam, author of *Bowling Alone* and professor at the John F. Kennedy School of Government at Harvard University (Saguaro Seminar, 2001). Over a period of 5 years, a diverse group of over 30 academic and practitioner participants, including Barack Obama, Ralph Reed, and George Stephanopoulos, met in 2-day face-to-face sessions in an attempt to develop strategies for connecting Americans in an effort to enhance the development of social capital.

The report contains many ideas and strategies for creating social capital and enhancing community engagement. Many of these strategies can be adapted for local city and county government application. Also contained in the report is a list of "150 Things You Can Do" as a guide for individual actions, some of which could be adapted as group activities.

Since the conclusion of the work that resulted in issuance of a final report titled "Better Together" (2001), the seminar has continued to focus in part on improving methodology and instruments to measure social capital. The seminar is also working on an update of survey data examining national levels of social capital.

Seattle

Beginning in 2001, the Seattle Commission on Electronic Communication established a direction. The goal statement recommended by the Seattle Commission on Electronic Communication is "To be a national leader in using technology to dramatically expand civic engagement and public discourse by transforming TVSea into a multimedia organization that provides compelling content and two-way communication opportunities." (Seattle.gov, 2004)

Seattle has coordinated efforts to enhance the city Web site, deliver a TV channel, free Internet access at public kiosks within many public buildings, development of e-commerce-type applications, and many other initiatives. A "democracy portal" has been created, and the Seattle.gov city Web site has won awards. These activities are directed by an ongoing strategic plan and coordinated efforts.

Claiming to be one of the most "wired" cities in the nation, the city is trying to increase two-way communication and thereby enhance civic engagement. Focus also involves activities to engage minority voices in video and interactive online discussions and debates. Programs to maximize accessibility to the Internet have been developed to enable increased participation.

Salt Lake City

Originally dubbed the Salt Lake City Greater Transparency or Collaborative Government Initiative, the program drafted and gained City Council endorsement of a guiding "Open Government Policy Statement." Later a revised final statement and policy implementation plan was adopted that now directs the activities of the program (Salt Lake City, 2009).

The work plan and guidelines cover such activities as a baseline assessment of current practices, paying attention to academic and other sources of best practices information, and protecting a "free thinking zone." Many of the identified activities mirror the path taken in Seattle.

One of the critical needs of the initiative, executive level support, has been achieved through the engagement and endorsement of the program by the City Council. A firm guiding policy endorsed by the City Council guides staff in their activities.

Progress reports have been published at increments of 30, 60, 90, 180, and 360 days. These reports highlight specific activities and provide information about the consistency between the guiding directives and the specific activities.

CURRENT CHALLENGES AND FUTURE IMPLICATIONS

Risk, Technology Adoption, and the Rate of Change

There is an enormous array of technologies available, both newly developed and evolving applications of older technologies. The rate of change can be a critical concern. Attractive, cutting-edge applications can appear to offer a range of solutions to uncomfortable political pressures. At the same time, as the common comment on innovation goes, "there is a lot of blood on the cutting edge."

The technology-adoption life cycle graphic in Figure 7.2, created by Ed Brenegar, (http://edbrenegar.typepad.com/leading_questions/technology_adoption_life_cycle/) illustrates the position of innovators in the cycle.

Innovators take on the greatest risk. Oftentimes project failures have great expense in resources as well as the loss of goodwill, public support, and political capital. For these reasons, it is frequently unfeasible for a city or county government to be seen as an innovator. Early adopters have the advantage of being close enough in time to benefit from the perception of being proactive and in a leadership position, with the benefit of the knowledge of project failures by innovators to avoid major pitfalls. New technologies are often unproven and need to be "debugged" before a public committal to their use is made.

In addition to avoiding the cutting edge, the pace of change is ever-increasing and can lead to a "jumping on the band wagon" approach to selecting technologies. Few if any could have predicted the surge of use in Facebook as more than a social networking tool. In one year, the number of hits to Facebook.com has exceeded the hits to the most used search engine, Google.com. In March of 2009, the weekly market share of visits were approximately 2.3% for Facebook and approximately 6.5% for Google. According to Dougherty (2010), by March of 2010, Facebook's market share exceeded Google's (7.07% to 7.03%, respectively).

Although a search engine and a social networking site are arguably apples and oranges, Facebook's evolution and maturation has made it a

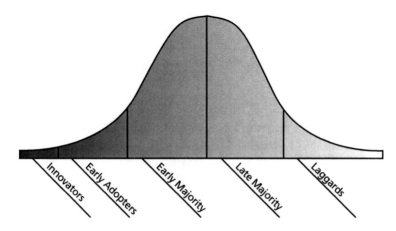

Figure 7.2 Technology adoption life cycle.

good bet for resource application in efforts to disseminate information. Several articles directed specifically at local government use of Facebook have been published (e.g., http://www.americancityandcounty.com/technology/local-government-social-media-20090408/index.html; http://www.insidefacebook.com/2009/11/05/10-ways-facebook-pages-can-help-local-governments-better-serve-their-constituents/). This illustrates the morphing capability of applications and the speed at which it can occur. Remembering that free-market applications are profit-driven entities is important, because functionality critical to enhancing citizen engagement could be lost if it does not create revenue.

Using a shared vision, a politically supported and executive-championed management team can resolve many project management issues that lead to failure. Protecting against insufficient budgets, project creep, change-order control, and evolving scopes are critical activities in managing project implementation.

Using technology to enable activities that build public trust, accountability, accessibility, and transparency can encourage citizen engagement. Targeted approaches tailored to unique community needs will be most effective. Involvement of all stakeholders, citizen, staff, and elected officials is required to maintain momentum.

While a focus on personalization can be an effective tool in engaging individuals and building the type of relationships that will create social capital, there is a delicate balance between familiarity and intrusion. This balance will vary with individuals, so flexible technological applications will be important. The use of data mining and knowledge-base building to breed familiarity and promote efficiency must be measured against community values and individual preferences. If processes can be built on that allow for gradually developing responses to citizens based on knowledge gained, the growth of the relationship can be managed.

Assessment: Efficiency, Effectiveness, and Value

Assessment is a critical area that should not be an afterthought. While there is a real need for better assessment instruments and methodologies, this void should not deter design and deployment of assessment systems. Program evaluation, resource allocation, and future direction are reliant upon feedback. Citizen satisfaction and perception will be important aspects to monitor, as well as quantifiable measures of improvements in relation to level of resources expended.

The increased accessibility of documents, information, video, and other media will bring increased need for accountability in their provision. Timeliness, equitable distribution of user fees or access charges, and responsiveness of staff will be concerns. It will become more challenging to archive and produce info in the sunshine. Maintaining control over information and the ability to produce and provide it under FOIA (Freedom of Information Act) requests will add expense to this new openness. This expense may be offset somewhat by the efficiencies created.

The Need to Measure

Robert Behn (2003), to which the phrase "What gets measured gets done" is often attributed, suggests there are eight purposes to measuring: "evaluate, control, budget, motivate, promote, celebrate, learn, and improve" (p. 381). The implication is that if something is not important enough to measure, it does not receive the attention necessary to be involved in a cycle of continuous improvement.

Data for general measures of political participation such as voting are easily collected. Social capital creation can be measured and trended over time using Putnam's Social Capital Index. Mattering can be assessed using Elliott, Kao, and Grant's (2004) Mattering Index. Correlations with desired engagement outcomes could be monitored. Better yet, the creation of a Citizen/Local Government Engagement Index could help prioritize resource allocation and policy adoption when deciding in which technologies local government resources should be invested and for what purposes. Although statistically immature, Rice (2001) created a Social Capital Values Index "by averaging the z-scores for three values (trust, political equality, and civic engagement).

There is a clear need for better instruments to measure engagement as conceptualized in this chapter. This area has been a recent focus of the Saguaro Seminar Project at Harvard. Better instruments and methodologies over time will help direct allocation of resources or investment decisions.

Sustainability

Convergence of work in agriculture, environmental stewardship, economics, land use, and community development has resulted in the emergence of a common notion of the concept of sustainability. In the arena of citizen engagement, sustainability becomes important as a framework for designing activities that can impact the way citizens relate with each other and engage with their local government.

Traditional communities often identify problems through citizen feedback to elected officials. Professional staff is then tasked with implementing solutions. The cycle then ends until a new problem is identified. Integration of issues is sometimes lost in the endless cycle of problem solving. Focusing on sustainability allows for transformation of the way citizens and elected officials work together to identify more global issues and develop responses that address the immediately visible symptoms as well as the underlying structural sources. New decision-making processes and relationship-building activities can increase citizen engagement and sustain the community through cultural and demographic changes and generational needs.

Demographic and Psychographic Variances and the Divide Between Citizen and Government Officials

More research is needed regarding the impact of technological initiatives, especially in the area of the engagement of underrepresented, disenfranchised, and marginally involved citizens. The social justice movement will likely be interested in the expansion of engagement by these groups. It will be important to understand cultural or psychographic factors that may prevent fully enhanced engagement. Nontechnological tactics may be required in order to fully engage some segments of the community.

Research by Aaron Smith (2010) of the Pew Research Center shows higher educated, higher income Americans are more likely to use social media and networking tools to receive information from government agencies. There are significant differences among racial/ethnic groups, income, and educational-level groupings when it comes to involvement in interactive participatory activities, desire to receive government information through social networking sites, and levels of trust in government.

Participation 2.0

The Internet as a tool of citizen/government engagement has evolved from an information resource and static one-way communication vehicle to service delivery and transaction enabling portals. Engagement between citizen and government has increased. Now two-way information exchange, collaborative problem solving, and solicitation of real-time interactive participation in decision-making processes are possible.

As the level of electronically distributed government increases and digital communities develop, local government leaders will be challenged to manage necessary resources, define how and why they choose to engage citizens electronically, and provide clarity about how citizen input will be used. Managing accessibility, enhancing literacy, and controlling interpretation of information loads that can become co-opted by well-organized messaging manipulators (an evolving specialty of its own) will become critical to insure balance and equitable participation.

CONCLUSION

There is credible evidence of a connection between social capital—especially the level of bridging social capital—and civic engagement as defined in this chapter. There also appear to be correlations between social capital and government performance and the enhancement of quality-of-life measures.

As long as the mission drives the activity rather than the technology being chosen for other reasons, activities that foster engagement can be supported and enhanced using technology. Helping citizens engage, create social capital, and improve their communities could be a wise investment of resources, even in lean financial times. Community-building work can be improved, and citizens can become more engaged in their city and county through the proper application of technology.

REFERENCES

Barth, J. E. (2007). Customer engagement and the operational efficiency of wine retail stores. *International Journal of Wine Business Research, 19*(3), 207–215.

Behn, R. D. (2003). Why measure performance? Different purposes require different measures. *Public Administration Review, 63*(5), 586–606.

Bennett, W. L. (2008). Changing citizenship in the digital age. In W. L. Bennett (Ed.), *Civic life online: Learning how digital media can engage youth.* The John D. and Catherine T. MacArthur Foundation Series on Digital Media and Learning. Cambridge, MA: MIT Press. Retrieved from http://www.mitpressjournals.org/doi/pdf/10.1162/dmal.9780262524827.001?cookieSet=1

Berman, D. (2000). We the e-people: Joe Mohen brings missionary zeal to the notion of online voting—and sees ways to make a buck at it. *Business Week Online.* Retrieved from http://www.businessweek.com/smallbiz/0002/ep3670042.htm

Beugelsdijk, S., & Smulders, S. (2003). *Bridging and bonding social capital: Which type is good for economic growth?* Paper presented at the Social Capital and Economic Development Conference, Tilburg University, Tilburg, Netherlands.

Department of Defense, Washington Headquarters Services. (2001, June). Federal voting assistance program. *Voting Over the Internet Pilot Project Assessment Report.* Retrieved from http://www.fvap.gov/resources/media/voi.pdf

Dougherty, H. (March 15, 2010). *Facebook reaches top ranking in US.* http://weblogs.hitwise.com/heather-dougherty/2010/03/facebook_reaches_top_ranking_i.html

Eggers, W. D. (2005). *Government 2.0: Using technology to improve education, cut red tape, reduce gridlock, and enhance democracy.* Lanham, MD: Rowman & Littlefield.

Elliott, G. C., Kao, S., & Grant, A. (2004). Mattering: Empirical validation of a social-psychological concept. *Self and Identity, 3,* 339–354.

Ellison, N. B., Steinfield, C., & Lampe, C. (2007). The benefits of Facebook friends: Social capital and college students' use of online social network sites. *Journal of Computer-Mediated Communication, 12*(4), 1143–1168. Retrieved from http://jcmc.indiana.edu/vol12/issue4/ellison.html

Farrell, K. (2009). Attorneys, legislators to pull plug on macro government's use of social Web sites? *naplesnews.com.* Retrieved July 2009, from http://www.naplesnews.com/news/2009/jul/07/attorneys-legislators-pull-plug marco-governments-/?printer=1/

Human Capital Institute. (2010). Social networking in government: Opportunities and challenges. *Human Capital Institute.* Retrieved from http://www.hci.org/

Kavanagh, S. C. (2007, February) Serving constituents, saving dollars: The cost-reduction potential of constituent relationship management. *Government Finance Review.* Retrieved from http://www.gfoa.org/downloads/Feb07main.pdf

Kirlin, M. (2003, March). The role of adolescent extracurricular activities in adult political engagement. *The Center for Information and Research on Civic Learning and Engagement.* Retrieved from http://www.civicyouth.org/PopUps/WorkingPapers/WP02Kirlin.pdf

Long, J. T, (2009). Local government 2.0 uses Facebook, Twitter to communicate with public. Retrieved from http://publicceo.com/index.php?option=com_content&view=article&id=1019:local-government-20-uses-facebook-twitter-to-communicate-with-public&catid=151:local-governments-publicceo-exclusive-&Itemid=20

Lu, J., & Chang, G. (2007). E-service intelligence: An introduction. *Studies in Computational Intelligence, 37,* 1–33.

McClenney, K., Marti, C. N., & Adkins, C. (2006). Student engagement and student outcomes: Key findings from community college survey of student engagement validation research. *Community College Leadership Program, The University of Texas at Austin.* Retrieved from http://www.ccsse.org/center/resources/docs/publications/CCSSE%20Validation%20Summary.pdf

McCullagh, D. (2010). Feds push for tracking cell phones. *CNET News.* Retrieved from http://news.cnet.com/8301-13578_3-10451518-38.html

McDonald, M. P., & Popkin, S. L. (2001). The myth of the vanishing voter. *The American Political Science Review, 95*(4), 963–974.

McKay, J. (2008). Wildfires ravaged Southern California, but reverse 911 and WebEOC helped evacuate 500,000. *Emergency Management.com.* Retrieved from http://www.emergencymgmt.com/disaster/Wildfires-Ravaged-Southern-California.html

Nielsen Report. (2009.) Global faces and networked places. *The Nielsen Report on Social Networking's New Global Footprint.* Retrieved from http://blog.nielsen.com/nielsenwire/wp-content/uploads/2009/03/nielsen_globalfaces_mar09.pdf

Opsahl, A. (2010). Backing up Twitter and Facebook posts challenges for governments. *Government Technology: Solutions for State and Local Government in the Information Age.* Retrieved from http://www.govtech.com/gt/738859

Pettingill, L. (2008). Engagement 2.0? How the new digital media can invigorate civic engagement. *GNOVIS Journal of Communications, Culture and Technology, 8*(3), 155–161.

Phillips, S. D., & Orsini, M. (2002). *Mapping the links: Citizen involvement in policy processes.* CPRN Discussion Paper No. F21. Canadian Policy Research Networks, Ottawa, Ontario Canada. Retrieved from http://www.eric.ed.gov/ERICDocs/data/ericdocs2sql/content_storage_01/0000019b/80/1a/e7/97.pdf

Phoenix Business Wire. (1999). Arizona democratic party selects votation.com to hold world's first legally binding public election over the Internet. Retrieved from http://www.thefreelibrary.com/Arizona+Democratic+Party+Selects+Votation.com+to+Hold+World%27s+First...-a058272337

Pieterson, W., Ebbers, W., & van Dijk, J. (2007). Personalization in the public sector: An inventory of organizational and user obstacles towards personalization of electronic services in the public sector. *Government Information Quarterly, 24*(1), 148–164.

Putnam, R. D. (1995). Bowling alone: America's declining social capital. *Journal of Democracy, 6*(1), 65–78. Retrieved from http://muse.jhu.edu.proxy-remote.galib.uga.edu/journals/journal_of_democracy/v006/6.1putnam.html

Putnam, R. D. (2000). *Bowling alone: The collapse and revival of American community.* New York, NY: Simon & Schuster.

Raill, S., & Hollander, E. (2006). How campuses can create engaged citizens: The student view. *Journal of College and Character, 7*(1), 4–5. Retrieved from http://www.collegevalues.org/pdfs/How%20Campuses%20Can%20Create%20Engaged%20Citizens.pdf

Rice, T. W. (2001). Social capital and government performance in Iowa communities. *Journal of Urban Affairs, 23*(3–4), 375–398.

Rosenberg, M., & McCullough, B. C. (1981) Mattering: Inferred significance and mental health. *Research in Community and Mental Health, 2,* 163–182.

Rowe, G., & Frewer, L. (2005). A typology of public engagement mechanisms. *Science Technology & Human Values, 30*(2), 251–290.

Saguaro Seminar on Civic Engagement in America. (2001). *Better together: The report.* Cambridge, MA: John F. Kennedy School of Government, Harvard University. Retrieved from http://www.bettertogether.org/thereport.htm; http://www.bettertogether.org/150ways.htm

Salt Lake City. (2009). *Open government initiative.* Retrieved from http://www.transparencyslcgov.com/Portals/0/Open%20Government%20Initiative%20-%20Proposed%20Work%20Plan.pdf

Sclair, B. (2009). Reverse 911 leads to guideline creation. *The Suburban Times.* Retrieved from http://www.thesubtimes.com/2009/11/29/reverse-911-leads-to-guideline-creation/

Seattle.gov. (2004). *New elements of democracy: Transforming civic engagement in Seattle.* Retrieved from http://www.cityofseattle.net/scec/DPArticle.htm

Sheedy, A., MacKinnon, M., Pitre, S., & Watling, J. (2008). *Handbook on citizen engagement: Beyond consultation.* Ottawa, ON: Canadian Research Policy Networks.

Smith, A. (2010). *Government online: The internet gives citizens new paths to services and information*. Pew Internet and American Life Project-A Project of the Pew Research Center. http://pewinternet.org/~/media//Files/Reports/2010/PIP_Government_Online_2010_with_topline.pdf

Smith, J. (2009). College students' Facebook use easing up over the summer, while parents logging on in record numbers. *Inside Facebook*. Retrieved from http://www.insidefacebook.com/2009/07/06/college-students-facebook-use-easing-up-over-the-summer-while-parents-logging-on-in-record-numbers/

Svanum, S., & Bigatti, S. (2009). Academic course engagement during one semester forecasts college success: Engaged students are more likely to earn a degree, do ot faster, and do it better. *Journal of College Student Development, 50*(1), 120–132.

Thompson, B. (n.d.). The evolution of relationship management. *Business Week Online*. Retrieved from http://www.businessweek.com/adsections/crm/evolution.html

Young, C. (2010, March 5). Duluth mayor to host live webcast to reach out to area. *Gwinnett Daily Post*, p. 4C.

CHAPTER 8

ENGAGING HISPANICS IN GOVERNANCE

A Social Constructivist Interpretation

Patria de Lancer Julnes
University of Baltimore

The United States is increasingly becoming a fully diverse society, with about a third of the population belonging to one of three minority groups—Hispanic, Black, and Asian, in order of size of the population. The rapid growth of the Hispanic population is contributing to this trend. As per the 2009 census estimates, Hispanics compose the largest minority group with 15.8% or 48.4 million people, which is expected to continue growing. Although this growth is occurring across the nation, it has especially spiked in parts of the country, such as the states in the Mountain West region, which have not been traditional magnets for Hispanics. Such diversity both complicates and necessitates efforts to engage citizens in governance.

In spite of the size and rapid growth of the Hispanic population, for a long time now Hispanics have been considered a *sleeping giant*, a label that, according to Cristina Beltran (2010), evokes the notion that Hispanics are "subjects on the cusp of political power and influence" (p. 3), and also a

The State of Citizen Participation in America, pages 195–224
Copyright © 2012 by Information Age Publishing
195

group that is "politically passive and difficult to mobilize: the giant who cannot be roused from its slumber" (p. 4). If we are to achieve the promise of democratic governance, in which citizens are allowed to be part of the deliberation on decisions that affect their well-being, we need to understand the barriers that keep minority groups from such deliberative processes and to develop strategies to address these barriers.

Efforts have been made to develop this understanding, but progress has been limited. One possibility is that progress requires doing more to understand how the perceived identities, or social constructions, of these populations interact with efforts to engage them in governance. To that end, this chapter addresses the barriers to engagement perceived by Hispanic people in Utah. As an elaboration of the work presented in de Lancer Julnes and Johnson (2011), this chapter builds on the barriers that are traditionally believed to preclude engagement, but recasts these barriers using a social constructivist approach to interpret findings.

The chapter begins with a review of the status of Hispanics in the United States, using census data to argue for the need to engage Hispanics in the process of governance. Following this discussion is a review of the traditional barriers to engagement and a discussion on the relevance of social constructivism, especially the theory of the social construction of target populations as developed by Schneider and Ingram (1993). The next section presents as a case example the engagement of Hispanics in governance in Utah, analyzing it through the theory of social construction of target populations. Utah is significant because it is one of the states that has experienced unprecedented growth in Hispanic population in the last decade. This growth represents opportunities and challenges for testing new theories and practices that can help to improve not only the status of Hispanics but also the practice of citizen engagement. The chapter concludes with suggestions for future research and for improving citizen engagement.

WHY HISPANICS?

In a recent book, journalist Jorge Ramos (2005) challenges the image of Hispanics as a sleeping giant, arguing that Hispanics not only are now able to decide closely contested electoral races, but also that because of their size, important decisions will require the support of Hispanics. Ramos predicts that the "Hispanic vote will cease to be a weightless player on the political scale, and instead become the veritable 'big boy' in states and regions where the Latino vote has historically congregated" (p. xviii). If the 2010 midterm elections are any indication, when for the first time three Hispanic candidates won top state-level posts, Ramos's predictions appear to be materializing.

Thus, the growth of the Hispanic population represents opportunities and challenges for policymakers, as they now need to think about the most appropriate ways to respond to the needs of this culturally and linguistically diverse group of citizens. Indeed, Ramos (2005) speculates that political parties and service organizations that do not take into account the needs of Hispanics stand to become irrelevant in the future. And yet, at this point, making such an argument based on the potential for political power of the Hispanic population may be futile. First, as contended by critics (see John, 2009; Moynihan, 2003), by itself, voting does not increase representation nor makes elected officials and administrators more responsive to citizen needs. What makes an impact is having a seat at the decision-making table, and citizens know this. As a case in point, in a recent study of people's willingness to participate in deliberative initiatives, Neblo et al. (2010) found that people want to participate, and that it is especially those who do not participate in "traditional partisan politics" who are much more likely to want to take part in deliberative initiatives (p. 567). According to the authors, part of the appeal is that deliberative initiatives represent an alternative to "'politics as usual'" (p. 567).

Second, according to the Pew Hispanic Center (2007), Hispanic voters lag behind other major racial groups. The Pew reported that even though Hispanics constituted 15.3% of the population of the United States, only 13% (5.6 million) of the total voted in the midterm election of 2006. Compare this to the White population who stand at 39% of the total population and Blacks with 27% of the total population. This entails that, in spite of many strides, the size of the Hispanic population does not, as of yet, automatically translate into more votes. Therefore, with the exception of places with a high concentration of eligible Hispanic voters, politicians interested in being elected may not see as a benefit having Hispanics on their side. The cost calculations may be too high, with some concluding that they gain more by opposing policies that benefit Hispanics.

Instead, perhaps at this point in time, the most compelling argument for decision makers (to pay heed to Hispanics) can be made based on statistics that paint a not-so-rosy picture of the social and economic conditions of this population. As one can deduce from the information below, in many respects Hispanic socioeconomic characteristics are most similar to those of Blacks, the second-largest minority in the country. But they also differ in important ways. Pew (2008a) reports that in 2008 in the United States, among the resident population of 25 and older, 23.5% of Hispanics (native and foreign born) had completed less than a 9th grade education, a rate significantly larger than that of Whites (3.2%) and Blacks (5.6%). Furthermore, fewer Hispanics over 25 had a college degree (12.9%) compared to Whites (30%) and Blacks (17.5%).

Pew (2008a) also reports that about 44% of Hispanics have a personal income of $20,000 or less, compared to about 32% of Whites and about 42% of Blacks. In contrast, only about 15% of Hispanics have a personal income that reaches or exceeds $50,000, compared to about 31% of Whites and about 18% of Blacks. Unless we make attempts to solve these issues, we may soon find ourselves with a huge minority population that is marginalized and unable to contribute to the economic growth and development of the country because of deeply rooted economic and social problems. This is particularly critical when we consider that the Hispanic population in the United States is expected to reach almost 130 million by 2050 (Pew, 2008b).

Given this background and the fact that voting may not be the most feasible approach to ensuring that there is adequate representation of Hispanics, the most promising approach may be to engage them in a deliberative process of governance in which they can be participants in policy development and decision making (Schachter, 1995). Whether eligible to vote or not, Hispanics have a stake in the communities where they reside, work, own businesses, or send their children to school and therefore should be able to take part in the process of governance. Such a broad understanding of citizenship, adopted by organizations like the Downtown Los Angeles Neighborhood Council, opens the door for more creative and effective solutions to problems affecting this community. As discussed below, this was the case of Midvale City, Utah (see de Lancer Julnes & Johnson, 2011).

However, in spite of its promise, participation of minorities in governance remains elusive. The reasons for this include the tools used to encourage participation, the structure of government, and social-economic characteristics (King, Feltey, & Susel, 1998). But little is known about issues that may affect specific minority groups such as Hispanics. Most research conducted on citizen participation refers to minorities as a general group, without differentiating in terms of ethnic background.

This chapter presents a study that begins to address the gap in the literature. Using the state of Utah as a case study, it describes findings of a series of in-person and telephone interviews with individuals who knew about the participation of Hispanics in the policymaking process in Utah. They were identified as key opinion leaders by others. Although some of these findings were discussed in de Lancer Julnes and Johnson (2011), this chapter takes a different theoretical approach in making sense of the dynamics involved in the engagement of Hispanics as perceived by Hispanic leaders. Using the theory of social constructivism as a backdrop, here we interpret the trends in terms of who participates among Hispanics, how they participate, in which policy areas they participate, and the perceived attitude of policymakers toward this participation. The framework developed by Schneider and Ingram (1993) about the social construction of target populations helps to tease out the nuances of these dynamics and provide a deeper understanding. Schneider and Ingram defined social construction of target populations as normative and evaluative "cultural characterizations or popular images of the persons or groups whose behavior and well-being are affected by public policy" (p. 334).

CITIZEN ENGAGEMENT REMAINS ELUSIVE

This section briefly explains the factors that have traditionally been found to preclude citizen engagement. It also posits that the social construction of citizens has an impact on citizen engagement efforts and further argues that the traditional factors need to be explored in the context of social constructions.

Traditional Barriers

As suggested earlier, effectively engaging citizens requires attention to a variety of factors. The first barrier addressed here is how much engagement decision makers seek. This is tightly intertwined with the approach that is chosen to facilitate participation or engagement. It is worth noting that even though the terms "citizen participation" and "citizen engagement" are often used interchangeably, these two terms are not identical. Aslin and Brown (2004) have distinguished the two by defining engagement as a deliberative process in which decisions are made and citizens are able to influence decisions that result in action.

This conceptualization is consistent with one of the most often cited conceptualizations of participation—that of Sherri Arnstein (1969), which distinguishes multiple levels of participation represented as a ladder, with each of the consecutive rungs representing a higher level of citizen influence in the decision-making processes. More specifically, Arnstein distinguished eight rungs that were grouped into one of three broad categories depending on the amount of power afforded to citizens: (a) Nonparticipation: the goal is simply to "'educate' or 'cure' participants" (p. 2); (b) Tokenism: citizens hear and are heard, but are not given any power to ensure that their views are taken into account; (c) Citizen power: citizens are able to negotiate with power holders and make decisions. Thus, for Arnstein, citizen engagement implies that power holders share decision-making power with citizens. This ladder also conveys moving up a rung, achieving greater levels of influence by citizens, and is increasingly difficult to facilitate.

Likewise, as described in de Lancer Julnes and Johnson (2011), the International Association for Public Participation (IAPP) has also adopted a working framework, called spectrum of participation, which is parallel to Arnstein's ladder and also based on the level of impact that the public is afforded through different mechanisms. This framework goes from the lowest level, or least involved form of participation—informing citizens—to the highest level, empowering citizens. These levels highlight how the differentiation between participation and engagement is useful in unmasking how much influence organizations allow the public to have. Distinguishing levels is also useful in determining what methods or approaches are effective in achieving the level of desired public influence. In large part, some activities are more likely than others to facilitate desired kinds of deliberative processes (Roberts, 2004). Thus, how engaged citizens are in the process of governance will depend on the participation approach or tool used by decision makers. As such, the method of engagement itself can become a barrier to engagement. One can further speculate that the construction of the target population whose involvement is sought may have an impact on both how much engagement is allowed and what method is used.

Table 8.1 shows the IAPP's spectrum along with Arnstein's (1969) broad categorizations of participation. To make comparisons easier, Arnstein's ladder is presented in reverse order so that the top portion of the table represents the lowest level and the bottom represents the highest level. The table also shows the methods of involvement, labeled modes of engagement, that are likely to facilitate each level, showing the lowest level at the top of the table and the highest at the bottom (IAPP, 2007; Petts & Leach,

TABLE 8.1   Modes of Engagement

Levels of Engagement		Modes of Engagement	
IAPP	**Arnstein's Ladder**	**Modes of Engagement**	
Inform	Nonparticipation	• Fact Sheets • Web sites • Open Houses	Participation (Easiest)
Consult	Tokenism	• Public Comment • Focus Groups • Surveys • Public Hearing	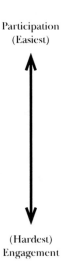
Involve		• Workshops • Deliberative Polling • Advisory Councils	
Collaborative		• Consensus Building • Participatory Decision	
Empower	Degrees of Citizen Power	• Citizen Jury • Referendum • Delegated Decision • Policy Boards	(Hardest) Engagement

2000). The notions of "easiest" and "hardest" are there to convey level of difficulty for both public leaders and citizens seeking engagement.

Commenting on the connections between modes of engagement and the levels in Arnstein's ladder, it is certainly true that any of the methods depicted in the table can be adapted to provide less or more opportunity for engagement. For example, synchronous tools such as web conferencing, chatting, and instant messaging can be used to achieve a level of engagement that goes beyond informing. Likewise, as will be shown later, public hearings can be used as a deliberative method that allows for real input. In reality, how much engagement is allowed will depend on what the intentions of the organizers of such hearings are. Nevertheless, based on the literature and current evidence, we can argue that open houses, which are good tools for providing information, would not be an approach that supports meaningful deliberation and hence a high level of public engagement. Similarly, citizens seeking to have a high impact on decision making will not be satisfied if the "engagement" mechanism is a mere fact sheet.

A second category of barriers relates to organizational factors in government. These include organizational arrangements and structure, trust of citizens, openness of administrators to citizen engagement, and elected officials' willingness to be collaborators and partners with citizens in the governance process (Barnes, 1999; King et al., 1998; King & Stivers, 1998; Petts, 2001; Thiel, 1999; Yang, 2005). Some organizational arrangements not only help to separate decision makers from administrators but also fuel mutual distrust between them and citizens, and lead decision makers to superficial commitments to democratic governance.

A third category commonly identified as a barrier to engaging minority groups are the socioeconomic characteristics of citizens. More specifically, issues associated with low social economic status such as lack of available transportation, time constraints, and other economic disadvantages, often act as barriers to engagement (King et al., 1998). Furthermore, evidence suggests that for the most part, citizens who take advantage of opportunities to influence the process of governance or who are often invited to do so tend to be older males, with higher levels of education and income, and whose trust in government is higher than the general citizenry (Marshall & Jones, 2005). Conversely, minority representation is often lacking in these efforts, and their absence is particularly noticeable in key policy decision-making bodies throughout government (Gladden & Oaks, 2007). Nevertheless, there are instances in which participation of minority members is higher and more successful. This is the case in geographic areas where there is a high concentration of a particular minority group (Musso, Weare, Jun, & Kitsuse, 2004).

Nontraditional Factors

A factor that may preclude effectively engaging citizens in governance, and particularly minorities, but that has not been explored in this context is how these groups are socially constructed. Social construction, or more appropriately social constructionism, refers to the theories used in the field of sociology that argue "that society is actively and creatively produced by human beings... The world is made or invented... Social worlds are interpretive nets woven by individuals and groups" (Marshall, 1998). These nets come to life in the form of labels and stereotypes. Closely related to labeling theorists, constructionists argue that there is no objective social reality, only that which is constructed. Thus, it follows that it is the public's interpretation of our acts that determines the outcome (Gergen, 2003, p. 42). These constructions, which Gergen calls "social reputation," or identity, are further reinforced by media representation, socialization, history, and linguistic tendencies and help to inform public policies and actions at a societal level. Significantly, the identities constructed to define groups can be detrimental to them in the political arena (Cohen, 1972; Goode & Ben-Yehuda, 2009; Zatz, 1987).

Consider, for example, the label "Hispanics." Beltran (2010) contends that the term, rooted in historical racism, has a homogenizing effect that is used by some who fear the growth of the Hispanic population to portray them as a foreign, culturally and racially "distinct group who resists assimilation and whose high birth rates and regressive cultural practices threaten to undermine the country's unity and civic values" (p. 7). Beltran joins scholars and the public who resist such derogatory constructions and attempt to create what Gergen (2003, p. 43) has referred to as "consciousness of identity politics—that is, deliberation on the ways in which group identities figure within the sociopolitical landscape."

As argued by Schneider and Ingram (1993) in their theory of social construction of target populations (and further supported by Nicholson-Crotty & Nicholson-Crotty, 2004 and Schroedel & Jordan, 1998, among others), social construction helps define in the minds of politicians who is to benefit from public policies and who is to receive the burdens. For example, Nicholson-Crotty and Nicholson-Crotty found that in the case of implementation of inmate health policy, the negative perception held by decision makers of this group rather than more objective criteria such as financial capacity was the key determinant of what little benefits inmates received. On the other hand, Schroedel and Jordan (1998) found that a positive construction of people with AIDS led policymakers to vote to allocate policy benefits to this target population. Conversely, a negative construction led to the casting of unfavorable votes.

Furthermore, Schneider and Ingram (1993) poignantly argued that social constructions affect who participates in the policy deliberation process. The authors contended that citizens internalize messages through their personal experience or exposure to the media that let them know whether they will be treated by government (a) as clients, and thus worthy of receiving attention and services; or (b) as objects whose behavior creates problems for others and, therefore, should either change or not come in contact with government to avoid being punished. As a result, groups who are labeled as dependents (e.g., children, mothers, disabled) or deviants (e.g., criminals, gangs, communists) often don't "mobilize or object to the distribution of benefits and burdens" (p. 344). One can argue that this is the case with minorities, both dependents and deviants, who, as suggested by Schneider and Ingram are stigmatized by a social reputation that carries to the policy process. This stigmatization is particularly damaging for those categorized as deviants, which unfortunately is how, in some circles, Hispanics tend to be perceived due to the immigration discourse.[2]

On the other hand, according to Schneider and Ingram (1993), groups whose social reputation is positively construed, the advantaged (e.g., elderly, business, scientists, and veterans) have a positive orientation toward government and tend to believe that "what is good for them is good for the country" (p. 344). These groups not only participate, but are encouraged to take advantage of their power to obtain benefits for themselves. Schneider and Ingram make the observation that others tend to believe that these groups deserve the benefits they get. The authors don't offer an explanation as to how the fourth group in their scheme, contenders, participates. There is no neat explanation for the behavior of this group or the benefits and burdens they receive, possibly because it is an ill-defined or amorphous category, which is presented as including such diverse groups as the rich, big unions, cultural elites, moral majority, and minorities.

In sum, there is a number of barriers commonly found to affect citizen participation and engagement, and particularly minorities. While it is helpful to know that these barriers still exist, applying a different lens can help us to obtain a more nuanced and actionable understanding of the phenomena. The lens proposed here is one provided by the theory of social construction of target populations. Even though some applications of the theory can have methodological limitations, such as a reliance on a dichotomous social construction of perception of population as positive or negative, Schroedel and Jordan (1988) contend that it is useful in confirming broad patterns of policy benefits and burdens to target populations. Given the nascent nature of the present research on Hispanic engagement, determining broad patterns is a useful first step for exploration.

A CASE EXAMPLE: ENGAGING HISPANICS IN UTAH

Traditionally, Hispanics have constituted a large share of the population in the southwest region of the United States and in states such as California, New York, and Illinois. However, in the last decade, the population has burgeoned in places such as Utah and other areas in the Intermountain West region, which now boast some of the country's fastest growth in the Hispanic population (Kandel & Kromartie, 2004; Guzman, 2001). In 2008, the Hispanic population in Utah approached 324,000 people, or 12% of the total population (Pew, 2008c).

As the Hispanic population in Utah continues to grow, the gap in key social and economic indicators between Hispanics and Whites should be of concern for policymakers. For example, mirroring the national trends described above, the Pew Hispanic Center (2008c) reports that about 18% of Hispanics in Utah age 25 and older have less than a high school diploma (compared to 6% for Whites); only 5% of Hispanics have completed college (compared to about 20% for Whites); and approximately 40% of Hispanics of all ages in Utah are uninsured (11% for Whites). Moreover, the percentage of Hispanics under 18 years of age living in poverty in Utah reaches 7% (compared to 4% for Whites); and the income differential for full-time, year-round workers is $12,000, with Hispanics having a median personal income of $26,478, compared to $38,699 for Whites. These statistics alone indicate that there is a need to pay attention to this population in Utah, as well as in the more traditional Hispanic areas of the United States.

Because of these concerns, in 2007 we conducted a study to find out what the government in Utah was doing to involve Hispanics in finding effective solutions to their pressing needs. The 27 in-person and telephone interviews targeted Hispanic and non-Hispanic individuals, identified by their peers as key opinion leaders. They were involved in Utah's Hispanic advocacy and service organizations as well as in policymaking positions. The latter included elected officials, public administrators, and agency personnel within Utah government. The Appendix provides the names and affiliations of these informants.

The reason for having a total of only 27 interviews is that no other individuals were identified by their peers as knowledgeable about the topic of this research. Thus, this research is based on a purposive snowball sample. Interview questions were designed to elicit responses to the following areas of interest:

- Policy areas in which government has made attempts to engage the Hispanic community,
- Modes of engagement,
- Barriers to engaging the Hispanic community,

- Engagement strategies that seem to have worked, and
- Policy areas in need of greater attention.

Those interviewed offered their opinions about each of these areas. Data were also gathered by observation of events and meetings sponsored by some of the agencies and service providers that took part in the study. In addition, the Web pages and archival information of the advocacy organizations included in the study were examined.

The next section of this chapter presents the findings of this research, interpreted using a social constructivist lens. It should be noted that this is one interpretation based on the available evidence. More research is needed not only in Utah but also in other parts of the country to validate the conclusions drawn here. However, while research on Hispanics is scant, the available research on policy that affects vulnerable populations seems to provide support for the interpretation of the evidence gathered for this research.

PARTICIPATION IN UTAH

Who Participates Among Hispanics

However well-intended, citizen participation efforts traditionally exclude individuals with lower levels of income, education, and time (King et al., 1998; Marshall & Jones, 2005). This appears to also be the case within groups when it comes to Hispanics in Utah. For example, according to informants in this study, the Hispanics engaged by government in Utah are highly educated, well-employed, and have the time to participate in government. In addition, the perception is that government feels comfortable regularly calling upon the same select group of citizens to participate as representatives of a community that exceeds 300,000 people. One informant stated that government "calls the people they know." This has resulted in Hispanics in Utah being represented by a small group of Hispanic elites and may explain why informants were unable to come up with more names of people who would be knowledgeable enough to participate in this study.

Some informants expressed concern about the ability of these elite, to which they too belonged, to represent the community, understand their needs, and assist government in being responsive to them. This suggests that more economically and educationally diverse leaders need to be identified and engaged in order to provide new insights and more meaningful representation of Hispanics' needs and values. For example, on the surface, it appears that at least these elite are being positively constructed and thus are being allowed to take advantage of opportunities to influence policy. But this is a rather simplistic assessment. The dynamics at work in Utah are complex and need to be explored in the context of how these individuals participate as well as their perceived barriers to participation. Indeed, context matters.

Level and Modes of Participation in Utah

Table 8.2 shows that the methods used in Utah to involve Hispanics in governance are mostly informational in nature. Table 8.2 is an expanded version of Table 8.1, showing the modes used in Utah to involve Hispanics, along with the level of engagement each mode is likely to facilitate. As shown in the table, the most common modes identified by informants were (informational) conferences, surveys, town hall forums, citizen advisory councils, and partnerships with community-based organizations. As implied by the level of engagement, none of these methods let Hispanics have decision-making power.

Conferences are important educational tools but do little to promote citizen engagement. Comparatively, these tools are easy to use and are a step in the right direction because they make information available to citizens about services in the community. However, these low-level tools in the hierarchy of participation may exclude citizens who are most in need of the information due to where and when they are held. In Utah, most of these conferences are held during the day and in the Salt Lake City area. This precludes participation by people who work or live in remote areas and whose work schedules tends to be less flexible.

Town hall forums and citizen advisory councils (CAC) have also been used to facilitate participation in governance by representatives of the Hispanic community. Deliberative town hall forums and CAC in Utah would normally be considered "tokenism" according to Arnstein's Ladder of Participation (1969) because citizens are able to hear and be heard by policymakers but are not provided with any decision-making ability. However, the Department of Human Services (DHS) has used town hall forums to assess performance and responsiveness to minority needs in a manner that allows for some public impact, though not public control.

According to one informant, the DHS started to conduct town hall forums because of recognition that the makeup of the state's population was changing, and the DHS was not meeting the needs of this new population. The information received from forum participants was taken into consideration in the development of the workforce diversification policies that came out of these town hall meetings. Since then, the DHS has held additional forums to receive feedback on their policy and its implementation. This approach allowed service providers and advocacy groups in the Hispanic community to give valuable feedback on DHS policy priorities. However,

TABLE 8.2 Level and Modes of Engagement

Levels of Engagement			
IAPP	Arnstein's (1969) Ladder	Modes of Engagement	Modes of Engagement in Utah
Inform	Nonparticipation	• Fact Sheets • Web sites • Open Houses	• Conferences
Consult	Tokenism	• Public Comment • Focus Groups • Surveys • Public Hearing	• Surveys
Involve		• Workshops • Deliberative Polling • Advisory Councils	• Advisory Councils • Deliberative Town Hall
Collaborative	Degrees of Citizen Power	• Consensus Building • Participatory Decision	• CBO Partnerships
Empower		• Citizen Jury • Referendum • Delegated Decision • Policy Boards	

Participation (Easiest) ⟷ (Hardest) Engagement

the successful use of town hall forums by the DHS is the exception rather than the rule in general. In the case of Utah, such usage of town hall forums was the result of enlightened administrators.

CACs are one of the most commonly used methods for giving Hispanics and other minorities a voice in Utah. CACs consist of individuals appointed by government to serve as representatives of their larger community. The governor,[3] state agencies,[4] and county governments[5] use this method to consult on specific issues or policies that affect each minority group.[6]

Informant comments revealed that members of Utah's Hispanic community see CACs as an inadequate form of citizen engagement. For some of our informants, "those positions [advisory councils] are there to placate the community." Informants recognized that they are being involved, but not at the level in which decisions are actually made, wherein they can feel in control of their destiny. Hispanic community leaders would like to see more Hispanics appointed to the various policy boards and commissions in the state because "that's where the power is," said one informant.

One tool that has allowed members of the Hispanic community to have an important impact on decisions is government partnerships with community-based organizations (CBO).[7] CBOs have proven to be a valuable tool for government to gain some legitimacy within the community and to facilitate enduring relationships with citizens. This is the case of Midvale, Utah, where the city government created a Community Building Community Coalition (CBC).

Midvale's CBC consists of citizen panels for each area of concern identified by needs-assessment surveys. In partnership with universities, community-based organization, and the citizen committees, the CBC put together a comprehensive plan for addressing infant mortality in the Hispanic community, which was approximately 12 per 1,000 live-births (Midvale Mayor Joann Seghini, personal communication, 2007). Using a neighbor-to-neighbor model, the city of Midvale identified and provided services to citizens who were in need of prenatal care and prenatal education. Because of Midvale's progressive efforts in directly involving citizens to identify problems and implement solutions, the infant mortality rate was cut in half.

If we take together the information on who participates and the modes by which Hispanics are engaged in Utah, we begin to form a picture of Hispanics that does not fit the powerful, but negatively constructed, category of "contenders" of Schneider and Ingram (1993), nor that of the positively constructed and powerful "advantaged," but one that more closely resembles the authors' "dependent" group category—powerless but positively constructed. According to the authors, policy tools used for these groups tend to be symbolic. The authors argue that there is little outreach to them by government, and they are often not encouraged to "devise their own solutions to problems but will have to rely on agencies to help them . . . because the dependents are not considered self-reliant" (p. 339). The treatment of this group is paternalistic and information tools are the most likely forms of resources given to them.

The social construction of target populations suggests that if Hispanics were constructed as "deserving, intelligent, and public-spirited (as we expect the powerful, positively viewed [advantaged] groups to be)" (Schneider & Ingram, p. 339), modes of engagement such as appointments to policy boards, which would give decision-making power to them, would be more often utilized by government in Utah. The efforts of the DHS with their forums and of Midvale with its CBC are the closest approximation to true citizen engagement in Utah and what social constructivists would consider a positive construction of Hispanics as able partners in the solution of problems that affect the community. However, in the opinion of informants, this positive construction is not consistent across policy areas, as will be seen below.

Attempts at Engagement by Policy Area

Policy areas in which Utah has made attempts to engage the Hispanic community have been traditionally focused on education, health care, and language-service policies. More recently, state agencies and local governments have put considerable effort into workforce diversification policies. As shown in Table 8.3, when informants were asked to identify the policy areas in which government has attempted to engage the Hispanic community, the top three were education (about 19% of comments), health care (about 17% of comments), and workforce diversification (about 13%).

TABLE 8.3 Attempts at Engagement by Policy Area

Policy Area	Percentage of Comments (n = 64)	Percentage of Informants (n = 27)[a]
Education	18.8	44.4
Health care	17.2	40.7
Workforce diversification	12.5	29.6
Language services	10.9	25.9
Public safety	9.4	22.2
Law enforcement	6.3	14.8
Cultural competency training	6.3	14.8
Other[b]	18.8	44.4

[a] Because each informant identified several policy areas, this does not add up to 100.
[b] Comments included in this category were so diverse that no clear pattern emerged.

The emphasis on education is consistent with the movement for school accountability nationwide, which has led to education policies that focus on increasing educational achievement. State and nationwide data show a wide achievement gap between Whites and Hispanics. Hispanics consistently score lower than their White counterparts in assessment tests. As a result, albeit ineffective, most of the education policy in Utah affecting Hispanics has largely been aimed at reducing this gap. According to the 2009 mathematics report of the National Center for EducationStatistics, in Utah, the gap between White and Hispanic 8th graders was 30 percentage points (Hemphill & Vanneman, 2011). This gap was significantly larger than the gap that existed in 1992 (22 percentage points). Similarly, the 2009 reading report card showed that the gap between White 8th and Hispanic 8th graders in Utah stood at 24 percentage points (Hemphill & Vanneman, 2011). But unlike the mathematics gap, the reading gap is relatively unchanged since 1998.

For the most part, the individuals interviewed believed that efforts to reduce the gap in Utah have been relatively unsuccessful. And one informant offered that there is "lack of skills preparation for minority kids entering the schools." Regretfully, the statistics presented above indicate that informants were perhaps correct in their negative assessment of the effectiveness of educational policy in Utah. According to another informant, the reason for this failure is that "Systematic change [in education] is taking place at the micro level and is piecemeal . . . it is informal and inconsistent." Policy efforts vary from district to district, from school to school, and there is no cohesiveness or consistency.

This failure appears to be why the commitment of the Utah State Office of Education (USOE) to serve Hispanic students has been questioned. One informant said that one of the things his organization did to bring attention to the issue was to deliver a letter to the governor stating their position of "no-confidence" in the Utah education system. "The State Office of Education is not paving the way or setting the standard to serve Latino students," said another informant, adding that "They (USOE) have articulated a position that these students are aliens, they are different, and they are alternative. We are the beneficiaries of immigrant labor and we will take these people's labor, but we don't want their problems and we don't want their kids." The perception of this and other informants seems to suggest that, consistent with social construction theory, and in spite of the political rhetoric on education accountability, this politically powerless and negatively perceived group will receive few benefits and little attention from government (Nicholson-Crotty & Nicholson-Crotty, 2004, p. 255).

In stark contrast, the perceptions among informants of engagement efforts and outcomes in the area of health care policy are more positive than in the area of education. Informants seemed optimistic about health care efforts in the state with some saying that Utah has put considerable effort into engaging minorities in health care policy. Efforts by the state to include Hispanics are in line with the recent recommendation by the Institute of Medicine to include minorities in public health efforts (Minkler, Blackwell, Thompson, & Tamir, 2003).

In 2004, the Utah Legislature passed a statute that mandated the creation of the Center for Multicultural Health (UCMH). The purpose of the UCMH is to eliminate racial and ethnic health disparities. The UCMH works through Utah's Minority Health Network (the Network), managed by nonprofit organization Comunidades Unidas, and is composed of health care providers, nonprofits, and community-based organizations. The Network coordinates a statewide effort to examine health disparities and to develop a strategic plan to address those disparities and ensure access to health care for minorities.

In addition, the UCMH works with local health departments and community-based organizations to make them better able to serve the different ethnic communities by providing them with "the proper tools to serve the minority community," said Mr. Owen Quinonez, director of UCMH. Part of what the UCMH does is to provide cultural sensitivity training to health care providers so they can work better with people from different cultural and ethnic communities. However, these efforts were viewed by some informants with skepticism. Many of them didn't think that cultural training helps in significant ways. One stated that "cultural training is an easy way out; simply another attempt to appease minority advocates."

Workforce diversification efforts, the third top policy area, are being implemented by some state agencies to better serve Utah's ethnic communities. The theory behind workforce diversification is that when agency personnel reflect the characteristics of the populations they serve, it increases government's capacity to respond to the needs of the population (Meier, 1993; Rourke, 1978; Selden, 1997; Selden & Selden, 2001). Indeed, a DHS informant said that they had found that the agency can better serve minority populations by having an ethnically diverse staff. As a result, the DHS has modified hiring and retention practices, and also now provides differential pay to bilingual employees.

Other levels of government also have efforts in place to diversify their workforce. Informants talked about how mayors at the county level (in Salt Lake County, Mayor Peter Corroon, 2004–present) and at the city level (Salt Lake City Mayor Rocky Anderson, 2000–2008) made progress in workforce diversification because their efforts had gone beyond simply having individuals who speak other languages. The work of these mayors focused on eliminating discrimination in the hiring process and on increasing the number of Hispanics, among other ethnic minorities, working for the city and county governments. According to one informant, the number of Hispanics in Salt Lake City has increased from 2% to about 12% (Robert "Archie" Archuleta, personal communication, 2007).

Informants also identified the policy issues that are most important for the Hispanic community and that needed greater attention from government. It was no surprise that the three top policy issues identified by informants were education (30% of informants), the appointment of Hispanics to policy boards and commissions (about 26% of informants), and health care (about 22% of informants). As discussed above, there have been some exemplars of attempts to involve Hispanics in seeking solutions to problems affecting their community, as was the case in health care. However, clearly the community doesn't feel engaged. They want to be empowered and given opportunities to be part of the decision-making bodies in government.

Other policy areas of interest, shown in Table 8.4, include immigration reform, ensuring that government provides a more welcoming environment, and having more accurate demographic information about minorities. That a welcoming environment was mentioned is not surprising given that, as will be discussed in the next section, there is a perception that government has a negative attitude toward Hispanics.

The strides made in Utah toward engagement in the areas of health care and workforce diversification are very positive. However, they continue to evoke the imagery of Hispanics as a dependent group, albeit positively construed in some instances and thus, worthy of some benefits. This is in stark contrast to the image in the area of education, which is more uniformly negative. Such a negative perception prevents the making and implementation of polices that more aggressively and directly address the problems affecting the Hispanic population.

TABLE 8.4 Policy Areas That Need Attention

Policy Area	Percentage of Comments (n = 3)	Percentage of Informants (n = 27)[a]
Education	24.2	29.6
Appointment of Hispanics to policy boards and commissions	21.2	25.9
Health care	18.1	22.2
Immigration reform	12.2	14.8
Providing a welcoming government environment	9.0	11.1
Updated demographic data	9.0	11.1
Other	6.0	7.4

[a] Because each informant identified several barriers, this does not add up to 100

Barriers to Engagement

We have seen that barriers commonly found to affect citizen participation in governance also affect the participation of Hispanics, but they offer limited explanation of the barriers encountered by this population. We gain a more nuanced understanding by taking into consideration social construction, as will be shown below. Two key sets of barriers are discussed below: characteristics of the Hispanic community and the culture of government.

Characteristics of the Hispanic Community

This category includes two important factors that illustrate the theory of social construction of target populations. The first is the lack of trust in and fear of government; and the second is factions within the community. Informants attributed Hispanics' lack of trust in and fear of government to a perceived hypocrisy on the part of government. According to informants, the Hispanic community believes that government tells them one thing but does another. One informant stated, "Government wants us to trust it, but what we experience is the opposite of trust." An example given by an informant is that the state tells Hispanics it wants them involved, but then outlaws their language by passing an English-only statute.[8]

In addition to the English-only statute, another government action that informants said contributed to the deterioration of trust in government and strengthened suspicions of racism by Hispanics was the passage in 2008 of the Illegal Immigration Bill (SB 81),[9] which turns local law enforcement agents into virtual federal immigration officials. For informants, these two government initiatives symbolized cultural intolerance. According to one legislator interviewed for this study, the biggest barrier to positively addressing minority issues "is the mentality of the Utah Legislature. It comes from a lack of understanding [of] what those issues mean in human terms to the people who are affected." In other words, the dehumanization of this population precludes effective policymaking.

Another compounding factor involved the raids in search of illegal immigrants conducted by the federal government in meat packing and other private businesses across the state and the nation that started in 2006. The reason was not that all Hispanics in Utah are illegal. Rather, the reasons are much more complex than this. First, informants said that Hispanics are subject to backlash from what appears to be an increasingly intolerant White population in Utah. The raids were accompanied by a slew of misinformation that tried to legitimize the raids by portraying the arrested individuals as "deviants." Not only did they break the law by entering the country illegally, but presumably, also stole law-abiding citizens' identities by illegally obtaining their social security numbers and using them to get employment. Second, the people arrested left behind families, often children who had no other relatives to take care of them and, as a result, became a burden on society. Third, opined informants, many Hispanics in Utah knew someone or were related to someone who was affected by the raids.

This author was living in one of the towns where the first of the raids occurred in Utah. She saw families shattered and people, both Hispanics and White, scared. While the entire community, including Whites, Hispanics, churches, government agencies, and human service nonprofit organizations, came together to help those made destitute by the raids, there were many locals (primarily White) who felt conflicted. On the one hand, they wanted to help the children and mothers left behind, but on the other hand, as expressed by an elderly friend of the author, they had no sympathy for those arrested. The friend remembered that once her identity was stolen, and it was an awful experience, it took her years to undo the damage done by the theft. Since those arrested were criminalized for supposedly stealing social security numbers, divested of their humanity, the locals couldn't and shouldn't feel sorry for them.

Considering other relevant characteristics of the community, some informants also identified intra-ethnic factions—and the associated in-fighting—as another barrier that precluded engagement of Hispanics by government. One informant said that Hispanics "are such a diverse population...we have new arrivals, multigenerational folks, those who have acculturated, and those who have not. It is difficult to come together with a consolidated voice." Factions appear to be centered on national identity and length of presence in the United States, which manifests itself in apparent conflict and resentment between Chicanos[10] and more recent immigrants from other countries in Latin America.

Some of the informants who were more recent immigrants felt that Chicanos are overrepresented in government engagement efforts. This creates friction because of the perception that the needs of multigenerational Chicanos are different from the needs of recent immigrant families. Furthermore, one of the informants stated that Chicanos have been fighting for Hispanic/minority rights in Utah since the 1960s. Thus, they seem to have developed a sense of ownership of Hispanic policy and civil rights discourses. As a result, when more recent immigrants are asked by government to represent Hispanics, they are often met with Chicano resentment.

The two factors discussed above are interrelated dynamics that, when viewed through a social construction lens, demonstrate not only the impact of social constructions on the public policy that affects Hispanics but also how social construction limits engagement of Hispanics. In these dynamics, we see first what appears to be a social construction or labeling of Hispanics as "deviants" (lawbreakers and misfits). This elicits what Cohen (1972) called "moral panic"; a concern over an issue that divides society into us and them, "leading actors to actively struggle against the threat in their midst" (Goode & Ben-Yahuda, 2009, p. 33). This is reflected in the language and immigration statutes enacted by Utah's legislators and the raids conducted by the federal government. And on a more personal level, the moral panic was also reflected in the comments made after the raids in our town by my elderly friend.

As argued by Schneider and Ingram (1993), even decision makers who disagree with the negative characterization of a population, in this case Hispanics, will not be eager to distribute benefits to this group, including such benefits as participation opportunities that lead to engagement. In this view, public officials are sensitive to both power and social construction. Thus, they rely on more symbolic tools that, in the words of an informant, are used just to "placate minorities." Furthermore, Schneider and Ingram (p. 336) contend that

> state officials develop maps of target populations based on both the stereotypes they themselves hold and those they believe to prevail among that segment of the public likely to become important to them.... They must explain and justify their policy positions to the electorate by articulating a vision of the public interest and then showing how a proposed policy is logically connected to these widely shared values.

Therefore, one can argue that the apparent experiences of Hispanics in Utah, including how they have been portrayed and stigmatized, may be responsible for their fear and distrust of government. What is more, the apparent stigmatization of Hispanics may be why over the years Hispanics appear to have adopted a position of passivity or partial withdrawal from the policy process, hence the "sleeping giant" metaphor. In turn, this becomes a self-fulfilling prophesy that appears to support views, such as those of Samuel Huntington (as quoted in Beltran, 2010), that Hispanics are apathetic, with little interest in civic engagement.

A second aspect of the dynamics described above has to do with the construction of Hispanics as a monolithic group. This "myth of unity" is what Cristina Beltran (2007) seeks to debunk in her book, *The Trouble With Unity*. She suggests that to understand and realize the political potential of Hispanics, we need to embrace the diversity within this group. The analysis of the interviews presented here supports Beltran's argument for the conception of Hispanics (she calls them Latinos and uses the term Latinidad—being Latin or Hispanic) in the same manner in which feminists conceive the category of women "as a permanent political contestation.... Latinidad ... as a political rather than merely descriptive category" (p. 9). The contestation among the Chicanos and other Hispanics from Latin America makes it clear that, as argued by Beltran, there is not such unity. While it is true that Hispanics as a group have a common core (e.g., language and history of colonization), it is also true that there are subgroups within (e.g., Argentineans, Bolivians, Dominicans, and Puerto Ricans) with different values, social class, and cultural experiences that make the notion of homogeneity incongruent with reality. Furthermore, the heterogeneity among Hispanics makes them more likely to compete in the policy arena for benefits. This was illustrated by the informant who talked about Chicanos resenting the appointment of other immigrants to fill political posts. In this instance, the benefit is perceived political power.

Culture in Government

It is significant that the culture in government was identified by informants as a major barrier. This culture is a product of the deeply rooted assumptions, values, and norms shared by those working in government, and it needs to be understood in the context of the local culture. The state of Utah has a homogeneous population (88% are White). This reality is mirrored in the composition of government workers who are now responsible for the needs of a rapidly growing diverse population. Furthermore, as explained in de Lancer Julnes and Johnson (2011), the people of Utah have had a complex and tense relationship with people of color. It wasn't until 1978 that the Church of Jesus Christ of Latter-Day Saints (LDS or Mormon Church), to which most people in Utah belong, allowed Blacks into the priesthood, a status available to "virtually all [White] males starting at age 12" (Dobner, 2008).

Based on informant responses, the barriers erected in Utah by the culture in government includes perceived attitudes of racism and tokenism toward Hispanics, as well as a perception of government agencies being intimidating and not creating a welcoming environment for Hispanics. Therefore, culture comes into play in how government approaches policymaking and service delivery. Recall that social constructions are cultural characterizations. For Hispanics, this is bad news in a society in which the culture leads to a propensity to construct for them a negative identity. Consider as an example what was noted by one informant when referring to the State Office of Education (USOE). The informant stated that "They work from a deficit-based model, meaning that there is something *wrong* with the [Hispanic] kids and they need to be fixed." If indeed this is how the USOE approaches its tasks, it is no wonder that policies to improve the educational performance of Hispanics have not worked.[11]

Significantly, according to Schneider and Ingram (1993), such construction of minorities by decision makers is not uncommon. In fact, when populations are constructed as "lazy or shiftless" and are believed to be minorities "who were responsible for their own plight" (p. 345), public officials feel justified in cutting benefits and allocating more burden to these populations. This is true not only for ethnic minorities but also for other groups perceived as powerless and who are negatively constructed, such as gays, inmates, and the poor (Schroedel & Jordan, 1998; Nicholson-Crotty and Nicholson-Crotty, 2004).

CONCLUSIONS

This chapter used the social construction of target-population theory of Schneider and Ingram (1993) to interpret results of interviews of key informants on efforts made in Utah to engage the Hispanic community. The application of this social constructivist lens helped to provide further explanations for the barriers to the engagement of Hispanics in the governance process in Utah. While the interpretations presented here are by no means conclusive, they provide support for the broad patterns predicted by Schneider and Ingram's theory and open a fertile ground for more research on participation in governance by Hispanics and other ethnic minorities, not only in Utah but also in other parts of the United States.

Three general conclusions can be drawn. The first is that among informants, the perception was that the social construction of Hispanics in Utah by the majority culture was largely negative. This construction impinges on how government deals with issues that affect the population, both in terms of the engagement efforts and policy response. Second, the social construction of Hispanics by this cultural majority doesn't match the social construction by Hispanics of themselves. Thus, we observe a mismatch of participation efforts as well as selective outreach and lack of understanding. On the other hand, the social construction of Hispanics by Hispanics may not always be helpful, as when the primary identification with their own countries of origin leads to negative images of those from other Latin countries. In emphasizing their real cultural diversity and disregarding their common interests, they may hurt the well-being of the overall Hispanic community. In light of these observations, we conclude with some suggestions for improving the engagement of Hispanics in governance.

The first suggestion is that to advance our understanding and the practice of citizen engagement, we need more research using a social constructivist framework that focuses on minority engagement, and particularly that of Hispanics. Questions to be explored include the following: How does the social construction of Hispanics vary from state to state or region to region, and how does this affect the way government approaches engagement efforts? To what extent does the social construction of Hispanics make them less likely to be engaged in governance? That is, in places where the Hispanic identity is negatively constructed, are they participating at a significantly lower rate than in places where they are positively constructed? If so, how can we change these negative constructions?

A second suggestion is that we need to further examine the construction of Hispanics as a homogenous unit of analysis. The results of the study presented here show that although Hispanics are viewed as a large and homogeneous mass, there is great diversity within this group, which complicates engagement. This diversity is not only reflected in the experiences of Hispanics but also in the way in which they are perceived by decision makers and the public in general—sometimes in a positive light, other times in a negative light. How might the competing notions of diversity and solidarity affect the social construction of Hispanic identity?

Another suggestion is that for participatory approaches to be effective in supporting representation and developing appropriate policies and programs, government needs to put more effort into human capacity building. Schneider and Ingram (1993) argued that benefits such as capacity building are usually made available to advantaged groups—positively constructed powerful citizens. A new narrative is needed for Hispanics; one that gives them a reputation of a population worthy and capable of taking advantage of opportunities. After all, government stands to greatly benefit from capacity-building activities that include eliminating the educational achievement gap between White and Hispanic students, for example. Capacity-building activities will increase the pool of talented and capable Hispanic citizens, providing government with fresh leaders to call upon to serve in various roles.

Finally, the diversity of the Hispanic population suggests that to increase participation and to ensure that a truly representative group of Hispanic citizens are being engaged, government needs to provide opportunities for different levels of engagement. Not all citizens want to or can be involved in the same manner, and yet many still want to be engaged in some way (Neblo et al., 2010; Berry, Portney, & Thomson, 1993). While some Hispanics may be satisfied with participating in low-level of engagement efforts, others seek greater engagement, such as that afforded when one is appointed to a policy board. Thus, differential approaches that capitalize on citizen skills, desire, and availability need to be used to reach a broader section of the community and ensure effective and meaningful engagement.

NOTES

1. The term "Hispanics" is consistent with the terminology used by the Census Bureau; however, the term "Latino" is used more often in day-to-day parlance. "Hispanic/Latino" describes people whose ancestry can be traced back to the Spanish-speaking countries of Latin America and the Caribbean.
2. It is worth noting that the concerns of being stigmatized raised by the immigration discourse are real for Hispanics. The 2010 report "Illegal Immigration Backlash Worries, Divides Latinos" by the Pew Hispanic Center (2010) cites immigration status as one of the leading reasons Hispanics believe they

are discriminated against. Respondents believed that due to the immigration backlash, all Hispanics, regardless of whether or not they were born in the United States, will be targets of discrimination.

3. The governor has four ethnic advisory councils: Asian, Hispanic, Black, and Pacific Islander.

4. Agencies with minority citizen advisory councils in Utah are the State Office of Education, the Utah Department of Health, and the Western Region of the Department of Child and Family Services.

5. Salt Lake County uses its Council on Diversity Affairs to address Hispanic and minority needs in the county.

6. Utah has five recognized ethnic groups: Asian, Hispanic, Black, Pacific Islander, and Native American.

7. Community-based organizations are nonprofits that provide social services to the public. CBOs are often reliant on government funds and can operate as a subcontractor to provide government functions (Fredericksen & London, 2000).

8. Utah Code Annotated § 63-13-1.5.

9. On May 11, the Associated Press (http://news.yahoo.com/s/ap/20110510/ap_on_re_us/us_utah_immigration) reported that another bill, Utah's HB 497, which has been described as "Arizona-style" because it allows police to verify the immigration status of someone they arrest if there is "reasonable suspicion the person is an illegal alien," was signed by the governor in March of 2011. It went into effect in May 2011, but shortly thereafter, a federal judge blocked its implementation. The judge in the case believes that the law would cause "irreparable damage" if allowed to stay in effect.

10. Chicano is a self-identifying term often used by Americans of Mexican descent to express a sense of ethnic pride and sometimes their political association.

11. Although attempts to interview USOE representatives were made, through multiple e-mails and an initial phone conversation, these efforts did not bear fruit.

APPENDIX

Interview Log

Interviewee	Title/Position	Date Interviewed
Luz Robles	Director, Utah Office of Ethnic Affairs (OEA)	8/14/2007
Jesse Soriano	Director, Utah Office of Hispanic/Latino Affairs (OEA)	8/14/2007
Frank Cordova	Executive Director, Utah Coalition of La Raza	8/14/2007
Leo Bravo	Director, Cache Hispanic/Multicultural Center	8/15/2007
Craig Petersen	Member, Cache County Council	8/15/2007
Hector Mendiola	Member, Hispanic Advisory Council	8/17/2007
Juan Carlos Vazquez	Member, Utah Hispanic Advisory Council	9/11/2007
Sabrina Morales	Executive Director, Comunidades Unidas	9/14/2007
Mauricio Agramont	Community Developer, Midvale City	9/14/2007
Diane Lovell	Community Liaison, Utah Department of Workforce Services	9/14/2007
Manuel Romero	Community Program Relations Manager, DHS	9/14/2007
Rebecca Chavez	Director, Community Affairs, Centro de la Familia de Utah	9/28/2007
Mark Wheatley	Utah State Representative, District 35	9/28/2007
Rebecca Sanchez	Director of Diversity Affairs, Salt Lake County	9/28/2007
Owen Quinonez	Director, Center of Multicultural Health, UDH	9/28/2007
Brent Platt	Director, Western Region, Department of Child and Family Services	10/3/2007
Lee Martinez	Utah Labor Commission	10/3/2007
Josie Valdez	Administrator, Salt Lake City Office of Diversity	10/3/2007
Robert "Archie" Archuleta	Utah Coalition of La Raza, Retired Teacher and School Administrator	10/16/2007
JoAnne Seghini	Mayor, Midvale City	10/16/2007
Rose Romero	Utah State Senator, District 7	10/19/2007
Marco Diaz	Central Committee Member, Utah Republican Party	11/9/2007
Tony Yapias	Former director of OEA	11/16/2007
Fred Fieff	Utah State Senator, District 1	11/16/2007
Carl Hernandez	Associate Dean, J. Ruben Clark School of Law, Brigham Young University, OEA Advisory Council	11/19/2007
Rosa Martinez	United Hispanics, St. George, UT	12/4/2007
Grace Huerta	Associate Professor Utah State University, College of Education	12/11/2007

REFERENCES

Arnstein, S. R. (1969). A ladder of citizen participation. *Journal of the American Institute of Planners, 35*(4), 216–224. Retrieved January 10, 2011, from http://lithgow-schmidt.dk/sherry-arnstein/ladder-of-citizen-participation.html

Aslin, H., & Brown, V. (2004). *Towards whole community engagement: A practical toolkit.* Murray-Darling Basin Commision. Canberra, ACT, Australia. Retrieved February, 2008, from http://publications.mdbc.gov.au/product_info.php?products_id=156

Barnes, M. (1999). Researching public participation. *Local Government Studies, 25*(4), 60–75.

Beltran, C. (2010). *The trouble with unity: Latino politics and the creation of identity.* New York, NY: Oxford University Press.

Berry, J. M., Portney, K. E., & Thomson, K. (1993). *The rebirth of urban democracy.* Washington DC: The Brookings Institution.

Cohen, S. (1972): *Folk devils and moral panics.* London, England: MacGibbon and Kee.

de Lancer Julnes, P., & Johnson, D. (2011). Strengthening efforts to engage the Hispanic community in citizen-driven governance: An assessment of efforts in Utah. *Public Administration Review, 71*(2), 221–231.

Frederickson, H. G. (1980). *New public administration.* Tuscaloosa: University of Alabama Press.

Gergen, K. J. (2003). *An invitation to social construction.* Thousand Oaks, CA: Sage.

Gladden, L., & Oaks, N. (2007). *Task Force on Minority Participation in the Environmental Community.* State of Maryland. Retrieved from http://aaenvironment.com/MDMINORITYTASKFORCEREPORT.pdf

Goode, E., & Ben-Yehuda, N. (2009). *Moral panics: The social construction of deviance* (2nd ed.). Oxford, England: John Wiley and Sons.

Guzman, B. (2001). *The hispanic population: Census 2000 brief.* Washington, DC: United States Census Bureau.

Hemphill, F. C., & Vanneman, A. (2011). *Achievement gaps: How hispanic and white students in public schools perform in mathematics and reading on the national assessment of educational progress (NCES 2011-459).* Washington, DC: National Center for Education Statistics, Institute of Education Sciences, U.S. Department of Education.

International Association for Public Participation. (2007). *IAP2: Spectrum of public participation.* Retrieved January 11, 2010, from http://www.iap2.org/associations/4748/files/IAP2percent20Spectrum_vertical.pdf

John, P. (2009). Can citizen governance redress the representative bias of political participation? *Public Administration Review, 69*(3), 494–516.

Kandel, W., & Kromartie, J. (2004). *New patterns of hispanic settlement in rural America.* United States Department of Agriculture. Retrieved from http://www.ers.usda.gov/publications/rdrr99/rdrr99.pdf

King, C. S., Feltey, K., & Susel, B. O. (1998). The question of participation: Toward authentic public participation in public administration. *Public Administration Review, 58*(4), 317–326.

King, C., & Stivers, C. (1998). Citizens and administrators: Roles and relationships. In C. King & C. Stivers (Eds.), *Government is us* (pp. 49–62). Thousand Oaks, CA: Sage.

Marshall, B., & Jones, R. (2005). Citizen participation in natural resource management: Does representativeness matter? *Sociological Spectrum, 25*(6), 715–737.

Marshall, G. (1998). Social constructionism: A dictionary of sociology. *Encyclopedia.com.* Retrieved January 11, 2011, from http://www.encyclopedia.com/doc/1O88-socialconstructionism.html

Meier, K. J. (1993). Representative bureaucracy: A theoretical and empirical exposition. *Research in Public Administration, 2*, 1–35.

Minkler, M., Blackwell, A., Thompson, M., & Tamir, H. (2003). Community-based participatory research: Implications for public health funding. *American Journal of Public Health, 93*(8), 1210–1213.

Moynihan, D. P. (2003). Normative and instrumental perspectives on public participation: Citizen summits in Washington, D.C. *American Review of Public Administration, 33*(2), 164–188.

Musso, J. A., Weare, C., Jun, K., & Kitsuse, A. (2004). Representing diversity in community governance: Neighborhood councils in Los Angeles. *Urban Institute Policy Brief.* Retrieved July, 2009, from http://www.usc.edu/schools/sppd/research/npp/nc_diversity.pdf

Neblo, M. A., Esterling, K. M., Kennedy, R., Lazer, P., David, M., & Sokhey, A. E. (2010). Who wants to deliberate—And why? *American Political Science Review, 104*(3), 566–583.

Nicholson-Crotty, J., & Nicholson-Crotty, S. (2004). Social construction and policy implementation: Inmate health as a public health issue. *Social Science Quarterly, 85*(2), 240–256. National Center for Education Statistics. Retrieved from http://nces.ed.gov/nationsreportcard/pdf/stt2007/2008470UT8.pdf

Petts, J. (2001). Evaluating the effect of deliberative process: Waste management case-studies. *Journal of Environmental Planning and Management, 44*(2), 207–226.

Petts, J., & Leach, B. (2000). Evaluating methods for public participation: Literature review. *R&D Technical Report: E135 Environment Agency.* Retrieved June 15, 2008, from http://www.environment-agency.gov.uk

Pew Hispanic Center. (2007). *The Latino electorate: A widening gap between voters and the larger Hispanic population in the U.S.* Retrieved January 12, 2011, from http://pewresearch.org/pubs/548/latino-electorate

Pew Hispanic Center. (2008a). *Statistical portrait of Hispanics in the United States.* Retrieved 2008, from http://pewhispanic.org/factsheets/factsheet.php?FactsheetID=58

Pew Hispanic Center. (2008b). *U.S. population projections: 2005–2050.* Retrieved from http://pewhispanic.org/reports/report.php?ReportID=85

Pew Hispanic Center. (2008c) *Demographic profile of Hispanics in Utah.* Retrieved 2008, from http://pewhispanic.org/states/?stateid=UT

Pew Hispanic Center. (2010). *Illegal immigration backlash worries, divides latinos.* http://www.pewhispanic.org/files/reports/128.pdf

Ramos, J. (2005). *The Latino wave: How Hispanics will elect the next American president* (2nd ed.). New York, NY: HarperCollins.

Roberts, N. (2004). Public deliberation in an age of direct citizen participation. *The American Review of Public Administration, 34*(4), 315–353.

Rourke, F. E. (1978). *Bureaucratic power in national politics (3rd ed.)*. Boston, MA: Little, Brown.

Schachter, H. L. (1995). Reinventing government or reinventing ourselves: Two models for improving government performance. *Public Administration Review, 55*(6), 530–537.

Schroedel, J. R., & Jordan, D. (1998). Senate voting and social construction of target populations: A study of AIDS policymaking 1987–1992. *Journal of Health Politics, Policy and Law, 3*(1), 107–132.

Schneider, A., & Ingram, H. (1993). The social construction of target populations: Implications for politics and policy. *The American Political Science Review, 87*(2), 334–347.

Selden, S. C. (1997). *The promise of representative bureaucracy: Diversity and responsiveness in a government agency*. Armonk, NY: M. E. Sharpe.

Selden, S. C., & Selden, F. (2001). Rethinking diversity in public organizations for the 21st century: Moving toward a multicultural model. *Administration and Society, 33*, 303–329.

Thiele, L. P. (1999). *Environmentalism for a new millennium: The challenge of coevolution*. New York, NY: Oxford University Press.

Yang, K. (2005). Public administrators' trust in citizens: A missing link in citizen involvement efforts. *Public Administration Review, 65*(3), 273–285.

Zatz, M. S. (1987). Chicano youth gangs and crime: The creation of amoral panic. *Crime, Law and Social Change, 11*(2), 129–158.

CHAPTER 9

ONLINE CITIZEN PARTICIPATION

A Case Study of Illinois Nonprofit Organizations

Alicia M. Schatteman
Northern Illinois University

The purpose of this chapter is to examine how technology, and specifically Web sites, support citizen participation in nonprofit organizations and thereby enhance civic engagement more broadly. According to the latest data, there were over 1.5 million nonprofits registered with the Internal Revenue Service (IRS) in 2008, an increase of 30% in 10 years (Wing, Roeger, & Pollak, 2010). Nonprofit organizations are a substantial part of the economy and provide a variety of public goods and services. For virtually any interest or issue, there is a nonprofit organization representing those interests. Some of us *seek out* organizations to further our interests, while others are *drawn into* organizations by personal experiences, friends, family or a nonprofit's marketing efforts. In either case, engagement with that organization can be sparked or supported by visits to the nonprofit's

The State of Citizen Participation in America, pages 225–238
Copyright © 2012 by Information Age Publishing
All rights of reproduction in any form reserved.

Web site. In this way, Web sites can spark and build community, thereby promoting citizen participation and community building. Web sites certainly help to define a community through promoting a nonprofit's mission, outlining the programs and services to support that mission or identifying how someone can get involved in the organization through volunteering or donating. The Web site can also be the forum itself to connect and engage individuals, volunteers, staff, board members, members, donors, visitors, clients, and so on. But if a Web site has this potential, are nonprofit organizations currently utilizing technology to engage their stakeholders and truly support citizen participation? This chapter seeks to answer this question by examining how 263 nonprofit organizations in northern Illinois use their Web sites to promote citizen participation.

A community can be a geographic place or a community that comes together for a specific issue. Smith, Kearns, and Fine (2005), authors of *Power to the Edges*, defined civic engagement as "the activities by which people participate in civic, community and political life and by doing so express their commitment to community" (p. 6). Technology enables citizens to more actively participate in the democratic process and governance of their communities (OECD, 2003). It has great potential to tie together people based on their interests and concerns, because consultation and discussion are not limited to the physical place. Online communication networks have the potential to create a strong sense of community and social ownership, high in social capital (Foth, 2003). In this way, there is the potential for us to become more connected to each other, increasing social capital and civic engagement. Nonprofit organizations support citizen participation by involving their stakeholders in service projects, providing direct service, or trying to influence support for their missions, to secure resources, or to influence public policy. Hall defined online citizen engagement as the use of information technology to "vitalize communities and mobilize social movements, enhance citizen efforts to join with others who share their views" and increase "their ability to access and disseminate information within communities" (2005, p. 3). In essence, it is the use of information technology to learn and practice civic engagement and/or political affairs.

LITERATURE REVIEW

The following literature will focus on the aspects with direct relevance to the topic of nonprofit organization use of online technology to support citizen participation. The first major area of this literature review is the extent to which nonprofits use Web sites—from staff and user perspectives. Some researchers have examined how the design of the Web sites supports citizen participation. Second, the literature review will analyze the research relating to how nonprofits are using technology to build and strengthen relationships and therefore encourage civic engagement.

Multiple Stakeholders Complicate Use of Information Technology

Just like other entities, nonprofit organizations have adopted new technologies to assist them with reaching their constituencies. This fact is complicated because nonprofits not only serve an identified population, such as teenage mothers or homeless families, but their stakeholders also include donors (which may or may not be their served population), volunteers, members, boards of directors, government officials, and staff. These stakeholders complicate any communication efforts made by nonprofits because of competing interests and information needs. It is certainly possible that a nonprofit may not be aware of the most effective means to reach them or consider it cost-prohibitive. Technology, however, has the potential to reach all of these various stakeholders in a cost-effective manner. Nonprofit Web sites could enhance "the participants' sense of inclusion in the organization and improve the organization's delivery of services" (Hardina, 2006, p. 7). Messages as well as Web experiences can be customized using 2.0 Web technology. To engage with the public, nonprofit organizations must first understand their stakeholder information needs and the best ways to engage them in the organization. Some of those needs may be for basic information, such as financial data or the listing of programs and services. However, to truly support citizen participation, nonprofits could offer ways both online and offline that directly connect that individual to the organization. This is an admitted challenge given the varying interests and needs of these stakeholder groups, but a challenge that could at least be partially met and supported through the use of information technologies. There is a limited amount of research in the use of Web technology by nonprofit organizations, which will be summarized here.

Organization Commitment to Web Presence

Some nonprofits are strategically using information technology to increase organizational capacity and effectiveness, including Web site capabilities (Hackler & Saxton, 2007). Some 77% of organizations surveyed had an organizational Web site. However, 32% of these Web sites are maintained or partially maintained by volunteers, 28% by an outside vendor, 24% by information systems staff, and 13% by communications staff. Hackler and Saxton (2007) suggest that who is responsible for maintaining the Web site may indicate whether the organization views the Web site as a communication tool, a technical tool, or a strategic tool. Larger nonprofits are more likely to measure the effectiveness of their information technology capabilities: "the data reflect that nonprofits do not relate IT to the bottom line as much as expected" (p. 479). Hackler and Saxton found that nonprofits with broad support among staff and boards of directors show the strongest association between the use of information technology and strategic management. According to the researchers' results, "only a small minority of nonprofits were using the Internet for strategic communications" (p. 480). Nonprofits are using information technology to support their work but only in its simplest form. Furthermore, most nonprofits are not taking advantage of Web technology to engage Web visitors to really build and enhance relationships. Reasons include lack of capacity and competency, as well as lacking leadership and resources.

Goatman and Lewis (2007) determined how a broad range of nonprofit organizations in the UK were using their Web sites and the attitudes of their staff toward their Web sites. Overall, 280 organizations from a broad range of causes responded to a mail survey. Larger organizations (those with fundraising incomes over £1 million) "expect their Web sites to make a greater contribution to several aspects of their work in terms of raising their profile, generating funds and enhancing their mission related work" (p. 37). Therefore, size does matter in terms of expectations and priority setting for nonprofit organizations. National organizations were also more enthusiastic about using their Web sites to span geographic distance to constituents. The same is true about expectations of using Web site technology to support fundraising efforts. "There was strong agreement that charities need Web sites, but a much lower level of agreement that charities would struggle to raise funds in the future if they did not have a Web site" (Goatman & Lewis, 2007, p. 41).

There are some nonprofits who understand the potential uses for online civic engagement. Kanter and Fine (2010) refer to these nonprofits as "networked," defined as "easy for outsiders to get in and insiders to get out...engage people in shaping and sharing their work in order to raise awareness of social issues, organize communities to provide services, or advocate for legislation" (p. 3). Building and supporting relationships with all stakeholders is viewed as a cultural shift not a resource drain (Kanter & Fine, 2010). The authors present a ladder of engagement beginning with listening, then sharing, fundraising (contributing) to creating something new. Their book offers several examples of organizations that have gone through these cultural changes to become a more open organization, but research needs to be done about the current state of nonprofits measured against their framework and the barriers prohibiting nonprofits from continuing up this ladder of engagement.

Research also shows that a lack of time and resources is commonly blamed for insufficient technological adoption by nonprofit organizations (Corder, 2001; Hackler & Saxton, 2007; Jaskyte, 2011; Saigal, 2008; Schneider, 2003;). However, is there more going on here than can be counted? One of the other challenges for nonprofit organizations to fully embrace technology and its potential to transform the ways they engage with members, donors, and supporters, is the ability of an organization to readily accept change. Gill (2010) suggests that nonprofits need to undergo a cultural transformation based on learning "that supports and encourages the collective discovery, sharing, and application of knowledge" (p. 5). Notoriously, nonprofits have focused on the provision of goods and services, constantly reacting to their environments without stopping for a breath, other than examining larger issues such as capacity. By creating a culture of learning, Gill suggests nonprofit organizations can "continually improve, achieve goals, and attain new possibilities" (p. 6). If nonprofits truly want to engage with citizens, then they need to create ways to support this cultural transformation. The culture and vision of an organization are critically important and ultimately are what draw resources into the organization to support their work. But to accept change, nonprofits must be open and willing to listen to constant feedback, including criticism. Hall (2005) found in his study of select nonprofit organizations that it is the willingness of organizations to see themselves as part of a larger community that ultimately makes them successful in their online participation efforts. Transformational leadership is also significant for technological innovation in nonprofit organizations, driving change from the top down and facilitating bottom-up innovation, according to Jaskyte (2011).

Building Credibility to Support Online Citizen Engagement

Designing nonprofit Web sites is more than about content and aesthetics. Web sites must be *used* and *useful* for users, in order to build credibility and a relationship with the organization. According to Metzger (2007), the users' sense of credibility is based on the look and feel of a Web site and the professionalism of the site. Nonprofit organizations need to keep this in mind if they want to attract and maintain relationships with their stakeholders. Fogg et al. (2001) studied how 1,400 stakeholders evaluated 51 different Web site elements to determine how the characteristics increased or decreased Web site credibility. They found that the characteristics ultimately fell into seven credibility factors: real-world feel, ease of use, expertise, trustworthiness, tailoring, commercial implications, and amateurism. Younger respondents were more critical of Web sites. Overall, "most people—regardless of age, gender, or other demographic factors—assess Web site credibility in similar ways" (Fogg et al., 2001, p. 67).

Virtual Accountability

Online accountability (or virtual accountability) is one aspect of the larger concept of accountability, important to supporting civic engagement. Some researchers (Saxton & Guo, 2009) have defined virtual accountability as having two dimensions: disclosure and dialogue. Overall, nonprofits are better at disclosing information than creating dialogue for true civic engagement. The most significant factors supporting higher online accountability were asset size (based on balance sheet assets) and board performance (Saxton & Guo, 2009).

Other researchers have determined that online accountability also has to do with Web characteristics of interactivity and multimedia orientation (Jo & Kim, 2003). The component of the Web site that actually supported higher accountability was the presence of interactive characteristics. "It appears that the enhancement of interactivity in a Web site would bring better relationships with publics" (Jo & Kim, 2003, p. 214). Therefore, Web sites that have more opportunities for visitors to interact with the organization have a higher potential to support and build civic engagement. Reingold argues that "public voice is learnable, a matter of consciously engaging with an active public rather than broadcasting to a passive audience" (2008, p. 101). Therefore, if nonprofits build better Web sites, they can teach and support civic engagement. Metzger (2007) calls for more research "on what users actually do to assess credibility" (p. 2087). Studies need to address possible discrepancies between self-reported Web site evaluations versus behavior (what we actually do).

However, online civic participation is not without its critics. Access to and use of the Internet has continued to rapidly expand "consistent with previous mass media" (Klotz, 2004, p. 27). However, there are still some gaps (such as the digital divide), which include age (Internet use declines with age), disability (visual, physical), socioeconomic status, and geographic location in the country (rural versus urban). But it is not just Internet adoption rates that we need to be concerned with; it is also the speed with at which Internet access is made. Broadband access means faster service with more power to see, download, and use large files with graphics and sound. Without broadband access, Internet users have very different experiences on Web sites and overall surfing (Klotz, 2004). This notion that online participation could reduce social equity and create thinner social bonds between individuals was also noted by Levine (2004). Critics also point out that there is little evidence that technology supports stakeholder relationships (Kent, Taylor, & White, 2003). Nonprofits are also restricted by how much they can actually voice the concerns of their stakeholders for fear of violating advocacy and lobbying rules prescribed by the IRS (Berry, 2005).

RESEARCH METHODS

This study encompassed what the U.S. Census Bureau defines as the Chicago-Naperville-Joliet, Illinois, Metropolitan Division, which includes Cook County, DeKalb County, DuPage County, Grundy County, Kane County, Kendall County, McHenry County, and Will County, as well as counties broadly across northern Illinois, adding Winnebago County, Boone County, Ogle County, Stephenson County, Lake County, and Kanakee County. A random sample of nonprofits from these counties was selected across all types of nonprofit organizations. Researchers evaluated each Web site based on a set of criteria adapted from the communications, public administration, and nonprofit literatures with regard to online accountability. These are

1. Posting of information
2. Listening Online: Initiating Dialogue
3. Supporting Online Engagement
4. Functionality and Usefulness

Data were collected using an online survey instrument, which was pretested for reliability. In fall 2010, nonprofit organizations were randomly selected in the northern Illinois area defined above. In total, 263 Web sites were ultimately analyzed. Some organizations do not have a Web site or the organization was deemed not to be a 501(c)(3) organization (tax exempt). The nonprofit organizations are equally distributed among nonprofit types including arts/culture, health, human services, and advocacy/social welfare. These nonprofit organizations are well-established, having been founded an average of 50 years ago, and most (83.5%) had paid staff.

RESULTS

This research sought to determine to what extent nonprofit organizations are currently utilizing information technology, and specifically their Web site, to support and enhance citizen participation.

Posting Information

In terms of Web communications by nonprofits, the Web sites were analyzed by researchers regarding how they are using the Web sites to simply post information or using one-way communication with constituents. See Table 9.1 for a summary of items found.

Nonprofit organizations are using use their Web sites to thank donors; those that do, thank mainly corporate sponsors (35.4%), individual donors (35.4%), major gift donors (25.6%), foundations (24.8%), government support (14.7%), and in-kind donations (17.1%). About a third (32.9%) of all nonprofit Web sites recognize volunteers in some way. Most nonprofit Web sites do not provide information about planned giving/bequests (67.8%) or corporate matching gift information (81.3%). About half (47.6%) of all Web sites studied have press releases issued by their organization and provide links to a news item about that organization in a media outlet (42.8%). However, of those with newsletters posted online, 37.7% of the newsletters are current within the last month, 34.4% are current within the last six months, 13.9% within the last year, and 13.9% are older than a year.

Listening Online: Initiating Dialogue

The Web sites were also reviewed to determine to what degree the Web sites promote two-way dialogue, a requirement for citizen participation. Nearly half (44.5%) of these organizations are membership-based, and of these, 69.3% provide information about how to join, but 27.2% have the ability to process membership payments online. Just over half (59%) allow

TABLE 9.1   Items Posted to Web Site

Item	Number	%
Mission	234	91.4
Annual Operating Budget	215	84.0
Location (address, directions, map)	214	83.9
Newsletter	127	50.4
Annual Report	80	32.0
Strategic Plan	34	13.7
Most Recent Web Site Update	30	11.7
Performance Measurement Results	15	6.2
Constitution/Bylaws	14	5.6
Board Meeting Minutes	8	3.2

visitors to register online for a program or event by accepting credit card payments online.

Social media has the great potential to build relationships. Over half (56.7%) of all Web sites link to social media pages. Of these, most link to Facebook (63.4%), Twitter (30.7%), and, to a much lesser degree, the social media Web sites of LinkedIn and YouTube. Few (10%) nonprofit Web sites have any audio content or Podcasts, and just about a third (34.4%) have video content. A small minority of nonprofit Web sites (6.0%) offer online surveys/polls on specific issues and of these, 7.1% have the results of these polls available online.

To promote citizen engagement with the organization, the Web site was analyzed to determine to what extent the site lists contact information for staff or the Board of Trustees (see the Figures 9.1 and 9.2).

Supporting Online Engagement

Third, sophisticated Internet users are accustomed to personalizing their browsing experiences using, for example, Web 2.0 technology. Over a quarter (26.5%) of Web sites utilize Web site design elements to personalize the web browsing experience. To really accomplish the goal of visitor customization requires a registration and log-in for the Web site. But most (63.5%) of all Web sites do not have a privacy or security statement

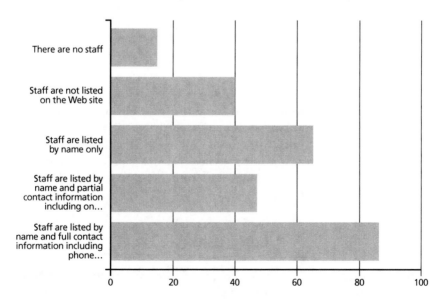

Figure 9.1 How can the staff be contacted?

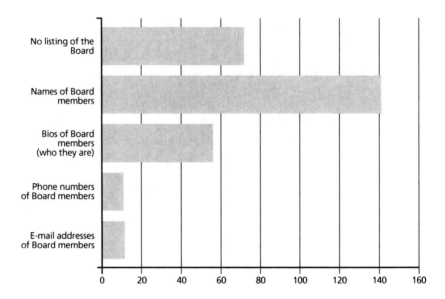

Figure 9.2 How can the Board be contacted?

posted on the Web site, which would assure potential users of the use and protection of their personal information. Over a quarter (26.5%) of Web sites have targeted audience links available on the home page so Web users could quickly get to the information they sought (such as members, youth, family, business, employees, etc.).

Functionality and Usefulness

Finally, the Web sites were reviewed to determine how user friendly the overall experience is, which would support a relationship with the organization. A basic search box is present on 29.3% of all Web sites, but of these, 66.4% actually work when tested by researchers. To do more advanced searches beyond keyword searches, just 18.2% of all Web sites have an advanced search function. Many nonprofits (68.6%) include Web links to other resources elsewhere.

CONCLUSIONS

This study sought to determine the extent to which nonprofit organizations are using their Web sites to support citizen participation. The analysis suggests that Web sites are currently being used almost purely as a form of one-way dialogue and further, they are fairly poor at that. Basic information is missing, incomplete, out-of-date, or difficult to find. Without basic, relevant, and updated information, citizens could be dissuaded from engaging with the organization at any level.

At a minimum, nonprofits need to be actively engaging their internal constituents, including staff, Boards of Trustees, donors, and members. In terms of external audiences, nonprofits also interact with the media, government officials, colleagues, potential members, potential donors, and the general public. It is this complicated accountability system that makes nonprofit Web sites even more critical to these efforts. It is the "public face" of the organization, visible to everyone in the world.

Nonprofit Web sites have the potential to attract and retain support. Potential donors often make a stop at the nonprofit's Web site first to learn about that organization, its history, programs, services, governance, management, and other information before they decide to get involved. Based on the Web site, that potential donor or potential volunteer may decide to "click away" and look elsewhere to spend their time or money, or get actively involved. Web site impressions are just as important, if not more important, than face-to-face first impressions. Web users are sophisticated and generally can navigate a site quickly. They will either be enticed to continue their stay and therefore learn more about how they can get involved, or they will leave and take their interests and assets to another organization. Although nonprofit organizations can never be sure how many Web visitors would actually turn into donors or supporters, they need to build Web sites with that intent. This should be a clear goal of Web site development and maintenance.

However, just building a Web site does not finish the job. Certain design features can encourage dialogue and support citizen participation, but nonprofit organizations need to be clear about what their stakeholders want and are comfortable using. Web site maintenance is also a critical component and often is a problem for nonprofit organizations struggling to make their operating budgets. And it's not just building the tools, we also have to teach individuals how to use them, and the debate is on as to whose responsibility that is; parents, schools, colleges, universities, communities, nonprofits. There is no point in building an engaging Web site if your constituents can't use the tools offered. We have to teach individuals to find their personal voice so that they can then find their public voice and fulfill the desire for broad civic participation.

Finally, citizen participation using nonprofit Web sites can connect multiple stakeholders to an organization in ways not previously possible (Hardina, 2006). However, what is needed is not necessarily more technology or more resources (although these are both required to some degree), but really, engaging with citizens isn't something you build (i.e., Web sites) but rather something you nurture, both off line (face-to-face) and online.

This case study is limited by the number of nonprofit organizations in the study (n = 263). The dataset needs to be expanded to include a larger number of nonprofit organizations from a broader geographic area. Considering the very limited resources of nonprofit organizations, it is not surprising that they are not able to invest in their Web sites, but there are also troubling signs beyond the economic concerns. What about their organizational culture? Do nonprofits need to adopt a culture that is more open and transparent; to open themselves up to the outside world?

Technology is constantly changing, so the tools that we use to engage our stakeholders are always changing, but unless nonprofit organizations truly commit to transparency and citizen participation, the technological tools are not worth the investment. Bimber (2000) also maintains that the Internet is not responsible for the radical transformation of our society but rather the access to information (Internet as a platform for that information). In effect, our information environment is changing. Ultimately it is the people behind the technology and those using the technology to engage that are important. Trust is still an important component of building relationships, and technology is not a substitute (Jo & Kim, 2003).

Nonprofit organizations serve the public's interest through incredibly difficult work under great financial constraints. They are also regulated by local, state, and the federal governments as well as reporting mandates to other funders such as individual donors and foundations. Their missions speak to some of society's greatest challenges and triumphs. Out of sheer necessity, they must solicit support for their work including raising funds, delivering programs and services, recruiting volunteers, and such. Currently, most of this work, particularly for small and medium nonprofits, is taking place using traditional media forms and not information technology. For many reasons already discussed, there is more potential to engage citizens in their work. Some are doing better than others and certainly should be lauded for their efforts. As the price of information technology continues to decline, and the professionalism of the nonprofit sector improves and the demand by their various stakeholders continues to increase, nonprofits will need to rethink their information technology strategies for civic engagement. There is huge potential for social marketing and other technological applications to support this 21st-century level of engagement. At the same time, IRS rules governing nonprofit advocacy and lobbying efforts will probably be redefined as the lines between engagement and advocacy become more blurred (Berry, 2005). Nonprofits give voice to many underrepresented groups, and information technology has the ability to support their personal and public voices if we let them. This may require a rethinking of how we fund nonprofit citizen engagement initiatives (which may not fit into the popular notion of project funding) or changing the rules regarding advocacy and lobbying capabilities now restricted by the IRS.

REFERENCES

Berry, J. (2005). Nonprofits and civic engagement. *Public Administration Review, 65*(5), 568–578.

Bimber, B. (2000). The study of information technology and civic engagement. *Political Communication, 17*(4), 329–333.

Corder, K. (2001). Acquiring new technology: Comparing nonprofit and public sector agencies. *Administration and Society, 33*(2), 194–219.

Fogg, B. J., Marshall, J., Laraki, O., Osipovich, A., Varma, C., Fang, N., . . . Treinen, M. (2001). What makes a Web site credible? A report on a large quantitative study. *Proceedings of ACM CHI 2001 conference on Human Factors in Computing Systems, 1,* 61–68. New York, NY: ACM.

Foth, M. (2003). "Connectivity Does Not Ensure Community: On Social Capital, Networks and Communities of Place," IRiRA 2003 Conference Track: Community Informatics.

Gill, S. (2010). *Developing a learning culture in nonprofit organizations.* Thousand Oaks, CA: Sage.

Goatman, A., & Lewis, B. (2007). Charity E-volution? An evaluation of the attitudes of UK charities towards website adoption and use. *International Journal of Nonprofit and Voluntary Sector Marketing, 12*(1), 33–46.

Hackler, D., & Saxton, G. (2007). The strategic use of information technology by nonprofit organizations: Increasing capacity and untapped potential. *Public Administration Review, 67*(3), 474–487.

Hall, P. D. (2005). *A question of empowerment: Information technology and civic engagement in New Haven, Connecticut.* Working Paper No. 30. The Hauser Center for Nonprofit Organizations and The John F. Kennedy School of Government, Harvard University.

Hardina, D. (2006). Strategies for citizen participation and empowerment in nonprofit community-based organizations. *Community Development, 37*(4), 4–17.

Jaskyte, K. (2011). Predictors of administrative and technological innovations in nonprofit organizations. *Public Administration Review, 71*(1), 77–86.

Jo, S., & Kim, Y. (2003). The effect of Web characteristics on relationship building. *Journal of Public Relations Research, 15*(3), 199–223.

Kanter, B., & Fine, A. (2010). *The networked nonprofit: Connecting with social media to drive change.* San Francisco, CA: Jossey-Bass.

Kent, M., Taylor, M., & White, W. (2003). The relationship between Web site design and organizational responsiveness to stakeholders. *Public Relations Review, 29*(1), 63–67.

Klotz, R. (2004). *The politics of Internet communication.* New York, NY: Rowman & Littlefield.

Levine, P. (2004). The Internet and civil society. In V. Gehring (Ed.), *The Internet in public life.* Lanham, MD: Rowman & Littlefield.

Metzger, M. (2007). Making sense of credibility on the Web: Models for evaluating online information and recommendations for future research. *Journal of the American Society for Information Science and Technology, 58*(13), 2078–2091.

Organisation for Economic Co-operation and Development (OECD). (2003). Engaging citizens online for better policy-making. *OECD Observer.* Paris Cedex, France. Retrieved March 2003, from www.oecd.org

Rheingold, H. (2008). Using participatory media and public voice to encourage civic engagement. In W. L. Bennett (Ed.), *Civic life online: Learning how digital media can engage youth* (pp. 97–118). Cambridge, MA: MIT Press.

Saigal, A. (2008). *A study on the impact of information technology use on nonprofit organizations.* Unpublished master's thesis. Grand Valley State University, Grand Rapids, Michigan.

Saxton, G., & Guo, C. (2009). Accountability online: Understanding the Web-based accountability practices of nonprofit organizations. *Nonprofit and Voluntary Sector Quarterly.*

Schneider, J. (2003). Small, minority-based nonprofits in the information age. *Nonprofit Management & Leadership, 13*(4), 383–399.

Smith, J., Kearns, M., & Fine, A. (2005). Power to the edges: Trends and opportunities in online civic engagement. *PACE Philanthropy for Active Civic Engagement, Denver, Colorado.* Retrieved from www.pacefunders.org

Wing, K., Roeger, K., & Pollak, T. (2010). *The nonprofit sector in brief: Public charities, giving, and volunteering.* Washington, DC: Urban Institute.

CHAPTER 10

VOLUNTARY ASSOCIATIONS, NONPROFIT ORGANIZATIONS, AND CIVIC ENGAGEMENT

Angela M. Eikenberry
University of Nebraska at Omaha

Courtney Jensen
Georgia Southern University

INTRODUCTION

Nonprofit organizations and voluntary associations have long been viewed as important institutions for promoting civic engagement and democracy in the United States. Nonprofit organizations are institutions designated by a state government as a nonprofit corporation and often, if an organization applies, by the Internal Revenue Service (IRS) as tax exempt. The term "nonprofit," then, designates a legal and regulatory status for an organization that does work typically related to the arts, education, health care, and social welfare. Nonprofit organizations can be quite diverse, ranging from small, human service organizations such as a local food bank; to large, federated organizations like the American Red Cross or Salvation Army; to substantially endowed universities, hospitals, and charitable foundations. The

The State of Citizen Participation in America, pages 239–260
Copyright © 2012 by Information Age Publishing

scale of the nonprofit sector has grown considerably in recent years—over 1.5 million organizations were registered with the IRS in 2008, an increase of 31% since 1998 (Wing, Roeger, & Pollack, 2010).[1] Voluntary associations predate, exist alongside, and sometimes become nonprofit organizations. These are made up of individuals who voluntarily come together to accomplish a purpose and range from informal associations such as book clubs and bible study groups to more formal organizations like the Kiwanis or the League of Women Voters.

There is much evidence, described below, to suggest that voluntary and nonprofit organizations engage citizens in civic life in various ways—through volunteering, giving, participating as members, and advocating for the interests of themselves and others. The outcome of this participation is often viewed as good for democracy, leading to a more pluralist, equitable society. However, as discussed further below, there is evidence this engagement is not always as it seems or can even lead to negative outcomes, such as distrust of others, the creation of illiberal groups like the Ku Klux Klan, unequal power relations among groups, and poor representation of constituent interests. Furthermore, because of changes in the broader political and social environment in recent years, many of these organizations have become more professionalized as they try to fill social service needs in the wake of government privatization, and marketized in their attempt to meet needs in the community. Simultaneously, the way citizens want to participate in these organizations is changing, making volunteering and giving more episodic and irregular, memberships more tenuous, and advocacy different in focus.

This chapter examines ways in which voluntary and nonprofit organizations do or do not promote civic engagement in the United States and the outcomes of this engagement. The next section presents standard views, largely drawn from Alexis de Tocqueville, of the effects of engagement through these organizations on individuals' civic skills and virtues, political participation, and representation. This is followed by more recent challenges to this perspective and then an examination of the changing landscape in which voluntary and nonprofit organizations operate. Next, taking these trends into consideration, the ways in which voluntary and nonprofit organizations engage citizens as givers and volunteers, members, and advocates are examined. Finally, conclusions and implications for political participation and public administration are discussed.

TOCQUEVILLE AND THE CIVIC ENGAGEMENT EFFECTS OF VOLUNTARY AND NONPROFIT ORGANIZATIONS

Views of voluntary and nonprofit organizations in the United States are often based on the writings of Alexis de Tocqueville (1835/2000). De Tocqueville believed that through voluntary associations, citizens learned civic virtues and skills, participated directly in governance, checked the power of government; and improved the quality and equality of representation in governance (Fung, 2003). De Tocqueville emphasized the "meaningful relationships that people develop and transform in the course of interaction in civic groups. Through "the reciprocal action of men one upon another" people's imaginations would grow bigger. Through that process, civic relationships would take on new definitions and purposes" (Lichterman, 2006, p. 534). Tocqueville also believed these groups could engage individuals "*routinely* in civic relationships over time, not merely sporadically" (p. 535, emphasis in original). Finally, Tocqueville believed such civic relationships could cultivate social capacity: "people's ability to work together organizing public relationships rather than ceding those relationships entirely to market exchange or administrative fiats of the state" (p. 535). In this context, civic virtues such as trust, moderation, compromise, and reciprocity could be learned; linking individuals' private interests to broader community interests (Dewey, 1927) and counteracting the processes of fragmentation and individualization within modern society (Durkheim, 1984/1933).

Voluntary and nonprofit organizations may also provide the motivation and capacity for individuals to take part in politics because they provide opportunities for "the acquisition of politically relevant resources and the enhancement of a sense of psychological engagement with politics" (Verba, Schlozman, & Brady, 1999, p. 4). Even when individuals pursue activities with no direct political content, such as chairing a committee to arrange a fundraising event, they have opportunities to develop organizational and communication skills that are relevant for politics (Almond & Verba, 1963; Verba et al., 1999). These organizations can also provide exposure to political cues and recruitment networks that facilitate political participation (Macleod et al., 1996; Rochon, 1998; Verba et al., 1999). For example, LeRoux (2007, p. 411) found nonprofit organizations can promote civic awareness and stimulate activity on the part of their clients and thus may be particularly well-suited to promoting participation by underrepresented groups. In addition, volunteer work in these organizations "makes people more aware of the structural nature of social problems and the need for political solutions" (Musick & Wilson, 2008, p. 461). Berger and Neuhaus (1977/1996) argued that voluntary groups can represent citizens by mediating between individuals and the "megastructures" of government and large corporations by providing "voice" for individual concerns.

CHALLENGING THE TOCQUEVILLIAN PERSPECTIVE

In recent years, there have been several challenges to Tocqueville's assertions or at least how his writings have been interpreted. For instance, while neo-Tocquevillians presume that voluntary associations lead to civic virtues such as generalized trust, Skocpol (1999, pp. 51–71) and others (Schneider, 2007, p. 594) have argued that civic engagement can stem from both distrust and trust. Kaufman (2002) shows that by encouraging Americans to bond together along gender, ethno-national, and ethno-religious lines, associationalism further disposed individuals

> to fear one another and thus to fear government itself—particularly any government program that might require the redistribution of income or collectivization of risk. The result was a nation with a rather bizarre sense of self, one rooted not in the benefits of citizenry or in the value of inclusion but in libertarian paranoia and mutual distrust. (p. 9)

Tamir (1998) similarly argues that "When allowed to associate, individuals quite often opt for illiberal, authoritarian, non-democratic options" (p. 219). There have been many examples of illiberal associations; for example, the Nazi movement during the Weimer Republic in Germany, the fascist movement in Italy, or the Ku Klux Klan in the United States all operated through or as illiberal voluntary groups that advocated hate, fascism, and bigotry (Berman, 1997; Chambers & Kopstein, 2001; Kwon, 2004; Sargent, 1995).

In relation to voluntary associations' promotion of political participation and representation, Warren (2001) argues that Tocqueville worked with a relatively simple bipolar model of state-civil society relations that did not consider associations work within fields of power relations. The Tocquevillian model "makes it difficult to conceive the (real) possibility that associational life might replicate, reinforce, and even enhance power relations among groups, even if they develop and reinforce egalitarian norms within associations" (p. 32). Tocqueville himself warned that such intermediary bodies often formed around special interests and not only diminished the sovereignty of the state but also favored propertied minorities with the resources to devote to their establishment and perpetuation (Hall, 1999, pp. 9–10; Whittington, 1998, p. 24).

This may explain why many existing studies have found that nonprofit organizations do not represent the interests of constituents and members to the degree often assumed. As Guo and Musso (2007) write,

> Many elections in membership organizations are characterized by low turnout rate and lack of democracy (Cnaan, 1991), and members may be marginalized in relation to board members and management (Lansley, 1996; Spear,

2004). Within the nonprofit sector, there has been a charge that many boards of directors are upper income, better educated, professional employers and managerial persons, whereas the community has little or no representation (e.g., Abzug & Galaskiewicz, 2001; Cnaan, 1991; DiMaggio & Anheier, 1990; Middleton, 1987). (p. 315)

This may be changing. Nonprofit organizations have recently begun programs to promote diversity by bringing in more women and individuals of color into leadership positions (Nielsen & Huang, 2009, p. 5); however, the voluntary sector still tends to reflect segregation in other domains of society (Moore & Whitt, 2000, p. 313). Guo and Musso (2007) also note that there is a complexity of representational mixes found in nonprofit organizations:

- *Substantive representation* occurs when an organization acts in the interest of its constituents, in a manner responsive to them. It is often measured by the congruence between leaders and constituents on issues of most importance.
- *Symbolic representation* occurs when an organization is trusted by its constituents as their legitimate representative.
- *Formal representation* occurs when formal organizational arrangements establish the ways in which its leaders are selected by its constituents. It focuses on elections and other relevant formal arrangements (e.g., rights of recall of leadership, etc.).
- *Descriptive representation* occurs when leaders of an organization mirror the (politically relevant) characteristics of its constituents.
- *Participatory representation* occurs when there is a direct, unmediated, and participatory relationship between an organization and its constituents. It highlights the importance of maintaining a variety of channels of communication with constituents.

They conclude that different types of nonprofit organizations may be more representative in certain dimensions but less representative in others.

THE CHANGING LANDSCAPE OF VOLUNTARY AND NONPROFIT ORGANIZATIONS

Some have suggested the associations Tocqueville wrote about were waning at the time of his visit; that is, he captured the decisive moment when an older tradition of charity and grassroots voluntary action was giving way to a new, modernist mode of voluntarism premised on contract and formal institutional structures (McGarvie, 2003, p. 93). By the 1840s, national associations rationalized the business of benevolence. They kept watch over huge sums of money through sophisticated cost-accounting; they replaced inefficient volunteers with paid agents recruited and trained for the job, and supervised them through a network of regional offices; and they relied on regular memos and reports to communicate with employees and on national magazines to publicize the cause to the public. (Gross, 2003, p. 43)

Thus, the rationalization and bureaucratization of voluntary organizations may have started long ago, affecting their ability to engage citizens.

Recent trends in the social, political, and economic environment may be exacerbating this and other affects of voluntary and nonprofit organizations on civic engagement. There have been at least three important social-political-economic trends taking place in the past few decades that have influenced voluntary and nonprofit organizations' ability to engage citizens. These are the shift to privatize the provision of public social services and increasing professionalization of voluntary and nonprofit organizations, a growing reliance on market-like activities to raise funds, and the detraditonalization of society.

Privatization and Professionalization

Since the early 1980s, governance in the United States has been motivated largely by an ideology that assumes political and economic life is a matter of individual freedom and initiative. Within this ideology, a free-market society and a minimal state are key objectives, achieved through the extension of the market to more and more areas of life, while the state is stripped of "excessive" involvement in the economy and provision of opportunities (Peters, 1996, pp. 22–28). The outcome has been a drive to privatize government and emphasize market-based and nongovernmental solutions to social problems. In this context, political leaders have looked to private, nongovernmental institutions as means to administer or replace public programs (Hacker, 2002, p. 7; Kettl, 1988; Milward & Provan, 2000; Salamon, 1995; Wolch, 1990).

While the government has grown to rely on these organizations to provide services, it has not provided adequate financial support and has also put extra accountability pressures on them. A recent study of human service nonprofit organizations (Boris, de Leon, Roeger, & Nikolova, 2010) found, for instance, that governments at the local, state, and national levels are persistently failing to pay the full costs for their contracts with nonprofit organizations, often pay late and change the terms of contracts midstream, and require complex contracting processes and reporting requirements. Simultaneously, exacerbated by the latest recession, nonprofit organizations have experienced growing demand for their services (Young & Salamon, 2002; Nonprofit Research Collaborative, 2010) without a significant increase in private charitable giving (Giving USA, 2010). The changes in social service provision have put more and more pressure on these organizations to become professionalized in their structure and programming.

Marketization

Voluntary and nonprofit organizations have responded to these pressures by adopting market-like approaches to raising funds. Between 1982 and 2002, commercial activities (program service revenue including government contracts, membership dues and assessments, income from special events, and profit from sales of inventory) among nonprofit organizations increased by 219% and grew as a percentage of their total revenue (Kerlin & Pollak, 2006). Nonprofit organizations have also entered into partnerships with for-profit corporations through such means as cause-related marketing;[2] that is, "profit-motivated giving that enables firms to contribute to nonprofit organizations while also increasing their bottom line by tying those contributions to sales" (Grau & Folse, 2007, p. 19). A well-known example is the "pink campaign" conducted by the Susan G. Komen Breast Cancer Foundation in partnership with several prominent multinational corporations in which part of the sales of a product goes to the charity.

In addition, voluntary and nonprofit organizations have escalated their use of "social enterprise" strategies, creating new business ventures that supposedly meet the organizations' "double bottom line" (social as well as financial). As with other initiatives mentioned above, this is not new; however, in the 1990s, "a vast array of influential funds and support networks arose to encourage nonprofits to embark on revenue-generating enterprises en masse, and in ways they never had before" (Seedco, 2007, p. 4), and the number of organizations attempting this strategy rose. This is evidenced by the data mentioned above regarding the growth of commercial income and also by a growing body of books, events, and experts helping and encouraging organization leaders to implement social enterprise practices (see, for example, Brinkerhoff, 2000; Dees, Emerson, & Economy, 2001, 2002). Board members and funders are increasingly urging nonprofit and voluntary organizations to be more entrepreneurial and self-supporting (Foster & Bradach, 2005), instead of having to rely on donors or the government for support.

Detraditionalization

Political scientists and public administrators have described the shift from state action to voluntary action as the "new governance" (Pierre,

2000; Rhodes, 1996). Sociologists argue this shift has helped to create a detraditionalized society; that is, a society that is characterized by the dissolution of traditional parameters and support systems such as social welfare institutions. The detraditionalization of society

> involves a shift of authority: from "without to within." It entails the decline of the belief in pre-given or natural orders of things. Individual subjects are themselves called upon to exercise authority in the face of the disorder and contingency which is thereby generated. (Heelas, 1996, p. 2)

In this context, individuals must make choices about everything: "lifestyles, partner types, politics and the like . . . [while] traditional structures of authority are no longer regarded as valid sources of norms" (Gundelach & Torpe, 1997, p. 54). Thus, this shift to a detraditionalized society is also a shift to a "risk society" in that individuals must increasingly rely on themselves rather than larger societal institutions, such as the welfare state, for survival (Beck, 1992; Ellison, 1997, p. 711). One reaction by individuals to this environment has been to seek out new identities and ways to cope with living in a detraditionalized society through engaging with other individuals, but in ways that match their personal interests, which are useful to their hectic lives and that they can control (Macduff, 2005; Wuthnow, 1994, 1998).

THE EFFECTS ON ENGAGEMENT IN VOLUNTARY AND NONPROFIT ORGANIZATIONS

The changing landscape in which voluntary and nonprofit organizations operate has influenced the ways and abilities of these organizations to engage citizens in relation to volunteering, giving, membership, and advocacy.

Volunteering

Americans have long been known for their generosity in giving time. In 2009, some 26.8% of adults volunteered for or through a nonprofit organization. This corresponds to 17.1 million volunteers with the average person spending 2.4 hours volunteering each day (Wing et al., 2010). Many more Americans volunteer informally helping friends and family. Data from the National Corporation for National and Community Service (Grimm et al., 2007) show that in 2006, people volunteered mainly in the areas of religion (35.3%), educational or youth services (27%), and social and community service (13.1%). The Bureau of Labor Statistics (2010) shows that in 2009, women (30.1%) volunteered more than men (23.3%); 35- to 44-year olds

(31.5%) and 45- to 54-year-olds (30.8%) had higher volunteering rates than those in their early 20s (18.8%) and those over 65 (23.9%); Whites were more likely to volunteer (28.3%) than African Americans (20.2%), Asians (19%), and Hispanics (14.7%); married individuals had higher volunteer rates (32.3%) than individuals that had never married (20.6%); and parents with children under the age of 18 (34.4%) were more likely to volunteer than individuals without children under the age of 18 (23.9%). Educational attainment also had a positive correlation, with higher volunteering rates for college graduates over the age of 25 (42.8%) than high school graduates (18.8%) and those with less than a high school diploma (8.6%).

The effects of the trends noted above on volunteering have been varied. The response by voluntary and nonprofit organizations to pressures for professionalization and accountability have been to focus on demonstrating efficiency and short-term effectiveness, which in turn has demanded greater emphasis on a professional, business orientation in operations. This can devalue the work of volunteers (Alexander, Nank, & Stivers, 1999, p. 462; Ryan, 1999). Alexander et al. (1999) note the focus and influence of government to do more with less "inevitably forces priorities to be set in terms of the bottom line rather than in terms of building social capital" and civic engagement (p. 462). As an example of this, Backman and Smith (2000, p. 369) describe an arts organization that eliminated its volunteer program because it was not considered to be "cost-effective."

In such an environment, when voluntary and nonprofit organizations do use volunteers, it is often through careful screening, training, indoctrination, and supervision, using volunteers for certain tasks that will not compromise organizational efficiency and administrative integrity. Lichterman (2006) calls this "plug-in style" volunteering. In an ethnographic study, Lichterman found that the effect for volunteers is typically little or no room for understanding voluntary effort within the context of larger political or policy issues. Volunteering today does not build meaningful relationships, strengthen "we-ness," or otherwise build up social capacity in ways Tocqueville imagined. Schneider (2007) has also found volunteering does not lead to greater civic engagement; rather, volunteers typically work toward a specific, not common good (p. 593).

Marketization activities also seem to have affected voluntary and nonprofit organizations' ability to enhance civic engagement through volunteering. In the past, the long-term survival of a voluntary organization depended on its capacity to sustain relationships with core constituencies, like community volunteers, thereby creating a network of social trust around the organization (Backman & Smith, 2000, p. 356). However, when these organizations rely on commercial revenue and entrepreneurial strategies, for example, there is less need to build these types of networks among constituencies, thus discouraging civic participation (Aspen Institute, 2001, p. 6).

Finally, detraditionalization also seems to have has an effect on volunteering. In the last decade, while the number of volunteers has increased, the total number of hours contributed has declined over the same period (Nunn, 2000). This may partially be due to a trend that has been described as "flexible" or "episodic" volunteering; volunteering that is sporadic, without ongoing commitment, and "often in the form of self-contained and time-specific projects" (Nunn, 2000, p. 116). For instance, in a 1998 "Giving and Volunteering Survey," the Independent Sector found that "41 percent of volunteers contributed time sporadically and considered it a one-time activity" (p. 117). To be sure, episodic volunteering is as old as volunteering itself, but it appears to be growing in use as a way for individuals to "give back" in the midst of busy and hectic lives, in their own way, and within the parameters of their own needs and interests (Hustinx & Lammertyn, 2003). As Macduff (2005) notes, "this shift in the behavior of volunteers occurs because the individual in the 21st Century is left to cobble together his or her own biography... [episodic] volunteering comes about because the individual in the postmodern era is a 'reflection' of the change in institutional conditions" (p. 55). Furthermore, Niemi and Chapman (1998) found in a study using 1996 National Household Education Survey data on the civic development of high school students that this irregular or infrequent volunteering had no influence on political knowledge.

Giving

Americans are said to be among the most generous when it comes to giving money. Among those who itemize taxes, 27.6% of American households gave charitable contributions in 2008. In 2009, Giving USA (2010) estimated individual giving was $227.41 billion, which includes estimated charitable deductions on tax returns filed and charitable giving by taxpayers who did not itemize deductions. In addition, charitable bequests were $23.8 billion, reflecting estimates for charitable deductions on estate tax returns filed in 2009 and giving by estates not filing federal estate tax returns.

With the privatization of social services and increasing professionalization and accountability demands, greater pressure has been put on philanthropy to fund basic social welfare needs. However, while charitable giving is substantial, this giving has remained stagnant over the past 40 years and does not necessarily go to areas most in need. During this time, giving accounted for about 2% of personal income and 2% of the U.S. Gross Domestic Product (GDP) (Burke, 2001, p. 187). Giving USA (2010) estimates charitable giving in 2009 was 2.1% of GDP. Recent data, from 2000 to 2005, shows there was virtually no change in the level of giving if measured in constant (inflation-adjusted) dollars, although the U.S. economy expanded by more than 12%, and total personal income increased by more than 7% (Urban Institute, 2006).

In addition, it is important to pay attention to where private giving goes: primarily to religious organizations (33%), education (13%), and grant-making foundations (10%), rather than to human services (9%) (Giving USA, 2010). A recent study conducted by the Center on Philanthropy at Indiana University (2007) found "less than one-third of the money individuals gave to nonprofits in 2005 was focused on the needs of the economically disadvantaged. Of the $250 billion in donations, less than $78 billion explicitly targeted those in need" (p. 2). Similarly, a 2007 study by the Institute for Jewish and Community Research found only 5% of total dollars from mega-gifts (gifts of $1 million dollars or more) went to social service groups (Tobin & Weinberg, 2007). These giving patterns reflect that people give to whom and to what they know and with which they are familiar and to causes with which they can identify and are physically or emotionally attached (Schervish & Havens, 2001). Thus, wealthy philanthropists, who provide the bulk of philanthropic dollars, give the majority of their donations to organizations from which they or their family benefit, such as the symphony, church, or their alma mater (Odendahl, 1990, p. 67; Ostrower, 1995) as well as to amenity services such as education, culture, and health (Wolpert, 1993, p. 7). Overall, most donations go to support "services that donors themselves use—and are not freely available to target the neediest and to sustain safety nets" (Wolpert, 1997, p. 101). Data also suggest organizations that rely heavily on philanthropic donations are less likely to serve the poor (Salamon, 1992).

During the past several decades, voluntary and nonprofit organizations have increasingly emphasized the use of more professionalized and "efficient" fundraising methods such as grant writing, work-place solicitation, telemarketing, direct-mail campaigns, telephone solicitation, donor-advised funds, and e-philanthropy, rather than more personal and volunteer-led methods of solicitation (McCully, 2008). These fundraising mechanisms may have generated substantial income, but they have also created "little stake in the organization or social connectedness for the individual" (Pratt, 1997, p. 251).

Finally, as with volunteering and indicative of the effects of detraditionalization, there have been changes in the way donors want to give. On the one hand, there are donors who want to be more engaged in their giving, some of whom emphasize collaboration across groups and sectors, partnering with funding recipients, and using hands-on, more donor-directed and unconventional modes of giving and volunteering that often focus on entrepreneurial problem-solving (Eikenberry, 2009; McCully, 2008; Ostrander, 2007). On the other hand are donors who want to be *less* engaged in their giving, either because they do not have enough time but want to do something to contribute to society betterment, or because they want more control over their everyday lives and how they do or do not participate in community activities (Eikenberry, 2009). These trends are apparent as well in the way individuals interact as members in voluntary and nonprofit organizations.

Membership

Professionalization, marketization, and detraditionalization have all played a role in changing the way citizens engage in voluntary and nonprofit organizations as members. Scholars have documented a shift from high-engagement, membership-based voluntary organizations in the U.S.—such as Kiwanis, Rotary, and the League of Women Voters—to on the one hand, the growth of value-based, low-engagement professional organizations, and on the other hand, to an expanding field of informal, self-organized, and decentralized initiatives. The first "are highly centralized and market-oriented, with a structural tendency to reduce the membership role to a type of 'vicarious commitment' by which individuals 'contract out the participation task to organizations'" (Hustinx & Lammertyn, 2003, p. 176). The latter have few institutional links transcending the local level, no clear center of authority, and often limited, project-oriented objectives.

Putnam (2000) has discussed the emergence of a new wave of national associational launchings in the United States that have dwarfed in volume traditional voluntary associations; however, these new organizations are a different breed of voluntary association, what he calls professionally led advocacy groups. These groups (such as the AARP, National Wildlife Federation, and Greenpeace) have narrow missions and few or no members or thin memberships based on computer-directed mailings to individuals who send checks and perhaps occasionally read a newsletter (p. 157). Within these groups, there is no longer face-to-face contact with membership—member ties are through common symbols, common leaders, and perhaps common ideals, but not with one another (p. 71). One of the consequences of this form of organization seems to be that more decisions are made by nonelected persons or organizational staff/professionals rather than the membership; democratic processes in general have less importance for the governance of the organization (Gundelach & Torpe, 1996). Putnam (2000, pp. 49–53) argues these organizations may not do much or enough to prepare citizens for their role in democratic society. Yet others argue that professional associations may have introduced alternative types of democratization:

> The increased level of education and changing make up of the individual into a more reflexive personality combined with new kinds of public participation

mean that the individual is politically engaged outside of the voluntary associations. Instead of a formal voluntary association discussions and identification with for instance other users take place in informal networks... this means that democratic socialization and democratic mobilization tend to take place in other social arenas than the voluntary associations. (Gundelach & Torpe, 1996, p. 15)

Ellison also concludes, considering changes in voluntary associations, that "by challenging the 'old order' and concepts of what makes a good citizen, there are more choices for people to engage with their community" (in Macduff, 2005, p. 56).

As opposed to traditional or professional associations, informal associations are less structured, smaller in scale, and more grassroots in nature. These include associations such as bible study groups, giving circles, and "network associations" (Borkman, 1999; Eikenberry, 2009; Gundelach & Torpe, 1996; Putnam, 2000; Wuthnow, 1994, 1998). Individuals who participate in these groups do not necessarily see themselves as members, or at least not "members for life," as in more formal associations (Wuthnow, 1994, 1998).

These informal groups and networks seem to promulgate a different kind of community than that discussed by Tocqueville as well. They may represent a "healthy development in democratic societies by establishing intersecting webs of allegiance" (Fine & Harrington, 2004, p. 343) and small-scale socialization "that is key to the development of democratic citizens" (Silver, 1990, p. 65). Yet some worry about the homogeneity, casualness, and self-interestedness of many of these groups. Small groups in particular seem to merely provide occasions for individuals to "focus on themselves in the presence of others" (Wuthnow, 1994, p. 319) and tend to discourage debate or criticism of others' opinions and explicitly rule out discussions of social and political issues. Because of this, they tend to extend trends that are already under way, without setting forth visions of a better world that could radically transform the way things are (Wuthnow, 1994, p. 319). Walsh (2004) found in an ethnographic study of small informal social groups that met on a regular basis that the informal public discussion within such groups can foster trust but also clarify social identities and *reinforce* exclusion. In addition, these groups do not require great social or personal sacrifice. Instead, they provide a kind of social interaction that busy, rootless people can grasp without making significant adjustments in their lifestyles and thereby allowing bonding to remain temporary (Wuthnow, 1998, p. 207); it is easy to walk away and not participate again (Wuthnow, 1998, p. 189).

Nevertheless, Wuthnow (1994) shows that self-help groups can extend their help to others outside their immediate circle. In a survey of small group members, nearly two in three said they have "worked with the group to help other people in need outside of the group" (p. 320). Almost as many claimed to have donated money to charitable organizations other than their church or synagogue, and half said they got involved in volunteer work in the community because of the group. Putnam and Feldstein (2003) have also shown the virtues of small groups for building social capital, especially if they are part of a larger federation that can help facilitate mixing and bridging among small groups (pp. 275–279).

Associating through loose connections may also bring about many benefits for individuals and contribute to democratic capacity building, such as

> becoming knowledgeable about their communities, taking an active interest in social and political issues, gaining greater confidence in their own abilities, acquiring social and civic skills, and learning how to be patient and trust others to do their part... it is also evident that their understanding of these traits is changing... Increasingly, good citizenship is... defined in terms of innovative skills that include networking, dealing with diversity, initiating new projects, and filling niches in an already crowded institutional environment. (Wuthnow, 1998, p. 166)

However, action within the context of loose connections can be much less effective in dealing with collective problems (Wuthnow, 1998, p. 110). Lichterman (2005) found in an ethnographic study of loose network organizations that busy, mobile individual participants in the network "could choose their niche, assuming that someone else was figuring out the bigger picture" (p. 68). Furthermore, loose network volunteering did not do much to build bridges to others, what Tocqueville saw as an important civic engagement aspect of voluntary associations. According to Lichterman, "volunteering in a loosely connected network gave me and other volunteers practice creating brief interpersonal—sometimes very impersonal—relationships. It did not teach us how to create more enduring bridges" (p. 83).

Advocacy

Another way in which voluntary and nonprofit organizations engage citizens is through advocacy work. Studies suggest these organizations engage in a wide range of activities, including testifying before legislative bodies, lobbying on behalf of or against proposed social-welfare legislation, and informally talking and meeting with policymakers about their organizations and the needs of their service population (LeRoux, 2007). A recent survey of 872 nonprofit organizations across the United States found 73% reported engaging in some type of policy advocacy or lobbying, 60% engaged in public policy efforts at least once a month, and 31% quarterly. Yet the survey also found 85% devoted only scant resources to lobbying or advocacy, and most relied on the least demanding forms of engagement (Salamon & Geller, 2008). This suggests that while these organizations' participation in advocacy efforts is substantial, the level and frequency of participation may not be enough to have a deep impact on the public policies that affect the constituents and causes these organizations represent. Focusing on human service organizations, Mosely (2010) concludes that advocacy is most commonly found in organizations that are relatively large in size, have professional leadership, strong collaborative ties, and high levels of government funding. Child and Grönbjerg (2007) also found that most nonprofits are ambivalent in their attitudes toward political advocacy, that those that engage in it do not see it as the primary purpose or mission, and that only a small percentage of nonprofit organizations dedicate considerable resources to advocacy (p. 276).

By playing a larger service-delivery role due to privatization, it appears that nonprofit organizations are increasingly consumed by the challenges of becoming competitive and professionalized providers and have less time and energy for advocacy work. Alexander et al. (1999, p. 460) found in a study of social service agencies that professionalized and market-oriented organizations shifted their focus from public goods such as research, teaching, advocacy, and serving the poor, to meeting individual client demands. Dart (2004) also found in a single-case study of a nonprofit in Canada, known for its strong mission-focus and business-like approach in its programs, that "other forms of valued service provisions and the enactment of other important pro-social values were diminished because of the need to focus on revenue-producing, mission-focused services" (p. 303).

Some nonprofits stay away from advocacy activities altogether because of concerns about losing tax-exempt status (Berry, 2005), while others have reduced advocacy efforts because they "are unsure if they could keep their contracts if they became critics of government or private sector contractors" (Skloot, 2000, p. 323). Recent action by the IRS to audit politically vocal nonprofit organizations suggests that there may be good cause for such worries (OMB Watch, 2006). Indicative of this and due to detraditionalization, the focus of advocacy efforts has changed in recent years—from material issues that improve standard of living (such as pensions, social security, taxation, subsidies, trade, economic regulation, and medical coverage) to postmaterial issues that focus on quality of life, such as environmental controls, consumer protection standards, and group rights (Berry, 1999).

CONCLUSIONS AND IMPLICATIONS FOR POLITICAL PARTICIPATION AND PUBLIC ADMINISTRATION

The discussion in this chapter shows there is general consensus that voluntary and nonprofit organizations play an important role in U.S. society and, since Tocqueville, have been viewed as important vehicles for civic engagement. However, nonprofit and voluntary organizations do not necessarily represent all interests and in some cases represent very narrow, socially unacceptable interests. While many types of voluntary and nonprofit organizations may expand civic skills and promote political participation, administrators should keep in mind that these groups are not a cure-all for expanding democracy and addressing social problems.

The landscape in which voluntary and nonprofit organizations operate has also changed considerably in recent years. Privatization, professionalization, marketization, and detraditionalization have all influenced how these organizations engage citizens and thus, the effect they have on political participation. Due to privatization and professionalization, voluntary and nonprofit organizations have become, for the most part, less focused on building community and grassroots action through volunteering, giving, membership, and advocacy. Marketization puts little to no value on these, and detraditionalization has served to fragment and individualize them further. Thus, Tocqueville's observations about voluntary organizations—that they expand civic relationships, engage individuals routinely in these relationships, and cultivate social capacity—seem very much in question. If citizens are not able to engage with organizations through volunteering, giving, becoming active members, or advocating, they have less opportunity for "the acquisition of politically relevant resources and the enhancement of a sense of psychological engagement with politics" as Verba, Schlozman, and Brady (1995, p. 4) found to be the case in their research more than a decade ago. Although the networks that facilitate political participation may still be intact, they are of a looser and more fragmented kind that do not necessarily provide any kind of unified or representative citizen voice. If citizens are less engaged with these organizations, it is difficult to see how voluntary and nonprofit organizations can adequately represent them in the ways described by Guo and Musso (2007)—substantive, symbolic, formal, descriptive, and participatory.

Awareness of these trends is important for public administrators, because looking to voluntary and nonprofit organizations as a means for civic engagement should be based on a realistic assessment of the degree to which they engage and represent citizens and promote civic and political engagement—and to what end. If government policies to contract out services to these organizations are done with the assumption that these organizations are more representative of the people or more closely embedded in the community, these assumptions may need to be reexamined. There was perhaps never a time when these organizations fully engaged citizens as Tocqueville believed and thus, perhaps never a time when civic voluntarism solved significant social problems. Rather, the true democratic value of voluntary and nonprofit organizations may be in their contributions to pluralism, when they enable freedom to associate, which is integral to free human life and to creating a democratic society (Warren, 2001; Rosenblum, 1998)—whatever the outcomes of such associations. If these organizations are made to address certain social ills, they may lose this freedom and thus democracy suffers. The implication is that the state may need to play a more, not less, significant role in providing for basic social well-being.

NOTES

1. This figure does not include nonprofits with less than $5,000 annual revenue. In addition, religious congregations do not need to register with the IRS (although many do).
2. Among corporate sponsors, cause-related marketing expenditures went from almost zero in 1983 to an estimated $1.3 billion in 2006.

REFERENCES

Alexander, J., Nank, R., & Stivers, C. (1999). Implications of welfare reform: Do nonprofit survival strategies threaten civil society? *Nonprofit and Voluntary Sector Quarterly, 28*(4), 452–475.

Almond, G. A., & Verba, S. (1963). *The civic culture: Political attitudes and democracy in five nations.* Princeton, NJ: Princeton University Press.

Aspen Institute. (2001, Summer). *The nonprofit sector and the market: Opportunities & challenges* (Publication No. 01-013). Washington, DC: Nonprofit Sector Strategy Group.

Backman, E. V., & Smith, S. R. (2000). Healthy organizations, unhealthy communities? *Nonprofit Management & Leadership, 10*(4), 355–373.

Beck, U. (1992) *Risk society: Towards a new modernity.* New Delhi, India: Sage.

Berger, P. L., & Neuhaus, R. J. (1996). *To empower people: From state to civil society* (2nd ed.). Washington, DC: AEI. (Original work published 1977)

Berman, S. (1997). Civil society and the collapse of the Weimar Republic. *World Politics, 49*(3), 401–429.

Berry, J. M. (1999). *The new liberalism: The rising power of citizen groups.* Washington, DC: Brooking Institution.

Berry, J. M. (2005). Nonprofits and civic engagement. *Public Administration Review, 65*(5), 568–578.

Boris, E. T., de Leon, E., Roeger, K. L., & Nikolova, M. (2010, October 7). *Human service nonprofits and government collaboration: Findings from the 2010 national survey of nonprofit government contracting and grants.* Washington, DC: Urban Institute. Retrieved December 27, 2010, from http://www.urban.org/publications/412228.html

Borkman, T. J. (1999). *Understanding self help/mutual aid: Experiential learning in the commons.* New Brunswick, CT: Rutgers University Press.

Brinkerhoff, P. C. (2000). *Social entrepreneurship: The art of mission-based venture development.* New York, NY: John Wiley & Sons.

Bureau of Labor Statistics. (2010). *Volunteering in the United States—2009* (USDL Publication No. USDL-10-0097). Washington DC: Bureau of Labor Statistics Press Office.

Burke, C. C. (2001). Nonprofit history's new numbers (and the need for more). *Nonprofit and Voluntary Sector Quarterly, 30*(2), 174–203.

Center on Philanthropy at Indiana University. (2007, Summer). Patterns of household charitable giving by Income Group, 2005. Prepared for Google. Indianapolis, IN: *The Center on Philanthropy at Indiana University.* Retrieved December 12, 2007 from http://www.philanthropy.iupui.edu/Research/Giving%20focused%20on%20meeting%20needs%20of%20the%20poor%20July%20 2007.pdf

Chambers, S., & Kopstein, J. (2001). Bad civil society. *Political Theory, 29,* 837–865.

Child, C. D., & Grönbjerg, K. A. (2007). Nonprofit advocacy organizations: Their characteristics and activities. *Social Science Quarterly, 88*(1), 259–281

Cnaan, R. A. (1991). Neighborhood-representing organizations: How democratic are they? *Social Science Review, 65*(4), 614–634.

Dart, R. (2004). Being "business-like" in a nonprofit organization: A grounded and inductive typology. *Nonprofit and Voluntary Sector Quarterly, 33*(2) 290–310.

Dees, J. G., Emerson, J., & Economy, P. (2001). *Enterprising nonprofits: A toolkit for social entrepreneurs.* New York, NY: John Wiley & Sons.

Dees, J. G., Emerson, J., & Economy, P. (2002). *Strategic tools for social entrepreneurs: Enhancing the performance of your enterprising nonprofit.* New York, NY: John Wiley & Sons.

de Tocqueville, A. (2000). *Democracy in America.* New York, NY: Bantam Books. (Original work published 1835)

Dewey, J. (1927). *The public and its problems.* Denver, CO: Allan Swallow.

Durkheim, E. (1984). The division of labor in society (W. D. Halls, trans.). New York, NY: Free Press. (Original work published 1933)

Eikenberry, A. M. (2009). *Giving circles: Philanthropy, voluntary association and democracy.* Bloomington: Indiana University Press.

Ellison, N. (1997). Towards a new social politics: Citizenship and reflexivity in late modernity. *Sociology, 31*(4), 697–717.

Fine, G. A., & Harrington, B. (2004). Tiny publics: Small groups and civil society. *Sociological Theory, 22*(3), 341–356.

Foster, W., & Bradach, J. (2005, February). Should nonprofits seek profits? *Harvard Business Review,* 92–100.

Fung, A. (2003). Associations and democracy: Between theories, hopes, and realities. *Annual Review of Sociology, 29*(1), 515–539.

Giving USA Foundation. (2010). *Giving USA 2010.* Glenview, IL: Author.

Grau, S. L., & Folse, J. A. G. (2007). Cause-related marketing: The influence of donation proximity and message-framing cues on the less-involved consumer. *Journal of Advertising, 36*(1), 19–33.

Grimm, R. Jr., Cramer, K., Dietz, N., Shelton, L., Dote, L., Manuel, C., & Jennings, S. (2007, April). *Volunteering in America: 2007 state trends and rankings in civic life.* Washington, DC: Corporation for National and Community Service.

Gross, R. (2003). Giving in America: From charity to philanthropy. In L. J. Friedman & M. D. McGarvie (Eds.), *Charity, philanthropy, and civility in American history* (pp. 29–48). Cambridge, England and New York, NY: Cambridge University Press.

Gundelach, P., & Torpe, L. (1996). *Voluntary associations: New types of involvement and democracy.* Paper presented at the ECPR Joint Sessions of Workshops, Oslo, Norway.

Gundelach, P., & Torpe, L. (1997). Social reflexivity, democracy and new types of citizen involvement in Denmark. In J. W. van Deth (Ed.), *Private groups and public life: Social participation, voluntary associations and political involvement in representative democracy* (pp. 47–63). London, England and New York, NY: Routledge.

Guo, C., & Musso, J. (2007). Representation in nonprofit and voluntary organizations: A conceptual framework. *Nonprofit and Voluntary Sector Quarterly, 36,* 308–326.

Hacker, J. S. (2002). *The divided welfare state: The battle over public and private social benefits in the United States.* Cambridge, MA: Cambridge University Press.

Hall, P. D. (1999). Resolving the dilemmas of democratic governance: The historical development of trusteeship in America, 1636–1996. In E. C. Lagemann (Ed.), *Philanthropic foundations: New scholarship, new possibilities* (pp. 3–42). Bloomington and Indianapolis: Indiana University Press.

Heelas, P. (1996). Introduction: Detraditionalization and its rivals. In P. Heelas, S. Lash, & P. Morris (Eds.), *Detraditionalization: Critical reflections on authority and identity* (pp. 1–20). Cambridge, MA: Blackwell.

Hustinx, L., & Lammertyn, F. (2003). Collective and reflexive styles of volunteering: A sociological modernization perspective. *Voluntas, 14*(2), 167–187.

Kaufman, J. (2002). *For the common good? American civic life and the golden age of fraternity.* New York, NY: Oxford University Press.

Kerlin, J. A., & Pollak, T. (2006). *Nonprofit commercial revenue: A replacement for declining government grants and private contributions?* Paper presented at the third annual United Kingdom Social Enterprise Research Conference, London, England.

Kettl, D. (1988). *Government by proxy.* Washington, DC: Congressional Quarterly Press.

Kwon, H. K. (2004). Associations, civic norms, and democracy: Revisiting the Italian case. *Theory & Society, 33*(2), 135–166.

LeRoux, K. (2007). Nonprofits as civic intermediaries: The role of community-based organizations in promoting political participation. *Urban Affairs Review, 42,* 410–422.

Lichterman, P. (2005). *Elusive togetherness: Church groups trying to bridge America's divisions.* Princeton, NJ: Princeton University Press.

Lichterman, P. (2006). Social capital or group style? Rescuing Tocqueville's insights on civic engagement. *Theory & Society, 35,* 529–563.

Macduff, N. (2005). Societal changes and the rise of the episodic volunteer. In J. L. Brudney (Ed.), *ARNOVA Occasional Paper Series, 1*(2), 49–61. Indianapolis, IN: Association for Research on Nonprofit Organizations and Voluntary Action.

McCully, G. (2008). *Philanthropy reconsidered: Private initiatives, public good, quality of life.* Bloomington, IN: AuthorHouse.

McGarvie, M. D. (2003). The *Dartmouth College* case and the legal design of civil society. In L. J. Friedman & M. D. McGarvie (Eds.), *Charity, philanthropy, and civility in American history* (pp. 91–105). Cambridge, England and New York, NY: Cambridge University Press.

McLeod, J. M., Daily, K., Guo. Z., Eveland, W. P., Jr., Bayer, J., Yang, S., & Wang, H. (1996). Community integration, local media use and democratic processes. *Communication Research, 23*(2), 179–209.

Milward, H. B., & Provan, K. (2000). Governing the hollow state. *Journal of Public Administration Research and Theory, 10*(2), 193–195.

Moore, G., & Whitt, J. A. (2000). Gender and networks in a local voluntary-sector elite. *Voluntas: International Journal of Voluntary and Nonprofit Organizations, 11*(4), 309–328.

Mosely, J. E. (2010). Organizational resources and environmental incentives: Understanding the policy advocacy involvement of human service nonprofits. *Social Service Review, 84,* 57–76.

Musick, M. A., & Wilson, J. (2008). *Volunteers: A social profile.* Bloomington: Indiana University Press.

Nielsen, S., & Huang, H. (2009). Diversity, inclusion, and the nonprofit sector. *National Civic Review, 98*(3), 4–8.

Niemi, R., & Chapman, C. (1998). *The civic development of 9th-through-12th grade students in the United States: 1996.* Washington, DC: National Center for Educational Statistics, U.S. Department of Education.

Nonprofit Research Collaborative. (2010). *November 2010 fundraising survey.* Washington, DC: Urban Institute.

Nunn, M. (2000). Building the bridge from episodic volunteerism to social capital. *The Fletcher Forum of World Affairs, 24*(2), 115–127.

Odendahl, T. (1990). *Charity begins at home: Generosity and self-interest among the philanthropic elite.* New York, NY: Basic.

OMB Watch. (2006, April 4). *IRS political audit program heats up.* Retrieved May 14, 2007, from http://www.ombwatch.org/article/articleview/3355/1/48?TopicID=1

Ostrander, S. A. (2007). The growth of donor control: Revisiting the social relations of philanthropy. *Nonprofit and Voluntary Sector Quarterly, 36,* 356–372.

Ostrower, F. (1995). *Why the wealthy give: The culture of elite philanthropy.* Princeton, NJ: Princeton University Press.

Peters, G. (1996). *The future of governing: Four emerging models.* Lawrence: University Press of Kansas.

Pierre, J. (Ed.). (2000). *Debating governance: Authority, steering and governance.* New York, NY: Oxford University Press.

Pratt, J. (1997). Bowling together: Fund raising practices and civic engagement. In D. F. Burlingame (Ed.), *Critical issues in fund raising* (pp. 247–255). New York, NY: John Wiley & Sons.

Putnam, R. D. (2000). *Bowling alone: The collapse and revival of American community.* New York, NY: Simon & Schuster.

Putnam, R. D., & Feldstein, L. M. (2003). *Better together: Restoring the American community.* New York, NY: Simon & Schuster.

Rawls, J. (1999). *A theory of justice.* Oxford, England: Oxford University Press. (Original work published 1971)

Rhodes, R. A. W. (1996). The new governance: Governing without government. *Political Studies, 44*(4), 652–667.

Rochon, T. (1998). *Culture moves: Ideas, activism, and changing values.* Princeton NJ: Princeton University Press.

Rosenblum, N. L. (1998). *Membership and morals: The personal uses of pluralism in America.* Princeton, NJ: Princeton University Press.

Ryan, W. P. (1999). The new landscape for nonprofits. *Harvard Business Review, 77,* 127–136.

Salamon, L. M. (1992). Social services. In C. T. Clotfelter (Ed.), *Who benefits from the nonprofit sector?* (pp. 134–173). Chicago, IL and London, England: University of Chicago Press.

Salamon, L. M. (1995). *Partners in public service: Government-nonprofit relations in the modern welfare state.* Baltimore, MD: Johns Hopkins University Press.

Salamon, L. M., & Geller, S. L. (2008). *Nonprofit America: A force for democracy.* Baltimore, MD: Johns Hopkins University Center for Civil Society Studies Institute for Policy Studies.

Sargent, L. T. (1995). *Extremism in America.* New York: New York University Press.

Schervish, P. G., & Havens, J. J. (2001). The mind of the millionaire: Findings from a national survey on wealth and responsibility. In *New directions for philanthropic fundraising: Understanding donor dynamics* (pp. 75–107). San Francisco, CA: Jossey-Bass.

Schneider, J. (2007). Connections and disconnections between civic engagement and social capital in community based nonprofits. *Nonprofit and Voluntary Sector Quarterly, 36*(4), 572–597.

Seedco Policy Center. (2007, June). *The limits of social enterprise: A field study & case analysis.* New York, NY: Author.

Silver, A. (1990). The curious importance of small groups in American sociology. In H. J. Gans (Ed.), *Sociology in America* (pp. 61–72). Newbury Park, CA: Sage.

Skloot, E. (2000). Evolution or extinction: A strategy for nonprofits in the marketplace. *Nonprofit and Voluntary Sector Quarterly, 29,* 315–324.

Skocpol, T. (1999). How Americans became civic. In T. Skocpol & M. Fiorina (Eds.), *Civic engagement in American democracy* (pp. 27–80). Washington, DC: Brookings Institution.

Tamir, Y. (1998). Revisiting the civic sphere. In A. Gutman (Ed.), *Freedom of association* (pp. 214–238). Princeton, NJ: Princeton University Press.

Tobin, G. A., & Weinberg, A. K. (2007). *Mega-gifts in American philanthropy: Giving patterns 2001–2003.* San Francisco, CA: Institute for Jewish and Community

Research. Retrieved February 20, 2008, from http://www.jewishresearch. org/PDFs/MegaGift.Web.07.pdf

Urban Institute. (2006). *The nonprofit sector in brief: Facts and figures from the nonprofit almanac 2007.* Washington, DC: Urban Institute.

Verba, S., Schlozman, K. L., & Brady, H. E. (1995). *Voice and equality: Civic voluntarism in American politics.* Cambridge, MA: Harvard University Press.

Walsh, K. C. (2004). *Talking about politics: Informal groups and social identity in American life.* Chicago, IL: University of Chicago Press.

Warren, M. E. (2001). *Democracy and association.* Princeton, NJ: Princeton University Press.

Whittington, K. E. (1998). Revisiting Tocqueville's America: Society, politics, and association in the nineteenth century. *American Behavioral Scientist, 42*(1), 21–32.

Wing, K. T., Roeger, K. L., & Pollack, T. H. (2010). *The nonprofit sector in brief: Public charities, giving, and volunteering, 2010.* Washington, DC: Urban Institute.

Wolch, J. R. (1990). *The shadow state: Government and voluntary sector in transition.* New York, NY: Foundation Center.

Wolpert, J. (1993). Decentralization and equity in public and nonprofit sectors. *Nonprofit and Voluntary Sector Quarterly, 22,* 281–296.

Wolpert, J. (1997). How federal cutbacks affect the charitable sector. In L. Staeheli, J. Kodras, & C. Flint (Eds.), *State devolution in America: Implications for a diverse society* (pp. 97–117). Thousand Oaks, CA: Sage.

Wuthnow, R. (1994). *Sharing the journey: Support groups and America's new quest for community.* New York, NY: Free Press.

Wuthnow, R. (1998). *Loose connections: Joining together in America's fragmented communities.* Cambridge, MA: Harvard University Press.

Wuthnow, R. (2002). The United States: Bridging the privileged and the marginalized? In R. D. Putnam (Ed.), *Democracies in flux: The evolution of social capital in contemporary society* (pp. 59–102). Oxford, England: Oxford University Press.

Young, D. R., & Salamon, L. M. (2002). Commercialization, social ventures, and for-profit competition. In L. M. Salamon (Ed.), *The state of nonprofit America* (pp. 423–446). Washington, DC: Brookings Institution.

PART IV

CITIZEN PARTICIPATION: INNOVATIVE CASES

CHAPTER 11

CITIZEN DELIBERATION ON HEALTH CARE COSTS

A Mock Courtroom Experiment[1]

Larkin Dudley
Virginia Tech

INTRODUCTION

The courthouse in America has become an icon for both justice and political fights (e.g., can you display the Ten Commandments?) as well as
notoriety (e.g., murders and feuds). In early America, the courthouse was
the gathering place for news and views as well as a prominent symbol of a
county's independence and its link to larger political bodies in the federalist system. Many courthouses contain not only the local court, the first
layer of the judicial system, but also the county administration offices, a link
to larger administrative structures, and the offices of elected policymakers
and public administrators, sometimes at the state level and sometimes the
national. As such, the courtroom experience has become a familiar venue
for all levels of government and a place for citizens to hear different sides
of an issue. Using the courthouse metaphor, this chapter reports on an
experiment to use the concept of courtroom drama to interest the public

The State of Citizen Participation in America, pages 263–281
Copyright © 2012 by Information Age Publishing

and policymakers in what citizens were saying about health care costs in the summer of 2009.

Different dimensions of this courthouse experiment are described. First, the citizen forums themselves are explained. Second, an experiment in a "mock courtroom" exercise is outlined in four regions and at the national level in the United States. Third, the two questions that guided the research are explained. The chapter concludes with reflections.

DELIBERATIVE FORUMS AND POLICY

The experiment in the mock courtroom reflects some of the directions in three strands of citizen participation scholarship. First, there is a robust literature on the importance of deliberation for democracy (see as a beginning, Dryzek, 2000; Guttman & Thompson, 1996). Within the research on deliberative democracy, according to Hauser (2004), the identification of a more complex notion of dialogue is one of the most important issues confronting the current scholarship around civic engagement. The forums reported here illustrate a complex concept of deliberation in that the forums combine both a problem-solving discourse, the more common type of forum in the United States, and sense-making dialogue. Both are important as forum participants often shift back and forth from one type to another within a single forum. The forums on health care costs were undertaken within the general questions of how meaning is generated in citizens' deliberative discourse and how that meaning can enhance our understanding of the framing of issues involved in a policy proposal, surface areas of disagreement, and illuminate how meaning is constructed. The making of meaning is particularly valuable at issue-definition stage, a time of building understanding of similarities and differences among relative perspectives (Hamilton & Willis-Toker, 2006; Mansbridge, 1983), and thus, the research on the forums here contributes to questions of how citizens make sense of policy issues (Buckler, 2007; Delli Carpini, Cook, & Jacobs, 2004; Jerit, 2008; Mathews, 1999; Putnam & Holmer, 1992; Tuler, 2000).

A second strain of scholarship has pondered whether and how the nuances of citizens' thinking in deliberation can be made more accessible to policymakers, media, and the general public. Studies from policy research on what influences legislative and executive policy decisions are somewhat inconclusive (Alter & Patterson, 2006; Bourdeaux, 2008; Canfield-Davis, Jain, Wattam, McMurty, & Johnson, 2010; Handley & Howell-Moroney, 2010; Hird, 2005; Koontz, 1999; Liu, Lindquist, Vedlitz, & Vincent, 2010; Weiss, 1993) and complicated by the assertion that politicians and the public may understand the issues and polarization in the legislative process differently (Fioriana & Samuel, 2009; Fioriana, Samuel, & Jeremy, 2006).

Much of the scholarly literature on how best to get information to poli-cymakers still agrees with J. G. March that there is an "elusive link" between information and decision strategies of policymakers (March, 1987). March argues, "Research reports produce diffuse changes in world views, rather than direct effects on decisions" (p. 157). To the extent that policy infor-mation enters the debate, legislators appear primarily to use it to defend existing ideas rather than to develop policy positions (Mooney, 1991; Shu-lock, 1999). In fact, many studies assert that legislators do not use available policy analysis to make decisions, but instead they use heuristics or cues with varying sets of cue-givers, such as other legislators or policy networks (for a concise summary of studies, see Bourdeaux, 2008).

With regard to the influence of citizens in policymaking, it is hard to interpret the results. Some find that governmental actors and various inter-est groups have relatively more influence in shaping local agendas than the general public, experts, and election-related actors (Liu et al., 2010), while others note the importance of the influence of fiscal impact, trust, and constituents on state policy decisions (Canfield-Davis et al., 2010); the differences in influences in state and national arenas (Koontz, 1999); and differences by how much administrators value citizen engagement in deci-sion making (Handley & Howell-Moroney, 2010).

Within the influences on policymakers, the difficulties of relaying infor-mation to policymakers and media are compounded for reports of forums because citizen deliberations reveal a complex balancing of values and opinions. Whereas opinion polls do not allow for in-depth understanding, reports from forums are best at revealing how citizens are naming and framing issues and what values they may hold. Since results from delib-eration are difficult to convey to those in policy (who are often focused on one specific issue) and to those in the media, (who have to convey information in 60-second sound bites), the experiment here centered on whether using a mock courtroom could be useful in presenting results to policymakers and media.

Third and finally, scholars of participation and deliberation have fo-cused on how solidified are publics on different issues. Daniel Yankelovich (1991) has been a pioneer in this arena with his work on public judgment. Yankelovich has critiqued the most often source of public opinion, opin-ion polls, as not indicating at which stage a particular issue has reached. According to Yankelovich, leaders may risk gridlock and frustration when attempting to communicate with the public without this information be-cause to communicate with the populace, a leader has to know from where people are coming, where they stand in their thinking now, and where they are headed. Yankelovich notes that the public struggles for years to rec-oncile conflicts about what should be done on policy issues. On different issues, the public may be somewhere along a continuum from just barely thinking about an issue to having considered alternatives and decided on a course of action. These insights from Yankelovich guided the formation of questions trying to gauge where the public was on considering the costs of health care in 2008–2009.

CONDUCTING FORUMS ON HEALTH CARE COSTS

For over 25 years, many thousands of citizens have gathered in small forums in schools, churches, community halls, and libraries throughout the national issue network to voice their ideas about what should be done in our country about pressing policy problems from troubled kids in school to the national deficit and most recently, health care costs (Stewart, 2009). Forums on health care costs, sponsored by the National Issues Forum and the Kettering Foundation, were conducted nationwide, including more than a thousand Americans in 40 states and the District of Columbia in 2008 and 2009. The forums intentionally drew from very different populations, for example, those with and without health care, employed and unemployed, all ages, retirees, students, rural and urban, different ethnic groups, and populations living all across the nation.

To engage participants in the hard work of making public decisions, the Kettering Foundation has developed a way of conducting public forums using issue books from the National Issues Forum (NIF). Various community groups, individuals, university centers, and associations organize forums around diverse public issues (Doble, 1996). Foundation publications emphasize that forum deliberation includes a comprehensive weighing of the tradeoffs and benefits of a policy issue by a concerned and informed public, different from a win-or-lose debate or a discussion with no concern for decision making. The informed deliberation is based on forum participants understanding the pros and cons of each alternative through examination of an issues book that outlines three or four different approaches to the issue and the assumptions and values of each approach based on extended research by the Kettering Foundation (Mathews & McAfee, 2003). Within each approach are the kernels for framing the issue in alternative ways. In the forums, citizens consider each approach, examine their concerns, and the costs, consequences, and trade-offs that may be incurred through following each approach. In doing so, forums surface how citizens are framing the issue, with what parts of an issue citizens are struggling, and the areas in which citizens see agreements and disagreements.

For the health care costs forums, the deliberation revolved around the issue book, "Coping With the Cost of Health Care: How Do We Pay for What We Need?" Three approaches to the issue included the arguments and consequences of Approach One, Reduce the Threat of Financial

Ruin, in which all would be required to have some sort of health insurance, somewhat of a modification of the existing system; Approach Two, Restrain Out of Control Costs, a focus on how to get prices of drugs, hospitals, and medical services under control; and Approach Three, Provide Coverage as a Right, which maintains that in one of the world's wealthiest nations, everyone should have a right to health care. Examples from the transcripts of these forums illustrate participants' efforts in orienting to essential differences and similarities of the approaches and the struggle among diverse perspectives from which new meanings emerge.[2] Excerpts below from forums give an idea of the types of thinking that occur (See Demortain, 2004 also). Each bulleted entry indicates a different speaker.

1. Participants below wrestle with whether health care is a societal problem or a personal problem and the "public" nature of health care:
   - "Everyone should have a right to appropriate or good health care."
   - "I do not know if I could agree with health care as a right for everyone."
   - "Who are you going to eliminate?"
   - "I do not know who would make that decision."
   - "I would not be comfortable for it to be mandated health care for everyone."
   - "Who would you leave out?"
   - "It fits into something . . . said earlier about is health care a societal problem. Is it a problem of the country as a whole rather than it just being a private problem?"
   - "I think the consequences immediately become a societal consequence and the evidence is where 30% of people depend on the hospital emergency room for their primary care."
   - "Yes, it is a social problem when kids are missing school for dental problems or poor nutrition or something like. Ten years down the road, 50 years down the road, these kids could be the one to cure cancer and save one of your grandchildren."

2. How much governmental intervention becomes an important part of the framing:
   - "I think we as Americans . . . don't want government intervention when it comes to a lot of these things. Until that mindset changes, I don't think you can find a solution because anytime the government jumps in we are like, 'Oh my god that is anti-American.'"
   - "But I think I agree that the government does need to guarantee that everybody has . . . ACCESS."
   - "I think . . . the real crux of the issue with this is the people who opt out and don't purchase health insurance. I think an area of

common ground was from most of us was ... back to the individual responsibility."

- "But there are problems with leaving it up to private insurance companies ... Because isn't a lot of the cost of the premiums to the insurance companies just paying for all of these administrators and people to tell you, 'No you can't get this done' or 'No we are not going to cover that' because they are trying to get a profit and deny people their claims?"

3. Participants wonder whether we should have a national standard or state-by-state:
   - "What about every state having different laws? What happens if you move?"
   - "That raises the idea of a national standard. If we had a national standard ... no matter where you move, you would always have certain health care that would be available to you."
   - "So then would that be better to then stay away from national standards and get closer to state-by-state?"
   - "I know what you are saying, but I think that if you were to take it state-by-state, it would encourage discrepancy between individual states."

4. Complicated Costs: In the dialogue here, the realization that the nature of costs is complicated becomes more obvious.
   - "But price ceilings never work; they always create shortages."
   - "But the current system is not working."
   - "The health system is very fragmented and in that fragmentation, a lot of the costs are administrative costs in health care because of insurance and the insurance companies themselves."
   - "I am not saying that we could not do without insurance. I am saying is the structure we have totally unnecessary? Could ... the care be delivered in a more efficient way is really what I am saying."

Although participants did begin with the stimulus of an issue booklet that outlined approaches to health care costs, the dialogues above illuminate participants' search for meaning, even though they began with a common referent. In the discussion of the issue under various frames, citizens told their personal experience and brought to the surface what was valuable to them. A growing sense of the complexity of the issue and a realization that others' views may have some validity resulted.

BEGINNING AN EXPERIMENT

Explaining the differences in the understandings that come from the deliberative forums from other types of public input to those who have never attended public forums, such as many policymakers and members of the media, has proven difficult. Political leaders typically receive calls, e-mails, or visits from individuals who want a specific outcome on a particular issue or who wish to register a complaint. As researcher Eric Giordano (2010) notes, "On many issues, constituents' opinions often contradict one another. So for lawmakers, more public participation often means more complaints and more people talking past each other."

Explanation of citizen views from public deliberation, however, move beyond this typical pattern of communication and report the way people talk with one another and together confront tough policy choices. Deliberation consists of conversations among citizens, not just one-way communication (citizens to decision makers or vice versa) as usually found in town halls. In deliberation, citizens become the problem solvers through working through difficult tradeoffs and making tough choices together, different from focus groups, which simply try to capture what people believe rather than have them work together toward decision making.

Believing in the importance of communicating the nuanced views of the tradeoffs citizens understand, the Kettering Foundation has not been satisfied with the results of communicating the public voice that emerges from such deliberation to policymakers, according to Philip Stewart (2009). Past efforts included bringing together former U.S. presidents, the media, and members of the policy community to Presidential Libraries to hear why public deliberation is important and to tell stories from the forums. Further, over nearly a dozen years, a TV program, *A Public Voice*, brought together elected officials, the media, and the policy community to discuss the public implications for relevant policy topics based on clips from public forum videos. Still, researchers felt there must be other effective ways to capture the attention of the public and the policy community.

Realizing that the sources of information regarded as useful by the policy community and media are usually opinion polls and analytical policy papers, methods already tried again and again, researchers sought other politically credible information sources. Court verdicts or decisions, particularly those of the U.S. Supreme Court, were suggested as a metaphor to "better raise awareness of the 'why' and more effectively articulate the 'what' of public deliberation to the policy community" (Stewart, 2009).

The courtroom metaphor thus became a key to this experiment with the idea of trying a mock courtroom at the national level and at five regional "centers for civic life," affiliated with Kettering research efforts and in the National Issues forum network. The goals of these centers for civic life include creating a stronger public voice, that is, a "more inclusive voice that would balance the voices coming from disparate interest groups," according to David Mathews (2010), Kettering president. From the 50 centers nationwide, 5 were asked to experiment with using a mock-courtroom format to present the results of regions to policymakers and the public. These were located at the Center for Public Administration and Policy, Virginia Tech; the Massachusetts Office of Dispute Resolution and Public Collaboration, University of Massachusetts; the Institute for Civic Discourse and Democracy, Kansas State University; the Wisconsin Institute for Public Policy and Service, University of Wisconsin system; and the Center for Voter Deliberation of Northern Virginia.

Among the research goals was to explore how a mock courtroom could communicate public thinking from deliberative forums to elected officials and the media. The difficulty of communicating citizens' nuanced understanding of issues to policymakers has been a struggle, according to both research literature (Mooney 1991; Shulock 1999) and practice (Stewart, 2009). The experiment would have a twofold focus: to evaluate how ready the public was to face the tradeoffs in health care costs and to focus on a method of communicating a public voice, developed through deliberative forums, to elected officials and the public. An assumption was made that the method and language of an appellate court decision may be readily recognized by public officials and the media. Thus, the research for the four civic life centers engaged in this experiment focused on two questions: In what ways does using a format of Appellate Court (panel of judges' deliberations and verdicts) contribute to understanding how results of public deliberation can be communicated to media and elected officials? A second related question was to understand Where are the citizens in these regions with regard to making a decision on health care costs, for example, at what stage is the public between just wishful thinking and commitment to a specific plan of action? To answer the two questions above, the centers also needed to collate the evidence on citizens' values and struggles in the health care cost deliberations.

COURTROOM EXPERIMENT

Four of the regional centers and Kettering affiliates at the national level designed sessions based on an appellate courtroom format.[3] After analyzing the forums, each of the regional centers at Kansas State, Virginia Tech, the University of Massachusetts, and the University of Wisconsin system took on the task of constructing a "courtroom" where two "advocates," acting in the roles of mock attorneys, debated how far along citizens who participated in the forums in their states were in their decisions on health care. With the guidance of regional center directors, these advocates (interns or graduate students) prepared rigorously through attending forums; analyzing written transcripts, audio and videotapes; writing and rewriting opening and rebuttal statements; and collaboratively preparing a script for the sessions.

At the regional and national level, the advocates prepared opposing arguments. With regional variation, most of the advocates argued the following: One advocate prepared an "optimistic" reading of the forums, arguing from the evidence of the forum deliberations that the public had moved along the stages of public judgment to consider the consequences of health care alternatives and was beginning to come to public judgment on the issues surrounding health care costs. The "optimistic case" was made on the basis that in the forums there was common ground for a belief in health care as a right ("social justice"); that this belief was enough to claim a shared sense of direction; and that participants favored a public option to coping with the costs of health care. The other advocate argued a "pessimistic" opinion based on the evidence from the forums that the public had not really considered the tradeoffs involved in the alternatives and was not yet at the stage of coming to judgment, but instead was only beginning to see contradictions and disagreements in health care cost alternatives. The advocates making the pessimistic case presented evidence from the forums that participants had not really found common ground yet and had not really yet faced up to the tradeoffs for different approaches. They maintained that it was true that many were favorable to reform, but had not yet worked through what reform really meant.

Each Center for Civic Life and the national presentation staged the courtroom with judges' panels composed of some combination of three to five high-level health care administrators, health policy experts, and elected officials.[4] In addition, each had representatives from the media participate in some role in order to gauge their response to the courtroom as an effective means of publicizing citizen views. Although wording differed among the four campus centers and the national presentation, all addressed the two questions: one, to what extent the citizens in their region were ready to accept the consequences, trade-offs, and costs of health care in supporting a health care plan; and two, how effective is the mock courtroom in highlighting the issues and in bringing those issues to the attention of policymakers and the public? Each of the regional centers presented the courtroom to a mixed audience of other officials, students, and citizens from the respective communities, while the national presentation included, in addition, representatives from national nonprofit organizations. The centers had their audiences formally evaluate the effects of the courtroom with a questionnaire or discussion and several, including the national presentation, prepared videotapes of the courtroom demonstrations for public television or other outlets in their regions.

With regional variations, the basic format included the moderator describing the forum design used in deliberative democracy and the three approaches to health care costs that were the topics of the forums. The two advocates gave opening statements explaining, respectively, their optimistic and pessimistic interpretations of their regional forums. Evidence and rebuttals were presented, and judges questioned the arguments and rendered a "verdict" of their opinion on how far along forum citizens were in considering the cost of health care. In some of the regional courtrooms and in the national presentations, excerpts from DVDs or representatives of the public forums were used as evidence for each attorney's argument. Because the advocates collaborated beforehand to ensure that the arguments were related and concise, the precision enabled complex issues to be presented in a fairly brief format.

EVALUATION OF THE MOCK COURTROOM AS EFFECTIVE COMMUNICATION

The audience, judges (elected officials and health care administrators), and the media representatives were asked to provide feedback on the effectiveness of this format in relaying citizen opinion to officials. Audiences, judges, and members of the media were positive on most dimensions of the courtroom drama. At all the centers, they gave very high evaluations on postcourtroom questionnaires to the performances of the advocates, judges' deliberations, and clarity of purpose, interest and novelty of the event. Audience members noted that the event changed their ideas about health care costs and opened their eyes to the deliberative methods. At one center, comments included

- "Goes beyond simply raising the issue, but [gives] evidence/logic behind opposing views."
- "I think it's a good way to show two sides of an important issue. It shows what alternatives there are in debatable issues and also allows the "jury" to see what groups of local people think. With local input, the people presenting ideas can figure out where else they need to elaborate."
- "I appreciated the structure because it provided detailed pros and cons for both opinions and thoroughly represented public opinion."
- "The presence of voting officials was the most important aspect of today's presentation." (Dudley, 2009)

In terms of a good way to articulate the issues, judges in all the centers noted that the format expressed most of the complexity in policy. Yet there were some reservations expressed. Several noted that public opinion is important, but also you need the experts and that you need broad representation in the forums to be sure to get opinions from all groups.

Can the mock courtroom assist in reaching policymakers and the media? Several of the judges who were state legislators in several of the different locations concluded that the mock courtroom did indeed capture their attention. Also, media representatives expressed the idea that one of the strengths of the mock courtroom was the ability to show multiple framings of the issue. However, several judges did note that one difficulty in relaying the results of forums is that groups who lobby are very focused on specific issues, and the public must be equally as focused to be heard. Further, they maintained that special interests do run government, unless the public gets really involved, and that it is always easier for legislators not to do something than to do something.

How can you make the media more interested in the courtroom debate? Several centers that televised their mock courtroom and were successful in having it aired over several public radio stations felt it had the potential to capture attention. However they agreed that working out a way to make it truly exciting to the viewing public would still take more time and creativity. Several of the media representatives felt the news angle still needed work, particularly suggesting that the forums themselves should be made more accessible to the media.

The researchers themselves concluded that as an event, the courtroom experience raised the interest of those present in deliberation and raised collective consciousness about the lack of deliberation in the public sphere. They concluded that the courtroom garnered political and media attention at a regional and state level. Yet they struggled with the question of effectiveness. Unresolved questions from representatives from the five centers included a question of whether using a courtroom's somewhat adversarial format conflicted with the idea of deliberation, which stresses reasoned judgment, not debate to win. The concern came from the fact that the deliberative forums stress looking at all sides of an issue, not focusing on the "win or lose" mentality that a courtroom represents. Although the researchers knew they were using the courtroom for dramatic effect, they still were concerned that it could misrepresent the deliberative nature of forums and instead give too simplistic an impression that the public either was following one advocate (public is ready) or the other (the public is not ready). Representatives from Kansas State (Mason-Imbody, 2009) noted that,

> Part of our goal is to communicate the results of public deliberations, and we find ourselves wanting to be positive in that "spin." So when an advocate argues that the public is not ready to act, even after having gone through a public deliberation, we worried about the impact of our overall message that deliberation was a positive, productive process. We also had concerns with

automatically connecting deliberation with action, which was inherent in how we framed our arguments (the public is ready to act vs. the public is not ready to act).

USING THE STAGES OF PUBLIC JUDGMENT: RESEARCH QUESTION TWO

Within these forums, one of the tasks of public deliberation is to help citizens get to more reflective opinions, or what Daniel Yankelovich (1991) called "public judgment." The path from just opinions to judgment may take a long time on any issue, for example, as long as a decade or more, and may be full of twists and turns (Kettering Foundation, 2007). However, once a public believes that something is happening, that could affect what they value; they may be able to move

> beyond wishful thinking and blaming others to face up to the course of actions or options that are available to them to solve the problem. A deliberative framework brings them face-to-face with unpleasant consequences, unwelcome costs, and tough trade-offs. Deliberation promotes weighing the options fairly and realistically... On any given issue, at any given point of time, citizens are at different points in the journey, and administrators who want to engage the public have to have a sense of where the public is and isn't. Trying to get people to face up to difficult trade-offs when they aren't really sure there is a problem is a mistake. (Kettering Foundation, 2007)

The ideas that guided the formation of research question two, in which citizens are making a decision on health care, were based in the work of Daniel Yankelovich (1991), discussed earlier in this chapter. For example, as Phil Stewart notes (2009), one of the reasons health care reform in 1993 did not succeed was because the public had not yet made the tough choices required. As this experiment began, the Obama administration had committed itself to major reform of our health care system with opinion polls suggesting that the public was ready to support this effort. However, as the debate itself eventually revealed, polls cannot always reflect whether citizens, indeed, have done the work of seriously weighing choices (Stewart, 2009).

Yankelovich (1991) notes that over a long period of time, the public may go in fits and starts through several stages of public opinion, and he describes seven possible stages within three overall orientations toward public issues. First, the public may only be engaging in *Consciousness Raising*, wherein they become aware of a problem (1. Dawning Awareness) and move toward a vague idea that something urgently needs to be fixed (2. Greater Urgency). When the public begins to focus on alternatives for solving the problems identified in a policy area, they may begin the process of *Working Through*, wherein they (3. Discover the Choices) and may first engage in (4. Wishful Thinking), wherin they do not deal with the difficult tradeoffs that must be made, until they begin (5. Weighing the Choices), wherein they look at the pros and cons of different alternatives, including dealing with feelings and ethical concerns. Finally, the public may come to *Resolution*, wherein they are ready to (6. Take a Stand Intellectually), grasping the consequences of their choices, or (7. Make a Responsible and Moral Choice), wherein they may accept inconsistencies and realities they do not like, but argue and act in defense of a greater good.

The researchers wanted to see how they could use the basic thinking of Yankelovich (1991) both to gauge where they thought the citizens were in the forums they facilitated and to have judges in the mock courtroom see if they felt the regional publics had really engaged the consequences of different alternatives. Although there were many nuances in the interpretation, the verdicts from the national courtroom and the regional ones maintained in general that citizen participants of recently held deliberative dialogue forums had not fully weighed the costs, consequences, and trade-offs of health care costs and were looking for more concrete policy options to evaluate (see Dudley, 2009; Giordano, 2010; Massachusetts Office of Dispute Resolution and Public Collaboration, 2010; Mason-Imbody, 2009). In terms of the stages of Yankelovich (1991), the citizens in these forums appear to be closer to Stage 4 (Wishful Thinking) on some dimensions and Stage 5 (Weighing the Choices) on others, according to the court deliberations and to audience opinions on questionnaires and in discussion.

None of the forums held by the centers were adjudged to have reached Resolution in Yankelovich's (1991) terms. The use of Yankelovich's specific seven stages was evaluated by the researchers at the center as too complex to convey to judges or the media in a short period. However the overall idea of Yankelovich of gauging where citizens are was still thought to be useful, but challenging. Foreshadowing the vitriolic debate that was yet to come in 2009–2010 on health care, the court in Massachusetts in 2009 gave excellent advice, which went unheeded (Massachusetts Office of Dispute Resolution and Public Collaboration, 2009):

> The court found that the forum participants reached common ground in their desire for access to quality, affordable health care for all, but the court raised concerns that once a policy is proposed issues will arise that may require the public to go back to working through the issues again. The court urged policymakers to take the process of health care reform slowly, to educate the public about how the reforms may be implemented, as the public is considered by the court to be in a relatively fragile state of judgment.

THE NEED FOR WORKING THROUGH

The findings from the regions were used by the regional advocates for a courtroom demonstration and were collated for two advocates in the role of "attorneys" who debated the questions in a mock courtroom demonstration in Washington, DC, for representatives from national nonprofits and other organizations. Results were combined in a final report distributed to policymakers and national administrators to inform them about the thinking of citizens on the issue. These results include questionnaire results from the participants, assessments of the forum moderators on the deliberation, and telephone interviews with forum moderators to better understand with what citizens are struggling. These evaluations of the judges, audiences, and researchers of the regional and national forum dovetail with the findings of the final report, *Public Thinking About Health Care: How Do We Pay for What We Need?* (Doble, Bosk, & DuPont, 2009), in which interpretation is made from more than a thousand Americans in National Issues Forums in 40 states and the District of Columbia. Researchers from Public Agenda analyzed a total of 1,095 postforum questionnaires filled out by forum participants. They conducted telephone interviews with moderators who led forums in 25 locations and conducted six research forums-focus groups, each with a demographically representative cross-section of up to a dozen people. The focus group sessions paralleled the other nationwide NIF forums in that participants viewed the starter video, deliberated together about the three choices, and filled out the postforum questionnaires.

The outcomes from these forums suggest that citizens see the issues surrounding health care costs with great personal urgency. The report notes that participants agreed that most important was the issue of cost, and health care should be available to all Americans, especially children. Many felt the whole system needed changing and endorsed wellness programs. Through analysis of the nuanced conversations, the researchers were able to demonstrate what values seem most in play: a concern for equality/fairness, for receiving more information, and for effectiveness/quality in health care.

The report (Doble et al., 2009) notes that, as forum participants deliberated, their comments illustrated some of the reasons why Americans think there is much wrong with our health care system and pointed to the changes and reforms Americans would like to see. At the same time, the forum results show how conflicted public thinking can be and suggest how much "working through" Americans need to do before reaching a stable, logically consistent public judgment about what a new health care system would involve.

In summary, the nationwide report (Doble et al., 2009) concludes that if the forums are any indication of the public's mood, the American people need two things in order to move the national dialogue forward: a clear set of policy choices with the trade-offs and pros and cons spelled out (including more information about health care in other countries); and the opportunity to deliberate about them. This is clearly an issue the people desperately want to address to define the common ground for decisive national and statewide actions that can deal with the rising cost of health care, according to this summary.[5]

The nationwide report was presented to both Congressional staff and to administrators at the Department of Health and Human Services. According to the presenters, the report was well-received and solicited questions about how citizens were thinking about health care. However there was no way to tell how the report may have influenced the ideas of those in the policy process.

One of the unique contributions of public deliberation could be to provide insights that policymakers need into "where the public is" on an issue. As Phil Stewart (2009) maintains, "If, as is often the case, public deliberation shows that the public is working on but has not yet fully resolved tough choices, as appears to be the case today respecting health-care reform, knowing this, policymakers can either delay action or act in ways that encourage and stimulate public thinking and deliberation."

REFLECTIONS ON THE COURTHOUSE EXPERIMENT

One conclusion from the experiment is that in forums, participants may gain a sense of their views, others' views, and how their own perspective relates to a range of values and opinions. The trade-offs participants are willing to make or the areas in which they believe they cannot compromise help reveal to them the parameters of their own beliefs and may lead them to public judgment, a new perspective that would be similar to a co-authoring among participants (Hamilton & Wills-Toker, 2006). In this sense, paying attention to words and the ideas in the forum makes us realize that the deliberation becomes a process of collaboratively generating meaning (Hamilton & Wills-Toker, 2006).

Although forum discourse often consists of many different views, in my experience as a moderator of over 30 forums and in agreement with Phillip Stewart (2005), deliberative dialogue rarely becomes acrimonious. There may be sharp disagreements, but the process leads to substantive and thoughtful discussion, as revealed here. Yet an important revelation is that the generation of meaning is messy, iterative, and that forum discussions may be only the beginning for most participants in forming their new meanings. Rather than always an immediate solidification of views, forums may be a beginning for further thinking, attention to the issues, and questioning of positions. The forums themselves may provide the public space in which citizens reach consensus on a particular frame, or the result may be a continuing discussion, a decision to engage other actions, or a seeking of other venues on the same topic.

As to research questions posed in this experiment, the researchers concluded for Question One that indeed the courtroom had captured state and regional legislators' attention, opened the way for relationships between the Civic Learning Centers and legislative offices, and helped gain media attention (and perhaps indirectly legislative attention) for citizen forums. However the difficulty of presenting the nuanced understanding of citizens in a political world of "yes or no" on specific policy issues still remains. For research Question Two, the researchers concluded that the public was still in the process of working through the issues, and that if legislators understood better where the public is in the process of reaching public judgment on issues, they could perhaps modify their approaches. In this case, citizens were not ready for the national "town halls," but instead would have benefited from more time to discuss the issues. In the final analysis, perhaps the most important lesson learned, according to Stewart (2009), was that

> "Where the public is" on an issue cannot be determined analytically or scientifically. It is, rather, a matter of judgment. Public thinking is far too nuanced, much too complex. Indeed, what might be most attractive and valuable to the media and policy community is demonstrating nuance and complexity in a compelling way.

As the reporting on the forums was taking place, events surrounding health care revealed that never had the need for reasoning, deliberating citizens become as apparent as in the health care cost debate. The town halls held across the country by members of Congress in their districts without a deliberative format did become acrimonious. In those town halls and in other demonstrations throughout the last 2 years, violence and uncivil dialogue escalated in our political debate. These events confirm our need to create situations in which citizens can thoughtfully deliberate and explore how to get informed citizen deliberations to the attention of policymakers at all levels of government. The importance of this need is accentuated in an opinion piece written by David Proctor and Erika Mason-Imbody (2009) after the Kansas State forums:

> We have found that it is possible to have conversations where every voice is heard, where emotions don't have to be checked at the door, and where elected officials agree to listen and then respond to what they are hearing. We invite you to join us in creating a stronger democracy. There is no better time for all of us to raise our voices and actions in support of what our democracy

can be. Not only is meaningful health care reform at stake, but the health of our democracy is as well. (Appendix)

NOTES

1. This chapter reports on the efforts of a group of researchers working in five different regional centers under the overall able leadership of Alice Diebel and Philip Stewart of the Kettering Foundation (www.kettering. org). Thanks to them and to the following researchers for allowing me to cite portions of their work in this report: Erika Imbody, Kansas State University; Lorraine Dellaport and Courtney Breese, University of Massachusetts; Eric Giordano, University of Wisconsin System; and Bill Corbett, the Center for Voter Deliberation, Northern Virginia. However, any errors or misunderstandings in the interpretation of the experiment are wholly mine and do not reflect the judgment of the Kettering Foundation or any of the researchers. Parts of this chapter were presented at the International Conference on Public Administration, Chengdu, China, and at the Southeastern Conference on Public Administration, Wilmington, N.C., 2010.

2. At least two forums of approximately 2 hours each from each of the regions were both transcribed and videotaped. Two of the transcripts from four of the centers—Virginia Tech, Kansas State, University of Wisconsin system, and University of Massachusetts—were loaded into NVivo 8 and analyzed by two different researchers at Virginia Tech to reveal with what themes citizens were struggling. Many other elements of the forums can be explored. These forums will be used along with others in future work to examine reasoned explanations, the sources participants used to buttress their arguments, their level of engagement with each other's statements, and how equal participation was.

3. The Northern Virginia Center used a different format and thus is not included in these findings.

4. Judges included a Democratic and Republican representative and a senator of the General Assembly in Virginia; a state supreme court justice, state legislator, and division medical director in Wisconsin; a state senator, health policy director, and vice president of health institute in Kansas; and a state legislator, a chief of surgery, and former federal employee and author in Massachusetts. Each also involved representatives of the media as judges or affiliates. Judges were selected by each Center for Civic Life with each trying for diversity in perspectives of the judges.

5. The report, with its carefully crafted conclusions, was released to the United States Congress in June 2009. A special session with representatives from the offices of members of Congress and another with members of the Department of Health and Human Services received very positive feedback. This then is another step in taking the results of citizens' forums and trying to get them into the mainstream of policy dialogues.

REFERENCES

Alter, J., & Patterson, J. (2006). Using a crystal ball instead of a rear-view mirror: Helping state legislators assess the future impacts of major federal legislation. *New Directions for Evaluation, 112,* 79–88.

Bourdeaux, C. (2008) Integrating performance information into legislative budget process. *Public Performance & Management Review, 31*(4), 547–569.

Buckler, S. (2007). Theory, ideology, rhetoric: Ideas in politics and the case of "community" in recent political discourse. *British Journal of Politics & International Relations, 9*(1), 36–54.

Canfield-Davis, K., Jain, S., Wattam, D., McMurtry, J., & Johnson, M. (2010). Factors of influence on legislative decision making: A descriptive study-update August 2009. *Journal of Legal, Ethical and Regulatory Issues, 13*(2), 55–69.

Delli Carpini, M., Cook, F. L., & Jacobs, L. R. (2004). Public deliberation, discursive participation, and citizen engagement: A review of the empirical literature. *Annual Review of Political Science, 7*(1), 315–344.

Demortain, D. (2004). Public organizations, stakeholders and the construction of publicness: Claims and defense of authority in public action. *Public Administration, 82*(4), 975–992.

Doble, J., Bosk, J., & DuPont, S. (2009). *Public thinking about health care: How do we pay for what we need?* Outcomes of the 2008 National Agenda Forums—A Public Agenda Report. Dayton, OH: Kettering Foundation.

Doble Research Associates. (1996) *The story of NIF: The effects of deliberation.* Dayton, OH: Kettering Foundation.

Dryzek, J. S. (2000). *Deliberative democracy and beyond: Liberals, critics, contestations.* New York, NY: Oxford University Press.

Dudley, L. (with Dulaney, E., & Herbst, D.) (2009, June 28). *Report to Kettering on local jury experiment from Virginia Tech.* Unpublished report, Kettering Foundation.

Fiorina, M. P., & Samuel, J. A. (2009). *Disconnect: The breakdown of representation in American politics.* Norman: University of Oklahoma.

Fiorina, M. P., Samuel, J. A., & Jeremy, C. P. (2006). *Culture wars? The myth of polarized America* (2nd ed.). New York, NY: Pearson Longman.

Giordano, E. (2010, February 26). *Coming to judgment on health care: An experiment in public deliberation: A report to the Kettering Foundation.* Unpublished report Kettering Foundation. Wisconsin Institute for Public Policy and Service.

Gutmann, A., & Thompson, D. (1996). *Democracy and disagreement.* Cambridge, MA: Belknap Press of Harvard University Press.

Hamilton, J. D., & Wills-Toker, C. (2006). Reconceptualizing dialogue in environmental public participation. *Policy Studies Journal, 34*(4), 755.

Handley, D. M., & Howell-Moroney, M. (2010). Ordering stakeholder relationships and citizen participation: Evidence from the community development block grant program. *Public Administration Review, 70*(4), 601–701.

Hauser, G. A. (2004). Introduction. In G. A. Hauser & A. Grimed (Eds.), *Rhetorical democracy: Discursive papers of selected engagement* (pp. 1–14). Mahwah, NJ: Lawrence Erlbaum.

Hird, J. (2005). *Power, knowledge, and politics: Policy analysis in the states.* Washington, DC: Georgetown University Press.

Jerit, J. (2008). Issue framing and engagement: Rhetorical strategy in public policy debates. *Political Behavior, 30*(1), 1–24.

Kettering Foundation. (2007, January) *Public administrators and citizens: What should the relationship be?* A Kettering Foundation report working draft.

Koontz, T. M. (1999) Citizen participation: Conflicting interests in state and national agency policy making. *Social Science Journal, 36*(3), 441–458.

Liu, X., Lindquist, E., Vedlitz, A., & Vincent, K. (2010). Understanding local policymaking: Policy elites' perceptions of local agenda setting and alternative policy selection. *The Policy Studies Journal, 38*(1), 69–91.

Mansbridge, J. J. (1983). *Beyond adversarial democracy.* Chicago, IL: University of Chicago Press.

March, J. G. (1987). Ambiguity and accounting: The elusive link between information and decision making. *Accounting, Organizations and Society, 12*(2), 153–168.

Massachusetts Office of Dispute Resolution and Public Collaboration. (2010). *Stages of judgment citizen court experiment report.* Unpublished report. Boston: University of Massachusetts, Kettering Foundation.

Mathews, D. (1999). *Politics for people: Finding a responsible public voice* (2nd ed.). Urbana: University of Illinois Press.

Mathews, D. (2010). *Foreword. Higher education exchange.* Dayton, OH: Kettering Foundation.

Mathews, D., & McAfee, N. (2003). *Making choices together: The power of public deliberation.* Dayton, OH: Kettering Foundation.

Mason-Imbody, E. (2009, October 16). *Coming to public judgment.* Institute for Civic Discourse and Democracy, Kansas State University. Unpublished report, Kettering Foundation.

Mooney, C. (1991). Information sources in state legislative decision making. *Legislative Studies Quarterly, 16*(3), 445–455.

Putnam, L., & Holmer, M. (1992). Framing, reframing and issue development. In L. Putnam & M. Roloff (Eds.), *Communication and negotiation.* London, England: Sage.

Procter, D. E., & Mason-Imbody, E. (2009, October 16). After national town halls [Guest column]. In E. Mason-Imbody, (Ed.), *Coming to public judgment* (Appendix). Institute for Civic Discourse and Democracy, Kansas State University. Unpublished report, Kettering Foundation.

Shulock, N. (1999). The paradox of policy analysis: If it is not used, why do we produce so much of it? *Journal of Policy Analysis and Management, 18*(2), 226–245.

Stewart, P. D. (2005). *Connecting the deliberative public to its elected representatives.* Research report on *A Public Voice.* Atlanta, GA: Kettering Foundation.

Stewart, P. D. (2009). Experiments in communicating the results of public deliberation. *Kettering Foundation.* Retrieved from www.kettering.org

Tuler, S. (2000). Forms of talk in policy dialogue: Distinguishing between adversarial and collaborative discourse. *Journal of Risk Research, 3*(1),1–17.

Weiss, C. H. (1993). Where politics and evaluation research meet. *Evaluation Practice, 14*(1), 93–106.

Yankelovich, D. (1991). *Coming to public judgment: Making democracy work in a complex world.* Syracuse, NY: Syracuse University Press.

CHAPTER 12

THE BENSON-AMES ALLIANCE

An Exercise in Urban Planning

Alan Kopetzky

INTRODUCTION

Civic engagement efforts have a long and uneven history in Omaha, Nebraska. Sometimes civic engagement has meant informing the public about a decision that has already been made. In other situations, the leaders of a project may be required to seek advice and input from citizens before implementing a plan of action. Many people are very cynical about the value of civic engagement activities, because it is rare when recommendations provided by the public are actually used in the program planning, development, and implementation of a project.

In the past, civic engagement usually meant voting in elections, running for public office, volunteering for a candidate running for public office, or serving as an appointee to an advisory board or special commission. In the 21st century, civic engagement is going through a period of transition. Two areas that have seen great change in civic engagement activities are the program planning and development process and the process of implement-

The State of Citizen Participation in America, pages 283–308
Copyright © 2012 by Information Age Publishing

ing public programs. Previously, civic engagement often meant a simple public hearing, in which information about a program was provided and a few questions were answered. Today civic engagement has become a major element in program planning and development. In the past, implementation meant that the government was going to do it! Now, many different organizations are often required to come together to plan and accomplish program implementation.

Among the reasons for increased civic engagement in program planning, development, and implementation processes is project complexity. Public programs and projects are larger, more complicated, and require more financing than ever before to address complex issues. This complexity makes it quite difficult for a single organization, acting alone, to fully address all the nuances of a particular project. Shorter time frames for project completion and implementation also demand a collaborative approach.

Among the trends in civic engagement is the growing number of community partnerships forming to address complicated issues. The originators for many of these partnerships mandate civic engagement and call for all stakeholders to be involved in the planning process. Often civic engagement activities are linked to funding. Public interest has increased in the local environment, because citizens feel like they can exert some level of control over local projects in order to maintain quality of life in their neighborhoods.

THE INDEX AND THE MATRIX

To evaluate civic engagement, this author developed the Index of Citizen Participation with five criteria that are significant indicators of the level of civic engagement in a project. (Note: For purposes of this case study, "citizen participation" will be used interchangeably with "civic engagement.") The Index arose from a series of interviews completed in the fall of 2008 with participants involved in the Benson-Ames Alliance project, including committee members, consultants, academics, and advisory personnel. The five criteria of the Index of Citizen Participation were the interviewee's most frequently mentioned traits for successful civic engagement.

1. The *number of citizens* participating in the project.
2. The *demographic representation* determines that the participants in a civic engagement effort adequately reflect the composition of the pool of stakeholders.
3. The *duration of the civic engagement* refers to its ongoing nature. Is civic engagement merely a single event or is it ongoing throughout a project?

4. The *variety of forums for participation* addresses the actual types and number of activities in the process. For a simple project, one type of activity may suffice. For a complex project, civic engagement activities may need to include focus groups, surveys, public meetings, presentations, and numerous other events.
5. The *use of the citizen input in the decision-making process* addresses the impact of the civic engagement efforts.

The Index of Citizen Participation is situational, meaning it has no set high, medium, and low levels of participation. The adequacy of the civic engagement effort is evaluated in relation to the type, complexity, and size of the project. Organizing a tree planting effort may require one or two public meetings to rally volunteers, whereas planning a new medical program for the elderly will require many different forums of participation over a long period of time.

This author has also developed a matrix for quick progress checks of the adequacy of civic engagement, using the two most important and frequently mentioned elements by interviewees (see Figure 12.1). The personal interviews consistently confirmed that representation by all stakeholders is paramount in planning civic engagement activities. Over 75% of those interviewed indicated the importance of involving enough of the right people in the civic engagement process. Over 70% of those interviewed indicated the crucial need to use citizen input in the decision-making process.

As the matrix in Figure 12.1 shows, Quadrant I represents the ideal situation of Full Citizen Participation with maximum stakeholder representation and good usage of citizen input in the decision-making process. All three of the other quadrants have significant problem areas.

Quadrant II, False Citizen Participation, reflects maximum stakeholder representation, but little citizen input used in the decision-making process.

	Input Used in Decision Making	Input Not Used in Decision Making
Stakeholders Well Represented	**Quadrant I** Full Citizen Participation	**Quadrant II** False Citizen Participation
Stakeholders Poorly Represented	**Quadrant III** Skewed Citizen Participation	**Quadrant IV** Non Participation

Figure 12.1 Matrix of citizen participation.

A situation falling into this quadrant would not demonstrate real civic engagement but merely an exercise in informing the public about a project.

Quadrant III, Skewed Citizen Participation, is a situation in which the information provided by stakeholders is actually used in the decision-making process, even though all groups of stakeholders are poorly represented. This is problematic, because it is difficult to determine if a project is actually meeting the needs of the public or merely meeting the needs of small special-interest groups.

Quadrant IV, Nonparticipation, would involve poor stakeholder representation and little or no use of citizen input in the decision-making process. This is the least desirable quadrant.

THE CITY OF OMAHA

Omaha is a city in eastern Nebraska, located on the Missouri River in the very center of the United States. The population of the greater Omaha metropolitan area, which includes parts of neighboring Iowa, is 838,856, with 525,044 people in Omaha proper and 315,812 in smaller cities and towns in the greater metropolitan area. The overall metro area has grown 9.4% in the past nine years. Additional growth of 2.3% is forecast by the year 2014 (www.uscensus2010.gov).

The ethnic makeup of the city is 75% White, 12.4% African American, 11% Hispanic, 1.4% Asian, 0.2% Native American, and 21.4% of the population is under the age of 20. Approximately 34.2% of the population is between the ages of 20 and 44, some 25.2% of the population is between the ages of 45 and 64. Overall, 11.2% of the residents are ages 65 or older (www.uscensus2010.gov).

The average household income is $67,576 per year. Median income is $59,130 per year, and per capita income is $26,013 per year. A total of 17.1% of the population earns less than $25,000 per year; 25.5% earn between $25,000 and $50,000. As much as 36.1% have earnings in the $50,000 to $100,000 per year range, and the remaining 22% have earnings in excess of $100,000 per year (www.uscensus2010.gov).

The quality of life is considered high in the Omaha Metro area. The cost of consumer goods and services and the cost of housing are below the national averages, with a wide selection of affordable housing. The number of high school graduates and college graduates from the area is above the national average. Omaha is home to several world-class medical facilities, as well as excellent cultural and recreational activities (www.cityofomaha.org).

Omaha is the headquarters of five Fortune 500 companies: Berkshire Hathaway, Union Pacific Railroad, ConAgra Foods, Peter Kiewit and Sons Inc., and Mutual of Omaha. The largest industry in the city is financial services, which includes the headquarters of TD Ameritrade and First National Bank of Omaha, the largest privately held bank in the country (www.cityofomaha.org).

Due to the presence of STRATCOMM military operations, the United States Weather Service, and the 55th Wing of the United States Air Force, defense-related industries are a crucial element of Omaha's economy. Transportation and manufacturing is also important, because of Omaha's central location, low energy costs, and excellent infrastructure. Agri-business is the principal form of manufacturing. Finally, the area has a large number of information technology enterprises (www.cityofomaha.org).

A HYBRID PLAN

Community development through coordinated urban planning is new to Omaha. The Omaha plan is a hybrid of the community development projects in Minneapolis, Minnesota, and Seattle, Washington. The Minneapolis Neighborhood Revitalization Program (NRP) started in 2002. The goal of the Minneapolis program is to develop neighborhood organizations to complete long-range neighborhood plans for revitalization with particular emphasis on developing adequate, low-cost housing for the poor and minorities. Forming partnerships is a key element in accomplishing this goal, because available government funding for the project is approximately $400 million, while the estimated project cost is over $2 billion (www.nrp.org).

The Minneapolis NRP uses a six-step process:

1. The neighborhood organization negotiates a participation agreement with the City of Minneapolis and selects a Steering Committee.
2. The Steering Committee creates a diverse civic engagement effort and gathers information.
3. The Steering Committee develops a draft plan.
4. Local citizens review the draft plan and provide feedback.
5. After modifications, the Steering Committee submits the plan to the necessary government agencies for approval.
6. The Steering Committee implements the plan. (www.nrp.org)

The Seattle Department of Neighborhoods is a city agency that manages an extensive set of programs administered through the Office of the Mayor.

The Department of Neighborhoods strives to bring government closer to the residents of Seattle by engaging them in civic participation; helping them to become empowered to make positive contributions to their communities; and by involving more of Seattle's underrepresented residents, including communities of color and immigrants, in civic discourse, processes, and opportunities. (www.scattle.gov)

In 1994, the Mayor's office introduced the "Involving all Neighbors" program to encourage civic engagement in addressing neighborhood issues. The city introduced the idea of "community connectors"—people who enjoy a challenge, who believe everyone can make a contribution, and who can build relationships within neighborhoods and communities (www. seattle.gov).

Omaha is in the beginning stages of expanding civic engagement as an important feature in urban development. The urban development project is part of an ongoing effort called Omaha by Design, an initiative of the Omaha Community Foundation. The Omaha Community Foundation is an organization looking for ways to develop a positive image for the City of Omaha and to improve the quality of life. The new program planning and development process closely resembles the NRP model in Minneapolis, but relies heavily on community connectors like those found in Seattle's program. The community connectors are necessary conduits to build essential relationships in the project areas (www.livelyomaha.org).

OMAHA BY DESIGN

The Omaha by Design comprehensive urban planning process was developed in conjunction with consultant Jonathan Barnett from Wallace, Roberts, and Todd. Mr. Barnett proposed a unique three-prong set of guidelines—Green Omaha, Civic Omaha, and Neighborhood Omaha— corresponding to three constituencies in the urban design process—environmentalists, civic and cultural organizations, and neighborhood activists. Green Omaha is concerned with issues such as flood control, park planning, tree planting, and general neighborhood beautification. Civic Omaha addresses the economic development of downtown Omaha and the conversion of business nodes on the main thoroughfares into full-fledged downtown areas. Neighborhood Omaha uses participative processes to develop urban neighborhood plans for each neighborhood in Omaha (Barnett, 2005, pp. 96–98).

Mr. Barnett did not propose anything that had not been tried successfully elsewhere in the country. The unique feature of the Omaha by Design process was the combination of activities involved. What evolved was an unusually ambitious, yet workable plan using the three previously mentioned elements (Barnett, 2005, pp. 93–97).

The City Planning Department divided the City of Omaha into 15 large neighborhoods, each containing 25,000 to 40,000 residents (www.ci.omaha.

ne.us). Each neighborhood will use a community collaborative process to develop a subarea plan that will become part of the City of Omaha's master plan for urban development. The City Planning Department, through the Office of the Mayor, will review the individual plans and negotiate any necessary modifications. The Planning Department will then submit the finished product to the Omaha City Council for approval.

Specific outcomes of the process include the formation of alliances between neighborhood associations and other government, public, and private organizations in the area. The ultimate objective of the collaboration is to implement the neighborhood development plan and bring it to completion. This is a long-term goal, taking up to 25 years to complete (www.bensonnebraska.com).

THE ORGANIZING AND STEERING COMMITTEES

The Benson-Ames Alliance Project began in early 2005 with the formation of an Organizing Committee brought together by Omaha by Design. The Organizing Committee consisted of a wide variety of people from the neighborhood, city government, local business, and the academic community. Omaha by Design worked diligently to make the committee as representative of the area as possible. To stimulate interest, Omaha by Design chose co-chairmen with excellent credentials—the Head of the City Planning Department and a former UNO Chancellor with a long history of community service (http://www.benson-ames.org/Background).

The Organizing Committee established goals, assessed data needs, and determined time frames for action. The overall goal of the Organizing Committee was to supervise creation of a subarea plan for the Benson-Ames portion of the city. The subarea plan is a long-term and comprehensive plan for an area's urban development, addressing numerous issues from economic development and housing needs to neighborhood beautification.

Developing the subarea plan required substantial participation from the area's residents, creating the need for extensive civic engagement. Another goal for the Organizing Committee was insuring that citizen input was identifiably present in the finished plan. The Organizing Committee developed a civic engagement strategy to guarantee substantial input from residents of the neighborhood.

The next goal of the Organizing Committee was the formation of an alliance consisting of all interested parties in the neighborhood, including local businessmen, neighborhood activists, civic leaders, area educators, religious leaders, environmentalists, and area residents. The Organizing Committee's work ended when the plan was approved, and the Steering Committee began the implementation process. The Steering Committee acted as a clearinghouse for all activities related to the realization of the subarea plan. To provide continuity, several members of the Organizing Committee joined the Steering Committee.

THE BENSON-AMES ALLIANCE

The City of Omaha determined the boundaries for the Benson-Ames Alliance area as part of the overall planning process. The boundaries are Sorenson Parkway on the north side, Fontenelle Boulevard on the east side, Western Avenue on the south side, and 72nd Street on the west side (see Figure 12.2).

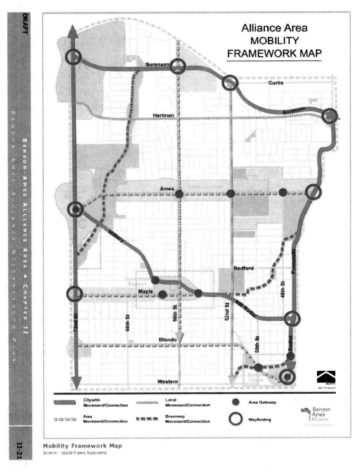

Figure 12.2 Mobility framework map. *Source:* Gould Evans Associates. Used with permission from Omaha by Design.

To develop the plan, the Organizing Committee hired Gould Evans Associates, LLC of Kansas City, Missouri, as the primary consulting firm. Two Omaha-based firms assisted Gould Evans: the Robert Peters Company and Ehrhart, Griffin and Associates (http://www.benson-ames.org).

The civic engagement process began in the summer of 2005 with a series of three focus groups conducted to obtain preliminary information about the strengths and concerns of the area's residents and to analyze the area's neighborhood association activity level.

The Benson-Ames area has eight active neighborhood associations with a total membership of approximately 1,000 people. All eight organizations participate in the Neighborhood Clean-Up Program. Most neighborhoods have already organized or are in the process of organizing neighborhood patrols. The Benson Association has had a neighborhood patrol for many years and was part of the founding effort with the Omaha Coalition of City Patrols. Many of the organizations have engaged in advocacy activities in conjunction with City Hall. For instance, the Hartman Avenue Association has attended Omaha City Council meetings and actively lobbied for change. They have seen a problematic apartment complex turned into a retirement center and have kept a developer out of the area who wanted to build a community of duplexes.

DEMOGRAPHIC REPRESENTATION

Researchers at the University of Nebraska at Omaha College of Public Affairs and Community Service (UNO CPACS) compiled an overview of the Benson-Ames Alliance area using data from the 2000 U.S. Census. The total population of the area is 36,875, composed of 15,543 households with an average of 2.37 persons per household. Males make up 47.5% (17,524) of the population, females are 52.5% (19,351) of the residents, and children under the age of 18 are 27.8% (10,247) of the residents. Adults between the ages of 18 and 64 are 60.6% (22,345) of the residents, and adults 65 and over are 11.6% (4,283) of the residents.

In terms of ethnicity, the residents in the Benson-Ames Alliance area are 67.5% (24,876) Caucasian, 26.4% (9,509) African American, 3.2% (1,195) Latino, 1.1% (402) Asian, and 0.6% (229) Native American. When compared to Omaha as a whole, the Benson-Ames Alliance area has twice as many African Americans and only half the average Latino population. Among the 15,543 households in the Benson-Ames Alliance area, 67.0% (9,925) are owner occupied, which is 7.4% greater than the rate of home ownership in Omaha as a whole. The remaining 33.0% (4,894) are rental properties, with 724 vacant houses in the area (U.S. Census, 2000).

RESIDENT SURVEY

The next step in the process was the Benson Residents Survey (BRS). Professional surveyors from the MSN Group conducted telephone interviews late in 2005, surveying a random sample of approximately 400 area residents. Principal topics included the residents' outlook for the neighborhood, positive and negative features, major issues that the alliance should address, and an evaluation of neighborhood services (Benson Residents Survey, 2005, p. 5).

Those surveyed had a largely positive view of their specific neighborhood: 75% of the respondents viewed their neighborhood as an ideal place to live and had no plans to move, while 86% of survey participants believed they were safe in their neighborhood (Benson Residents Survey, 2005, pp. 7–11).

Approximately half of all respondents believed their neighborhood would be changing in the next 5 years. One third of the respondents believed that the neighborhood would go downhill with a concurrent decline in the housing stock. Only 11% believed the neighborhood would improve (Benson Residents Survey, 2005, pp. 11–13).

When asked to identify the best thing about the Benson-Ames Alliance area, 33% of the respondents said it was the neighborhoods and the people, 31% stated that it was Benson-specific characteristics, and 27% stated it was the geographic location.

One third of those surveyed viewed crime and violence as the worst feature of the area and the most important issue to address. No specific type of criminal activity was identified. Respondents saw this as an issue occurring evenly throughout the area.

Alliance residents were very satisfied with fire service, police service, educational facilities, and health care in the area. The condition of streets, sidewalks, and trails, and the lack of entertainment options caused the most dissatisfaction (Benson Residents Survey, pp. 23–24).

THE BUSINESS SUMMARY

The UNO Center for Public Administration Research (CPAR) compiled a report about the 807 businesses in the Benson-Ames Alliance area. Businesses fall into the following categories:

- *23.4% Service industries:* churches, barber and beauty shops, auto body shops, and household goods repair shops.
- *17.6% Retail trade:* car dealerships, gas stations, automotive parts stores, pharmacies, antique shops, sporting goods, and miscellaneous stores.

- *13.4% Health care and social assistance:* doctor's offices, daycare centers, counseling centers, dentists, and other health care providers.
- *6.1% Food service:* fast food restaurants, 15 full service restaurants, bars (CPAR, 2005).
- *2.9% Financial institutions:* banks, financial service businesses
- *36.6% Other*

THE 2005 OMAHA NEIGHBORHOOD SCAN

As part of the Omaha Neighborhood Scan, students evaluated 625 properties in the Benson-Ames Alliance area in the fall of 2005. The students used automated scanners to record the data for storage and processing. The purpose of this inventory was to determine the rehabilitation needs of structures in the area, identify geographical differences in the neighborhood, and to estimate the overall costs of renewal (Omaha Neighborhood Scan, 2005, p. 6).

The scan found major code violations in 51.4% of the properties, most of them safety issues. The largest problem found in 25.0% of the properties was the lack of handrails and guardrails on homes or homes with improper or unsafe rails. Sidewalk and driveway repairs were required in 80 homes. Two other areas of concern included the 75 homes with inoperable motor vehicles parked on the lawn or sitting idly on the street and 42 homes with excessive weeds (Omaha Neighborhood Scan, 2005, p. 7).

THE VISIONING PROCESS

In February 2006, Gould Evans conducted a series of public meetings. They led participants through a "visioning process," in which they brainstormed about the positive and negative aspects of living in the Benson-Ames neighborhood. After identifying issues, they discussed how the positive aspects could be enhanced and the negative aspects eliminated. Finally, participants voted to prioritize the various solutions they had developed to make the Benson-Ames area a better place to live.

Participants identified many positive aspects of the area, citing the historic nature and the "small town in the big city" atmosphere most frequently. Participants mentioned that the neighborhood was filled with good starter homes with a wide variety of housing styles. Several brought up the beautiful established trees and the landscaped medians along some of the roads. Many residents appreciated the convenience of the area, noting that one can drive anywhere in Omaha in about 20 minutes. Participants commented favorably about many other positive attributes of the area, including the beautiful library, good schools, fine churches, green parks, excellent medical services, the strong police presence, and the number of civic organizations.

The participants identified many negative aspects of the area, including poor crosswalks, unkempt rental properties, congested intersections, storm sewers that overflowed into roadways, and inadequate parking. One attendee noted that the Northwest Radial Highway had fewer ruts 60 years ago as a dirt road than it does today as a major thoroughfare. Another woman complained of "too many loose dogs with attitude" running in her neighborhood. Lastly, one participant stated that she did not like the solution to the parking problem on her street. Apparently her neighbors were paving their front yards to have adequate parking and then painting the concrete green to resemble grass. She was not fooled by the green paint and thought it was quite unattractive!

In addition to the conducting public meetings and conferencing with the Organizing Committee, the Gould Evans consultants made an extensive tour of the neighborhood and met with several community groups.

THE MAY 2006 OPEN HOUSE SURVEY

The Gould Evans consultants returned to Omaha in May 2006 and held a large open house at the local high school, where they shared preliminary plans for improving the Benson-Ames Alliance area. The plan targeted four areas of the neighborhood and addressed issues of housing, economic development, public safety, recreation, and aesthetics. Attendees evaluated the plans, questioned the consultants, and provided feedback by written survey.

The consultants presented three possible development frameworks. The first framework, the *Traditional Retail Approach*, addressed retail development on the area's main streets. The second framework, the *City Plan Approach*, used nodes of development for revitalizing the proposal area. A node is a multipurpose development meant to serve a specific geographic location. The third framework, the *Regional Community Approach*, concentrated primarily on overall neighborhood development. Open house participants chose the City Plan Approach (Benson-Ames Open House Survey, 2006).

Next, the consultants presented ideas about linking the Benson-Ames area internally and linking the area to the rest of Omaha. Finally, the consultants presented plans to convert underutilized spaces to multipurpose spaces. Attendees were excited about the linkage and space usage plans. In addition to the open house, the consultants made presentations to various community groups and gathered feedback regarding the preliminary plan. They used the feedback to refine the plan and make their final recommendations (Benson-Ames Open House Survey, 2006).

THE FINAL RECOMMENDATIONS

In August 2006, the consultants hosted a second open house and presented highlights of the final plan. They distributed printed and CD-ROM copies of the final recommendations to all attendees. In August and September of 2006, the City Planning Commission reviewed the plan and made recommendations for clarifications and adjustments. At their October 2006 meeting, the Omaha City Council approved the Benson-Ames Alliance Sub-Area Plan and made it part of the master plan for the City of Omaha.

As their final task, the Organizing Committee established a permanent Steering Committee with a chair, vice-chair, and five subcommittees: Business Affairs, Finance/Development, Marketing/Public Relations, Neighborhood Affairs, and a Nominating Committee (http://www.benson-ames.org).

While the project is ongoing, the Steering Committee meets bimonthly. Subcommittees meet on the alternate months. Currently, the Steering Committee is managing a landscaping project to make streets more attractive, an analysis of retail and housing needs, and a community-branding project to determine how to market the area's attractions. In the northwestern section of the neighborhood, they have just begun the Cole Creek Storm Water Demonstration Project. This will be a model project for how to address storm water flooding issues in neighborhoods all over Omaha (http://www.benson-ames.org).

THE BENSON-AMES ALLIANCE PLAN

Diversity is the most important and unique feature of the Benson-Ames neighborhood, with diversity of population, economic conditions, physical environment, and development. This rich combination of attributes is enhanced by the presence of a large number of community resources, like stores, educational facilities, and houses of worship (Benson-Ames Alliance, 2006, sec. II, p. 3).

The plan's vision for the Benson-Ames area provides sustainable commercial centers with safe, attractive linkages between them. The vision makes heavy use of the idea that Benson-Ames has a small-town feel in the big city. The plan recommends physical changes to "foster unique communities within a larger community" (Benson-Ames Alliance, 2006, sec. II, pp. 3–4).

The plan features six objectives:

1. To support the consolidation of existing commercial strip mall development into mixed-use commercial, residential, and public space community destinations.

2. To create unique, identifiable community centers that will enhance the special character of the neighborhood.
3. To encourage smart, sustainable development and urban forms and patterns that increase the quality of life in the Benson-Ames area.
4. To promote development patterns that encourage walking and a vibrant street life in the neighborhood.
5. To improve the connecting routes and circulation patterns to facilitate the smooth flow of multimodal traffic throughout the area.
6. To encourage diversified residential development with an emphasis on alternative forms of housing, including townhomes, condominiums, patio homes, and multiple-unit residences (Benson-Ames Alliance, 2006, sec. II, pp. 4–6).

MIXED-USE SPACES

The first objective addresses the effective use of land in the Benson-Ames Alliance area. The principal recommendation suggests the creation of nine areas of development or "centers." The plan uses International Council for Shopping Center (ICSC) standards as guidelines for the development of two convenience centers, three neighborhood centers, and four community centers (see Figure 12.3) (Benson-Ames Alliance, 2006, sec. II, pp. 9–11).

A *convenience center* is a small commercial area that provides commercial services only. Typical facilities in a convenience center include convenience stores, gas stations, small retail spaces, and offices. The ICSC guidelines encourage convenience centers near high-density residential structures. Convenience centers should complement rather than compete with community centers and neighborhood centers. The coverage area of a convenience center should be less than 10 acres. Centers should be at least one mile apart (Benson-Ames Alliance, 2006, sec. II, p. 12).

A *neighborhood center* is larger than a convenience center and contains mixed-use facilities, like retail and service space of less than 3,000 square feet per establishment, religious institutions of less than five acres, a neighborhood school, and possibly a small-scale park and community center. The surrounding area supports the neighborhood center with medium-density residential property, including single-family dwellings, apartments, and townhomes. Neighborhood centers should not exceed 30 acres. Buildings should be no higher than three stories. Centers should be no closer than two miles apart (Benson-Ames Alliance, 2006, sec. II, pp. 12–13).

A *community center* is a general shopping area with many types of businesses, including large (over 40,000 square feet) retail spaces, grocery stores, medical and educational facilities, major auto service centers, restaurants, and large-scale civic and cultural institutions. These areas should contain

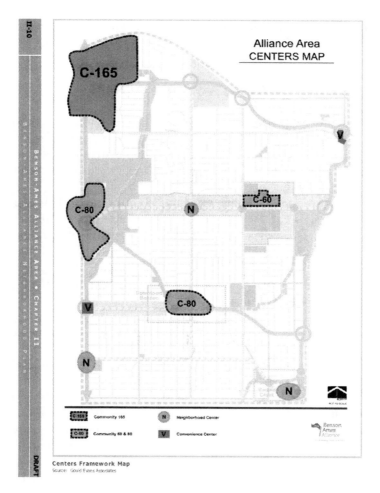

Centers Framework Map
Source: Gould Evans Associates

Figure 12.3 Centers framework map. *Source:* Gould Evans Associates. Used with permission from Omaha by Design.

a mixture of residential structures featuring large, high-density, multi-unit housing. The size of a community center should be no larger than 165 acres. Units should not exceed six stories in height. Centers should be at least five miles apart (Benson-Ames Alliance, 2006, sec. II, pp. 13–15).

The planners believe that these nine centers will provide an even distribution of service in the alliance area. The map in Figure 12.3 shows the location of all of the various centers. Six of the nine centers are located on the periphery of the project area, because centers generally need to be on a major street in an area with adequate access and minimal disruption of quieter residential streets. The other three centers provide service coverage to areas farther inside the Benson-Ames Alliance boundaries (Benson-Ames Alliance, 2006, sec. II, pp. 9–15).

UNIQUE COMMUNITY CENTERS

The consultants selected four areas for significant development: Downtown Benson, the Ames Avenue Corridor, the area around 72nd Street and Military Avenue, and the Saddle Creek area. These four areas will each be developed into unique identifiable community centers (Benson-Ames Alliance, 2006, sec. II, p. 29).

The plan proposes an ambitious project for Downtown Benson: an old retail area in the south central section of the Benson-Ames Alliance area. Turning a tired, somewhat charming area into a citywide destination filled with specialty shops, unique restaurants, and clubs is at the heart of the plan. The plan maintains the "small-town mainstreet" atmosphere of the Maple Street business corridor and the surrounding city blocks (see Figure 12.4) (Benson-Ames Alliance, 2006, sec. II, pp. 31–34).

The plan addresses several issues. Parking is a major issue, especially when turning the area into a commercial, retail, and entertainment destination. The proposal advocates a better delineation of on-street parking, as well as the construction of several new parking lots and two multilevel parking structures (Benson-Ames Alliance, 2006, sec. II, pp. 31–34).

Emphasizing the handsome and historic nature of the neighborhood is an excellent way to enhance the reputation and beauty of the area. While many buildings have century-old details, not all buildings have maintained their historic storefronts. The plan suggests redesigning these buildings with a historic look and feel using significant amounts of transparent glazing and stone masonry work (Benson-Ames Alliance, 2006, sec. II, pp. 31–34).

The main floors of buildings will be devoted to commercial, retail, and entertainment space. The plan encourages developers to use the upper lev-

Figure 12.4 Downtown Benson in its current condition.

els for small offices and residential facilities. Buildings should have a zero setback from the street, except for small areas to accommodate entries, outdoor dining, courtyards, and public plazas. Major pedestrian intersections would be enhanced with decorative pavement to make intersections more attractive (Benson-Ames Alliance, 2006, sec. II, pp. 31–34).

The plan recommends placement of higher-density housing developments in the area, with a large series of townhomes north of Downtown Benson and a combination of high-density apartments, townhomes, and duplexes south of Downtown Benson. The destination quality of the area would bring in a new group of residents interested in alternatives to the single-family home (Benson-Ames Alliance, 2006, sec. II, pp. 31–34).

Finally, the plan recommends a series of gateways, arches, and decorative signage at major entry points to the area. These neighborhood delineators would establish borders for the area and introduce the neighborhood as a historic place (Benson-Ames Alliance, 2006, sec. II, pp. 31–34).

SUSTAINABILITY RECOMMENDATIONS

The plan recommends sustainable neighborhood improvement giving consideration to three specific concepts: *conservation areas, stabilization areas,* and *reestablishment areas* (Benson-Ames Alliance, 2006, sec. II, pp. 15–17).

Conservation areas are well-maintained with little unused or vacant space. They are physically sound and economically viable and have only minor rehabilitation needs. The many conservation areas in the Benson-Ames neighborhood are characterized by high-quality housing, often with a historic character. Guidelines for management of these areas focus on preventing decline by promoting quality development that fits into the historic character of the neighborhood, proactively enforcing codes to protect the physical appearance of these areas, and carefully maintaining public facilities and streets. Neighborhood organizations would need to work diligently to retain neighborhood churches, schools, and historic facilities (Benson-Ames Alliance, 2006, sec. II, p.17).

Stabilization areas show signs of initial decline in physical appearance and economic viability. The Benson-Ames neighborhood has stabilization areas characterized by lesser quality housing units, many with code violations. The primary purpose is to prevent continued decline. Recommendations for stabilization include improvement of community services, like police and fire protection, public space and infrastructure maintenance and enhancement, and increased code enforcement. City planning efforts must address the infill of vacant lots. Finally, financial incentive programs would be necessary to attract private investment money (Benson-Ames Alliance, 2006, sec. II, pp. 17–18).

Reestablishment areas show signs of extensive deterioration and prolonged neglect. The Benson-Ames neighborhood has reestablishment areas characterized by low-quality housing with visible damage to foundations and roofs. These areas also have a large number of abandoned buildings and vacant lots overgrown with weeds and strewn with debris. Reestablishment areas often house poor residents without the physical capital and social organization needed to address their numerous problems. Social programs, like job training, education, and counseling services, are necessary and should complement physical development (Benson-Ames Alliance, 2006, sec. II, pp. 18–19).

Recommendations for reestablishment include working with the City of Omaha to acquire and prepare land for redevelopment, improved code enforcement, and the creation of targeted programs to promote major repair and renovation. This often includes targeted incentives like low-interest loans and the creation of tax-increment financing zones. Finally, the enhancement of community services is essential to retain residents and attract newcomers to the area (Benson-Ames Alliance, 2006, sec. II, pp. 18–19).

VIBRANT STREET LIFE

The plan encourages walking and a vibrant street life. To accomplish this objective, the consultants have developed recommendations for the area at 72nd Street and Military Avenue, an 80-acre triangular piece of land bordered on the east by Military Avenue, on the south by Cole Creek, and on the west by 72nd Street. The plan turns this portion of land into a mixed-use community center that will provide services to multiple neighborhoods in the Benson-Ames area, including retail business, commercial space, restaurants, entertainment facilities, and a hotel or motel (see Figure 12.5) (Benson-Ames Alliance Plan, 2006, sec. II, pp. 42–46).

The area's main challenge and its main asset is its proximity to Cole Creek. The plan addresses flooding issues along the creek. Once the flooding is controlled, the area adjacent to the creek can be developed into a landscaped, tree-lined pedestrian and bicycle trail with access to the development area. The trail's green space would act as a buffer between the development and adjacent neighborhoods (Benson-Ames Alliance, 2006, sec. II, pp. 42–46).

An important feature would be a mixed-use commercial and residential development at the edge of the creek. This development would incorporate construction of a restaurant with terraces overlooking the creek and high-density residential facilities with balconies that have scenic views of the trail (Benson-Ames Alliance, 2006, sec. II, pp. 42–46).

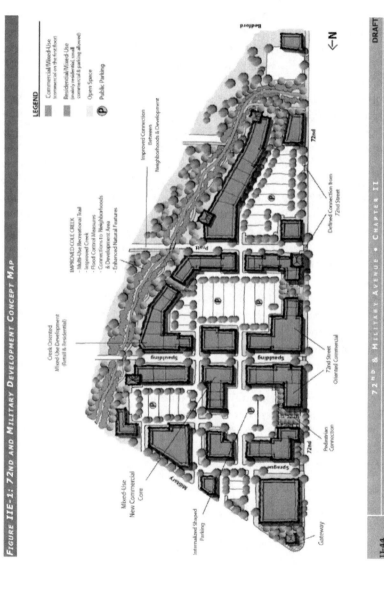

Figure 12.5 72nd and Military development concept map.

CIRCULATION RECOMMENDATIONS

The plan designates four major thoroughfares as *citywide corridors*, major roadways that serve a citywide function. These would have no on-street parking, minimal access to private drives, and bicycle paths separated from the street by landscape elements. Access to facilities in these areas should be through shared-use access points at mid-blocks, alleyways, or side streets to minimize traffic congestion (Benson-Ames Alliance, 2006, sec. II, pp. 20–23).

The plan identifies five streets as *area corridors*, minor arterial streets as compared to citywide corridors. These streets would have five lanes for motor vehicles, two lanes going each way with a turn lane in the middle, plus two smaller lanes for bicycles. On-street parking would be limited to areas where it does not interfere with traffic flow. Like citywide corridors, access off these streets would be through mid-block entrances, exits, alleyways, and side streets (Benson-Ames Alliance, 2006, sec. II, pp. 23–24).

The plan recognizes three streets as *local streets*, minor arterial roads that connect neighborhoods to area and citywide corridors. *Local streets* would have a two- or three-lane configuration with designated off-street parking and bicycle paths (Benson-Ames Alliance, 2006, sec. II, pp. 24–25).

All other streets are viewed as *neighborhood streets*, intended to facilitate transportation through residential areas. These streets would have on-street parking and sidewalks with landscape features separating them from the streets (Benson-Ames Alliance, 2006, sec. II, p. 25).

The Benson-Ames neighborhood currently has three stretches of greenway, bicycle and pedestrian pathways removed from roadways that are used as connecting routes and recreational trails by neighborhood residents. The plan recommends significant enhancements to provide increased mobility and improve aesthetics. The circulation section of the plan concludes with a recommendation for ornamental signage at key intersections on the perimeter to uniquely identify and draw people into the Benson-Ames Alliance area (Benson-Ames Alliance, 2006, sec. II, pp. 25–27).

DIVERSIFIED RESIDENTIAL DEVELOPMENT

Throughout the plan, the consultants advocate an increase in alternative forms of housing, including apartments, condominiums, townhomes, and duplexes. The purpose of the housing alternatives is to bring in younger, single, and more affluent people, so that the area continues to grow and thrive. The new housing additions could all be designed in styles that enhance the antique character of the neighborhood.

THE NEXT STEPS

The report from the consulting committee concludes with a brief section about the next steps in the implementation process. The first recommendation is to cultivate leadership on the Benson-Ames Alliance Steering Committee. The consultants encourage the use of the Steering Committee as the primary organization for implementation. According to the consultants, the Steering Committee needs to continue to recruit and develop leadership for implementation activities. They also call for continued training of leaders through the Alliance Academy, which is a training program offered through the Neighborhood Center of Greater Omaha. Omaha by Design should continue to support the leadership team (Benson-Ames Alliance, 2006, sec. III, pp. 1–9).

The implementation process is truly about partnerships, so it should be a priority of the Steering Committee to develop partnerships. The Steering Committee also needs to continue to cultivate a good working relationship with the City of Omaha Planning Department. The recommendations in the plan are meant to develop the unique character of the Benson-Ames area. Many of the recommendations will require rezoning efforts and will have to comply with city ordinances, so working closely with the city is imperative (Benson-Ames Alliance, 2006, sec. III, pp. 1–9).

USING THE INDEX TO EVALUATE CIVIC ENGAGEMENT IN THE BENSON-AMES ALLIANCE

Criteria One: The Number of Participants Involved in the Process

The survey company interviewed 387 people during the 2005 Benson Residents Survey. A total of 25 people participated in the focus groups and about 200 people in the visioning process. Most of the people attending the May 2006 and August 2006 open houses were participants in the visioning process. This means approximately 625 people were involved in the civic engagement efforts or about 2.5% of the adult population of the Benson-Ames Alliance area.

These numbers show an adequate percentage of civic engagement for the planning process, because the participants had homogenous opinions about the assets, needs, and issues for the area. Information provided by the random survey matched the information provided by the neighborhood activists in the focus groups and by participants in the visioning process. Similar results from all activities increase the validity of the information gathered. While the number appears adequate for the planning process, it is low for the implementation process, because large sections of the Benson-Ames Alliance area have no neighborhood association activity and minimal representation. For purposes of implementation, the number of participants was only about 200. This is less than 1% of the area's total population. It is not realistic to include those surveyed by telephone in the final number. Capacity building, or recruiting new participants and resources, is necessary if the implementation process is to succeed. The low participation rate indicates a need for capacity building in the implementation phase of the project.

Criteria Two: The Demographic Comparison

The demographic comparison is quite difficult in this case, as it is based solely on the personal observations of this researcher, because no demographic data was collected from any of the civic engagement activities.

From this author's general perception, the citizen participants were moderately representative of the area as a whole, with a few major issues. One underrepresented group was African Americans. African Americans make up 26% of the population in the Benson-Ames Alliance area, but less the 25% of the attendees of each civic engagement event were African American. However, representation on the Organizing and Steering Committees does appear to mirror the demographics of the area, since over 26% of the membership is African American.

Another group that was underrepresented was renters. Through observation and informal discussion with attendees in the focus groups and public meetings, it was evident that very few renters attended. This researcher did not actually meet or talk with a single renter at any of the sessions. No renters are part of the Organizing or Steering Committees. All residents on these two committees are homeowners.

At the public meetings, there was an overrepresentation of retirees and an underrepresentation of young families. This is logical because retirees have more time to devote to volunteer organizations and community activities, but is something to address in the future.

Overall, the demographics of the citizen participants mirror the demographics of the total area at a moderate level of representation, since many groups are well-represented in the process, but several important groups were underrepresented. In the future, the Benson-Ames Alliance needs to track demographic information and work on capacity building to insure that citizen participants better match the demographics of the area.

Criteria Three: Is the Civic Engagement Ongoing?

The project rates high in this area. Civic engagement did not just occur at the beginning of the process. It has not been a one-time or sporadic activity. The Steering Committee and subcommittees continue to hold civic engagement events and communicate with neighborhood residents through the Benson-Ames Alliance Web site. Citizens significantly represent residents in the alliance area as members of the Organizing and Steering Committees. New citizens come into the process as the Steering Committee establishes new subcommittees.

Results of the interviews and surveys support the idea that civic engagement needs to occur early in the program planning, development, and implementation processes. They also supported the idea that civic engagement needs to be implemented by the developers of the program or a third-party organization. In the Benson-Ames Alliance, Omaha by Design was the third-party developer of the process.

One significant issue with good civic engagement is cost. The Benson-Ames Alliance experience showed that good civic engagement is expensive. Between consultant fees and survey expenses, the completion of the Benson-Ames Alliance Sub-Area Plan cost approximately $500,000. Several interview respondents believe that in order to have effective ongoing civic engagement, organizers need to find the money to pay for someone to oversee the process. In the Benson-Ames Alliance project, Omaha by Design played that vital role of bringing people together, providing forums and funding for civic engagement, and moving the planning process to completion.

Criteria Four: The Number and Variety of Civic Engagement Forums

The Benson-Ames Alliance made use of several different types of civic engagement activities, including focus groups, surveys, and public meetings. This case shows a positive relationship between surveys and focus groups, and surveys and public meetings, since all three methods of civic engagement produced the same results.

The combination of the telephone survey and public meetings was particularly effective in cross-checking results for civic engagement activities. The survey was conducted with interviews of randomly selected people throughout the entire Benson-Ames Alliance area. Neighborhood activists and interested parties attended the public meetings. It is unlikely that a large share of those participating in the telephone survey attended the public meetings. The agreement between the telephone survey participants and the activists about the assets, issues, and needs of the area indicates they were assessed in a reliable manner.

Criteria Five: Was the Information Gathered Through Civic Engagement Activities Used in the Decision-Making Process?

The consultants used a significant amount of citizen input in the creation of the final subarea plan for the Benson-Ames area. One issue of concern that citizens identified in all forums was the poor condition of sidewalks and roads in the area. The plans for the area include significant enhancements to streets and sidewalk repair. Plans for the whole area call for the elimination of code violations. Poor sidewalk conditions are one of the most prominent code violations, according to the Omaha Neighborhood Scan. The plan also recommends enhancements to streets in the area to insure good traffic flow and connection within the area and to the city at-large.

The plans suggest improvements and extensions of recreational trails throughout the area, an issue identified frequently in the 2005 Benson Resident Survey, focus groups, and public meetings. Residents want increased recreational facilities and better ways to use alternative modes of transportation, such as bicycling.

For residents of the northwestern section of the Benson-Ames Alliance, flooding from Cole Creek is a major issue during rainstorms and a long-term problem. The Benson-Ames Alliance Steering Committee has already unveiled plans to control flooding in the area. The flood control plans will serve as a demonstration project, providing a model for other areas of the city where flooding is a problem.

The recommendations address capacity building to increase leadership and civic engagement in the Benson-Ames Alliance area. The plan specifically states that the Steering Committee is responsible for developing leadership during the implementation process. The plan also recommends the use of the Alliance Academy for training purposes. Most of the focus group participants had been to Alliance Academy training and felt that the experience was extremely valuable.

The plans for the four target areas demonstrate where the consultants used citizen input. The Downtown Benson area had several citizen-generated requests, including plans to address the parking issues in the area and the very popular idea of turning Downtown Benson into an entertainment center. Since many citizens identified the blighted Ames Street corridor as a problem area, the consultants selected it as a target area for development. Citizens strongly supported the plan to convert the current drainage ditch into a scenic trail at 72nd & Military Avenue. Finally, many citizens were happy to see plans to convert the rundown industrial buildings in the Saddle Creek Road area into an interesting shopping destination. The Steering Committee for the Benson-Ames area project receives high marks for using citizen input in their recommendations.

USING THE MATRIX TO EVALUATE CIVIC ENGAGEMENT IN THE BENSON-AMES ALLIANCE

Using the Matrix of Citizen Participation, the civic engagement process would appear in the first quadrant, Full Citizen Participation, bordering Quadrant III, Skewed Participation. The Steering Committee used citizen input in many positive ways in the development of the plan. However, some representational issues exist regarding the low number of African Americans, renters, and young families involved in the process. Organizers would need to bring in missing stakeholders in order to be centered in the Full Citizen Participation quadrant of the Matrix.

CONCLUSION

The Benson-Ames Alliance provided an excellent opportunity to view civic engagement in action. Overall, the Benson-Ames Alliance is performing well in their civic engagement efforts. The plan shows high levels of ongoing civic engagement, a good number of forums for civic engagement, and significant use of citizen input in the process. Organizers need to bring in more people for the implementation process, especially underrepresented stakeholders. The Matrix of Citizen Participation shows civic engagement at a level just inside the first quadrant, Full Citizen Participation.

Civic engagement can be time-consuming and costly, but it is important in the development of a project. Major strategic projects usually require major civic engagement. This case shows the value of community collaboration and consultants in creating a strong comprehensive plan for growth.

REFERENCES

Barnett, J. (2005, Spring/Summer). Omaha by design. *Harvard Design Magazine, 22.*

Bayor, R.H. (1982). *Neighborhoods in urban America.* Port Washington, NY: National University Publications.

Benson-Ames Alliance. (2006). *The Benson-Ames Alliance Plan.*

Benson Resident Survey. (2005). *The Benson Residents Survey.*

Center for Public Affairs Research. (2005). *Business Summary Report.* University of Nebraska at Omaha.

The Omaha Neighborhood Scan. (2005). *The Omaha Neighborhood Scan.*
U.S. Census. (2000) Washington, DC: U.S. Census Bureau.

WEBSITES

Retrieved April 14, 2007, from http://assist.needed.org-7
Retrieved May 7, 2007, from http://download.tdconline.dk/pub/kongehuset
Retrieved June 30, 2005, from http://www.bensonnebraska.com
Retrieved May 4, 2007, from http://www.livelyomaha.org/History-Background.html
Retrieved January 18, 2009, from http://www.benson-ames.org
Retrieved December 18, 2010, from www.cityofomaha.org
Retrieved May 3, 2007, from www.cityofseattle.net/neighborhoods
      or www.seattle.gov
Retrieved May 7 2007, from www.nrp.org
Retrieved May 7 2007, from www.sen.org
Retrieved May 7 2007, from www.SNGi.org
Retrieved January 5, 2011, from www.uscensus2010.gov

CHAPTER 13

DELIBERATIVE POLLING

Theoretical and Methodological Issues of Civic Engagement

Jeremy Harris Lipschultz
The University of Nebraska at Omaha

Use of the Internet—Web sites, blogs, wikis, Facebook, Twitter, and other methods—has transformed contemporary American and global politics by dispersing state and media control (Garrett & Danziger, 2011). As media author Ken Auletta has observed, the "great paradox" is that "growing concentration" of media ownership has been *countered* by easy-to-use technologies as a "democratic instrument...that basically challenges companies" (Lipschultz, 2011, p. 272). At the same time, private interaction has been extended to public "crowdsourcing" behavior: "Virtually anyone has the potential to plug in valuable information" (Greengard, 2011, p. 20). Online collaboration and computer-mediated communication (CMC)—identity formation, interaction opportunities, and community building—introduced a challenge to the traditional powers of government and politics (Barnes, 2003; Lipschultz, 2008). Digital relationships vary greatly in strength and depth, and these may be related to social capital, social ties,

The State of Citizen Participation in America, pages 309–323
Copyright © 2012 by Information Age Publishing
All rights of reproduction in any form reserved.

and our ability to differentiate communicator purpose and motivation (Brown, 2011).

The election of Barack Obama in 2008, for example, ushered in a "digital technology" era in which political campaigns may use huge e-mail lists to go directly to one of every five voters (Kenski, Hardy, & Jamieson, 2010, p. 305). In the years since that election, the spread of information among small and relatively private groups of family and friends has moved into the public sphere through much larger social networks, Facebook being the largest online congregation space with somewhere between 500 million and 1 billion active users in 2011. Randi Zuckerberg of Facebook sees social networking as social space for activism and change:

> Through social media, people not only donate money, but even more importantly, their reputation and identity. Each time someone clicks "like" or joins a cause on Facebook, they are broadcasting that message to hundreds of their friends, and aligning themselves with a particular issue . . . the awareness generated from that simple action has a ripple effect and has the potential to recruit some extremely engaged volunteers and donors in the future. (Vericat, 2010, p. 177)

Rapid publication of Facebook posts, Zuckerberg suggests, may fill a void in face-to-face conversation lost for social or political reasons: "I believe that Facebook's ability to occupy the space of a free and unmoderated media and civil space will bring many more opportunities for meaningful democratic change" (p. 178). These online social networks may be depicted through visualization that illuminates "clear patterns" of affiliation and communication (Langlois, Elmer, McKelvey, & Devereaux, 2009, p. 425). Still, the relatively recent popularity of constructing large online social networks that may be built upon a collection of weak "acquaintances and other people with shallower connections" (Brown, 2011, p. 31), does not reduce the need for richer engagement.

The construct of citizen participation implies that there are social and technological vehicles available that allow interested citizens to exercise various levels of participatory behavior within a given political system. In the United States, however, the 20th century came and went with few formal mechanisms available. Broadcasting, for example, is regulated by the Federal Communications Commission (FCC); however, the FCC's Fairness Doctrine, which required talk shows to seek balance through significant competing points of view, was eliminated by the Commission in the late 1980s. Congressional attempts to reconstruct it failed to receive presidential support. The resulting environment is one in which extreme political positions may became the new norm on talk radio and unregulated cable television channels (McGregor, 2011): "Fearful that a new fairness doctrine would jeopardize popular conservative talk shows and religious programming, Republicans in Congress proposed legislation that would prohibit the FCC from reinstating the doctrine" (p. 211).

Free Expression and Media

At the informal level, the American model began with the lonely pamphleteer, gained access to big media through newspaper "Letters to the Editor," and eventually offered citizens unprecedented access to others through the World Wide Web in the 1990s. The Internet age brought us the art of blogging (Rettberg, 2008) and promotion of opinion on social media channels (Mathison, 2009), such as Twitter (Pogue, 2009) and Facebook (Lipschultz, 2011): "As new and newer media allow individuals to take on the role of publisher (through use of blogs, podcasts, Twitter and Facebook postings, and location based sites), there are new freedoms *and* new responsibilities" (p. 243). Citizens enter the conversation on any "controversial issue of public importance" (Joint Statement, 1998) amid a flood of emotionally charged opinions that at least sometimes do not reflect the factual evidence. While charged opinions are nothing new—President Lincoln and the Founders before him suffered the effects of partisan attacks—political blogs seem to have brought us back around to them following an era that was moderated through professional media and norms of objectivity. While this model of the 1960s through the 1980s was imperfect because of such limited access, it tended to support so-called civility within established political-media systems. Perhaps this was due, in part, to civil unrest beyond the doors of power. Whatever the reason, the Internet is a game changer.

Public opinion in the current political environment may be triggered by social media diffusion of new ideas (Rogers, 2003). In this dynamic social and political environment, policies involving use of technology tend to lag far behind entrepreneurial innovation (Genachowski, 2010). Additionally, protection of First Amendment rights through court decisions restricts government from imposing draconian limitations on the free flow of ideas or strict procedures of moderating a civil dialogue, so defined (Lipschultz, 2000). Instead, anyone with a computer or access to one, media literacy skills and knowledge to participate, and a will to activate views may enter the online arena. Further, national borders do not bound the Internet. Wikileaks, a site devoted to the practice of protecting anonymous whistleblowers of corruption, operated at a global level. Computer servers may be located in unregulated locations, and this helped spark uprisings in Iran (2009), Egypt, Libya, Syria, and Oman (2011) that played out in real time on Twitter. Motadel (2011) has referred to "Waves of Revolution" that expand "political mass mobilisation" through coordinated "messages against tyranny" (pp. 3–4). While these high-profile examples of instantaneously mediated revolts represent an exaggerated form of citizen participation, it is more common for public affairs issues to occupy a quieter and more enduring place within civic and political life. To the extent that people come together offline as family, friends, and colleagues, they may be able to engage in somewhat private and frank conversations about controversial public issues, even using strong language that may violate online terms of service agreements. So while online sites such as Facebook have responded to complaints from other users by filtering caustic content, offline spaces present opportunities to confront uninformed opinion. One such issue, immigration, has been a staple of recent political campaigns and elections.

Immigration as a Test Case

A controversial and contentious issue in the United States has been what Congress should do about immigration policy. The presence of undocumented workers coming across the U.S.-Mexico border—in some cases filling job openings in the midst of rising unemployment figures—has given rise to criticism of policy and the promotion of new laws, such as those passed in Arizona. Analysts point out that half of immigrant workers come to the United States from Mexico, but the public, confused by a lack of issue education and superficial media coverage, may not be able to distinguish between legal and illegal workers. In states such as Nebraska, public opinion may ignore the contributions immigrants have made in promoting the local economy by doing hard-to-fill jobs:

> People used to read newspapers and listen to the news regularly; today, headlines and the ten-second sound bites may form the depth of news knowledge . . . The Internet and blogosphere have contributed to negative attitudes about immigration, as they quickly and widely disseminate myths and misconceptions, as well as vitriolic commentary. (Strategic Discussions for Nebraska 2008, p. 4)

Research on how people use media and obtain gratification from content date from the 1940s, and it has been found that prior motivations and selectivity impact potential influences on social issues (Baran & Davis, 2000, p. 256). In brief, the public seeks information that reinforces goals, needs, and orientations. From a social utility perspective, we often talk about what we read, see, and hear. In the view of Dominick (2009), media use has "conversational currency" because "media provide a common ground for social conversations" (p. 40). While such conversations typically happen within one's primary groups, it is also possible to bring people together in social settings that are designed to cultivate and develop beliefs about public issues. Such conversation is one way to activate engagement of citizens on important public issues.

Deliberative Polling

In response to the limitations of public opinion polls, which tend to emphasize large and *often uninformed* views, the deliberative polling method has been conceptualized as a response to overgeneralization. To represent informed opinion in a democracy, Fishkin's group developed a deliberative poll method that includes a system to first provide people with information on public issues *before* seeking their opinions (Luskin, Fishkin, & Jowel, 2002). Deliberative polling can be used "when policy makers or the media want citizen input on subjects as diverse as health care, immigration, or foreign policy" (Fishkin & Rosell 2004, p. 55). A daylong event may provide people with an opportunity to learn about complexities of issues. Additionally, deliberative polls often have been paired with the videotaping for a later public television broadcast. While this approach does not offer much group privacy, a measure of intimacy can be achieved through division of the sample into several small group discussions. The results of deliberative polls provide researchers with information about opinion formation in "a quasi-experiment" (Fishkin & Luskin, 2005, p. 188). Further, the discovery of informed opinion on a controversial issue, such as immigration, is designed to provide policymakers with valuable information in advance of possible legislation. From a communication perspective, deliberative polls not only address the problem of uninformed public opinion, they also may trigger democratic interest among a disinterested public (Sturgis, Roberts, & Allum, 2005, p. 30).

Deliberative polls may be related to the civic engagement and participation movement that seeks to broaden public discussion beyond political elites and mass media. While a deliberative poll can produce group effects by changing opinion in more than one direction, the focus on a single issue "can translate into sizeable shifts in the distribution of collective preferences" (Sturgis, 2003, p. 474). In the case of immigration, some of the important context for the public involves immigrants filling minimum wage or subminimum wage jobs in "primarily the agricultural, construction, manufacturing, hospitality and domestic-work sectors" (Murphey, 2006, p. 339). As such, arguments often are reduced to the problem of illegal immigration versus the need to fill jobs that are unappealing to most citizens. In Nebraska, the meat packing industry, agriculture, and construction provide ample opportunities for legal and illegal immigrants to find work. Against this backdrop, as well as a concurrent and intense national immigration debate, a 2007 deliberative poll in Omaha sought to explore the issue.

Researchers have been interested in the usefulness of media information about immigration, credibility of news sources for deliberative poll participants, and the overall impact of the deliberative poll approach on those attending an event. As an alternative to public opinion polling, deliberative polls also now stand in stark contrast to the Facebook-style social network and media sharing in that there is issue focus and an extended amount of time devoted to the issue.

The Omaha Project

Some 100 Omaha residents gathered on the University of Nebraska at Omaha campus to engage in a *By The People: Dialogues in Democracy* deliberation (University of Nebraska Public Policy Center, 2007). The local project was part of a larger national PBS television dialogue research effort. The deliberative polling methodology was developed in the United States in 1996 and has been adopted by researchers in various foreign countries (Center for Deliberative Democracy, 2010). In brief, research subjects are administered a pre-event survey, attend local discussions, and then are surveyed again following the small group and large group deliberations. Media questions were asked within the context of a broader collection of data before the deliberative dialogue. The University of Nebraska Public Policy Center contracted with the University of Nebraska-Lincoln Bureau of Sociological Research (BOSR) to recruit participants from within the Omaha city limits. BOSR began with 3,091 random telephone numbers, oversampling African American and Hispanic/Latino neighborhoods. In September 2007, BOSR sent 2,120 prenotification letters and then made contact through telephone calls and contact with 1,956 households in the sample. Of these, 542 respondents completed the pre-event survey, 179 agreed to attend the deliberation, 89 indicated they might attend, and 274 declined. BOSR followed up with two informational mailings and telephone calls. Participants were given a briefing booklet summarizing the various Nebraska immigration issues. A total of 189 individuals agreed to participate, including 10 from the original uncertain group. In the end, a total of 100 actually attended the October 14, 2007, event. While participants constituted a nonprobability sample, they reflected a diverse group of Omahans on a wide range of demographic variables and were similar to other deliberative polling groups across the nation. Out of these participants, 51% identified themselves as Democrats, 21% as Republicans, 23% as Independents, and 5% as Other. Local and national survey questions were focused on immigration and civic engagement (University of Nebraska Public Policy Center, 2007). The focus of pre-event survey questions was on the usefulness of media sources in the coverage of the global immigration issue.

Respondents participated in 1 of 10 breakout discussion groups on is-sues related to immigration. One Nebraska public television camera crew, one Omaha public television crew, and one research team member with a handheld camera (a total of three) roamed the 10 discussions seeking examples of conflict and consensus. Additionally, one student note-taker was present in each room. Trained moderators guided the discussion us-ing a framework of small group deliberation and diversity offered by ran-dom group assignment (Abdel-Monem, Bingham, Marincic, & Tompkins, 2010). Afterward, postevent survey questions asked for information on the amount of attention respondents paid to media. Additionally, a postevent focus group explored public opinion on the credibility of various news sources. During the final survey, participants who expressed an interest in mass media issues were asked to remain to participate in a postevent focus group. Six participants agreed to do so and responded to a set of structured focus group questions.

Bringing Together Media and Immigration Opinions

The pre-event survey data revealed a broad range of useful media types. While there was an emphasis on traditional media, usefulness of Internet news was increasing. The respondents were asked which best described their view of media coverage on the immigration issue: "News media are more liberal on the issue than my personal view" (7.9%); "News media are more conservative on the issue than my personal view" (32.7%); "News me-dia mirror my personal view on the issue" (34.7%); "Don't know" (24.7%). The results suggested a higher proportion of liberal-leaning responses. A majority of respondents used television (86.1%), radio (55.4%), and news-papers (54.5%) on a daily basis. Television, newspapers, and radio also were seen as the most credible news sources for information about the immigration issue. Among participants, 15.8% found television very cred-ible, and 53.5% found it fairly credible. Newspapers, magazines, and radio showed similar patterns. The Internet, which was lowest in overall cred-ibility scores, still had 6.9% of poll participants finding it very credible and 39.6% fairly credible.

At the deliberative poll event—a daylong set of sessions on a Sunday in October a year before the 2008 presidential election—participants were randomly assigned into 10 different discussion groups. Participants com-pleted a second survey about immigration and civic engagement issues. At this point, participants were given written and video briefing materi-als about immigration issues in Nebraska. The groups then convened for breakout sessions moderated by trained discussion leaders. Nebraska Edu-cational Telecommunications (NET) and the Omaha research group videotaped some of the discussions, moving from group to group. Additionally, trained note-takers summarized all discussion. In general, the group discussions focused on the following topics: undocumented immigrants, education, language, employment, economic impact identification of workers, health insurance, and social security. Mass media were rarely mentioned.

At the end of small group sessions, the 100 participants reconvened at a plenary that featured a state lawmaker, an immigration attorney, and a professor. A television moderator from NET led the discussion that was videotaped for a later broadcast. At the end of the final session, participants completed a postevent survey about immigration and civic engagement issues.

A postevent survey reflected a balance between media use and interpersonal talk about the immigration issue after participation in the deliberative polling. Discussing immigration issues with other citizens in the community led 38.8% of participants to pay closer attention to media stories; 46.6% of participants to talk more than usual with family, friends or co-workers; and 31.1% of participants to seek more information. Our team's postevent focus group provided insights from those participants who expressed interest in staying for one additional hour to talk further about media issues. We found that political orientation and media interest varied across this group.

Media, Immigration, and Social Context

Six participants who expressed an interest in media issues stayed after the polling event had ended and took part in a focus group. There were three men and three women. Among men, all three were Caucasian, with two under 50 years of age and one older than 50. Among women, one was Latina, one was African American, and one was Caucasian. In terms of age, one was under 50 while the other two women were over 50. Focus group members were asked for their perceptions of the prime media source for the public's information about immigration. Specifically, they were asked, "Which media is your primary information source when it comes to immigration?" Four of the six focus group members mentioned television (that included cable television news, public television news, and local television news), one mentioned newspapers, and one mentioned the Internet. All three females responded that it was television, while males mentioned television along with newspapers and Internet sites. The heavy Internet user, Peter, sampled major national newspapers as well as the entire political spectrum. Similarly, a heavy cable television news user, David, mentioned CNN, Fox, and MSNBC. One focus group member, Ruby, mentioned only television generically and would not be more specific. Two other group members, Donna and Lonnie, mentioned the convenience of cable television news. The primary newspaper user, Joseph, was interested in local issues.

Further, respondents also were asked, "Which media do you think are most influential?" Four respondents pointed to cable television news, one to newspaper, and one to network television news:

Peter: "I still think major newspapers such as *The New York Times* and *Washington Post* are the most influential. I believe local newspapers are the most influential in their own markets. I tend to dismiss local TV news because it tends to be pretty superficial."

Ruby: "I try to read the local newspaper, and I thought they were the most influential, but my kids don't read the paper or watch TV, but they get all their information over the Internet, and they seem as well-informed from that as my husband and I are."

Focus group members were also asked, "Which media do you think are most reliable and least reliable?" Three of the six focus group members perceive the local newspaper as most reliable, and four of the six members perceive the Internet as least reliable. For example, Joseph, was a heavy local newspaper user and this influenced him: "To me the farther you are away from a story, the less accurate you're going to be . . . The Internet, without a doubt. Anybody can put anything on there without accreditation or follow-up, or back-up, or supporting documentation." But Donna was the only focus group member emphasizing the Internet as the most reliable source:

Donna: "There was a time you couldn't believe anything in the National Enquirer, but now it's like I make sure I get in the aisle where it's sold . . . There is a lot of truth on the Internet, because people are not afraid. There's a sense of anonymity. They'll say things on there they can back up."

All six participants agreed that talk radio is one of the least reliable media sources. Focus group members were asked to look beyond mass media and describe other good sources for immigration information: "Besides media, who or what do you consider a good source on immigration topics? Why?" Focus group members emphasized the value of personal experience and observation of local immigrants. Additionally, they talked about obtaining information through their local schools, churches, and visits to ethnic restaurants:

David: "This is a radical idea, but immigrants just might be a good source of information . . . or just something as simple as visiting 24th Street on a regular basis or visiting the restaurants. There is no substitute for personal experience. . . . or for firsthand experiences and contact. Show me somebody like a teacher or somebody in social services, and I'll show you somebody that I'd like to listen to."

Joseph: "If you want to know about immigration or the latest scoop, go ask someone who's in the process, or is hiding from the process, or is looking to find out about the process."

Ruby, a Latina focus group member, was the only participant of the six currently living in a predominantly immigrant area of Omaha. Her daughters attended a local high school and brought information about immigrants home. She synthesized a multitude of observations about immigrants over time:

Ruby: "Watching how they live, and realizing that their customs are not the same as ours, but if you give them a chance and sit back, they watch to see what we are doing, and they try to live the same way we are."

Another focus group member, Donna, hires immigrants and talks to them about issues. Finally, four of the six focus group members had some connection to the local school system and explained that this led to learning about immigration issues.

There were two final questions asked of focus group members. First, they were asked, "After hearing opinions expressed today, which of you, if any, may reevaluate the quality of information from your preferred media sources?" Nobody said they would. Second, they were asked, "After hearing what you heard today, will you go out and seek a different source of media information?" Donna, a cable television news user, responded that Peter, an Internet user, had convinced her to go look at some of his suggested Web sites.

Deliberative Polling in an Age of Social Media

While the deliberative poll produced some evidence of short-term effects in terms of citizens learning about the immigration issue, attitudes about media credibility, based upon the focus group, appeared to be well-established before the event and based on personal experiences. These beliefs may also have influenced the course of dialogue within the deliberative poll event. The method proved valuable for exploring in-depth views about controversial issues. Although a deliberative polling event is conducted with a relatively small number of people, the results reflect the context of an intense, daylong interaction on a specific issue. Education may reduce public confusion about the immigration issue, and the deliberative polling approach offers useful context. Structured discussion appeared to promote formation of opinions on controversial aspects of the immigration problem. Such discussion may trigger civic engagement and allow for public sentiments to reach media and lawmakers.

Participants utilized deliberative poll briefing facts to help frame their discussions. They reported that the traditional media remained most useful, but this was in combination with Internet sources. Radio, television, and newspapers were judged as the most credible news sources on the immigration issue. The postevent focus group highlighted the importance of both elite national news media, particularly newspapers and cable television networks, and the local newspaper. The Internet served as a supplemental source for additional information. The deliberative poll appeared to have some impact on participant interest in media stories about immigration and their desire to talk about the issue with others. The activation of civic engagement on important public issues goes beyond what typically happens in private settings in which news is consumed. Citizens process media stories, but it is civic conversation that helps people articulate their views. The Omaha event led to short-term crystallization of opinions.

However, waning media and public interest in the immigration issue followed because of the 2008 presidential election and the worsening global economy. Among competing issues for political, media, and public agendas, the immigration issue and its possible solutions took a backseat to the more pressing issues of the day.

Future work should study opinion formation over time, across a wider range of political viewpoints. A limitation of the current work was that the attendees of the deliberative poll event leaned slightly liberal in their overall political perspectives. In the end, states such as Nebraska have less control over immigration law than the federal government. The deliberative polling method may be valuable as a mechanism for measuring and using national public opinion on important issues. Deliberative polling suffers from its weak connections in early research to media theory, which is extensive and rich. Further, the polling method itself is challenging to practice in a way that ensures representative samples, reliable data, strict scientific controls, and linkages to established approaches for determining validity of data through theory and systematic observation. It instead offers similarity to qualitative methods, which favor generation of explanatory depth.

Deliberation and the Future

The deliberative polling event was unique as a method for people to gain and process information on a contentious social issue. In the case of immigration, small group researchers were able to measure that participants perceived group satisfaction, effectiveness, and quality; expressed common views of the positive aspects of engaging in a diverse yet respectful group;

and perceived that hearing different opinions triggered learning (Abdel-Monem et al., 2010). Among the most salient opinions about the immigration issue was "I used to think it was just crazy to offer drivers licenses to illegal aliens, and now I think totally opposite" (p. 762). Overall, participants came away from the process observing that the immigration issue is more complex than portrayed in mass media.

More than 3 years after the deliberative polling event, Facebook activity had spread across wide sectors of the U.S. population. Among some social networks with Facebook or other sites, political discussion is common and ongoing. In these cases, links to news stories may spark a dialogue. While political discussion makes up relatively small proportions of social media on Facebook networks, it is more common among those using the less popular but also less restricted Twitter social networks (Pew Research Center, 2011). One can envision a social network as a place where opinions are activated by distribution of news, information, data, and opinion. At the same time, salience of a particular social issue such as immigration reflects the rise and fall of news cycles and various social contexts. How this deliberation influences governance depends upon the participation of lawmakers. In the Omaha project, for example, one state senator agreed to participate in one of the panels near the end of the day to take questions along with a professor and an immigration lawyer. The impact of his participation and listening to a group of somewhat informed citizens would be difficult to gauge. Extended to social networks, elected politicians appear more likely to send out information than to engage in meaningful exchange of ideas with their constituents. Similar to town hall meetings in local communities, representatives appear to be more adept at sharing what they know about a given legislative session than to answer questions from the public, take in and consider new ideas, and practice what television host David Susskind called "the lively art of conversation." It is more than an art form when it produces consensus through collaborative techniques that have the potential to steer society away from contentious disagreements, and society off the path of supporting laws based upon uninformed opinion, incomplete information, and mediated hyperbole.

Toward Media Literacy

The Internet has led some authors to emphasize the importance of digital literacy skills, information literacy skills, technology literacy, and visual literacy as significant elements in understanding media literacy today. Shapiro and Hughes (1996) asked what individuals need to know to be considered competent and literate in an information society:

As we witness not only the saturation of our daily lives with information organized and transmitted via information technology, by the way in which public
issues and social life increasingly are affected by information-technology issues—from intellectual property to privacy and the structure of work to entertainment, art and fantasy life—the issue of what it means to be information-
literate becomes more acute for our whole society. (p. 1)

Silverblatt (1995) organizes media literacy around four prime aspects of
message interpretation: process, context, framework, and production values. He builds upon this through a definition of media literacy that has five
elements:

1. An awareness of the impact on the individual and society;
2. An understanding of the process of mass communication;
3. The development of strategies with which to analyze and discuss
   media messages;
4. An awareness of media content as a "text" that provides insight into
   our contemporary culture and ourselves;
5. The cultivation of an enhanced enjoyment, understanding, and appreciation of media content.

Silverblatt (1995) expands the traditional print literacy definition to include all forms of mass media. Therefore, concerns such as content, form,
and impact are essential to understanding how people develop critical
awareness about media within a historical, cultural, and international context (Silverblatt & Zlobin, 2004). When it comes to a long-running discussion of a controversial issue, such as the reform of immigration laws, perhaps a variety of settings are needed to offer new information and opinions.
Deliberative polling is one method that could be incorporated along with
traditional polling and media, and the social media environment that is
now present. The more people are willing to be informed on important
issues, the more likely decision makers will have social space to seek innovative compromises through collaboration. New communication technologies allow individuals to advance ideas in the absence of traditional news
media support or promotion.

REFERENCES

Abdel-Monem, T., Bingham, S., Marincic, J., & Tompkins, A. (2010). Deliberation
and diversity: Perceptions of small group discussions by race and ethnicity.
Small Group Research, 41(6), 746–776.

Baran, S. J., & Davis, D. K. (2000). *Mass communication theory: Foundations, ferment,
and future.* Belmont, CA: Wadsworth/Thomson.

Barnes, S. B. (2003). *Computer-mediated communication: Human-to-human communication across the Internet.* Boston, MA: Allyn and Bacon.

Brown, A. (2011, March–April). Relationships, community, and identity in the new virtual society. *The Futurist, 29–31,* 34.

Center for Deliberative Democracy. (2010). Research papers. *Stanford University.* Retrieved September 22, 2011, from http://cdd.stanford.edu/research

Dominick, J. R. (2009). *The dynamics of mass communication* (10th ed.). New York, NY: McGraw-Hill.

Fishkin, J. S., & Luskin, R. C. (2005). Broadcasts of deliberative polls: Aspirations and effects. *British Journal of Political Science, 36*(1), 184–188.

Fishkin, J. S., & Rosell, S. A. (2004). Choice dialogues and deliberative polls: Two approaches to deliberative democracy. *National Civic Review, 93*(4), 55–63.

Garrett, R. K., & Danziger, J. N. (2011, March). The Internet electorate. *Communications of the ACM, 54*(3), 117–123.

Genachowski, J. (2010, October 15). *U.S. Senate Committee on Small Business and Entrepreneurship* [FCC chair's response]. Retrieved May 10, 2011, from http://fjallfoss.fcc.gov/edocs_public/attachmatch/DOC-302374A1.pdf

Greengard, S. (2011). Following the crowd. *Communications of the ACM, 54*(2), 20–22.

Joint Statement. (1998). *Join statement of Commissioners Powell and Furchtgott-Roth.* FCC General Docket No. 83-484. Retrieved from http://www.fcc.gov/Speeches/Furchtgott_Roth/Statements/sthfr834.html

Kenski, K., Hardy, B. W., & Jamieson, K. H. (2010). *The Obama victory: How media, money, and message shaped the 2008 election.* New York, NY: Oxford University Press.

Langlois, G., Elmer, G., McKelvey, F., & Devereaux, Z. (2009). Networked publics: The double articulation of code and politics on Facebook. *Canadian Journal of Communication, 34*(3), 415–434.

Lipschultz, J. H. (2000). *Free expression in the age of the Internet: Social and legal boundaries.* Boulder, CO: Westview.

Lipschultz, J. H. (2008). *Broadcast and Internet indecency: Defining free speech.* New York, NY: Routledge.

Lipschultz, J. H. (2011). New communication technologies. In W. W. Hopkins (Ed.), *Communication and the law* (2011 ed., pp. 243–273). Northport, AL: Vision.

Luskin, R. C., Fishkin, J. S., & Jowell, R. (2002). Considered opinions: Deliberative polling in Britain. *British Journal of Political Science, 32*(3), 455–487.

Mathison, D. (2009). *Be the media.* New Hyde Park, NY: Natural E Creative Group.

McGregor, M. A. (2011). Broadcast regulation. In W. W. Hopkins (Ed.), *Communication and the law* (2011 ed., pp. 197–220). Northport, AL: Vision.

Motadel, D. (2011). Waves of revolution. *History Today, 61*(4), 3–4.

Murphey, D. D. (2006). If past is prologue: Americans' future "guilt" about today's use of low-pay immigrant labor. *Journal of Social, Political & Economic Studies, 31*(3), 339–365.

Pew Research Center. (2009, June 24). Strong public interest in Iranian election protests: Many know Iranians using Internet to get message out. *Pew Research Center.* Retrieved April 16, 2010, from http://people-press.org/report/525/strong-public-interest-in-iranian-election-protests

Pogue, D. (2009). *The world according to Twitter.* New York, NY: Blackdog & Levanthal.

Rettberg, J. W. (2008). *Blogging.* Cambridge, England: Polity.

Rogers, E. (2003). *Diffusion of innovations* (5th ed.). New York, NY: Free Press.

Shapiro, J. J., & Hughes, S. K. (1996, March/April). Information literacy as a liberal art: Enlightenment proposals for a new curriculum. *EDUCOM Review, 31*(2), 31–35.

Silverblatt, A. (1995). *Media literacy: Keys to interpreting media messages.* Westport, CT: Praeger.

Silverblatt, A., & Zlobin, N. (2004). *International communications: A media literacy approach.* Armonk, NY: M.E. Sharpe.

Strategic Discussions for Nebraska. (2008). *Immigration in Nebraska.* Lincoln: College of Journalism and Mass Communications, University of Nebraska-Lincoln.

Sturgis, P. (2003). Knowledge and collective preferences: A comparison of two approaches to estimating the opinions of a better informed public. *Sociological Methods Research 31*(4), 453–485.

Sturgis, P., Roberts, C., & Allum, N. (2005). A different take on the deliberative poll. *Public Opinion Quarterly, 69*(1), 30–65.

University of Nebraska Public Policy Center. (2007). *By the people: Dialogues in democracy, immigration and Nebraska.* Lincoln: University of Nebraska Public Policy Center.

Vericat, J. (2010). Accidental activists: Using Facebook to drive change. *Journal of International Affairs, 64*(1), 177–180.

CHAPTER 14

CITIZEN PARTICIPATION AND PERFORMANCE

A Model for Citizen-Based Government and Performance Management

Marc Holzer
Rutgers University–Newark

Lauren Bock Mullins
Rutgers University–Newark

Citizen-based government, or government that is fueled by and acts on the needs and demands of the people, should be an important justification for the implementation of both performance budgeting and performance-based management; but it is often overlooked. As de Lancer Julnes and Holzer argue, "Although practitioners will accord lower importance or status to responding to constituents' demands as an objective for strategic planning, it is clear that these demands and pressures underlie most of the other objectives for strategic planning," (de Lancer Julnes & Holzer, 2008, p. 68). This is not surprising, considering that Ammons and King found

The State of Citizen Participation in America, pages 325–347
Copyright © 2012 by Information Age Publishing
All rights of reproduction in any form reserved.

even productivity improvement is not on the top of administrators' priority lists, falling fourth behind fiscal crisis, capital improvements, and economic development (Ammons & King, 1983).

De Lancer Julnes and Holzer (2008) designate a list of four other factors that inhibit citizen-driven government:

CHALLENGES FOR CITIZEN-BASED GOVERNMENT

1. Agency reluctance to implement a power-sharing culture.
2. Citizen-based government conflicts with hierarchy and specialization of bureaucracy.
3. Public managers lack of training in skills for citizen/customer surveys.
4. Public managers' deficiencies in collaboration, negotiation, and conflict resolution (skills necessary for productive citizen engagement). (p. 84)

This list of challenges can be expanded to a fifth point: citizen-based government is not a top priority for public managers, even when they are implementing performance improvement initiatives, versus other priorities such as identifying goals; building infrastructure (as transparency Web sites); collecting relevant, recent, and accurate data; and getting the bureaucracy onboard/motivating staff. Perhaps the major reason why citizen-based government is not a priority is that public sector issues are so complex that the concept of enveloping citizens in the process becomes marginalized, if brought to the table at all. And so within this complexity of public sector concerns, policy pitfalls, and political quagmires, there is a lack of a citizen-based government culture. This is partly due to lack of public sector advertising, public education promoting citizen-based government, and citizen-based government motivation by public employees.

Further, citizen-based government is not a priority to the extent that public managers have enough trouble implementing the performance management programs they have, and often fail to implement them due to problems such as insufficient funding; they are, therefore, unprepared to further complicate the process by adding in a citizen participation component.

We also must wonder if bureaucrats are reluctant to include citizens in the process because they fear the difficulty involved in potential outcomes. When you are serving a diverse constituency, the demands and interests are likely to be a cumbersome undertaking.

Kwak identifies unintended consequences of performance measurement—problematic implementation factors—as tunnel vision, suboptimization, myopia, measure fixation, misrepresentation, gaming, and ossification. In addition, he cites the "Performance Paradox," meaning "incongruence between reported Performance Indicators and actual performance itself," (Kwak, 2006, p. 97).

Since government cannot legally advertise itself as does the private sector, it is difficult to get the word out to the public in order to educate them about their civic responsibilities as Schachter's (1997) citizen-owners, suggesting that in the future, public education institutions might somehow instill this in the curriculum for the benefit of all constituents as well as future government leaders and bureaucrats. It is difficult to expect people to want to do citizen-based government if they do not have an appreciation for what citizen-based government is. Perhaps then, the motivation for performance improvement would no longer be exclusively cost cutting; rather, there would be ample room for public participation. Perhaps strengthening and promoting interest groups established to promote citizen-based government would also be useful assets in bridging this gap.

This chapter will provide an overview of theory on how citizen participation has been linked to performance improvement, followed by a discussion of a sample of relevant case studies as to how these concepts have played out in real-world examples, and then will offer a theoretical model for citizen-based government as a catalyst for performance-based management.

LITERATURE

In their introductory chapter of Citizen-Driven Government Performance, Holzer and Rhee (2006) define performance measurement as "an advanced management tool that is becoming more and more sophisticated and systematic" (Holzer & Rhee, 2006, p. 1) and explain how it factors in a wide range of needs deriving from various government levels and communities requiring diverse services. Holzer and Rhee then introduce a model of five concepts for achieving enhanced productivity as follows:

- Measuring for Performance

  In terms of performance measurement, the most successful agencies are those that use the techniques... in order to move from subjective, personal measures of performance to objective, empirical measures. To maximize productivity and success, agencies should establish goals and measure results, using multiple measures of internal capacities, outputs (services), and outcomes (impacts). Performance-measurement tools allow agencies to effectively estimate and justify resource requirements, and when appropriate, reallocate resources. And agencies can involve employees in the process to motivate them to improve their performance.

- Managing for Quality

  Managing for quality requires top management support, employee empowerment and teamwork. Employees must be adequately trained and recognized for their contributions. Managing for quality demands a customer focus, an emphasis on long-term strategic planning, and a commitment to measurement, analysis, and quality assurance.

- Developing Human Resources

  One key part of managing for quality is developing human resources. Quality managers need to recruit the best and brightest, and then provide them with systematic training and ongoing employee assistance. The best managers recognize the value of diversity, and they build services by building teams within the organization. They understand the importance of balancing the needs of employees and the needs of the organization.

- Adapting Technologies

  Managers should not be afraid to use automation to enhance productivity. The most innovative and effective agencies willingly adapt cost-effective applications and crosscutting techniques in order to accomplish their goals. When used well, technology can allow agencies to provide open access to data and to deliver services and information in response to the public's demands.

- Building Partnerships

  In order to enhance productivity, innovation, and performance, agencies should look for appropriate opportunities to form partnerships. Collaborating with other public-sector entities, members of the private sector, nonprofit organizations, citizens and volunteers can help agencies improve their performance. (Holzer & Rhee, 2006, pp. 3–4)

Despite the accessibility of these performance-improvement tools to public managers, due to lack of citizen engagement in planning, data generation, and decision making, the public sector often fails to succeed in performance improvement. To what extent is this failure directly related to lack of citizen engagement in the process? In other words, why is citizen involvement important when it comes to performance improvement?

De Lancer Julnes (2006) discusses the importance of citizen participation, offers examples of models, citing the spectrum, from low to high, of participation developed by the International Association for Public Participation (IAPP):

1. Inform: to provide the public with balanced and objective information to assist them in understanding the problems, alternatives and or solutions
2. Consult: to obtain public feedback on analysis, alternatives and or decisions

3. Involve: To work directly with the public throughout the process to ensure that public issues and concerns are consistently understood and considered
4. Collaborate: to partner with the public in each aspect of the decision, including the development of alternatives and the identification of the preferred solution.
5. Empower: to place final decision-making in the hands of the public. (http://www.iap2.org.au/spectrum.pdf, as cited by de Lancer Julnes, 2006, p. 165).

De Lancer Julnes says citizen participation incorporated in performance management programs is mutually beneficial to citizens and governments—governments gain trust, legitimacy, and responsive/accountable perceptions, while citizens get empowerment, value for their taxes, and a sense of community.

Yang reminds us of Berman and Wang's (2000) work that says performance measurement relies on stakeholder support, while involving citizens in the process of performance management is a good tool for democracy; "Informing stakeholders about government performance is consistent with the democratic spirit of transparency and informed citizenship" (Yang, 2008). In her study of trained-observer ratings, Mark says, "The perspective of a stakeholder will always be a little different from the view of a professional" (Mark, 2008). Mark also reinforces the idea that including volunteers in civic engagement can help to make "historically disenfranchised" citizens feel empowered (Mark, 2008). Yang cautions,

> Without stakeholder involvement, performance measurement may be guided by bureaucratic interests and the technocratic logic and produce numbers that external stakeholders cannot understand. In turn, when elected officials and citizens are better informed about government performance, they are more likely to participate. (Yang, 2008)

Based on such theories, it seems likely that citizen involvement in performance improvement efforts would be a win-win, but in reality, the relationship between the two concepts proves to be a delicate one, fraught with challenges.

While adoption of performance management has been widespread in the U.S. public sector, there is much work to be done to bring stakeholders into the equation (Yang, 2008). Holzer identifies three roadblocks to citizen-driven government performance: lack of patience by politicians due to their focus on reelection, reluctance to uncover pricey problems, and the issue of experts not being able to clearly communicate results to stakeholders (Holzer, 2005). Nevertheless, there are also various theories as to why the system might break down even if the government has its act together, such as citizens may not participate, and if they do, it is difficult to ensure sustained participation. Depending on the type of information presented and how it is presented, citizens may opt in or out. Yang (2008) cites Epstein, Coates, and Wray (2006), who say citizen participation is likely when negative information about performance is communicated in a way that interests them.

Riccucci reminds us that ever since the National Performance Review (NPR) (beginning on March 3, 1993) and the 1993 Government Performance and Results Act (GPRA), much research has been done about performance measurement, "But in the frenzy of implementing performance measurement programs, governments have lost sight of the fact that it is extraordinarily difficult to measure government outputs" (Riccucci, 2006, p. 78). She cites the problems of goal and customer identification in relation to this process, and she additionally discusses the difference in how public sector considerations play out when linking citizens to performance improvement. "Unlike in the private sector, the government is bound by values of democratic governance, including equity, due process, and responsiveness to the general public," (Riccucci, 2006, p. 81). While she is a proponent of citizen-driven measures, citing various examples of literature that attest to performance measurement having increased accountability, she cautions that citizens who are active in governance are more likely to be educated and in-the-know about government processes, which may result in the incorporation of only certain interests, adding equity concerns. Considering the challenges involved in measurement, accountability, and equity, she posits that the ideal setting for performance management is municipal government, because of its closer access to citizen participation.

The complexity of implementation is also a problem. Yang (2008) cites three issues involved in implementing stakeholder-centered performance measurement:

1. Technical/conceptual: Why is there a need for stakeholder involvement? This framework specifies how public organizations can get different stakeholders involved, in different steps of performance management, in different ways and for different reasons. All of these factors need to be carefully thought out in order to construct an appropriate plan.
2. Organizational: How can managers use resources to make stakeholder-centered performance management happen? Unfortunately, since performance measurement is often implemented to reduce cost, there is often a lack of resources for bringing in stakeholders and also a lack of training. There is an emphasis on the importance of leadership to spearhead these efforts and sustain them (Berman & Wang, 2000; McDavid & Hawthorn, 2006; Melkers & Willoughby,

2001, as cited in Yang 2008). Getting citizens involved in performance measures also requires a pliable organizational culture.
3. Institutional: Performance management and citizen participation rely on major changes in the institution.

Mark (2008) discusses the potential problems involved when implementing performance management with a citizen focus; for example, the potential for pushback from public officials who are concerned that measuring performance could lead to being punished for circumstances beyond their control.

Regardless of this litany of obstacles, the future of citizen involvement in performance management is not as bleak as it might seem. Halachmi argues that civil society organizations can play a role in promoting citizen-driven government. He predicts that

> a better developed civil society facilitates better use of the finite resources that are available to a given polity. Thus, greater safety and security which result from a better performance by civil society-based organizations may indicate better governance, and thus better government performance." (Halachmi, 2006, p. 15)

Berman (2006) recommends the use of citizen surveys to link citizens to government performance, and while he warns that such surveys are complicated and costly, he believes they may be a better tool for engaging citizens in the performance process, as opposed to public hearings, elections, and such.

Price says, "increased initiatives that stress citizen participation, evaluation, and performance measurement have been instrumental in improving public sector productivity by heightening the awareness and importance of citizen-based performance initiatives" (Price, 2006, p. 111), and that much of this education has happened through nonprofit agencies, academic institutions, and citizens themselves. Price notes a global movement to promote and increase citizen-based government, citing Rutgers University-Newark's National Center for Public Performance, which offers a performance measurement and citizen participation certificate through a Sloan Foundation initiative, as well as Canada's Public Service 2000 federal initiative, as appropriate examples of "high leverage projects," (Price, 2006, p. 122).

What then, do we have left to learn? Having considered much of the convergent literature on citizen participation and performance management, the picture of exactly how these concepts can be collaboratively joined for the benefit of all stakeholders becomes clearer; but like an elaborate watercolor painting, the colors merge, fade, and bleed into one another when we factor in the tribulations associated with development, implementation, and outcomes for all involved parties, leaving us with the potential for various interpretations. Holzer and Kloby (2008) contend that while there are some instances of "citizen-driven performance measurement," there is more theory out there than sustained, real-world examples of implementation. According to Ryan's work on performance measurement in relation to public education, "public engagement has not been studied systematically" (Ryan, 2008), and so there remains a need to go beyond case studies to systematically examine exactly how public engagement works in relation to performance measurement. However, until that research is done, we must rely on case studies as supplements to the theory in order to frame a more vibrant and accurate picture.

CASE STUDIES

The following case studies illustrate the benefits of citizen-driven performance measurement in the United States by providing specific illustrative examples of citizen involvement in the development and implementation of performance initiatives.

Ho (2011) conducted a case study of the performance management and budgeting program in Indianapolis ("Indystat," modeled after Baltimore's Citistat) to see if performance data could have an impact on subdepartmental funding decisions. Ho statistically analyzed the budgets of 41 departments and agencies from 2008 to 2010, conducted interviews of officials involved in the initiative, and sat in on Indystat meetings to record observations. The qualitative data was gathered to see how performance information is used in conversations about the budget. Regression results showed that the variation of program budgets is significantly and positively correlated with the variation of the departmental budget; the more performance measures a department reported to IndyStat, the more intradepartmental budget changes took place in the department. Ho also found, to his amazement, that program budget variation was negatively correlated with the number of outcome measures used. He explains this regression result by postulating that perhaps departments with more outcome-based measures are more progressive in management style and more focused on the community, which increases trust in government and alleviates the likelihood of outside intervention. Further, he finds that departments with more outcome-based measures might better be able to justify certain programs and their importance to policy goals, which could lead to less volatility in the budget process and more stable program budgets. This case study shows that performance-based budgeting (PBB) can actually work in practice, and that performance information could be effectively used to make program decisions.

Krueathep's case study of Chattanooga, Tennessee, (2010, p. 3) illustrates how the city went from treating citizens as customers to government partners through a system of three major management systems, initiated by Mayor Bob Corker, who created the Office of Performance Review when he realized there was no way of tracking government performance because they lacked sufficient data. The 3-1-1 system, which traces government response to information from citizen calls; ChattanoogaRESULTS (http://www.chattanooga.gov/office_performance_review/1449.htm), modeled after CitiStat; and ChattanoogaCITIZEN, a project funded by the Alfred P. Sloan Foundation to get citizens involved in creating performance measures for their municipal government, were all quite successful. ChattanoogaRESULTS and 3-1-1 provided direct citizen access to city government and helped keep city managers focused on their achievements or lack thereof. ChattanoogaRESULTS also developed political support, redefined the organization, and encouraged IT and staff commitment. Then, to take citizen involvement even further, the city implemented ChattanoogaCITIZEN, which involved citizen deliberation, shared authority and responsibilities, and citizen collaboration with government officials. This third step, implementing ChattanoogaCITIZEN, is really what transformed the model from citizen-as-customer to citizen-as-partner.

The case of Chattanooga proves that a well-developed measurement system is a difficult but worthwhile project to link citizens more closely to government for beneficial outcomes. The documents describing Chattanooga-RESULTS, on the City of Chattanooga's Web site, stress the importance of measuring successes, which can be beneficial to government employees; it is really a win-win situation, helping to improve performance and encouraging positive views of citizen participation.

The Collaborative Governance Council in Minnesota (http://www.osa.state.mn.us/default.aspx?page=20100702.000) was the result of a bipartisan plan by the 2010 Minnesota state legislature to create a council that would make recommendations for the legislature and governor so as to increase collaboration in government. Members included representatives from city, county, town, and school board governing bodies, as well as representatives from the Minnesota Chamber of Commerce, AFSCME, Education Minnesota, and SIEU. All meetings were open to the public, and materials pertaining to the meetings were posted on the State Auditor's Web site. Often citizens, lobbyists, and chamber representatives were in attendance at the nine meetings that were convened. The focus of the Council was on looking at areas of collaboration in local government such as technology, shared services, joint purchasing, and joint powers agreements. They found that local governments wanted better ways to deliver services in a more efficient and effective way and were able to give recommendations based on their findings. Impediments to collaboration were identified as finance, mistrust, and power. They also found that the main ingredient for successful collaborations is communication on a regular basis among all community stakeholders, including city, town, chamber, nonprofits, businesses, and schools. They reported that building relationships would be crucial to improving trust and eliminating power and financial disagreements. This case is a good example of how much could be accomplished through citizen participation in collaboration with local government, even when there is no allocated funding for staff (see Collaborative Governance Council Legislative Report 2011, http://www.osa.state.mn.us/other/councils/CollaborativeGovernance/Collaborative_Governance_Council_Legislative_Report.pdf).

King County's collaboration, the Committee to End Homelessness, in Seattle, Washington (http://cehkc.org/), includes the Funders Group, which was named one of the Top 25 "Innovations in American Government" by the Kennedy School of Government in May 2011. This collaboration is 3 years into its 10-year plan and has realized much success. Their Web site includes extensive details about the program, including quarterly reports, news, and highlights. The Committee to End Homelessness is structured as follows:

- Governing Board: 20 elected officials, business people, and community faith leaders from various parts of the county.
- Consumer Advocacy Council: a group of homeless people who either currently are homeless or have at one time been homeless; they provide information on best ways to run the system and represent the homeless needs and interests of the county.
- Interagency Council: the executive director and department director level personnel from the various organizations involved in the collaboration effort in King County; they focus on how to change current programs to better serve the needs of the homeless community.
- The Funders Group: they coordinate the funding by setting priorities and timelines; this group is composed of representatives from the public and nonprofit groups who provide major homeless services and housing funding. Members come from the housing authority, donor foundations, and the United Way of King County.

The committee enjoys staff support for implementation from the King County Department of Community and Human Services, and the funding comes from United Way of King County, the City of Seattle, and other sources. Three committees divided by population (targeting single adults, families, and young adults) provide assistance. Public relations increases awareness and education about homelessness and is responsible for the annual report and Web site, and the South King County Forum on Homelessness and the Eastside Homelessness Advisory Committee focus on regional solutions aimed at local needs.

The separate groups work together and support each other. For example, the Funders Group considers policy recommendations from the Interagency Council and other divisions and then develops an annual work plan to make sure their strategies will help make progress toward attaining the goals contained in the 10-year plan. They have sought to fully embed "best practices" into the process, and have seen much success in improving efficiency and meeting goals, rather than spending money on a system that was not working as well as it could. This case serves as a robust example of how county stakeholders can organize around a cause to produce favorable results, accomplished in a way that might not be possible without such a collaborative effort of a large group of stakeholders.

The Boulder County Human Services Strategic Plan in Boulder, Colorado (http://www.bouldercolorado.gov/files/boulder_county_human_services _strategic_plan.pdf), also referred to as "Building Caring Livable Communities," is a winner of the 2010 National Association of Counties Achievement Awards (http://www.naco.org/programs/recognition/ Pages/2010AchievementAwards.aspx) and is an example of how citizen participation can be folded into government strategic plans to improve performance. In 2006, the Human Services Coordinating Council appointed a steering committee to coordinate human services planning to improve the county funding in human services; they also founded an organization that would serve as a consulting team. Building a strategic plan was a community-based approach, beginning with a 2-day event called "Future Search," in which 64 community leaders got together, including business people, human service providers, policymakers, and educators, to sit down and identify the county's priority needs as well as opportunities. Based on seven priority areas, action groups were set up to focus on each of these areas, and the action groups were open to any community member, meeting between two and five times to generate benchmarks and strategies. Four community forums were held, as well as a nonprofit/funder summit, to help develop the strategic plan. A public Web site was created to track the progress of the strategic initiative.

Manoharan's case study of the New York Public Interest Research Group's (NYPIRG) Straphangers Campaign (Manoharan, 2010, p.17), which began in 1979, traces the success of a citizen-driven program meant to make the NYC subway system cleaner and more reliable, at a point in time when such conditions were deplorable. The campaign became known for its State of the Subways report cards. These report cards based their findings on six different measures that were developed with the help of stakeholder input. Overall, the campaign was successful in making the subway system a better place for citizens. This case study was a positive example of the importance of advocacy groups to improving citizen participation, the importance of measuring both inputs and outputs, and the importance of information communication tools, such as the Internet, for publishing reports and obtaining citizen feedback (http://www.straphangers.org/).

In the case study of the Dayton, Ohio, project (Harris, 2001, p. 7), Harris describes how Dayton's citizen participation system of seven Priority Boards wanted to select indicators of quality of life and publish an annual report while also developing citizen participation indicators. Harris recommends that any community looking to implement a similar project should have commitments from three types of organizations: city government; a powerful citizen group in the community; and academic assistance to provide technical, design, and organizational skills. Harris says that four of the seven Priority Boards have reaped early rewards from the strategic planning process, but that the true success lies in the sustainability of the Priority Boards, which will be fueled by further citizen recruitment as citizens witness board progress. According to the City of Dayton Web site, this program has increased responsiveness and aligned service delivery with priorities of citizens. The site states,

> To address today's problems and face the challenges of the future, citizens must participate directly in the solution of ALL community problems. This will include building the economic base, restoring and maintaining neighborhood vitality and fostering the quality of life for all citizens. More and more, it will require community involvement in human and social service arenas to address issues of self-sufficiency, families and children. (http://www.cityofdayton.org/departments/pcd/cp/Pages/PriorityBoards.aspx)

Coates and Ho's case study on "Citizen-Initiated Performance Assessment" in Iowa was funded by the Alfred P. Sloan Foundation in 2001 (Coats & Ho, 2010, p. 12) and involved citizens, city council members, and departmental staff of nine cities in developing and using performance measures for evaluation. Lessons learned from this project are that such a program can increase public accountability, that public communication plays an important role, that citizens have an interest in comparative performance measurement, that measures should be reported to neighborhoods so they are applicable to the citizens of that area, and that public reporting of performance measurements is useful and can be done cheaply with the use of the Internet.

Harris and Holzer's case study on the Street Smoothness Project in the City of New York (Harris & Holzer, 2001, p.16) was an initiative by the Fund for the City of New York's Center on Municipal Government Performance. It began with representative focus groups of people who were asked four pertinent questions in order to develop performance measures. The first of its kind in the nation, this project used a "Profilometer" to get laser technology reads of the conditions of roads, and then this data was transformed into a "City Roughness Index." The program enjoyed short- and long-term benefits, which include a new performance measurement system that the public deemed serious, transference of government engineering evaluations to public use evaluations, objective measures of streets, and public and governmental access to important information on the streets throughout the city. This project is an example of how citizen participation can be translated directly into practical, focused success.

Steele and Holzer's case study of the CitiScan Project in Connecticut shows how technology in the hands of everyday citizens can be a good tool for government service evaluation (Steele & Holzer, 2001, p. 19). In Hartford, Connecticut, neighborhood groups helped figure out which measures would be important to focus on and decided on a list of 35 measures. They then gave a group of high school students digital cameras, special software, and handheld computers to take a survey of the parks in the area. Using technology for documentation, they were able to give the city government a detailed account of park conditions. Although there was local government disinterest in the program, and community leaders' time was limited for data collection and meetings, among other benefits to the community, they found that the participating students saw their neighborhoods in a new way, neighborhood groups now had better data for leverage, and nonprofit groups were now taking on responsibility for handling problems like graffiti. This case is a good example of how, despite lack of interest, it is possible to work around the government to collect and report data.

Apsel's case study takes up the topic of Insideschools.org, an online guide to public schools in New York City, which is sponsored by Advocates for Children of New York and was funded by the Alfred P. Sloan Foundation to help parents learn about legal rights, get advice, or complain to a school. Measures such as enrollment, attendance, graduation rates, test scores, and ethnic breakdown are accessible for 1,200 schools, but it also provides school descriptions and reviews based on interviews with parents and school visits. Parents are also able to post comments. Apsel points out, "This feature serves as a sort of electronic town hall meeting where citizens-parents, students, teachers and community members come together to share information about their experience in a particular school, its curriculum, or its leadership," (Apsel, 2001, p. 22). This site is meant to assist parents in making educated decisions for their children and to make schools more accountable while also making sure city and state performance indicators are balanced. The site also provides "articles, opinions and advice" (http://insideschools.org/). This case is a good example of how citizen participation can be enhanced by technology and how such participation can serve as a platform for accountability of government agencies and services.

Similar to the theoretical literature linking performance and citizen participation, the case studies highlighted in this chapter provide insight into not only the difficulties involved in the process, but the promise in developing and implementing performance management programs in the public sector with thorough citizen involvement, not simply in a symbolic way, but in a real and practical way, and how such programs can benefit all involved stakeholders. These real-world examples transcend national boundaries, and the lessons learned could be applicable to any government, depending on the particular circumstances.

THEORETICAL MODEL

Having considered the theoretical literature and case studies aforementioned, it might be worthwhile to envision a model to integrate citizen-based government and performance management (see Figure 14.1). In order to promote citizen participation in government, it is essential that the public education system incorporate proper education on this subject in a way that will create a public spirit of participation and an understanding of the importance of community involvement in government in relation to performance. Programs such as the CitiScan project in Hartford are a good example of a case-based learning so that high school students might learn the importance and effectiveness of individually getting involved in their local governments. Service learning or internship opportunities could be offered at the high school and college levels for students to take part in community groups that engage in processes such as developing performance measures to see how deliberation and collaboration play out. Another way to incorporate it into the curriculum, even as early as grade school, would be an Earth Day–type initiative in which instead of learning about the environment and preserving the Earth's natural resources, students would learn how civic involvement in performance management programs helps to enhance democracy, hold governments accountable, and build a strong sense of community.

By educating young people about what citizen participation is in relation to performance management, and how it can be a useful tool for them and their communities, we stand to gain not only responsible and contributive members of society, but future government leaders and bureaucrats who might better understand and appreciate the need to have programs that combine citizen participation and performance management. Again, it is difficult to expect people to want to do citizen-based government if they do not have an appreciation for what citizen-based government is. The motivation for performance improvement would then be expanded across the board beyond mere cost cutting.

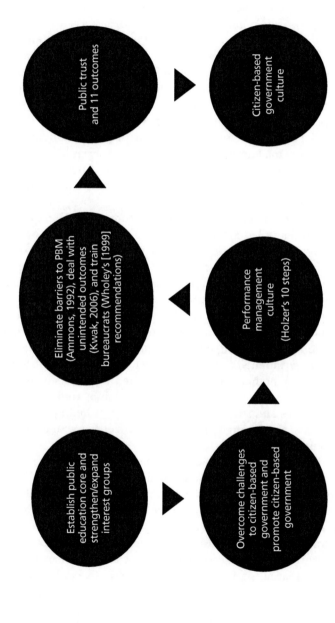

Figure 14.1 A model for citizen-based government and performance management.

Then if a strong and focused public education curriculum was to be combined with the strengthening and promotion of interest groups established to promote citizen-based government, this would help foster the grassroots development of a performance management culture. The cases discussed above tell us how private organizations helped citizens organize for the sake of the common good, despite government indifference. Strengthening such interest groups will be a complex task, involving not only citizens, but funding. Perhaps certain interest groups could consider joining together in collaborative agreements to share resources and ideas, while university programs such as Rutgers NCPP could provide programs such as seminars developed specifically to educate citizen participation interest groups on shared services, strategic planning, advertising, and recruitment. Even individual citizens or small groups of citizens can have a significant impact by creating grassroots organizations such as Courage to Connect NJ (http://www.couragetoconnectnj.org/), a nonprofit organization that promotes public engagement and shared services.

Developing a performance management culture would help to bring the discussion to dinner tables, making performance measurement and citizen participation household concepts. Performance measurement combined with citizen engagement would no longer be optional for governments; rather, it would be just the way things are done—business as usual. This would make related programs more innovative by building on past successes and trying out new options and ideas; obligatory in the sense that it would be unheard of for a government to not incorporate such programs; and sustainable to provide long-term outcomes, as opposed to the current potpourri of governments cherry-picking what techniques, if any, they would like to use. Whether the authority of the programs stemmed from legislation, the executive or management leadership would matter little since infrastructures and systems would likely already be in place and ripe for improvements. Not having to reinvent the wheel every time a new party takes over would be a boon.

Thus, having a performance management culture would potentially lead to elimination of performance management barriers that Ammons warns of, which include environmental, organizational, and personal barriers (see Table 14.1). Barriers that can often be overcome or circumvented often remain, and so must somehow be managed (Ammons, 1992).

Properly training bureaucrats to do performance management (Wholey, 1999) is one way to promote the importance of citizen participation. Wholey recommends that all staff and managers receive five different areas of training:

- Recognizing political and bureaucratic contexts for performance-based management;

TABLE 14.1   Common Barriers to Productivity Improvement in the Public Sector

Environmental Barriers[a]

Absence of market pressures

Political factors that influence decision making

Public's lack of patience with operational changes

Lack of enthusiasm for gradual gains

Dominant preference for the status quo

Productivity's lack of political appeal

Short time horizon of politicians and top administrators

Subordination of efficiency to secondary status

Limited options for achieving economies of scale

Procurement and personnel procedures

Legal restrictions and court rulings

Anti-innovation and antiproductivity effects of some grants and other intergovernmental programs

Intergovernmental mandating of expenditures

Organizational Barriers[b]

Bureaucratic socialization process

Lack of accountability

Focus on output rather than outcomes

Perverse reward system

"Spend it or lose it" budget rules

Inadequate management commitment to productivity

Barriers to monetary incentive plans

Union resistance

Perceived threat to job security

Excessive layers of middle management

Supervisory resistance

Ambiguous objectives

Reluctance to abandon

Insufficient analytic skills or analytic staffing

Inadequate cost-accounting systems

Inadequate performance data within/across jurisdictions

Inadequate performance evaluation/appraisal

Inadequate dissemination of program information and reluctance to use what is known

Fragmentation of government

Bureaucratic rigidities, including an extreme focus on rules and procedures

Fragmented authority or uncertainty about where decisions can be made

Turf-protecting tactics

Inadequate research, development, and experimentation

Requirement of large initial investment for productivity improvement efforts

Performance myths

Overselling productivity

(continued)

TABLE 14.1 Common Barriers to Productivity Improvement in the Public Sector (continued)

Personal Barriers[c]

  Inadequate control of time/workday

  Conceptual confusion

  Risk avoidance

  Proclivity to "paralysis by analysis"

  Managerial alibis

---

[a] Barriers common to virtually all public sector operations (i.e., obstacles that are part of the public sector environment).

[b] Barriers found at varying degrees in many public sector organizations (i.e., obstacles whose presence and magnitude are likely to vary from one organization to another).

[c] Barriers that stem from traits, attitudes, and behavior of individuals.

Source: Ammons, 1992

- Defining mission, goals, and strategies for achieving goals;
- Measuring, evaluating, and reporting on performance;
- Using performance information;
- Reinforcing performance-based management (Wholey, 1999, p. 72).

Once strategically armed with the proper skills, staff and management alike will have an easier time accomplishing performance management in a way that is productive and useful; this would likely lessen resistance to such programs.

Another important part of the performance management culture would be to educate managers and staff on Holzer and Lee's (2001) multistep strategy. These prescriptions were created with the expectation that they would be molded and adjusted to fit each specific organization and set of circumstances; they stand to serve as a basic guide for organizations that are implementing performance management. They are

Step 1. *Clarifying Goals and Obtaining Support:* Productivity programs must agree upon, and have commitments to, reasonable goals and objectives, adequate staff and resource support, and organizational visibility. The full cooperation of top management and elected officials is a prerequisite to success.

Step 2. *Locating Models:* Because productivity is an increasing priority of government, existing projects can suggest both successful paths and ways to avoid potential mistakes. Models are available from computer networks, the professional literature, and at conferences.

Step 3. *Identifying Promising Areas:* As a means of building a successful track record, new productivity programs might select as targets those functions continually faced with large backlogs, slipping deadlines, high turnover, or many complaints. Because personnel costs are the largest expenditure for most public agencies, improved morale, training, or working conditions might offer a high payoff. Organizations might also target functions in which new techniques, procedures, or emerging technologies seem to offer promising paybacks.

Step 4. *Building a Team:* Productivity programs are much more likely to succeed as bottom-up rather than top-down or externally directed entities. Productivity project teams should include middle management, supervisors, employees, and union representatives. They might also include consultants, clients, and representatives of advocacy groups. If employees are involved in looking for opportunities, then they are likely to suggest which barriers or obstacles need to be overcome; what tasks can be done more efficiently, dropped, or simplified; which workloads are unrealistically high or low.

Step 5. *Planning the Project:* Team members should agree on a specific statement of scope, objectives, tasks, responsibilities, and time frames. This agreement should be detailed as a project management plan, which should then be updated and discussed on a regular basis.

Step 6. *Collecting Program Data:* Potentially relevant information should be defined broadly and might include reviews of existing databases, interviews, budgets, and studies by consultants or client groups. A measurement system should be developed to collect data on a regular basis, and all data should be supplied to the team for regular analysis. The validity and usefulness of such information should be constantly monitored.

Step 7. *Modifying Project Plans:* Realistic decisions, based on continuing team discussions of alternative approaches and data, must be made about program problems, opportunities, modifications, and priorities. For instance, would a problem be solved best through the more intensive use of technology, improved training, better supervision, or improved incentives?

Step 8. *Expecting Problems:* Projects are more likely to succeed if they openly confront and then discuss potential misunderstandings, slippages, resource shortages, client and employee resistance, and so on. Any such problem, if unaddressed, can cause a project to fail.

Step 9. *Implementing Improvement Actions:* Implementation should be phased in on a modest basis and without great fanfare. Projects that are highly touted, but then do not deliver as expected, are more likely to embarrass top management (and political supporters), with predictable consequences. Projects that adopt a low profile are less likely to threaten key actors, especially middle management and labor.

Step 10. *Evaluating and Publicizing Results:* Measurable success, rather than vague claims, is important. Elected officials, the press, and citizen groups are more likely to accept claims of success if they are backed up by hard data. "Softer" feedback can then support such claims. Particularly important in providing evidence of progress are timely data that reflect cost savings, additional services, independent evaluations of service levels, client satisfaction, and reductions in waiting or processing times.

Once a society has developed a performance management culture, it will get closer to reaching the coveted goal of "Public Trust," which Goodsell calls the "pinnacle byproduct" of public administration (Goodsell, 2006, p. 67).

Other beneficial outcomes, typically expected of good performance management, include accountability, responsiveness, openness, diversity, comparability, complexity, reporting, resources, and accuracy (de Lancer Julnes & Holzer, 2008). Additionally, representative democracy might be considered a tenth outcome because "enlisting citizens in policy deliberation sends the message that government is interested in promoting and supporting a representative democracy" (de Lancer Julnes & Holzer, 2008, p. 84).

Another outcome of a performance management culture fueled by citizen-based government is that more research might well be conducted to add to theory and best practice knowledge. And finally, the combination of increased trust, along with the eleven beneficial outcomes (above), will lead to a strong citizen-based government culture. Such a culture would benefit all stakeholders, because an inclusive, collaborative community is a productive one.

CONCLUSION

What, then, is the added value of citizen participation as a critical resource for improving the performance of public organizations? Several possibilities, vis à vis the challenges identified at the beginning of this chapter, appear to form such an agenda:

1. Because citizens have a great deal of evaluative "data" to offer in terms of their experiences and critiques of public service delivery, agencies need to overcome their reluctance to share power insofar as "information is power." That is, agencies are only advantaged by real-world data and cases that citizens might offer, and power is a barrier to that data sharing. The cases in this chapter are evidence that citizen participation is widespread, works, and contributes to performance improvement.

2. Citizen-based government is, more specifically, a threat to the bureaucracy in terms of rigid hierarchy and specialization of functions. But so what? Intelligent bureaucracies should welcome the participation of citizens, even as untrained observers, because their perspectives offer insights that desk-bound bureaucrats cannot possibly imagine.

3. Even public managers who are open to citizen feedback lack requisite training. This suggests that citizen groups should take the initiative to connect public servants with capacity-building resources such as short courses, but might also suggest that a citizen group, university, or foundation establish an online certificate that could help improve the capacities of public managers in this regard.

4. Further, beyond the survey research or interviewing skills necessary to obtain valid and reliable citizen feedback, public managers need to master specific sets of skills, such as collaboration with citizen volunteers, negotiation with citizen groups, and conflict-resolution strategies that would foster consensus.

5. Overall, then, the culture of public management has to change from one that assumes that citizens are annoyances to a more progressive and productive concept of citizens as partners. Public bureaucracies are increasingly seeking ways to do more with less. Given that they commonly have far fewer financial resources than they recently controlled, citizen-based government offers substantial and valuable resources—human and informational—that cannot be ignored. Involving citizens is a win-win strategy, an avenue for data- and case-driven analysis, and a partnership that can only help improve agency productivity and performance.

REFERENCES

Ammons, D. N. (1992). Productivity barriers in the public sector. In M. Holzer (Ed.), *Public productivity handbook* (pp. 117–136). New York, NY: Marcel Dekker.

Ammons, D. N., & King. J. C. (1983). Productivity improvement in local government: Its place among competing priorities. *Public Administration Review, 43*(2), 113–120.

Apsel, D. (2001). Inside schools-advocates for children: Lessons from New York City. In *Citizen-driven government performance: Case studies and curricular resources* (pp. 22–23). Newark, NJ: Rutgers University. Reprinted with permission from the *PA Times*, monthly newspaper of the American Society for Public Administration (ASPA), www.aspanet.org.

Berman, E. M. (2006). The art and science of doing citizen surveys. In M. Holzer & S-K. Rhee (Eds.), *Citizen-driven government performance* (pp. 91–110). Newark, NJ: Rutgers University.

Berman, E. M., & Wang, X. (2000). Performance measurement in U.S. counties: Capacity for reform. *Public Administration Review 60*(5), 409–420.

Coats, P., & Ho, A. T-K. (2001). Citizen-initiated performance assessment: Lessons from Iowa. In *Citizen-driven government performance: Case studies and curricular resources* (pp. 12–13). Newark, NJ: Rutgers University. Reprinted with permission from the *PA Times*, monthly newspaper of the American Society for Public Administration (ASPA), www.aspanet.org.

de Lancer Julnes, P. (2006). Engaging citizens in governance-for-results: Opportunities and challenges. In M. Holzer, & S-K. Rhee (Eds.), *Citizen-driven government performance* (pp. 161–187). Newark, NJ: Rutgers University.

de Lancer Julnes, P., & Holzer, M. (Eds.). (2008). *Performance measurement: Building theory, improving practice.* Armonk, NY: M.E. Sharpe.

Goodsell, C.T. (2006). A new vision for public administration. In M. Holzer & E. Charbonneau (Eds.), *Public management & administration illustrated, Vol. I English (A volume in a multi-lingual collection of diagrams)* (p. 67). Newark, NJ: Rutgers University.

Halachmi, A. (2006). Civil society organizations and citizen driven performance measurement. In M. Holzer, & S-K. Rhee (Eds.), *Citizen-driven government performance* (pp. 15–50). Newark, NJ: Rutgers University.

Harris, G. L. A. (2001). Quality of life indicators: Lessons from Dayton, Ohio. In *Citizen-driven government performance: Case studies and curricular resources* (pp. 6–7). Newark, NJ: Rutgers University. Reprinted with permission from the *PA Times*, monthly newspaper of the American Society for Public Administration (ASPA), www.aspanet.org.

Harris, G. L. A., & Holzer, M. (2001). Straphanger's campaign: Lessons from transit in New York City. In *Citizen-driven government performance: Case studies and curricular resources* (pp. 14–15). Newark, NJ: Rutgers University. Reprinted with permission from the *PA Times,* monthly newspaper of the American Society for Public Administration (ASPA), www.aspanet.org.

Ho, A. T-K. (2011). PBB in American local governments: It's more than a management tool. *Public Administration Review, 71,* 391–401.

Holzer, M., & Kloby, K. (2008). Helping government measure up: Models of citizen-driven government performance measurement initiatives. In P. de Lancer Julnes, F. Stokes Berry, M. P. Aristigueta, & K. Yang (Eds.), *International handbook of practice-based performance management* (pp. 257–281). Los Angeles, CA: Sage.

Holzer M., & Lee, S. H. (2004). Mastering public productivity and performance improvement: From a productive management perspective. In M. Holzer & S-H. Lee (Eds.). *Public productivity handbook* (2nd ed.). New York, NY: Marcel Dekker.

Holzer, M., & Rhee, S-K. (Eds.). (2006). *Citizen-driven government performance.* Newark, NJ: Seoul Development Institute and the National Center for Public Performance, Rutgers University.

Krueathep, W. (2010). From passive participation to participatory deliberation: The case of evolving performance management system in Chattanooga, TN. In M. Holzer, D. Kong, & D. Bromberg (Eds.), *Citizen participation: Innovative and alternative modes for engaging citizens: Cases from the United States and South Korea* (pp. 3–16). Newark, NJ: Rutgers University.

Kwak, S. (2006). Consequences of performance measurement. In M. Holzer & E. Charbonneau (Eds.), *Public management & administration illustrated, Vol. 1: English (A volume in a multi-lingual collection of diagrams)* (p. 57). Newark, NJ: Rutgers University.

Manoharan, A. (2010). Citizen-driven government performance: The straphangers campaign New York City. In M. Holzer, D. Kong, & D. Bromberg (Eds.), *Citizen participation: Innovative and alternative modes for engaging citizens: Cases from the United States and South Korea* (pp. 17–24). Newark, NJ: Rutgers University.

Mark, K. (2008). Experience with trained observers in transition and developing countries: Citizen engagement in monitoring results. In P. de Lancer Julnes, F. Stokes Berry, M. P. Aristigueta, & K. Yang (Eds.), *International handbook of practice-based performance management* (pp. 233–256). Los Angeles, CA: Sage.

Price, B. E. (2006). Evaluation, citizen engagement, and performance measurement tools to make government more productive. In M. Holzer & S-K. Rhee (Eds.), *Citizen driven government performance* (pp. 111–128). Newark, NJ: Rutgers University.

Riccucci, N. M. (2006). Integrating citizen-driven measures and performance improvement. In M. Holzer & S-K. Rhee (Eds.), *Citizen-driven government performance* (pp. 77–90). Newark, NJ: Rutgers University.

Ryan, K. E. (2008). Performance measurement and educational accountability: The U.S. case. In P. de Lancer Julnes, F. Stokes Berry, M. P. Aristigueta, & K. Yang (Eds.), *International handbook of practice-based performance management* (pp. 213–232). Los Angeles, CA: Sage.

Schachter, H. L. (1997). *Reinventing government or reinventing ourselves: The role of citizen owner in making a better government.* Albany: State University of New York Press.

Steele, L., & Holzer, M. (2001). City Scan project: Lessons from Hartford, Connecticut. In *Citizen-driven government performance: Cases studies and curricular resources* (pp. 18–19). Newark, NJ: Rutgers University. Reprinted with permission from the *PA Times*, monthly newspaper of the American Society for Public Administration (ASPA), www.aspanet.org.

Wholey, J. (1999). Performance-based management: Responding to the challenges. In P. de Lancer Julnes, & M. Holzer (Eds.), *Performance measurement: Building theory, improving practice* (p. 72). Armonk, NY: M.E. Sharpe.

Yang, K. (2008). Making performance measurement relevant: Informing and involving stakeholders in performance measurement. In P. de Lancer Julnes, F. Stokes Berry, M. P. Aristigueta, & K. Yang (Eds.), *International handbook of practice-based performance management* (pp. 173–188). Los Angeles, CA: Sage.

CHAPTER 15

AN ANALYSIS
OF COLLABORATIVE
GOVERNANCE MODELS
IN THE CONTEXT
OF SHARED SERVICES

**Marc Holzer, Lauren Bock Mullins, Rusi Sun,
and Jonathan Woolley**
Rutgers University–Newark

INTRODUCTION

In the face of economic crises, limited resources and crippling federal and state budgetary cuts of extraordinary proportions, it has become increasingly important to consider ways in which government can sustain itself while inching its way out of a deficit, and without sacrificing quality service delivery. For this reason, collaborative governance, which joins public and private forces to accomplish common goals for the community, provides a fertile ground for exploration into innovative and efficient ways to create and implement public policy. Considering current economic constraints, it is also useful to consider how important collaborative governance can be in

The State of Citizen Participation in America, pages 349–384
Copyright © 2012 by Information Age Publishing
All rights of reproduction in any form reserved.

promoting and implementing initiatives such as shared services (Holzer & Fry, 2011) in order to conserve resources.

For a long time, citizens have been primarily considered as the users of public services and products. However, their roles have greatly changed. Recent years have witnessed citizens taking a more active role in decision-making processes in governments of all levels throughout the world. Therefore it is assumed that the government should not only make an effort to achieve "better responsiveness to citizens as clients," but also to develop and maintain "effective collaboration with them as partners" (Vigoda, 2002, p. 527). This practice has been extensively documented in the literature. In reviewing it, it is not surprising that citizen involvement can happen at various stages of governmental administration. The Porto Alegre project, one of five cases of participatory governance in Fung and Wright's study (2001), illustrates the impact of citizen participation programs on budget development. Citizen participation can also make a difference in ecosystem management and environmental planning (Brody, 2003; Leach, 2006; see also Ansell, 2003; Moore & Koontz, 2003; Soma & Vatn, 2009). Moreover, it is obvious that local governments tend to involve a large number and diverse group of residents to solve community related problems such as education, health, and so on (Lasker, 2003).

Citizen participation has been defined as "the process by which members of a society (those not holding office or administrative positions in government) share power with public officials in making substantive decisions and in taking actions related to the community" (Roberts, 2004, p. 320). These decisions and actions are aimed at influencing both the direction of public policy and its execution. "Many public services require for their execution the active involvement of the general public and, especially, those who are to be the direct beneficiaries of the service" (Whitaker, 1980, p. 242). One successful means of achieving this, Whitaker explains, is "citizens and agents interacting to adjust each other's service expectations and actions" (1980, p. 242). Citizens often do this by forming organizations to further their interests on that particular issue in the belief they will be able to collectively achieve goals that would be difficult for them to achieve individually.[1] In fact, this practice is so common[2] that Zimmerman and Rappaport, in their study regarding a sense of empowerment among people participating in community organizations, used a definition of citizen participation "as involvement in any organized activity in which the individual participates without pay in order to achieve a common goal" (Zimmerman & Rappaport, 1988, p. 726). "Collaborative local action," as Cuthill and Fien (2005) have noted, "is the visible expression of [a] community and local government relationship" (p. 75).

Thus, citizen participation allows residents of a jurisdiction to express their relative satisfaction with the performance of government services—

a manifestation of Whitaker's view of "citizens and agents interacting to adjust each other's service expectations and actions" (1980, p. 242). "As government services continue to devolve, and an array of different entities are providing public services, citizen participation offers answers to issues of democratic accountability" (Holzer & Bromberg, 2011, pp. 1–2). Numerous organizations started by concerned citizens have graded the performance of local governments regarding their delivery of services; quality-of-life issues in Seattle (Bromberg & Charbonneau, 2011) and transit agency performance in both New York (Manoharan, 2011) and Philadelphia (Woolley, 2011) are just three of many instances in which citizen-based organizations have critiqued service delivery by governments in their respective jurisdictions and have provided suggestions for the improvement of those services. In sum, they are doing what Donahue (2004) describes as governance, doing "what government does (though not always directly or on its own)" (p. 2).

Thus, these citizen-based organizations are providing governance. Ansell and Gash (2008) define collaborative governance as

> a governing arrangement where one or more public agencies directly engage non-state stakeholders in a collective decision-making process that is formal, consensus-oriented, and deliberative and that aims to make or implement public policy or manage public programs or assets. (p. 544)

By providing information about service administration and management, these citizen-based organizations are providing governance. Indeed, this form of citizen-based collaborative governance has become more important in recent years as responsibility for government service delivery has often been decentralized ("Central to governance theory is the idea that state power has become 'de-centred' and is now exerted through plural institutions" [Newman, Barnes, Sullivan, & Knops, 2004, p. 217]). Civil society organizations can help lead to greater public productivity (Halachmi, 2005), which is especially important when one considers how performance measurements are typically based on inputs rather than on outcomes that correspond to citizen satisfaction (Cohn Berman, 2006). Since citizen involvement has been shown to increase public productivity (Price, 2005), it follows that a form of collaborative governance that fosters citizen involvement would also have potential to improve performance. Thus, collaborative governance provides a vehicle for citizen involvement in ways that can be beneficial to all.

The importance of collaborative governance as an opportunity for citizen participation also emerges when one considers, as de Lancer Julnes notes, "Engaging citizens in policy deliberation sends the message that government is interested in promoting and supporting a representative democracy" (2005, p. 175). Furthermore, collaborative governance could miss the mark if it is not citizen focused; that is, citizen involvement becomes critical to a successful and appropriate use of that approach. After all, public service is not merely a "bottom line." It is useful, therefore, to consider how citizen-based groups can resolve community issues through collaborative governance.

Methodology

With this goal in mind, the study upon which this chapter is based entailed a thorough investigation of innovative collaborative governance models at the local and regional level, with a focus on citizen involvement and a potential application of that problem-solving capacity in the context of shared services. We identified and ranked models of collaborative governance to determine the most appropriate models for forming a problem-solving citizen council to serve as a catalyst for community reform and improvement. We researched examples of collaborative governance models that deal with shared services through publications, case studies, the Internet, news clippings, and videos. After choosing 21 best practice organizations in the United States and Canada based on the capacity for citizen involvement and a shared services context, we created a more refined checklist of criteria with which to compare and evaluate each organization. These criteria focused on issues such as the method of funding the organization, the source of the organization's members and/or personnel, the amount of citizen involvement in the organization, the comparative amount of citizen focus by the organization, the amount of satisfaction felt by citizens about the organization, and overall success of the organization in achieving its goals. In order to rank the 21 cases, we selected key criteria from the checklist and compared totals of the aggregate number of key characteristics present in each case. These key characteristics collectively serve as a measure of the success of implementation of each program. Thus, these totals created an automatic ranking system, with the highest-numbered totals representing cases with "best features."

Using a chart we prepared from those criteria, each organization was then evaluated based upon its relative merits. Some of the rejected organizations, however, had one or two features rarely seen among the good role models and that were considered important in organizational development; using the chart meant we could identify these key features without having to use those entire organizations as role models. Thus, the evaluation chart allowed for a great deal of flexibility (see the chart in Appendix 3).

After analyzing the group of selected cases, three separate models combining best practices were devised as recommendations for the development of future collaborative governance models. Three different researchers collaborated on the analysis of cases.

Other issues, including whether or not the organization had shown a particular record of innovation, whether the organization had received an award, the geographical scope of the organization, and the organization's interest in the promotion of the sharing of services among government entities were also considered. To help ensure the effectiveness of this evaluation chart, we then asked an expert (K. Yang, personal communication, June 2011) on citizen engagement to briefly review the criteria we had chosen. That expert pronounced the criteria list to be "comprehensive," but suggested adding a category regarding the use of social media. This was duly added, as were two other categories regarding Internet usage that we ourselves constructed.

The case descriptions in Appendix 1 provide an overview of the organizations, including structure, function, funding, and other information relevant to helping create our models. After analyzing the group of selected cases, the research team devised three separate models. Diagrams of the organizational structures of each model are also provided below.

Analysis

The cases we collected through different channels appear to be the best representation of collaboration involving citizen participation and shared services in the United States and Canada. They vary considerably in terms of their initiation, location, size, service delivered, funding resources, organizational structure, function, and management. Therefore it is helpful to summarize the primary characteristics of successful practice of collaborative governance and shared services as well as the basic components of its governance and administration based on the review of these cases. Moreover, reviewing these practices helps to provide a basis for proposing three models in the following section.

The summary proceeds in four parts. First, the initiator of collaboration will be discussed. This is important since the initiator would determine the structure of the collaboration, the composition of a governance board/committee, and the sources of funding. Then we will discuss the organizational structure in terms of what kind of collaborative governance structure could maximize representation of the whole population and provide access to mutual benefits such as shared services.

The next aspect of collaboration pertains to funding sources. We identify the tendency that no matter who is the initiator of the collaboration, the type of services, the population and the areas served are more likely to influence the amount of resources they can attain.

Finally, specific managerial strategies that each case uses were analyzed to see what practices are important in order to determine their success, besides effective governance structure, sufficient funding, or strong support from a locality, and other government entities.

Initiators

Among the cases listed in Appendix 1, the collaborations are either initiated by grassroots agencies, by a group of citizens in the related neighborhood, or by governments. The programs identified by agencies are often about the provision of a service whose benefit is confined to a relatively small geographic area, such as public education, recreation, or public health. Therefore, the primary aim is to increase citizen accessibility and improve the quality of public service in the locality. For example, the DC Promise Neighborhood Initiative (DCPNI, 2010) started from a small group of community residents and other active supporters who made the effort to discuss how neighbors could collectively promote school success and access to college for neighborhood children.

Citizens often identify opportunities for collaboration and cooperation at the grassroots level. In the case of Montana's Blackfoot River Watershed (Harvard Kennedy School, 2011), a network of community-based partnerships was developed by the U.S. Fish and Wildlife Service and is made up of citizens and representatives from state and federal natural resource agencies. Over 660 partners are involved in collaboration, each with different sets of interests. The cooperation between landowners, conservationists, and government allowed for improved management of the watershed.

The Structure of Shared Service Initiatives

When higher levels of government decide to develop collaborative governance and shared services, it is almost always the case that the delivery of services by the private sector is insufficient and costly. Those services and goods that are characterized as "public goods," such as road maintenance, fire, emergency, courts, or services that mainly focus on improving the cost-effectiveness of government administration, are targets of opportunity for sharing services across vast geographic areas and multiple agencies. For example, the Collaborative Governance Council in Minnesota (Office of the Minnesota State Auditor, 2011) is a statewide initiative backed by legislation termed "Minnesota 2010." The focus of the Council is on looking at areas of collaboration in local government such as technology, shared services, joint purchasing, and joint powers agreements. The primary purpose is to find a better way to deliver services more efficiently and effectively. More-over, the Shared Services Initiative of Sussex County, NJ (Sussex County, 2011) is another government created collaborative governance program which attempted to reduce the duplication of services and facilitate cost savings in a time of financial uncertainty.

The Structure of Collaborative Governance Practices

The essential aspect that determines the successful implementation and management of collaborative governance and shared services is the gov-ernance structure of the organization. The effectiveness of a governance structure relies considerably on the appropriate composition of political authorities, administrative professionals, and citizens. According to the Washington State Shared Service Model 2009, the organizational structure should make sure that, "1) critical business decisions are made in a timely manner; 2) services are deployed in ways that produce planned results; 3) the needs of consumers, provider agencies, and other stakeholders are sat-isfied by each service," (Washington State, 2009, p. 11).

As a result, whether collaborations are initiated by grassroots agencies or by governments, governance structures with extensive citizen participation often, but not always, consist of similar components. A three-tier structure is most often used, incorporating (Washington State, 2009): (a) one overall control body in which the authorities are centralized, such as a Govern-ing Board or Steering Committee. This entity is mainly in charge of goal setting, strategy development, funding, and management to ensure that the shared services are implemented in ways that produce the desired level of performance and benefit; (b) an Advisory Committee as a body that is responsible for developing specific plans prescribing how the service is provided and that oversees the collaborative process in order to design, implement, and operate a given shared service. It recruits members from both organizations, providing service and groups of service users. In the case of DCPNI, the Advisory Committee is composed of neighborhood resi-dents, local elected officials, education policy experts, and executives from local foundations and corporations, who bring different advantages and tools to the table; (c) finally, a User Committee is necessary for each shared service. The User Committee functions as the citizen feedback loop on per-formance and operations, and provides necessary suggestions for further improvement of a given public service.

Moreover, through strengthening the interaction between service provid-ers, consumer agencies, and governmental employees, the User Committee plays an important role in maintaining the extensive participation in the whole process of shared services delivery. Besides the current consumers of shared services, it is argued that the User Committee "should consider membership from potential consumers to help ensure as broad a view of the service as possible" (Washington State, 2009, p. 31). That committee structure is evident in one of our cases: King County collaboration to End Homelessness in Seattle (Committee to End Homelessness, 2011). In this shared services program, a group of people with experience being homeless offers ideas and opinions to inform best practices and represent the needs of the homeless. The general governance structure is illustrated by Figure 15.1.

Single-level governance can be identified from some cases in which the services are initiated by governments, especially those services at city-level governments. Planning departments at the county or municipal governments are often in charge of the development and implementation of programs. For example, in Westchester County, New York (Westchester County, 2011), the government is focused on consolidating several basic services at the county level; the planning department identifies the key fields in which the possible shared services opportunities lie and creates a variety of shared services programs to encourage the agencies of city governments to make use of those opportunities.

Figure 15.1 Governance structure of shared service. *Source:* Washington State Shared Services Model (http://dis.wa.gov/WA_shared_services_model.pdf).

Moreover, in the presence of sufficient support from government, some shared services programs have established a special position to resolve issues and coordinate participants in the process of shared services operations. For example, Sussex County, New Jersey, has developed a specific department that is in charge of shared services programs. The position of shared services coordinator was initially supported by funds from the state of New Jersey Department of Community Affairs. The duties of the Shared Services Coordinator include "1) to make contact with all of the municipal officials and initiate discussion on possible shared service opportunities; 2) act as a third party negotiator for contracts and services; 3) facilitate the expertise of county employees to review proposed municipal projects/public entity service contracts" (Sussex County, 2011).

Funding Sources

The cases of collaborative governance models we collected vary considerably in terms of their funding sources. Most of the grassroots collaborations obtain their funding from governmental grants, such as DC Promise Neighborhood Initiative, which is one of 20 national recipients of the U.S. Department of Education's Promise Neighborhood Planning Grants. Some obtain funding from for-profit organizations and individual donations.

The government-initiated programs have simpler sources of funding. The primary support often comes from governments, especially the parent organizations or agencies. This is not surprising as these services are more likely to be public goods, which the government has the responsibility to provide. For example, shared services at the county or local levels in Westchester and Sussex counties are more about infrastructure construction and public works. Their primary purpose is to save government operational costs and improve the decision-making process. Most of these programs, therefore, are financed solely by governments.

Since we did not have complete access to financial documents and related information about the operation of these shared services agencies, our analysis is somewhat limited in terms of funding. However, judging by the amount of grant funding each type of shared service program can obtain, our team found that no matter who is the initiator of the collaboration, the type of services, the population, and that areas served can influence the amount of resources they can attain. That is, programs such as ecological preservation and environmental protection are more likely to have large investments by government agencies. For example, the Think Salmon Collaborative Watershed Governance Initiative in Canada (Pacific Salmon Foundation, 2011) was initiated by nonprofit organizations dedicated to preserving wild salmon in British Columbia. Preserving wild salmon in British Columbia requires great investments of money and human resources, which can hardly be supported by any single organization or individual, therefore the local and federal governments play essential roles in financing them. This collaborative service got a $21 million fund established by British Columbia's Ministry of the Environment in 2002. Its parent organization, the Fraser Salmon and Watersheds Program, attained a $10 million grant (half in cash, half in services) from the federal government.

Managerial Strategy

Besides the three aspects discussed in the preceding part—the initiator, the governance structure and the funding sources—another characteristic of collaborative governance that substantially influences the effectiveness and success of its implementation and operation is the specific managerial approach to shared service implementation. Since there is no one size-fits-all suggestion for organizational administration, we list several key points that our team considers to be helpful for improving program performance.

First, some shared services programs make great efforts to track their service performance through measurable indicators and report performance information on their Web sites. It is argued that strategic use of performance measurement is essential to organizational goal-setting and improvement planning. Moreover, reporting performance data also contributes to the strengthening of the collaborative nature of shared services, which creates a venue for the communication among the different stakeholders. Therefore, cases such as DCPNI (2010) and MetroGIS (2010) are actively involved in the performance measurement system. DCPNI even seeks technical support from external institutes for performance measurement. The Urban Institute is the DCPNI data and evaluation partner and will take the lead in overseeing the development of the database, monitoring data quality, and producing regular performance reports for key project and program indicators. Moreover, the MetroGIS at Minnesota also operates a performance-evaluation system, which assesses whether the value and services created is consistent with customer needs. It also continually updates their performance-measurement plan and reports annually based on the results of diagnostic tools measuring the effectiveness of goals and plans in previous years.

Second, shared services have a lot to do with maintaining favorable public relations. Developing close partnerships with the external environment is substantially important, particularly in the era of networking governance. Therefore, during the implementation of shared services programs, the cooperative relationship between stakeholders makes it helpful for important goals to be achieved in which the risk of conflict will be substantially reduced. In the case of King County (Committee to End Homelessness, 2011), a thorough public relations approach, including distribution of an annual report and continually updating and expanding the Web site, have improved the organization's image and sustainability.

Finally, in recent years we have witnessed a diffusion of strategic management in public organizations by strengthening the linkage between goal-setting and performance-tracking. By developing long-term plans along with short-term goals, the shared services programs would have a better understanding about the extent to which the desired level of performance has been achieved. In our cases, some of them even take shared services as one of the important priorities for their strategic planning. For Boulder County, Colorado (Boulder County Human Services, n.d.), building a strategic plan was a community-based approach. They began with an event called "Future Search," gathering together 64 leaders from the community to put together a list of opportunities. Based on seven priority areas identified, action groups were established to create timelines and strategies to carry out work toward achieving goals.

In sum, based on the analysis of the key aspects of shared services, we can conclude that (a) the shared services in these cases are initiated by grassroots agencies and citizens in the related neighborhood or governments; (b) no matter whether the service programs are initiated from grassroots or by government, the governance structure often consists of three basic components even though the specific names varies: Governing Board, Advisory Committee, and User Committee; (c) shared services programs make use of various citizen-based strategies to improve their managerial capacity and effectiveness, such as enhancing public relations, tracking service provisions publicly through performance measurement systems, and utilizing strategic planning processes that involve citizens.

RECOMMENDATIONS

Based on the previous analysis of cases, three model organizations have been devised for future collaborative governance templates. Model A postulates the organization having a very low financial base. Model B postulates a better level of financial security. Model C postulates a moderate level of funding and a known ability to cooperate with local government.

Model A

We conceived of the first model keeping in mind that funding might be difficult to come by during the early stage of an organization, especially if

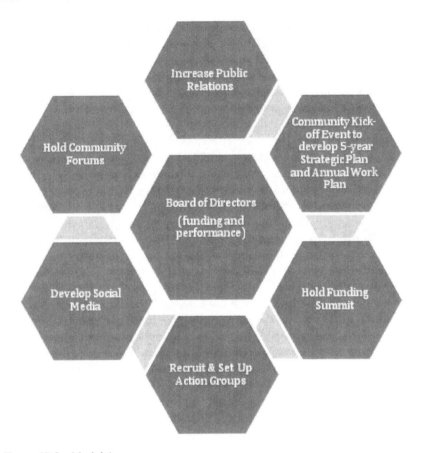

Figure 15.2 Model A.

it is initiated by citizens as opposed to government. To this end we recommend a model that can be effective but does not require a large amount of funding from the onset (see Figure 15.2). The structure might begin with a Board of Directors (that you already have) as the "control center" of the council. The Board of Directors would oversee all projects of the council as it expands, with a focus on generating/seeking funding.

As we saw in the Boulder County case (Boulder County Human Services, n.d.), we recommend building a strategic plan through a community-based approach, beginning with an event in which community leaders might agree upon a prioritized list of needs. The results of this meeting will allow the Board of Directors to identify the main areas in which action is needed. From there, action groups of volunteers can be recruited, to think of ideas, and plan strategy for different projects. For example, categories of action groups may include shared services and education initiatives. Another consideration might be holding regular community forums and a funding conference to attract and gather possible donors to discuss ideas and get them involved.

Like the King County case (Committee to End Homelessness, 2011), we recommend an increase in public relations (increased awareness about the collaboration, publishing an annual report and generating timely Website updates); developing a 5-year plan, and then an annual work plan, to make sure board strategies will help make progress toward the goals for the plan; and incorporating "best practices" into the implementation process. In addition to tracking the progress of the council on a Web site, social media connections (i.e., creating a Facebook and Twitter account) would help empower the council.

Model B

Model B is a combination of various techniques to involve several stakeholders (see Figure 15.3). The Depot Town Community Development Foundation (Depot Town Community Development Foundation, 2011) has pursued a policy of developing an Advisory Council of six members separate from its Board of Directors. These advisory councilors were often recruited by the original board members and generally have similar financial resources to that of the board's members. By recruiting them, the board achieved two forms of additional buy-in to the organization: personal and financial. Their involvement as advisory councilors meant they knew their opinions would be listened to, which in turn, encouraged them to

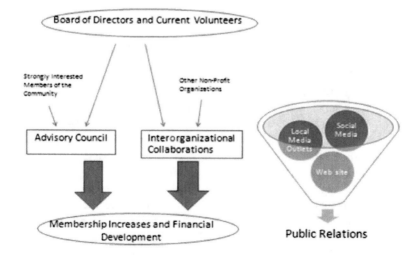

Figure 15.3   Model B.

make additional efforts to support the organization including soliciting additional volunteers and financial contributors. It also encouraged them to contribute financially themselves. Recruiting additional members (and financial contributors) by developing an advisory council, strongly influential to but hierarchically junior to the board of directors, could be useful. This in turn would then be used to recruit additional volunteers and donors. Not only would this increase the capacity of the collaboration, but each involved person would serve as a symbol, providing word-of-mouth "advertising" in practice.

Interorganizational collaborations among nonprofits have become a successful method of achieving an organization's goals in recent years, particularly when grant money is involved. In addition to the Depot Town Community Development Foundation, the Think Salmon Collaborative Watershed Governance Initiative (Pacific Salmon Foundation, 2011) and the St. Margaret's Bay Stewardship Association (St. Margaret's Bay Stewardship Association, 2008) have used partnerships with other organizations to obtain grant money they might not have been able to obtain individually. In addition, as the Depot Town Community Development Foundation has found, interorganizational cooperation helps raise an organization's profile among both other nonprofits and local governments (Depot Town Community Development Foundation, 2011). Similarly, the St. Margaret's Bay Stewardship Association has worked with the equivalents of local Chambers of Commerce, thus allowing it to achieve buy-in to its plan from organizations that might otherwise have opposed them.

Cultivating political contacts will also be helpful, along with soliciting community input. Conducting occasional focus groups with ordinary citizens would allow access to information only citizens have. More importantly, however, they would also serve two other purposes. First, they would help spread the word about the collaboration among the community, perhaps resulting in additional volunteers or additional donations. Second, having a focus group's endorsement of the collaboration will help convince local politicians and local town administrators to pursue this option. Some of the cases researched in this study, such as the Stanislaus Recreation Stakeholders (Sacramento State Center for Collaborative Policy, n.d.a) and the Pathway 2007 Lake Tahoe Restoration Project (Sacramento State Center for Collaborative Policy, n.d.b), both of which occurred in California, used the facilities and expertise of Sacramento State University for an extended period of time to effect this.

An additional issue to consider is the need to increase awareness in the community regarding the collaboration. In essence, this means improving the organization's public relations efforts. If people do not know of the organization's existence, not only will they not know to make use of the organization for the community's needs, they will not know they can donate financially to the organization. Additionally, efforts to contact the public through social media networks should also be implemented, as should efforts to develop relationships with local news media outlets.

Model C

The third model was created keeping in mind that once collaboration took place, the public service it delivered would influence a wide range of geographical areas (i.e., the service is very professional and technical, such as GIS data or watershed, etc.) Therefore, we recommend an alternative model (see Figure 15.4) to illustrate the characteristics mentioned above.

Besides the board of directors, which serves as the control and representative body, an Executive Committee that is responsible for implementation and intellectual support would be set up. The Executive Committee could be composed of professionals and relevant groups from nonprofit and for-profit organizations. What differentiates this model is that the Executive Committee should be led by government officials; having more government officials serving on the committee could strengthen buy-in from political and administrative officials.

Furthermore, if services provided are complicated, several working groups that aim to fulfill different goals can be developed, such as is the practice in DCPNI. These subgroups could be composed of a representative of neighborhood residents, appropriate experts, funders, service providers, and policymakers. They could meet frequently according to the progress of

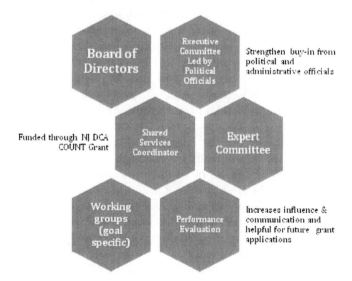

Figure 15.4 Model C.

the program. Their function would be to develop a specific plan to implement and monitor program operations and collect data.

Moreover, if the service provided requires special expertise, a professional committee can be developed as a supplementary organization to the executive agency to provide specific technical advice when the programs or policies do not work well due to practical problems. This committee can also play a role as a forum for information and knowledge-sharing, as in the case of MetroGIS Minnesota (MetroGIS, 2010).

The evaluation of program performance requires attention. This serves as a tool to facilitate communication between citizens and public organizations. Therefore, periodically reviewing the cost, output, and outcomes of shared services and reporting that evaluative data on a Web site would enhance that interaction and help to build mutual trust.

CONCLUSION

This chapter has examined various collaborative governance models in the United States and Canada. It is based on 21 cases, extracting the common themes and strategies used. These common themes and strategies could substantially assist the creation of future effective collaborative governance models beyond the three hypothetical models proposed herein. Different best practices should be chosen and combined carefully, based on each situation; not all collaborative governance models will work everywhere.

By collecting and analyzing evidence of successful collaborative governance, we can contribute to community knowledge about this phenomenon, which can be a useful resource for grassroots collaborative governance initiatives. Future research to continually track innovative trends in collaborative governance models will allow for extraction of best practices and analysis of what is actually successful over time. By researching and publishing such a compendium, we stand to gain shared knowledge of innovations that could very well benefit the entire community.

When citizens are at the heart of collaborative governance initiatives, there is more of a chance that the initiative will be focused on what is important for the community in terms of goals. On the other hand, government entities will get support and information they would not otherwise enjoy. The cases highlighted in this chapter tell the story of collaborative governance as a real, tested means to manage public services and policies. Where government alone fails or falls short, collaborative governance has the ability to regenerate progress. As more and more collaborative governance models surface, there will be more evidence of the power and potential this form of governance holds, and more real-world examples of how involved citizens can collaborate with government and private entities in significant ways to improve the efficiency and effectiveness of services to the public.

APPENDIX 1: CASE DESCRIPTIONS

Case I: DC Promise Neighborhood Initiative (DCPNI)

The DCPNI was developed to promote the accessibility of students to better public education and to improve their academic achievement in the community. These communities consist of seven neighborhoods in Ward 7, where 37% of the children are from low-income families. The unemployment rate is up to 30%. The students' performance is rated lower than the average school district in DC.

To achieve its goal and mission, the DCPNI develops collaboration of stakeholders to provide support for students in education by bettering the community environment, school environment, and student health. In 2011, DCPNI won a grant from the U.S. Department of Education's Promise Neighborhood Planning, totaling $500,000. Thus far, Cesar Chavez Parkside High School has reported an increase in student reading and math scores by 9% and 20%, respectively.

The governance structure of the DCPNI is developed basically on two tiers: the Advisory Board and different working groups for each of collaboration goal. Moreover, special institutional arrangements also play an important role in ensuring citizen participation in the whole process of collaboration. A video about collaboration can be found at the DCPNI (2010) home page.

Case II: Lake Norman Community Development Council (LNCDC)

The LNCDC in Davidson, North Carolina, involves nonprofits, government officials, members of the faith community, and residents of the North Mecklenburg/South Iredell community. They focus on the issues including housing, health care, education, and family; they develop different programs for each goal and attain funding from various resources. For example, two health agencies—the Ada Jenkins Center in Davidson and Solomon House in Huntersville—help prevent diabetes in the Lake Norman communities.

The structure of the LNCDC has changed over time due to their expansive focus (see Figure 15.5). It started with five subcommittees (Health, Housing, Transportation, Families in Crisis, Education), then added two

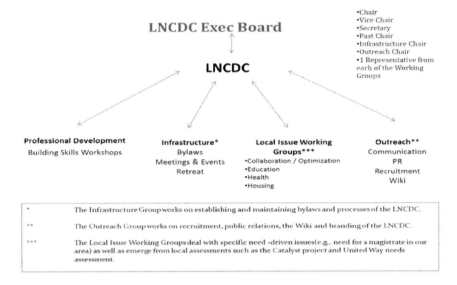

Figure 15.5 The general structure of the LNCDC.

more in 2005—Latino Outreach and Transitional Housing. In 2006–2008, the number dropped to four—Education, Health, Housing, and Social Issues. In 2009–2010, it "decommissioned" committees in favor of "action teams."

Case III: Models of Community Engagement, Minnesota Department of Health

The Minnesota Department of Health (2011) highlights three models for community engagement, civic engagement, community involvement and participation (see Table 15.1).

Case IV: Jefferson County Community Network, Washington State

The Jefferson County Community Network (n.d.) is a quasi-governmental agency. Its primary goal is to bring agencies, schools, community groups and parents together to work on preventing child abuse and youth substance abuse. They are part of a DSHS (Washington State Department of Social and Health Services) agency called the Family Policy Council, which works with Networks in other counties and represent them at the state level. The Jefferson County Health Department also receives funding from Wash-

TABLE 15.1   Models of Community Engagement

Models	Development	Purpose	Focus
Asset-Based Community Development	Developed by John McKnight and John Kretzmann	Discover a community's capacities and assets and to mobilize those assets for community improvement.	It discovers the strengths of a community and how to bring those strengths to bear in community improvement activities
Association for Community Health Improvement	Conceived in 2002 as a successor to three national community health initiatives	Strengthen community health through education, peer networking, and the dissemination of practical tools	Convenes and supports leaders from the health care, public health, community and philanthropic sectors to identify and achieve shared community health goals
Cultural Complementarity	Developed in 1993 by the Greater Twin Cities United Way	Put diverse people working together, valuing the attributes that such diversity brings to the group, in a combined effort to attain mutually agreed-upon goals that would be difficult to accomplish via separate efforts	Circle consensus

ington State's Community Mobilization Program to focus on the prevention of youth substance abuse and violence prevention.

The Jefferson County Community Network helps communities improve their prevention service. To achieve this primary goal, they operate different programs, activities, and forums and provide funding to other local groups. Moreover, the network provides consultant services to local programs regarding grant-writing as well as training services concerning program evaluation, and such. Finally they maintain community partnerships.

The Community Network is governed by a policy board of citizen volunteers and local agency representatives. They also employ one part-time staff member. For the flowchart of the organization structure of JCCN, please see Jefferson County Community Network (n.d.).

Case V: King County Collaboration to End Homelessness in Seattle

The Funders Group in the King County collaboration was named one of the Top 25 "Innovations in American Government" by the Kennedy School of Government as of May 2011; this collaboration is in its third year of the 10-year plan.

The Committee to End Homelessness is structured as follows:

- Governing Board: 20 leaders to plan and gather resources; members include elected officials, business people, and community leaders in different areas of King County.
- Consumer Advocacy Council: a group of people with experience being homeless; they provide expertise about homeless needs.
- Interagency Council: the executive director and department director level staff from the organizations involved in the collaboration; they focus on how to improve current programs.
- The Funders Group: they coordinate the funding; this group is composed of representatives from the public and nonprofit groups who provide funding.

The committee gets staff support from the King County Department of Community and Human Services, and the funding comes from United Way of King County, the City of Seattle, and other sources. Other committees that support them include three population committees (targeting single adults, families, and young adults), public relations (increases awareness and handles the annual report and Web site), and the South King County Forum on Homelessness and the Eastside Homelessness Advisory Committee (focuses on regional solutions aimed at local needs).

The separate groups work together. The Funders Group considers policy recommendations from the Interagency Council and other divisions and then develops a work plan each year to make sure their strategies are on target for progress toward specific goals laid out in the 10-year plan. They rely on best practices and have enjoyed much success in improving their implementation. To access a video on what their 10-year plan means to the community, go to http://www.cehkc.org/plan10/video.aspx. For more information, see Committee to End Homelessness (2011).

Case VI: Boulder County Human Services Strategic Plan in Boulder

In 2006, the Human Services Coordinating Council set up a steering committee to coordinate planning to improve funding in human services.

They founded an organization to provide a consulting team to help build this strategic plan through a community-based approach. They kicked off the initiative with a 2-day event called "Future Search," in which 64 community leaders pinpointed priorities. Based on seven priority areas that were identified, they then set up action groups that were open to the community, which would meet between two and five times to gather information. There were also four community forums held along with a nonprofit/funder summit. A Web site was created to track the progress of the initiative. For more information, see Boulder County Human Services (n.d.).

Case VII: Collaborative Governance Council in Minnesota

The 2010 Minnesota state legislature created a council to make recommendations for the legislature and governor to improve government collaboration. There was no funding or staff provided, but representatives from city, county, town, and school board governments as well as representatives from the Minnesota Chamber of Commerce, AFSCME, Education Minnesota, and SIEU were involved. There were various community members in attendance at the nine meetings held. The focus of the Council was to focus on areas of collaboration in local government, including technology, shared services, joint purchasing, and joint powers agreements. They found local governments were interested in finding better ways to deliver services with efficiency and effectiveness.

Despite this being a statewide initiative backed by legislation, the simple model and concept of gathering together members from various city organizations for a series of meetings with a common purpose and organized agenda could result in a fruitful outcome. For more information, see Office of the Minnesota State Auditor (2011).

Case VIII: Montana's Blackfoot River Watershed

This network has found a way to become a model of conservation. This was a surprising success in the western United States, where tensions between various stakeholders are inevitable. This grassroots cooperative system has created many improvements. In 1993, stakeholders joined together to create the Blackfoot Challenge, a nonprofit organization to promote cooperative conservation efforts in the watershed. So far, they have helped to conserve 90,000 acres of private lands, among other accomplishments. This example was cited in Weber (2009). For more information, see Harvard Kennedy School Ash Center for Democratic Governance and Innovation (2011).

Case IX: CALFED Bay Delta Program

The CALFED Bay-Delta Program is a collaboration of 25 state and federal organizations to improve California's water supply and the health of the San Francisco Bay/Sacramento-San Joaquin River Delta, the most vital source of water in California. In 2000, a 30-year plan for the delta was drafted, and the involved state and federal agencies promised to implement the plan. In 2002, the California Bay-Delta Authority was created to make sure implementation occurred, and in 2004 Congress adopted the plan. They have an Independent Science Board of engineers and scientists to help with policy decisions. This case was cited in O'Leary, Gerard, & Blomgren Bingham (2006). For more information, see CALFED Bay-Delta Program Archived Website (2007).

Case X: Sacramento Transportation and Air Quality Collaborative by the Sacramento Center for Collaborative Policy

The Sacramento Transportation and Air Quality Collaborative consists of 100 citizens who have come together to deal with transportation and related air pollution problems in the Sacramento area. The citizens involved represent businesses, public agencies, community groups, underprivileged populations, local neighborhoods, and the environment. It was started and sponsored by 11 public agencies and seeks to develop recommendations for Stakeholder Boards' use.

The Sacramento Transportation and Air Quality Collaborative was cited in O'Leary et al. (2006). For more information, see Sacramento Transportation and Air Quality Collaborative (2011).

Case XI: Think Salmon Collaborative Watershed Governance Initiative

Think Salmon is a project of the Fraser Salmon and Watersheds Program, which in turn is managed by two Canadian nonprofits dedicated to preserving wild salmon in British Columbia—the Pacific Salmon Foundation and the Fraser Basin Council.

In 2008, this project was launched to promote collaborative governance regarding the watersheds of British Columbia. The provincial government had recently released a plan regarding salmon preservation, so the timing seemed right to deal with the issue. In November 2008, a workshop was conducted on collaborative watershed governance. This created a consensus among environmentalists, native tribal leaders, and other stakeholders on how to proceed, and to continue dialog and engagement among each other. The stakeholders have begun working toward creating collective action for building a framework for more collaborative processes in watershed management. One key success of this project was achieving the support of a key politician, the former Lieutenant Governor.

This project was funded by a $60,000 grant from the Living Rivers Trust Fund, a $21 million fund established by British Columbia's Ministry of the Environment in 2002. Think Salmon's parent organization, the Fraser Salmon and Watersheds Program, is the result of a $10 million grant from the Living Rivers Trust Fund and a $10 million grant (half in cash, half in services) from the federal government. Between 2006 and 2010, the Fraser Salmon and Watersheds Program distributed $12.2 million to 275 projects, including Think Salmon's Collaborative Watershed Governance Initiative. For more information, see Pacific Salmon Foundation (2011).

Case XII: St. Margaret's Bay Stewardship Association

This is a nonprofit volunteer association in Nova Scotia dedicated to speaking on behalf of local residents regarding commercial development, environmental preservation, and reforming regional municipal bylaws pertaining to St. Margaret's Bay, Nova Scotia. The association has a 15-member Board of Directors and claims 500 supporters. The organization was established in 2003.

During the spring of 2008, the organization hosted a conference of local residents, soliciting their views on various social, environmental, and political options regarding the future of the Bay area. The association subsequently authored a position paper on regional issues based upon resident views. A follow-up meeting in 2009 regarding neighborhood development attracted people from 35 local organizations. A similar meeting in April 2010 helped the organization create substantial pressure to reform the relevant local ordinances.

The organization is also a member of the Nova Scotia Coastal Coalition, which is working to develop clear legislation regarding the demarcation of coastal preservation responsibilities. Through the Coastal Coalition's efforts, a recent memorandum was signed by the federal and provincial governments to work together in resolving this issue.

The association has the advantage of working closely with other regional and environmental groups in Nova Scotia, from which it draws some of its key supporters. It has also worked on issues affecting preservation of the region's natural character with the local Chamber of Commerce and Tourism Board, thus allowing it to receive buy-in from groups some might view as natural antagonists to coastal preservation. These factors give it a key advantage, since it makes it easier to access information about fundraising in the environmental nonprofit sector.

In 2007, the association raised over $1 million for the public purchase and management of an island in St. Margaret's Bay for preservation purposes. In 2008, the association established an endowment fund to maintain historic properties on the island. The organization recently received grants from the Aspotogen Heritage Trust, EcoAction, and the Nova Scotia Heritage Trust, enabling it to establish environmental heritage and stewardship programs in 2010. For more information, see St. Margaret's Bay Stewardship Association (2008).

Case XIII: Depot Town Community Development Foundation

This nonprofit, located in Ypsilanti, Michigan, seeks to help community members access economic, educational, civic, and recreational opportunities in the Ypsilanti area. To that end, it has partnered with various local and regional governments, as well as with other nonprofits, with a view to creating strategic partnerships toward the furthering of its goals. It has also partnered with private corporations.

The core of this organization is roughly the same size as that of many local community foundations (and is centered on one city much as many community foundations are). It has a Board of Directors consisting of five members and an executive director, who reports to the board. These six people are supplemented by an Advisory Board of 10 members, none of whom are members of the Board of Directors. This 16-person structure could serve as a blueprint for the future structural development of a typical small, young, community foundation, since the original nucleus of Depot Town was the similar in size to that of a typical new, startup community foundation. The initial members were able to involve other potential stakeholders as advisory members, who then helped create the resources necessary both to promote a larger role in the community and to recruit larger involvement from other organizations and governments.

The organization has partnered with various organizations in the Ypsilanti area. These efforts have allowed it to solicit funding from sources it might not have otherwise have been able to achieve on its own. This has important implications for a small, developing community foundation, indicating that cooperating with other foundations in the vicinity (for instance, in the same county) may increase its ability to raise funds. The organization has also been able to raise funds from organizations it has partnered with.

An example of raising funds from an organization it was partnering with is the Ypsilanti Area Community Foundation. In 2007, for instance, the Ypsilanti Area Community Foundation gave Depot Town a $2,000 grant regarding a parks project. Since, in 2007, Depot Town was still a growing organization, $2,000 represented a sizeable grant. However, the receipt of this grant allowed the organization to help build its reputation among other Michigan grantors. For more information, see Depot Town Community Development Foundation (2011).

Case XIV: Oakland 2025

This is a project of the Oakland Planning and Development Corporation, an organization that is dedicated to improving the Oakland neighborhood of Pittsburgh, Pennsylvania, by promoting community engagement, neighborhood preservation and investment, and job placement programs. As part of its community engagement programs, the Oakland Planning and Development Corporation developed Oakland 2025, a citizen-driven community planning process that is designed to develop common themes for planners to take into account as well as to help community members discuss ideas that matter, build relationships, and develop ideas for positive change. The process, which is still ongoing, involves over 100 local citizens, businessmen, and commuters, ranging in age from young adults to retirees, divided into eleven focus groups led by 25 moderators. The focus groups were conducted in various sections of the Oakland neighborhood and totaled 110 hours. They identified seven themes—some planning-related, some quality-of-life-related—for city officials to focus on. Additional meetings to help influence city policy are scheduled for the near future.

This program is a project of the Oakland Planning and Development Corporation, but is also supported by the Oakland Neighborhood Partnership Program. The Oakland Neighborhood Partnership Program, in turn, is funded by the Pennsylvania Department of Community and Economic Development Neighborhood Assistance Tax Credit Program. It has also received investments from Dollar Bank, PNC Bank, and the University of Pittsburgh Medical Center Health Plan. For more information, see Oakland Planning and Development Corporation (2010).

Case XV: Portsmouth Listens

Portsmouth Listens is a collaborative effort to provide grassroots citizen input on the updating of the Master Plan of Portsmouth, New Hampshire. Volunteers solicit public input on the city's future, which is then communicated to city officials. The city's Planning Board now views Portsmouth Listens as an integral part of the Master Plan updating process.

Portsmouth Listens uses focus groups to solicit public input. These focus groups consist of 8 to 15 members of the public, led by a moderator. These focus groups meet for two hours per week for approximately one month. The responses of the members of the public of each group are then combined and forwarded to city officials in a report. There are two rounds of focus groups: Phase I deals with general issues and Phase II deals with specific areas of concern raised during Phase I. A separate report is issued to city officials (and the public) after the completion of both Phases I and II. For more information, see Portsmouth Listens (n.d.).

Case XVI: Pathway 2007 Lake Tahoe Restoration Project

The goal of this project was to coordinate long-term development and ecological strategies for the water of Lake Tahoe and for the people who partake of and/or reside near the lake. The project was a cooperative project of the U.S. Forest Service, the Tahoe Regional Planning Agency, and environmental regulators from California and Nevada. The project includes a large public outreach component to include stakeholders who are not part of government agencies. This outreach solicited public input on the issues surrounding planning in the Lake Tahoe Basin. It was also used to help design other public policy issues regarding Lake Tahoe and the surrounding area. This outreach lasted from 2004 to 2007 and was facilitated by Sacramento State University's Center for Collaborative Policy. For more information, see Sacramento State Center for Collaborative Policy (n.d.b).

Case XVII: Stanislaus Recreation Stakeholders

This is a community group whose mission is to enhance recreation opportunities in California's Stanislaus National Forest. The group's primary goal is to reduce conflict between different types of recreational activities. They also seek to minimize the effect of all types of recreational activities upon the environment. The Forest Supervisor of Stanislaus National Forest has agreed to take the group's recommendations into consideration.

Stanislaus Recreation Stakeholders had its beginnings in 2002, when Sacramento State University's Center for Collaborative Policy helped form a small design team, which then conducted a 1-day work session with local stakeholders regarding the park's recreational opportunities. Within a year, this had become a formal collaborative process involving over 150 stakeholders. Because it was recognized that not all stakeholders personally partake of recreational activities in the park, the stakeholders include environmental and community representatives (such as homeowners) as well as representatives of various recreational pursuits. One particular area of interest is the Forest Service's rules about how and where motorized vehicles may be used in the park; resolving potential conflicts between vehicle users and non–vehicle users has been an interest of both stakeholders and the Forest Supervisor. Stanislaus Recreation Stakeholders continues to receive meeting and facility support from the Center for Collaborative Policy. For more information, see Sacramento State Center for Collaborative Policy (n.d.a) and U.S. Forest Service (2006).

Case XVIII: Shared Services and Programs in Westchester, NY

To reduce the cost of service delivery, increase the efficiency of government administration and improve the decision making process of the municipalities, the Planning department of Westchester County created a variety of shared service programs for the city-level governments. These programs include purchasing, printing, IT, public works, and emergency services, among others. For more information, see Westchester County (2011).

Case XIX: Shared Services Among New York's Local Governments

Many municipalities around New York State have already developed collaboration through formal or informal arrangements, which result in up to $765 million savings statewide. This report can be considered as the summary and evaluation of the shared services practice in New York State. It presents several examples of services that are most influential at the local government level such as public safety, public works and justice court, and so on. It discusses the pros and cons of using consolidated service delivery in enhancing the public performance, especially during these times of fiscal uncertainty, while it also reinforces the potential challenges and resources that are available. For more information, see New York State, Office of the State Comptroller (2009).

Case XX: Shared Services Initiatives of Sussex County, NJ

Sussex County has developed a specific department that is in charge of shared service programs. They have a position of Shared Service Coordinator supported by funds of the State of New Jersey Department of Consumer Affairs, COUNT Grant. This coordinator facilitates every step of development and implementation of consolidated services in Sussex County. These shared services have produced great cost savings.

Sussex County has initiated several shared service programs, which can be categorized into four types that vary in terms of the relationship with the governmental agencies involved:

1. County to municipality/public entity
   - All health services countywide
   - Winter road maintenance services
2. Municipal to municipal
   - Animal control
   - Tax assessing
   - Tax collecting
3. Municipality to county
   - Prosecutors office, Narcotics Task Force officers
4. County to county
   - Meals on Wheels (Passaic)
   - Purchasing co-ops (with Morris County)
   - Youth shelter (Morris County)

For more information, see Sussex County (2011).

Case XXI: MetroGIS Minnesota

The MetroGIS is the winner of 2002 Exemplary Systems in Government (ESIG) Award, Enterprise Systems category. It aims to provide regional sharing of geographic information among the 7-county Minneapolis-St. Paul metropolitan area. (For an illustration of the organizational structure, see Figure 15.6.) It serves as a forum in which the local and regional governments—along with other participants in state and federal government, academic institutions, nonprofit organizations, and businesses—collaborate voluntarily. The MetroGIS began its concept from the Minnesota GIS/LIS State Conference in September 1995, where wide needs of data that are essential to the business and community development and great opportunity to consolidate a regional GIS were identified. In the same year, MetroGIS approved the basis for its management mission, five initial strate-

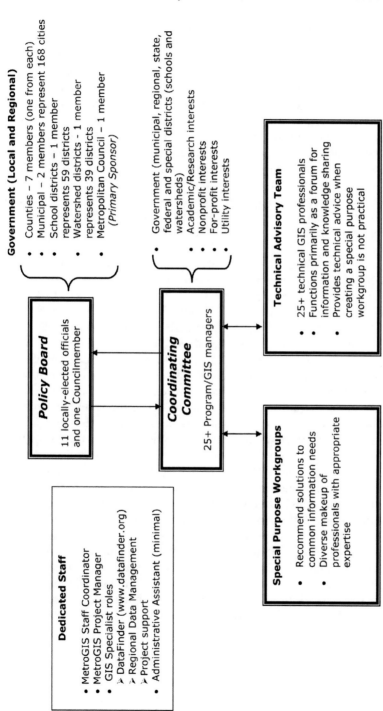

Government (Local and Regional)

- Counties – 7 members (one from each)
- Municipal – 2 members represent 168 cities
- School districts – 1 member
  represents 59 districts
- Watershed districts - 1 member
  represents 39 districts
- Metropolitan Council – 1 member
  (Primary Sponsor)

- Government (municipal, regional, state,
  federal and special districts (schools and
  watersheds)
- Academic/Research interests
- Nonprofit interests
- For-profit interests
- Utility interests

Policy Board

11 locally-elected officials
and one Councilmember

**Coordinating
Committee**

25+ Program/GIS managers

Technical Advisory Team

- 25+ technical GIS professionals
- Functions primarily as a forum for
  information and knowledge sharing
- Provides technical advice when
  creating a special purpose
  workgroup is not practical

Special Purpose Workgroups

- Recommend solutions to
  common information needs
- Diverse makeup of
  professionals with appropriate
  expertise

Dedicated Staff

- MetroGIS Staff Coordinator
- MetroGIS Project Manager
- GIS Specialist roles
  ➤ DataFinder (www.datafinder.org)
  ➤ Regional Data Management
  ➤ Project support
- Administrative Assistant (minimal)

Figure 15.6 MetroGIS organizational structure illustrated.

gic design projects, and an initial organizational structure. The time from 1996 to 2001 was spent refining the structure and function of MetroGIS. Since 2001, this collaborative agency has expanded into an institution that includes several hundred people representing a wide variety of agencies and organizations whose interests include counties; cities; metropolitan, state, and federal agencies; school districts; watershed districts; nonprofit groups; private organizations; utilities; research organizations; education professionals; and private citizens. To achieve their goals and strengthen the collaboration between different stakeholders, a system of participative processes were employed to guarantee the effective operation of the Metro-GIS, which led to huge success. This collaborative commitment is incorporated in the effort to develop a mission statement, priority functions (also referred to as "products and services," beginning with the 2002 Business Planning efforts), and identifying a priority of common business information needs.

In terms of funding, the MetroGIS attains substantial support from two main resources: the Metropolitan Council and the National Spatial Data Infrastructure (NSDI) program. In 2001, it attained an NSDI Web Mapping Service (WMS) grant of $18,700; in 1998, it got NSDI benefits of $48,000; and an NSDI Framework Demonstration grant of $100,000 in 1998.

The governance structure of MetroGIS relies on three tiers: the Policy Board, Coordinating Committee, Customer Committees, including Special Purpose Workgroups and a Technical Advisory Committee. The Board is composed of 12 elected/executive officials representing eleven key Metro-GIS stakeholder organizations: each of the seven metropolitan counties, the Association of Metropolitan Municipalities (AMM), the Metropolitan Chapter of the Minnesota Association of Watershed Districts (MAWD), Technology Information Educational Services (TIES–school districts), and the Metropolitan Council. The Coordinating Committee, composed of approximately 25 managers and administrators from a cross-section of interests and organizations, recommends courses of action to the Policy Board concerning design, implementation, and operation of MetroGIS. The Technical Advisory Team members are people with broad expertise and perspective, including GIS and other relevant organizational policy, data access, data content, and data standards backgrounds. The Special Purpose Workgroups are also composed of professionals with related expertise. It has attempted to address issues and problems that come out at the each step of shared services. For more information, see MetroGIS (2010).

APPENDIX 2: CASE RANKING RESULTS

The ranking numbers from 0–7 represent the aggregate number of criteria each case satisfied. Cases with higher numbers satisfied more of the criteria.

Case	Ranking
MN Dept of Health	0
Salmon	1
Lake Tahoe	1
Stanislaus Recreation	2
Oakland	2
Depot	2
Collaborative Governance in MN	2
Portsmouth	3
CALFED	3
Montana Blackfoot	3

These cases are ranked as the top 11 cases.

Case	Ranking
Westchester	4
New York City	4
Sussex County	4
Boulder County	5
Sacramento	5
St. Margaret's Bay	5
Jefferson County	5
Lake Norman	5
King County	6
MetroGIS	7
D.C. Promise	7

APPENDIX 3: RANKING CHART

Case Number	Case Title	Concerned with Shared Services	Whether it has individual volunteers	Includes people it's designed to help	Whether it is initiated by citizens	Founding from individual donations	Success of implementation	Cost savings	Shared services provided	Other non-financial goals	Total
I	D.C. Promise Neighborhood Initiative	X	X	X		X	X		X	X	7
II	Lake Norman Community Development Council	X	X				X		X	X	5
III	Models of Community Engagement, MN Dept. of Health	X	X				X		X	X	5
IV	Jefferson County Community Network, WA	X	X	X			X		X		5
V	King County Collaboration to End Homelessness in Seattle	X	X	X		X	X			X	6
VI	Boulder County Human Services Strategic Plan, CO	X	X	X			X			X	5
VII	Collaborative Governance Council in Minnesota	X					X				2
VIII	Montana's Blackfoot River Watershed		X				X			X	3
IX	CALFED Bay Delta Program		X				X			X	3
X	Sacramento Transportation and Air Quality Collaborative by the Sacremento Center for Collaborative Policy	X	X	X			X			X	5
XI	Think Salmon collaborative Watershed Governance Initiative									X	1
XII	St. Margaret's Bay Stewardship Association		X	X	X	X				X	5
XIII	Depot Town Community Development Foundation			X	X						2
XIV	Oakland 2025			X		X					2
XV	Portsmouth Listens		X	X						X	3
XVI	Pathway 2007 Lake Tahoe Restoration Project						X				1
XVII	Stanislaus Recreation Stakeholders			X		X					2
XVIII	Shared Service and Programs in Westchester, NY	X					X	X	X		4
XIX	Shared Services Among New York's Local Governments	X					X	X	X		4
XX	Shared Services Initiatives of Sussex County, NJ	X					X	X	X		4
XXI	MetroGIS Minneapolis-St. Paul Metropolitan Area	X	X	X			X	X	X	X	7

NOTES

1. This has been going on since the republic's founding. Macedo et. al. (2005) quotes de Tocqueville as saying that "citizens organize at the slightest pretext: 'If some obstacle blocks the public road halting the circulation of traffic, the neighbors at once form a deliberative body'" (p. 119).
2. For instance, citizen-initiated groups form the largest proportion of watershed groups in Ohio (Moore & Koontz, 2003).

REFERENCES

Ansell, C. (2003). Community embeddedness and collaborative governance in the San Francisco Bay area environmental movement. In M. Diani & D. McAdam (Eds.), *Social movements and networks: Relational approaches to collective action.* New York, NY: Oxford University Press. Retrieved from http://scholar.google. com/scholar?q=collaborative+governance&hl=en&as_sdt=1%2C31&as_ sdtp=on

Ansell, C., & Gash, A. (2008). Collaborative governance in theory and practice. *Journal of Public Administration Research and Theory, 18*(4), 543–571.

Boulder County Human Services. (n.d.). *Building caring and livable communities for all: 2008–2013 Boulder County Human Services strategic plan.* Retrieved on September 15, 2011, from http://www.bouldercolorado.gov/files/boulder_ county_human_services_strategic_plan.pdf

Brody, S. D. (2003). Measuring the effects of stakeholder participation on the quality of local plans based on the principles of collaborative ecosystem management. *Journal of Planning Education and Research, 22*(4), 407–419.

Bromberg, D., & Charbonneau, E. (2011). Sustainable Seattle: The sustainable indicators and the sustainable urban neighborhood initiative. In M. Holzer, D. Kong, & D. Bromberg (Eds.), *Citizen participation: Innovative and alternative models for engaging citizens* (pp. 55–73). Newark, N.J.: National Center for Public Performance.

Cohn Berman, B. (2006). *Listening to the public: Adding the voice of the people to government performance measurement and reporting.* New York: Fund for the City of New York.

CALFED Bay-Delta Program Archived Website. (2007). State of California. *Ca.gov* Retrieved September 15, 2011, from http://calwater.ca.gov/

Committee to End Homelessness. (2011). *King county ten year plan to end homelessness.* Retrieved September 15, 2011, from http://cehkc.org/

Cuthill, M., & Fien, J. (2005). Capacity building: Facilitating citizen participation in local governance. *Australian Journal of Public Administration, 64*(4), 63–80.

DC Promise Neighborhood Initiative. (2010). *DC Promise Neighborhood Initiative.* Retrieved September 15, 2011, from http://www.dcpni.org/

de Lancer Julnes, P. (2005). Engaging citizens in governance-for-results: Opportunities and challenges. In M. Holzer & S-K. Rhee (Ed.), *Citizen-driven government performance.* Newark, NJ: Rutgers University.

Depot Town Community Development Foundation. (2011). *Welcome to the Depot Town Community Development Corporation!* Retrieved June 3, 2011, from http://www.depottowncdc.org/

Donahue, J. (2004). *On collaborative governance* (Corporate social responsibility initiative working paper no. 2). Cambridge, MA: John F. Kennedy School of Government, Harvard University.

Fung, A., & Wright E. O. (2001). Deepening democracy: Innovations in empowered participatory governance. *Politics & Society, 29,* 5–41.

Halachmi, A. (2005). Civil society organizations and citizen driven performance measurement. In M. Holzer and S-K. Rhee (Ed.), *Citizen-driven government performance.* Newark, NJ: Rutgers University.

Harvard Kennedy School, Ash Center for Democratic Governance and Innovation. (2011). *Grass roots conservation.* Retrieved September 15, 2011, from http://www.innovations.harvard.edu/awards.html?id=39701

Holzer, M., & Bromberg, D. (2011). *Introduction.* In M. Holzer, D. Kong, & D. Bromberg (Eds.), *Citizen participation: Innovative and alternative models for engaging citizens* (pp. 1–4). Newark, NJ: National Center for Public Performance.

Holzer, M., & Fry, J. (2011). *Shared services and municipal consolidation: A critical analysis.* Alexandria, VA: Public Technology Institute.

Jefferson County Community Network. (n.d.). *Jefferson County Community Network.* Retrieved September 15, 2011, from http://www.jeffcocommunitynetwork.org/aboutjccn

Lake Norman Community Development Council. (2011). *LNCDC Welcome.* Retrieved September 15, 2011, from http://lncdc.pbworks.com/w/page/8714106/LNCDC-Welcome

Lasker, R. D. (2003). Broadening participation in community problem solving: A multidisciplinary model to support collaborative practice and research. *Journal of Urban Health: Bulletin of the New York Academy of Medicine, 80*(1), 14–60.

Leach, W. D. (2006). Collaborative public management and democracy: Evidence from Western watershed partnerships. *Public Administration Review, 66*(s1), 100–110.

Macedo, S., et. al. (2005). Associational life and the nonprofit and philanthropic sector. In *Democracy at risk: How political choices undermine citizen participation, and what we can do about it* (pp.117–154). Washington, DC: Brookings Institution.

Manoharan, A. (2011). Citizen-driven government performance: The straphangers campaign New York City. In M. Holzer, D. Kong, & D. Bromberg (Eds.), *Citizen participation: Innovative and alternative models for engaging citizens* (pp. 37–51). Newark, NJ: National Center for Public Performance.

MetroGIS. (2010). Retrieved September 15, 2011, from http://www.metrogis.org/

Minnesota Department of Health. (2011). *Models of community engagement.* Retrieved September 15, 2011, from http://www.health.state.mn.us/communityeng/intro/models.html

Moore, E., & Koontz, T. (2003). A typology of collaborative watershed groups: Citizen-based, agency-based, and mixed partnerships. *Society and Natural Resources, 16,* 451–460.

Newman, J., Barnes, M., Sullivan, H., & Knops, A. (2004). Public participation and collaborative governance. *Journal of Social Policy, 33,* 203–223.

New York State, Office of the State Comptroller. (2009, November). *Shared services among New York's local governments: Best practices and tips for success.* Retrieved September 15, 2011, from http://www.osc.state.ny.us/localgov/pubs/research/sharedservices.pdf

Oakland Planning and Development Corporation. (2010). *Oakland 2025: Planning Oakland's future.* Retrieved June 12, 2011, from http://www.opdc.org/programs-services/plan-partner/2011-community-plan/

Office of the Minnesota State Auditor. (2011). *Collaborative governance council legislative report 2011.* Retrieved September 15, 2011, from http://www.osa.state.mn.us/other/councils/CollaborativeGovernance/Collaborative_Governance_Council_Legislative_Report.pdf

O'Leary, R., Gerard, C., & Blomgren Bingham, L. (2006, December). Introduction to the symposium on collaborative public management. *PAR, 66*(Suppl. s1), 6–9.

Pacific Salmon Foundation. (2011). *Think salmon.* Retrieved June 3, 2011, from http://www.thinksalmon.com/

Portsmouth Listens. (n.d.). *Process and people.* Retrieved June 12, 2011, from http://www.portsmouthlistens.org/people.htm

Price, B. E. (2005). Evaluation, citizen engagement, and performance measurement tools to make government more productive. In M. Holzer & S-K. Rhee (Ed.), *Citizen-driven government performance.* Newark, NJ: Rutgers University.

Roberts, N. (2004). Public deliberation in an age of direct citizen participation. *The American Review of Public Administration, 34*(4), 315–353.

Sacramento State Center for Collaborative Policy. (n.d.a). *Community dialogue: Stanislaus recreation stakeholders.* Retrieved June 12, 2011, from http://www.csus.edu/ccp/jun14.htm

Sacramento State Center for Collaborative Policy. (n.d.b). *Lake Tahoe restoration project.* Retrieved June 12, 2011, from http://www.csus.edu/ccp/Lake_Tahoe/index.stm

Sacramento State Center for Collaborative Policy. (2004, June). *Stakeholder collaborative process feasibility assessment report: Lake Tahoe Basin, California and Nevada.* Retrieved June 12, 2011, from http://www.csus.edu/ccp/Lake_Tahoe/Final%20P7%20Assessment%20Report%209-24-04%20v6.pdf

Sacramento Transportation and Air Quality Collaborative. (2011). *Sacramento State Center for Collaborative Policy.* Retrieved September 15, 2011, from http://www.csus.edu/ccp/SacTAQC/index.stm

Soma, K., & Vatn, A. (2009). Local democracy implications for coastal zone management: A case study in southern Norway. *Land Use Policy, 26*(3), 755–762.

St. Margaret's Bay Stewardship Association. (2008). Retrieved June 3, 2011, from http://www.heartofthebay.ca/

Sussex County. (2011). *Department of Central and Shared Services.* Retrieved September 15, 2011, from http://www.sussex.nj.us/cit-e-access/webpage.cfm?TID=7&TPID=10991&Print=1

U.S. Forest Service. (2006, September). *Stanislaus National Forest route designation project: Update, 1*(1). Retrieved June 12, 2011, from http://www.csus.edu/ccp/jun14/2006-09-newsletter.pdf

Vigoda, E. (2002). From responsiveness to collaboration: Governance, citizens, and the next generation of public administration. *Public Administration Review, 62*(5), 527–540.

Washington State Shared Services Model. (2009). *Reorganizing Washington state government.* Retrieved September 15, 2011, from http://dis.wa.gov/WA_shared_services_model.pdf

Weber, E. P. (2009). Explaining institutional change in tough cases of collaboration: "Ideas" in the Blackfoot Watershed. *Public Administration Review, 69*(2), 314–327.

Westchester County. (2011). *Shared services and programs.* Retrieved September 15, 2011, from http://planning.westchestergov.com/about-us/shared-services

Whitaker, G. P. (1980). Coproduction: Citizen participation in service delivery. *Public Administration Review, 40*(3), 240–246. doi:10.2307/975377

Woolley, J. (2011). Clean Air Council: An effort to evaluate the Southeastern Pennsylvania Transportation Authority. In M. Holzer, D. Kong, & D. Bromberg (Eds.), *Citizen participation: Innovative and alternative modes for engaging citizens* (pp. 77–92). Newark, NJ: National Center for Public Performance.

Zimmerman, M. A., & Rappaport, J. (1988). Citizen participation, perceived control, and psychological empowerment. *American Journal of Community Psychology, 16*(5), 725–750.

PART V

RESEARCH REFLECTIONS

CHAPTER 16

RESEARCHING PARTICIPATION THROUGH INTERPRETIVE PHENOMENOLOGY

The Case of Neighborhood Organizing

María Verónica Elías
Eastern Washington University

Deliberation and collaborative action are crucial for the creation and recreation of democratic governance (Barber, 1984; de Sousa Briggs, 2008; Follett, 1918/1923, 1925; Gaventa & Barrett, 2010; Kathi & Cooper, 2005; Kemmis, 1990; King & Stivers, 1998; Lindblom & Woodhouse, 1993; Stivers, 1990, 1994; Stone, 2001; Wamsley & Wolf, 1996). Public deliberation and civic engagement hold the potential to overcome the current "dark times" in public administration (Stivers, 2008a), characterized by a heightened sense of fear, a retreat of people into their private spaces, and the concomitant disappearance of the public realm, understood as *vita activa* (Arendt, 1958). The call to bring the public spaces of deliberation back to life is far from recent (Arendt, 1958; Barber, 1984; Follett, 1918/1923; Stivers, 2008a). Public deliberative practices not only contribute to a more

The State of Citizen Participation in America, pages 387–414

democratic governance process but also to a more effective and potentially more efficient one (de Sousa Briggs, 2008). Finally, deliberative governance prompts citizens—once initiated in an ongoing deliberation—to continue to engage in public discourse on a regular basis (de Sousa Briggs, 2008; Follett, 1918/1923), developing citizenship skills and fomenting civic virtue (Follett, 1918/1923). As people engage in deliberation, they learn about others' viewpoints and experiences hence taking a dynamic stance on problem definition, agenda setting, and resource allocation plans (de Sousa Briggs, 2008; Forester 1989, 1999, 2009; Hummel & Stivers, 1998; Kathi & Cooper, 2005; King & Stivers, 1998).

However, how can researchers access people's deliberative experiences and collaborative practices? Understanding social events or phenomena constitutes a contested epistemological and ontological quandary. In fact, the question of *how we know what we know* invariably brings the researcher face-to-face with the possibility that there may be multiple ways to access knowledge and to judge each methodology's validity claim or assumption of truth. Invariably, under different epistemological approaches the researcher asks certain questions and gathers the data in specific ways. She also approaches the "subjects" of study differently, and, as a result, reaches unique findingsand conclusions (Yanow & Schwartz-Shea, 2006). For instance, a straightforward approach to access people's community engagement knowledge would be to ask questions directly to the participants about their collaborative experiences when dealing with public issues (R. P. Hummel, personal communication, November 25, 2007; Hummel & Stivers, 1998).

Neighborhood groups' participants who get together to deliberate on a regular basis with the purpose of making sense of shared situations know firsthand what it takes to transition from distant or opposing ideas to collaborative and integrative processes. Community process (Follett, 1918/1923) prompts participants to engage in a continuous deliberation which integrates individual ideas into new, collectively constituted, understandings of a shared reality. Phenomenological investigation helps unveil important but often neglected dimensions in the study of deliberative democracy: the dynamics of community processes as expressed by those who experience them firsthand.

Social science researchers utilize multiple approaches to gain an understanding on issues of civic engagement and collaborative democracy. Qualitative researchers have used a wide array of methods, from case study generalizations and grand theorizing, to modeling ideal deliberative types. While many "qualitative" studies use data collected from primary or secondary sources through surveys and structured interviews, for example, their analyses tend to follow the quantitative methods' steps and procedures. In that sense, studies that count the frequency of topics or issues that appear in the interviews, add quantitative analyses (statistical analyses of survey responses through computer-assisted software) to make survey or interview findings more rigorous and robust, and generalize the research results, are abundant. Interpretive studies, on the other hand, seek word-based data to understand intersubjective or *social reality*, which, as Camilla Stivers (2008b) notes,

> Is the reality that emerges from the interactions among people in a shared space. It spans several levels of consciousness, including explicit, tacit, and unconscious. It is talk and action, whether collaborative or competitive. It produces, sustains, and transforms shared (or disputed) meanings, norms, and understandings about what is going on, carried primarily but not exclusively in language. (p. 1010)

This chapter makes a case for interpretive phenomenology as a research approach that helps unveil the dynamics of deliberative processes, that is, the "levels of consciousness," the "shared or disputed meanings, norms and understandings" of a people's intersubjective reality (Stivers, 2008b). Interpretive methodologies seek people's meanings of their collaborative experiences in their own terms through stories and anecdotes. As Stivers (2008b) persuasively argues, unveiling intersubjective meanings requires an epistemology that focuses on "explicating the meaning of the social situation for the people in it," rather than seeking causal explanations (p. 1011). Allowing the phenomenon under study to express itself in its own terms (Heidegger, 1962; R. P. Hummel, personal correspondence, December 15, 2007) may reveal civic engagement and collaborative practices under a new light. The participants' experiences with collaboration could enrich the dialogue about participation and democratic governance as they have firsthand knowledge on the issues discussed and the deliberative process. In that context, the question of how to gather the data about intersubjective experiences inexorably arises. Through interpretive phenomenology the researcher gains a keen understanding about the phenomenon of collaboration by listening to people's stories and observing them interact.

The discussion in this chapter refers to neighborhood group members' stories in the same way that professor Ralph P. Hummel (1991) speaks of the importance and value of managers' stories to understand and make sense of always-changing and unpredictable situations in the public administrator's everyday work. In essence, what neighborhood group members know is especially important in understanding deliberative democracy as it happens in actual group processes. Accessing people's experiential knowledge would allow public administrators to understand public issues and concerns from people's viewpoints, as they encounter them on a daily basis. A collaborative process that involves all players not only fosters a more democratic governance process, but it also helps focus attention on the most excruciating problems from quite different perspectives.

This discussion draws from the evidence gathered in a case study (Elías, 2008) of people's experiences in five neighborhood improvement associations in Akron, Ohio. Through an interpretive epistemological, the case study exemplified a research process that was both shaped and validated by its participants. Starting from open-ended and lengthy interviews, to the interpretation of the narratives, the research evolved a new understanding of collaborative practices in neighborhoods based on people's actual experiences.

The first section of this chapter will discuss the basic tenets of interpretive epistemology, with an emphasis on phenomenology (Flyvbjerg, 2006; Harmon, 1981; Hycner, 1985; Taylor, 1971; van Manen, 1990; Yanow, 2000, 2004; Yanow & Schwartz-Shea, 2006) and its advantages in studying collaborative practices in the context of community processes (Follett, 1918/1923; 1919). Next, the chapter will reflect on a case study (Elías, 2008) of neighborhood improvement groups' practices, in which the researcher pursued interpretive phenomenology as a mode of inquiry.

The underlying argument is that interpretive phenomenology as an approach to study social reality can unveil important and otherwise unknown aspects of the phenomenon under investigation. This chapter posits that researching "community process" (Follett, 1918/1923; 1919) from an interpretive phenomenology lens allows the participants' own terms and shared meanings to shape the research process in ways that can reveal new dimensions of collaborative endeavors. Finally, the author reflects on the contributions of interpretive phenomenology to the deliberative democracy and participatory democracy dialogue.

INTERPRETIVE PHENOMENOLOGY AS A WAY OF KNOWING

A close look at a sample of recent empirical research in the area of deliberative democracy and civic engagement shows a predominance of studies that, in seeking generalization and replicability of the results, privilege the standards of rigor of quantitative methods (Askim & Hanssen, 2008; de Lancer Julnes & Johnson, 2011; Handley & Howell-Moroney, 2010; LeRoux, 2009; Weeks, 2000).

Understood today as conglomerating all non-quantitative studies, "qualitative" research, broadly conceived, tends to follow positivistic assumptions and the standards of rigor of quantitative methods (Yanow & Schwartz-Shea, 2006). They rely on structured interviews, surveys, focus groups, and Q-sort to gather data about the social world. The distinction between qualitative research, thus understood, and *interpretive* research, which focuses on understanding the social or human world as perceived, understood, and made sense of by their very participants, is far from insignificant. In fact, interpretive theorists Dvora Yanow and Peregrine Schwartz-Shea (2006) speak of such difference (between qualitative and interpretive studies) as "both in procedure and in rationales... reflecting differences in ontological and epistemological presuppositions" (p. xv), that is, distinct philosophical and worldview assumptions to understand human and social prolegomena. Interpretive researchers support their studies on ethnographic, participant-observer, ethnomethodological, semiotic, narrative, phenomenological, discourse analysis, and other similar approaches (Yanow & Schwartz-Shea, 2006).

While mainstream qualitative studies enjoy a greater attention than interpretive methodologies, traditional qualitative research presents some gaps in the study and understanding of deliberative democracy and collaborative practices. In searching for reliability, consistency, and unbiased results, researchers select their study populations through stratified or random sampling techniques. They may utilize structured interviews and surveys, and analyze the data through quantitative content analyses with numerical controls—counting the frequency of comments (de Lancer Julnes & Johnson, 2011)—and qualitative analysis of interviews using software aids. In assessing the levels of citizen participation (understood as citizens' input in government decisions), researchers use a wide range of quantitative analysis techniques, from basic to highly complex statistical analyses, including logistic regression (Askim & Hanssen, 2008) and ordered probit regression (Handley & Howell-Moroney, 2010). Yet other studies seek to model the "ideal" conditions for deliberative democracy (by researching particular cases), which could be tested and replicated in other settings (Weeks, 2000). While these studies aim to generate robust data and statistically significant results, which could later be generalized and replicated, they lack from the contextual details and richness of the social situation under study and the richness of deliberation as lived and expressed by the participants in their own terms. Finally, they fall short of accessing the intersubjective meanings, norms, and understandings of particular collaborative experiences, which can shed light on how deliberative practices happen in particular contexts and in all their dimensions (Stivers, 2008b).

Interpretive phenomenology fills in those gaps by asking the people (otherwise called our "subjects of research") about the context-specific dynamics of the situation. The interpretive phenomenologist seeks to access people's *meanings* of their lived experiences to explicate social phenomena in their full complexities. To that end, she allows the participants' stories and actions to "mold" the investigation's path and findings, mediated by the researcher's interpretation of "word data" (Hycner, 1985; Taylor, 1971; Yanow& Schwartz-Shea, 2006). In short, accessing the richness and complexity of the particular situations can help us understand collaborative practices in ways not captured by other methodological approaches or levels of analysis. The detail and depth of people's descriptions regarding their lived experiences constitutes the data of phenomenological research that can inform the collaborative governance dialogue. The "thick" descriptions, when systematically and rigorously interpreted and explicated (Flyvbjerg, 2006; Hycner, 1985; Taylor, 1971; Yanow & Schwartz-Shea, 2006) provide a new viewpoint on the dynamics of collaborative processes, which might otherwise remain unexplored and misunderstood.

Interpretive research has developed in disciplinary foci such as community development and participatory planning (Flyvbjerg, 1998; Forester, 2009), pedagogy (van Manen, 1990), nursing and health care (Aston & Meagher-Stewart, 2009; Yeung, Passmore, & Packer, 2008), public organizations (Maynard-Moody & Musheno, 2003; Yanow, 1997) and policy analysis (Wagenaar, 2011; Yanow, 1997).[2]

A mode of inquiry beyond traditional methods (i.e., technical rationality) is necessary to capture the complexities of social reality as enacted in intersubjective practices (Harmon, 1981; Heidegger, 2005; Hummel & Stivers, 1998; Hycner, 1985; Schutz, 1967; Stivers, 2008b; Taylor, 1971; van Manen, 1990; Yanow, 2000, 2004, 2007). How can we access the citizens' knowledge about their participatory experiences in public affairs? What lessons can researchers and practitioners learn from people's collaborative practices and the meanings that they evolve in the process? Put differently, *how does collaborative governance occur from the viewpoints of those who regularly take part in them?* These have been relatively neglected questions in the Public Administration field (Elías, 2010). A dialogue about such quandary is important in order to gain a better understanding of actual practices of civic engagement.

People's stories become the foundation of an interpretive research inquiry. Without a priori (researcher-formulated) categorizations, people's lived experiences of collaboration shed light on our understanding of shared governance. Interpretive phenomenology, hence, seeks to reveal people's meanings of their lived experiences in their own terms[3] (Flyvbjerg, 2006; Heidegger, 1962; Husserl, 1970; Hycner, 1985; Schutz, 1967; Taylor, 1971; van Manen, 1990).

Through participant observation and in-depth interviews, interpretive phenomenologists look for meaning through an understanding of people's hands-on, experiential, knowledge, in this case, of collaborative practices. More importantly, insofar as interpretive phenomenology seeks the subjects' interpretations of their lived collaborative experiences, that approach could help democratize a research that *is* about democracy (Ansley & Gaventa, 1997). Therefore, a phenomenological research of civic engagement and collaboration could bridge some of the gaps in the understanding of deliberative democracy as, so far, presented through a positivistic lens. Some of those gaps result from what is lost when qualitative data is processed and analyzed in a laboratory-like setting, in a way that strictly seeks objective and neutral results that can be generalized and replicated in other scenarios.[4]

Another advantage of using interpretive phenomenology in deliberative democracy research is that by asking people to relate their experiences in their own terms, as well as by observing citizens' collaborative practices, important reflections evolve. People's stories ensure a great deal of detail regarding the settings and contexts in which the collaborative experiences take place—what Clifford Geerts (1973) called "thick description" (p. 6)—which can shed light into the inner dynamics of collaborative processes. Finally, this methodological approach gives rise to a new understanding of the research problem in the light of the person living and understanding the phenomenon from *within*, as expressed or relived by the doer and as observed by the researcher-observer.

With the purpose of unveiling the intricacies of social problems, interpretive methodologies inquire about the participants' multifaceted interpretations of a reality that they share. Scholars versed in this approach argue that important dimensions of social life cannot be fully "captured" by mimicking the research methods used in the physical and natural sciences (Harmon, 1981; Taylor, 1971; Yanow 2004; Yanow & Schwartz-Shea, 2006). Instead, interpretive methodologies, such as phenomenology, ethnography, and hermeneutics acknowledge the different intersubjective meanings, which can most clearly be understood by inquiring the specific communities of meaning (Yanow, 2000). Understanding those unique meanings requires a standpoint epistemology, an approach to knowing that privileges the participants' viewpoints from which they can express the meanings of situations or experiences in their own terms and from their particular viewpoints (Heidegger, 2005; Schutz, 1967; Yanow, 2000, 2007, 2009).

Through a systematic and reasoned process to explicate narratives and non-numerical data, interpretive phenomenology seeks the free flow of the phenomenon under investigation—in this case, the neighborhood improvement processes—without imposing any *a priori* boundaries or predefined categories of analysis (Flyvbjerg, 2006; Hummel, 1991, 1998; Hycner, 1985; Taylor, 1971; van Manen, 1990; Yanow, 2000, 2004). The unit of analysis of interpretive studies is the face-to-face encounter, more so than the individual person or group of people (Harmon, 1981). In this process, the researcher proceeds from a careful design of open-ended questions to a sequence of interpretive stages. The purpose is to understand people's meanings of their lived communal experiences as participants articulate those meanings in their own terms.

Case studies allow an interpretation of intersubjective meanings about collaborative experiences within a specific context. Formal generalization is only one of many ways by which people create and accumulate knowledge. That new knowledge may not always be formally generalized does not mean that it cannot be crucial in the collective process of knowledge accumulation in a given field or in a society (Flyvbjerg, 2006). In fact, a purely descriptive phenomenological case study without any attempt to generalize can certainly be of value in the process of scientific discovery and has often helped cut a path toward scientific innovation in different fields (Flyvbjerg, 2006, p. 76). An attempt to interpret intersubjective meanings in light of a common reality that groups of people share is what interpretive methodologies can contribute to the scholarly dialogue about community process and civic engagement in public administration and policy. The following section presents an example of how interpretive phenomenology works in a real-life case study of collaboration and shared governance.

INTERPRETING COMMUNITY PROCESS: A CASE STUDY

A research project that looked at the intersubjective experiences of communal politics illustrates how interpretive phenomenology can help reveal shared meanings about what is common among people and in their own terms (Hummel, 1991). Through a case study (Elías, 2008), the researcher sought to understand, and bring new appreciation for, the concept of community through the *practices* and narrations of neighborhood improvement groups. The researcher conducted 23 in-depth interviews with active neighbors from five neighborhood associations of west Akron, Ohio. She also pursued multiple observations of the associations' meetings and activities. By means of a systematic and rigorous interpretive process, the researcher reconceptualized "community" via the meanings of the participants' lived experiences (Elías, 2008, 2010). The findings shed light on important dynamics of governance from the ground up in the neighborhood associations investigated. Furthermore, the study suggested that practitioners and scholars could greatly benefit from accessing the active neighbors' hands-on knowledge about collaborative practices and ultimately engage in a more democratic and intelligent decision-making process (Lindblom & Woodhouse, 1993; Stone, 2001).

Case Study and Method

The neighbors first created the neighborhood associations in the Highland Square neighborhood of west Akron, Ohio, as a response to particular issues striking the neighborhood and its inhabitants, such as economic stagnation, surmounting criminal activity, abandoned housing, as well as other socioeconomic problems crystallized in the needs of children, the elderly, and the homeless in that area of town. Abiding by the criterion that the groups' main aim was to engage in joint efforts to improve some aspect/s of their neighborhood, the researcher selected the participants to interview through a snowballing technique.[5] A second criterion was ontological: by investigating neighborhood groups, the researcher could test Follett's (1981/1923, 1919) community process theory in light of the meanings that the participants could evolve through their hands-on experiences in everyday communal practices.

The qualities of the Highland Square neighborhood of west Akron made the neighborhood organizations thereby established a good test of Follett's (1918/1923, 1919) community process due to the diversity of neighborhood associations as well as to the neighborhood's long engagement tradition. The diversity of the neighborhood and its heterogeneous character were also salient, from its architecture to the people's diverse occupations and hobbies. A historical and dense urban area of west Akron that developed during the mid-1950s during the industrial tire-manufacturing boom, Highland Square stands today as a distinct artistic spot for eclectic interests. This neighborhood has earned a reputation for the bohemian and artsy lifestyle of its people. It houses businesses such as a neighborhood theater, local restaurants and coffee shops, and events like arts and holiday festivals, among other attractions. Another outstanding characteristic of the neighborhood is its mixed land uses, featuring an intertwined residential and business dynamic that sets the neighborhood apart from others in town. The neighbors have a wide range of socioeconomic, educational, and religious backgrounds, as well as ethnic origins. However, as the reader will later uncover, what the neighbors share is a sense of deep care for the place and its people, the enrichment by the arts and social events, and the responsibility for the well-being of all neighbors. With the purpose of protecting the identities of the study's subjects the author has replaced the real names of interviewees and groups with pseudonyms.

The neighborhood associations studied were renamed as "Miraflores," "Pagoda," "Campinha," and "Manizales." As their members expressed, they all work with the purpose of improving the quality of life broadly understood in the Highland Square neighborhood, on the west side of the city of Akron, Ohio. Miraflores and Campinha are the two neighborhood organizations with the longest tradition in the study area, while, at the time the study took place, Pagoda and Manizales were in their incipient organizational stages. The neighborhood association Miraflores is a nonprofit organization that works through different subcommittees, each of which deals with a specific issue (i.e., Crime and Safety, Housing and Historic Preservation, Beautification, among other ad hoc subcommittees). The Campinha group is a neighborhood organization that nucleates the neighbors of a few streets in Highland Square. People meet frequently to talk about issues and concerns common to their area. Furthermore, they undertake projects to clean up streets; erase graffiti; beautify gardens; watch for criminal activity; provide social, recreational, and educational programs for the neighbors; and socialize, among other activities.

The researcher opted for a research methodology that would bring storytelling to the center of the inquiry. Through face-to-face interviews, this approach could most appropriately capture people's meanings about their communal experiences. The researcher conducted 23 interviews with active neighbors from five neighborhood associations on the west side of Akron, as stated above. A thorough two-stage interpretation process ensued, which was then compared with Mary Parker Follett's (1918/1923, 1919) theory of community process. As a result, a reconceptualization of Follett's community process emerged from the interpretation process of people's stories of their lived experiences.

Interpretive Stages

The interview questions sought to get people to describe their experiences by means of detailed stories rather than to define or conceptualize their practices (see Appendix for interview instrument). After transcribing the narratives, the researcher began to explicate them via two levels of interpretation (Hycner, 1985). Through multiple readings of the raw stories in the first interpretation phase, the investigator sought to "capture" the neighbors' interpretations of their own lived experiences. The next and second interpretive level was the researcher's interpretation of the people's narratives (Yanow & Schwartz-Shea, 2006). Seeking large and encompassing themes, the researcher grouped "units of general meaning" (Hycner, 1985, p. 280) as they stemmed directly from interpretations of the detailed narratives and stories. Then the researcher moved onto the following step, allowing the "units of meaning relevant to the research question" (Hycner, 1985, p. 284) to "show" themselves in their own terms; to appear in the interpretation process. In this stage, the researcher allocated the units of general meaning to those themes or units that could clearly shed light on the research question.[6]

Finally, and later in the research process, the neighbors themselves validated the new, larger, themes presented to them as a synthesis of the study's findings. The participants' positive feedback on the final themes and findings constituted the first validity check of the study, as interpretive philosopher Richard Hycner (1985) posits, "the first validity check is the participants themselves. They are able, at an experiential level to validate the findings of the research, that is, whether the findings are valid for them" (p. 297).

The researcher asked the participants whether the findings "rang true" to them. A doctoral dissertation committee with experienced phenomenologists provided a further validity check. They looked at the narratives and the researcher's interpretation and provided useful feedback to the researcher. The epistemic community, or community of meaning, can finally validate the interpretive phenomenological study. The ultimate goal of any interpretive research is to broaden the dialogue about the issue under study to the larger audience (Hycner, 1985).

Interpretation and Findings[7]

This section seeks to use the case study findings—or "units of meaning relevant to the research question" (Hycner, 1985, p. 284)—to make a case for interpretive phenomenology as a way of knowing important information about deliberative democracy. A number of themes emerged from the interpretation of people's stories compiled through interviews. The stories revealed the dynamism and change of neighborhood group associations in a rich manner. As discussed above, interpretive methodology is advantageous insofar as it allows the research participants to reveal their intersubjective meanings of neighborhood collaborative processes in their own terms. The final aim is to inform administrators and scholars about otherwise unknown dynamics of civic engagement at the neighborhood association level. What follows is a discussion of the grand themes as they emerged from interpreting people's stories and their actions.

Co-Creation and Shared Action

The interview narratives revealed the dynamics of the group's deliberative practices by pointing at shared ideas and actions. For instance, a neighbor talked of her experience of having an idea, which, thanks to the group deliberation, was transformed and enriched into a new "group idea," which, in turn, translated into shared group action:

> So Jennifer had this idea. She expressed it either here or over across the street where we had the holiday festival, and people *came together* to help others in the community. So it's having a sense of place that draws people together, to have a way of communicating...So I think if we have this Main Street program, that would tie the whole neighborhood together. (Juliet, Pagoda)

Co-creating social life through the improvement of different aspects of the neighborhood appeared, as well, in the meaning of this excerpt: "Seeing people come together and watch out for crime being solved effectively and having something effective happen, has been the best experience" (Gary, Miraflores). In Gary's comment, we can see the element of surprise connoted by the superlative he uses ("the best experience"), which reflects the pleasure of accomplishing with others what would have otherwise seemed impossible. Moreover, this co-creation—this bringing something new into being with the group—meant a unique experience for the neighbor.

Neighborhood Collaboration: Dynamism and Change

In asking the participants about their experiences, the researcher discovered people's meanings about collaboration. The following story makes a case for how deliberative practices bring people's synergies together to create a new unity of purpose:

> I realized that we have a great array of people in the neighborhood, and I realized how rich we are. We have senior citizens who are architects or were in the war. Or from people who have kids, you learn what other people's needs are. As a group, we need to do something about it. **So, being involved in the group has really opened my eyes to what the various issues are in the different constituencies.** And it has made me very passionate about the neighborhood. I really love this neighborhood, I love this area. If someone would contact me and say, "I live in this area and I need help with such and such," I would do anything I could to help them get in touch with whomever they need to. **Being involved in the neighborhood has made me a stronger advocate for the area and for the people living in it.** (Laura, Campinha)

In the passage above, Laura notes that by being an active member of the neighborhood association, she was able to better relate to the problems and concerns of the people living in her neighborhood and understand their struggles and the group's potential and strength to change negative situations. The neighborhood group practices also helped her appreciate the potential innate in people's diverse knowledge, rich backgrounds, and expertise that could benefit the neighborhood as a whole. Finally, this story points to the importance of understanding where in life each neighbor is coming from in order to be able to grasp people's realities, concerns, and hopes, and relate personally to them. Another neighbor conveys that meaning as follows: "At the tree-lighting in the Legion, I was *amazed* to see how other people have it worse than me, even though I'm unemployed" (Jennifer, Pagoda).

The neighbors' stories echo and expand Follett's (1918/1923, 1919) group processes understood as a "unifying activity" of the dynamism and change of life itself. She argued that the flow of lived experience does not abandon itself, but rather evolves into "the new flow" of lived experience endlessly (1919, p. 582). As can be seen in the participants' stories, the collaborative practices prompted the participants to learn together, generating a new, shared knowledge.

Practical Politics as Shared Power

Instead of attempting to suppress conflict—a term usually charged with a negative connotation—the neighbors argued that respecting people's different viewpoints and capitalizing on them was paramount to get people involved in the neighborhood association's activities on a regular basis. Multiple examples in this case study reveal how people's experiences can reveal—in the participants' own terms—something new about conflictive situations in deliberative processes and participative practices, which would otherwise remain unknown. In fact, people do work through the tensions and struggles characteristic of working with others by turning what appears to be negative at first sight into something positive and constructive. The following story points to the advantage of having different people and ideas to achieve a fruitful group process experience:

> There is *no* one leader; there is a kind of commune-like arrangement or community where everybody accepts a good amount of responsibility of what happens. **So it doesn't matter who is chairing the meeting; what matters is what everyone brings to the table. I don't know if we would be successful if there was only one leader,** we *are* successful because there is *not* just one leader. We have 40 to 50 very different personalities that happen to live in the same area. (Nick, Campinha)

This story brings life to the idea that differences among people are positive insofar as, through deliberation, they evolve new ways to come to terms with a situation and to solve problems collectively. Such quality is crucial for the creation of the public space, of community process (Arendt, 1958; Follett, 1918/1923, 1919).

In the case of shared power, a neighbor asserted that "community is what a good family should be: You don't always think alike, but you always care about each other" (Juliet, Pagoda). In this sense, politics is clearly the finding of common ground amidst difference. It does not mean that people agree all the time, or even that discussions happen in an orderly fashion.

Responsibility in local governance emerged in people's stories as a concern needing compromised, shared attention and action. A participant argued that rather than waiting for the government to solve public problems, the neighbors should recognize that *they* are the city, *they* make the town, and in interacting with others, *they* constitute and reconstitute—they embody—government:

> It's a little frustrating because many people think that the city is *some* entity that has unlimited wealth and that is there to clean up after you. And each of

us make up the city, so it's not like the city is somebody else that is going to come and clean the street signs and scrape the sidewalks. It is your street, you know? You pay the taxes to get the streets repaired and the lights up, so I think that **you really have to take ownership. You feel a strong sense of ownership because you know that most things that are going to get done is because the group is going to do it, otherwise it won't get done.** (Jerry, Campinha)

The neighbors' narratives can be interpreted as an expansion of Follett's (1925) "power-with" into a more encompassing "power-to," or a power collectively enacted from within the group process. In this sense, and as the story above suggests, the moment that a group is strongly or univocally headed, the richness of the diversity fades away. The following story illustrates this point:

The best [experience we had] was a couple of months ago with a landlord, a very hard and controversial issue, all the way up to the City Council. They could rule in our favor or against us. The issue was the number of tenants he had in his property. He had six, and we wanted him to bring his unit down to two families, just like the zoning code says. If you let him have six, then everyone else will have six and then you have the crime problem . . . So four or five of our neighbors stood up and spoke, and literally, because of what *they* said, they changed the councilmen's minds. And they voted and voted in our favor! That was very big. That was a success story. The citizens stood up, and the council listened to us. That was very big. The worst issue was in the beginning, when our councilman didn't know who we were before he had gotten our city district. Nobody would listen; they didn't want to listen to us. We went about it in another way; we did it on our own. We went to Columbus, raised the money, put in the application and we got the grant. Once we got it, now they [city councilmen] felt different, and now they were with us. . . It's basic human nature. So it's a tricky business; it's listening and knowing exactly what you want and a constant dialogue, communicating what you want, even when you are on the same side of an issue. (Amelia, Miraflores)

Amelia's story recounted that the members of the neighborhood group Miraflores pushed a zoning issue before the City Council for many years until it successfully passed. This story also teaches us other lessons. Compromise is not a choice when a difficult and controversial decision is to be made between two or more groups (in this case, the neighborhood association and the City Council). A successful process required Follett's (1918/1923) "integration" rather than "compromise" ("compromising would have resulted in a bad precedent," Laura, Campinha).

The success of this story emerges from the neighbors' long-standing deliberative tradition and commitment to the zoning issue pointed out above, in Amelia's story, along with the city council members' willingness to begin "to hear" what the neighbors had to say in their own terms ("the citizens stood up and councilmen listened," Amelia, Miraflores). Noteworthy is the neighbor's reflection on the controversial nature of civic engagement through their own deliberative experiences that involved conflicting issues and contested values. Furthermore, this story illustrates the importance of the group "sticking together" for what they believed needed to be said. In the process, a shared power (power-to) emerged. This victory, in which the neighbors managed differences with public officials by "fighting them out" until they found common ground is a great example of Follett's (1918/1923) community process, and offers food for thought regarding what deliberative democracy and joint participative action can achieve.

The participants' stories and the ensuing interpretation can inform democratic-theory scholars and practitioners of the unique dynamics of intersubjective dynamics in neighborhood groups and collaborative governance. To get to the findings and lessons that these stories suggest, an interpretive phenomenological approach was crucial to understanding collaborative situations as lived and experienced by the doers, and in their own terms.

Neighborliness: A Shared Construction of the Polis

The neighbors' stories pointed to their meanings of neighborliness as more than a shared physical entity. They understood their place as a collectively constructed process based on creating new and shared ideas amidst individual differences—a place that unites people and a vision that evolves over time. The following story makes this point clear:

> Community is where people work together; take pride in where they live and in their neighbors, work toward pulling people together rather than dividing people. **To have central accord is an important part of community, where people know they can find their friends; to have a place where people can express themselves; a *place* where if a neighbor is in need, other neighbors might find out about it.** There is a person that comes in here, her name is Jennifer. She is not working right now but she waited until her check came in at Christmastime in order to help a family that came to the neighborhood festival without proper clothing, and had babies and they didn't have all the things they needed to exist. And Jennifer *saw* that and she was spending her own money to help them. And so I thought "Gosh, if Jennifer is doing this . . . ," so I gave her some money, and then Mike gave her some money, and Becky then gave her some money, and someone else gave her a dollar, and so forth. **So Jennifer had this idea,** she expressed it either here or over across the street where we had the holiday festival, **and people *came together* to help others** in their community. (Juliet, Pagoda)

The conception of the public space as what is constructed in the coming-together-with-others (Arendt, 1958) gains content and meaning in the participants' own terms as stories. In fact, Juliet's story discussed above brings new meaning to the idea of "public space"—a place that is constructed *with* others in the coming together of all and over time; it is driven by the sense of care and the need to help and protect those who suffer hardships. In this sense, the neighborhood becomes the basic unit of deliberation and group process because that is where people connect with themselves and with others and where they find meaning in life.

The neighbors reflected on how group interactions and collaboration prompted its members to value the neighborhood as a meaningful place to live and develop and value themselves as people driven by larger and common goals that transcended their single individualities. In this sense, the group members illuminated the understanding of deliberative democracy by means of their shared meanings about their collaborative experiences:

> By being involved in the group, I actually feel that I really belong to it more than I ever had...I feel *more* part of the neighborhood being part of the group. I feel that I have more to offer now that I am involved. I can bring out other people in the neighborhood and get them more involved. It is nice to have more diversity. (Jennifer, Pagoda)

This phenomenological inquiry found that since life is lived at the neighborhood level, people have the possibility to deliberate and articulate most eloquently public concerns and needs *in neighborhoods*. The neighbors are best equipped to pursue a constructive and useful deliberation process because they are most fully acquainted with, and aware of, the potential, resources and needs of the area they inhabit and care for. Neighbors enjoy a unique angle on the situations that happen in their lived spaces. That is, neighbors possess the firsthand, experiential knowledge vital to mobilizing change. Policymakers could take advantage of such knowledge in understanding public issues as seen through the eyes of those who experience them daily.

Evolving the Common Good

The participants' stories show that neighbors come together to create a better place for everybody. Note how the group members work together to improve their neighborhood, enhance what they like about it, and resolve unwanted situations:

> A group of us got together because we cared about our neighborhood; we loved living in the neighborhood, and we had common concerns. **We decided to form this group so that we could work together to enhance what we liked about it and to better the things we thought that were problems.** The reason we did that is that we got tired of just sort of sitting there and expecting the police, the city, and everyone expecting them to solve problems...We were

worried about crime; we wanted to improve the values of our homes, and we wanted to protect what was there. (Amelia, Miraflores)

An interpretive epistemology revealed that through deliberative democracy, people not only learn about the value of caring for others but also about the *process* of coming to terms as a group with common difficulties and obstacles and joining in practices to overcome them. The group process may not lead to a consensus, but the joint resolution or group idea that arises from the process of integrating differences is one in which all have a part in its creation. Therefore, "learning in the doing" appears in people's stories as a core value of working with others over time toward evolving the common good for the neighborhood:

> A few of us felt that we could not wait for the city to do everything. So some of us decided that we would break up into little committees to clean up things, and we decided that no one should have to do that by themselves. So we formed the beautification committee that I was part of. I just wanted to participate. I don't want to have someone else decide what happens at our street. It is important to help out. (Jerry, Campinha)

Jerry discovered that joining forces with others led to greater improvements in the neighborhood than what he might have achieved by himself alone. Learning-in-the-doing emerges as a "relevant theme" (Hycner, 1985) inasmuch as it broadens the concept of civic engagement to a process that, over time, becomes both a habit of co-creation of new, shared practices and a "civic capacity" (de Sousa Briggs, 2008).

Freedom: Discovering Life Through "Group Process"

One of the highest values of the group process, as expressed by the participants, is the attainment of freedom and finding the meaning of life through the group. The following story illustrates how making sense of a shared neighborhood reality is a process born within the group and utterly related to "others":

> [Being part of the neighborhood group] is probably one of the most rewarding things that I did in my whole life. Learning that you can take up an idea and make it happen, even when everybody is looking at you and says, "You want to do what?" and just being persistent and saying "Yeah," and enlisting people and getting them engaged in the idea. Those are skills that translate anywhere. . . . It was like everybody showed up, did their part, had a really good time, and sat back afterwards and said, "Wasn't that fun?! Let's do it again!" And that—in a small scale—is what makes the neighborhood work: It is people doing their work and saying, "It worked, that was fun; let's do it again." (Mary, Pagoda)

Mary's reflection that the group wanted to "do it again" is in line with the idea that in joining with others, we discover the larger will (Follett, 1918/1923), and true freedom (Arendt, 2005). In fact, the greatest discovery of the interpretive study was that people are *being constituted* by and while interacting with others as a creative and dynamic process. As the stories relate, the neighbors make sense of life situations through collaborative practices based on the interweaving of ideas and a shared meaning and understanding of the situation at hand, thus creating "interpretive communities" (Yanow, 2000, 2009).

Interpersonal Benefits

Another theme that emerged from this case study—aiming to unveil the meanings that people evolve when they collaborate to achieve public and shared ends—is the benefits arising from working with others, which may transcend the realm of the neighborhood and move into the participants' personal lives—intersubjectively constituted. People's lives were transformed by their genuine care for others (note the abovementioned story on helping a family in need). In the process of getting together and deliberating on a regular basis, people create close bonds among each other and with different public administrators and other agents with whom they interact. The following narrative shows that developing relationships among neighbors is as important (if not more so) than simply keeping the neighborhood in good shape and healthful:

> We are not just concerned about the neighborhood but about the neighbors as well. I think there are different depths of layers of community. At the most basic, it's just a shared interest about our houses and making our neighborhood look nice; but then it goes deeper than that as you grow with the group. (Laura, Campinha)

Shared struggles create shared bonds among group members, as well as a sense of pride for what they have created jointly as a group. Taking pride in the group practices means for this neighbor to value one another in a genuine way:

> I would say the best thing [about working with the group] has been doing chores with my neighbors, like—it may not sound so much fun—planting flowers, or I don't really enjoy scraping stickers off of signs, but **being together with your neighbors, and doing things together so that when you are done you feel proud, it makes you feel good.** And I think that's the best part of it. It is sharing the community feeling. I don't even think of them being neighbors but as being friends; that we are doing it because we care. (Jerry, Campinha)

Likewise, another neighbor talks about the benefits of having joined the neighborhood organization: "I think that the neighborhood group has helped me keep connected to my neighborhood, and become drafted into participating. I do more now for my neighborhood than what I would have done otherwise" (Paul, Miraflores).

Other interpersonal benefits appeared, as the discovery that life "now makes sense;" sharing activities and endeavors with fellow neighbors, such as launching joint business enterprises, seeking to run for public office, working in the nonprofit and voluntary sectors, and collaborating with different agencies, among other interpersonal projects. This neighbor reflects on his experience of discovering "nice" people in the area through the neighborhood group and wanting to spend time with them. He also points to the access to new information and opportunities that the neighborhood group facilitated in its members:

> I'd say I have pretty good connections in the neighborhood, in terms of interactions with other people. It definitely increased them to another level. So it definitely makes you feel good about the neighborhood. It makes you aware about activities, like the garden tour. I had never gone to a garden tour until I joined the group. I went on the garden tour last year and **I had a blast! So it's helped increase my involvement in my community, in my daily life, and it has helped my connections with other people that I *didn't* know before.** And the people who usually join these groups are nice people; people who you would want to know. So I am happy about that...So I think that there are **added benefits to it, also political opportunities.** I was on the City Council years ago, and if I ever decided to run for office, this is a strong political base too. (Paul, Miraflores)

As these stories portray, in working together, people evolve mutual trust and confidence. Furthermore, they gain freedom at both a personal level and as a group through daily activities that involve the fellow other. Collaborative practices instilled in the participants a shared sense of care for others, which for the neighbors, translated into ownership of the place and pride in the group's evolving dynamics. Through a group process à la Follett (1918/1923, 1919), the neighbors create and re-create a new reality, vital and effective; a consequence of their deliberative practices and joint endeavors.

As the stories illustrated above, new and richer group ideas emerged as meaningful interplays among the participants. That is, the process of building competencies or abilities intersubjectively became more complex and intertwined as people met and discussed the ideas further and anew. The neighbors' stories show that creative thinking in neighborhood associations summarizes what Follett (1918/1923) described as the process of "integration," or the creative joint experience of coming together and bearing an idea as a whole through the "back and forth" of the deliberative practices. As the participants noted, group process becomes highly conditioned by who participates in each meeting or activity: "the members of a group are reciprocally conditioning forces none of which acts as it would act if any one member were different or absent" (Follett, 1918/1923, p. 31).

INTERPRETING PEOPLE'S MEANINGS OF COMMUNITY PROCESS: LESSONS LEARNED

A better understanding of deliberative democracy and collaborative endeavors at the neighborhood level was possible by means of an interpretive epistemology, which privileged people's meanings of their lived experiences to guide the research interpretation and findings. The stories of people's collaborative experiences and the meanings they evolve are crucial in finding out the details and inner dynamics that lead to a shared governance process that is in fact more democratic and potentially more efficient. Therein resides the advantages of interpretive phenomenology as a foundational logic of inquiry in any study of deliberative democracy and participative practice that aims at revealing intersubjective meanings.

As the stories above conveyed, people's meanings of their collaborative experiences allow researchers and practitioners to discover the detail and richness of community processes, as the protagonists of the case study discussed in this chapter vividly expressed in their own terms. Interpretation of shared meanings through storytelling emerges as an important tool to understand the contextual circumstances of people's experiences about collaborative practices.

The stories showed that the neighbors' shared meanings of collaboration fell in line with Follett's (1918/1923) community process theory, especially with what relates to the "coming together with others" through "creative thinking" to work together to understand and solve common problems, as well as in the notion of a shared place that the neighbors care for. Moreover, the neighbors' stories spoke for the group's abilities to adapt to the constant dynamism and change of situations by integrating different desires into a "resolution" arrived at by all in an ongoing process of deliberation. In fact, the stories showed that the groups were able to cope with the uncertainty of a continuously changing membership, as well as with multiple struggles, which further strengthened the existing ties and bonds among group members.

People's stories illustrated that the common good was the *leitmotif* of the group to achieve joint practices. The neighbors pointed to their convictions to push forward group ideas, such as street clean-ups, neighborhood watches to prevent crime, enforcing local zoning laws, and social activities, among other projects. The ultimate group goal was the well-being and health of the neighborhood, the city at-large, and its people. Likewise, the interpretive phenomenological approach used in this investigation revealed that "power-to" emerged from *within* the group in the back-and-forth process of deliberation.

The "operational" dynamics and implications of the meaning of politics showed themselves in practical and concrete terms by asking the participants about their experiences, through their storytelling. That is, the interpretive methodology used in this case study unveiled the practical know-how of deliberative experiences in neighborhood groups. It showed that integration of ideas built a genuine joint process founded on the shared commitment to the well-being of the neighborhood and its people.

Other findings that the neighbors brought to light through their stories were the meanings of interpersonal benefits and other gains related to being active in neighborhood improvement practices. Some of those benefits, as they pointed out, were new friendships, caring for the neighborhood more than before, feeling an utter sense of "belonging to the place and a common objective," and of "caring for others."

The finding of personal freedom through the group is probably one of the most meaningful discoveries of this phenomenological study. It points directly to the idea that practical politics—as deliberation based on differences—brings people together in creating a new, shared reality in which the person finds life's ultimate meaning *through* the group's activities and in the presence of and exchanges with others (Arendt, 1958, 2005; Follett, 1918/1923; Stivers, 2008a).

The neighborhood groups interviewed believed that both formal and informal interactions with other groups, agencies, and public officials strengthened their relationships over time. In fact, the story of the zoning code ordinance showed that the neighbors stood up for themselves, although they were willing to listen and deliberate with the officials, while the latter eventually became willing to listen attentively to the neighbors (Forester, 1981). Discussing concerns over time enabled a shared power between public officials and the neighbors in the decision-making process. The neighbors also referred to these relationships as important benefits to influence formal and informal policy decision processes locally, more pointedly when the participants had a voice in the political "game" to get things done. An example is the neighbors' success in the zoning issue passed in the neighborhood association's favor. The deliberative process with the city officials led the neighbors to feel like valued citizens and key actors in resolving the zoning issue at hand, which was very "personal" to them.

An interpretive approach—which was both methodologically systematic and rigorous—sought to gain access to the neighbors' intersubjective meanings about shared processes and goals. Interpreting and explicating people's stories in terms of their meanings illuminated and expanded otherwise abstract conceptualizations about community process (Elías, 2008, 2010). Phenomenological interpretation allowed for further thinking and dialogue about the potential of neighborhood group processes to construct more inclusive and participatory governance.

Some limitations of interpretive phenomenology in the study of civic engagement and deliberative practices are that it may not be used for large-scale studies. Interpretive approaches capture best the meanings evolved in relatively "small" groups of people due to the intrinsic meanings evolved in each group, or "interpretive community" (Yanow, 2000), which makes any interpretation context-specific. Moreover, since interpretive approaches utilize in-depth interviews, lengthy transcriptions, and multilevel interpretation processes, they are more feasible in smaller population samples. In addition, interpretive studies cannot be generalized or replicated to other settings or populations. Since each context and situation is unique in their own right, they can seldom be used as benchmarks or categories against which to judge other situations, contexts, experiences, and events. Insofar as the researcher takes an active role in the phenomenological study, either as a participant-observer, as a listener of stories, or interpreting "thick descriptions" that ensue from those activities, this epistemology might be seen as presenting a problem of "intrusion" with the subjects of study, the data, and even the study results. "Bracketing out"[8] can prevent the immediate tendency to categorize stories and meanings while observing people deliberate and act, when listening, transcribing and interpreting stories. To "correct" for possible misinterpretations of a story due to one's observationalinvolvement in it, the interpretive phenomenologist is encouraged to ask researchers in her "epistemic community" for feedback (Yanow, 2001, 2006).

Important questions—such as how to govern the administrative state democratically, the meaning of the public space, who should participate in the policy dialogue and in decision-making processes—must be addressed from various perspectives. If scholars and practitioners are seriously committed to a democratic governance process that involves multiple perspectives, they should take into greater account the meanings that citizens evolve when they work together and with public officials. The quest for shared meaning in everyday situations could help public administrators understand the intersubjective experiences of collaborative processes to create a more intelligent (i.e., more democratic) public administration and policy process (Lindblom & Woodhouse, 1993).

REFLECTION

What is the value of interpretive epistemologies to public administrators as they seek to understand and promote collaborative governance? The methods of interpretive phenomenology allow the experiential knowledge of neighbors to emerge in their own terms as reflections of their own lived experiences. As does political theorist M. P. Follett (1918/1923, 1919), the participants of the exemplar case study (Elías, 2008) prompt researchers to consider that the social world, intersubjectively constituted, requires unique and specific ways of accessing it, of knowing it (Flyvbjerg, 2006; Harmon, 1981; Hummel & Stivers, 1998; Hycner, 1985; Stivers, 2008b; Taylor, 1971; van Manen, 1990; Yanow, 2004, 2007, 2009). Interpretive epistemologies, such as phenomenology, are adequate to access the meanings that evolve through collaborative experiences (Elías, 2010).

The case study showed that expanding the dialogue about community and deliberative democracy to nonacademic arenas has the potential to create a richer and more encompassing scholarship about the practice of grassroots democracy. People's experiences are vital for understanding and making concrete people's meanings of a shared reality in the public realm. Through interpretive phenomenology, scholars and practitioners could retrieve from anonymity this "forgotten man" of the social sciences (Schutz, 1967, pp. 6–7), that is, the neglected articulations of people's intersubjective experiences, as in neighborhood improvement groups.

The case study discussed in this chapter (Elías, 2008) showed that understanding communal experiences in the participants' own terms brought experiential and hands-on meaning to otherwise abstract speculations about community process and grassroots democracy at the neighborhood level (Hummel, 1991, 1998). Grounding concept-formation in people's experiences, public administration scholars and practitioners would be able to understand from different and unexplored perspectives different ways to govern democratically and inclusively.

Although interpretive researchers may not generalize the results of context-bound interpretations, in-depth case studies do bring to light the richness and detail characteristic of life itself by means of stories, anecdotes, and metaphors (Hummel, 1991, 1998; Stone, 2001; Yanow, 2004, 2007, 2009). Attentively listening to people's storytelling and direct observations of groups' meetings and activities can help researchers gain an understanding of people's intersubjective experiences and the meanings they evolve from them. Interpretive phenomenology, thus, has the advantage of allowing the phenomenon under investigation to show itself in its own terms when appropriately addressed (Heidegger, 1962).

At the local level and from the viewpoint of the different constituencies, that research approach could help tackle complex public problems from a diversity of perspectives. Consequently, interpretive phenomenology could be a useful tool for practitioners to frame public policies in a more inclusive and thus meaningful way, understanding that ultimately, a large and diverse constituency will have to live with the actual application of the policies.

Taking into account the diverse "communities of meaning" (Yanow, 2000), public administrators can foster a participatory public policy process that is reflective of their constituencies' aims and aspirations, and thus, a genuine practice of democratic governance.

APPENDIX

Interview Questions[9]

1. How did you become a member of this group?
2. What usually happens at your meetings?
3. Can you give me an example of an issue that you have dealt with? Can you describe what it's been like working on that issue?
4. Has there been a time when the group members did not agreed with an issue? How have you dealt with it?
5. How has your work in the group changed the way you feel about your neighborhood?
6. Is there any person in your group whose presence or absence would make a difference? If so, how?
7. What is the trick to be a member of this group? What does it take to be a leader?
8. If you were to sum up your experiences of being involved in your neighborhood group, what would you say?
9. For you personally, what have been the best and the worst experiences that you have dealt with, whatever "best" and "worst" mean to you?
10. Can you describe your group's interactions with government officials or agencies?
11. What is the best experience you have had interacting with government in an issue of your neighborhood group? What is the worst?
12. What does "community" mean to you?

NOTES

1. The purpose of that case study (Elías, 2008) was to understand the collaborative experiences in the participants' own terms and to reflect on those findings in light of Follett's (1918/1923, 1919) theory of community process.
2. For an in-depth discussion on the interpretive epistemologies and their place in today's social science research, see Yanow & Schwartz-Shea, 2006.
3. Even though the researcher conducts an interpretation of the interview narratives and observations, she ought to keep the terms used by the participants as intact as possible.

4. Methodological individualism emphasizes objectivity and neutrality as the only way to achieve reliable results, and thus scientific findings. This is based on the idea that the researcher can separate herself from the social world, which she attempts to make clear.

5. A detailed discussion of the protocol used in this phenomenological research (as well as the raw interview transcriptions and interpretations) can be found in Elías (2008).

6. Allowing the "units of general meaning" as well as the "units of meaning relevant to the research question" to emerge demands a systematic approach that begins by listening attentively to the recordings many times, followed by their transcription, and finally, reading them many times. When explicating the themes or units of meaning, it is crucial that the researcher utilizes the participants' own terms in defining concepts or making sense of ideas (Elías, 2008, 2010).

7. The doubled emphasis (*italics* and/or **bold**) within some quotes in this chapter, is to draw the reader's attention in two different ways. First, the *italicized words/phrases* convey the emphases that the neighbors themselves allocated to their storytelling as they narrated their experiences. Second, with the **bold emphasis on words/phrases**, the author seeks to emphasize some sections (or the entirety) of the emerging themes as she interpreted people's narratives, utilizing people's own terms.

8. "Bracketing out" refers to a conscious setting aside of the researcher's quick tendency to categorize and analyze people's stories and observing the phenomenon as lived by people, at the same time as these are being gathered.

9 These questions are from a previous study by the author (Elías, 2008).

REFERENCES

Ansley, F., & Gaventa, J. (1997). Researching for democracy and democratizing research. *Change, 29*(1), 46–53.

Askim, J., & Hanssen, G. S. (2008). Councillors' receipt and use of citizen input: Experience from Norwegian local government. *Public Administration, 86*(2), 387–409.

Aston, M., & Meagher-Stewart, D. (2009). Public health nurses' primary health care practice: Strategies for fostering citizen participation. *Journal of Community Health Nursing, 26*, 24–34.

Arendt, H. (1958). *The human condition.* Chicago, IL.: University of Chicago Press.

Arendt, H. (2005). *The promise of politics.* New York, NY: Schocken.

Barber, B. (1984). *Strong democracy: Participatory politics for a new age.* Berkeley and Los Angeles: University of California Press.

de Lancer Julnes, P., & Johnson, D. (2011). Strengthening efforts to engage the Hispanic community in citizen-driven governance: An assessment of efforts in Utah. *Public Administration Review, 71*(2), 221–231.

de Sousa Briggs, X. (2008). *Democracy as problem solving: Civic capacity in communities across the globe.* Cambridge, MA: MIT Press.

Elías, M. V. (2008). *Community: An experience-based critique of the concept.* Unpublished doctoral dissertation. The University of Akron, Ohio.

Elías, M. V. (2010). Governance from the ground up: Rediscovering Mary Parker Follett. *Public Administration and Management, 15*(1), 9–45.

Flyvbjerg, B. (1998). *Rationality and power: Democracy in practice.* Chicago, IL: University of Chicago Press.

Flyvbjerg, B. (2006). *Making social science matter.* Cambridge, MA: Cambridge University Press.

Follett, M. P. (1918/1923). *The new state: Group organization the solution of popular government.* New York, NY: Longman Green.

Follett, M. P. (1919). Community is a process. *The Philosophical Review, 28*(6), 576–588.

Follett, M. P. (1925). Power. In H. C. Metcalf & L. Urwick (Eds.), *Dynamic administration. The collected papers of Mary Parker Follett* (pp. 95–116). New York, NY: Harper.

Forester, J. (1981). Questioning and organizing attention: Toward a critical theory of planning and administrative practice. *Administration and Society, 13,* 161–205.

Forester, J. (1989). *Planning in the face of power.* Berkeley: University of California Press.

Forester, J. (1999). *The deliberative practitioner: Encouraging participatory planning processes.* Cambridge, MA: MIT Press.

Forester, J. (2009). *Dealing with differences. Dramas of mediating public disputes.* New York, NY: Oxford University Press.

Gaventa, J., & Barrett, G. (2010). *So what difference does it make? Mapping the outcomes of citizen engagement.* IDS Research Summary of IDS Working Paper 347. Brighton, England: IDS.

Geertz, C. (1973). Thick description: Toward an interpretive theory of culture. In *The interpretation of cultures* (pp. 3–32). New York, NY: Basic.

Handley, D. M., & Howell-Moroney, M. (2010). Ordering stakeholder relationships and citizen participation: Evidence from the community development block grant program. *Public Administration Review, 70*(4), 601–609.

Harmon, M. (1981). *Action theory for public administration.* New York, NY: Longman.

Heidegger, M. (1962). *Being and time.* New York, NY: Harper.

Heidegger, M. (2005). *Introduction to phenomenological research.* Bloomington: Indiana University Press.

Hummel, R. P. (1991). Stories managers tell: Why they are as valid as science. *Public Administration Review, 51,* 31–41.

Hummel, R. P. (1998). Practice illuminating theory. *Administrative Theory & Praxis, 20,* 150–158.

Hummel, R. P., & Stivers, C. (1998). Government isn't us: The possibility of democratic knowledge in representative government. In C. S. King, C. Stivers, & Collaborators, *Government is us: Public administration in an anti-government era* (pp. 28–48). Thousand Oaks, CA: Sage.

Husserl, E. (1970). *The crisis of European sciences and transcendental phenomenology. An introduction to phenomenological philosophy.* Evanston, IL: Northwestern University Press.

Hycner, R. (1985). Some guidelines for the phenomenological analysis of interview data. *Human Studies, 8,* 279–303.

Kathi, P. C., & Cooper, T. (2005). Democratizing the administrative state: Connecting neighborhood councils and city agencies. *Public Administration Review, 65*(5), 559–567.

Kemmis, D. (1990). *Community and the politics of place.* Norman: University of Oklahoma Press.

King, C. S., Stivers, C., & Collaborators. (1998). *Government is us: Public administration in an anti-government.* Thousand Oaks, CA: Sage.

LeRoux, K. (2009). Paternalistic or participatory governance? Examining opportunities for client participation in nonprofit social service organizations. *Public Administration Review, 69*(3), 504–517.

Lindblom, C., & Woodhouse, E. (1993). *The policymaking process.* Englewood Cliffs, NJ: Prentice-Hall.

Maynard-Moody, S., & Musheno, M. (2003). *Cops, teachers, counselors: Stories from the front lines of public service.* Ann Arbor: University of Michigan Press.

Schutz, A. (1967). *The phenomenology of the social world.* Evanston, IL: Northwestern University Press.

Stivers, C. (1990). The public agency as polis: Active citizenship in the administrative state. *Administration & Society, 22*(1), 86–105.

Stivers, C. (1994). The listening bureaucrat: Responsiveness in public administration. *Public Administration Review, 54*(4), 364–369.

Stivers, C. (2008a). *Governance in dark times: Practical philosophy for public service.* Washington, DC: Georgetown University Press.

Stivers, C. (2008b). Public administration's myth of Sisyphus. *Administration & Society, 39*(8), 1008–1012.

Stone, D. (2001). *Policy paradox: The art of political decision making.* New York, NY: W.W. Norton.

Taylor, C. (1971). Interpretation and the sciences of man. *The Review of Metaphysics, 25*(1), 3–51.

van Manen, M. (1990). *Researching lived experience. Human science for an action sensitive pedagogy.* Albany: State University of New York Press.

Wagenaar, H. (2011). *Meaning in action. Interpretation and dialogue in policy analysis.* Armonk, NY: M.E. Sharpe.

Wamsley, G. L., & Wolf, J. F. (Eds.). (1996). *Refounding democratic public administration: Modern paradoxes, postmodern challenges.* Thousand Oaks, CA: Sage.

Weeks, E. C. (2000). The practice of deliberative democracy: Results from four large-scale trials. *Public Administration Review, 60*(4), 360–372.

Yanow, D. (1997). *How does a policy mean? Interpreting policy and organizational action.* Washington, DC: Georgetown University Press.

Yanow, D. (2000). *Conducting interpretive policy analysis.* Thousand Oaks, CA: Sage.

Yanow, D. (2004, September). *How do I know what I'm going to find before I get into the field? Hypotheses, variables, measurement and other philosophical issues.* Paper presented at the annual meeting of the American Political Science Association, Chicago, IL.

Yanow, D. (2007). Interpretation in policy analysis: On methods and practice. *Critical Policy Analysis, 1*(1), 109–121.

Yanow, D. (2009). Ways of knowing: Passionate humility and reflective practice in research and management. *The American Review of Public Administration, 39,* 579–601.

Yanow, D., & Schwartz-Shea, P. (2006). *Interpretation and method: Empirical research methods and the interpretive turn.* Armonk, NY: M.E. Sharpe.

Yeung, P. H. Y., Passmore, A. E., & Packer, T. L. (2008). Active citizens or passive recipients: How Australian young adults with cerebral palsy define citizenship. *Journal of Intellectual and Developmental Disability, 33*(1), 65–75.

CHAPTER 17

SOCIAL PSYCHOLOGICAL BARRIERS TO COMMUNICATIVE RATIONALITY

A Critical Look at Public Participation

Walter F. Kuentzel
University of Vermont

Curtis Ventriss
University of Vermont and *Johns Hopkins University*

THE PROBLEM WITH RATIONAL DELIBERATION

The literature on environmental planning and policy almost universally tells a "good news" story about public participation in environmental decision making (Hart, 1984; Roberts, 2004). Stakeholder involvement in environmental problem solving is the new currency of managerial decision making (Chase, Decker, & Lauber, 2004; Thompson, Forster, Werner, & Peterson, 2010), incorporating the foundations of discursive de-

The State of Citizen Participation in America, pages 415–444
Copyright © 2012 by Information Age Publishing
415

mocracy envisioned in theories of communicative rationality (Habermas, 1984; Hajer, 1995). This emerging culture of public involvement aspires to be inclusive, collaborative, rationally deliberative, and receptive to a broad horizon of ideas in its problem-solving approach to contemporary complex environmental challenges. From this perspective, effective governance relies on Habermas' (1984) principle of the "ideal speech act," in which people can deliberate as equals in a fair and open context without fear of embarrassment, patronization, or reprisal. The ideal speech act assumes that deliberative compromise and decision making in civil society produces better outcomes than the expert decision-making process that was central to the progressive/modernist approach of the 20th century. The "bad news" story about public participation, however, comes with a closer examination of how people come together to deliberate. We argue in this chapter that the ideal speech act is socially psychologically naïve. Deliberative groups in certain contexts can produce "better" outcomes, but more often they do not, for a host of social psychological reasons that have received little scholarly attention.

We have argued elsewhere (Ventriss & Kuentzel, 2005) that contemporary public participation has failed to realize its transformative potential as envisioned by Habermas' theory of communicative rationality and instead has acquiesced to "enlightened business as usual" (Harvey, 2000). Habermas' (1984) theory rejected the popular notion that contemporary society was evidence for the failure of modernity, that is, a postmodernity. Rather, he viewed contemporary society as the next historical step in a transformation from instrumental rationality to communicative rationality; from a state-centered bureaucratic society to a collaborative and discursive form of civil society; from the expert-driven "high priest" model of decision making to deliberative public participation as the centerpiece of contemporary problem solving. Habermas' theory of communicative rationality has provided a resonating diagnosis of the contemporary world for the public participation literature. His theory, however, was short on prescription. Because of this, we have argued that contemporary public participation has generally failed to play its role in societal transformation because it frames questions and seeks solutions within existing institutions and prevailing market ideologies. The result is a "politics of policy containment" (Ventriss, 2002) that exerts a selective filter on agenda setting, participant inclusion, group leadership/authority, relevant knowledge, and influence in the participatory process. It is a process that is rarely conducive to nurturing a fair and open "ideal speech act," and instead is one more tool of instrumental decision making through interest group compromise.

Ventriss and Kuentzel (2005) argued *in theory* why collaborative groups in a public participation context often fail to meet their transformative potential. What was missing from that analysis was why participatory groups *in practice* often fail to meet their transformative potential. We maintain that the public participation literature's shortcomings are rooted in its implicit reliance on a utilitarian framework of individual self-interest. The problem with this framework is best illustrated by Garrett Hardin's "Tragedy of the Commons" (1968), which has been highly influential in environmental management and policy circles. Hardin famously argued that environmental problems are, at their root, problems of human behavior. Out of self-interest, individuals will typically claim as many of the commonly held resources as possible: land, air, water, wind, scenic beauty, wildlife, recreational experiences, and so on. Because personal utility drives individual behavior, society risks overuse and eventual degradation of its natural environment. Hardin's solution to the dilemma of the commons was "mutual coercion, mutually agreed," which fit beautifully with the existing mandate of a managerial state (coercion or regulation) and with the principles of public participation (mutual agreement or compromise). "Mutual coercion, mutually agreed," like the "ideal speech act" however, was socially psychologically naïve. Hardin's solution—coordinated behavior bounded by normative constraint—had long been a foundational principle of social psychology. In short, Hardin's diagnosis of human behavior was simplistic, and his solution even in the 1960s was passé. The social psychology literature is packed with reasons why "mutual agreement" in public participation must traverse a minefield of behavioral contingency to produce what are often ambivalent outcomes.

Our argument is drawn from a range of theories in social psychology, which is a science of interaction and by extension a science of deliberation. Social psychology has a lot to say about public opinion, performance, power, and influence in the public sphere. Moreover, it suggests a host of reasons why fairness and openness in the public participation process may be an ideal rarely achieved. This chapter will review the social psychological minefields that are inherent in the public participation process. Specifically, social psychology can speak to three questions and challenges that face public participation. First, who does and who does not participate? The goal of public participation is to treat "stakeholder" interests as equal. Yet participants rarely come to the table as equals, and there are many individual differences that predispose some to engage and others to remain disengaged, despite equal interest. Second, is deliberation and rational argumentation always better? Habermas argues that deliberative speech produces progressive compromise that moves a debate beyond the "mere subjectivity" of the individual thought process (1984). Yet social psychology demonstrates that individual cognition and perception is far more complex and consequential than "mere subjectivity," and that argumentation is subject to contingencies of influence, conformity, and persuasion that can short-circuit "rational" compromise. Finally, are groups really better at solving environmental dilemmas and conflicts? Social psychology has demonstrated as many barriers as enablers to group performance, and the forces at work in intergroup conflict make compromise an elusive target. Before examining these three questions, however, we first review the "good news" story that is told in the public participation literature, and examine its unquestioned assumption that public participation is better for achieving instrumentally rational ends.

The "Good News" Story in Public Participation

Active public participation in civic affairs has always been closely associated with promoting and ultimately encouraging citizen governance as a democratic ideal (Frederickson, 1982; Hart, 1984; Roberts, 2004; Ventriss, 1989). According to Benjamin Barber (1984, p. 24), robust public participation can lead to what he referred to as strong democracy as a way of abating the influence of thin democracy, which he defined in these sharply worded terms:

> Oblivious to that essential human interdependency that underlies all political life, thin democratic politics is at best a politics of static interest, never a politics of transformation; a politics of bargaining and exchange, never a politics of invention and creation; and a politics that conceives of women and men at their worst (in order to protect them from themselves), never at their potential best (to help them become better than they are).

Barber touches upon a key point that is, at least, implicit in much of the participatory literature: that public participation can mitigate the tendency in modern liberalism to facilitate the "apolitical individual" who becomes primarily a creature of appetite and sheer passion, corrupted by both apathy and anomie. Put bluntly, public participation, if done correctly, can arrest the further atomization of citizenship wherein citizens subordinate their public responsibilities into either rampant materialism or, more troubling, civic privatism (Ventriss, 2011). Public participation becomes viewed as part and parcel of a process that can reconnect a citizenry in confronting the powerful forces that have come to dominate modern politics.

However, as Terry Cooper (1980) has argued in his classic analysis of a community organization in southeast Los Angeles (observed over an 11-year period), there is a proclivity for these citizen groups to become a mere mirror image of the public agency they are dealing with. In short, in order to become effective with their dealings with public agencies, citizens groups eventually adopt the language, technical rationality, and bureaucratic perspectives of such agencies. To confront this vexing tendency, Cooper claimed that public organizations must actually cultivate a positive relationship with such neighborhood organizations as a valuable source of input as well as hiring community liaisons to work closely with communities in forging a "communication link."

Notwithstanding the validity of Cooper's analysis, the good news concerning public participation has, generally speaking, exhibited the following substantive attributes: (a) Direct participation is developmental (it fosters an active, public-spirited moral character); (b) Direct citizen participation is educative (it helps develop the attitudes and skills of democratic citizenship that encourage a deliberative process in civic affairs); (c) Direct citizen participation is therapeutic and integrative (it can achieve psychic rewards and a strong sense of political efficacy); (d) Direct citizen participation is legitimating (it produces administrative and political stability within the modern polity); (e) Direct citizen participation is protective of freedom (it increases control over their lives and environment and fosters the protection of their freedom). (Roberts, 2004, pp. 323–324).

While Roberts and others have pinpointed many of the prevailing arguments (pro and con) about public participation, there is a troubling issue that is often overlooked: many of the substantive values associated with democracy—equality and participation—stand in sharp opposition to the instrumental values of hierarchy, specialization, and impersonality ascribed to the modern bureaucracy (Thompson, 1983). If indeed this is correct, how is it possible to foster a genuine public participation that would confront the political, economic, and societal *leitmotifs* that can distort or reify the role of substantive rationality in democratizing political and economic systems? (Adams & Balfour, 2008; Tussman, 1974; Ventriss, 1998, 2011).

While the discussion here about the good news of public participation is hardly exhaustive, public participation has the merit of reawakening in us the realization that "when citizens' voices are muted by manipulation and moneyed interests, that adversarial democracy, by putting citizen against citizen, threatens the commonwealth and our collective future" (Roberts, 2004, p. 344). But is there more to this story? Do the barriers to public participation run deeper than class conflict or bureaucratic manipulation of its citizenry? Are there other reasons for citizens to be skeptical of a stakeholder-driven public participation process?

Who Participates and Who Does Not?

From a "good news" perspective, the fundamental task of effective public participation is to "rev up" the cognitive engines of self-interested stakeholders to generate a momentum of new and innovative ideas, alternatives, and solutions. All people have to do in a public participation setting is to show up with an open mind ready to talk about and wrestle with the problem at hand. Social psychology, however, provides ample evidence to indicate that many, if not most, self-interested stakeholders never show up. Research on volunteerism has shown that a small minority of people (roughly 5%) are actively involved in neighborhood volunteer work in the United States (Oliver, 1984), and they tend to be "career" volunteers. Research on group performance also shows that even when people do show up to participate in a group function, a minority of group members often perform the majority of the group tasks (Rich, 1980), and the free-rider phenomenon (Latane, Williams, & Harkins, 1979) is always a threat to effective group performance. Why then do people with seemingly clear interests in an issue choose not to participate? Moreover, why do many people who do show up contribute very little besides their presence to the process and outcome of the participatory event? We argue that even though the principles of communicative rationality and discursive democracy guarantee equality among all people in the public participation process, social psychology demonstrates that human behavior varies widely, and people never *participate* in equivalent ways. We offer behavioral explanations for nonparticipation by stakeholders in a public participation process that draws from literature on (a) the self and social structure and (b) attitude structure and attitude strength.

"Stakeholder" Differences

Personality Constraints

Rational actor models of human behavior assume that all stakeholders in an environmental dispute or controversy will know and can articulate their interests. Social psychology makes it clear, however, that there is wide variation in the way people know, perceive, and communicate their interests. At the heart of these differences lies the concept of self-representation (Baumeister, 1999; Swann & Bossun, 2010): self-perception, identity, and self-esteem. There is a variety of reasons related to personality and self-concept that leads people to avoid public participation settings even when they have an obvious interest or stake in the outcome. For example, the recent literature on social cognitive neuroscience (Leiberman, 2010) has produced a growing body of research on the role of the amygdala region of the brain in emotional recognition and response. Specifically, research has demonstrated variation among individuals in their response to unfamiliar faces (Schwartz, Wright, Shin, Kagan, & Rauch, 2003). Those with an active amygdala response to a novel face respond with higher levels of anxiety and fear, while those with a less active amygdala response show no indication of fear. This finding is, in effect, a neurological shyness response that for some can make talking in front of strangers in a public meeting a frightening experience. Of course, small samples in these studies make it difficult to say how many people in a population fear group situations. Moreover, fear of public speaking is something that can be overcome. Nevertheless, Borden (1980) states that "the fear of speaking before a group may be the most prevalent fear that people admit experiencing" (p. 100). Consequently, having a stake in an issue may be an insufficient force to overcome fear of the novel, unfamiliar social setting of a public participation context.

Another factor that has bearing on people's willingness to engage in public participation settings is variation in self-perception or self-image. The concept of self refers to a set of more or less stable mental representations that define the key behavioral and cognitive characteristics of a person. Psychology typically thinks of these representations as personality traits or dispositions. One frequently studied, though controversial, personality type is the authoritarian personality (Adorno, Frenkel-Brunswik, Levinson, & Sanford, 1950), which describes forceful, take-charge types of people who are more likely to exaggerate their own competence in the face of other people's perceived shortcomings. This type of individual is much more likely to dominate public participation settings, while those with more reserved or easygoing personalities are more likely to acquiesce to or withdraw from the "muscle flexing" power displays of the authoritarian.

Another example of personality research is the literature on variations in the way people typically employ inferential vs. intuitive reasoning (Wegner & Bargh, 1998) in everyday life. This framework argues that some people tend to be more systems oriented in their thinking, drawing on linear cause-and-effect observations and probabilistic logic in directing their everyday affairs toward desired ends. Other people tend to rely more on hunches, thought "incubation" (Dijksterhuis, 2010), automaticity, priming, and affect to negotiate everyday affairs in less goal-directed ways. Public participation in the context of environmental planning and policymaking relies on inferential goal-directed thinking. Therefore, those whose cognitive style is more intuitive can find themselves on the outside looking in with little to add to a discourse that likely has been framed around instrumental problem solving.

A third example of the role of personality traits in public participation is found in White's notion of effectance (1959). He argued that a key element in explaining behavioral variation was a person's desire to have an effect on one's world. Working from the humanist perspective in psychology, he believed that humans were motivated to avoid passive acquiescence to the events and normative conditions of the world that "happen to us." Instead, the psychologically "healthy" individual is motivated to actively shape thoughts, events, and the environment in which he/she lives. Research in this tradition has demonstrated that people vary in their effectance motivation (Harter, 1978). Consequently, those with a stronger effectance disposition should be more likely to engage in public participation activities, while those with a stronger acquiescence disposition will be less likely, even when stakeholder relevance is constant.

Identity Salience

Psychology through much of the 20th century has focused its attention on what William James (1890/1950) called the "me" dimension of self-representation, which describes a person's generally stable characteristics that can be observed across time and context. During the same era, social psychology has mostly focused its attention on James's "I" dimension, which describes the emergent qualities of the acting self as its self-representations progressively change to fit the particular social circumstance. Goffman's (1959) dramaturgical version of role theory argued that people assume and enact certain roles in a given situation, that each comes with normative expectations for behavior and loosely defined scripts and story lines, and that most are presented in good faith between competent actors. He maintained that people could readily take on and off roles as the situations changed. One could move easily from a work role, into a family role at home, into a political role at a town council meeting, and into a leisure role at the bowling alley. The main point was that social interaction was a role-making process that carried with it clear socially structural properties that were reproduced and occasionally altered and remade by acting individuals.

Most early symbolic interaction research stressed the dynamic qualities of self-representation that were expressed in the changing scenes and changing roles that one could slip on and slip off with relative ease. By the late 1970s, however, social psychology began to shift back toward James's concept of "me" in describing self-representations. Turner's (1978) notion of the role-person merger argued that roles are not simply put on and then taken off just to match the demands of a given situation. Rather, when people assume a repertoire of roles, some roles become favored roles, some roles are more comfortable than others, and some roles make more sense to the actor. When this happens, people assume favored roles that bleed across different situations and contexts. That is, they merge the role-play and role expectations with their self-representation. Stryker (1980) called this process identity salience, in which the role identities one enacts in everyday life become ranked on a salience continuum—some role identities are called up across multiple situations, while others are rarely used. Identity salience builds when individuals develop "intensive commitment" to the identity. The identity becomes central to one's lifestyle, and the individual chooses identity-related behaviors at the expense of other potentially more appropriate activities. Identity salience also increases with extensive commitment, in which one enacts identity-related behaviors around an expanding social circle of people who support and encourage the preferred role identity.

In Oliver's (1984) research on volunteerism, she described the small minority of the population who does most of the volunteer work in the United States as lifestyle or career volunteers. In many cases, volunteers may often invest themselves personally in their activity, building a progressively more salient identity as a volunteer. If this is true, the public participation process could be suffering from serious sampling bias. Public participation as a form of volunteerism may be attracting only a small minority of stakeholders who have made personal investments in an identity formulated around a specific environmental issue or around a "civically engaged" or "socially responsible" identity. The rest of the stakeholders whose representations of self revolve around alternative identities such as family, religion, or work may be preoccupied with other important role expectations to give much attention to public participation controversies. Moreover, the division of labor within a public participation process can create a variety of roles and role expectations that some marginal participants are unwilling to assume.

Self-Efficacy

One final example of behavioral differences among individuals is the concept of self-efficacy (Bandura, 1977). One of the most robust findings in social psychology is the notion of a self-enhancement motive. This motive drives people to seek out positive and confirming information about one's self-representation. While there is plenty of controversy about the role of negative self-information in the self-enhancement literature (e.g., the "better than average effect" in Swann & Bosson, 2010), the concept supports the notion that people want to think of themselves as capable and likeable people in whatever social circumstance they enter. Research indicates that self-efficacy and self-esteem vary widely across individuals (Brown, 1998; Deci & Ryan, 1995) and over time, and as many as 30% of the U.S. population hold negative self-representations (Swann & Bosson, 2010). Environmental controversies are often complex scientific and social dilemmas. Public participation therefore assumes a certain degree of knowledge and understanding. The human capital requirements of the public participation process assume a certain degree of capability and understanding, which attracts some, but may well be off-putting to many other stakeholders who must deal with self-doubt, inexperience, and ambivalence.

Attitude Structure

Thus far in this chapter, we have asked two primary questions: Why don't many stakeholders participate in public deliberations over environmental controversies? and Why do many who show up to public participation events add very little to the deliberations? The previous section on stakeholder differences primarily addressed the first question. The attitude literature from social psychology has much to say about both questions.

Attitude Strength

During the early 1930s, LaPierre traveled around the western United States with a Japanese couple, during a time of widespread distrust and prejudice against Asian Americans. During their travels, only two restaurants refused service to the traveling party. When he returned home, LaPierre wrote letters to each of the 251 restaurants and hotels they had visited, informing them that he would be traveling with an Asian couple and inquiring if they would serve Asians. About half the establishments responded, and 92% wrote back saying no, they would *not* serve Asians (LaPiere, 1934). LaPierre's study unleashed 5 decades of research trying to settle the question of why attitudes (as expressed by business people's willingness to serve Asians) were poor predictors of behavior. As a result, attitudes have become perhaps the most widely studied concept in social psychology.

Two widely studied concepts from the attitude literature that are important to our purposes here are attitude strength and attitude ambivalence. Attitudes have been defined in a multitude of ways (Banaji & Heiphetz, 2010), but most definitions agree that an attitude is a cognitive response expressed along a continuum of positive to negative toward some person, object, or issue (Petty & Cacciopo, 1981). Those responses combine a set of beliefs with an affective or emotional component and a set of behavioral intentions or action tendencies toward the attitude object (Zanna & Rempel, 1988). This tripartite conceptualization of an attitude (beliefs, affect, behavioral intention) is a widely used framework for describing structure in the way humans evaluate objects in the world.

Heberlein (1981) used a passage from Aldo Leopold's *Sand County Almanac* (1949) describing why Leopold favored white pine trees to birch trees in managing his central Wisconsin farm. Heberlein used the passage to show both a vertical and a horizontal structure in Leopold's attitude statement, "I am in love with pines." At the foundational level, Leopold articulates a series of values that inform his attitude, such as family security (pines are worth more), significance (pines live twice as long), and social recognition (a woodlot of distinction). Next, is a series of cognitive beliefs about the attitude object such as, "I planted the pine, the birch planted itself" and "Neighbors have no pines and plenty of birches." Finally, Leopold articulated a set of preferred choices that followed directly from his values and beliefs, such as "Having pines produces more income" and "It's better to take care of longer-living trees." Heberlein argues that attitudes are strongest when they are well-grounded in a linked vertical structure of values, beliefs, and preferred choices. Equally important in attitude strength is the horizontal structure. The more values, beliefs, and preferred choices that inform an attitude object, the less likely it will change, and the more likely it will predict behavior. Heberlein states that many of our attitudes are weakly held attitudes because they may lack a set of core values on which they are grounded. Moreover, attitudes can be weakly held because they are based on single beliefs, that is, people often have not given much consideration to certain attitude objects.

Others (Krosnick, Boninger, Chuang, Berent, & Carnot, 1993; Raden, 1985) have elaborated on the attitude-strength concept by examining variations in other cognitive components of attitudes. Krosnick et al. (1993) reviewed a series of attitude-strength components such as emotional intensity, certainty, importance, extremity, interest, direct experience, and accessibility. The collective point of this research is that attitudes are not simply discrete evaluations about an attitude object. Instead, attitudes combine a complex array of cognitive "data points" or components with an equally complex process of evaluation, preference, and behavioral intentions.

Variation in attitude strength then helps explain nonparticipation in a public participation setting. Some people simply have not given much thought to the controversy or issue at hand. Without much knowledge about the topic, it is difficult for someone to develop a strong attitude about an issue that might then stimulate participation, much less remedial action. Environmental issues are also oftentimes quite complex, so even if the outcome of a public participation process has a clear impact on a stakeholder, the chances of effective participation are slim when the vertical and horizontal structure of an individual's attitude is weak.

Can stakeholders be brought "up to speed" on complex environmental issues through education? It is successful only to a point. The goal of public education is to provide information to either inform or persuade someone on an issue. However, information addresses only the belief component of attitude structure. Education tends to ignore values in its programs, except insofar as the education incorporates the values of the educator. This approach, however, does not guarantee that the recipient of the educational message shares the values implicit in the message. Moreover, education has even less control over the subsequent evaluation one makes of the attitude object.

Attitude Ambivalence

A concept closely related to attitude strength that has received increasing attention over the past 20 years is attitude ambivalence. One of the most common errors made by managers and decision makers when using attitude research is the "majority rules fallacy." This fallacy derives from a "polling culture" (Macnaghten & Urry, 1998) in which policymakers look for the ratio of a population that "agrees/disagrees" or "supports/opposes" a particular proposal. To estimate this ratio, policymakers frequently collapse the 5-point scale used to measure attitude items into a dichotomous ratio. Public participation often relies on this simplified version of public attitudes to help identify stakeholders in the selection process. However, the distribution of most attitude measures typically resemble a normal curve. There is a minority, often vocal, who is opposed, and another minority, often equally vocal, who is in favor. In between, however, are the masses who don't know, who don't care, or who are rationally ambivalent. The majority in most measures of attitudes are people whose attitude structure is poorly developed—they have given little thought to the issue. They also are people whose attitude strength is weak—they have little personal investment in the issue (McGrane, 2010). Attitude ambivalence recognizes that most people in a population are either relatively apathetic about an issue and invest fewer cognitive resources into the attitude object or have considered a variety of beliefs about an attitude object and are unable to make a conclusive evaluation about the object—they are rationally ambivalent.

Public participation efforts must therefore guard against overrepresentation by the extremes. It is difficult to conceive of a fair and open public participation process when the participants are a well-spoken (or outspoken) minority with the greatest personal investment in the issue, and most others do not think of themselves as stakeholders and might be content to acquiesce to the will of the minority.

"Merely Subjective"

The "central experience" in Habermas' theory of communicative action is "the unconstrained, unifying, consensus-bringing force of argumentative speech, in which different participants overcome their merely subjective views" (Habermas 1984, p. 10). This experience of deliberative communication in civil society is transformative because it reforms the expert-driven, high-priest model of bureaucratic decision making in society—a "recolonization of the lifeworld." However, this quote indicates that his hierarchy of knowledge and reasoning remains mostly unchanged from its modernist formulation. Rational, communicatively generated knowledge is superior to individual subjectivity and impression-based knowledge of everyday life. This hierarchy is problematic for social psychology. In this section, we critically analyze this hierarchical assumption about cognition and perception by drawing from two major social psychological traditions, including literature on social cognition, and influence and conformity.

Social Cognition

At the heart of modernism is the assumption that reason and science are gradually dispensing with uncertainty. Controlled observation and systematic thinking helps us progressively recognize order and predictability in the world. For Habermas, communicative rationality is the primary extension of progressive reason in the late modern age that produces knowledge and coherence in contemporary life (Habermas, 1984). The main criticism of the project of modernity, however, is that scientific advances have produced an ever-expanding horizon of ambiguity (Bauman, 2002). Solving one set of problems through science and reason tends to produce and compound a whole new set of problems. For some theorists, the primary challenge of life in the late modern age is less about knowledge production and more about coping with ambiguity and uncertainty (Gergen, 1991). Social cognition is a branch of social psychology that has specifically tackled this problem of ambiguity in human perception and cognition (Fiske & Taylor, 1984).

Social cognition originated out of research in the 1950s from behavioral economics, which examined decision making within the context of rational actor models. Its primary goal was to optimize decision making by understanding the way individuals calculate the benefits and costs of a given action to produce a desired outcome. Perhaps the most robust finding that came out of this research on benefit maximization is that individual reason and judgment is full of contingency. Instead of making optimal decisions, individuals are better characterized as making "satificing" decisions (Simon, 1963), or decisions that are considered satisfactory given the circumstances. This was some of the first behavioral research that documented the limits of reason in everyday human affairs.

Research beginning in the 1970s took this "limits to reason" argument even further by arguing that human judgment is frequently flawed. The research program originated by Kahneman and Tversky and others (1974, 1982) was founded on the notion that human judgment is often biased by the use of heuristics, which are mental shortcuts employed in a variety of circumstances, which help relieve the cognitive burden of judgmental tasks. For example, the availability heuristic describes the ease with which someone can bring something to mind. It is easier to associate cold weather and heavy snow with evidence against climate change rather than searching weather records for annual average temperatures over the past 100 years or finding annual data on the spring ice-free dates of local lakes. Another example is the representativeness heuristic (Kahneman & Tversky, 1972), in which people will classify a specific object or situation according to how similar it is to a typical case. It is easier to think of a dairy farmer with a thousand acres and 1,200 cows as a corporate farmer interested only in profits and unconcerned about environmental impacts to the local watershed rather than paying attention to the farmer's state-mandated requirements or voluntary installments of waste management BMPs. The literature on cognitive heuristics has thrived since the 1970s, generating empirical evidence on the variety of ways individual cognition is frequently less than "rational" and sometimes suboptimal in producing the most beneficial outcomes.

This research casts a cautionary shadow upon Habermas' "unifying, consensus-bringing force of argumentative speech" (1984). The public participation process requires a commitment of time and mental effort from those involved to move beyond this natural inclination toward heuristic cognitive shortcuts. It is unclear, however, the degree to which people are willing or able to invest the cognitive effort to think as expansively and creatively as Habermas' ideal speech act requires.

Social cognition has formalized this "limits to rationality" literature into a broader framework that draws from phenomenological theories of perception. From this perspective, cognition is a process of mediation between *noemena,* or the undifferentiated blur of the perceived world and *phenomena,* or the named objects and events carved out of individual experience in the world (Husserl, 1973). Cognition is the process of "bracketing" bits and pieces of the perceptual blur into a world of "things" that can be selectively identified or constructed, described in a coherent way, and predicted or manipulated toward a certain outcome. This phenomenological approach assumes, however, that objects are not simply given for our perception. Rather, individuals bracket "objects" in a variety of ways for a variety of reasons (e.g., Putnam's [1983] discussion of men's perception of cats and women's perception of cats* or "cats prime"). It is this differential bracketing process that generates argument. On the one hand, there are normative pressures toward standardization of what is considered "objective." On the other hand, however, there are always alternative ways to bracket those standardized objects in new and different ways. For Habermas (1984), this argumentative process leads to compromise by establishing new and hopefully better ways to think about objects in the world. For social cognition, however, compromise may be fleeting, lasting only as long as it takes for someone else to come along who brackets the world in a different, more resonating way. Putnam (1983) argues that with an accelerating pace of globally diverse ideas in circulation within civil society, compromise is no longer a realistic goal of argumentative speech. Argument itself becomes the goal and with it, a parallel expansion of understanding *and* ambiguity.

Within this theoretical framework, social cognition describes the process of cognition in the context of how individuals must deal with complexity and ambiguity in the contemporary world. The literature describes cognition as an ongoing interplay between high-effort cognition and low-effort cognition (Fiske & Taylor, 1984). High-effort cognition is often referred to as the "naïve scientist" or "naïve psychologist" framework of thinking.

It is, in effect, the bracketing process of individual thinking. In bracketing out conceptions of objects, events, people, or self in the world, individuals naturally construct cause-and-effect explanations of the world. "Why did the water in the lake turn green?" "Why is he being so loud?" "Why am I always so lazy?" Individuals, in effect, use the "methods" of scientific observation to make sense of their world. For social cognition, cause-and-effect explanations are not necessarily correct, practical, or useful (Aronson, Wilson, & Akert, 2010). People often base their explanations on a limited set of observations, and they may not always perceive things the same way each time. The question, then, that might just as easily be asked of argumentative speech is, "How can we overcome our 'merely rational' views?" The point, however, is that during times of high-effort cognition, people are actively bracketing the world in ways that lend a sense of order and recognizability, and in ways that serve a given purpose for the individual.

High-effort cognition from this perspective is founded in ambivalence and presents a fundamental challenge for public participation. Communicative rationality relies on the assumption that the integration of a diversity of ideas will produce better outcomes. Admittedly, it may help us better manipulate the "complex systems" that society has collectively bracketed out of the *noemena* of the world. However, this assumption is a $2 + 2 = 4$ approach to argumentative collaboration, or a "two heads are better than one" kind of assumption. High-effort cognition within the social cognition tradition, however, challenges public participation to be vigilant for the possibility that "2" might be a nice number, but "green" is the more important factor, a process that may never come close to a compromise or a progressive outcome.

Low-effort thinking, or the "cognitive miser" framework, is the second form of cognition within the social cognition tradition (Fiske & Taylor, 1984). Because of the complexity and ambiguity of the perceptual world, people seek ways to reduce their cognitive load and simplify the mental tasks of everyday life. In addition to the heuristic thinking described above, people employ schemas (Hastie, 1981) and scripts (Langer, 1975) in the ways they process the world. Schemas are the prototypical ways individuals cognitively represent and organize the world. For example, many of our biological colleagues assume that because environmental problems are people problems, they must "educate the public" about their negative effects on environmental health. Educating the public is a schema that carries with it a certain set of assumptions about the world and prescriptions about human behavior. An "educate the public" schema initiates a process of selective attention to the world, in which one brackets the world in a specific way that ignores or makes irrelevant certain types of perception. This means that often, other technical or structural solutions to environmental problems may be disregarded or never considered. Langer (1975) argues that language reflects these streamlined processes of the cognitive miser in the everyday scripts and societal discourses (Hajer, 1995) we use to talk about our mental representations of the world. The "population bomb" (Erlich, 1968) is a well-entrenched script used to argue that overpopulation is a ticking time-bomb of environmental catastrophe. The Zero Population Growth movement uses a different type of script from that of the ecological economists, who are seeking ways to solve environmental problems through existing market structures. The point is that individuals frequently choose minimal exertion in their cognitive efforts. They are frequently selective in their perceptions and tend to fit specific observations into generalized representations of the world.

The cognitive miser framework in social cognition also suggests that individuals not only rely on generalizations to reduce their cognitive load, but human cognition also exhibits a variety of automatic mental processes that have received recent attention, including incubation or unconscious thinking, intuition, imitation and behavioral priming, and preconscious processing (Dijksterhuis, 2010). Social cognition has also studied the way people establish routine actions in everyday life that lend comfort and security in an ambiguous world (Giddens, 1991) or that reflect a process of skill acquisition that makes certain behaviors automatic and second nature.

From a social cognition perspective, the idea that argumentative speech in a public participation context enables people to "overcome their merely subjective views" is socially psychologically problematic. Habermas (1984) assumes a hierarchy of cognitive processes in which objective thinking is better than subjective thinking. Social cognition, however, argues that there is nothing to be "overcome" in argumentative speech. People use both high-effort and low-effort processes of cognition. Both types are the material of any public participation debate in which people bring their schemas, stereotypes, and "half-baked" ideas to the table. Argumentative speech may indeed produce better understanding, but the social cognition literature would insist that one type of thinking is no better than the other for generating useful outcomes.

Influence and Conformity: Merely Rational?

The literature on influence, persuasion, and conformity offers an even greater challenge to Habermas' (1984) ideal of argumentative speech in the public participation process. During World War II, the U.S. Department of Defense began funding research on influence and persuasion (Asch, 1957; Hoveland, Janis, & Kelley, 1953) to help with propaganda campaigns and cope with "brainwashing" among returning POWs. Since that time, the literature on persuasion and attitude change has been one of the defining pillars of social psychology during the second half of the 20th century. The earliest research in this tradition assumed a rational-actor framework and focused on the properties of the message and the processes of attention, processing, and retention (Hoveland et al., 1953). However, the literature soon turned its attention to group influences on the individual, which in many ways challenged the rational-actor, benefit-optimizing model of individual behavior. Moscovici (1985) argues that "all individuals are rational in their behavior, but taken collectively... each of us... readily complies with authority; goes along with the opinions of friends or relations and accepts the views of the newspaper; and adapts personal tastes, speech, and attire to the fashions of the day" (p. 347). Moscovici states that individuals "cease to be rational" in settings of collective interaction. We would refine that statement by saying that individuals frequently suspend the conventions of individual observation and evidence-based reason and are readily willing to submit to the influence of others. Social psychology has amply demonstrated the conditions under which individuals will often abrogate individual reason to the influence of others. The challenge for the public participation process therefore may be to find ways to "overcome the merely rational tendencies" of group influence and conformity.

Conformity

One of the most famous experiments in social psychology was a study by Solomon Asch on individual conformity to the group (Asch, 1951, 1955). Asch brought a single subject into a room full of confederates. The experimenters projected a series of four vertical lines on the wall. One line on the left was the reference line, while three lines on the right were the comparison lines. One of the three was the same length as the reference line, while the other two were different lengths. Each person in the room was then asked to say out loud which line from the three was the same length as the reference line. Confederates were instructed to answer correctly for the first two trials, but then to answer incorrectly for the remaining trials. Asch found that the subject conformed to the incorrect responses of the group in 33% of the trials.

Asch's conformity experiment has been well-replicated over the years, and there have been numerous variations on the theme. The autokinetic effect is a property in the pupil of the eye that makes a single dot of light projected in a dark room appear to move slightly, even though the light is stationary. Sherif (1936), even before Asch, placed a subject in a room of confederates and asked them to estimate the distance in inches that they thought light moved across the wall. Subjects conformed to group estimates, even when the estimates were extreme. The smoke-filled room experiment (Latane & Darley, 1968) was a test of the passive bystander effect. This study placed subjects in a room to fill out a questionnaire, as smoke from what was apparently an adjacent kitchen began to seep under the door and into the room where the subject sat. Half the subjects were placed alone in the room to fill out the questionnaire, and the other half were placed in a room full of confederates who were instructed to pay no attention to the smoke. In the alone trials, 75% of the subject reported the smoke to the experimenter. In the group trials, only 10% of the subjects reported the smoke to the experimenter. Finally, Milgram's (1974) famous experiments placed a subject in front of a machine that ostensibly delivered shocks to the confederate on the other side. The subject was to ask the confederate a series of quiz questions. For each wrong answer, the subject was to deliver a series of progressively more powerful shocks up to a debilitating 450 volts. Confederates were instructed to follow their wrong answers with progressive responses from discomfort to pain to agony. The experimenter stood over the shoulder of subject, and with each shock and protest from the subject, the experimenter calmly stated that it was important for the subject to complete the experiment. Milgram found that two thirds of the subjects completed the experiment to the highest level of shock.

Why do people exhibit this tendency toward conformity? Some suggest a "group psychology" effect in which "those who conform tend to have lower self-esteem, greater need for social support or social approval, a need for self-control, lower IQ, high anxiety, feelings of self-blame and insecurity in the group, feelings of inferiority in the group, and an authoritarian personality" (Hogg, 2010, p. 1180). Others characterize this tendency to conform as a need for dependence in which individuals find satisfaction and security in obedience (Marlow & Gergen, 1969). One way of characterizing variation across groups is to characterize people along a personality continuum of inner-directed (autonomous) to outer-directed (heteronomous) (Rotter, 1966). Research shows that autonomous individuals are less likely to conform to group pressure and are more receptive to textual efforts at influence, whereas heteronomous individuals are more likely to respond to group pressure and verbal messages. Perhaps Giddens (1991) has theorized this tendency toward conformity best by arguing that people find comfort and satisfaction in routine and normative structure ("ontological security"). Conformity to social structure exists because interacting individuals create and continually reproduce shared expectations that produce a sense of coherence and order about the world.

Therefore, while birds of a feather may indeed flock together, this research tradition shows a pervasive effect whereby "people who flock together become birds of a feather" (Moscovici, 1985, p. 378). Moreover, in spite of an individual's best observation, judgment, sense of responsibility, and ethics, the tendency to conform to others is a powerful impulse and often disconnected from evidence-based rationality. It is a paradox of everyday life: "While group conformity commonly prevents the individual from giving his or her best, the only way that people can fulfill themselves as human beings is by participating in group life" (Moscovici, 1985; p. 379). Consequently, it becomes difficult to know in a public participation context whether argumentative speech has generated a reasoned compromise or simply conformity to a prevailing view.

Influence

Conformity is only half the story, however. If conformity were the exclusive impulse of human behavior, there would be no ambiguity and ambivalence in everyday life. There would be no need for communicative rationality. There would only be deviants needing proper socialization into the stable norms and values of a group or society. Instead, it is readily apparent that uncertainty, conflict, and change are well-infused into the everyday affairs of civil society. Communicative rationality argues that groups can best "sort out" the confusion and conflict through reasoned argumentation. Innovative solutions that resonate among a group then emerge from the conversation, creating new or revised norms and preferences for the conduct of everyday life. The social psychology literature, however, would indicate that reasoned argument is often absent in the influence process, and that problem solving and innovative solutions are hardly inevitable outcomes or expressions of group adaptation and social change. Instead, the influence process is subject to a variety of contextual constraints inherent in social interaction. If we think of conformity and innovation as two ends of a continuum, these constraints of the influence process are just as likely to cause a retreat back toward conformity as they are to move the group toward innovation.

The influence literature in social psychology makes it clear that *what* is said is not the sole component and perhaps not even the most important feature of a communicative act. This literature shows that the *how* and the *who* of argumentation and debate are equally important. Moscovici's review of influence and conformity (1985) builds off of Goffman's (1959) notion of "gestures given" (the delivered content of a communication) and "gestures given off" (the style and affect of communication), and similar to Petty and Cacciopo's two-factor theory of persuasion (1986). The behavioral style "given off" in a group setting is reflected in a variety of verbal and nonverbal expressions such as sitting at the head of the table, speaking without hesitation, speaking with assured confidence, maintaining eye contact while speaking, and expecting positive outcomes. Those who exhibit these behavioral styles are perceived to sound more authoritative and influential (Ridgeway, Berger, & Smith, 1985). Moscovici discusses three broad types of behavioral style that are important to the influence process; autonomy, consistency, and rigidity.

First, messages are more influential when they are perceived to come from an autonomous source. An autonomous source is perceived to be one who delivers an independently considered argument relatively free of outside bias, who delivers information objectively without persuasive intent, and who is relatively impartial without a clear interest in the outcome. In face-to-face interaction, the well-reasoned "lone wolf" observer can be more influential than the passionate partisan. In the context of groups, an autonomous majority will exert greater influence on a minority than a conformist majority. That is, an argument put forth by individuals who have independently come to the same conclusion exerts more influence on others than a majority that has acquiesced to a "party line." Individuals who find themselves at variance with the majority will feel less constrained to challenge the party line than they would to challenge the independent judgments of the majority. Consequently, the pressures to conform could be particularly great surrounding environmental controversies when arguments based on the science of presumably independent sources is the currency of public debate. It is not clear, however, whether science necessarily produces the most innovative solutions to environmental problems.

A second behavioral style important to the influence process is consistency (Moscovici, 1985). Consistency refers to the certainty, commitment, and singleness of purpose with which an argument is made. Arguments made with a string of qualifications or a hesitant manner have less influence than those made with an uncompromising assurance. Consistency is communicated as a refusal to compromise, which "stems from the fact that the individual thinks, and gives the impression of thinking, that he knows the truth, that he knows what is right and wrong" (p. 361). It is, in short, a quality of charisma that exudes confidence and an unwavering commitment to the certainty of one's argument. In a group context, research has shown that it is more than simply a numerical majority that influences the minority on an issue. Rather, it is the unanimity of the majority that has the most influence. As soon as an individual from the majority breaks with the group opinion, collective consistency is compromised, and the minority is less likely to be swayed by the majority position. A consistent behavioral style employed in environmental disputes in which ambiguity is common is likely to exert a powerful pull toward conformity and missed opportunity for innovative solutions.

Moscovici's third behavioral style is rigidity (1985). Rigid arguments are those that come across as inflexible in spite of countervailing evidence. Rigidity is most often found when competing views of a debate are polarized, and one's latitude of rejection (or the chances of being influenced) is small (Sherif, Sherif, & Nebergall, 1965). Dogmatism has set in and the chances of changing one's mind about an issue are almost nonexistent. Research on rigidity and influence is mixed. It has shown that extreme positions are more influential than moderate positions, because they force others to pause and think about how someone else could hold such a divergent position from one's own. However, flexible positions are more influential than the sort of dogmatic arguments made by those at the extremes. While rigid arguments can influence some by the "power of conviction," dogmatic appeals to truth are unlikely to generate much conformity and also unlikely to stimulate much innovation.

Influence is also the product of *who* has standing in a discussion or debate. Research has documented that hierarchy in groups is often the product of external status cues that individuals bring to a group that typically become powerful mediators in the influence process (Moscovici, 1985). Expectation-states theory (Berger & Zelditch, 1998) argues that group members bring a variety of specific and diffuse status characteristics that determine performance expectations in group processes. Performance expectations are derived from a group process whereby members evaluate the potential quality of each group member's contribution. They then will defer to those who they collectively believe will make the most valuable contribution. Once formed, these performance expectations typically shape group behavior in a self-fulfilling manner (Correll & Ridgeway, 2006). These performance expectations are based on a variety of socially significant characteristics that individuals bring to the group, the perceived rewards that an individual can bring to the group, and the mechanisms of behavioral style (i.e., confidence and charisma) that the individual displays. A hydrologist has a specific status privilege as the "expert" in a group concerned with agricultural runoff into streams and lakes, whereas a male CEO of a nuclear power plant may have a diffuse status privilege over a female school teacher in a group concerned about local property tax increases. Experts and men are status characteristics that typically allow individuals to exert more influence in a group. But experts often bring an "educate the public" mentality to the group that can be more conformist than innovative, and being male does not guarantee effectiveness. Yet externally attributed position or standing influences groups in ways that compromise the rational argumentation of Habermas' ideal speech act (1984).

Finally, the size of the majority and the size of the minority have a bearing on conformity and influence. One might expect that the relationship between the size of a majority and influence would be positive and linear. However, research has shown that influence increases only to a majority of three people (Moscovici, 1985). Beyond that point, the influence on the minority is the same. In other words, a majority of four is as influential as a majority of eight. Conversely, the smaller the minority, the stronger the tendency is to conform. The minority however, is not always at the mercy of the majority. Research has shown that the minority can influence the majority in the absence of any explicit norms, tasks, or group goals. The minority can choose the "black sheep" role by denying consensus to the group and by arguing with consistent and repeated messages against the majority. Such minority challenges give pause to the majority and under certain circumstances can bring about incremental change to the normative structure of the group.

The persuasive power of groups described here demonstrates that communicative rationality, as envisioned by Habermas (1984) is not enough to guarantee positive change. Reasoned argument is, of course, the foundation of public participation. Yet reason is mediated by a host of group pressures toward conformity, and any public participation effort is faced with a variety of personality and group dynamics that interact in often unpredictable ways with group performance and outcomes. So if the tendency of groups is toward conformity, public participation that encourages fair and open discussion that educates the stakeholders and moves them toward a congenial consensus may not be sufficient to generate effective solutions to environmental problems. It may be that public participation practitioners need to find ways to facilitate group conflict and minority challenges that move people out of their comfort zone of conformity to explore ideas, subjectivities, and solutions on the edges of public discourse.

Are Groups Better?

Finally, we ask a simple question in this section: Do groups really produce better outcomes? It is an unquestioned assumption in the public participation literature that "two heads are better than one," and that diverse viewpoints combined with collaborative problem solving can produce better solutions. The literature reviewed above, however, indicates that group problem solving is laced with a mix of potentially counterproductive group dynamics. These group interaction dynamics may also give rise to a variety of collectively expressed group behaviors that can produce "process loss" in the overall performance of a group.

Social facilitation is one example of behavior in groups in which the presence of other people can stimulate a higher degree of individual focus on a task out of the knowledge that others are evaluating one's performance. This is Mead's (1934) classic notion of "taking the perspective of the other." An individual imagines the scrutiny with which others in the group perceive one's efforts. Social facilitation can be a double-edged sword. On the one hand, the presence of others can motivate effective performance on simple or familiar tasks. On the other hand, if the task is complex or unfamiliar, this can leave the individual flustered and less effective than had they performed the task in isolation (Zajonc, 1968).

This social-facilitation effect can also be mediated by the type of task that must be performed in a group setting. If the task is additive, working as a group produces better outcomes. Complex tasks in which clear responsibility for simpler subtasks is divided more or less equally means that individuals are less likely to be overwhelmed and more likely to be motivated to pull their own weight and make effective contributions to group outcomes. Group productivity in additive tasks is the sum of individual contributions that are easily motivated by the normative pressure of the group. Group performance on conjunctive or disjunctive tasks, however, might have a moderating effect on the total group effort and output (Michener & Delemater, 1999). A conjunctive task is one in which performance is limited by the weakest or least proficient member of the group, such as a sports team or musical group. In these types of settings, the weakest member of a group may "drag down" the performance of more skilled group members and moderate the overall performance of the group. A disjunctive task is one in which performance is the product of the most proficient member of the group, such as a rescue team trying to locate an avalanche victim before it is too late. Disjunctive tasks, in which the strongest member of the group "carries the load" for the others, are especially susceptible to "social loafing" (Latane et al., 1979). If the strongest member comes up short in performance, the whole group then suffers. In sum, groups in a public participation context can indeed facilitate positive deliberation and solutions. The point, however, is that groups are just as likely to perform suboptimally given the task and given the abilities and motivation of group members.

There are other forms of social loafing that operate independently of the evaluative presence of others. The earliest studies of group behavior, if not social psychology, examined the "crowd" effect (LeBon, 1896; Tarde, 1890) wherein people in the presence of others take on a social contagion in which individuals relax their individual standards of behavior to engage in impulsive or violent group activities. Contemporary examples include crowd violence at sporting events or student behavior during spring break on the beach in Cancún. The process of deindividuation occurs when responsibility for action is removed from the individual and spread throughout a large anonymous crowd. Without the spotlight of individual evaluation, people then engage in behaviors they would never dream of doing alone.

While crowd behavior is typically not task oriented, the diffusion of responsibility among group members is the foundation of other forms of social loafing that occurs in more goal-directed groups. The Ringelmann effect (1913) demonstrated that when a group pulls on a rope in a tug-of-war, each individual in the group exerts less overall effort than if they were pulling alone. Sharing responsibility in a group without the fear of individual performance evaluation produces less individual effort. One need not speak up frequently in a watershed advisory committee meeting when others actively direct and control the proceedings. It may even lead to the free-rider effect, in which becoming "lost" in a group means that individuals can share in the rewards of group performance without the burden of making a contribution. Thus, collective group performance does not guarantee better results because there is frequently the tendency to relax one's effort and even relax one's commitment to the task in the presence of others.

There are other forms of process loss that are inherent in the group interaction process as well. Brainstorming sessions often produce less than satisfying results because of a process known as production blocking (Diehl & Stroebe, 1987). The typical convention in group brainstorming sessions is turn-taking to present one's ideas. As participants wait their turn, they first of all must mentally rehearse their ideas so that their presentation comes off as competent. The discussion at hand can also be distracting, so that attention to other ideas may be limited. Rehearsing also limits the production of new ideas that may arise out of the discussion. In situations such as these, argumentative rationality may produce more episodic talking points than generative and integrated solutions.

Effective group communication is always a challenge for task performance. Process loss can obviously occur when group members fail to listen or fail to hear each other. It may occur when group members refuse to give "standing" or legitimacy to other individuals in the group. It may occur when one person dominates the proceedings and others learn to ignore the messages of the individual or minority coalition. Another problem of communication in groups is the failure to share unique information (Wittenbaum & Park, 2001). Groups have a tendency to focus discussion on shared information or information that members already know rather than to draw out information that only some members know.

At its extreme, these basic communication challenges can lead to "groupthink" (Janis, 1982) and group polarization (Palmer & Loveland, 2008). Groupthink is a process of group performance wherein rational deliberation and the balanced consideration of alternatives is overwhelmed when groups feel overconfident and immune to failure, are convinced they are right, and are convinced of their shared consensus and commitment. These traits of group arrogance lead them to discount warnings and counterarguments and to stereotype their out-group adversaries. It also causes groups to silence dissention from within and to guard against ideas that may break the perceived certainty of their position. So while these types of groups may be highly cohesive, the pressure toward conformity comes at the cost of innovation and effective problem solving.

In addition to potential structural deficits in group performance, research also has shown that groups can encourage exaggerated outcomes that may be harmful. Group polarization has demonstrated that group deliberation has a tendency to produce riskier or more conservative decisions (about investments or regulations) than what individuals would judge as appropriate. This concept assumes that the shared responsibility for a group outcome will pressure groups into decisions or judgments that are more extreme than a member's individual conclusion. When individuals in a group are inclined to be conservative, group deliberation will lead them to even more conservative recommendations. When individuals are inclined to take more risks, group deliberation will lead them to even riskier outcomes—the "risky shift."

So, are groups better? They can be. Reasoned argumentation serves a useful and potentially transformative function. But public participation as mandated by many resource management agencies is more like public participation for its own sake. It cannot realize its transformative potential without a better understanding of group dynamics and group behavior. The social psychology of groups makes it abundantly clear that the "rationality" of groups can also be counterproductive for innovation, integration, and problem solving.

ENVIRONMENTAL CRISIS AND THE DILEMMA
OF PUBLIC PARTICIPATION

The narrative of many environmental discourses is a story of crisis. The hubris of our anthropocentric belief in perpetual progress has brought human kind to the brink of environmental disaster. Global climate change, peak oil, toxic pollution, extinction of species, deforestation, and overpopulation are narratives whose solution requires society to make hard decisions about resource allocation and possibly dramatic changes to the status quo. At the same time, these stories are overlaid onto resource management agencies and decision-making authorities who are constrained by their own set of public and legislative mandates and operational procedures. While the stories are calling for a structural overhaul, the decision makers are limited to incremental change within existing social structures through conflict resolution, public education, and consensus making. The lessons from social psychology indicate that these incremental changes are not typically achieved through the sort of passionate and committed form of argumentation that Habermas (1984) envisioned. Rather, these incremental changes from the public participation process more typically come from a tendency toward ambivalence, cognitive shortcuts, and conformity. If predictions of environmental catastrophe are true, then decision makers need to find ways to facilitate conflict in the public participation process. Communicative rationality is most effective when it elicits the sort of collective "gut-wrenching" examination of environmental dilemmas that comes from careful and committed argumentation, and that seeks solutions outside the collective "comfort zone" of existing managerial procedures and social structures.

REFERENCES

Adams, G., & Balfour, D. (2008). *Unmasking administrative ethics.* Armonk, NY: M.E. Sharpe.

Adorno, T. W., Frenkel-Brunswik, E. Levinson, D. J., & Sanford, R. N. (1950). *The authoritarian personality.* New York, NY: Harper.

Aronson, E., Wilson, T. D., & Akert, R. M. (2010). *Social Psychology* (7th ed.). Upper Saddle River, NJ; Pearson/Prentiss Hall.

Asch, S. E. (1951). Effects of group pressure upon the modification and distortion of judgments. In H. Guetzkow (Ed.), *Groups, leadership, and men.* Pittsburgh, PA: Carnegie.

Asch, S. E. (1955). Opinions and social pressure. *Scientific American, 193,* 31–35.

Asch, S. E. (1957). An experimental investigation of group influences. *Symposium on preventive and social psychiatry.* Water Reed Army Institute of Research. Washington, DC: U.S. Government Printing Office.

Bandura, A. (1977). Self-efficacy: Toward a unifying theory of behavioral change. *Psychological Review, 84,* 191–215.

Barber, B. (1984). *Strong democracy.* Berkeley: University of California Press.

Bauman, Z. (2002). *Society under siege.* Cambridge, England: Polity.

Baumeister, R. F. (1999). The nature and structure of the self: An overview. In R. F. Baumeister (Ed.), *The self in social psychology* (pp. 1–20). Philadelphia, PA: Psychology.

Benaji, M. R., & Heiphetz, L. (2010) Attitudes. In S. T. Fiske, D. T. Gilbert, & Lindzey, G. (Eds.) *Handbook of social psychology* (5th ed.). Hoboken, NJ: John Wiley & Sons.

Berger, J., & Zelditch, M. (1998). *Status, power, and legitimacy: Strategies and theories.* New Brunswick, NJ: Transaction.

Borden, R. I. (1980). Audience influence. In P. B. Paulus (Ed.), *Psychology of group influence.* (pp. 99–132). Hillsdale, NJ: Erlbaum.

Brown, J. D. (1998). *The self.* New York, NY: McGraw-Hill.

Chase, L. C., Decker, D. J., & Lauber, B. (2004). Public participation and wildlife management: What do stakeholders want? *Society & Natural Resources, 17*(7), 629–639.

Cooper, T. (1980). Bureaucracy and community organization: The metamorphosis of a relationship. *Administration and Society, 11,* 418–444.

Correll, S. J., & Ridgeway, C. L. (2006). Expectation states theory. In J. Delemater (Ed.), *Handbook of social psychology* (pp. 29–52). New York, NY: Springer.

Deci, E. L., & Ryan, R. M. (1995). Human autonomy: The basis for true self-esteem. In M. H. Kernis (Ed.), *Efficacy, agency, and self-esteem* (pp. 31–49). New York, NY: Plenum.

Diehl, M., & Stroebe, W. (1987). Productivity loss in brainstorming groups: Toward the solution of a riddle. *Journal of Personality and Social Psychology, 53*(3), 497–509.

Dijksterhuis, A. (2010). Automaticity and the unconscious. In S. T. Fiske, D. T. Gilbert, & G. Lindzey (Eds.), *Handbook of social psychology* (5th ed., pp. 589–628). Hoboken, NJ: John Wiley & Sons.

Ehrlich, P. R. (1968). *The population bomb.* New York, NY: Ballantine.

Fiske, S. T., & Tayler, S. E. (1984). *Social cognition.* New York, NY: Random House.

Frederickson, H. G. (1982). The recovery of civism in public administration. *Public Administration Review, 42*(6), 501–507.

Gergen, K. J. (1991) The saturated self: Dilemmas of identity in contemporary life. New York, NY: Basic.

Giddens, A. (1991). *Modernity and self-identity: Self and society in the late modern age.* Stanford, CA: Stanford University Press.

Goffman, E. (1959). *The presentation of self in everyday life.* New York, NY: Doubleday.

Habermas, J. (1984). *The theory of communicative action.* Boston, MA: Beacon.

Hajer, M. A. (1995) *The politics of environmental discourse: Ecological modernization and the policy process.* Oxford, England: Oxford University Press.

Hardin, G. (1968). The tragedy of the commons. *Science, 162,* 1243–1248.

Hart, D. K. (1984). The virtuous citizen, the honorable bureaucrat, and public administration. *Public Administration Review, 44,* 111–120.

Harter, S. (1978). Effectance motivation reconsidered: Toward a developmental model. *Human Development, 21*(1), 34–64.

Harvey, D. (2000). *Spaces of hope.* Berkeley: University of California Press.

Hastie, R. (1981) Schematic principle in human memory. In E. T. Higgins, C. P. Herman, & M. P. Zanna (Eds.), *Social cognition: The Ontario symposium* (Vol. 1, pp. 39–88). Hillsdale, NJ: Erlbaum.

Heberlein, T. A. (1981). Environmental attitudes. *Journal of Environmental Policy, 2,* 241–272.

Hogg, M. A. (2010). Influence and leadership. In S. T. Fiske, D. T. Gilbert, & G. Lindzey (Eds.), *Handbook of social psychology* (5th ed., pp. 589–628). Hoboken, NJ: John Wiley & Sons.

Hoveland, C. I., Janis, I. L., & Kelley, H. H. (1953). *Communication and persuasion: Psychological studies of opinion change.* New Haven, CT: Yale University Press.

Husserl, E. (1973). *Cartesian meditations: An introduction to phenomenology.* The Hague, The Netherlands: Martinus Nijhoff.

James, W. (1890/1950). *The principles of psychology.* New York, NY: Dover.

Janis, I. L. (1982). *Groupthink: Psychological studies of policy decisions and fiascoes* (2nd ed.). Boston, MA: Houghton Mifflin.

Kahneman, D., & Tversky, A. (1972). Subjective probability: A judgment of representativeness. *Cognitive Psychology, 3*(3), 430–454.

Kahneman, D., Tversky, A., & Slovic, P. (1982). *Judgment under uncertainty: Heuristics and biases.* Cambridge, NY: Cambridge University Press.

Krosnick. J. A., Boninger, D. S., Chuang, Y. C., Berent, M. K., & Carnot, C. G. (1993). Attitude strength: One construct or many related constructs? *Journal of Personality and Social Psychology, 65*(6), 1132–1151.

LaPiere, R. T. (1934). Attitudes vs. actions. *Social Forces, 13,* 230–237.

Langer, E. J. (1975). The illusion of control. *Journal of Personality and Social Psychology, 32,* 311–328.

Latane, B., & Darley, J. M. (1968) Group inhibition of bystander intervention in emergencies. *Journal of Personality and Social Psychology, 10*(3), 215–221.

Latane, B., Williams, K., & Harkins, S. (1979). Many hands make light work: The causes and consequences of social loafing. *Journal of Personal Sociology and Psychology, 37*(6), 822–832.

LeBon, G. (1896). *The crowd: A study of the popular mind.* London, England: Unwin.

Leiberman, M. D. (2010). Social cognitive neuroscience. In S. T. Fiske, D. T. Gilbert, & G. Lindzey (Eds.), *Handbook of social psychology* (5th ed., pp. 143–193). Hoboken, NJ: John Wiley & Sons.

Leopold. A. (1949) *A Sand county almanac.* New York, NY: Oxford University Press.

Macnaghten, P. & Urry, J. (1998). *Contested natures.* London, England: Sage.

Marlow, D., & Gergen, K. (1969). Personality and social interaction. In G. Lindzey & E. Aronson (Eds.), *The handbook of social psychology* (2nd ed., pp. 590–665). Reading, MA: Addison-Wesley.

McGrane, J. A. (2010). *Unfolding ambivalence: The conceptualisation and measurement of ambivalent attitudes in psychology.* Saarbrücken, Germany: Lambert Academic.

Mead, G. H. (1934). *Mind, self, and society: From the standpoint of a social behaviorist.* Chicago, IL: University of Chicago Press.

Michener, H. A., & Delemater, J. D. (1999). *Social psychology* (4th ed.). New York, NY: Harcourt Brace College.

Milgram, S. (1974). *Obedience to authority.* New York, NY: Harper & Row.

Moscovici, S. (1985). Social influence and conformity. In G. Lindzey & E. Aronson (Eds.), *Handbook of social psychology* (3rd ed., pp. 347–412). New York, NY: Random House.

Oliver, P. (1984). "If you don't do it, nobody else will." Active and token contributors to local collective action. *American Sociological Review, 49*(5), 601–610.

Palmer, J., & Loveland, J. (2008). The influence of group discussion on performance judgments: Rating accuracy, contrast effects, and halo. *Journal of Psychology: Interdisciplinary and Applied, 142*(2), 117–130.

Petty, R. E., & Cacioppo, J. T. (1981). *Attitudes and persuasion: Classic and contemporary approaches.* Dubuque, IA: Westview.

Petty, R. E., & Cacioppo, J. T. (1986). *Communication and persuasion: Central and peripheral routes to attitude change.* New York, NY: Springer-Verlag.

Putnam, H. (1983). *Realism and reason.* Cambridge, MA: Cambridge University Press.

Raden, D. (1985). Strength-related attitude dimensions. *Social Psychology Quarterly, 48*(4), 312–330.

Rich, R. C. (1980). The dynamics of leadership in neighborhood organizations. *Social Science Quarterly, 60,* 570–587.

Ridgeway, C. L., Berger, J., & Smith, L. (1985). Nonverbal cues and status: An expectation states approach. *American Journal of Sociology, 90*(5), 955–978.

Ringelmann, M. (1913). Recherches sur les moteurs animes: Travail de l'homme. *Annales de l'Istitute National Agronomique, 2*(12), 1–40.

Roberts, D. (2004). Public deliberation in an age of direct citizen participation. *American Review of Public Administration, 34*(4), 315–353.

Rotter, J. B. (1966). Generalized expectancies for internal versus external control of reinforcement. *Psychological Monographs, 180*(1), 1–28.

Schwartz, C. E., Wright, C. I., Shin, L. M., Kagan, J., & Rauch, S. L. (2003). Inhibited and uninhibited infants "grown up": Adult amygdalar response to novelty. *Science, 300,* 1952–1953.

Sherif, M. (1936). *The psychology of social norms.* New York, NY: Harper & Row.

Sherif, C. W., Sherif, M., & Nebergall, R. E. (1965). *Attitude and attitude change: The social judgment-involvement approach.* Philadelphia, PA: W.B. Saunders.

Simon, H. A. (1963). Economics and psychology. In S. Koch (Ed.), *Psychology: A study of a* science (pp. 715–752). New York, NY: McGraw-Hill.

Stryker, S. (1980). *Symbolic interactionism: A social structural version.* Menlo Park, CA: Benjamin/Cummings.

Swann, W. B., & Bosson, J. K. (2010). Self and identity. In S. T. Fiske, D. T. Gilbert, & G. Lindzey (Eds.), *Handbook of social psychology* (5th ed., pp. 589–628). Hoboken, NJ: John Wiley & Sons.

Tarde, G. (1890). *Les lois de l'imitation. Etude sociologique.* Paris, France: Alcan.

Thompson, D. F. (1983). Bureaucracy and democracy. In G. Duncan (Ed.), *Democratic theory and practice.* Cambridge, MA: Cambridge University Press.

Thompson, J. L, Forster, C. B., Werner, C., & Peterson, T. R. (2010). Mediated modeling: Using collaborative processes to integrate scientist and stakeholder knowledge about greenhouse gas emissions in an urban ecosystem. *Society and Natural Resources, 23,* 742–757.

Turner, R. H. (1978). The role and the person. *American Journal of Sociology, 84*(1), 1–23.

Tussman, J. (1974). *Obligation and the body politic.* New York, NY: Oxford University Press.

Tversky, A., & Kahneman, D. (1974). Judgment under uncertainty: Heuristics and biases. *Science, 185,* 1124–1131.

Ventriss, C. (1989). Toward a public philosophy of public administration: A civic perspective of the public. *Public Administration Review, 49*(2), 173–179.

Ventriss, C. (1998). Political democratic thought and contemporary American public administration. *American Review of Public Administration, 28*(3), 227–245.

Ventriss, C. (2002). The rise of the entrepreneurial state governments in the United States: The dilemma of public governance in an era of globalization. *Administrative Theory and Praxis, 24*(1), 81–102.

Ventriss, C. (2011/in press). Democratic citizenship and public ethics: The importance of civic stewardship in an era of public distrust and cynicism. *Journal of Public Integrity.*

Ventriss, C., & Kuentzel, W. F. (2005). Critical theory and the role of citizen involvement in environmental decision making: A re-examination. *International Journal of Organization Theory and Behavior, 8*(4), 519–539.

Wegner, D. M., & Bargh, J. A. (1998). Control and automaticity in social life. In S. T. Fiske & D. T. Gilbert (Eds.), *The handbook of social psychology* (pp. 446–496). New York, NY: McGraw-Hill.

White, R. W. (1959). Motivation reconsidered: The concept of competence. *Psychological Review, 66*(5), 297–333.

Wittenbaum, G. M., & Park, E. S. (2001). The collective preference for shared information. *Current Directions in Psychological Science, 10*(2), 72–75.

Zanna, M. P., & Rempel, J. K. (1988). Attitudes: A new look at an old concept. In D. Bar-Tal & A. W. Kruglanski (Eds.), *The social psychology of attitudes* (pp. 315–334). New York, NY: Cambridge University Press.

Zajonc, R. B. (1968). The attitudinal effects of mere exposure. *Journal of Personality and Social Psychology, 9*(Monograph suppl. no. 2, Pt. 2), 1–27.

PART VI

CONCLUSION

CHAPTER 18

THEORY BUILDING AND TESTING IN CITIZEN PARTICIPATION RESEARCH

Reflection and Conjecture

Kaifeng Yang
Florida State University

The purpose of this book is to provide an accurate, balanced, and up-to-date assessment of the practice—and to a lesser degree, research—of citizen participation in the United States. Our excellent contributors have covered a wide range of issues on citizen participation, such as the presidential policy on citizenship (e.g., Bryer), the use of technology (e.g., Barnes & Williams; Lipschultz; Schatteman), the role of media (e.g., Crow & Stevens), the problem of representation (e.g., de Lancer Julnes; Eikenberry & Jensen; Sharp), the innovation of participation tools (e.g., Barnes & Williams; Dudley; Lipschultz), the concern about transparency (Piotrowski & Liao), the effect of participation (e.g., Kopetzky; Sharp; Holzer & Mullins), and deliberative participation and its barriers (Dudley; Kuetzel & Ventriss), among others. Moreover, the chapters touch on different levels or types

The State of Citizen Participation in America, pages 447–464
Copyright © 2012 by Information Age Publishing
All rights of reproduction in any form reserved.

of organizations: federal government (e.g., Piotrowski & Liao; Bryer), state governments (e.g., de Lancer Julnes), local governments (e.g., Sharp; Crow & Stevens; Holzer & Mullins), nonprofits (e.g., Schatteman; Eikenberry & Jensen), and collaborative partnerships (e.g., Kopetzky; Holzer, Mullins, Sun & Woolley). The list of issues and organizational types is not exhaustive, but together the chapters depict a nice picture of the citizen participation landscape in the United States.

Each of the chapters summarizes what we know on an aspect of citizen participation and points to future research questions. Together, what can we learn from the chapters in terms of theory building and testing in citizen participation research? Despite the risk of oversimplification and omission, this concluding chapter discusses the conceptualization of citizen participation, the role of theory in citizen participation research, methodology, and the relationship between theory and practice. The discussion is perhaps biased by my own theoretical interest, but it seves as a modest spur to induce others to come forward with valuable contributions.

CONCEPTUALIZING CITIZEN PARTICIPATION

The issue of definition and conceptualization is of great importance to theory building and testing. Theory starts with concepts, which must be clearly defined to ensure that the phenomenon studied by the researchers is the same, the research results can be compared, and as a result, knowledge can be accumulated. This issue is particularly relevant for citizen participation research because citizen participation may mean very different things (Arnstein, 1969; Jacobs, Cook, & Delli Carpini, 2009; Yang & Callahan, 2005). In her chapter, Sharp points out four reasons why acknowledging differences in types of participation is important. First, while some types of participation might have declined historically over time, others might have increased. Second, the factors shaping participation might differ across the types. Third, the capacity of governmental and nongovernmental organizations to mobilize participation might differ across the types. Finally, the impact of participation might depend on the type of participation.

While some of the chapters do not give a clear definition of citizen participation, many do, and the definitions are varied. Comparing the definitions is complicated by the fact that the same term might mean different things among different authors. For example, Sharp cites Zukin, Keeter, Andolina, Jenkins, and Delli Carpini (2006) to differentiate between political engagement and civic engagement, treating two concepts as interchangeable with political participation and civic participation, respectively. Many authors similarly do not differentiate between "participation" and "engagement." De Lancer Julnes, in contrast, submits that engagement is

more substantive than participation, referring to the former as a deliberative process in which citizens are able to influence decisions that result in
action. One can also debate about whether there is a difference between
"public" participation and "citizen" participation, as strictly speaking, the
"public" includes not only citizens but also media and other nongovernmental social groups.

Nevertheless, if we concentrate on the substantive instead of semantic
meaning of the concepts, there are three general conceptions of citizen
participation that can be differentiated by their scope. Adopted by some
of the chapters, the broadest conception refers to citizen participation in
political, administrative, civic, associational, and even interactive efforts or
activities. For Bryer, as an example, civic engagement, civic participation,
public engagement, public involvement, and public participation are treated as the same, as they all reflect citizenship. Sharp uses the term "political
participation" as "any form of involvement in community affairs that has
the potential to shape the allocation of public resources or the resolution
of community issues."

A narrower conception denotes citizen participation as citizens' participation in the political and administrative arena, which is in contrast to
citizens' involvement in voluntary organizations or associational activities.
For example, Nishishiba, Banyan, and Morgan use the phrase "citizen participation" to "denote the relationship between citizens and their legally
constituted governing institutions," while they use the term "civic engagement" to "denote the relationship between citizens and voluntary associations in civic society as well as the relationship between voluntary associations and the legally constituted governing institutions." This is similar to
Zukin et al.'s (2006) distinction between political engagement and civic engagement. This conception is shared by Holzer, Mullins, Sun, and Woolley
(who cite Roberts, 2004), Barnes and Williams, as well as those who rely on
Arnstein's (1969) conceptualization of participation types (e.g., de Lancer
Julnes; Piotrowski & Liao). Arnstein emphasizes "participation of the governed in their government" and treat citizen participation as "a categorical
term for citizen power."

The third conception is the narrowest in scope. In his chapter, Kopetzky
writes that while traditionally, the concept "meant voting in elections, running for public offices, volunteering for a candidate running for public
office, or serving as an appointee," he uses it to mean participation and
partnerships in the program planning, development, and implementation. This conception is used in the literature by some public administration scholars as an "administrative" perspective of citizen participation. It
focuses on citizen participation in the administrative processes (e.g., Berman, 1997; King & Stivers, 1998; Koontz, 1999; Thomas, 1995; Yang & Callahan, 2005, 2007). For example, King, Felty, and Susal (1998) refer to it

as "the role of the public in the process of administrative decision making" (p. 317), and Wang (2001) uses it as "involvement in making service delivery and management decisions" (p. 322; see also Yang & Callahan, 2005). An "administrative" conception is not to argue that politics and administration can be separated; rather, it is to separate electoral participation from nonelectoral participation. This separation is rooted in Langton's (1978) categorization of four types of participation: (a) citizen action such as lobbying and protest, (b) citizen involvement such as public hearings and citizen surveys, (c) electoral participation such as voting and campaigning for political candidates, and (d) obligatory participation such as paying taxes and performing jury duty.

If the second and third conceptions are juxtaposed, it seems that electoral participation, civic participation, and administrative participation are three relatively separate participatory terrains or arenas. The existence of multiple conceptions of citizen participation does not prevent us from advancing theory as long as we clearly define what we mean by the term in each project and consciously map out the interrelationships among the different terrains of citizen participation. Much is still to be done toward this end.

First and foremost, more research should be conducted to further establish the construct validity of civic participation and administrative participation. To convince people that they are indeed different from electoral participation, they need to have high levels of discriminant validity—the degree to which one construct is indeed distinct from other related constructs. They need to have a different set of antecedents and consequences, or different relationships with the same set of explanatory and impact variables. For instance, while voter turnout and citizen engagement in networks of social groups have declined (Putnam, 2000; Verba, Schlozman, Brady, & Nie, 1993), there is evidence that working informally with others on community problems has increased (Jacobs et al., 2009). It has been argued that younger generations have become more cynical about elections and thus choose to give up electoral participation and turn to civic participation. More research is necessary to further validate this finding, to assess whether civic participation and electoral participation have different explanatory variables, mobilization potential, and governing impact, and to evaluate how the two types of participation affect each other.

These research questions can be applied to administrative participation too. What has been the trend of administrative participation? If people distrust elections, would they be more likely to participate in administrative decision making and management processes? Are active civic participants and administrative participants the same group of people? Would administrative participation have different explanatory variables, mobilization potential, and governing impact? Although the public administration literature has started to examine administrative participation via quantitative modeling (e.g., Yang & Callahan, 2007), conscious efforts to compare with the other two types of participation are still lacking. For example, in local governments, would the forms of government have different effects on the three types of participation? Studies have found that the effect of community size on electoral participation is still a puzzle, with conflicting empirical evidence and theoretical arguments in the political science and urban politics literature (Kelleher & Lowery, 2004). How would community size affect civic and administrative participation?

Going one step further, one could question whether administrative participation is better treated as a set of different subtypes of participation such as participatory budgeting, participation planning, and community policing. In statistical terms, while those subtypes share some common variance, their unique variance may significantly outweigh the common variance. That is, the distinction among the subtypes may be too large to be ignored in theory building and explanation. The literature has shown that the level of participation varies across functional areas (Wang, 2001; Yang & Callahan, 2005). The literature also has different streams of studies dealing with, for example, participatory budgeting, participation planning, and community policing. However, few studies have consciously compared across these subtypes of participation. Do they involve different theoretical mechanisms? Do they require different theories? How are they related?

The discussions above are around the single dimension of subject area or arena. The discussions would be further complicated if another dimension is added to explore the difference between face-to-face and Web-based participation. For example, traditional voting and online voting have been studied separately as researchers start to evaluate the effects of the Internet on electoral participation (Bimber, 2001; Tolbert & McNeal, 2003). It is possible that the Internet will stimulate online voting without improving the overall voter turnout because it might simply attract some traditional voters and turn them into online voters. It is also possible that the Internet increases the overall voter turnout because it improves information dissemination and sharing among the potential voters. Civic participation and administrative participation, or their subtypes, can also occur face-to-face and online. Take administrative participation as an example. Are online participants different from their face-to-face counterparts? Do the two participation modes tend to generate different results? More studies are necessary to assess whether the two modes are theoretically distinct in a meaningful way. If they are, we need to find out how public officials strategically use the two modes.

The fact that citizen participation practice contains distinctive types and subtypes speaks to the futility of developing general or grand theories of citizen participation. Different theories might be necessary to explain different types or subtypes of participation. Alternatively, we need to develop more midrange theories that provide an integrative framework for a circumscribed aspect of citizen participation based on clearly formulated, verifiable statements of relationships between variables. Midrange theory is a form of theory midway between unified theories that seek to explain all uniformities at one end of the theory spectrum and working hypotheses at the other end (Merton, 1968). More than 4 decades ago, Caiden (1971) lamented that many public administration studies aim to either build grand theories or deal with unique practices, specific organizations, and special cases. As a response, developing midrange theories is identified by Perry (1991) as a central strategy for building public administration theory.

THE ROLE OF THEORY

The importance of theory to the scientific endeavor cannot be overstated. Contribution to theory has increasingly been used as a standard for top public administration journals. Theories help organize our thoughts, generate coherent explanations, and improve predictions. When the Public Management Research Association broke away from the American Society for Public Administration, one of the criticisms leveled against "traditional" public administration research was the lack of theory development (Bozeman, 1993; see also Houston & Delevan, 1990; McCurdy & Cleary, 1984). Today, most researchers recognize the diverse and complex nature of citizen participation and would not attempt to develop grand theories. They also pay attention to theory development, although the degree and actual contributions vary.

It should be noted that the use of theory applies to both quantitative and qualitative research in most circumstances. While the pursuit of theory-driven research might sometimes be taken to mean rigorous quantitative model testing, it applies to qualitative inquires. There is an argument that some qualitative research does not need theory because the researchers are supposed to dive into the practice without preset assumptions and derive theories from the ground. This is probably true when the subject is so novel that it has never been realized or observed in the past, but given such a subject, the same argument can be applied to quantitative research as well. In most research we do, no researcher can start a project without any influence from some previous theories. In Elías's chapter, for example, an inductive study based on interpretive phenomenology generated very rich qualitative data, but to interpret the lessons learned, Elías uses Follett's (1918/1923) community process theory.

What constitutes a theory is often debatable. Generally there are two types of theories. One is normative, directing people on what they "should" do or what is normatively desirable. The other is explanatory and explains a social process by identifying "what variables are important and for what reasons," specifying "how they are interrelated and why," and demonstrating "the conditions under which they should be related or not related" (Campbell, 1990).

Normative theories of citizen participation are frequently referred to in the chapters of this book, such as Barber's (1984) theory of strong democracy, Frederickson's (1982) theory of public administration civism, and Habermas's (1984) theory of communicative action. The chapter by Nishishiba, Banyan, and Morgan is primarily based on constitutional theories, and the chapter cannot be more theoretical and cannot be more strikingly provocative. By relying on the founding thoughts and tracing the civic engagement traditions in the United States, the three authors propose that the issue of citizen participation be understood in the context of ensuring democratic liberty and observing an enduring four-way tension among the need for government competence, popular sovereignty, the preservation of minority rights, and an engaged citizenry. To develop and demonstrate their citizen engagement and nonprofit engagement models in the United States, they use informative and straightforward two-by-two tables. Their conclusions, that the viability of a democracy does not necessarily depend on the robustness of its associational life and that the amount and kind of participation in one sector has consequences for participation in other sectors, are consistent with those of other chapters. Indeed, Nishishiba et al.'s development of a constitutional theory of citizen participation exemplifies how normative theorizing should be conducted.

The emphasis of this chapter is more on explanatory theories, as most of the other chapters are empirical, ask empirical questions, or are based the empirical literature. A brief review is offered below regarding two related issues: what existing theories are used and what new theories or constructs are developed. On the former, many of the "empirical" chapters do not rely on one or more explanatory theories, as their main purpose is not to explain but to describe and introduce. However, the attention to theory is apparent in other chapters. Some chapters use existing citizen participation theories to help organize and interpret. For instance, Sharp mentions three theoretical approaches that explain who participates in politics and civic affairs: (a) the one that emphasizes attitudes, values, and other psychological predispositions; (b) the one that emphasizes individual self-interests and rational choices; and (c) the political mobilization theory proposed by Rosenstone and Hansen (1993). To various degrees, the chapters by Sharp, Eikenberry and Jensen, and Crow and Stevens all rely on the mobilization theory to organize the argument or structure the writing. Dudley's chapter touches on organizational theory and decision-making theory, but her major contribution seems to hinge upon Yankelovich's (1991) process theory of public judgment. Elías's chapter primarily borrows Follett's (1918/1923) community process theory to help explain the findings.

The existing theories of citizen participation should continue to be used in future inquires. As demonstrated in the previous section, there are many unanswered questions regarding civic participation, administrative participation, and their subtypes. The existing theories are useful guidelines for studying those questions. Although they are largely developed to explain electoral participation and some aspects of civic participation, they are great starting points for theorizing and modeling on administrative participation issues.

An important way to make a theoretical contribution is to borrow existing theories in other research domains to explain citizen participation issues. De Lancer Julnes's chapter, for example, creatively extends Schneider and Ingram's (1993) theory of social construction of target populations into the study of participation among Hispanics in Utah. The theory has been used to explain issues in policy design, policy implementation, and legislative voting, among other areas, but it has rarely been used to explain citizen participation. Coincidentally, a recent paper presented at the 11th Annual Public Management Research Conference also attempts to use the Schneider and Ingram framework to explain why some state agencies are more open to public input than others (Neshkova & Guo, 2011).

Unlike de Lancer Julnes, who turns to the policy analysis literature, Kuentzel and Ventriss apply a variety of theories from social psychology to explore the limits of communicative rationality in a public participation setting. The theories used include attitude structure, attitude ambivalence, social cognition, influence and conformity, and group performance. Kuentzel and Ventriss argue that social psychology theories can help address three questions and challenges that face public participation: (a) Who does and who does not participate? (b) Is deliberation and rational argumentation always better? and (c) Are groups really better at solving policy dilemmas and conflicts? Indeed, participation is a social process in which citizens interact with officials, citizens, and other players. The understanding of that process can be facilitated by knowledge and theory about the cognition, attitude, and behavior of all individual players, as well as group dynamics among the players and the outcome produced by the dynamics. Future citizen participation research should pay more attention to the research in psychology, social psychology, and organizational behavior, building a microlevel (individual and group) foundation of citizen participation theories. This is not to advocate for methodological individualism; instead, this is a call for attention to the social mechanisms that link citizens, officials, and other players in producing participation outcomes.

Similarly, in a recent article, Yang and Pandey (2011) call for more use of mainstream organizational theories to enrich citizen involvement studies. Although the citizen involvement literature acknowledges the importance of administrative systems in shaping citizen participation, how organizational variables affect participation outcomes is still underexplored. Applying public organizational theories can provide a more sophisticated description and explanation of the relationships. The implementation of citizen participation activities reflects an organizational adaption process. Organizational arrangements determine what information citizens seek, how they process the signals, and how they act upon their perceived reality. This echoes the marketing literature on companies' market orientation, which finds that the effect of market orientation on organizational performance depends on organization characteristics such as learning ability, strategic flexibility, innovativeness, and industry type (Yang & Pandey, 2007). As Yang and Pandey (2011) conclude, "Bridging the citizen participation literature and the recent public management literature would offer great opportunities to advance theory development in both research domains" (p. 889).

Another, perhaps more difficult, form of theory development is creating new theoretical constructs, categories, typologies, and/or frameworks to help explain social phenomena. This book includes at least three chapters that engage in such theory development. One is the chapter by Nishishiba, Banyan, and Morgan, as mentioned above. Another is the chapter by Piotrowski and Liao, who create a typology of four variants of information quantity and usability: overload, ideal, opaque, and pseudo. The typology helps explain that transparency does not generate more citizen participation if the information released by government is not usable by citizens. By "usable" the authors mean whether the information is accurate, accessible, complete, understandable, timely, and free or low cost. Two dimensions of the two-by-two typology are not something unheard of by transparency or participation researchers, but pulling them together and building a systematic framework is novel. Piotrowski and Liao's work shows that creating new theoretical constructs or typologies might not require racking one's brain and searching for terms that have not been created. Instead, abstracting practical wisdom in a systematic and theoretical way might well suffice. Similarly, the three models identified in the chapter by Holzer, Mullins, Sun, and Woolley are not based on pure theoretical deduction, but on abstractions from the practice. By studying 21 best practice organizations in the United States and Canada, based on the capacity for citizen involvement in a shared service context, the authors differentiate three general models of collaborative governance depending on the focal organization's financial base and ability to cooperate.

METHODOLOGICAL DIVERSITY

The methodology used in the chapters of this book reflect the current state of research in public administration studies on citizen participation. Except the 3 largely conceptual chapters (Nishishiba, Banyan, & Morgan; Kuetzel & Ventriss; Barnes & Williams) and 2 review chapters (Sharp; Eikenberry & Jensen), all other 11 chapters, which are firsthand studies, are based on variants of qualitative methods. Specifically, case study is used by 8 chapters either as a stand-alone case or as part a mixed methodology (e.g, Crow & Stevens); content analysis is used in 2 chapters (Bryer; Schatteman), and interpretative phenomenology is used in 1 chapter (Elías).

Case study, perhaps the most widely used method in the existing empirical citizen participation literature, is also the dominant method among the empirical chapters of this book. In all, 3 out of 11 are based on a single case—the chapters by de Lancer Julnes, Kopetzky, and Lipschultz. Another five are based on multiple cases—the chapters by Dudley; Piotriowski and Liao; Holzer and Mullins; Holzer, Mullins, Sun, and Woolley; and by Crow and Stevens. For some chapters, the case method is used in the way that Yin (1984) recommends, as the authors develop a theory first and then apply the case(s) to illustrate the theory, reflecting more of a deductive approach (e.g., de Lancer Julnes; Piotriowski & Liao). Other chapters use more of an inductive approach, finding patterns and models from the cases (e.g., Holzer & Mullins; Holzer, Mullins, Sun, & Woolley; Dudley). Notably, even for those largely inductive case studies, the authors review the literature and provide theoretical background information (to various degrees) at the beginning of the chapters. This may not be the actual sequence of thinking for inductive inquiries, but it reflects what readers and reviewers expect to read. It makes clear what theoretical contributions a study has. As shown in the chapters, both types of case methods can help theory development by building new constructs or models. The de Lancer Julnes chapter is a good example of the former type and the Holzer, Mullins, Sun, and Woolley chapter is a good example for the latter.

A careful reading of the two review chapters (Sharp; Eikenberry & Jensen) indicates that in political science, the research on political/electoral participation includes a significant number of quantitative studies with multivariate model testing. Such studies in public administration do exist (e.g., Yang, 2005; Yang & Callahan, 2007), but they are much less salient than political science. As Yang and Pandey (2011) observe, public administration scholars have proposed compelling prescriptive models of citizen participation, but these models have rarely been tested with large-scale data. Public administration scholars have used case studies to illustrate how citizen participation can work in a particular government, with a particular mechanism, or in a particular policy area, but what remains untested is how participation as a general strategy can improve decision making.

Take King's (2011) edited volume, *Government is Us 2.0*, as an example. Excluding the two introduction chapters and one conclusion chapter, the rest of the 10 chapters include 3 conceptual ones and 7 empirical ones (or with notable empirical components). All of the 7 empirical ones are based on case studies, with 5 of them making up the book's third section, titled as "Stories of Practice."

There are many reasons why the methodological choice by public administration researchers on citizen participation has been the way it is. Case research, for example, has the strength of the likelihood of generating novel theories and the strength of exploring new contexts or emerging topics. More generally, many scholars believe that public administration is not a science, and the efforts to make it so through the application of quantitatively based empirical research are bound to be fruitless (Stivers, 2000). Riccuci (2008) concludes that "striving to apply ontologies, epistemologies, and methodologies of the natural sciences will not produce better research and will not improve the field of public administration; they are, in effect, inappropriate" (p. 9). The public administration research on citizen participation is perhaps more so than other public administration subfields because it is linked with normative values, subjective experiences, and often a sense of emancipation. It is partly for this reason that in her chapter, Elías argues for more interpretive studies as a way to unveil the dynamics of participation processes via participants' own intersubjective meanings.

However, there are equally significant arguments for more scientific studies of public administration (Bozeman, 1993; Gill & Meier, 2000). The debate between Herbert Simon and Dwight Waldo over the desirability of a science of public administration has dragged on into our time (Harmon, 1989). A more viable approach to me is to be more tolerant of methodological diversity, recognizing the strengths and weaknesses of all methods, and understanding that the nature of the problem dictates the choice of methods. After applying multivariate statistics, Yang and Pandey (2011) conclude:

> Future citizen participation research will benefit from integrating normative, qualitative, and quantitative inquiries. Testing a multivariate model helps us reveal the complex relationships among the variables, despite the fact that quantitative designs, particularly survey research with cross-sectional data, have limitations. With such testing, it is straightforward to demonstrate the relative importance of the explanatory variables and the potential interactive effects. This is not to downplay the importance of normative inquiry or qualitative design. Indeed, the theory and hypothesis development of this article is grounded in the normative and qualitative literature, our results are largely consistent with the literature, and some of our intriguing findings may well need qualitative inquiries to validate in future. What we argue is that combin-

ing normative, qualitative, and quantitative inquiries will greatly advance our understanding. Current citizen involvement studies, unlike the political science literature on electoral participation, have not fully taken advantage of quantitative designs. (p. 889)

An arguably more fundamental issue is methodological rigor. Methodological diversity is important to the extent that the research problems are diverse and multifaceted. Methodological rigor, however, is always a critical concern regardless of ontologies, epistemologies, and methodologies. One aspect of rigor is to what extent the research convincingly advances theory development and illuminates the problem. To this end, it is reasonable to state that both qualitative and quantitative studies on citizen participation in the current public administration literature have room to improve and can learn from each other. Unfortunately, the two camps often seem to be intolerant of each other, talking past each other or simply dismissing the criticism from the other side.

For example, in order to generate good theory from case study research, many steps should be considered or followed to increase validity and reliability (Strauss, 1987; Yin, 1984). Eisenhardt (1989) outlines eight steps:

1. *Getting Started* by defining the research question and possibly develop *a priori* constructs;
2. *Selecting Cases* by using theoretical sampling;
3. *Crafting Instruments and Protocols* by using multiple data-collection methods, multiple investigators, and combining qualitative and quantitative data;
4. *Entering the Field* by using overlapped data collection and analysis and adopting flexible and opportunistic data-collection methods;
5. *Analyzing Data* with within-case analysis and cross-case pattern search;
6. *Shaping Hypotheses* with iterative tabulation of evidence for each construct, replication logic across cases, and evidence for "why" behind relationships;
7. *Enfolding Literature* with comparison with similar and conflicting literatures;
8. *Reaching Closure* with theoretical saturation when possible.

Quite often, many public administration publications based on case research either are not based on such a rigorous process or do not report the process in a clear way. Quantitative publications face the challenge of rigor as well, such as the issues about poor data reporting (Wright, Manigault, & Black, 2004), simplistic modeling (Houston & Delevan, 1990), lack of methodological sophistication (Gill & Meier, 2000), lack of rigorous measurement model testing (Coursey & Pandey, 2007), a-theoretical research (Perry, 1991), and overreliance on cross-sectional data (Wright et al., 2004).

THEORIZING AND PRACTICING

Admittedly, theory building and testing is not the sole purpose of social science research. Identifying a significant new problem or observing an emerging pattern from practice or data is sometimes more important for human inquiry than developing an explanatory theory for it. Moreover, public administration scholars have the responsibility to not only advance knowledge but also contribute to practice. Among them, those who study citizen participation are perhaps one of the groups who value this responsibility the most. After all, the citizenship value applies to us as scholar-citizens. This indicates the importance of anchoring research with practice. Lewin's (1945) statement that "nothing is so practical as a good theory" captures this point well.

On that aspect, the authors and chapters of this book well-reflect the citizen participation subfield as a whole. Some of the chapters are based on the authors' direct participation in a project, such as Dudley's participation in the mock courtroom experiment, Kopetzky's involvement in the Benson-Ames Alliance, and Lipschultz's organization of the deliberative polling project. Elías's chapter is based on her participatory observations of the local community and its participants. Some chapters are based on projects that aim to find workable solutions or models from the practice before disseminating them to governments and the public (e.g., Holzer & Mullin; Holzer, Mullins, Sun, and Woolley). Other chapters may not be directly based on such practice-centered projects, but many of the authors are active citizens in their community. This is a strength of the citizen participation subfield. Active participation by the scholars helps advance both practice and theory. Good theory is not built through finding holes in the literature but through an engagement with problems in the real world.

Citizen participation has some everlasting tensions or dilemmas, such as those between representation and ability, between representative democracy and participatory democracy, between instrumental and normative focuses, and among state, civil society, and the market. These tensions are identified in some of the chapters (e.g., Nishishiba, Banyan, and Morgan). In the meantime, such tensions are often manifested as unique problems or challenges in different contexts. An active participation in (or attention to) the changing practice helps scholars identify the most pressing problems and the most feasible solutions. Across the chapters, several such pressing issues emerge. I take only two of the issues for example below.

One issue is citizen participation in collaborative network governance. While Holzer and his colleagues identify different structures and models for collaborative governance, which includes an active role of citizens, several other chapters caution about the impact of partnerships, associations, and privatization on citizen participation. Nishishiba, Banyan, and Morgan, for example, arrive at this point by historical thinking, while Sharp, as well as Eikenberry and Jensen, refers to the empirical findings from the literature. In their introduction to the *Public Administration Review* symposium on collaborative management, O'Leary, Gerard, and Bingham (2006) differentiate between collaborative public management and participatory governance. The former is "a concept that describes the process of facilitating and operating in multiorganizational arrangements to solve problems that cannot be solved or easily solved by single organizations" (p. 7). The latter is "the active involvement of citizens in government decision making." They emphasize that these two concepts are different. In their concluding essay, Bingham and O'Leary (2006) point out:

> For the most part, the literature on collaborative public management and collaboration does not generally address—or often even mention—the role of the citizen or the public as distinct from the public, private, or nonprofit organizational participants in a network or collaborative. Similarly, the literature on civic engagement and public participation does not generally address the cross-sector context and institutional framework within which civic engagement takes place. When we discuss how collaborative networks relate to democracy, we tend to focus on the rule of law, not the role of the public. As a result, we do not yet have a higher-order theory to help public managers make informed choices about the participants, goals, likely outcomes, design, implementation, evaluation, or institutionalization of collaborative governance. (p. 161)

Another cross-cutting issue is the role of information and communication technologies (ICTs), particularly the Web-based technologies. The chapter by Barnes and Williams describes the opportunities and challenges in applying technology to enhance citizen involvement in local governments. The chapter by Schatteman discusses online citizen participation by comparing the Web sites of nonprofit organizations. The Piotrowski and Liao chapter includes two cases that are based on technologies: USASpending.gov and the 1-800-Medicare helpline. The Holzer and Mullins chapter uses the cases of the Fund for the City of New York's Center on Municipal Government Performance and the CitiScan Project in Connecticut, showing how laser technology, digital cameras, and handheld computers are used to enable citizens to participate in performance management. The other chapter by Holzer and his colleagues includes the use of Web sites and social media in evaluating the best practice organizations.

Not covered in the book, however, is the more substantive literature on the relationship between ICTs and citizen participation, an issue that has generated great theoretical controversies (Barber, 1998–1999; Kamarck & Nye, 1999, 2002; Thomas, 2004). Both the development of ICTs and the increasing demand for citizen participation can be considered as ongoing revolutions, but the two revolutions have largely been studied separately: "relatively little attention has been paid until recently to the interaction of the two revolutions, especially to how the information revolution may impact public involvement" (Thomas, 2004, p. 68). The interwoven development of ICTs, participation, and administrative institutions is a great minefield to be explored.

CONCLUDING REMARKS

The chapters in this book touch on many frontier issues of citizen participation and contribute to our understanding of the complexity of citizen participation. They also point to many future questions. Albert Einstein allegedly once said, "As our circle of knowledge expands, so does the circumference of darkness surrounding it." It is clear that there are many unanswered questions, as well as a need for better theory development and more methodological rigor. The existence of room for improvement in such an important research area is exciting for students of public administration. What's more exciting is that participation is an issue that government and citizens face every day in dealing with the most significant and challenging issues of our time. What is the role of citizen participation in emergency management and disaster response? What are citizen participation issues in a global economy? Would citizen participation help us overcome the current financial or budgetary crisis? For all those important issues, how can we make citizen voice better heard? How can we make sure that citizen liberty and well-being are carefully and fairly considered? These issues are exciting for public administration scholars and students.

REFERENCES

Arnstein, S. (1969). A ladder of citizen participation. *Journal of the American Planning Association, 35*(4), 216–224.

Barber, B. R. (1984). *Strong democracy.* Berkeley: University of California Press.

Barber, B. R. (1998-1999). Three scenarios for the future of technology and strong democracy. *Political Science Quarterly, 113*(4), 573–589.

Berman, E. (1997). Dealing with cynical citizens. *Public Administration Review, 57*(2), 105–123.

Bimber, B. (2001). Information and political engagement in America: The search for effects of information technology at the individual level. *Public Research Quarterly, 54*(1), 53–67.

Bingham, L., & O'Leary, R. (2006). Conclusion: Parallel play, not collaboration: Missing questions, missing connections. *Public Administration Review, 66*(Suppl.), 161–167.

Bozeman, B. (1993). Introduction: Two concepts of public management. In B. Bozeman (Ed.), *Public management* (pp. 1–5). San Francisco, CA: Jossey-Bass.

Caiden, C. (1971). *The dynamics of public administration: Guidelines to current transformations in theory and practice.* New York, NY: Holt, Rinehart and Winston.

Campbell, J. P. (1990). The role of theory in industrial and organizational psychology. In M. D. Dunnette & L. M. Hough (Eds.), *Handbook of industrial and organizational psychology, 1,* 39–74. Palo Alto, CA: Consulting Psychologists.

Coursey, D., & Pandey, S. (2007). Content domain, measurement, and validity of the red tape concept. *American Review of Public Administration, 37*(3), 342–361.

Eisenhardt, K. (1989). Building theories from case study research. *Academy of Management Review, 14*(4), 532–550.

Follett, M. P. (1918/1923). *The new state:* **G***roup organization the solution of popular government.* New York, NY: Longman Green.

Frederickson, H. G. (1982). The recovery of civism in public administration. *Public Administration Review, 42*(6), 501–508.

Gill, J., & Meier, K. (2000). Public administration research and practice: A methodological manifesto. *Journal of Public Administration Research and Theory, 10*(1), 157–199.

Habermas, J. (1984). *The theory of communicative action.* Boston, MA: Beacon.

Harmon, M. (1989). The Simon/Waldo debate: A review and update. *Public Administration Quarterly 12*(4), 437–451.

Houston, D., & Delevan, S. (1990). Public administration research: An assessment of journal publications. *Public Administration Review, 50*(6), 674–681.

Jacobs, L. R., Cook, F. L., &. Delli Carpini, M. X. (2009). *Talking together.* Chicago, IL: University of Chicago Press.

Kamarck, E. C., & Nye, J. S. (Ed.). (1999). *Democracy.com? Governance in a networked world.* Hollis, NH: Hollis.

Kamarck, E. C., & Nye, J. S. (Ed.). (2002). *Governance.com: Democracy in the information age.* Washington, DC: Brookings Institution.

Kelleher, C., & Lowery, D. (2004). Political participation and metropolitan institutional contexts. *Urban Affairs Review, 39*(6), 720–757.

King, C. S. (Ed.). (2011). *Government is us 2.0.* Armonk, NY: M.E. Sharpe.

King, C. S., Feltey, K. M., & Susel, B. (1998). The question of participation: Toward authentic public participation in public administration. *Public Administration Review, 58*(4), 317–326.

King, C. S., & Stivers, C. (1998). *Government is us.* Thousand Oaks, CA: Sage.

Koontz, T. M. (1999). Administrators and citizens: Measuring agency officials' efforts to foster and use public input in forest policy. *Journal of Public Administration Research and Theory, 9*(2), 251–280.

Langton, S. (1978). What is citizen participation? In S. Langton (Ed.), *Citizen participation in America* (pp. 13–24). Lexington, MA: Lexington.

Lewin, K. (1945). The research center for group dynamics at Massachusetts Institute of Technology. *Sociometry, 8,* 126–135.

McCurdy, H., & Cleary, R. (1984). Why can't we resolve the research issue in public administration? *Public Administration Review, 44*(1), 49–55.

Merton, R. K. (1968). *Social theory and social structure.* New York, NY: Free Press.

Neshkova, M., & Guo, H. (2011, June 2–4). *Explaining the patterns of public participation in agency decision-making.* Paper presented at the 11th annual Public Management Research Conference, Syracuse University, New York.

O'Leary, R., Gerard, C., & Bingham, L. (2006). Introduction to the symposium on collaborative public management. *Public Administration Review, 66*(Suppl.), 6–9.

Perry, J. L. (1991). Strategies for building public administration theory. *Research in Public Administration, 1,* 1–18.

Putnam, R. D. (2000). *Bowling alone: The challenge and revival of American community.* New York, NY: Simon & Schuster.

Riccucci, N. (2008). The logic of inquiry in the field of public administration. In K. Yang & G. Miller (Eds.), *Handbook of research methods in public administration* (pp. 3–12). Boca Raton, FL: Taylor & Francis.

Roberts, N. (2004). Public deliberation in an age of direct citizen participation. *The American Review of Public Administration, 34*(4), 315–353.

Rosenstone, S. J., & Hansen, J. M. (1993). *Mobilization, participation, and democracy in America.* New York, NY: Macmillan.

Schneider, A., & Ingram, H. (1993). The social construction of target populations: Implications for politics and policy. *The American Political Science Review, 87*(2), 334–347.

Stivers, C. (2000). *Bureau men, settlement women: Construction public administration in the progressive era.* Lawrence: University Press of Kansas.

Strauss, A. (1987). *Qualitative analysis for social scientists.* Cambridge, England: Cambridge University Press.

Thomas, J. C. (1995). *Public participation in public decisions.* San Francisco, CA: Jossey-Bass.

Thomas, J. C. (2004). Public involvement in public administration in the information age. In M. Mälkiä, A. Anttiroko, & R. Savolainen (Eds.), *eTransformation in governance: New directions in government and politics* (pp. 67–84). Hershey, PA: Idea Group.

Tolbert, C., & McNeal, R. (2003). Unraveling the effects of the Internet on political participation? *Political Research Quarterly, 56*(2), 175–185.

Verba, S., Schlozman, K. L., Brady, H., & Nie, N. H. (1993). Citizen activity: Who participates? What do they say? *American Political Science Review, 87*(2), 303–318.

Wang, X. (2001). Assessing public participation in U.S. cities. *Public Performance & Management Review, 24*(4), 322–336.

Wright, B., Manigault, L., & Black, T. (2004). Quantitative research measurement in public administration: An assessment of journal publications. *Administration & Society, 35*(6), 747–764.

Yang, K. (2005). Public administrators' trust in citizens: A missing link in citizen involvement efforts. *Public Administration Review, 65*(3), 273–285.

Yang, K., & Callahan, K. (2007). Citizen involvement efforts and bureaucratic responsiveness. *Public Administration Review, 67*(2), 249–264.

Yang, K., & Callahan, K. (2005). Assessing citizen involvement efforts by local government. *Public Performance & Management Review, 29*(2), 191–216.

Yang, K., & Pandey, S. (2007). Public responsiveness of government organizations: Testing a preliminary model. *Public Performance & Management Review, 31*(2), 215–240.

Yang, K., & Pandey, S. (2011). Further dissecting the black box of citizen participation: When does citizen involvement lead to good outcomes? *Public Administration Review, 71*(6), 880–892.

Yankelovich, D. (1991). *Coming to public judgment: Making democracy work in a complex world.* Syracuse, NY: Syracuse University Press.

Yin, R. (1984). *Case study research: Design and methods.* Newbury Park, CA: Sage.

Zukin, C., Keeter, S., Andolina, M., Jenkins, K., & Delli Carpini, M. X. (2006). *A new engagement?* New York, NY: Oxford University Press.

ABOUT THE CONTRIBUTORS

Margaret Banyan is assistant professor in the Division of Public Affairs at Florida Gulf Coast University. Dr. Banyan focuses on research and practice in the areas of civic infrastructure, special district and intergovernmental relations, public transit, sustainability, and community planning. She has published chapters, book reviews, and articles in *Public Administration Review, Administrative Theory and Praxis, Encyclopedia of Governance*, and four editions of *The Roads to Congress*. Dr. Banyan also serves as a Senior Faculty Associate in the FGCU Southwest Florida Center for Public and Social Policy, where she consults with local communities in the areas of land use and strategic planning.

Bill Barnes is currently serving as assistant to the Director of Public Works for the City of Suwanee, Georgia, a *Money* magazine "Top 10 Best Places to Live" in America, and Georgia Municipal Association "City of Excellence" award-winning city. Bill enjoyed a 20-year career in higher education administration, serving as Assistant Dean of Students at the Georgia Institute of Technology, prior to transitioning to local government service, first in process improvement and now in public works administration. Bill earned a BBA at Columbus State University, MEd from Mississippi State University, and MPA from the University of Georgia.

Thomas Bryer is assistant professor in the School of Public Administration at the University of Central Florida and Director of the Center for Public and Nonprofit Management. His teaching and research focuses on public participation with government, citizen engagement, cross-sector collabo-

The State of Citizen Participation in America, pages 465–471
Copyright © 2012 by Information Age Publishing
All rights of reproduction in any form reserved.

ration, and ethics. His work has appeared in *Public Administration Review, Journal of Public Administration Research and Theory, Administrative Theory & Praxis, Public Performance and Management Review, Journal of Public Affairs Education, American Review of Public Administration, International Journal of Public Participation, Journal of Homeland Security and Management, Public Administration and Management, Policy & Internet, Public Integrity,* and *International Journal of Organization Theory and Behavior.* He also has published chapters in peer-reviewed books and award-winning teaching simulations.

Deserai Anderson Crow is associate director of the Center for Environmental Journalism and assistant professor in the Environmental Studies Program at the University of Colorado Boulder. She is also affiliated with the Center for Science & Technology Policy Research. Her research interests include local environmental policy change, citizen participation, mass media influence on environmental issues, and institutional change, with a particular focus on property rights regime change and Western water law. Her previous work focuses on how media, experts, interest groups, and citizens influence environmental policy decisions at local and statewide levels. She earned her doctorate from Duke University's Nicholas School of the Environment and Earth Sciences (2008).

Patria de Lancer Julnes, PhD, is professor and director of the Doctor of Public Administration Program in the School of Public and International Affairs at the University of Baltimore. Patria's research focuses on performance measurement, accountability, and citizen-driven governance. Her articles have appeared in *Public Administration Review, Public Performance and Management Review, Evaluation,* and Revista del CLAD *Reforma y Democracia,* among others. She is the author of the book *Performance-Based Management Systems: Effective Implementation and Maintenance* (CRC Press), and lead co-editor of the *International Handbook of Practice-Based Performance Management* (Sage), *and Performance Measurement: Building Theory, Supporting Practice* (M.E. Sharpe). Patria is past co-chair of ASPA's Center for Accountability and Performance and currently serves as managing editor of the *International Review of Public Administration.*

Dr. Larkin Dudley, associate professor emerita, has moderated citizen forums for over 12 years. As associate professor at the Center for Public Administration and Policy, Virginia Tech, Blacksburg, Virginia, she has taught and published articles and book chapters on citizen participation and public policy. She continues to teach public policy courses at Virginia Tech and is active in research on citizen participation, deliberative democracy, and public management.

Angela M. Eikenberry is associate professor in the School of Public Administration at the University of Nebraska at Omaha, where she also serves as the advisor for the nonprofit concentration in the MPA program. Before returning to graduate school, Dr. Eikenberry was a development and grant writing consultant. Her main research interests include philanthropy and nonprofit organizations and their role in democratic governance. She has published articles in numerous academic journals, and her research has been featured on NPR's *All Things Considered* and in the *Stanford Social Innovation Review*. Her book, *Giving Circles: Philanthropy, Voluntary Association, Democracy* (Indiana University Press), won the CASE 2010 John Grenzebach Research Award for Outstanding Research in Philanthropy, Published Scholarship.

María Verónica Elías is assistant professor of public administration at Eastern Washington University. Her research focuses on deliberative democracy and collaborative governance, with an emphasis on community process and grassroots organizing. She utilizes interpretive phenomenology to investigate collaboration from the viewpoints and experiences of its participants. Dr. Elías is a research fellow of the Institute of Applied Phenomenology in Science and Technology led by Professor Ralph P. Hummel and housed in Canal Fulton, Ohio, and Spruce Head, Maine.

Marc Holzer (MPA, PhD, University of Michigan) is founding dean of the School of Public Affairs and Administration and Board of Governors Professor of Public Affairs and Administration at Rutgers University's Newark Campus. He is a Fellow of the National Academy of Public Administration. Since 1975, he has directed the National Center for Public Performance. Dr. Holzer is past president of the American Society for Public Administration and is a recipient of several national and international awards in the field, including the Distinguished Research Award from the National Association of Schools of Public Affairs and Administration and the American Society for Public Administration, 2009; the Sweeney Academic Award from the International City Management Association, 2005; ASPA's Charles H. Levine Memorial Award for Demonstrated Excellence in Teaching, Research and Service to the Community, 2000. At Rutgers he has received University awards for Research (2001), Public Service (2002), and Human Dignity (2004). He is the editor-in-chief of the Public Performance and Management Review and has published over 200 books, articles, and reports.

Courtney Jensen is assistant professor of public administration at Georgia Southern University. In 2011 she earned a PhD degree at the University of Nebraska at Omaha, where her dissertation, *Foundations and Racial Inequality: A Discourse Analysis,* explored how foundations understand and address racial inequality in the United States. Her areas of research and teaching interest include racial equality, the role of philanthropic institutions in democratic societies, race and public administration, foundations and minority philanthropy. She holds an MPA from Eastern Washington University and a BA in political science from the University of Washington.

Alan Kopetzky earned his PhD in public administration from the University of Nebraska at Omaha in December 2009, where he taught courses in public administration. Through his 22 years of experience in state government, Dr. Kopetzky has realized the importance of building effective public-private partnerships in community development processes.

Walter Kuentzel, PhD, is associate professor in the Rubenstein School of Environment and Natural Resources, and a former Visiting Research Fellow at the Policy Institute, Trinity College Dublin. Dr. Kuentzel's research interests include social psychology of the environment, rural community change, and social psychology of leisure.

Yuguo Liao is a PhD candidate in the School of Public Affairs and Administration at Rutgers University-Newark. His main research interests are citizen participation, bureaucratic behavior, and government performance improvement.

Jeremy Harris Lipschultz, PhD, is professor and director of the School of Communication at the University of Nebraska at Omaha. He is a Senior Fellow in the Center for Collaboration Science, a Fellow in the Center for Great Plains Studies, and Reviews Editor for *Journalism & Mass Communication Educator*. He previously served as co-editor for *Studies In Media & Information Literacy Education (SIMILE)*. Dr. Lipschultz has published six books and more than 100 articles on mass communication. His work has been cited by numerous law reviews, and he has been interviewed by major national and international news media about government regulation of media and new technologies. He currently blogs for the *Huffington Post*.

Douglas Morgan is professor emeritus of public administration in the Mark O. Hatfield School of Government, Portland State University. He is the author and/or co-author of several monographs and articles on public service leadership and ethics, including *Foundations of Public Service* (M.E Sharpe), *Public Service Leadership: Leading from Where You Sit* (forthcoming from M.E. Sharpe), *Foundations of Local Public Budgeting* (forthcoming from M.E. Sharpe), *Performance Governance and Leadership: A Chinese-American Comparative Perspective* (a joint venture with the Lanzhou School of Public Management). His article on "What Middle Managers Do" received the Louis Brownlow Award from the American Society of Public Administration. He currently serves as director of the Executive MPA Program in the Center for Public Service in the Hatfield School of Government and works on collaborative leadership development programs in China and Vietnam.

Lauren Bock Mullins is a doctoral student in the School of Public Affairs and Administration at Rutgers University's Newark campus. Her research interests include public management, women and family policy, performance measurement and improvement, and citizen participation. She is currently writing her dissertation on the effects of family responsibility discrimination on career advancement and will be an assistant professor at Long Island University's C.W. Post campus in fall 2012.

Masami Nishishiba is assistant professor in the Division of Public Administration in the Mark O. Hatfield School of Government, Portland State University. Her areas of interest include civic capacity, cultural competence, project management, local government, and research methods. Her work has appeared in the *Journal of Public Affairs Education, Journal of Public Affairs*, and *Journal of Applied Communication Research*. She is a lead author of the English/Japanese bilingual book *Project Management Toolkit: A Strategic Approach to New Local Governance* [*Chihou Gyoursei wo Kaeru 'Project Management Toolkit': Jichitai Shokuin no Tameno Shin-Shigotojutsu*]. She also serves as associate director of the Center for Public Service in the Hatfield School of Government, where she oversees a number of professional training programs and applied research projects.

Suzanne Piotrowski is associate professor of public affairs and administration at Rutgers University-Newark. Her research focuses on non-mission-based values in public administration, including administrative transparency and ethics. Her books include *Governmental Transparency in the Path of Administrative Reform* and *Governmental Transparency and Secrecy: Linking Literature and Contemporary Debate.* Professor Piotrowski founded and moderates the International Transparency and Secrecy Research Network listserv. She has widely published in journals such as *Public Administration Review, American Review of Public Administration,* and *Journal of Public Administration Research and Theory.*

Hindy Lauer Schachter is professor in the School of Management at New Jersey Institute of Technology. She is the author of *Reinventing Government or Reinventing Ourselves: The Role of Citizen Owners in Making a Better Government* (SUNY Press, 1997), *Frederick Taylor and the Public Administration Community: A Reevaluation* (SUNY Press, 1989), and *Public Agency Communication: Theory and Practice* (Nelson Hall, 1983). Her articles have appeared in *Public Administration Review, Administration and Society, International Journal of Public Administration, Public Administration Quarterly,* and other journals. She served as book review editor of *Public Administration Review* from 2009 to 2011.

Alicia Schatteman is assistant professor in the Division of Public Administration and also teaches for the new Center for NGO Leadership and

Development at Northern Illinois University. She had 12 years of experience working in the nonprofit and public sectors in Canada and the United States before graduating with her PhD from the School of Public Affairs and Administration at Rutgers University-Newark. Her research interests address issues of financial and performance management of nonprofit organizations.

Elaine B. Sharp is professor in the Department of Political Science at the University of Kansas. Her research and teaching interests include urban politics and policymaking, public opinion, and morality politics. She is the author of *Morality Issues and City Politics* (University Press of Kansas, 2005), *The Sometime Connection: Public Opinion and Social Policy* (State University of New York Press, 1999) and *Does Local Government Matter? How Urban Policies Shape Civic Engagement* (University of Minnesota Press, in press). Her recent articles on urban research topics focus on racial tolerance, policing, local political culture, the participation effects of urban programs, and local government sustainability programs; they have appeared in *Social Science Quarterly, State and Local Government Review, Justice Quarterly,* and *Urban Affairs Review.*

J. Richard Stevens is assistant professor in journalism and mass communication at the University of Colorado, Boulder. His research delves into the intersection of ideological formation and media message dissemination. This work comprises studies investigating how science is communicated to news consumers, how cultural messages are formed and passed through popular media, how technology infrastructure affects the delivery of media messages, how communication technology policy affects democratic processes, and related studies in how media and technology platforms are changing American public discourse. He earned his doctorate at the University of Texas at Austin's School of Journalism (2004).

Rusi Sun is currently a doctoral student in public administration at Rutgers University at Newark. Her research interests include public management; public performance measurement and improvement; social equity and diversity, as well as health policy.

Curtis Ventriss is professor of public policy in the Rubenstein School of Environment and Natural Resources, and adjunct professor of policy studies, Johns Hopkins University. He has published several books and has written over 100 articles. He has been a visiting professor at the University of Southern California, Johns Hopkins University, and the University of Oxford. He has also served as the associate editor of the Public Administration Review.

Brian N. Williams is associate professor in the Department of Public Administration and Policy at the University of Georgia, after previous faculty appointments at Florida State University and Vanderbilt University. His primary areas of research explore the relationships between bureaucratic units and communities, in general, and community and problem-oriented policing efforts within communities of color, in particular. He earned his AB, MPA, and PhD degrees at the University of Georgia and is the author of *Citizen Perspectives on Community Policing: A Case Study in Athens, Georgia* (SUNY Press), among other research articles, book chapters, and government reports.

Jonathan Woolley is a financial and policy analyst specializing in public transportation, capital infrastructure, citizen participation, and performance measurement. He has worked in corporate, nonprofit, and public finance; served on oversight bodies in municipal government dealing with issues extending from recycling to ethics; been affiliated with various advocacy groups working on transportation; and has offered testimony in New York, New Jersey, and Pennsylvania on transportation and budgetary concerns. He is currently pursuing a doctorate at Rutgers University's School of Public Affairs and Administration, where he is researching capital infrastructure projects at airports.

Kaifeng Yang is professor and PhD director of the Askew School of Public Administration and Policy, Florida State University. He is the managing editor of *Public Performance & Management Review* and a co-editor of the International Civic Engagement Book Series for Information Age Publishing. His research interests include citizen participation, performance and public management, and organizational theory. He has widely published in leading journals such as *Public Administration Review* and *Journal of Public Administration Research and Theory*.

INDEX

A

Active citizens, 9–11
Administrator–conceived deliberation, 11–12
American Revolution, 23–24
American Society for Public Administration (ASPA), 3
AmeriCorps, 70
Assessment instruments, 188–189
Associational engagement model, 32–33

B

Barriers to minority civic participation, 199–201, 213–217
Behavioral styles, 433—435
Benson Residents Survey, 292
Benson–Ames Alliance, 284, 289–291
  business profile, 292–293
  civic engagement in, 303–307
  demographics of, 291
Benson–Ames Alliance Plan, 295–303
Bill of Rights, 28

C

Center for New Democratic Processes, 13
Citizen engagement/participation, 164–165, 182–185, 350–351
  principles of, 168
  with local government, 169–170
Citizen panels, 12–13
Citizen participation
  conceptualization of, 448–452
  in environmental policymaking, 134–136, 145–148
  theory of, 452–455
Citizen Relationship Management (CRM), 173–175
Citizen survey, 8–9
Citizen-based government, 325ff
  challenges for, 326–327
Citizen-based organizations, 351
Citizen-centered democracy, 28–29
Citizen-driven performance measurement, 7, 327–332
  case studies of, 332–338
  theoretical model of, 338–344

The State of Citizen Participation in America, pages 473–477
Copyright © 2012 by Information Age Publishing

CPSIA information can be obtained at www.ICGtesting.com
Printed in the USA
LVOW08s1001180914

404701LV00001B/10/P